Worlds of History

A Comparative Reader

Volume Two: Since 1400

Worlds of History

A Comparative Reader

Volume Two: Since 1400

Fourth Edition

Kevin Reilly
Raritan Valley College

Bedford/St. Martin's
Boston • New York

To those who taught me to think historically: Eugene Meehan, Donald Weinstein, and Peter Stearns; and to the memory of Warren Susman and Traian Stoianovich

For Bedford/St. Martin's

Publisher for History: Mary V. Dougherty
Executive Editor for History: Traci Mueller Crowell
Director of Development for History: Jane Knetzger
Senior Developmental Editor: Heidi L. Hood
Production Editor: Katherine Caruana
Production Supervisor: Jennifer Peterson
Executive Marketing Manager: Jenna Bookin Barry
Editorial Assistant: Jennifer Jovin
Copyeditor: Susan Zorn
Senior Art Director: Anna Palchik
Text Design: Janis Owens
Photo Research: Lisa Jelly Smith
Cover Design: Billy Boardman
Cover Art: Rigaud V. Benoit, *Fishing Scene,* Haiti, 20th c. Manu Sassoonian/
    Art Resource, N.Y.; Utagawa Kuniyoshi, *Fine view of Mount Fuji from
    Tsukuda-jima* from *Thirty-six views of Mount Fuji from Edo,* 19th c.
    Victoria and Albert Museum, London/Art Resource, N.Y.
Cartography: Mapping Specialists, Ltd.
Composition: MPS Limited, A Macmillan Company
Printing and Binding: Haddon Craftsmen, Inc., an RR Donnelley & Sons Company

President: Joan E. Feinberg
Editorial Director: Denise B. Wydra
Director of Marketing: Karen R. Soeltz
Director of Editing, Design, and Production: Susan W. Brown
Assistant Director of Editing, Design, and Production: Elise S. Kaiser
Managing Editor: Elizabeth M. Schaaf

Library of Congress Control Number: 2010920450

5   4   3   2   1   0
f   e   d   c   b   a

For information, write: Bedford/St. Martin's, 75 Arlington Street,
Boston, MA 02116   (617-399-4000)

ISBN-10: 0-312-54988-1
ISBN-13: 978-0-312-54988-6

Preface

This new edition of *Worlds of History* offers affirmation of past success along with an opportunity to introduce some of the vast new scholarship that is bringing an ever receding past into sharper focus. The format, however, is the same that has worked to great acclaim in previous editions. Teaching introductory world history to college students for forty years has helped me appreciate three enduring truths that provide the framework for this book. The first is that any introductory history course must begin by engaging the students, as they sit before us in their remarkable diversity. The second is that the virtually infinite scope of the subject of world history can best be organized and presented topically and comparatively, thus addressing the interests of our students while respecting the integrity of the field. The third is that students need to learn to think historically, critically, and independently — goals that the study of history is ideally suited to realize. Adopters and reviewers have commented that this strategy has resulted in readings especially effective at piquing student interest and engaging students' minds. This new edition aims to maintain that high level of reader interest for today's students, who face an even greater number of calls on their attention. Accordingly, I have added controversial new studies (on, for instance, Judaism and Islam), a broader representation of new scholarship on sexuality, and a greater range of visual materials. The effort at making *Worlds of History* more accessible, however, has not dumbed it down. There are still more selections from the "great books," presented at greater length and with more annotation, than found elsewhere. I have also continued to carefully word selection introductions so that they cannot become an alternative to reading the source. Finally, I have continued to use the selections to show teachers and students how the study of history can not only teach broad trends and comparative experiences, but also develop what the Romans used to call "habits of mind" and what we today call "critical thinking skills."

The primary and secondary source selections in this reader address specific topics that I believe can impart a general understanding of world history while helping students develop critical thinking skills. The reader's format helps students (and instructors) make sense of the overwhelming richness and complexity of world history. As a framework, the reader has a **thematic and topical organization** that is also chronological, with each chapter focusing on a captivating topic within a particular time period. These topics are constructed to elucidate the major processes and themes most commonly taught in world history courses. Into these thematic chapters I've woven a **comparative approach**, examining two or more cultures at a time. In some chapters students can trace parallel developments in separate regions, such as the rise of ancient urban civilizations in Mesopotamia, Egypt, and Mexico in Volume One, or the advent of nationalism in Japan, India, and the Islamic world in Volume Two. In other cases students examine the enduring effects of contact and exchange between cultures, as in Volume One's chapter on Mongol and Viking raiding and settlements from the tenth to the fourteenth centuries, or Volume Two's chapter on the scientific revolution in Europe, the Ottoman Empire, the Americas, and Asia. To help students grapple with the diverse sources and cultures, a specific **critical thinking focus** in each chapter builds students' ability to analyze, synthesize, and interpret sources one step at a time.

A wealth of **pedagogical tools** helps students unlock the readings and hone their critical thinking skills. Each chapter begins with "**Historical Context**," an introduction to the chapter's topic that sets the stage for directed comparisons among the readings. A separate "**Thinking Historically**" section follows, which introduces a particular critical thinking skill—such as asking about author, audience, and agenda or distinguishing causes of change—that are designed to mine the chapter's selections. Headnotes preceding each selection provide additional context, while document-specific "Thinking Historically" paragraphs pose questions to encourage close analysis of the selections using the critical thinking skill introduced at the beginning of the chapter. **Explanatory gloss notes** and **pronunciation guides** throughout ensure comprehension of the readings. A set of "**Reflections**" that both summarizes and extends the chapter's lessons concludes each chapter.

To enrich the instructor's experience teaching with this reader, I have written an **instructor's resource manual** (*Editor's Notes for Worlds of History*). Available online at **bedfordstmartins.com/reilly/catalog** this manual provides the rationale for the selection and organization of the readings, suggestions for teaching with the documents, and information about additional resources, including films and Internet sites. In addition, all maps from the book are available in Make History at **bedfordstmartins.com/makehistory** where they can be downloaded for presentation.

■ NEW TO THIS EDITION

While I am continually testing selections in my own classroom, I appreciate input from readers and adopters, and I want to thank them for their many suggestions for exciting new chapters and selections. Having incorporated some of this feedback, I think those who have used the reader previously will find the fourth edition even more geographically and topically comprehensive, interesting, and accessible to students.

More than one-third of the new selections are on regions and topics from Latin America to Africa and on new theories on the Koran to women and science during the Enlightenment, which have allowed me to introduce fresh material into each volume. In addition, I have included five new chapters that explore the Chinese and Roman empires (Chapter 4); gender, sex, and love in the classical era (Chapter 5); the spread of Christianity, Buddhism, and Islam (Chapter 7); the Cold War and the Third World (Chapter 26); and the environment, population, and resources in the contemporary world (Chapter 27). With these new chapters I have also included five new "Thinking Historically" exercises: "Distinguishing Ideas from Actions and Understanding Their Relationship"; "Asking about Author, Audience, and Agenda"; "Understanding Continuity and Change"; "Finding a Point of View in Word Selection"; and "Evaluating Arguments."

Another exciting change to this edition is the inclusion of 20 percent more maps and images with more visuals acting as "documents," thereby increasing the reader's emphasis on the importance of nonwritten sources as historical evidence. Nine chapters now incorporate visual evidence, including Egyptian wall paintings in Chapter 2, Fayum portraits of women in Chapter 5, images of the Black Death in Chapter 12, new illustrations of medieval cities in Chapters 13, images of humans and the environment in Chapter 14, contrasting views of Amerindians and new illustrations of cross-Atlantic slavery in Chapter 16, new anatomical drawings on the Scientific Revolution in Chapter 19, Japanese images of Westernization in Chapter 23, and World War I propaganda posters, including new posters aimed at women on the home front, in Chapter 24.

Two more changes to this edition of *Worlds of History* have, I hope, made the reader text more accessible. First, I have expanded the popular explanatory gloss notes so students may read the documents with deeper appreciation. Second, due to favorable reception in the third edition, I have included more terms in the running pronunciation guide at the base of the page. This sounds out difficult-to-pronounce terms and names and should help students discuss the sources with greater confidence.

I am not a believer in change for its own sake; when I have a successful way of teaching a subject, I am not disposed to jettison it for something new. Consequently, many of my most satisfying changes are incremental: a better translation of a document, the addition of a newly discovered source, or additional questions to further inspire critical thinking. In some cases I have been able to further edit a useful source, retaining its muscle, but providing room for a precious new find. I begin each round of revision with the conviction that the book is already as good as it can get. And I end each round with the surprising discovery that it is much better than it was.

■ ACKNOWLEDGMENTS

A book like this cannot be written without the help and advice of a vast army of colleagues and friends. I consider myself enormously fortunate to have met and known such a large group of gifted and generous scholars. Some were especially helpful in the preparation of this new edition. They include W. Nathan Alexander, Troy University; Stanley Arnold, Northern Illinois University; Alan Barenberg, Columbus State University; Richard Bowler, Salisbury University; Michael Cardinal, Heartland Community College; Michael Clinton, Gwynedd-Mercy College; William D. Coleman, McMaster University; Clayton J. Drees, Virginia Wesleyan College; Paul Gillingham, University of North Carolina–Wilmington; Steven A. Glazer, Graceland University; Dale Griepenstroh, Chula Vista High School (CA); Gillian Hendershot, Grand Valley State University; Marianne Holdzkom, Southern Polytechnic State University; Megan Jones, University of Delaware; Dana Lightfoot, University of Texas at El Paso; Edward H. Lykens, Middle Tennessee State University; Eric Martin, Lewis-Clark State College; Thomas W. Maulucci, Jr., American International College; Eben Miller, Southern Maine Community College; Peter A. Ngwafu, Albany State University; Neal Palmer, Christian Brothers University; Elizabeth Peifer, Auburn University–Montgomery; Thomas Porter, North Carolina A&T State University; Dana Rabin, University of Illinois; Linda Rodish, Mesquite High School (AZ); Mary Louise Shell, Etowah High School (GA); George D. Sussman, LaGuardia Community College; Sarah Trembanis, Immaculata University; Jason Treter, National University; Julie Turner, Miami University of Ohio; Gary Vargas, Mt. San Jacinto College; Alfred Martin Wainwright, The University of Akron; Andrew Walzer, Los Angeles City College; Krista Webb, Woodstock High School (GA); James Whidden, Acadia University; Andrew Kier Wise, Daemen College; and Jack Zevin, Queens College.

Over the years I have benefited from the suggestions of innumerable friends and fellow world historians. Among them: Michael Adas, Rutgers University; Jerry Bentley, University of Hawai'i; David Berry, Essex County Community College; Edmund (Terry) Burke III, University of California–Santa Cruz; Catherine Clay, Shippensburg University; the late Philip Curtin, Johns Hopkins University; S. Ross Doughty, Ursinus College; Ross Dunn, San Diego State University; Marc Gilbert, Hawai'i Pacific University; Steve Gosch, University of Wisconsin–Eau Claire; Gregory Guzman, Bradley University; Brock Haussamen, Raritan Valley College; Allen Howard, Rutgers University; Sarah Hughes, Shippensburg University; Karen Jolly, University of Hawai'i; Stephen Kaufman, Raritan Valley College; Maghan Keita, Villanova University; Craig Lockard, University of Wisconsin–Green Bay; Pat Manning, University of Pittsburgh; Adam McKeown, Columbia University; John McNeill, Georgetown University; William H. McNeill, University of Chicago;

Gyan Prakash, Princeton University; Lauren Ristvet, University of Pennsylvania; Robert Rosen, University of California–Los Angeles; Heidi Roupp, Aspen High School; John Russell-Wood, Johns Hopkins University; Lynda Shaffer, Tufts University; Ira Spar, Ramapo College; Robert Strayer, California State University–Monterey Bay; Robert Tignor, Princeton University; and John Voll, Georgetown University.

I also want to thank the people at Bedford/St. Martin's. Joan Feinberg and Denise Wydra remained involved and helpful throughout, as did Mary Dougherty, Traci Mueller Crowell, and Jane Knetzger. Adrianne Hiltz provided invaluable help in reviewing the previous edition, and Jennifer Jovin coordinated the development of the instructor's manual, ensured the book's maps all appeared online in *Make History*, and provided invaluable behind-the-scenes support for the reader. I want to thank my production editor, Katherine Caruana, for overseeing the entire production process of design, copyediting, and page composition. I would also like to thank Susan Zorn for copyediting, Billy Boardman for the cover design, Kim Cevoli for designing promotional materials, and Jenna Bookin Barry for expertly marketing the book. Finally, my deepest appreciation goes to Senior Editor Louise Townsend for her editorial guidance through the first half of the revision and Senior Editor Heidi Hood for completing the process, challenging everything again, and forcing me to make it a better book than I had any right to expect.

None of this would have been possible if I had not been blessed in my own introduction to history and critical thinking at Rutgers in the 1960s with teachers I still aspire to emulate. Eugene Meehan taught me how to think and showed me that I could. Traian Stoianovich introduced me to the world and an endless range of historical inquiry. Warren Susman lit up a room with more life than I ever knew existed. Donald Weinstein guided me as a young teaching assistant to listen to students and talk with them rather than at them. And Peter Stearns showed me how important and exciting it could be to understand history by making comparisons. I dedicate this book to them.

Finally, I want to thank my own institution, Raritan Valley College, for nurturing my career, allowing me to teach whatever I wanted, and entrusting me with some of the best students one could encounter anywhere. I could not ask for anything more. Except, of course, a loving wife like Pearl.

Kevin Reilly

Introduction

Throughout both volumes of this reader you have a lesson in world history, which deals with a particular historical period and topic. Some of the topics are narrow and specific, covering events such as the Black Death and World War I in detail, while others are broad and general, such as the spread of universal religions and globalization.

As you learn about historical periods and topics, you will also be learning to explore history by analyzing primary and secondary sources systematically. The "Thinking Historically" exercises in each chapter encourage habits of mind that I associate with my own study of history. They are not necessarily intended to turn you into historians but, rather, to give you skills that will help you in all of your college courses and throughout your life. For example, the first chapter leads you to become more perceptive about time, the passage of time, measuring time, and the time between events, all of which are useful throughout life. Similarly, a number of chapters help you in various ways to distinguish between fact and opinion—an ability as necessary for work, on a jury, in the voting booth, and in discussions with friends as it is in the study of history.

World history is nothing less than everything ever done or imagined, so we cannot possibly cover it all; we are forced to choose among different places and times in our study of the global past. Our choices do include some particular moments in time, like the one in 111 c.e. in the first half of this reader, when the Roman governor of Bithynia consulted Emperor Trajan about proper treatment of Christians, but our attention will be directed toward much longer periods as well. And while we will visit particular places in time like Imperial Rome in the second century or Africa in the nineteenth century, typically we will study more than one place at a time by using a comparative approach.

Comparisons can be enormously useful in studying world history. When we compare cities globally in the religious origins of Christians and Buddhists, the raiding and trading of Vikings and Mongols, the scientific revolution in Europe and Japan, and the Cold War in Cuba and Afghanistan, we learn about the general and the specific at the same time. My hope is that by comparing some of the various worlds of history, a deeper and more nuanced understanding of our global past will emerge. With that understanding, we are better equipped to make sense of the world today and to confront whatever the future holds.

Contents

17. State and Religion: Asian, Islamic, and Christian States, 1500–1800 636

In this chapter, we view the relationship between religion and political authority through the prism of Chinese, Japanese, South Asian, and Western experience in the early modern period. By examining the competing and sometimes cooperating dynamics between church and state in the past, we explore the history of an issue much debated in our own time and gain new insights on church-state relations today.

20. Enlightenment and Revolution: Europe, the Americas, and India, 1650–1850 752

> The eighteenth-century Enlightenment applied scientific reason to politics, but reason meant different things to different people and societies. What were the goals of the political revolutions produced by the Enlightenment? A close reading of the period texts reveals disagreement and shared dreams.

21. Capitalism and the Industrial Revolution: Europe and the World, 1750–1900 785

Modern society has been shaped dramatically by capitalism and the industrial revolution, but these two forces are not the same. Which one is principally responsible for the creation of our modern world: the economic system of the market or the technology of the industrial revolution? Distinguishing different "causes" allows us to gauge their relative effects and legacies.

22. Colonized and Colonizers: Europeans in Africa and Asia, 1850–1930 826

Colonialism resulted in a world divided between the colonized and the colonizers, a world in which people's identities were defined by their power relationships with others who looked and often spoke differently.

The meeting of strangers and their forced adjustment to predefined roles inspired a number of great literary works that we look to in this chapter for historical guidance.

23. Westernization and Nationalism: Japan, India, Turkey, and Egypt, 1860–1950 868

Western colonialism elicited two conflicting responses among the colonized — rejection and imitation. Sometimes both cohered in the same individual or movement. Exploring this tension through the visual and written sources in this chapter reveals much about the historical process and helps us appreciate the struggles of peoples torn between different ideals.

How could governments, armies, and ordinary people commit such un-speakable acts? How can we recognize the unbelievable and understand the inexcusable?

26. The Cold War and the Third World: China, Vietnam, Cuba, and Afghanistan, 1945–1989 981

The Cold War was not only a conflict between the United States and the Soviet Union in which both superpowers avoided direct military confron-tation; it was also a series of hot wars and propaganda battles, often played out with surrogates, for the creation of a new "postcolonial" world order and the control of an emerging "Third World." A war of words is a good place to look for hidden political meanings.

27. Resources and Environment: The Case of Water, 1945 to the Present 1019

As world population almost tripled since World War II, the carrying capacity of the planet remained the same. New technologies, consumer goods, and material aspirations multiplied the stress of numbers. Would there be enough essential resources or serious shortages? Without neglecting obvious vital resources like oil, we focus our attention on the fundamental needs of food and water. Different arguments have been made about the impact of population, economic, and political forces in causing the pressures we face. We need to evaluate these arguments in order to determine what can be done.

28. Globalization, 1960 to the Present 1050

Globalization is a word with many meanings and a process with many causes. What are the forces most responsible for the shrinking of the world into one global community? Do the forces of globalization unite or divide us? Do they impoverish or enrich us? We undertake the study of process to answer these questions.

LIST OF MAPS

15

Overseas Expansion in the Early Modern Period

China and Europe, 1400–1600

■ HISTORICAL CONTEXT

Between 1400 and 1500, the balance between Chinese and European sea power changed drastically. Before 1434, Chinese shipbuilding was the envy of the world. Chinese ships were larger, more numerous, safer, and better outfitted than European ships. The Chinese navy made frequent trips through the South China Sea to the Spice Islands, through the Indian Ocean, and as far as East Africa and the Persian Gulf (see Map 15.1). Every island, port, and kingdom along the route was integrated into the Chinese system of tributaries. Goods were exchanged, marriages arranged, and princes taken to visit the Chinese emperor.

In the second half of the fifteenth century, the Chinese navy virtually disappeared. At the same time, the Portuguese began a series of explorations down the coast of Africa and into the Atlantic Ocean. In 1434 Portuguese ships rounded the treacherous Cape Bojador, just south of Morocco, and in 1488 Bartolomeu Dias rounded the Cape of Good Hope. Vasco da Gama sailed into the Indian Ocean, arriving in Calicut the following year. And in 1500 a fortuitous landfall in Brazil by Pedro Cabral gave the Portuguese a claim from the western Atlantic to the Indian Ocean. By 1512 Portuguese ships had reached the Bandas and Moluccas — the Spice Islands of what is today eastern Indonesia.

Beginning in 1492, after the defeat of the Moors (Muslims) and the voyages of Columbus, the Spanish claimed most of the Western Hemisphere until challenged by the Dutch, English, and French. European control in the Americas penetrated far deeper than in Asia, where it was limited to enclaves on the coast and where European nations were in an almost perpetual state of war with each other. Taken together, the nations of Western Europe dominated the seas of the world after 1500 (see Map 15.2).

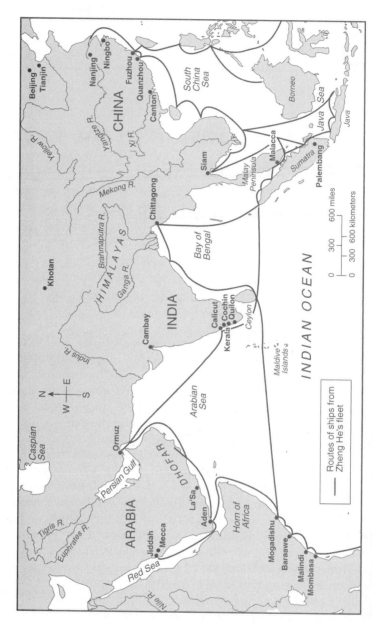

Map 15.1 Chinese Naval Expeditions, 1405–1433.

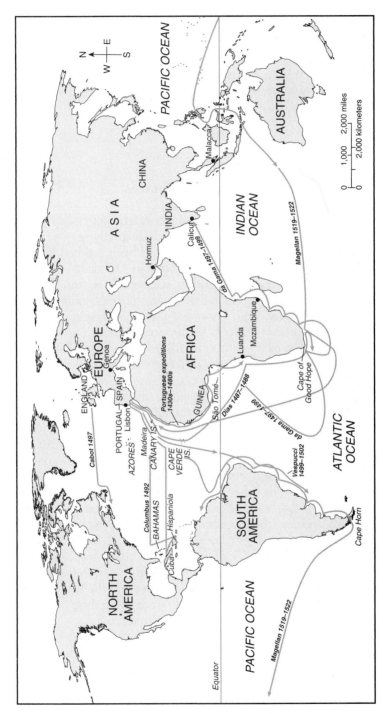

Map 15.2 European Overseas Exploration, 1430s–1530s.

What accounts for the different fortunes of China and Europe in the fifteenth century? Were the decline of China and the rise of Europe inevitable? Probably no objective observer of the time would have thought so. In what ways were the expansions of China and Europe similar? In what ways were they different? Think about these questions as you reflect on the readings in this chapter.

■ THINKING HISTORICALLY

Reading Primary and Secondary Sources

This chapter contains both primary and secondary sources. *Primary sources* are actual pieces of the past and include anything — art, letters, essays, and so on — from the historical period being studied. If a future historian were to study and research students in American colleges at the beginning of the twenty-first century, some primary sources might include diaries, letters, cartoons, music videos, posters, paintings, e-mail messages, blogs and Web sites, class notes, school newspapers, tests, and official and unofficial records. *Secondary sources* are usually books and articles *about* the past — interpretations of the past. These sources are "secondary" because they must be based on primary sources; therefore, a history written after an event occurs is a secondary source.

In your studies, you will be expected to distinguish primary from secondary sources. A quick glance at the introductions to this chapter's selections tells you that the first article is written by a modern journalist in 1999 and the last is written by a modern environmentalist, taken from his book published in 1991. These are both secondary sources since they are modern interpretations of the past rather than documents from the past. The other selections in this chapter are such documents, or primary sources. The second selection is an account of the great fifteenth-century Chinese admiral Zheng He's* voyage to Southeast Asia written by someone who was there, Ma Huan, a member of the crew. The third selection is similarly a participant's account of the voyage of the first European fleet to reach South Asia, that of Vasco da Gama at the end of the fifteenth century. These and the fourth selection, a letter penned by Christopher Columbus more than five hundred years ago, are firsthand accounts of worlds long past.

Having determined whether selections are primary or secondary sources, we also explore some of the subtle complexities that are overlooked by such designations.

---

* jung HUH

Note: Pronunciations of difficult-to-pronounce terms will be given throughout the book. The emphasis goes on the syllable appearing in all capitals. [Ed.]

NICHOLAS D. KRISTOF

1492: The Prequel

Almost a century before Columbus, Zheng He, a eunuch admiral in the
court, sailed from China with three hundred ships and twenty-eight
thousand men. His fleet stopped at ports in the Indian Ocean and
journeyed as far as the east coast of Africa. Nicholas Kristof travels to
the East African island of Pate to find traces of these fifteenth-century
Chinese sailors. What types of evidence is he seeking? What does
Kristof's brief history suggest about China, India, and Europe and their
roles in the making of the modern world? How would today's world be
different if Chinese ships had reached the Western Hemisphere before
Columbus?

THINKING HISTORICALLY

In his secondary account of Zheng He's voyages, Kristof alludes to certain
possible primary sources. What sorts of primary sources are available to
historians interested in reconstructing the life and voyages of Zheng He?
What primary sources are not available? Why are they not available? Has
Kristof's recent voyage led to the discovery of a new primary source?

From the sea, the tiny East African island of Pate, just off the Kenyan
coast, looks much as it must have in the 15th century: an impenetrable
shore of endless mangrove trees. As my little boat bounced along the
waves in the gray dawn, I could see no antennae or buildings or even
gaps where trees had been cut down, no sign of human habitation, nothing but a dense and mysterious jungle.

The boatman drew as close as he could to a narrow black-sand
beach, and I splashed ashore. My local Swahili interpreter led the way
through the forest, along a winding trail scattered with mangoes, co-
conuts, and occasional seashells deposited by high tides. The tropical
sun was firmly overhead when we finally came upon a village of stone
houses with thatched roofs, its dirt paths sheltered by palm trees. The
village's inhabitants, much lighter-skinned than people on the Kenyan
mainland, emerged barefoot to stare at me with the same curiosity with
which I was studying them. These were people I had come halfway
around the world to see, in the hope of solving an ancient historical
puzzle.

Source: Nicholas D. Kristof, "1492: The Prequel," *New York Times Magazine*, June 6, 1999,
6, 80:1.

"Tell me," I asked the first group I encountered, "where did the people here come from? Long ago, did foreign sailors ever settle here?" The answer was a series of shrugs. "I've never heard about that," one said. "You'll have to ask the elders."

I tried several old men and women without success. Finally the villagers led me to the patriarch of the village, Bwana Mkuu Al-Bauri, the keeper of oral traditions. He was a frail old man with gray stubble on his cheeks, head, and chest. He wore a yellow sarong around his waist; his ribs pressed through the taut skin on his bare torso. Al-Bauri hobbled out of his bed, resting on a cane and the arm of a grandson. He claimed to be 121 years old; a pineapple-size tumor jutted from the left side of his chest.

"I know this from my grandfather, who himself was the keeper of history here," the patriarch told me in an unexpectedly clear voice. "Many, many years ago, there was a ship from China that wrecked on the rocks off the coast near here. The sailors swam ashore near the village of Shanga — my ancestors were there and saw it themselves.

"The Chinese were visitors, so we helped those Chinese men and gave them food and shelter, and then they married our women. Although they do not live in this village, I believe their descendants still can be found somewhere else on this island."

I almost felt like hugging Bwana Al-Bauri. For months I had been poking around obscure documents and research reports, trying to track down a legend of an ancient Chinese shipwreck that had led to a settlement on the African coast. My interest arose from a fascination with what to me is a central enigma of the millennium: Why did the West triumph over the East?

For most of the last several thousand years, it would have seemed far likelier that Chinese or Indians, not Europeans, would dominate the world by the year 2000, and that America and Australia would be settled by Chinese rather than by the inhabitants of a backward island called Britain. The reversal of fortunes of East and West strikes me as the biggest news story of the millennium, and one of its most unexpected as well.

As a resident of Asia for most of the past thirteen years, I've been searching for an explanation. It has always seemed to me that the turning point came in the early 1400s, when Admiral Zheng He sailed from China to conquer the world. Zheng He (pronounced JUNG HUH) was an improbable commander of a great Chinese fleet, in that he was a Muslim from a rebel family and had been seized by the Chinese Army when he was still a boy. Like many other prisoners of the time, he was castrated, his sexual organs completely hacked off, a process that killed many of those who suffered it. But he was a brilliant and tenacious boy who grew up to be physically imposing. A natural leader, he had the good fortune to be assigned, as a houseboy, to the household of a great prince, Zhu Di.

In time, the prince and Zheng He grew close, and they conspired to overthrow the prince's nephew, the Emperor of China. With Zheng He as one of the prince's military commanders, the revolt succeeded and the prince became China's Yongle Emperor. One of the emperor's first acts (after torturing to death those who had opposed him) was to reward Zheng He with the command of a great fleet that was to sail off and assert China's pre-eminence in the world.

Between 1405 and 1433, Zheng He led seven major expeditions, commanding the largest armada the world would see for the next five centuries. Not until World War I did the West mount anything comparable. Zheng He's fleet included twenty-eight thousand sailors on three hundred ships, the longest of which were four hundred feet. By comparison, Columbus in 1492 had ninety sailors on three ships, the biggest of which was eighty-five feet long. Zheng He's ships also had advanced design elements that would not be introduced in Europe for another 350 years, including balanced rudders and watertight bulwark compartments.

The sophistication of Zheng He's fleet underscores just how far ahead of the West the East once was. Indeed, except for the period of the Roman Empire, China had been wealthier, more advanced, and more cosmopolitan than any place in Europe for several thousand years. Hangzhou, for example, had a population in excess of a million during the time it was China's capital (in the twelfth century), and records suggest that as early as the seventh century, the city of Guangzhou had 200,000 foreign residents: Arabs, Persians, Malays, Indians, Africans, and Turks. By contrast, the largest city in Europe in 1400 was probably Paris, with a total population of slightly more than 100,000.

A half-century before Columbus, Zheng He had reached East Africa and learned about Europe from Arab traders. The Chinese could easily have continued around the Cape of Good Hope and established direct trade with Europe. But as they saw it, Europe was a backward region, and China had little interest in the wood, beads, and wine Europe had to trade. Africa had what China wanted — ivory, medicines, spices, exotic woods, even specimens of native wildlife.

In Zheng He's time, China and India together accounted for more than half of the world's gross national product, as they have for most of human history. Even as recently as 1820, China accounted for 29 percent of the global economy and India another 16 percent, according to the calculations of Angus Maddison, a leading British economic historian.

Asia's retreat into relative isolation after the expeditions of Zheng He amounted to a catastrophic missed opportunity, one that laid the groundwork for the rise of Europe and, eventually, America. Westerners often attribute their economic advantage today to the intelligence, democratic habits, or hard work of their forebears, but a more important reason may well have been the folly of fifteenth-century Chinese rulers. That is why I came to be fascinated with Zheng He and set out earlier this year to retrace his journeys. I wanted to see what legacy, if any, remained of his achievement, and to figure out why his travels did not remake the world in the way that Columbus's did.

Zheng He lived in Nanjing, the old capital, where I arrived one day in February. Nanjing is a grimy metropolis on the Yangtze River in the heart of China. It has been five centuries since Zheng He's death, and his marks on the city have grown faint. The shipyards that built his fleet are still busy, and the courtyard of what had been his splendid seventy-two-room mansion is now the Zheng He Memorial Park, where children roller-skate and old couples totter around for exercise. But though the park has a small Zheng He museum, it was closed — for renovation, a caretaker told me, though he knew of no plans to reopen it.

I'd heard that Zheng He's tomb is on a hillside outside the city, and I set out to find it. It wasn't long before the road petered out, from asphalt to gravel to dirt to nothing. No tomb was in sight, so I approached an old man weeding a vegetable garden behind his house. Tang Yiming, seventy-two, was still lithe and strong. His hair was gray and ragged where he had cut it himself, disastrously, in front of a mirror. Evidently lonely, he was delighted to talk, and offered to show me the path to the tomb. As we walked, I mentioned that I had read that there used to be an old Ming Dynasty tablet on Zheng He's grave.

"Oh, yeah, the old tablet," he said nonchalantly. "When I was a boy, there was a Ming Dynasty tablet here. When it disappeared, the Government offered a huge reward to anyone who would return it — a reward big enough to build a new house. Seemed like a lot of money. But the problem was that we couldn't give it back. People around here are poor. We'd smashed it up to use as building materials."

A second mystery concerned what, if anything, is actually buried in Zheng He's tomb, since he is believed to have died on his last voyage and been buried at sea. So I said in passing that I'd heard tell the tomb is empty, and let my voice trail off.

"Oh, there's nothing in there," Tang said, a bit sadly. "No bones, nothing. That's for sure."

"How do you know?"

"In 1962, people dug up the grave, looking for anything to sell. We dug up the ground to one and a half times the height of a man. But there was absolutely nothing in there. It's empty."

The absence of impressive monuments to Zheng He in China today should probably come as no surprise, since his achievement was ultimately renounced. Curiously, it is not in China but in Indonesia where his memory has been most actively kept alive. Zheng He's expeditions led directly to the wave of Chinese immigration to Southeast Asia, and in some countries he is regarded today as a deity. In the Indonesia city of Semarang, for example, there is a large temple honoring Zheng He, located near a cave where he once nursed a sick friend. Indonesians still pray to Zheng He for a cure or good luck.

Not so in his native land. Zheng He was viewed with deep suspicion by China's traditional elite, the Confucian scholars, who made sure to destroy the archives of his journey. Even so, it is possible to learn something about his story from Chinese sources — from imperial archives and even the memoirs of crewmen. The historical record makes clear, for example, that it was not some sudden impulse of extroversion that led to Zheng He's achievement. It grew, rather, out of a long sailing tradition. Chinese accounts suggest that in the fifth century a Chinese monk sailed to a mysterious "far east country" that sounds very much like Mayan Mexico, and Mayan art at that time suddenly began to include Buddhist symbols. By the thirteenth century, Chinese ships regularly traveled to India and occasionally to East Africa.

Zheng He's armada was far grander, of course, than anything that came before. His grandest vessels were the "treasure ships," 400 feet long and 160 feet wide, with nine masts raising red silk sails to the wind, as well as multiple decks and luxury cabins with balconies. His armada included supply ships to carry horses, troop transports, warships, patrol boats, and as many as twenty tankers to carry fresh water. The full contingent of 28,000 crew members included interpreters for Arabic and other languages, astrologers to forecast the weather, astronomers to study the stars, pharmacologists to collect medicinal plants, ship-repair specialists, doctors, and even two protocol officers to help organize official receptions.

In the aftermath of such an incredible undertaking, you somehow expect to find a deeper mark on Chinese history, a greater legacy. But perhaps the faintness of Zheng He's trace in contemporary China is itself a lesson. In the end, an explorer makes history but does not necessarily change it, for his impact depends less on the trail he blazes than on the willingness of others to follow. The daring of a great expedition ultimately is hostage to the national will of those who remain behind.

In February I traveled to Calicut, a port town in southwestern India that was (and still is) the pepper capital of the world. The evening I arrived, I went down to the beach in the center of town to look at the coastline where Zheng He once had berthed his ships. In the fourteenth and fifteenth centuries, Calicut was one of the world's great ports, known to the Chinese as "the great country of the Western ocean." In the early fifteenth century, the sight of Zheng He's fleet riding anchor in Calicut harbor symbolized the strength of the world's two greatest powers, China and India.

On this sultry evening, the beach, framed by long piers jutting out to sea, was crowded with young lovers and ice-cream vendors. Those piers are all that remain of the port of Calicut, and you can see at a glance that they are no longer usable. The following day I visited the port offices, musty with handwritten ledgers of ship visits dating back nearly a century. The administrator of the port, Captain E. G. Mohanan, explained matter-of-factly what had happened. "The piers got old and no proper maintenance was ever carried out," he said, as a ceiling fan whirred tiredly overhead. "By the time we thought of it, it was not economical to fix it up." So in 1989, trade was halted, and one of the great ports of the world became no port at all.

The disappearance of a great Chinese fleet from a great Indian port symbolized one of history's biggest lost opportunities — Asia's failure to dominate the second half of this millennium. So how did this happen?

While Zheng He was crossing the Indian Ocean, the Confucian scholar-officials who dominated the upper echelons of the Chinese Government were at political war with the eunuchs, a group they regarded as corrupt and immoral. The eunuchs' role at court involved looking after the concubines, but they also served as palace administrators, often doling out contracts in exchange for kickbacks. Partly as a result of their legendary greed, they promoted commerce. Unlike the scholars — who owed their position to their mastery of two thousand-year-old texts — the eunuchs, lacking any such roots in a classical past, were sometimes outward-looking and progressive. Indeed, one can argue that it was the virtuous, incorruptible scholars who in the mid-fifteenth century set China on its disastrous course.

After the Yongle Emperor died in 1424, China endured a series of brutal power struggles; a successor emperor died under suspicious circumstances and ultimately the scholars emerged triumphant. They ended the voyages of Zheng He's successors, halted construction of new ships, and imposed curbs on private shipping. To prevent any backsliding, they destroyed Zheng He's sailing records and, with the backing of the new emperor, set about dismantling China's navy.

By 1500 the Government had made it a capital offense to build a boat with more than two masts, and in 1525 the Government ordered the destruction of all oceangoing ships. The greatest navy in history, which a century earlier had 3,500 ships (by comparison, the United States Navy today has 324), had been extinguished, and China set a course for itself that would lead to poverty, defeat, and decline.

Still, it was not the outcome of a single power struggle in the 1440s that cost China its worldly influence. Historians offer a host of reasons for why Asia eventually lost its way economically and was late to industrialize; two and a half reasons seem most convincing.

The first is that Asia was simply not greedy enough. The dominant social ethos in ancient China was Confucianism and in India it was caste, with the result that the elites in both nations looked down their noses at business. Ancient China cared about many things — prestige, honor, culture, arts, education, ancestors, religion, filial piety — but making money came far down the list. Confucius had specifically declared that it was wrong for a man to make a distant voyage while his parents were alive, and he had condemned profit as the concern of "a little man." As it was, Zheng He's ships were built on such a grand scale and carried such lavish gifts to foreign leaders that the voyages were not the huge money spinners they could have been.

In contrast to Asia, Europe was consumed with greed. Portugal led the age of discovery in the fifteenth century largely because it wanted spices, a precious commodity; it was the hope of profits that drove its ships steadily farther down the African coast and eventually around the Horn to Asia. The profits of this trade could be vast: Magellan's crew once sold a cargo of twenty-six tons of cloves for ten thousand times the cost.

A second reason for Asia's economic stagnation is more difficult to articulate but has to do with what might be called a culture of complacency. China and India shared a tendency to look inward, a devotion to past ideals and methods, a respect for authority, and a suspicion of new ideas. David S. Landes, a Harvard economist, has written of ancient China's "intelligent xenophobia"; the former Indian Prime Minister Jawaharlal Nehru referred to the "petrification of classes" and the "static nature" of Indian society. These are all different ways of describing the same economic and intellectual complacency.

Chinese elites regarded their country as the "Middle Kingdom" and believed they had nothing to learn from barbarians abroad. India exhibited much of the same self-satisfaction. "Indians didn't go to Portugal not because they couldn't but because they didn't want to," mused M. P. Sridharan, a historian, as we sat talking on the porch of his home in Calicut.

The fifteenth-century Portuguese were the opposite. Because of its coastline and fishing industry, Portugal always looked to the sea, yet rivalries with Spain and other countries shut it out of the Mediterranean trade. So the only way for Portugal to get at the wealth of the East was by conquering the oceans.

The half reason is simply that China was a single nation while Europe was many. When the Confucian scholars reasserted control in Beijing and banned shipping, their policy mistake condemned all of China. In contrast, European countries committed economic suicide selectively. So when Portugal slipped into a quasi-Chinese mind-set in the sixteenth century, slaughtering Jews and burning heretics, and driving astronomers and scientists abroad, Holland and England were free to take up the slack.

When I first began researching Zheng He, I never thought I'd be traveling all the way to Africa to look for traces of his voyages. Then I came across a few intriguing references to the possibility of an ancient Chinese shipwreck that might have left some Chinese stranded on the island of Pate (pronounced PAH-tay). One was a skeptical reference in a scholarly journal, another was a casual conversation with a Kenyan I met a few years ago, and the third was the epilogue of Louise Levathes's wonderful 1994 book about China's maritime adventures, "When China Ruled the Seas." Levathes had traveled to Kenya and found people who believed they were descended from survivors of a Chinese shipwreck. So, on a whim and an expense account, I flew to Lamu, an island off northern Kenya, and hired a boat and an interpreter to go to Pate and see for myself.

Pate is off in its own world, without electricity or roads or vehicles. Mostly jungle, it has been shielded from the twentieth century largely because it is accessible from the Kenyan mainland only by taking a boat through a narrow tidal channel that is passable only at high tide. Initially I was disappointed by what I found there. In the first villages I visited, I saw people who were light-skinned and had hair that was not tightly curled, but they could have been part Arab or European rather than part Chinese. The remote villages of Chundwa and Faza were more promising, for there I found people whose eyes, hair, and complexion hinted at Asian ancestry, though their background was ambiguous.

And then on a still and sweltering afternoon I strolled through the coconut palms into the village of Siyu, where I met a fisherman in his forties named Abdullah Mohammed Badui. I stopped and stared at the man in astonishment, for he had light skin and narrow eyes. Fortunately, he was as rude as I was, and we stared at each other in mutual surprise before venturing a word. Eventually I asked him about his background and appearance.

"I am in the Famao clan," he said. "There are fifty or one hundred of us Famao left here. Legend has it that we are descended from Chinese and others.

"A Chinese ship was coming along and it hit rocks and wrecked," Badui continued. "The sailors swam ashore to the village that we now call Shanga, and they married the local women, and that is why we Famao look so different."

Another Famao, with the same light complexion and vaguely Asian features, approached to listen. His name was Athman Mohammed Mzee, and he, too, told of hearing of the Chinese shipwreck from the elders. He volunteered an intriguing detail: The Africans had given giraffes to the Chinese.

Salim Bonaheri, a fifty-five-year-old Famao man I met the next day, proudly declared, "My ancestors were Chinese or Vietnamese or something like that." I asked how they had got to Pate.

"I don't know," Bonaheri said with a shrug. Most of my conversations were like that, intriguing but frustrating dead ends. I was surrounded by people whose appearance seemed tantalizingly Asian, but who had only the vaguest notions of why that might be. I kept at it, though, and eventually found people like Khalifa Mohammed Omar, a fifty-five-year-old Famao fisherman who looked somewhat Chinese and who also clearly remembered the stories passed down by his grandfather. From him and others, a tale emerged.

Countless generations ago, they said, Chinese sailors traded with local African kings. The local kings gave them giraffes to take back to China. One of the Chinese ships struck rocks off the eastern coast of Pate, and the sailors swam ashore, carrying with them porcelain and other goods from the ship. In time they married local women, converted to Islam, and named the village Shanga, after Shanghai. Later, fighting erupted among Pate's clans, Shanga was destroyed, and the Famao fled, some to the mainland, others to the village of Siyu.

Every time I heard the story about the giraffes my pulse began to race. Chinese records indicate that Zheng He had brought the first giraffes to China, a fact that is not widely known. The giraffe caused an enormous stir in China because it was believed to be the mythical qilin, or Chinese unicorn. It is difficult to imagine how African villagers on an island as remote as Pate would know about the giraffes unless the tale had been handed down to them by the Chinese sailors.

Chinese ceramics are found in many places along the east African coast, and their presence on Pate could be the result of purchases from Arab traders. But the porcelain on Pate was overwhelmingly concentrated among the Famao clan, which could mean that it had been inherited rather than purchased. I also visited some ancient Famao graves that looked less like traditional Kenyan graves than what the Chinese call "turtle-shell graves," with rounded tops.

Researchers have turned up other equally tantalizing clues. Craftsmen on Pate and the other islands of Lamu practice a kind of basket-weaving that is common in southern China but unknown on the Kenyan mainland. On Pate, drums are more often played in the Chinese than the African style, and the local dialect has a few words that may be Chinese in origin. More startling, in 1569 a Portuguese priest named Monclaro wrote that Pate had a flourishing silk-making industry — Pate, and no other place in the region. Elders in several villages on Pate confirmed to me that their island had produced silk until about half a century ago.

When I asked my boatman, Bakari Muhaji Ali, if he thought it was possible that a ship could have wrecked off the coast near Shanga, he laughed. "There are undersea rocks all over there," he said. "If you don't know exactly where you're going, you'll wreck your ship for sure."

If indeed there was a Chinese shipwreck off Pate, there is reason to think it happened in Zheng He's time. For if the shipwreck had predated him, surviving sailors would not have passed down stories of the giraffes. And if the wreck didn't occur until after Zheng He, its survivors could not have settled in Shanga, since British archeological digs indicate that the village was sacked, burned, and abandoned in about 1440 — very soon after Zheng He's last voyage.

Still, there is no hard proof for the shipwreck theory, and there are plenty of holes in it. No ancient Chinese characters have been found on tombs in Pate, no nautical instruments have ever turned up on the island, and there are no Chinese accounts of an African shipwreck. This last lacuna might be explained by the destruction of the fleet's records. Yet if one of Zheng He's ships did founder on the rocks off Pate, then why didn't some other ships in the fleet come to the sailors' rescue?

As I made my way back through the jungle for the return trip, I pondered the significance of what I'd seen on Pate. In the faces of the Famao, in those bits of pottery and tantalizing hints of Chinese culture, I felt as though I'd glimpsed the shadowy outlines of one of the greatest might-have-beens of the millennium now ending. I thought about the Columbian Exchange, the swap of animals, plants, genes, germs, weapons, and peoples that utterly remade both the New World and the Old, and I couldn't help wondering about another exchange — Zheng He's — that never took place, yet could have.

If ancient China had been greedier and more outward-looking, if other traders had followed in Zheng He's wake and then continued on, Asia might well have dominated Africa and even Europe. Chinese might have settled in not only Malaysia and Singapore, but also in East Africa, the Pacific Islands, even in America. Perhaps the Famao show us what the mestizos of such a world might have looked like, the children of a hybrid culture that was never born. What I'd glimpsed in Pate was the highwater mark of an Asian push that simply stopped — not for want of ships or know-how, but strictly for want of national will.

All this might seem fanciful, and yet in Zheng He's time the prospect of a New World settled by the Spanish or English would have seemed infinitely more remote than a New World made by the Chinese. How different would history have been had Zheng He continued on to America? The mind rebels; the ramifications are almost too overwhelming to contemplate. So consider just one: This magazine would have been published in Chinese.

2

MA HUAN

The Overall Survey of the Ocean's Shores

The voyages of Zheng He were well documented at the time. In addition to twenty to thirty thousand crewmen on the three-hundred-ship fleet of the first voyage, the admiral included scientists, artists, and other specialists to record the voyage. Most of these primary sources are lost, but the notes of three voyages by one crew member, Ma Huan, a Muslim carpenter and translator, have survived in his book, *The Overall Survey of the Ocean's Shores*. Ma Huan organized his "Overall Survey" by countries. This brief reading includes Ma Huan's account

Source: Ma Huan, Ying Lai Sheng-Lan, "The Overall Survey of the Ocean's Shores" [1433], ed. and trans. Feng Ch'eng Chun with an introduction by J. V. G. Mills © Hakluyt Society, 1970. Reprinted: (Bangkok: The White Lotus Press, 1979), 102–9, 113–14.

of the kingdom of Siam (modern Thailand) and part of his account of Malacca, a town on the Malay Peninsula that had only recently become an important port and the capital of a Muslim sultanate. What does this selection tell you about the purposes and operation of the Chinese expeditions? How do you think people in these countries would have responded to the Chinese?

THINKING HISTORICALLY

Most of the "Overall Survey" is systematic in presentation, giving an outline for each country. This excerpt departs somewhat from that model to provide more insight into Ma Huan as an author. What do you think of him as author and observer? How reliable does he seem? What other primary sources would you like to have to test Ma Huan?

The Country of Hsien Lo

[Siam, Thailand]

Travelling from Chan city[1] towards the south-west[2] for seven days and nights with a fair wind, the ship comes to the estuary at New Strait Tower[3] and enters the anchorage; then you reach the capital.

The country is a thousand *li* in circumference, the outer mountains [being] steep and rugged, [and] the inner land wet and swampy. The soil is barren and little of it is suitable for cultivation.[4] The climate varies — sometimes cold, sometimes hot.

The house in which the king resides is rather elegant, neat, and clean.[5] The houses of the populace are constructed in storeyed form; in the upper [part of the house] they do not join planks together [to make a floor], but they use the wood of the areca-palm, which they cleave into strips resembling bamboo splits; [these strips] are laid close together and bound very securely with rattans; on [this platform] they spread rattan mats and bamboo matting, and on these they do all their sitting, sleeping, eating, and resting.

---

[1] Champa, Central Vietnam. . . .

[2] This direction is most misleading, since, according to the sailing instructions, Chinese ships sailed south, then south-west, then north-west, then north.

[3] . . . The sailing directions indicate that the estuary in question was that of Maenam Mae Klong (Meklong river), about 38 miles west of Maenam Chao Phraya (Bangkok river).

[4] . . . Ma Huan is almost certainly wrong; in contrast, Fei Hsin says that the fields were fertile. Annual floods covert the central region into a very fertile plain. . . .

[5] The capital was then at Ayutthaya, about 35 miles north of the modern Bangkok on the Maenam Chao Phraya. The royal palace, built by King Ramadhipati (Rama Thibodi) in 1350, is to a great extent in ruins. In Ma Huan's time the rulers were Int'araja (1408–24) and Boromoraja II (1424–48). . . .

As to the king's dress: he uses a white cloth to wind round his head; on the upper [part of his body] he wears no garment; [and] round the lower [part he wears] a silk-embroidered kerchief, adding a waist-band of brocaded silk-gauze. When going about he mounts an elephant or else rides in a sedan-chair, while a man holds [over him] a gold-handled umbrella made of *chiao-chang* leaves,[6] [which is] very elegant. The king is a man of the So-li race,[7] and a firm believer in the Buddhist[8] religion.

In this country the people who become priests or become nuns are exceedingly numerous; the habit of the priests and nuns is somewhat the same as in the Central Country;[9] and they, too, live in nunneries and monasteries, fasting and doing penance.

It is their custom that all affairs are managed by their wives; both the king of the country and the common people, if they have matters which require thought and deliberation — punishments light and heavy, all trading transactions great and small — they all follow the decisions of their wives, [for] the mental capacity of the wives certainly exceeds that of the men.

If a married woman is very intimate with one of our men from the Central Country, wine and food are provided, and they drink and sit and sleep together. The husband is quite calm and takes no exception to it; indeed he says "My wife is beautiful and the man from the Central Country is delighted with her." The men dress the hair in a chignon, and use a white head-cloth to bind round the head [and] on the body they wear a long gown. The women also pin up the hair in a chignon, and wear a long gown.

When a man has attained his twentieth year, they take the skin which surrounds the *membrum virile*, and with a fine knife shaped like [the leaf of] an onion they open it up and insert a dozen tin beads inside the skin; [then] they close it up and protect it with medicinal herbs. The man waits till the opening of the wound is healed; then he goes out and walks about. The [beads] look like a cluster of grapes. There is indeed a class of men who arrange this operation; they specialize in inserting and soldering these beads for people; [and] they do it as a profession.

If it is the king of the country or a great chief or a wealthy man [who has the operation], then they use gold to make hollow beads, inside which a grain of sand is placed, and they are inserted [in the *membrum virile*]; [when the man] walks about, they make a tinkling sound, and this is regarded as beautiful. The men who have no beads inserted are people of the lower classes. This is a most curious thing.

[6] . . . A waterproof matting made from the leaves of screw-pines.

[7] Probably Ma Huan means merely that the king was of Indian descent.

[8] . . . The people of Thailand received their religion, art, science, and writing originally from India. . . . Hinayana (Theravada) Buddhism was accepted as the national religion in the thirteenth century and was firmly established by the end of the fourteenth. . . .

[9] China. [Ed.]

When men and women marry, they first of all invite a Buddhist priest to escort the groom to the woman's family-house; and then they direct the Buddhist priest to take some of the maiden's virginal blood and dab it on the man's forehead; this [ceremony] is called *li shih*. After that the marriage is consummated. Three days later they again invite a Buddhist priest and the relatives and friends, and, bearing areca-nut and a decorated boat and other such things, they escort the husband and wife back to the man's family-house, where they prepare wine, play music, and entertain the relatives and friends.

As to their funeral-rites: whenever a man of wealth and standing dies, they take quicksilver and pour it inside the abdomen [of the corpse] and bury it; when one of the poorer classes dies, they carry the corpse to the wilds by the sea-side, and place it on the edge of the sand; subsequently golden-coloured birds as large as geese — more than thirty, or fifty, of them — gather in flight in the sky; they descend, take the flesh of the corpse, devour it completely, and fly away; [and] the people of the [dead man's] family weep over the bones which remain, then cast them away in the water and return home. They call this "bird-burial." They also invite a Buddhist priest to celebrate a mass, chant liturgies, and worship Buddha, and that is all.

When you travel something over two hundred *li*[10] to the north-west from the capital, there is a market-town called Upper Water,[11] whence you can go through into Yün nan [province] by a back-entrance. In this place there are five or six hundred families of foreigners; all kinds of foreign goods are for sale; red *ma-ssu-k'en-ti*[12] stones are sold in great numbers here; this stone is inferior to the red *ya-ku*, [and] its brightness resembles that of a pomegranate seed. When the treasure-ships of the Central Country come to Hsien Lo,[13] [our men] also take small boats and go to trade [at Upper Water].

The country produces yellow *su* incense, Lo-ho *su* incense, laka-wood, sinking incense, rose-wood, cardamoms, chaulmoogra seeds,[14] dragon's blood,[15] liana nodes,[16] sapan-wood, "flower tin,"[17] elephants'

---

[10] About 67 miles.

[11] . . . If Ma Huan's distance is roughly correct, this must be Lopburi, approximately 27 miles north of Ayutthaya. . . .

[12] A variegated, lusterless stone like garnet. [Ed.]

[13] Thailand.

[14] . . . The discovery of chaulmoogra oil for the treatment of leprosy had been made by the fourteenth century. . . .

[15] . . . Meaning "sap, resin, gum." Since the true dragon's blood was a product of the Arab countries, . . . Ma Huan probably refers to "false dragon's blood," and this, . . . was probably gum-kino, a red gum produced by the rosewood *Pterocarpus indicus*. However, Ma Huan may allude to another resin which today passes under the name of dragon's blood; this is obtained from palms of the genus *Daemonorhops* and certain other genera. . . .

[16] . . . Lianas or rattans are the stems of climbing plants of the genus *Calamus* and certain other genera. . . .

[17] . . . Might mean tin in certain forms used in trade. . . .

teeth, kingfishers' feathers, and other such things. This sapan-wood is as abundant as firewood, and for colour decidedly superior to the product of other countries. The unusual animals are white elephants, lions,[18] cats, and white mice. The varieties of vegetables are the same as in Chan city. For wines they have rice wine and coconut wine; both are distilled spirits; [and] the price is very cheap. Oxen, goats, fowls, ducks, and other such domestic animals — all these they have.

The language of the country somewhat resembles the local patois as pronounced in Kuang tung [province].[19] The customs of the people are noisy and licentious. They like to practise fighting on water, [and] their king constantly despatches his commanders to subject neighbouring countries.

In trading they employ cowries as money for current use; optionally, gold, silver, and copper coins may all be used; but the copper coins of the successive dynasties in the Central Country are not in use.

The king regularly sends chiefs who take sapan-wood, laka-wood, and other such valuable things, and bring them as tribute to the Central Country.

The Country of Man-La-Chia[20]

[malacca]

From Chan City[21] you go due south, and after travelling for eight days with a fair wind the ship comes to Lung ya strait; after entering the strait you travel west;[22] [and] you can reach [this place] in two days.

Formerly this place was not designated a "country"; [and] because the sea [hereabouts] was named "Five Islands," [the place] was in consequence named "Five Islands." There was no king of the country; [and] it was controlled only by a chief. This territory was subordinate to the jurisdiction of Hsien Lo; it paid an annual tribute of forty *liang*[23]

---

[18] If Ma Huan really means lions, they must have been imported from elsewhere. But, like Polo, he may have meant tigers.

[19] The Thai language has many characteristics similar to those of Chinese, and linguists classify it as belonging to the Chinese–Thai branch of the Sino-Tibetan family; the script, however, is aligned with early Mon or Khmer scripts of Indian origin. . . .

[20] . . . Malacca, port on the west coast of the Malay peninsula, 2° 12′ N, 102° 15′ E; in Ma Huan's time politically unimportant, but of considerable, and rapidly increasing, importance as an entrepôt of international trade, where for the first time the commerce of the world's major trade-route, between Venice and the Molucca islands, was concentrated in one central point according to a definite plan. . . .

[21] Champa; Central Vietnam.

[22] The true direction is north-west.

[23] The equivalent of 40 liang was 47.96 ounces troy weight. . . .

of gold; [and] if it were not [to pay], then Hsien Lo would send men to attack it.[24]

In the seventh year of the Yung-lo [period], [the cyclic year] *chi-ch'ou*, the Emperor ordered the principal envoy the grand eunuch Cheng Ho[25] and others to assume command [of the treasure-ships], and to take the imperial edicts and to bestow upon this chief two silver seals, a hat, a girdle and a robe. [Cheng Ho] set up a stone tablet and raised [the place] to a city; [and] it was subsequently called the "country of Man-la-chia."[26] Thereafter Hsien lo did not dare to invade it.[27]

The chief, having received the favour of being made king,[28] conducted his wife and son,[29] and went to the court at the capital[30] to return thanks and to present tribute of local products. The court also granted him a sea-going ship, so that he might return to his country and protect his land.

On the south-east of the country is the great sea; on the north-west the sea-shore adjoins the mountains. All is sandy, saltish land. The climate is hot by day, cold by night. The fields are infertile and the crops poor; [and] the people seldom practise agriculture.

There is one large river whose waters flow down past the front of the king's residence to enter the sea;[31] over the river the king has constructed a wooden bridge, on which are built more than twenty bridge-pavilions, [and] all the trading in every article takes place on this [bridge]. . . .

Whenever the treasure-ships of the Central Country arrived there, they at once erected a line of stockading, like a city-wall, and set up towers for the watch-drums at four gates; at night they had patrols of police carrying bells; inside, again, they erected a second stockade, like a small city-wall, [within which] they constructed warehouses

---

[24] Thailand still controlled the east coast of the Malay peninsula down to, and including, Singapore; it remained the inveterate enemy of Malacca.

[25] Zheng He in older Wade-Giles system. [Ed.]

[26] . . . On his third expedition, Cheng Ho would have reached Malacca in 1410, and he then raised the town in status to a *ch'eng*, "city."

[27] . . . Malacca did not finally repudiate its vassalage to Thailand until after 1488. . . . But Thailand still claimed suzerainty over the whole peninsula when the Portuguese captured Malacca in 1511, and the four northern states of Malaya, that is, Kelantan, Trengganu, Kedah, and Perlis, acknowledged the supremacy of Thailand until 1909. . . .

[28] The chief was the founder and first king of Malacca; in the *Ming shih* he is called "Pai-li-mi-su-la," that is, Permiçura (Parameswara); he took the title of Sultan Iskandar Shah . . . about 1413.

[29] Or "wives and sons"; the Chinese text is imprecise.

[30] They would have returned on the ship of Cheng Ho, who reached Nanking on 6 July 1411. . . .

[31] The Malacca river.

and granaries; [and] all the money and provisions were stored in them. The ships which had gone to various countries returned to this place and assembled; they marshalled the foreign goods and loaded them in the ships; [then] waited till the south wind was perfectly favourable. In the middle decade of the fifth moon they put to sea and returned home.[32]

Moreover, the king[33] of the country made a selection of local products, conducted his wife and son, brought his chiefs, boarded a ship and followed the treasure-ships;[34] [and] he attended at court [and] presented tribute.[35]

[32] In 1433 the fifth moon began on 19 May. . . . In May southerly winds become frequent in the central part of Malacca strait, and the south-west monsoon is considered to blow from June to September.

[33] In 1433 the king was Sri Maharaja (1424–44), second king of Malacca, son of the founder and first king of Malacca.

[34] The king did not reach Nanking till the autumn, and as Cheng Ho reached Peking on 22 July, the king must have followed in his own ship.

[35] . . . It was as part of a tribute-present from Malacca that spectacles were first introduced into China in 1410.

3

Journal of the First Voyage of Vasco da Gama

In 1497 the Portuguese seaman Vasco da Gama led a fleet of four ships around the southern tip of Africa into the Indian Ocean, which they reached the following year. He benefited from the experience of Bartolomeu Dias, who ten years before had negotiated the rough waters of the South African Cape. But Dias had returned to Portugal. Da Gama continued up the African coast and sailed across the Indian Ocean to the port of Calicut, the center of a kingdom that encompassed much of the modern state of Kerala in southwest India. What seem to have been the motives of Portugal and da Gama in sailing to South Asia? How were the Portuguese intentions similar to, and different from, those of China earlier in the century? How would you compare the preparation and behavior of Chinese and Portuguese crews? How would you explain the differences between Chinese and Portuguese voyages?

Source: *A Journal of the First Voyage of Vasco da Gama, 1497–1499*, trans. and ed. E. G. Ravenstein (London: Hakluyt Society, 1898), 48–59, 60–63.

THINKING HISTORICALLY

We do not know the identity of the author of this document. He was one of the officers or crewmen who sailed on this voyage, however, and many of their names are known to us. What indications do you have that they spanned a wide range of Portuguese society?

The fact that the author was a witness does not mean that he gets everything right. What does he miss? What might have caused him to be misled? Generally, primary sources get more things right than wrong. How do you know this is true for this selection? How do we determine where a primary source is reliable and where it is not?

Calicut

[*Arrival.*][1] That night[2] [May 20] we anchored two leagues from the city of Calicut, and we did so because our pilot mistook *Capua*,[3] a town at that place, for Calicut. Still further there is another town called *Pandarani*.[4] We anchored about a league and a half from the shore. After we were at anchor, four boats (*almadias*) approached us from the land, who asked of what nation we were. We told them, and they then pointed out Calicut to us.

On the following day [May 21] these same boats came again alongside, when the captain-major[5] sent one of the convicts[6] to Calicut, and those with whom he went took him to two Moors from Tunis,[7] who could speak Castilian and Genoese. The first greeting that he received was in these words: "May the Devil take thee! What brought you hither?" They asked what he sought so far away from home, and he told them that we came in search of Christians and of spices. They said: "Why does not the King of Castile, the King of France, or the Signoria of Venice send thither?" He said that the King of Portugal would not consent to their doing so, and they said he did the right thing. After this conversation they took him to their lodgings and gave him wheaten

---

[1] Brackets enclose editorial additions of translator, Ravenstein, unless otherwise indicated. [Ed.]

[2] Afternoon (*a tarde*), according to Glenn J. Ames, *Em Nome de Deus* (Leiden: Brill, 2009), 70. [Ed.]

[3] Kappatt, a village about 7 miles north of Calicut. [Ed.]

[4] About 14 miles north of Calicut. [Ed.]

[5] Da Gama. [Ed.]

[6] The crew included a number of "convict-exiles," men who had been convicted of a crime punishable by death who were pardoned by the king to sail as adventurers and live out their lives overseas. Da Gama wanted such people in his crew to create a permanent presence overseas. [Ed.]

[7] Likely Muslim exiles from Spain after the defeat of the last Muslim stronghold in Granada by Christians in 1492. [Ed.]

bread and honey. When he had eaten he returned to the ships, accompanied by one of the Moors, who was no sooner on board, than he said these words: "A lucky venture, a lucky venture! Plenty of rubies, plenty of emeralds! You owe great thanks to God, for having brought you to a country holding such riches!" We were greatly astonished to hear his talk, for we never expected to hear our language spoken so far away from Portugal.

[*A description of Calicut.*] The city of Calicut is inhabited by Christians.[8] They are of tawny complexion. Some of them have big beards and long hair, whilst others clip their hair short or shave the head, merely allowing a tuft to remain on the crown as a sign that they are Christians. They also wear moustaches. They pierce the ears and wear much gold in them. They go naked down to the waist, covering their lower extremities with very fine cotton stuffs. But it is only the most respectable who do this, for the others manage as best they are able.

The women of this country, as a rule, are ugly and of small stature. They wear many jewels of gold round the neck, numerous bracelets on their arms, and rings set with precious stones on their toes. All these people are well-disposed and apparently of mild temper. At first sight they seem covetous and ignorant.

[*A messenger sent to the King.*] When we arrived at Calicut the king was fifteen leagues away. The captain-major sent two men to him with a message, informing him that an ambassador had arrived from the King of Portugal with letters, and that if he desired it he would take them to where the king then was.

The king presented the bearers of this message with much fine cloth. He sent word to the captain-major bidding him welcome, saying that he was about to proceed to Calicut. As a matter of fact, he started at once with a large retinue.

[*At Anchor at Pandarani, May 27.*] A pilot accompanied our two men, with orders to take us to a place called Pandarani, below the place [Capua] where we anchored at first. At this time we were actually in front of the city of Calicut. We were told that the anchorage at the place to which we were to go was good, whilst at the place we were then it was bad, with a stony bottom, which was quite true; and, moreover, that it was customary for the ships which came to this country to anchor there for the sake of safety. We ourselves did not feel comfortable, and the captain-major had no sooner received this royal message than he ordered the sails to be set, and we departed. We did not, however, anchor as near the shore as the king's pilot desired.

---

[8] There were Christians in southern India, but the population was overwhelmingly Hindu. [Ed.]

When we were at anchor, a message arrived informing the captain-major that the king was already in the city. At the same time the king sent a *bale*,[9] with other men of distinction, to Pandarani, to conduct the captain-major to where the king awaited him. This *bale* is like an *alcaide*, and is always attended by two hundred men armed with swords and bucklers. As it was late when this message arrived, the captain-major deferred going.

[*Gama goes to Calicut.*] On the following morning, which was Monday, May 28th, the captain-major set out to speak to the king, and took with him thirteen men, of which I was one.[10] On landing, the captain-major was received by the *alcaide*, with whom were many men, armed and unarmed. The reception was friendly, as if the people were pleased to see us, though at first appearances looked threatening, for they carried naked swords in their hands. A palanquin[11] was provided for the captain-major, such as is used by men of distinction in that country, as also by some of the merchants, who pay something to the king for this privilege. The captain-major entered the palanquin, which was carried by six men by turns. Attended by all these people we took the road of Calicut, and came first to another town, called Capua. The captain-major was there deposited at the house of a man of rank, whilst we others were provided with food, consisting of rice, with much butter, and excellent boiled fish. The captain-major did not wish to eat, and as we had done so, we embarked on a river close by, which flows between the sea and the mainland, close to the coast. The two boats in which we embarked were lashed together, so that we were not separated. There were numerous other boats, all crowded with people. As to those who were on the banks I say nothing; their number was infinite, and they had all come to see us. We went up that river for about a league, and saw many large ships drawn up high and dry on its banks, for there is no port here.

When we disembarked, the captain-major once more entered his palanquin. The road was crowded with a countless multitude anxious to see us. Even the women came out of their houses with children in their arms and followed us.

[*A Christian Church.*][12] When we arrived [at Calicut] they took us to a large church, and this is what we saw: —

The body of the church is as large as a monastery, all built of hewn stone and covered with tiles. At the main entrance rises a pillar of bronze

---

[9] Governor. [Ed.]

[10] We know the names of about half of the thirteen, but not which of them is the author. [Ed.]

[11] An enclosed chair carried on poles front and rear. [Ed.]

[12] The translator, Ravenstein, who supplied this heading, added a note: "This 'church' was, of course, a pagoda or temple." [Ed.]

as high as a mast, on the top of which was perched a bird, apparently a cock.[13] In addition to this, there was another pillar as high as a man, and very stout. In the center of the body of the church rose a chapel, all built of hewn stone, with a bronze door sufficiently wide for a man to pass, and stone steps leading up to it. Within this sanctuary stood a small image which they said represented Our Lady.[14] Along the walls, by the main entrance, hung seven small bells. In this church the captain-major said his prayers, and we with him.[15]

We did not go within the chapel, for it is the custom that only certain servants of the church, called *quafees*,[16] should enter. These *quafees* wore some threads passing over the left shoulder and under the right arm, in the same manner as our deacons wear the stole. They threw holy water over us, and gave us some white earth,[17] which the Christians of this country are in the habit of putting on their foreheads, breasts, around the neck, and on the forearms. They threw holy water upon the captain-major and gave him some of the earth, which he gave in charge of someone, giving them to understand that he would put it on later.[18]

Many other saints were painted on the walls of the church, wearing crowns. They were painted variously, with teeth protruding an inch from the mouth, and four or five arms.

Below this church there was a large masonry tank, similar to many others which we had seen along the road.

[*Progress through the Town.*] After we had left that place, and had arrived at the entrance to the city [of Calicut] we were shown another church, where we saw things like those described above. Here the crowd grew so dense that progress along the street became next to impossible, and for this reason they put the captain-major into a house, and us with him.

The king sent a brother of the *bale*, who was a lord of this country, to accompany the captain-major, and he was attended by men beating drums, blowing *anafils* and bagpipes, and firing off matchlocks. In conducting the captain-major they showed us much respect, more than is shown in Spain to a king. The number of people was countless, for in addition to those who surrounded us, and among whom there were two thousand armed men, they crowded the roofs and houses.

---

[13] Ravenstein (1898) believes the bird to be a Hindu war-god. Ames (2009) suggests it was an image of Garuda, the bird-god who carried Vishnu, the creator-god of the Hindu trinity. [Ed.]

[14] Possibly Mari, a local deity, protector from smallpox. [Ed.]

[15] Another source reports that at least one of the crew did not believe it was a Christian church. He is said to have knelt next to Vasco da Gama and said: "If this is the devil, I worship the True God" (Ames, 2009, 76). [Ed.]

[16] Ames (2009) suggests that this term for Brahman priests was either the Arabic *quadi* (judge) or *kafir* (unbeliever). [Ed.]

[17] Possibly ash from burnt cow dung. [Ed.]

[18] Did da Gama's refusal to anoint himself with ash mean he questioned the legitimacy of ritual or church? [Ed.]

[*The King's Palace.*] The further we advanced in the direction of the king's palace, the more did they increase in number. And when we arrived there, men of much distinction and great lords came out to meet the captain-major, and joined those who were already in attendance upon him. It was then an hour before sunset. When we reached the palace we passed through a gate into a courtyard of great size, and before we arrived at where the king was, we passed four doors, through which we had to force our way, giving many blows to the people. When, at last, we reached the door where the king was, there came forth from it a little old man, who holds a position resembling that of a bishop, and whose advice the king acts upon in all affairs of the church. This man embraced the captain-major when he entered the door. Several men were wounded at this door, and we only got in by the use of much force.

[*A Royal Audience, May 28.*] The king[19] was in a small court, reclining upon a couch covered with a cloth of green velvet, above which was a good mattress, and upon this again a sheet of cotton stuff, very white and fine, more so than any linen. The cushions were after the same fashion. In his left hand the king held a very large golden cup [spittoon], having a capacity of half an almude [8 pints]. At its mouth this cup was two palmas [16 inches] wide, and apparently it was massive. Into this cup the king threw the husks of a certain herb which is chewed by the people of this country because of its soothing effects, and which they call *atambor*.[20] On the right side of the king stood a basin of gold, so large that a man might just encircle it with his arms: this contained the herbs. There were likewise many silver jugs. The canopy above the couch was all gilt.

The captain, on entering, saluted in the manner of the country: by putting the hands together, then raising them towards Heaven, as is done by Christians when addressing God, and immediately afterwards opening them and shutting fists quickly. The king beckoned to the captain with his right hand to come nearer, but the captain did not approach him, for it is the custom of the country for no man to approach the king except only the servant who hands him the herbs, and when anyone addresses the king he holds his hand before the mouth, and remains at a distance. When the king beckoned to the captain he looked at us others, and ordered us to be seated on a stone bench near him, where he could see us. He ordered that water for our hands should be given us, as also some fruit, one kind of which resembled a melon, except that its outside was rough and the inside sweet, whilst another kind of fruit resembled a fig, and tasted very nice. There were men who prepared these fruits for them; and the king looked at them eating, and smiled; and talked to the servant who stood near him supplying him with the herbs referred to.

[19] Manivikraman Raja. [Ed.]
[20] Betel-nut. [Ed.]

Then, throwing his eyes on the captain, who sat facing him, he invited him to address himself to the courtiers present, saying they were men of much distinction, that he could tell them whatever he desired to say, and they would repeat it to him (the king). The captain-major replied that he was the ambassador of the King of Portugal, and the bearer of a message which he could only deliver to him personally. The king said this was good, and immediately asked him to be conducted to a chamber. When the captain had entered, the king, too, rose and joined him, whilst we remained where we were. All this happened about sunset. An old man who was in the court took away the couch as soon as the king rose, but allowed the plate to remain. The king, when he joined the captain, threw himself upon another couch, covered with various stuffs embroidered in gold, and asked the captain what he wanted.

And the captain told him he was the ambassador of a King of Portugal, who was Lord of many countries and the possessor of great wealth of every description, exceeding that of any king of these parts; that for a period of sixty years his ancestors had annually sent out vessels to make discoveries in the direction of India, as they knew that there were Christian kings there like themselves. This, he said, was the reason which induced them to order this country to be discovered, not because they sought for gold or silver, for of this they had such abundance that they needed not what was to be found in this country. He further stated that the captains sent out traveled for a year or two, until their provisions were exhausted, and then returned to Portugal, without having succeeded in making the desired discovery. There reigned a king now whose name was Dom Manuel, who had ordered him to build three vessels, of which he had been appointed captain-major, and who had ordered him not to return to Portugal until he should have discovered this King of the Christians, on pain of having his head cut off. That two letters had been intrusted to him to be presented in case he succeeded in discovering him, and that he would do so on the ensuing day; and, finally, he had been instructed to say by word of mouth that he [the King of Portugal] desired to be his friend and brother.

In reply to this the king said that he was welcome; that, on his part, he held him as a friend and brother, and would send ambassadors with him to Portugal. This latter had been asked as a favor, the captain pretending that he would not dare to present himself before his king and master unless he was able to present, at the same time, some men of this country.

These and many other things passed between the two in this chamber, and as it was already late in the night, the king asked the captain with whom he desired to lodge, with Christians or with Moors? And the captain replied, neither with Christians nor with Moors, and begged as a favor that he be given a lodging by himself. The king said he would order it thus, upon which the captain took leave of the king and came to where the men were, that is, to a veranda lit up by a huge candlestick. By that time four hours of the night had already gone.[21] . . .

[*Presents for the King.*] On Tuesday, May 29, the captain-major got ready the following things to be sent to the king, viz., twelve pieces of *lambel*,[22] four scarlet hoods, six hats, four strings of coral, a case containing six wash-hand basins, a case of sugar, two casks of oil, and two of honey.[23] And as it is the custom not to send anything to the king without the knowledge of the Moor, his factor, and of the *bale*, the captain informed them of his intention. They came, and when they saw the present they laughed at it, saying that it was not a thing to offer to a king, that the poorest merchant from Mecca, or any other part of India, gave more, and that if he wanted to make a present it should be in gold, as the king would not accept such things. When the captain heard this he grew sad, and said that he had brought no gold, that, moreover, he was no merchant, but an ambassador; that he gave of that which he had, which was his own [private gift] and not the king's; that if the King of Portugal ordered him to return he would intrust him with far richer presents; and that if King Camolim[24] would not accept these things he would send them back to the ships. Upon this they declared that they would not forward his presents, nor consent to his forwarding them himself. When they had gone there came certain Moorish merchants, and they all depreciated the present which the captain desired to be sent to the king.

When the captain saw that they were determined not to forward his present, he said, that as they would not allow him to send his present to the palace he would go to speak to the king, and would then return to the ships. They approved of this, and told him that if he would wait a short time they would return and accompany him to the palace. And the captain waited all day, but they never came back. The captain was very wroth at being among so phlegmatic and unreliable a people, and intended, at first, to go to the palace without them. On further consideration, however, he thought it best to wait until the following day. The men diverted themselves, singing and dancing to the sound of trumpets, and enjoyed themselves much.

[*A Second Audience, May 30.*] On Wednesday morning the Moors returned, and took the captain to the palace, and others with him. The palace was crowded with armed men. Our captain was kept waiting with his conductors for fully four long hours, outside a door, which was only opened when the king sent word to admit him, attended by two men only, whom he might select. The captain-major said that he desired to

---

[21] Four hours after sunset, or about 10 P.M. [Ed.]

[22] Striped cloth. [Ed.]

[23] The ships had been loaded by Bartolomeu Dias (1451–1500), who used such goods effectively in trading with Africans. [Ed.]

[24] Camorim (with a soft *c*) is a version of the king's title, more often written as Zamorin or Samorin, meaning ruler of the coasts or king of the seas. [Ed.]

have Fernao Martins with him, who could interpret, and his secretary. It seemed to him, as it did to us, that this separation portended no good.

When he had entered, the king said that he had expected him on Tuesday. The captain-major said that the long road had tired him, and that for this reason he had not come to see him. The king then said that he had told him that he came from a very rich kingdom, and yet had brought him nothing; that he had also told him that he was the bearer of a letter, which had not yet been delivered. To this the captain rejoined that he had brought nothing, because the object of his voyage was merely to make discoveries, but that when other ships came he would then see what they brought him; as to the letter, it was true that he had brought one, and would deliver it immediately.

The king then asked what it was he had come to discover: stones or men? If he came to discover men, as he said, why had he brought nothing? Moreover, he had been told that he carried with him the golden image of a Santa Maria. The captain-major said that the Santa Maria was not of gold, and that even if she were he would not part with her, as she had guided him across the ocean, and would guide him back to his own country. The king then asked for the letter. The captain said that he begged as a favor, that as the Moors wished him ill and might misinterpret him, a Christian able to speak Arabic should be sent for. The king said this was well, and at once sent for a young man, of small stature, whose name was Quaram. The captain-major then said that he had two letters, one written in his own language and the other in that of the Moors;[25] that he was able to read the former, and knew that it contained nothing but what would prove acceptable; but that as to the other he was unable to read it, and it might be good, or contain something that was erroneous. As the Christian was unable to *read* Moorish, four Moors took the letter and read it between them, after which they translated it to the king, who was well satisfied with its contents.

The king then asked what kind of merchandise was to be found in his country. The captain said there was much corn,[26] cloth, iron, bronze, and many other things. The king asked whether he had any merchandise with him. The captain-major replied that he had a little of each sort, as samples, and that if permitted to return to the ships he would order it to be landed, and that meantime four or five men would remain at the lodgings assigned them. The king said no! He might take all his people with him, securely moor his ships, land his merchandise, and sell it to the best advantage. Having taken leave of the king the captain-major returned to his lodgings, and we with him. As it was already late no attempt was made to depart that night.

[25] Arabic. [Ed.]

[26] Corn had already been transplanted from the Americas by this time, but the author more likely meant wheat (Ames, 2009, 83). [Ed.]

CHRISTOPHER COLUMBUS

Letter to King Ferdinand and Queen Isabella

Christopher Columbus sent this letter to his royal backers, King Ferdinand and Queen Isabella of Spain, on his return in March 1493 from his first voyage across the Atlantic. (See Map 15.3.)

An Italian sailor from Genoa, Columbus, in 1483–1484, tried to convince King John II of Portugal to underwrite his plan to sail across the western ocean to the spice-rich East Indies. Relying on a Florentine map that used Marco Polo's overstated distance from Venice to Japan across Asia and an understated estimate of the circumference of the globe, Columbus believed that Japan lay only 2,500 miles west of the Portuguese Azores. King John II rejected the proposal because he had more accurate estimates indicating that sailing around Africa was the shorter route, as the voyages of Bartolomeu Dias in 1488 and Vasco da Gama in 1497–1499 proved.

Less knowledgeable about navigation, the new Spanish monarchs, Ferdinand and Isabella, supported Columbus and financed his plan to sail west to Asia. In four voyages, Columbus touched a number of Caribbean islands and the coast of Central America, settled Spaniards on Hispaniola (Española), and began to create one of the largest empires in world history for Spain — all the while thinking he was near China and Japan, in the realm of the Great Khan whom Marco Polo had met and who had died hundreds of years earlier.

In what ways was the voyage of Columbus similar to that of da Gama? In what ways was it similar to that of Zheng He? In what ways was it different from both of these voyages? Taking the voyages of da Gama and Columbus together, what were the differences between Chinese and European expansion?

THINKING HISTORICALLY

Because this document comes from the period we are studying and is written by Columbus himself, it is a primary source. Primary sources have a great sense of immediacy and can often seem to transport us directly into the past. However, involvement when reading does not always lead to understanding, so it is important to

---

Source: "First Voyage of Columbus," in *The Four Voyages of Columbus*, ed. Cecil Jane (New York: Dover, 1988), 1–18.

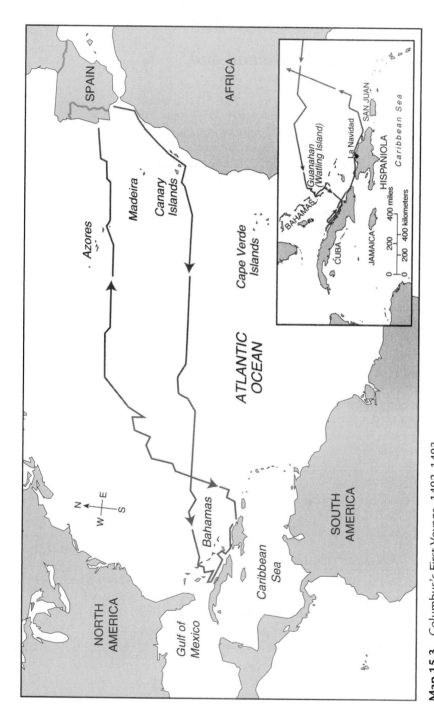

Map 15.3 Columbus's First Voyage, 1492–1493.

Source: Lawrence V. Mott.

think critically about the source and the writer's intended audience as we read. First we must determine the source of the document. Where does it come from? Is it original? If not, is it a copy or a translation? Next, we must determine who wrote it, when it was written, and for what purpose. After answering these questions, we are able to read the document with a critical eye, which leads to greater understanding.

The original letter by Columbus has been lost. This selection is an English translation based on three different printed Spanish versions of the letter. So this text is a reconstruction, not an original, though it is believed to be quite close to the original.

The original letter was probably composed during a relaxed time on the return voyage before its date of February 15, 1493—possibly as early as the middle of January—and sent to the Spanish monarchs from Lisbon in order to reach them by the time Columbus arrived in Barcelona.

What does Columbus want to impart to Ferdinand and Isabella? First and foremost, he wants them to know that he reached the Indies, that the voyage was a success. And so, the letter's opening sentence tells us something that Columbus certainly did not intend or know. We learn that on his return in 1493, Columbus thought he had been to the Indies when in fact he had not. (It is due to Columbus's confusion that we call the islands he visited the West Indies and Native Americans "Indians.")

Knowing what the author wants a reader to believe is useful information because it serves as a point of reference for other statements the author makes. The success of Columbus's voyage is a case in point. Columbus does not admit to the loss of one of his ships in his letter, nor does he explain fully why he had to build a fort at Navidad and leave some of his crew there, returning home without them. Clearly, Columbus had reason to worry that his voyage would be viewed as a failure. He had not found the gold mines he sought or the Asian cities described by Marco Polo. He thought he had discovered many spices, though only the chili peppers were new. Notice, as you read this letter, how Columbus presents his voyage in the best light.

Aside from what Columbus intends, what facts do you learn from the letter about Columbus, his first voyage, and his encounter with the New World? What seems to drive Columbus to do what he does? What is Columbus's attitude toward the "Indians"? What does Columbus's letter tell us about the society and culture of the Taino* — the people he met in the Caribbean?

* TY noh

Sir, As I know that you will be pleased at the great victory with which Our Lord has crowned my voyage, I write this to you, from which you will learn how in thirty-three days, I passed from the Canary Islands to the Indies with the fleet which the most illustrious king and queen, our sovereigns, gave to me. And there I found very many islands filled with people innumerable, and of them all I have taken possession for their highnesses, by proclamation made and with the royal standard unfurled, and no opposition was offered to me. To the first island which I found, I gave the name *San Salvador*, in remembrance of the Divine Majesty, Who has marvellously bestowed all this; the Indians call it "Guanahani."* To the second, I gave the name *Isla de Santa María de Concepción*; to the third, *Fernandina*; to the fourth, *Isabella*; to the fifth, *Isla Juana*, and so to each one I gave a new name.

When I reached Juana, I followed its coast to the westward, and I found it to be so extensive that I thought that it must be the mainland, the province of Catayo. And since there were neither towns nor villages on the seashore, but only small hamlets, with the people which I could not have speech, because they all fled immediately, I went forward on the same course, thinking that I should not fail to find great cities and towns. And, at the end of many leagues, seeing that there was no change and that the coast was bearing me northwards, which I wished to avoid, since winter was already beginning and I proposed to make from it to the south, and as moreover the wind was carrying me forward, I determined not to wait for a change in the weather and retraced my path as far as a certain harbour known to me. And from that point, I sent two men inland to learn if there were a king or great cities. They travelled three days' journey and found an infinity of small hamlets and people without number, but nothing of importance. For this reason, they returned.

I understood sufficiently from other Indians, whom I had already taken, that this land was nothing but an island. And therefore I followed its coast eastwards for one hundred and seven leagues to the point where it ended. And from that cape, I saw another island, distant eighteen leagues from the former, to the east, to which I at once gave the name "Española." And I went there and followed its northern coast, as I had in the case of Juana, to the eastward for one hundred and eighty-eight great leagues in a straight line. This island and all the others are very fertile to a limitless degree, and this island is extremely so. In it there are many harbours on the coast of the sea, beyond comparison with others which I know in Christendom, and many rivers, good and large, which is marvellous. Its lands are high, and there are in it very many sierras and very lofty mountains, beyond comparison with the island of Teneriffe. All are most beautiful, of a thousand shapes, and all are accessible and

---

* gwah nah HAH nee

filled with trees of a thousand kinds and tall, and they seem to touch the sky. And I am told that they never lose their foliage, as I can understand, for I saw them as green and as lovely as they are in Spain in May, and some of them were flowering, some bearing fruit, and some in another stage, according to their nature. And the nightingale was singing and other birds of a thousand kinds in the month of November there where I went. There are six or eight kinds of palm, which are a wonder to behold on account of their beautiful variety, but so are the other trees and fruits and plants. In it are marvellous pine groves, and there are very large tracts of cultivatable lands, and there is honey, and there are birds of many kinds and fruits in great diversity. In the interior are mines of metals, and the population is without number. Española is a marvel.

The sierras and mountains, the plains and arable lands and pastures, are so lovely and rich for planting and sowing, for breeding cattle of every kind, for building towns and villages. The harbours of the sea here are such as cannot be believed to exist unless they have been seen, and so with the rivers, many and great, and good waters, the majority of which contain gold. In the trees and fruits and plants, there is a great difference from those of Juana. In this island, there are many spices and great mines of gold and of other metals.

The people of this island, and of all the other islands which I have found and of which I have information, all go naked, men and women, as their mothers bore them, although some women cover a single place with the leaf of a plant or with a net of cotton which they make for the purpose. They have no iron or steel or weapons, nor are they fitted to use them, not because they are not well built men and of handsome stature, but because they are very marvellously timorous. They have no other arms than weapons made of canes, cut in seeding time, to the ends of which they fix a small sharpened stick. And they do not dare to make use of these, for many times it has happened that I have sent ashore two or three men to some town to have speech, and countless people have come out to them, and as soon as they have seen my men approaching they have fled, even a father not waiting for his son. And this, not because ill has been done to anyone; on the contrary, at every point where I have been and have been able to have speech, I have given to them of all that I had, such as cloth and many other things, without receiving anything for it; but so they are, incurably timid. It is true that, after they have been reassured and have lost their fear, they are so guileless and so generous with all they possess, that no one would believe it who has not seen it. They never refuse anything which they possess, if it be asked of them; on the contrary, they invite anyone to share it, and display as much love as if they would give their hearts, and whether the thing be of value or whether it be of small price, at once with whatever trifle of whatever kind it may be that is given to them, with that they are content. I forbade that they should be given things so worthless as fragments of broken crockery and scraps of broken glass, and ends of straps, although when they were able to get them, they fancied that they possessed the best jewel in the world. So it was found that a sailor for a strap received gold to the weight of two and a half *castellanos*, and others much more for other things which were worth much less. As for new *blancas*,[1] for them they would give everything which they had, although it might be two or three *castellanos'* weight of gold or an *arroba*[2] or two of spun cotton. . . . They took even the pieces of the broken hoops of the wine barrels and, like savages, gave what they had, so that it seemed to me to be wrong and I forbade it. And I gave a thousand handsome good things, which I had brought, in order that they might conceive affection, and more than that, might become Christians and be inclined to the love and service of their highnesses and of the whole Castilian nation, and strive to aid us and to give us of the things which they have in abundance and which are necessary to us. And they do not know any creed and are not idolaters; only they all believe that power and good are in the heavens, and they are very firmly convinced that I, with these ships and men, came from the heavens, and in this belief they everywhere received me, after they had overcome their fear. And this does not come because they are ignorant; on the contrary, they are of a very acute intelligence and are men who navigate all those seas, so that it is amazing how good an account they give of everything, but it is because they have never seen people clothed or ships of such a kind.

And as soon as I arrived in the Indies, in the first island which I found, I took by force some of them, in order that they might learn and give me information of that which there is in those parts, and so it was that they soon understood us, and we them, either by speech or signs, and they have been very serviceable. I still take them with me, and they are always assured that I come from Heaven, for all the intercourse which they have had with me; and they were the first to announce this wherever I went, and the others went running from house to house and to the neighbouring towns, with loud cries of, "Come! Come to see the people from Heaven!" So all, men and women alike, when their minds were set at rest concerning us, came, so that not one, great or small, remained behind, and all brought something to eat and drink, which they gave with extraordinary affection. In all the island, they have very many canoes, like rowing *fustas*,[3] some larger, some smaller, and some are larger than a *fusta* of eighteen benches. They are not so broad, because they are made of a single log of wood, but a *fusta* would not keep up with them in rowing, since their speed is a thing incredible. And in these they navigate among all those islands, which are innumerable, and carry

---

[1] Spanish copper coins. [Ed.]

[2] A unit of weight (about 25 pounds) indicated by the @ symbol. [Ed.]

[3] Fast ships with oars and sails, probably of Arab origin. [Ed.]

their goods. One of these canoes I have seen with seventy and eighty men in her, and each one with his oar.

In all these islands, I saw no great diversity in the appearance of the people or in their manners and language. On the contrary, they all understand one another, which is a very curious thing, on account of which I hope that their highnesses will determine upon their conversion to our holy faith, towards which they are very inclined.

I have already said how I have gone one hundred and seven leagues in a straight line from west to east along the seashore of the island Juana, and as a result of that voyage, I can say that this island is larger than England and Scotland together, for, beyond these one hundred and seven leagues, there remain to the westward two provinces to which I have not gone. One of these provinces they call "Avan," and there the people are born with tails; and these provinces cannot have a length of less than fifty or sixty leagues, as I could understand from those Indians whom I have and who know all the islands.

The other, Española, has a circumference greater than all Spain, from Colibre, by the sea-coast, to Fuenterabia in Vizcaya, since I voyaged along one side one hundred and eighty-eight great leagues in a straight line from west to east. It is a land to be desired and, seen, it is never to be left. And in it, although of all I have taken possession for their highnesses and all are more richly endowed than I know how, or am able, to say, and I hold them all for their highnesses, so that they may dispose of them as, and as absolutely as, of the kingdoms of Castile, in this Española, in the situation most convenient and in the best position for the mines of gold and for all intercourse as well with the mainland here as with that there, belonging to the Grand Khan, where will be great trade and gain, I have taken possession of a large town, to which I gave the name *Villa de Navidad*, and in it I have made fortifications and a fort, which now will by this time be entirely finished, and I have left in it sufficient men for such a purpose with arms and artillery and provisions for more than a year, and a *fusta*, and one, a master of all seacraft, to build others, and great friendship with the king of that land, so much so, that he was proud to call me, and to treat me as, a brother. And even if he were to change his attitude to one of hostility towards these men, he and his do not know what arms are and they go naked, as I have already said, and are the most timorous people that there are in the world, so that the men whom I have left there alone would suffice to destroy all that land, and the island is without danger for their persons, if they know how to govern themselves.

In all these islands, it seems to me that all men are content with one woman, and to their chief or king they give as many as twenty. It appears to me that the women work more than the men. And I have not been able to learn if they hold private property; what seemed to me to appear was that, in that which one had, all took a share, especially of eatable things.

In these islands I have so far found no human monstrosities, as many expected, but on the contrary the whole population is very well-formed, nor are they negros as in Guinea, but their hair is flowing, and they are not born where there is intense force in the rays of the sun; it is true that the sun has there great power, although it is distant from the equinoctial line twenty-six degrees. In these islands, where there are high mountains, the cold was severe this winter, but they endure it, being used to it and with the help of meats which they eat with many and extremely hot spices. As I have found no monsters, so I have had no report of any, except in an island "Quaris," the second at the coming into the Indies, which is inhabited by a people who are regarded in all the islands as very fierce and who eat human flesh. They have many canoes with which they range through all the islands of India and pillage and take as many as they can. They are no more malformed than the others, except that they have the custom of wearing their hair long like women, and they use bows and arrows of the same cane stems, with a small piece of wood at the end, owing to lack of iron which they do not possess. They are ferocious among these other people who are cowardly to an excessive degree, but I make no more account of them than of the rest. These are those who have intercourse with the women of "Matinino," which is the first island met on the way from Spain to the Indies, in which there is not a man. These women engage in no feminine occupation, but use bows and arrows of cane, like those already mentioned, and they arm and protect themselves with plates of copper, of which they have much.

In another island, which they assure me is larger than Española, the people have no hair. In it, there is gold incalculable, and from it and from the other islands, I bring with me Indians as evidence.

In conclusion, to speak only of that which has been accomplished on this voyage, which was so hasty, their highnesses can see that I will give them as much gold as they may need, if their highnesses will render me very slight assistance; moreover, spice and cotton, as much as their highnesses shall command; and mastic, as much as they shall order to be shipped and which, up to now, has been found only in Greece, in the island of Chios, and the Seignory sells it for what it pleases; and aloe wood, as much as they shall order to be shipped, and slaves, as many as they shall order to be shipped and who will be from the idolaters. And I believe that I have found rhubarb and cinnamon, and I shall find a thousand other things of value, which the people whom I have left there will have discovered, for I have not delayed at any point, so far as the wind allowed me to sail, except in the town of Navidad, in order to leave it secured and well established, and in truth, I should have done much more, if the ships had served me, as reason demanded.

This is enough . . . and the eternal God, our Lord, Who gives to all those who walk in His way triumph over things which appear to be impossible, and this was notably one; for, although men have talked or have written of these lands, all was conjectural, without suggestion of ocular evidence, but amounted only to this, that those who heard for the most part listened and judged it to be rather a fable than as having any vestige of truth. So that, since Our Redeemer has given this victory to our most illustrious king and queen, and to their renowned kingdoms, in so great a matter, for this all Christendom ought to feel delight and make great feasts and give solemn thanks to the Holy Trinity with many solemn prayers for the great exaltation which they shall have, in the turning of so many peoples to our holy faith, and afterwards for temporal benefits, for not only Spain but all Christians will have hence refreshment and gain.

This, in accordance with that which has been accomplished, thus briefly.

Done in the caravel,[4] off the Canary Islands, on the fifteenth of February, in the year one thousand four hundred and ninety-three.

At your orders.   El Almirante.

After having written this, and being in the sea of Castile, there came on me so great a south-south-west wind, that I was obliged to lighten ship. But I ran here to-day into this port of Lisbon, which was the greatest marvel in the world, whence I decided to write to their highnesses. In all the Indies, I have always found weather like May; where I went in thirty-three days and I had returned in twenty-eight, save for these storms which have detained me for fourteen days, beating about in this sea. Here all the sailors say that never has there been so bad a winter nor so many ships lost.

Done on the fourth day of March.

[4] Sailing ship, in this case the *Santa Maria*. [Ed.]

5

KIRKPATRICK SALE

The Conquest of Paradise

In this selection from his popular study of Columbus, Sale is concerned with Columbus's attitude toward nature in the New World. Sale regards Columbus as a symbol of European expansion. If Columbus is distinctly European, what is Sale saying about European expansion? How and what does Sale add to your understanding of the similarities and differences between Chinese and European expansion?

Source: Kirkpatrick Sale, *The Conquest of Paradise* (New York: Penguin, 1991), 92–104.

Was Columbus much different from Zheng He? Or were the areas and peoples they visited causes for different responses? Vasco da Gama visited the same areas as Zheng He. How similar, or different, was da Gama from Zheng He? If da Gama was a better symbol of European expansion, how different was the European experience from the Chinese?

THINKING HISTORICALLY

Clearly, this selection is a secondary source; Sale is a modern writer, not a fifteenth-century contemporary of Columbus. Still, you will not have to read very far into the selection to realize that Sale has a distinct point of view. Secondary sources, like primary ones, should be analyzed for bias and perspective, and the author's interpretation should be identified.

Sale is an environmentalist and a cultural critic. Do his beliefs and values hinder his understanding of Columbus, or do they inform and illuminate aspects of Columbus that might otherwise be missed? Does Sale help you recognize things you would not have seen on your own, or does he persuade you to see things that might not truly be there?

Notice how Sale uses primary sources in his text. He quotes from Columbus's journal and his letter to King Ferdinand and Queen Isabella. Do these quotes help you understand Columbus, or do they simply support Sale's argument? What do you think about Sale's use of the Spanish *Colón** for *Columbus*? Does Sale "take possession" of Columbus by, in effect, "renaming" him for modern readers? Is the effect humanizing or debunking?

Notice how Sale sometimes calls attention to what the primary source did *not* say rather than what it did say. Is this a legitimate way to understand someone, or is Sale projecting a twentieth-century perspective on Columbus to make a point?

Toward the end of the selection, Sale extends his criticism beyond Columbus to include others. Who are the others? What is the effect of this larger criticism?

Admiral Colón spent a total of ninety-six days exploring the lands he encountered on the far side of the Ocean Sea—four rather small coralline islands in the Bahamian chain and two substantial coastlines of what he finally acknowledged were larger islands—every one of which he "took possession of" in the name of his Sovereigns.

The first he named San Salvador, no doubt as much in thanksgiving for its welcome presence after more than a month at sea as for the Son

* koh LOHN

of God whom it honored; the second he called Santa María de la Concepcíon, after the Virgin whose name his flagship bore; and the third and fourth he called Fernandina and Isabela, for his patrons, honoring Aragon before Castile for reasons never explained (possibly protocol, possibly in recognition of the chief sources of backing for the voyage). The first of the two large and very fertile islands he called Juana, which Fernando [Columbus's son] says was done in honor of Prince Juan, heir to the Castilian throne, but just as plausibly might have been done in recognition of Princess Juana, the unstable child who eventually carried on the line; the second he named la Ysla Española, the "Spanish Island," because it resembled (though he felt it surpassed in beauty) the lands of Castile.

It was not that the islands were in need of names, mind you, nor indeed that Colón was ignorant of the names that native peoples had already given them, for he frequently used those original names before endowing them with his own. Rather, the process of bestowing new names went along with "taking possession of" those parts of the world he deemed suitable for Spanish ownership, showing the royal banners, erecting various crosses, and pronouncing certain oaths and pledges. If this was presumption, it had an honored heritage: It was Adam who was charged by his Creator with the task of naming "every living creature," including the product of his own rib, in the course of establishing "dominion over" them.

Colón went on to assign no fewer than sixty-two other names on the geography of the islands—capes, points, mountains, ports—with a blithe assurance suggesting that in his (and Europe's) perception the act of name-giving was in some sense a talisman of conquest, a rite that changed raw neutral stretches of far-off earth into extensions of Europe. The process began slowly, even haltingly—he forgot to record, for example, until four days afterward that he named the landfall island San Salvador—but by the time he came to Española at the end he went on a naming spree, using more than two-thirds of all the titles he concocted on that one coastline. On certain days it became almost a frenzy: on December 6 he named six places, on the nineteenth six more, and on January 11 no fewer than ten—eight capes, a point, and a mountain. It is almost as if, as he sailed along the last of the islands, he was determined to leave his mark on it the only way he knew how, and thus to establish his authority—and by extension Spain's—even, as with baptism, to make it thus sanctified, and real, and official. . . .

This business of naming and "possessing" foreign islands was by no means casual. The Admiral took it very seriously, pointing out that "it was my wish to bypass no island without taking possession" (October 15) and that "in all regions [I] always left a cross standing" (November 16) as a mark of Christian dominance. There even seem to have been certain prescriptions for it (the instructions from the Sovereigns speak of "the administering of the oath and the performing of the rites prescribed in such cases"), and Rodrigo de Escobedo was sent along as secretary of the fleet explicitly to witness and record these events in detail.

But consider the implications of this act and the questions it raises again about what was in the Sovereigns' minds, what in Colón's. Why would the Admiral assume that these territories were in some way *un*possessed—even by those clearly inhabiting them—and thus available for Spain to claim? Why would he not think twice about the possibility that some considerable potentate—the Grand Khan of China, for example, whom he later acknowledged (November 6) "must be" the ruler of Española—might descend upon him at any moment with a greater military force than his three vessels commanded and punish him for his territorial presumption? Why would he make the ceremony of possession his very first act on shore, even before meeting the inhabitants or exploring the environs, or finding out if anybody there objected to being thus possessed—particularly if they actually owned the great treasures he hoped would be there? No European would have imagined that anyone—three small boatloads of Indians, say—could come up to a European shore or island and "take possession" of it, nor would a European imagine marching up to some part of North Africa or the Middle East and claiming sovereignty there with impunity. Why were these lands thought to be different?

Could there be any reason for the Admiral to assume he had reached "unclaimed" shores, new lands that lay far from the domains of any of the potentates of the East? Can that really have been in his mind—or can it all be explained as simple Eurocentrism, or Eurosuperiority, mixed with cupidity and naiveté? . . .

Once safely "possessed,"[1] San Salvador was open for inspection. Now the Admiral turned his attention for the first time to the "naked people" staring at him on the beach—he did not automatically give them a name, interestingly enough, and it would be another six days before he decided what he might call them—and tried to win their favor with his trinkets.

> They all go around as naked as their mothers bore them; and also the women, although I didn't see more than one really young girl. All that I saw were young people [*mancebos*], none of them more than 30 years old. They are very well built, with very handsome bodies and very good faces; their hair [is] coarse, almost like the silk of a horse's tail, and short. They wear their hair over their eyebrows, except for a little in the back that they wear long and never cut. Some of them paint themselves black (and they are the color of the Canary Islanders, neither black nor white), and some paint themselves white, and some red, and some with what they find. And some paint their faces, and some of them the whole body, and some the eyes only, and some of them only the nose.

It may fairly be called the birth of American anthropology.

---

[1] Given Spanish names. [Ed.]

A crude anthropology, of course, as superficial as Colón's descriptions always were when his interest was limited, but simple and straightforward enough, with none of the fable and fantasy that characterized many earlier (and even some later) accounts of new-found peoples. There was no pretense to objectivity, or any sense that these people might be representatives of a culture equal to, or in any way a model for, Europe's. Colón immediately presumed the inferiority of the natives, not merely because (a sure enough sign) they were naked, but because (his society could have no surer measure) they seemed so technologically backward. "It appeared to me that these people were very poor in everything," he wrote on that first day, and, worse still, "they have no iron." And they went on to prove their inferiority to the Admiral by being ignorant of even such a basic artifact of European life as a sword: "They bear no arms, nor are they acquainted with them," he wrote, "for I showed them swords and they grasped them by the blade and cut themselves through ignorance." Thus did European arms spill the first drops of native blood on the sands of the New World, accompanied not with a gasp of compassion but with a smirk of superiority.

Then, just six sentences further on, Colón clarified what this inferiority meant in his eyes:

> They ought to be good servants and of good intelligence [*ingenio*].
> . . . I believe that they would easily be made Christians, because it seemed to me that they had no religion. Our Lord pleasing, I will carry off six of them at my departure to Your Highnesses, in order that they may learn to speak.

No clothes, no arms, no possessions, no iron, and now no religion—not even speech: hence they were fit to be servants, and captives. It may fairly be called the birth of American slavery.

Whether or not the idea of slavery was in Colón's mind all along is uncertain, although he did suggest he had had experience as a slave trader in Africa (November 12) and he certainly knew of Portuguese plantation slavery in the Madeiras and Spanish slavery of Guanches in the Canaries. But it seems to have taken shape early and grown ever firmer as the weeks went on and as he captured more and more of the helpless natives. At one point he even sent his crew ashore to kidnap "seven head of women, young ones and adults, and three small children"; the expression of such callousness led the Spanish historian Salvador de Madariaga to remark, "It would be difficult to find a starker utterance of utilitarian subjection of man by man than this passage [whose] form is no less devoid of human feeling than its substance."

To be sure, Colón knew nothing about these people he encountered and considered enslaving, and he was hardly trained to find out very much, even if he was moved to care. But they were in fact members of an extensive, populous, and successful people whom Europe, using its own peculiar taxonomy, subsequently called "Taino" (or "Taíno"), their own word for "good" or "noble," and their response when asked who they were. They were related distantly by both language and culture to the Arawak people of the South American mainland, but it is misleading (and needlessly imprecise) to call them Arawaks, as historians are wont to do, when the term "Taino" better establishes their ethnic and historical distinctiveness. They had migrated to the islands from the mainland at about the time of the birth of Christ, occupying the three large islands we now call the Greater Antilles and arriving at Guanahani (Colón's San Salvador) and the end of the Bahamian chain probably sometime around A.D. 900. There they displaced an earlier people, the Guanahacabibes (sometimes called Guanahatabeys), who by the time of the European discovery occupied only the western third of Cuba and possibly remote corners of Española; and there, probably in the early fifteenth century, they eventually confronted another people moving up the islands from the mainland, the Caribs, whose culture eventually occupied a dozen small islands of what are called the Lesser Antilles.

The Tainos were not nearly so backward as Colón assumed from their lack of dress. (It might be said that it was the Europeans, who generally kept clothed head to foot during the day despite temperatures regularly in the eighties, who were the more unsophisticated in garmenture — especially since the Tainos, as Colón later noted, also used their body paint to prevent sunburn.) Indeed, they had achieved a means of living in a balanced and fruitful harmony with their natural surroundings that any society might well have envied. They had, to begin with, a not unsophisticated technology that made exact use of their available resources, two parts of which were so impressive that they were picked up and adopted by the European invaders: *canoa* (canoes) that were carved and fire-burned from large silk-cotton trees, "all in one piece, and wonderfully made" (October 13), some of which were capable of carrying up to 150 passengers; and *hamaca* (hammocks) that were "like nets of cotton" (October 17) and may have been a staple item of trade with Indian tribes as far away as the Florida mainland. Their houses were not only spacious and clean — as the Europeans noted with surprise and appreciation, used as they were to the generally crowded and slovenly hovels and huts of south European peasantry — but more apropos, remarkably resistant to hurricanes; the circular walls were made of strong cane poles set deep and close together ("as close as the fingers of a hand," Colón noted), the conical roofs of branches and vines tightly interwoven on a frame of smaller poles and covered with heavy palm leaves. Their artifacts and jewelry, with the exception of a few gold trinkets and ornaments, were based largely on renewable materials, including bracelets and necklaces of coral, shells, bone, and stone, embroidered cotton belts, woven baskets, carved statues and chairs, wooden and shell utensils, and pottery of variously intricate decoration depending on period and place.

Perhaps the most sophisticated, and most carefully integrated, part of their technology was their agricultural system, extraordinarily productive and perfectly adapted to the conditions of the island environment. It was based primarily on fields of knee-high mounds, called *conucos*, planted with *yuca* (sometimes called manioc), *batata* (sweet potato), and various squashes and beans grown all together in multicrop harmony: The root crops were excellent in resisting erosion and producing minerals and potash, the leaf crops effective in providing shade and moisture, and the mound configurations largely resistant to erosion and flooding and adaptable to almost all topographic conditions including steep hillsides. Not only was the *conuco* system environmentally appropriate — "conuco agriculture seems to have provided an exceptionally ecologically well-balanced and protective form of land use," according to David Watts's recent and authoritative *West Indies* — but it was also highly productive, surpassing in yields anything known in Europe at the time, with labor that amounted to hardly more than two or three hours a week, and in continuous yearlong harvest. The pioneering American geographical scholar Carl Sauer calls Taino agriculture "productive as few parts of the world," giving the "highest returns of food in continuous supply by the simplest methods and modest labor," and adds, with a touch of regret, "The white man never fully appreciated the excellent combination of plants that were grown in conucos."

In their arts of government the Tainos seem to have achieved a parallel sort of harmony. Most villages were small (ten to fifteen families) and autonomous, although many apparently recognized loose allegiances with neighboring villages, and they were governed by a hereditary official called a *kaseke* (*cacique,** in the Spanish form), something of a cross between an arbiter and a prolocutor, supported by advisers and elders. So little a part did violence play in their system that they seem, remarkably, to have been a society without war (at least we know of no war music or signals or artifacts, and no evidence of intertribal combats) and even without overt conflict (Las Casas reports that no Spaniard ever saw two Tainos fighting). And here we come to what was obviously the Tainos' outstanding cultural achievement, a proficiency in the social arts that led those who first met them to comment unfailingly on their friendliness, their warmth, their openness, and above all — so striking to those of an acquisitive culture — their generosity.

"They are the best people in the world and above all the gentlest," Colón recorded in his *Journal* (December 16), and from first to last he was astonished at their kindness:

* kah SEEK

They became so much our friends that it was a marvel. . . . They traded and gave everything they had, with good will [October 12].

I sent the ship's boat ashore for water, and they very willingly showed my people where the water was, and they themselves carried the full barrels to the boat, and took great delight in pleasing us [October 16].

They are very gentle and without knowledge of what is evil; nor do they murder or steal [November 12].

Your Highnesses may believe that in all the world there can be no better or gentler people . . . for neither better people nor land can there be. . . . All the people show the most singular loving behavior and they speak pleasantly [December 24].

I assure Your Highnesses that I believe that in all the world there is no better people nor better country. They love their neighbors as themselves, and they have the sweetest talk in the world, and are gentle and always laughing [December 25].

Even if one allows for some exaggeration — Colón was clearly trying to convince Ferdinand and Isabella that his Indians could be easily conquered and converted, should that be the Sovereigns' wish — it is obvious that the Tainos exhibited a manner of social discourse that quite impressed the rough Europeans. But that was not high among the traits of "civilized" nations, as Colón and Europe understood it, and it counted for little in the Admiral's assessment of these people. However struck he was with such behavior, he would not have thought that it was the mark of a benign and harmonious society, or that from it another culture might learn. For him it was something like the wondrous behavior of children, the naive guilelessness of prelapsarian[2] creatures who knew no better how to bargain and chaffer and cheat than they did to dress themselves: "For a lacepoint they gave good pieces of gold the size of two fingers" (January 6), and "They even took pieces of the broken hoops of the wine casks and, like beasts [como besti], gave what they had" (Santangel Letter).[3] Like beasts; such innocence was not human.

It is to be regretted that the Admiral, unable to see past their nakedness, as it were, knew not the real virtues of the people he confronted. For the Tainos' lives were in many ways as idyllic as their surroundings, into which they fit with such skill and comfort. They were well fed and well housed, without poverty or serious disease. They enjoyed considerable leisure, given over to dancing, singing, ballgames, and sex, and expressed themselves artistically in basketry, woodworking, pottery, and

---

[2] Before the Fall. In other words, before the time, according to the Old Testament, when Adam and Eve sinned and were banished by God from the Garden of Eden. [Ed.]

[3] Santangel was the minister of Ferdinand and Isabella who received the letter. [Ed.]

jewelry. They lived in general harmony and peace, without greed or cov-
etousness or theft. . . .

It is perhaps only natural that Colón should devote his initial attention to the handsome, naked, naive islanders, but it does seem peculiar
that he pays almost no attention, especially in the early days, to the
spectacular scenery around them. Here he was, in the middle of an old-
growth tropical forest the likes of which he could not have imagined
before, its trees reaching sixty or seventy feet into the sky, more varieties
than he knew how to count much less name, exhibiting a lushness that
stood in sharp contrast to the sparse and denuded lands he had known
in the Mediterranean, hearing a melodious multiplicity of bird songs and
parrot calls — why was it not an occasion of wonder, excitement, and
the sheer joy at nature in its full, arrogant abundance? But there is not a
word of that: He actually said nothing about the physical surroundings
on the first day, aside from a single phrase about "very green trees" and
"many streams," and on the second managed only that short sentence
about a big island with a big lake and green trees. Indeed, for the whole
two weeks of the first leg of his voyage through the Bahamas to Cuba, he
devoted only a third of the lines of description to the phenomena around
him. And there are some natural sights he seems not to have noticed at
all: He did not mention (except in terms of navigation) the nighttime
heavens, the sharp, glorious configurations of stars that he must have
seen virtually every night of his journey, many for the first time.

Eventually Colón succumbed to the islands' natural charms as he
sailed on — how could he not? — and began to wax warmly about how
"these islands are very green and fertile and the air very sweet" (October
15), with "trees which were more beautiful to see than any other thing
that has ever been seen" (October 17), and "so good and sweet a smell
of flowers or trees from the land" (October 19). But his descriptions are
curiously vapid and vague, the language opaque and lifeless:

> The other island, which is very big [October 15] . . . this island is very
> large [October 16] . . . these islands are very green and fertile
> [October 15] . . . this land is the best and most fertile [October 17] . . .
> in it many plants and trees . . . if the others are very beautiful, this is
> more so [October 19] . . . here are some great lagoons . . . big and little
> birds of all sorts . . . if the others already seen are very beautiful and
> green and fertile, this one is much more so [October 21] . . . full of
> very good harbors and deep rivers [October 28].

You begin to see the Admiral's problem: He cares little about the
features of nature, at least the ones he doesn't use for sailing, and even
when he admires them he has little experience in assessing them and
less acquaintance with a vocabulary to describe them. To convey the
lush density and stately grandeur of those tropical forests, for example,
he had little more than the modifiers "green" and "very": "very green

trees" (October 12), "trees very green" (October 13), "trees . . . so green and with leaves like those of Castile" (October 14), "very green and very big trees" (October 19), "large groves are very green" (October 21), "trees . . . beautiful and green" (October 28). And when he began to be aware of the diversity among those trees, he was still unable to make meaningful distinctions: "All the trees are as different from ours as day from night" (October 17), "trees of a thousand kinds" (October 21), "a thousand sorts of trees" (October 23), "trees . . . different from ours" (October 28), "trees of a thousand sorts" (November 14), "trees of a thousand kinds" (December 6).

Such was his ignorance — a failing he repeatedly bemoaned ("I don't recognize them, which gives me great grief," October 19) — that when he did stop to examine a species he often had no idea what he was looking at. "I saw many trees very different from ours," he wrote on October 16, "and many of them have branches of many kinds, and all on one trunk, and one twig is of one kind and another of another, and so different that it is the greatest wonder in the world how much diversity there is of one kind from the other. That is to say, one branch has leaves like a cane, and another like mastic, and thus on one tree five or six kinds, and all so different." There is no such tree in existence, much less "many of them," and never was: Why would anyone imagine, or so contrive, such a thing to be?

Colón's attempts to identify species were likewise frequently wrong-headed, usually imputing to them commercial worth that they did not have, as with the worthless "aloes" he loaded such quantities of. The "amaranth" he identified on October 28 and the "oaks" and "arbutus" of November 25 are species that do not grow in the Caribbean; the "mastic" he found on November 5 and loaded on board to sell in Spain was gumbo-limbo, commercially worthless. (On the other hand, one of the species of flora he deemed of no marketable interest — "weeds [*tizon*] in their hands to drink in the fragrant smoke" [November 6] — was tobacco.) Similarly, the "whales" he spotted on October 16 must have been simply large fish, the "geese" he saw on November 6 and again on December 22 were ducks, the "nightingales" that kept delighting him (November 6; December 7, 13) do not exist in the Americas, and the skulls of "cows" he identified on October 29 were probably not those of land animals but of manatees.

This all seems a little sad, revealing a man rather lost in a world that he cannot come to know, a man with a "geographic and naturalistic knowledge that doesn't turn out to be very deep or nearly complete," and "a limited imagination and a capacity for comparisons conditioned by a not very broad geographic culture," in the words of Gaetano Ferro, a Columbus scholar and professor of geography at the University of Genoa. One could not of course have expected that an adventurer and sailor of this era would also be a naturalist, or necessarily even have some genuine interest in or curiosity about the natural world, but it is a disappointment nonetheless that the Discoverer of the New World turns out to be quite so simple, quite so inexperienced, in the ways of discovering his environment.

Colón's limitations, I hasten to say, were not his alone; they were of his culture, and they would be found in the descriptions of many others — Vespucci, Cortés, Hawkins, Juet, Cartier, Champlain, Ralegh — in the century of discovery to follow. They are the source of what the distinguished English historian J. H. Elliott has called "the problem of description" faced by Europeans confronting the uniqueness of the New World: "So often the physical appearance of the New World is either totally ignored or else described in the flattest and most conventional phraseology. This off-hand treatment of nature contrasts strikingly with the many precise and acute descriptions of the native inhabitants. It is as if the American landscape is seen as no more than a backcloth against which the strange and perennially fascinating peoples of the New World are dutifully grouped." The reason, Elliott thinks, and this is telling, may be "a lack of interest among sixteenth-century Europeans, and especially those of the Mediterranean world, in landscape and in nature." This lack of interest was reflected in the lack of vocabulary, the lack of that facility common to nature-based peoples whose cultures are steeped in natural imagery. Oviedo, for example, setting out to write descriptions for his *Historia General* in the next century, continually threw his hands up in the air: "Of all the things I have seen," he said at one point, "this is the one which has most left me without hope of being able to describe it in words"; or at another, "It needs to be painted by the hand of a Berruguete or some other excellent painter like him, or by Leonardo da Vinci or Andrea Mantegna, famous painters whom I knew in Italy." Like Colón, visitor after visitor to the New World seemed mind-boggled and tongue-tied trying to convey the wonders before them, and about the only color they seem to have eyes for is green — and not very many shades of that, either. . . .

■ REFLECTIONS

It is difficult to ignore moral issues when considering explorations and explorers. The prefix *great* is used liberally, and words like *discovery* and *courage* readily fit when describing "firsts" and "unknowns." However, celebratory images, national myths, and heroic biographies inevitably breed skepticism. Sometimes the result is an opposite assessment. Kirkpatrick Sale charges Columbus with arrogance, ignorance, and insufficient curiosity. Chinese historians of the last twenty years have swung from ignoring to celebrating the voyages of Zheng He, and some more recently have criticized Zheng He for military suppression of those in the lands his fleet visited.

On the matter of preparation, the difference between the Chinese and European voyages is especially striking. Da Gama at least brought an Arabic interpreter, though the absence of valuable gifts undermined the success of the voyage. The floating Chinese scientific laboratories, traveling experts, sages, and interpreters contrast starkly with the lack of a single artist or naturalist on board Columbus's ships. But the inability to distinguish shades of green is not a moral failure. We might say that Columbus's voyage was premature, Zheng He's meticulously planned and prepared. Like the designers of a modern aircraft, the Chinese built in redundancies: separate compartments that could fill with water without sinking the ship, more rice and fresh water than they would need, experts to find plants that might cure diseases yet unknown. By contrast, Columbus seems like a loose cannon, unaware of where he was going or where he had been, capable of lighting a match inside a dark powder shed.

These were, and in many ways still are, the differences between Chinese and European (now Western) scientific innovation. No European king could organize an enterprise on the scale of Zhu Di. No Chinese emperor had reason to sanction an experimental voyage into the unknown. The domain of the emperor was the known world, of which he was the center. In the Europe of closely competing princes, a Columbus could hatch a personal scheme with minimal supervision and barely sufficient funding and the consequences could still be — indeed, were — momentous. (See Chapter 16.) Was such a system irresponsible? Today, as we begin to probe the heavens around us, even as we tamper with technologies that change the balance of natural forces on Earth, we might consider whether the Confucian scholars of six hundred years ago were on to something when they burned the ships and destroyed all the records of their age of great discovery.

Primary sources are not limited to artifacts, images, and old written records, however. In the recent phase of celebrating the memory of Zheng He, the Chinese claimed as their own a young woman from Kenya, Mwamaka Sharifu, who looked like some of the people Kristof saw in 1999. Chinese-African faces on the coast of East Africa are evidence of contact, but not of contact in 1421. Combined, however, with family stories, DNA tests, local histories, and archaeological finds, a single living primary source may become the basis for a new interpretation of a broader history. In the case of Mwamaka Sharifu, members of her family, and other residents of coastal Somalia and Kenya, the evidence has proved convincing.

16

Atlantic World Encounters

*Europeans, Americans, and Africans,
1500–1850*

European expansion in the Atlantic that began with Portuguese
voyages along the African coast in the 1440s and Columbus's discovery
of the Americas in 1492 created a new Atlantic zone of human contact
and communication that embraced four continents and one ocean.
Nothing prior—neither the Chinese contacts with Africa in the early
fifteenth century, nor the expansion of Islam throughout Eurasia in
the almost thousand years since the Prophet Muhammad's death in
632—had so thoroughly and so permanently changed the human and
ecological balance of the world.

Sub-Saharan Africa had already been integrated into the world of
Eurasia by 1450. African populations became more mixed as peoples
from the Niger River area migrated east and south throughout the
continent during the fifteen hundred years before the arrival of the
Portuguese. Muslims from North Africa and the Middle East aided or
established Muslim states and trading ports south of the Sahara in East
and West Africa after 1000. Cultural and technical innovations of the
Middle East, like the literacy that came with Islam, penetrated slowly,
and the spread of the many plants and animals of the Northern Hemisphere was slowed by the Sahara and equator. However, microbes
traveled swiftly and easily from Eurasia to Africa, creating a single
set of diseases and immunities for the peoples of the Afro-Eurasian
Old World.

The peoples of the Americas, having been isolated ecologically
for more than a thousand years, were not so fortunate. The arrival of
Europeans and Africans in the Americas after 1492 had devastating
consequences for Native American populations. Old World diseases like

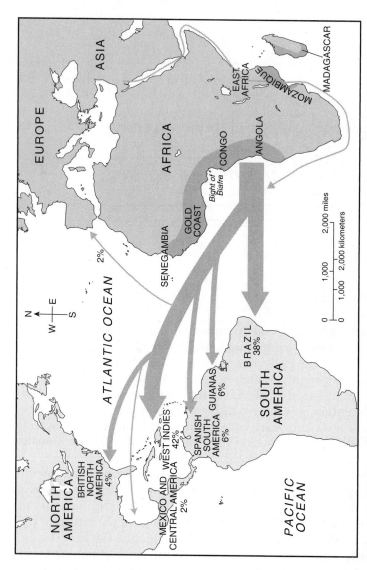

Map 16.1 The Atlantic Slave Trade.

smallpox were responsible for millions of Native American deaths—a tragedy of far greater scope than the casualties caused by wars. To work the mines and plantations of the New World, Europeans used Indian labor, but increasingly, especially for lowland plantations, they used African slaves (see Map 16.1). By 1850 the combination of Indian "die-off" and African and European migration resulted in vastly different populations in the Americas. On some Caribbean islands and in plantation areas like northeastern Brazil, Indian populations were entirely replaced by Africans. At the same time, European animals (for example, goats, cattle, horses) multiplied in the absence of natural predators.

The new Atlantic ecological system was not a uniform zone, however. Coastal regions in Western Europe and towns on the eastern seaboard of the Americas prospered, while American interiors and African populations in Africa stagnated or declined. The Atlantic Ocean became a vast lake that united port cities and plantations with sailing ships that carried African slaves to the Caribbean, Caribbean sugar and rum to North American and European industrial ports, and guns, pots, and liquor to the African "Slave Coast."

Thus, the Atlantic world was integrated with the Old World. Trade routes that began in Boston or Bahia, Brazil, stretched across Eurasia and around southern Africa into the Indian Ocean and the China Sea. Crops that had previously been known only to Native Americans—corn, potatoes, and tomatoes—fueled population explosions from Ireland to China and graced the tables of peasants and princes in between. What began as an effort by European merchants to import Asian spices directly became after 1650 (as European tastes for pepper and Asian spices moderated) a new global pantry of possibilities.

In this chapter, we will read selections that describe this new global dynamic. We will read of Europeans in the Americas and in West Africa and examine European depictions of natives from both North and South America. We will also explore some of the African and American responses to this European expansion. When studying these accounts and images, notice how individuals at the frontier of a new age understood and treated each other. Consider how these exchanges, so apparently fortuitous and transitory at the time, changed the face of the world.

■ THINKING HISTORICALLY

Comparing Primary Sources

By comparing and contrasting one thing with another, we learn more about each, and by examining related works in their proper context, we learn more about the whole of which they are part. In the first chapter we compared China and Europe or Chinese and European expansion in the fifteenth century. In this chapter we look at the Atlantic world, specifically at Europeans in Africa and the Americas. We begin with three views of the Spanish conquest of Mexico—separate accounts by the Spanish conquistadors, by the Mexicans, and by a Dominican friar. The fourth selection juxtaposes two European depictions of Native Americans.

The final four selections examine encounters between Europeans and Africans and the development of the Atlantic slave trade. Did Europeans treat Africans differently from the way they treated Native Americans? If so, why?

1

BERNAL DÍAZ

The Conquest of New Spain

Bernal Díaz del Castillo was born in Spain in 1492, the year Columbus sailed to America. After participating in two explorations of the Mexican coast, Díaz joined the expedition of Hernán Cortés to Mexico City in 1519. He wrote this history of the conquest much later, when he was in his seventies; he died circa 1580, a municipal official with a small estate in Guatemala.

The conquest of Mexico did not automatically follow from the first Spanish settlements in Santo Domingo, Hispaniola, and then Cuba in the West Indies. The Spanish crown had given permission for trade and exploration, not colonization. But many Spaniards, from fortune-seeking peasant-soldiers to minor nobility, were eager to conquer their own lands and exploit the populations of dependent Indians.

Cortés, of minor noble descent, at the age of nineteen sailed to the Indies, where he established a sizeable estate on the island of Hispaniola. When he heard stories of Montezuma's gold, he was determined to find the fabled capital of the Aztec Empire, Tenochtitlán* (modern Mexico City). He gathered more than five hundred amateur soldiers, eleven ships, sixteen horses, and several pieces of artillery, then sailed across the Caribbean and Gulf of Mexico and there began the long march from the coast up to the high central plateau of Mexico.

* teh NOHCH teet LAHN

Source: Bernal Díaz, *The Conquest of New Spain*, trans. J. M. Cohen (Baltimore: Penguin Books, 1963), 217–19, 221–25, 228–38, 241–43.

The Aztecs were new to central Mexico, arriving from the North American desert only about two hundred years before the Spanish, around 1325. By 1500 they had established dominion over almost all other city-states of Mexico, ruling an empire that stretched as far south as Guatemala and as far east as the Maya lands of the Yucatan Peninsula.

Aztec power relied on a combination of old and new religious ideas and a military system that conquered through terror. The older religious tradition that the Aztecs adopted from Toltec culture centered on Quetzalcoatl* — the feathered serpent, god of creation and brotherhood, whose nurturing forces continued in Aztec society in a system of universal education and in festivals dedicated to life, creativity, and procreation. But the Aztecs also worshiped Huitzilopochtli,† a warrior-god primed for death and sacrifice, who was given dominant status in the Aztec pantheon. Huitzilopochtli (rendered "Huichilobos"‡ in this selection) was a force for building a powerful Aztec Empire. Drawing on the god's need for human sacrifice — a need not unknown among religions of central Mexico (or Christians) — Montezuma's predecessors built altars to Huitzilopochtli at Tenochtitlán, Cholula, and other sites. The war-god required a never-ending supply of human hearts, a need that prompted armies to ever-more remote sections of Central America in search of sacrificial victims and that created an endless supply of enemies of the Aztecs, among them, the Tlaxcalans.

With the help of his Indian captive and companion Doña Marina — called La Malinche§ by some of the Indians (thus, Montezuma sometimes calls Cortés "Lord Malinche" in the selection) — Cortés was able to communicate with the Tlaxcalans and other Indians who were tired of Aztec domination. On his march toward Tenochtitlán, Cortés stopped to join forces with the Tlaxcalans, perhaps cementing the relationship and demonstrating his resolve through a brutal massacre of the people of Cholula, an Aztec ally and archenemy of the Tlaxcalans. By the time Cortés arrived at Tenochtitlán, Montezuma knew of the defeat of his allies at Cholula.

This selection from Bernal Díaz begins with the Spanish entry into Tenochtitlán. What impresses Díaz, and presumably other Spanish conquistadors, about the Mexican capital city? What parts of the city attract his attention the most? What conclusions does he draw about Mexican (or Aztec) civilization? Does he think Spanish civilization is equal, inferior, or superior to that of Mexico?

---

* keht zahl koh AH tuhl
† wheat zee loh po ACHT lee
‡ wee chee LOH bohs
§ lah mah LEEN cheh   A variation on "Marina." In contemporary Mexico a traitor is often called a "Malinchisto."

Díaz gives us a dramatic account of the meeting of Cortés and Montezuma. What do you think each is thinking and feeling? Do you see any signs of tension in their elaborate greetings? Why are both behaving so politely? What do they want from each other?

Notice how the initial hospitality turns tense. What causes this? Is either side more to blame for what happens next? Was conflict inevitable? Could the encounter have ended in some sort of peaceful resolution?

THINKING HISTORICALLY

Remember, we are going to compare Díaz's view with a Mexican view of these events. From your reading of Díaz, does he seem able to understand the Mexican point of view? Would you call him a sympathetic observer?

When Cortes saw, heard, and was told that the great Montezuma was approaching, he dismounted from his horse, and when he came near to Montezuma each bowed deeply to the other. Montezuma welcomed our Captain, and Cortes, speaking through Doña Marina, answered by wishing him very good health. Cortes, I think, offered Montezuma his right hand, but Montezuma refused it and extended his own. Then Cortes brought out a necklace which he had been holding. It was made of those elaborately worked and coloured glass beads called *margaritas*, . . . and was strung on a gold cord and dipped in musk to give it a good odour. This he hung round the great Montezuma's neck, and as he did so attempted to embrace him. But the great princes who stood round Montezuma grasped Cortes' arm to prevent him, for they considered this an indignity.

Then Cortes told Montezuma that it rejoiced his heart to have seen such a great prince, and that he took his coming in person to receive him and the repeated favours he had done him as a high honour. After this Montezuma made him another complimentary speech, and ordered two of his nephews who were supporting him, the lords of Texcoco and Coyoacan, to go with us and show us our quarters. Montezuma returned to the city with the other two kinsmen of his escort, the lords of Cuitlahuac and Tacuba; and all those grand companies of *Caciques*[1] and dignitaries who had come with him returned also in his train. . . .

On our arrival we entered the large court, where the great Montezuma was awaiting our Captain. Taking him by the hand, the prince led him

[1] kah SEEK Chiefs. [Ed.]

to his apartment in the hall where he was to lodge, which was very richly furnished in their manner. Montezuma had ready for him a very rich necklace, made of golden crabs, a marvellous piece of work, which he hung round Cortes' neck. His captains were greatly astonished at this sign of honour.

After this ceremony, for which Cortes thanked him through our interpreters, Montezuma said: "Malinche, you and your brothers are in your own house. Rest a while." He then returned to his palace, which was not far off.

We divided our lodgings by companies, and placed our artillery in a convenient spot. Then the order we were to keep was clearly explained to us, and we were warned to be very much on the alert, both the horsemen and the rest of us soldiers. We then ate a sumptuous dinner which they had prepared for us in their native style.

So, with luck on our side, we boldly entered the city of Tenochtitlán or Mexico on 8 November in the year of our Lord 1519.

The Stay in Mexico

. . . Montezuma had ordered his stewards to provide us with everything we needed for our way of living: maize, grindstones, women to make our bread, fowls, fruit, and plenty of fodder for the horses. He then took leave of us all with the greatest courtesy, and we accompanied him to the street. However, Cortes ordered us not to go far from our quarters for the present until we knew better what conduct to observe.

Next day Cortes decided to go to Montezuma's palace. But first he sent to know whether the prince was busy and to inform him of our coming. He took four captains with him: Pedro de Alvarado, Juan Velazquez de Leon, Diego de Ordaz, and Gonzalo de Sandoval, and five of us soldiers.

When Montezuma was informed of our coming, he advanced into the middle of the hall to receive us, closely surrounded by his nephews, for no other chiefs were allowed to enter his palace or communicate with him except upon important business. Cortes and Montezuma exchanged bows, and clasped hands. Then Montezuma led Cortes to his own dais, and setting him down on his right, called for more seats, on which he ordered us all to sit also.

Cortes began to make a speech through our interpreters, saying that we were all now rested, and that in coming to see and speak with such a great prince we had fulfilled the purpose of our voyage and the orders of our lord the King. The principal things he had come to say on behalf of our Lord God had already been communicated to Montezuma through his three ambassadors, on that occasion in the sandhills when he did us the favour of sending us the golden moon and sun. We had then told him that we were Christians and worshipped one God alone, named

Jesus Christ, who had suffered His passion and death to save us; and that what they worshipped as gods were not gods but devils, which were evil things, and if they were ugly to look at, their deeds were uglier. But he had proved to them how evil and ineffectual their gods were, as both the prince and his people would observe in the course of time, since, where we had put up crosses such as their ambassadors had seen, they had been too frightened to appear before them.

The favour he now begged of the great Montezuma was that he should listen to the words he now wished to speak. Then he very carefully expounded the creation of the world, how we are all brothers, the children of one mother and father called Adam and Eve; and how such a brother as our great Emperor, grieving for the perdition of so many souls as their idols were leading to hell, where they burnt in living flame, had sent us to tell him this, so that he might put a stop to it, and so that they might give up the worship of idols and make no more human sacrifices—for all men are brothers—and commit no more robbery or sodomy. He also promised that in the course of time the King would send some men who lead holy lives among us, much better than our own, to explain this more fully, for we had only come to give them warning. Therefore he begged Montezuma to do as he was asked.

As Montezuma seemed about to reply, Cortes broke off his speech, saying to those of us who were with him: "Since this is only the first attempt, we have now done our duty."

"My lord Malinche," Montezuma replied, "these arguments of yours have been familiar to me for some time. I understand what you said to my ambassadors on the sandhills about the three gods and the cross, also what you preached in the various towns through which you passed. We have given you no answer, since we have worshipped our own gods here from the beginning and know them to be good. No doubt yours are good also, but do not trouble to tell us any more about them at present. Regarding the creation of the world, we have held the same belief for many ages, and for this reason are certain that you are those who our ancestors predicted would come from the direction of the sunrise. As for your great King, I am in his debt and will give him of what I possess. For, as I have already said, two years ago I had news of the Captains who came in ships, by the road that you came, and said they were servants of this great king of yours. I should like to know if you are all the same people."

Cortes answered that we were all brothers and servants of the Emperor, and that they had come to discover a route and explore the seas and ports, so that when they knew them well we could follow, as we had done. Montezuma was referring to the expeditions of Francisco Hernandez de Cordoba and of Grijalva, the first voyages of discovery. He said that ever since that time he had wanted to invite some of these men to visit the cities of his kingdom, where he would receive them and do them honour, and that now his gods had fulfilled his desire, for we were in his house, which we might call our own. Here we might rest and enjoy ourselves, for we should receive good treatment. If on other occasions he had sent to forbid our entrance into his city, it was not of his own free will, but because his vassals were afraid. For they told him we shot out flashes of lightning, and killed many Indians with our horses, and that we were angry *Teules*,[2] and other such childish stories. But now that he had seen us, he knew that we were of flesh and blood and very intelligent, also very brave. Therefore he had a far greater esteem for us than these reports had given him, and would share with us what he had.

We all thanked him heartily for his . . . good will, and Montezuma replied with a laugh, because in his princely manner he spoke very gaily: "Malinche, I know that these people of Tlascala with whom you are so friendly have told you that I am a sort of god or *Teule*, and keep nothing in any of my houses that is not made of silver and gold and precious stones. But I know very well that you are too intelligent to believe this and will take it as a joke. See now, Malinche, my body is made of flesh and blood like yours, and my houses and palaces are of stone, wood, and plaster. It is true that I am a great king, and have inherited the riches of my ancestors, but the lies and nonsense you have heard of us are not true. You must take them as a joke, as I take the story of your thunders and lightnings."

Cortes answered also with a laugh that enemies always speak evil and tell lies about the people they hate, but he knew he could not hope to find a more magnificent prince in that land, and there was good reason why his fame should have reached our Emperor.

While this conversation was going on, Montezuma quietly sent one of his nephews, a great *Cacique*, to order his stewards to bring certain pieces of gold, which had apparently been set aside as a gift for Cortes, and ten loads of fine cloaks which he divided: the gold and cloaks between Cortes and the four captains, and for each of us soldiers two gold necklaces, each worth ten pesos, and two loads of cloaks. The gold that he then gave us was worth in all more than a thousand pesos, and he gave it all cheerfully, like a great and valiant prince.

As it was now past midday and he did not wish to be importunate, Cortes said to Montezuma: "My lord, the favours you do us increase, load by load, every day, and it is now the hour of your dinner." Montezuma answered that he thanked us for visiting him. We then took our leave with the greatest courtesy, and returned to our quarters, talking as we went of the prince's fine breeding and manners and deciding to show him the greatest respect in every way, and to remove our quilted caps in his presence, which we always did.

[2] Gods. [Ed.]

The great Montezuma was about forty years old, of good height, well proportioned, spare and slight, and not very dark, though of the usual Indian complexion. He did not wear his hair long but just over his ears, and he had a short black beard, well-shaped and thin. His face was rather long and cheerful, he had fine eyes, and in his appearance and manner could express geniality or, when necessary, a serious composure. He was very neat and clean, and took a bath every afternoon. He had many women as his mistresses, the daughters of chieftains, but two legitimate wives who were *Caciques* in their own right, and when he had intercourse with any of them it was so secret that only some of his servants knew of it. He was quite free from sodomy. The clothes he wore one day he did not wear again till three or four days later. He had a guard of two hundred chieftains lodged in rooms beside his own, only some of whom were permitted to speak to him. When they entered his presence they were compelled to take off their rich cloaks and put on others of little value. They had to be clean and walk barefoot, with their eyes downcast, for they were not allowed to look him in the face, and as they approached they had to make three obeisances, saying as they did so, "Lord, my lord, my great lord!" Then, when they had said what they had come to say, he would dismiss them with a few words. They did not turn their backs on him as they went out, but kept their faces towards him and their eyes downcast, only turning round when they had left the room. Another thing I noticed was that when other great chiefs came from distant lands about disputes or on business, they too had to take off their shoes and put on poor cloaks before entering Montezuma's apartments; and they were not allowed to enter the palace immediately but had to linger for a while near the door, since to enter hurriedly was considered disrespectful. . . .

Montezuma had two houses stocked with every sort of weapon; many of them were richly adorned with gold and precious stones. There were shields large and small, and a sort of broadsword, and two-handed swords set with flint blades that cut much better than our swords, and lances longer than ours, with five-foot blades consisting of many knives. Even when these are driven at a buckler or a shield they are not deflected. In fact they cut like razors, and the Indians can shave their heads with them. They had very good bows and arrows, and double and single-pointed javelins as well as their throwing-sticks and many slings and round stones shaped by hand, and another sort of shield that can be rolled up when they are not fighting, so that it does not get in the way, but which can be opened when they need it in battle and covers their bodies from head to foot. There was also a great deal of cotton armour richly worked on the outside with different coloured feathers, which they used as devices and distinguishing marks, and they had casques and helmets made of wood and bone which were also highly decorated with feathers on the outside. They had other arms of different kinds which I will not mention through fear of prolixity, and workmen skilled in the manufacture of such things, and stewards who were in charge of these arms. . . .

I have already described the manner of their sacrifices. They strike open the wretched Indian's chest with flint knives and hastily tear out the palpitating heart which, with the blood, they present to the idols in whose name they have performed the sacrifice. Then they cut off the arms, thighs, and head, eating the arms and thighs at their ceremonial banquets. The head they hang up on a beam, and the body of the sacrificed man is not eaten but given to the beasts of prey. They also had many vipers in this accursed house, and poisonous snakes which have something that sounds like a bell in their tails. These, which are the deadliest snakes of all, they kept in jars and great pottery vessels full of feathers, in which they laid their eggs and reared their young. They were fed on the bodies of sacrificed Indians and the flesh of the dogs that they bred. We know for certain, too, that when they drove us out of Mexico and killed over eight hundred and fifty of our soldiers, they fed those beasts and snakes on their bodies for many days, as I shall relate in due course. These snakes and wild beasts were dedicated to their fierce idols, and kept them company. As for the horrible noise when the lions and tigers roared, and the jackals and foxes howled, and the serpents hissed, it was so appalling that one seemed to be in hell. . . .

When our Captain and the Mercedarian friar realized that Montezuma would not allow us to set up a cross at Huichilobos' *cue*[3] or build a church there, it was decided that we should ask his stewards for masons so that we could put up a church in our own quarters. For every time we had said mass since entering the city of Mexico we had had to erect an altar on tables and dismantle it again.

The stewards promised to tell Montezuma of our wishes, and Cortes also sent our interpreters to ask him in person. Montezuma granted our request and ordered that we should be supplied with all the necessary material. We had our church finished in two days, and a cross erected in front of our lodgings, and mass was said there each day until the wine gave out. For as Cortes and some other captains and a friar had been ill during the Tlascalan campaign, there had been a run on the wine that we kept for mass. Still, though it was finished, we still went to church every day and prayed on our knees before the altar and images, firstly because it was our obligation as Christians and a good habit, and secondly so that Montezuma and all his captains should observe us and, seeing us worshipping on our knees before the cross—especially when we intoned the Ave Maria—might be inclined to imitate us.

It being our habit to examine and inquire into everything, when we were all assembled in our lodging and considering which was the best place for an altar, two of our men, one of whom was the carpenter

[3] The temple of the sun-god, who demanded human sacrifice. [Ed.]

Alonso Yañez, called attention to some marks on one of the walls which showed that there had once been a door, though it had been well plastered up and painted. Now as we had heard that Montezuma kept his father's treasure in this building, we immediately suspected that it must be in this room, which had been closed up only a few days before. Yañez made the suggestion to Juan Velazquez de Leon and Francisco de Lugo, both relatives of mine, to whom he had attached himself as a servant; and they mentioned the matter to Cortes. So the door was secretly opened, and Cortes went in first with certain captains. When they saw the quantity of golden objects—jewels and plates and ingots—which lay in that chamber they were quite transported. They did not know what to think of such riches. The news soon spread to the other captains and soldiers, and very secretly we all went in to see. The sight of all that wealth dumbfounded me. Being only a youth at the time and never having seen such riches before, I felt certain that there could not be a store like it in the whole world. We unanimously decided that we could not think of touching a particle of it, and that the stones should immediately be replaced in the doorway, which should be blocked again and cemented just as we had found it. We resolved also that not a word should be said about this until times changed, for fear Montezuma might hear of our discovery.

Let us leave this subject of the treasure and tell how four of our most valiant captains took Cortes aside in the church, with a dozen soldiers who were in his trust and confidence, myself among them, and asked him to consider the net or trap in which we were caught, to look at the great strength of the city and observe the causeways and bridges, and remember the warnings we had received in every town we had passed through that Huichilobos had counselled Montezuma to let us into the city and kill us there. We reminded him that the hearts of men are very fickle, especially among the Indians, and begged him not to trust the good will and affection that Montezuma was showing us, because from one hour to another it might change. If he should take it into his head to attack us, we said, the stoppage of our supplies of food and water, or the raising of any of the bridges, would render us helpless. Then, considering the vast army of warriors he possessed, we should be incapable of attacking or defending ourselves. And since all the houses stood in the water, how could our Tlascalan allies come in to help us? We asked him to think over all that we had said, for if we wanted to preserve our lives we must seize Montezuma immediately, without even a day's delay. We pointed out that all the gold Montezuma had given us, and all that we had seen in the treasury of his father Axayacatl, and all the food we ate was turning to poison in our bodies, for we could not sleep by night or day or take any rest while these thoughts were in our minds. If any of our soldiers gave him less drastic advice, we concluded, they would be senseless beasts charmed by the gold and incapable of looking death in the eye.

When he had heard our opinion, Cortes answered: "Do not imagine, gentlemen, that I am asleep or that I do not share your anxiety. You must have seen that I do. But what strength have we got for so bold a course as to take this great lord in his own palace, surrounded as he is by warriors and guards? What scheme or trick can we devise to prevent him from summoning his soldiers to attack us at once?"

Our captains (Juan Velazquez de Leon, Diego de Ordaz, Gonzalo de Sandoval, and Pedro de Alvarado) replied that Montezuma must be got out of his palace by smooth words and brought to our quarters. Once there, he must be told that he must remain as a prisoner, and that if he called out or made any disturbance he would pay for it with his life. If Cortes was unwilling to take this course at once, they begged him for permission to do it themselves. With two very dangerous alternatives before us, the better and more profitable thing, they said, would be to seize Montezuma rather than wait for him to attack us. Once he did so, what chance would we have? Some of us soldiers also remarked that Montezuma's stewards who brought us our food seemed to be growing insolent, and did not serve us as politely as they had at first. Two of our Tlascalan allies had, moreover, secretly observed to Jeronimo de Aguilar that for the last two days the Mexicans had appeared less well disposed to us. We spent a good hour discussing whether or not to take Montezuma prisoner, and how it should be done. But our final advice, that at all costs we should take him prisoner, was approved by our Captain, and we then left the matter till next day. All night we prayed God to direct events in the interests of His holy service. . . .

2

The Broken Spears: The Aztec Account of the Conquest of Mexico

This Aztec account, one of several written by native priests and wise men of the encounter between the Spanish and the Indians of Mexico, was written some years after the events described. Spanish Christian monks helped a postconquest generation of Aztec Nahuatl* speakers translate the illustrated manuscripts of the conquest period. According to this account, how did Montezuma respond to Cortés?

*nah WAH tuhl

Source: *The Broken Spears: The Aztec Account of the Conquest of Mexico*, ed. Miguel Leon-Portilla (Boston: Beacon Press, 1990), 64–76.

Was Montezuma's attitude toward the Spanish shared by other Aztecs? How reliable is this account, do you think, in describing Montezuma's thoughts, motives, and behavior?

THINKING HISTORICALLY

How does the Aztec account of the conquest differ from that of the Spanish, written by Díaz? Is this difference merely a matter of perspective, or do the authors disagree about what happened? To the extent to which there are differences, how do you decide which account to believe and accept?

Speeches of Motecuhzoma and Cortes

When Motecuhzoma[1] had given necklaces to each one, Cortes asked him: "Are you Motecuhzoma? Are you the king? Is it true that you are the king Motecuhzoma?"

And the king said: "Yes, I am Motecuhzoma." Then he stood up to welcome Cortes; he came forward, bowed his head low and addressed him in these words: "Our lord, you are weary. The journey has tired you, but now you have arrived on the earth. You have come to your city, Mexico. You have come here to sit on your throne, to sit under its canopy.

"The kings who have gone before, your representatives, guarded it and preserved it for your coming. The kings Itzcoatl, Motecuhzoma the Elder, Axayacatl, Tizoc, and Ahuitzol ruled for you in the City of Mexico. The people were protected by their swords and sheltered by their shields.

"Do the kings know the destiny of those they left behind, their posterity? If only they are watching! If only they can see what I see!

"No, it is not a dream. I am not walking in my sleep. I am not seeing you in my dreams. . . . I have seen you at last! I have met you face to face! I was in agony for five days, for ten days, with my eyes fixed on the Region of the Mystery. And now you have come out of the clouds and mists to sit on your throne again.

"This was foretold by the kings who governed your city, and now it has taken place. You have come back to us; you have come down from the sky. Rest now, and take possession of your royal houses. Welcome to your land, my lords!"

When Motecuhzoma had finished, La Malinche translated his address into Spanish so that the Captain could understand it. Cortes replied in his strange and savage tongue, speaking first to La Malinche: "Tell

---

[1] Montezuma (earlier spelling). [Ed.]

Motecuhzoma that we are his friends. There is nothing to fear. We have wanted to see him for a long time, and now we have seen his face and heard his words. Tell him that we love him well and that our hearts are contented."

Then he said to Motecuhzoma: "We have come to your house in Mexico as friends. There is nothing to fear."

La Malinche translated this speech and the Spaniards grasped Motecuhzoma's hands and patted his back to show their affection for him.

Attitudes of the Spaniards and the Native Lords

The Spaniards examined everything they saw. They dismounted from their horses, and mounted them again, and dismounted again, so as not to miss anything of interest.

The chiefs who accompanied Motecuhzoma were: Cacama, king of Tezcoco; Tetlepanquetzaltzin, king of Tlacopan; Itzcuauhtzin the Tlacochcalcatl, lord of Tlatelolco; and Topantemoc, Motecuhzoma's treasurer in Tlatelolco. These four chiefs were standing in a file.

The other princes were: Atlixcatzin [chief who has taken captives];[2] Tepeoatzin, the Tlacochcalcatl; Quetzalaztatzin, the keeper of the chalk; Totomotzin; Hecateupatiltzin; and Cuappiatzin.

When Motecuhzoma was imprisoned, they all went into hiding. They ran away to hide and treacherously abandoned him!

The Spaniards Take Possession of the City

When the Spaniards entered the Royal House, they placed Motecuhzoma under guard and kept him under their vigilance. They also placed a guard over Itzcuauhtzin, but the other lords were permitted to depart.

Then the Spaniards fired one of their cannons, and this caused great confusion in the city. The people scattered in every direction; they fled without rhyme or reason; they ran off as if they were being pursued. It was as if they had eaten the mushrooms that confuse the mind, or had seen some dreadful apparition. They were all overcome by terror, as if their hearts had fainted. And when night fell, the panic spread through the city and their fears would not let them sleep.

In the morning the Spaniards told Motecuhzoma what they needed in the way of supplies: tortillas, fried chickens, hens' eggs, pure water, firewood, and charcoal. Also: large, clean cooking pots, water jars, pitchers, dishes, and other pottery. Motecuhzoma ordered that it be sent to

[2] Military title given to a warrior who had captured four enemies.

them. The chiefs who received this order were angry with the king and no longer revered or respected him. But they furnished the Spaniards with all the provisions they needed—food, beverages, and water, and fodder for the horses.

The Spaniards Reveal Their Greed

When the Spaniards were installed in the palace, they asked Motecuhzoma about the city's resources and reserves and about the warriors' ensigns and shields. They questioned him closely and then demanded gold.

Motecuhzoma guided them to it. They surrounded him and crowded close with their weapons. He walked in the center, while they formed a circle around him.

When they arrived at the treasure house called Teucalco, the riches of gold and feathers were brought out to them: ornaments made of quetzal feathers, richly worked shields, disks of gold, the necklaces of the idols, gold nose plugs, gold greaves,[3] and bracelets and crowns.

The Spaniards immediately stripped the feathers from the gold shields and ensigns. They gathered all the gold into a great mound and set fire to everything else, regardless of its value. Then they melted down the gold into ingots. As for the precious green stones, they took only the best of them; the rest were snatched up by the Tlaxcaltecas. The Spaniards searched through the whole treasure house, questioning and quarreling, and seized every object they thought was beautiful.

The Seizure of Motecuhzoma's Treasures

Next they went to Motecuhzoma's storehouse, in the place called Totocalco [Place of the Palace of the Birds],[4] where his personal treasures were kept. The Spaniards grinned like little beasts and patted each other with delight.

When they entered the hall of treasures, it was as if they had arrived in Paradise. They searched everywhere and coveted everything; they were slaves to their own greed. All of Motecuhzoma's possessions were brought out: fine bracelets, necklaces with large stones, ankle rings with little gold bells, the royal crowns, and all the royal finery—everything that belonged to the king and was reserved to him only. They seized these treasures as if they were their own, as if this plunder were merely a stroke of good luck. And when they had taken all the gold, they heaped up everything else in the middle of the patio.

[3] Leg armour. [Ed.]
[4] The zoological garden attached to the royal palaces.

La Malinche called the nobles together. She climbed up to the palace roof and cried: "Mexicanos, come forward! The Spaniards need your help! Bring them food and pure water. They are tired and hungry; they are almost fainting from exhaustion! Why do you not come forward? Are you angry with them?"

The Mexicans were too frightened to approach. They were crushed by terror and would not risk coming forward. They shied away as if the Spaniards were wild beasts, as if the hour were midnight on the blackest night of the year. Yet they did not abandon the Spaniards to hunger and thirst. They brought them whatever they needed, but shook with fear as they did so. They delivered the supplies to the Spaniards with trembling hands, then turned and hurried away.

The Preparations for the Fiesta

The Aztecs begged permission of their king to hold the fiesta of Huitzilopochtli.[5] The Spaniards wanted to see this fiesta to learn how it was celebrated. A delegation of the celebrants came to the palace where Motecuhzoma was a prisoner, and when their spokesman asked his permission, he granted it to them.

As soon as the delegation returned, the women began to grind seeds of the *chicalote*.[6] These women had fasted for a whole year. They ground the seeds in the patio of the temple.

The Spaniards came out of the palace together, dressed in armor and carrying their weapons with them. They stalked among the women and looked at them one by one; they stared into the faces of the women who were grinding seeds. After this cold inspection, they went back into the palace. It is said that they planned to kill the celebrants if the men entered the patio.

The Statue of Huitzilopochtli

On the evening before the fiesta of Toxcatl, the celebrants began to model a statue of Huitzilopochtli. They gave it such a human appearance that it seemed the body of a living man. Yet they made the statue with nothing but a paste made of the ground seeds of the chicalote, which they shaped over an armature of sticks.

When the statue was finished, they dressed it in rich feathers, and they painted crossbars over and under its eyes. They also clipped on its

[5] Aztec war-god. See Introduction to selections. [Ed.]
[6] Edible plants also used in medicines. [Ed.]

earrings of turquoise mosaic; these were in the shape of serpents, with gold rings hanging from them. Its nose plug, in the shape of an arrow, was made of gold and was inlaid with fine stones.

They placed the magic headdress of hummingbird feathers on its head. They also adorned it with an *anecuyotl*, which was a belt made of feathers, with a cone at the back. Then they hung around its neck an ornament of yellow parrot feathers, fringed like the locks of a young boy. Over this they put its nettle-leaf cape, which was painted black and decorated with five clusters of eagle feathers.

Next they wrapped it in its cloak, which was painted with skull and bones, and over this they fastened its vest. The vest was painted with dismembered human parts: skulls, ears, hearts, intestines, torsos, breasts, hands, and feet. They also put on its *maxtlatl*, or loincloth, which was decorated with images of dissevered limbs and fringed with amate paper. This *maxtlatl* was painted with vertical stripes of bright blue.

They fastened a red paper flag at its shoulder and placed on its head what looked like a sacrificial flint knife. This too was made of red paper; it seemed to have been steeped in blood.

The statue carried a *tehuehuelli*, a bamboo shield decorated with four clusters of fine eagle feathers. The pendant of this shield was blood-red, like the knife and the shoulder flag. The statue also carried four arrows.

Finally, they put the wristbands on its arms. These bands, made of coyote skin, were fringed with paper cut into little strips.

The Beginning of the Fiesta

Early the next morning, the statue's face was uncovered by those who had been chosen for that ceremony. They gathered in front of the idol in single file and offered it gifts of food, such as round seedcakes or perhaps human flesh. But they did not carry it up to its temple on top of the pyramid.

All the young warriors were eager for the fiesta to begin. They had sworn to dance and sing with all their hearts, so that the Spaniards would marvel at the beauty of the rituals.

The procession began, and the celebrants filed into the temple patio to dance the Dance of the Serpent. When they were all together in the patio, the songs and the dance began. Those who had fasted for twenty days and those who had fasted for a year were in command of the others; they kept the dancers in file with their pine wands. (If anyone wished to urinate, he did not stop dancing, but simply opened his clothing at the hips and separated his clusters of heron feathers.)

If anyone disobeyed the leaders or was not in his proper place they struck him on the hips and shoulders. Then they drove him out of the patio, beating him and shoving him from behind. They pushed him so hard that he sprawled to the ground, and they dragged him outside by the ears. No one dared to say a word about this punishment, for those who had fasted during the year were feared and venerated; they had earned the exclusive title "Brothers of Huitzilopochtli."

The great captains, the bravest warriors, danced at the head of the files to guide the others. The youths followed at a slight distance. Some of the youths wore their hair gathered into large locks, a sign that they had never taken any captives. Others carried their headdresses on their shoulders; they had taken captives, but only with help.

Then came the recruits, who were called "the young warriors." They had each captured an enemy or two. The others called to them: "Come, comrades, show us how brave you are! Dance with all your hearts!"

The Spaniards Attack the Celebrants

At this moment in the fiesta, when the dance was loveliest and when song was linked to song, the Spaniards were seized with an urge to kill the celebrants. They all ran forward, armed as if for battle. They closed the entrances and passageways, all the gates of the patio: the Eagle Gate in the lesser palace, the Gate of the Canestalk and the Gate of the Serpent of Mirrors. They posted guards so that no one could escape, and then rushed into the Sacred Patio to slaughter the celebrants. They came on foot, carrying their swords and their wooden or metal shields.

They ran in among the dancers, forcing their way to the place where the drums were played. They attacked the man who was drumming and cut off his arms. Then they cut off his head, and it rolled across the floor.

They attacked all the celebrants, stabbing them, spearing them, striking them with their swords. They attacked some of them from behind, and these fell instantly to the ground with their entrails hanging out. Others they beheaded: they cut off their heads, or split their heads to pieces.

They struck others in the shoulders, and their arms were torn from their bodies. They wounded some in the thigh and some in the calf.

They slashed others in the abdomen, and their entrails all spilled to the ground. Some attempted to run away, but their intestines dragged as they ran; they seemed to tangle their feet in their own entrails. No matter how they tried to save themselves, they could find no escape.

Some attempted to force their way out, but the Spaniards murdered them at the gates. Others climbed the walls, but they could not save themselves. Those who ran into the communal houses were safe there for a while; so were those who lay down among the victims and pretended to be dead. But if they stood up again, the Spaniards saw them and killed them.

The blood of the warriors flowed like water and gathered into pools. The pools widened, and the stench of blood and entrails filled the air. The Spaniards ran into the communal houses to kill those who were hiding. They ran everywhere and searched everywhere; they invaded every room, hunting and killing.

3

BARTOLOMÉ DE LAS CASAS
The Devastation of the Indies

Las Casas (1484–1566) emigrated with his father from Spain to the island of Hispaniola in 1502. Eight years later he became a priest, served as a missionary to the Taino of Cuba (1512), attempted to create a utopian society for the Indians of Venezuela, and became a Dominican friar in 1522. Repelled by his early experience among the conquistadors, Las Casas the priest and friar devoted his adult life to aiding the Indians in the Americas and defending their rights in the Spanish court. This selection is drawn from his brief history, *The Devastation of the Indies*, published in 1555. The work for this book and a larger volume, *In Defense of the Indians*, presented his case against Indian slavery in the great debate at the Spanish court at Valladolid in 1550. Along with his monumental *History of the Indies*, published after his death, the writings of Las Casas constituted such an indictment of Spanish colonialism that Protestant enemies were able to argue that Catholic slavery and exploitation of the "New World" was worse than their own, a dubious proposition that became known as "the Black Legend." What do you make of this account by Las Casas? Does he exaggerate, or is it likely that these events happened?

THINKING HISTORICALLY

Compare this account with the two previous selections. Do you think the Spanish treated the people of Hispaniola and Mexico differently? Do these three readings offer different interpretations of the role of Christianity in the Americas?

Source: Bartolomé de Las Casas, *The Devastation of the Indies: A Brief Account,* trans. Herma Briffault (Baltimore: Johns Hopkins University Press, 1992), 32–35, 40–41.

This [Hispaniola][1] was the first land in the New World to be destroyed and depopulated by the Christians, and here they began their subjection of the women and children, taking them away from the Indians to use them and ill use them, eating the food they provided with their sweat and toil. The Spaniards did not content themselves with what the Indians gave them of their own free will, according to their ability, which was always too little to satisfy enormous appetites, for a Christian eats and consumes in one day an amount of food that would suffice to feed three houses inhabited by ten Indians for one month. And they committed other acts of force and violence and oppression which made the Indians realize that these men had not come from Heaven. And some of the Indians concealed their foods while others concealed their wives and children and still others fled to the mountains to avoid the terrible transactions of the Christians.

And the Christians attacked them with buffets and beatings, until finally they laid hands on the nobles of the villages. Then they behaved with such temerity and shamelessness that the most powerful ruler of the islands had to see his own wife raped by a Christian officer.

From that time onward the Indians began to seek ways to throw the Christians out of their lands. They took up arms, but their weapons were very weak and of little service in offense and still less in defense. (Because of this, the wars of the Indians against each other are little more than games played by children.) And the Christians, with their horses and swords and pikes began to carry out massacres and strange cruelties against them. They attacked the towns and spared neither the children nor the aged nor pregnant women nor women in childbed, not only stabbing them and dismembering them but cutting them to pieces as if dealing with sheep in the slaughter house. They laid bets as to who, with one stroke of the sword, could split a man in two or could cut off his head or spill out his entrails with a single stroke of the pike. They took infants from their mothers' breasts, snatching them by the legs and pitching them headfirst against the crags or snatched them by the arms and threw them into the rivers, roaring with laughter and saying as the babies fell into the water, "Boil there, you offspring of the devil!" Other infants they put to the sword along with their mothers and anyone else who happened to be nearby. They made some low wide gallows on which the hanged victim's feet almost touched the ground, stringing up their victims in lots of thirteen, in memory of Our Redeemer and His twelve Apostles, then set burning wood at their feet and thus burned them alive. To others they attached straw or wrapped their whole bodies in straw and set them afire. With still others, all those they wanted to capture alive, they cut off their hands and hung them round the victim's neck, saying, "Go now, carry the message," meaning, Take the news to the Indians who have fled to

---

[1] The island that today includes the Dominican Republic and Haiti. [Ed.]

the mountains. They usually dealt with the chieftains and nobles in the following way: they made a grid of rods which they placed on forked sticks, then lashed the victims to the grid and lighted a smoldering fire underneath, so that little by little, as those captives screamed in despair and torment, their souls would leave them.

I once saw this, when there were four or five nobles lashed on grids and burning; I seem even to recall that there were two or three pairs of grids where others were burning, and because they uttered such loud screams that they disturbed the captain's sleep, he ordered them to be strangled. And the constable, who was worse than an executioner, did not want to obey that order (and I know the name of that constable and know his relatives in Seville), but instead put a stick over the victims' tongues, so they could not make a sound, and he stirred up the fire, but not too much, so that they roasted slowly, as he liked. I saw all these things I have described, and countless others.

And because all the people who could do so fled to the mountains to escape these inhuman, ruthless, and ferocious acts, the Spanish captains, enemies of the human race, pursued them with the fierce dogs they kept which attacked the Indians, tearing them to pieces and devouring them. And because on few and far between occasions, the Indians justifiably killed some Christians, the Spaniards made a rule among themselves that for every Christian slain by the Indians, they would slay a hundred Indians. . . .

Because the particulars that enter into these outrages are so numerous they could not be contained in the scope of much writing, for in truth I believe that in the great deal I have set down here I have not revealed the thousandth part of the sufferings endured by the Indians, I now want only to add that, in the matter of these unprovoked and destructive wars, and God is my witness, all these acts of wickedness I have described, as well as those I have omitted, were perpetrated against the Indians without cause, without any more cause than could give a community of good monks living together in a monastery. And still more strongly I affirm that until the multitude of people on this island of Hispaniola were killed and their lands devastated, they committed no sin against the Christians that would be punishable by man's laws, and as to those sins punishable by God's law, such as vengeful feelings against such powerful enemies as the Christians have been, those sins would be committed by the very few Indians who are hardhearted and impetuous. And I can say this from my great experience with them: their hardness and impetuosity would be that of children, of boys ten or twelve years old. I know by certain infallible signs that the wars waged by the Indians against the Christians have been justifiable wars and that all the wars waged by the Christians against the Indians have been unjust wars, more diabolical than any wars ever waged anywhere in the world. This I declare to be so of all the many wars they have waged against the peoples throughout the Indies.

After the wars and the killings had ended, when usually there survived only some boys, some women, and children, these survivors were distributed among the Christians to be slaves. The *repartimiento* or distribution was made according to the rank and importance of the Christian to whom the Indians were allocated, one of them being given thirty, another forty, still another, one or two hundred, and besides the rank of the Christian there was also to be considered in what favor he stood with the tyrant they called Governor. The pretext was that these allocated Indians were to be instructed in the articles of the Christian Faith. As if those Christians who were as a rule foolish and cruel and greedy and vicious could be caretakers of souls! And the care they took was to send the men to the mines to dig for gold, which is intolerable labor, and to send the women into the fields of the big ranches to hoe and till the land, work suitable for strong men. Nor to either the men or the women did they give any food except herbs and legumes, things of little substance. The milk in the breasts of the women with infants dried up and thus in a short while the infants perished.

4

European Views of Native Americans

Las Casas's sympathetic view of the Indians was hardly one shared by the average Frenchman, Italian, or Scot. Indeed, many Europeans harbored fantastical and negative notions about the inhabitants of the "New World," envisioning them as wild and cannibalistic, savage and ruthless toward their enemies. Reinforcing this impression were images that circulated throughout Europe during the sixteenth and seventeenth centuries, such as this engraving from the 1590s, part of a series by Flemish engraver Theodore de Bry, based on paintings by an artist who had accompanied a French expedition to Florida a few decades earlier. Figure 16.1 shows the alleged cannibalistic practices by natives supposedly witnessed by the explorers. What is going on in this picture? It is likely that de Bry made adjustments to his engravings from the originals to please potential buyers. If so, what does this tell us about the expectations of European audiences about the Americas and their inhabitants?

Almost seventy-five years later, a very different set of no less remarkable images emerged from a Dutch colony in northeastern Brazil. Count Johan Maurits, the humanist governor general of the colony from 1636 to 1644, brought several artists and scientists with him to observe and record the region's flora and fauna as well as its inhabitants. Johan Maurits, who was fascinated by the local peoples and their cultures, commissioned from artist Albert Eckhout a number of

Figure 16.1 Cannibalism, Engraving by Theodore de Bry.

Source: Scene of Cannibalism, from 'Brevis Narratio', engraved by Theodore de Bry (1528–98) 1564 (coloured engraving), Le Moyne, Jacques (de Morgues) (1533–88) (after)/ Service Historique de la Marine, Vincennes, France/Giraudon/The Bridgeman Art Library.

still-lifes and group and individual portraits, including one showing a female Tapuya Indian (see Figure 16.2). According to Dutch accounts, the Tapuya were more warlike and less "civilized" than some of the other local peoples — for example, they sometimes consumed their dead instead of burying them. Aside from the body parts this woman carries in her hand and in her bag, what other signs of this warlike tendency do you see in Figure 16.2? Look closely at the many interesting details in this painting. What does the artist seem to be interested in showing?

THINKING HISTORICALLY

What are the differences in style and content between Figures 16.1 and 16.2, and how do you account for them? Which of the following factors do you think is most important in explaining their differences: chronology, agenda of the artist, the potential audience for the image, the setting in which they were produced? What might be the

Figure 16.2 Tapuya Indian, by Albert Eckhout.
Source: The Granger Collection, New York.

pitfalls for students of history in comparing these two images? How do you reconcile Las Casas's account in the previous source with the scene portrayed in Figure 16.1? Which source would you consider more reliable, and why? Which source would a sixteenth-century Spaniard have considered more reliable, and why? Consider how women are depicted in these works. What differences and similarities do you see? What might that tell us about European notions of women and gender in the New World?

NZINGA MBEMBA

Appeal to the King of Portugal

Europeans were unable to conquer Africa as they did the Americas until the end of the nineteenth century. Rivers that fell steeply to the sea, military defenses, and diseases like malaria proved insurmountable to Europeans before the age of the steamship, the machine gun, and antimalarial quinine. Before the last half of the nineteenth century, Europeans had to be content with alliances with African kings and rulers. The Portuguese had been the first to meet Africans in the towns and villages along the Atlantic coast, and they became the first European missionaries and trading partners.

Nzinga Mbemba, whose Christian name was Affonso, was king of the West African state of Congo (comprising what is today parts of Angola as well as the two Congo states) from about 1506 to 1543. He succeeded his father, King Nzinga, a Kuwu who, shortly after his first contact with the Portuguese in 1483, sent officials to Lisbon to learn European ways. In 1491 father and son were baptized, and Portuguese priests, merchants, artisans, and soldiers were provided with a coastal settlement.

What exactly is the complaint of the king of Congo? What seems to be the impact of Portuguese traders (called "factors") in the Congo? What does King Affonso want the king of Portugal to do?

THINKING HISTORICALLY

This selection offers an opportunity to compare European expansion in the Americas and Africa. Portuguese contact with Nzinga Mbemba of the Congo was roughly contemporaneous with Spanish colonialism in the Americas. What differences do you see between these two cases of early European expansion? Can you think of any reasons that Congo kings converted to Christianity whereas Mexican kings did not?

Compare the Europeans' treatment of Africans with their treatment of Native Americans. Why did Europeans enslave Africans and not, for the most part, American Indians?

Sir, Your Highness [of Portugal] should know how our Kingdom is being lost in so many ways that it is convenient to provide for the necessary remedy, since this is caused by the excessive freedom given by

Source: Basil Davidson, *The African Past* (Boston: Little, Brown, and Company, 1964), 191–94.

your factors and officials to the men and merchants who are allowed to come to this Kingdom to set up shops with goods and many things which have been prohibited by us, and which they spread throughout our Kingdoms and Domains in such an abundance that many of our vassals, whom we had in obedience, do not comply because they have the things in greater abundance than we ourselves; and it was with these things that we had them content and subjected under our vassalage and jurisdiction, so it is doing a great harm not only to the service of God, but to the security and peace of our Kingdoms and State as well.

And we cannot reckon how great the damage is, since the mentioned merchants are taking every day our natives, sons of the land and the sons of our noblemen and vassals and our relatives, because the thieves and men of bad conscience grab them wishing to have the things and wares of this Kingdom which they are ambitious of; they grab them and get them to be sold; and so great, Sir, is the corruption and licentiousness that our country is being completely depopulated, and Your Highness should not agree with this nor accept it as in your service. And to avoid it we need from those [your] Kingdoms no more than some priests and a few people to teach in schools, and no other goods except wine and flour for the holy sacrament. That is why we beg of Your Highness to help and assist us in this matter, commanding your factors that they should not send here either merchants or wares, because it is *our will that in these Kingdoms there should not be any trade of slaves nor outlet for them.*[1] Concerning what is referred above, again we beg of Your Highness to agree with it, since otherwise we cannot remedy such an obvious damage. Pray Our Lord in His mercy to have Your Highness under His guard and let you do for ever the things of His service. I kiss your hands many times.

> At our town of Congo, written on the sixth day of July.
> João Teixeira did it in 1526.
> The King. Dom Affonso.
> [On the back of this letter the following can be read:
> To the most powerful and excellent prince Dom João, King our Brother.]

Moreover, Sir, in our Kingdoms there is another great inconvenience which is of little service to God, and this is that many of our people [*naturaes*], keenly desirous as they are of the wares and things of your Kingdoms, which are brought here by your people, and in order to satisfy their voracious appetite, seize many of our people, freed and exempt men; and very often it happens that they kidnap even noblemen and the

---

[1] Emphasis in the original.

sons of noblemen, and our relatives, and take them to be sold to the white men who are in our Kingdoms; and for this purpose they have concealed them; and others are brought during the night so that they might not be recognized.

And as soon as they are taken by the white men they are immediately ironed and branded with fire, and when they are carried to be embarked, if they are caught by our guards' men the whites allege that they have bought them but they cannot say from whom, so that it is our duty to do justice and to restore to the freemen their freedom, but it cannot be done if your subjects feel offended, as they claim to be.

And to avoid such a great evil we passed a law so that any white man living in our Kingdoms and wanting to purchase goods in any way should first inform three of our noblemen and officials of our court whom we rely upon in this matter, and these are Dom Pedro Manipanza and Dom Manuel Manissaba, our chief usher, and Gonçalo Pires our chief freighter, who should investigate if the mentioned goods are captives or free men, and if cleared by them there will be no further doubt nor embargo for them to be taken and embarked. But if the white men do not comply with it they will lose the aforementioned goods. And if we do them this favor and concession it is for the part Your Highness has in it, since we know that it is in your service too that these goods are taken from our Kingdom, otherwise we should not consent to this. . . .

Sir, Your Highness has been kind enough to write to us saying that we should ask in our letters for anything we need, and that we shall be provided with everything, and as the peace and the health of our Kingdom depend on us, and as there are among us old folks and people who have lived for many days, it happens that we have continuously many and different diseases which put us very often in such a weakness that we reach almost the last extreme; and the same happens to our children, relatives, and natives owing to the lack in this country of physicians and surgeons who might know how to cure properly such diseases. And as we have got neither dispensaries nor drugs which might help us in this forlornness, many of those who had been already confirmed and instructed in the holy faith of Our Lord Jesus Christ perish and die; and the rest of the people in their majority cure themselves with herbs and breads and other ancient methods, so that they put all their faith in the mentioned herbs and ceremonies if they live, and believe that they are saved if they die; and this is not much in the service of God.

And to avoid such a great error and inconvenience, since it is from God in the first place and then from your Kingdoms and from Your Highness that all the goods and drugs and medicines have come to save us, we beg of you to be agreeable and kind enough to send us two physicians and two apothecaries and one surgeon, so that they may come with their drug-stores and all the necessary things to stay in our kingdoms, because we are in extreme need of them all and each of them. We shall do them all good and shall benefit them by all means, since they are sent by Your Highness, whom we thank for your work in their coming. We beg of Your Highness as a great favor to do this for us, because besides being good in itself it is in the service of God as we have said above.

6

CAPTAIN THOMAS PHILLIPS

Buying Slaves in 1693

Phillips, the captain of the English ship *Hannibal*, arrived at the African port of Ouidah (Whydah) in what is today Benin to purchase slaves for transport and sale in the West Indian islands of St. Thomas and Barbados. From this part of his journal, we can see that the Captain is well versed in the procedures for buying slaves on the African coast. What sorts of preparations has he made for the purchase? How does he go about making the purchase? What does this selection tell you about the African slave trade?

THINKING HISTORICALLY

The circumstances by which Europeans encountered Africans were clearly different from those by which they encountered Native Americans. What are these differences, and how do they account for differences in their attitudes toward Africans and Indians?

This day got our canoos and all things else ready, in order to go ashore to-morrow to purchase our slaves.

May the 21st. This morning I went ashore at Whidaw, accompany'd by my doctor and purser, Mr. Clay, the present captain of the *East India Merchant*, his doctor and purser, and about a dozen of our seamen for our guard, arm'd, in order here to reside till we could purchase 1300 negro slaves, which was the number we both wanted, to compleat 700 for the *Hannibal*, and 650 for the *East India Merchant*, according to our agreement in our charter-parties with the Royal African Company; in

Source: Capt. Thomas Phillips' Journal, in *Churchill's Collection of Voyages*, vol. 6, London, 1746. Reprinted in George Francis Dow, *Slave Ships and Slaving*, originally published by the Marine Research Society, Salem, MA, 1927. Reprinted by Dover Press, 2002, 58–64.

procuring which quantity of slaves we spent about nine weeks, during which time what observations my indisposition with convulsions in my head, &c. would permit me to make on this country, its trade, manners, &c. are as follows, viz. . . .

Our factory, built by Captain Wiburne, Sir John Wiburne's brother, stands low near the marshes, which renders it a very unhealthy place to live in; the white men the African Company send there, seldom returning to tell their tale; 'tis compass'd round with a mud wall, about six foot high, and on the south-side is the gate; within is a large yard, a mud thatch'd house, where the factor[1] lives, with the white men; also a storehouse, a trunk for slaves, and a place where they bury their dead white men, call'd, very improperly, the hog-yard; there is also a good forge, and some other small houses: To the east are two small flankers of mud, with a few popguns and harquebusses,[2] which serve more to terrify the poor ignorant negroes than to do any execution. . . .

This factory, feared as 'tis, proved very beneficial to us, by housing our goods which came ashore late, and could not arrive at the king's town where I kept my warehouse, ere it was dark, when they would be very incident to be pilfer'd by the negro porters which carry them, at which they are most exquisite; for in the day-time they would steal the cowries,[3] altho' our white men that attended the goods from the marine watched them, they having instruments like wedges, made on purpose to force asunder the staves of the barrels, that contain'd the cowries, whereby the shells dropt out; and when any of our seamen that watch'd the goods came near such porters, they would take out their machine, and the staves would insensibly close again, so that no hole did appear, having always their wives and children running by them to carry off the plunder; which with all our threats and complaints made to the king, we could not prevent, tho' we often beat them cruelly, and piniar'd some, but it was all one, what was bred in the bone, &c. whatever we could do would not make them forbear.

The factory prov'd beneficial to us in another kind; for after we had procured a parcel of slaves, and sent them down to the sea-side to be carry'd off, it sometimes proved bad weather, and so great a sea, that the canoos could not come ashore to fetch them, so that they returned to the factory, where they were secured and provided for till good weather presented, and then were near to embrace the opportunity, we sometimes shipping off a hundred of both sexes at a time.

We had our cook ashore, and eat as well as we could, provisions being plenty and cheap; but we soon lost our stomachs by sickness, most of my men having fevers, and myself such convulsions and aches in my

[1] Manager or agent. [Ed.]
[2] Firearms with a long barrel and a cord to ignite powder. [Ed.]
[3] Shells used as currency. [Ed.]

head, that I could hardly stand or go to the trunk without assistance, and there often fainted with the horrid stink of the negroes, it being an old house where all the slaves are kept together, and evacuate nature where they lie, so that no jakes[4] can stink worse; there being forced to sit three or four hours at a time, quite ruin'd my health, but there was no help.

When we were at the trunk, the king's slaves, if he had any, were the first offer'd to sale, which the cappasheirs[5] would be very urgent with us to buy, and would in a manner force us to it ere they would shew us any other, saying they were the Reys Cosa,[6] and we must not refuse them, tho' as I observed they were generally the worst slaves in the trunk, and we paid more for them than any others, which we could not remedy, it being one of his majesty's prerogatives. Then the cappasheirs each brought out his slaves according to his degree and quality, the greatest first, &c. and our surgeon examined them well in all kinds, to see that they were sound wind and limb, making them jump, stretch out their arms swiftly, looking in their mouths to judge of their age; for the cappasheirs are so cunning, that they shave them all close before we see them, so that let them be never so old we can see no grey hairs in their heads or beards; and then having liquor'd them well and sleeked with palm oil, 'tis no easy matter to know an old one from a middle-aged one, but by the teeths decay. But our greatest care of all is to buy none that are pox'd, lest they should infect the rest aboard; for tho' we separate the men and women aboard by partitions and bulk-heads, to prevent quarrels and wranglings among them, yet do what we can they will come together, and that distemper which they call the yaws, is very common here, and discovers itself by almost the same symptoms as the *Lues Venerea*[7] or clap does with us; therefore our surgeon is forc'd to examine the privities of both men and women with the nicest scrutiny, which is a great slavery, but what can't be omitted. When we had selected from the rest such as we liked, we agreed in what goods to pay for them, the prices being already stated before the king, how much of each sort of merchandize we were to give for a man, woman, and child, which gave us much ease, and saved abundance of disputes and wranglings, and gave the owner a note, signifying our agreement of the sorts of goods; upon delivery of which the next day he receiv'd them; then we mark'd the slaves we had bought in the breast, or shoulder, with a hot iron, having the letter of the ship's name on it, the place being before anointed with a little palm oil, which caused but little pain, the mark being usually well in four or five days, appearing very plain and white after.

When we had purchased to the number of 50 or 60, we would send them aboard, there being a cappasheir, intitled the captain of the slaves, whose care it was to secure them to the waterside, and see them all

---

[4] British slang for a latrine. [Ed.]
[5] Slave handlers appointed by the African king. [Ed.]
[6] The African king's special slaves. [Ed.]
[7] Venereal disease (STD). [Ed.]

off; and if in carrying to the marine any were lost, he was bound to make them good to us, the captain of the trunk being oblig'd to do the like, if any run away while under his care, for after we buy them we give him charge of them till the captain of the slaves comes to carry them away: There are two officers appointed by the king for this purpose, to each of which every ship pays the value of a slave in what goods they like best for their trouble, when they have done trading. . . .

There is likewise a captain of the sand, who is appointed to take care of the merchandise we have come ashore to trade with, that the negroes do not plunder them. . . .

When our slaves were come to the sea-side, our canoos were ready to carry them off to the longboat, if the sea permitted, and he convey'd them aboard ship, where the men were all put in irons, two and two shackl'd together, to prevent their mutiny, or swimming ashore.

The negroes are so wilful and loth to leave their own country, that they have often leap'd out of the canoos, boat and ship, into the sea, and kept under water till they were drowned, to avoid being taken up and saved by our boats, which pursued them; they having a more dreadful apprehension of Barbadoes than we can have of hell, tho' in reality they live much better there than in their own country; but home is home, &c. . . . We had about 12 negroes did wilfully drown themselves, and others starv'd themselves to death; for 'tis their belief that when they die they return home to their own country and friends again.

The best goods to purchase slaves here are cowries, the smaller the more esteemed; for they pay them all by tale, the smallest being as valuable as the biggest, but take them from us by measure or weight, of which about 100 pounds for a good man-slave. The next in demand are brass neptunes or basons, very large, thin, and flat; for after they have bought them they cut them in pieces to make anilias or bracelets, and collars for their arms, legs and necks. The other preferable goods are blue paper sletias, cambricks or lawns, caddy chints, broad ditto, coral, large, smooth, and of a deep red, rangoes large and red, iron bars, powder and brandy.[8]

With the above goods a ship cannot want slaves here, and may purchase them for about three pounds fifteen shillings a head, but near half the cargo value must be cowries or booges, and brass basons, to set off the other goods that we buy cheaper, as coral, rangoes, iron, &c. else they will not take them; for if a cappasheir sells five slaves, he will have two of them paid for in cowries, and one in brass, which are dear slaves; for a slave in cowries costs us above four pounds in England; whereas a slave in coral, rangoes, or iron, does not cost fifty shillings; but without the cowries and brass they will take none of the last goods, and but small

---

[8] Sletias were cloths, also called silesias, after their probable origin; cambricks were fine white linens from Cambray, Flanders; chints referred to chintz, an Indian cotton with brightly-colored design, usually flowers; broad referred to broad cloths; lawns were linens from Laorn, France; rangoes were beads. [Ed.]

quantities at best, especially, if they can discover that you have good store of cowries and brass aboard . . . therefore every man that comes here, ought to be very cautious in making his report to the king at first, of what sorts and quantities of goods he has, and be sure to say his cargo consists mostly in iron, coral, rangoes, chints, &c. so that he may dispose of those goods as soon as he can. . . .

7

Images of African American Slavery

The visual record of slavery in the Americas is dominated by images rendered by members of the slave-owning societies; few images by slaves themselves exist. Nevertheless, much can be learned about the circumstances of slavery from the illustrations that do exist. Figure 16.3 shows a sale of slaves in Africa that was not atypical. Who are the slaves? Who is selling them? Who is buying them?

The work and living conditions of slaves varied among countries and slaveholders. Many slaves were put to work on large plantations to help with large-scale production, while others worked in smaller operations or as house servants and were sometimes hired out to work in other locations by their masters. A fortunate few were eventually granted their freedom after years of dedicated labor. Figure 16.4 depicts plantation work in Martinique in the early nineteenth century. Published in a traveler's account of the Americas, the text accompanying this image reads: "The slaves are called to work by the plantation bell at 6 in the morning, each person takes his hoe to the field under the supervision of overseers, either European or Creole; in a single line, they work in unison while chanting some African work song; the overseers occasionally use the whip to increase the work pace; at 11 the bell sounds, they take a meal, then resume their work until 6 in the evening." What does this image tell you that you might not have known about slavery?

Slaves were sold at auction both upon arrival from Africa and sometimes when being sold by their owners. Figure 16.5 illustrates a slave auction in Brazil in the 1830s. Do slaves appear to be in high demand here? What does this image suggest to you about the cost and care of slaves in Brazil? Figure 16.6 offers a contrasting scene from a British newspaper of slaves awaiting sale in the United States. The article from the *Illustrated London News* reads: "The accompanying engraving represents a gang of Negroes exhibited in the city of New Orleans, previous to an auction, from a sketch made on the spot by our artist. The men and women are well clothed, in their Sunday best—the men in blue cloth . . . with beaver hats; and the women in calico dresses, of more or less brilliancy, with silk bandana handkerchiefs bound round their

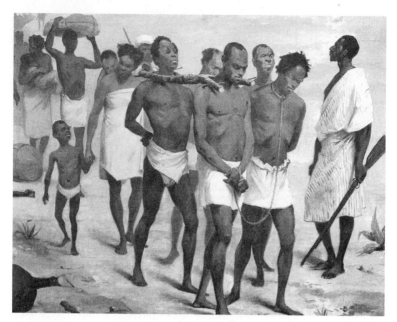

Figure 16.3   Buying Slaves in Africa, Late 1700s or Early 1800s.

Source: Rue des Archives / The Granger Collection, New York.

Figure 16.4   Plantation Work, Martinique, 1826.

Source: Field Gang at work in Martinique, 1826, NW0313, Special Collections, University of Virginia Library.

Figure 16.5   Slave Market, Rio de Janeiro, Brazil, 1830s.
Source: Snark/Art Resource, NY.

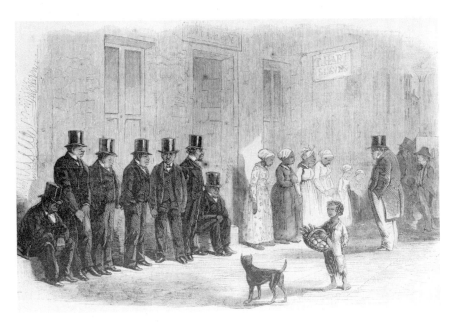

Figure 16.6   Slaves Awaiting Sale, New Orleans, 1861.
Source: A Slave-Pen at New Orleans—Before the Auction, from *Harper's Weekly*, 24th January 1863 (engraving) (b & w photo), American School (19th century) / Library of Congress, Washington D.C., USA / The Bridgeman Art Library.

heads. . . . they stand through a good part of the day, subject to the inspection of the purchasing or non-purchasing passing crowd. . . . An orderly silence is preserved as a general rule at these sales, although conversation does not seem to be altogether prohibited." What does this image suggest to you about slavery in New Orleans in 1861?

THINKING HISTORICALLY

These four images of African slavery in the Americas are selected out of thousands of paintings, engravings, and drawings, almost all done by Europeans who held varying attitudes toward slavery. Even if they accurately depict what the European artist saw at a particular moment in a particular place, we should be careful to avoid making generalizations based on a single image. Nevertheless, often a primary source, written or visual, prompts new questions rather than answers to old ones. What questions occur to you when you view these images?

8

FREDERICK DOUGLASS

Narrative of the Life of an American Slave

This is a selection from America's most famous slave narrative. Frederick Douglass (1818–1895) was a slave in Maryland and Virginia. After his escape in 1838, Douglass became a leading orator and newspaper publisher on behalf of the abolitionist movement. He also spoke out for the rights of women, Native Americans, immigrants, and even Irish home rule. His autobiographical *Narrative*, published in 1845, was so popular that he had to temporarily flee to Britain to avoid arrest as a fugitive slave.

In this selection, Douglass recalls his life as a twelve-year-old slave. What does his story tell you about the lives of slaves in the United States? What social and cultural factors most influenced the life of an American slave? How, according to Douglass, was the life of a city slave different from that of a slave on a plantation?

Douglass wrote his autobiography to inform people in pre–Civil War America about the injustices and horrors of slavery. It served

Source: Frederick Douglass, *Narrative of the Life of Frederick Douglass, An American Slave*, chaps. 6–7, available at The Free Library, http://douglass.thefreelibrary.com/Narrative-of-the-Life-of-Frederick-Douglass-An-American-Slave.

as an important document in the abolitionist movement. He was writing from the perspective of a person in his mid-twenties about his life at the age of twelve. How did learning to read change Douglass's attitude toward slavery and freedom? Why would a written source like this be such a potent force in the abolitionist movement?

THINKING HISTORICALLY

Compare this narrative with the images in the previous selection. Which pictures of slavery most resemble Douglass's experience? How was the life of a slave different from that of Indians? How were they treated differently?

Very soon after I went to live with Mr. and Mrs. Auld, she very kindly commenced to teach me the A, B, C. After I had learned this, she assisted me in learning to spell words of three or four letters. Just at this point of my progress, Mr. Auld found out what was going on, and at once forbade Mrs. Auld to instruct me further, telling her, among other things, that it was unlawful, as well as unsafe, to teach a slave to read. To use his own words, further, he said, "If you give a nigger an inch, he will take an ell. A nigger should know nothing but to obey his master—to do as he is told to do. Learning would ~spoil~ the best nigger in the world. Now," said he, "if you teach that nigger (speaking of myself) how to read, there would be no keeping him. It would forever unfit him to be a slave. He would at once become unmanageable, and of no value to his master. As to himself, it could do him no good, but a great deal of harm. It would make him discontented and unhappy." These words sank deep into my heart, stirred up sentiments within that lay slumbering, and called into existence an entirely new train of thought. It was a new and special revelation, explaining dark and mysterious things, with which my youthful understanding had struggled, but struggled in vain. I now understood what had been to me a most perplexing difficulty—to wit, the white man's power to enslave the black man. It was a grand achievement, and I prized it highly. From that moment, I understood the pathway from slavery to freedom. . . . Though conscious of the difficulty of learning without a teacher, I set out with high hope, and a fixed purpose, at whatever cost of trouble, to learn how to read. . . . That which to him was a great evil, to be carefully shunned, was to me a great good, to be diligently sought; and the argument which he so warmly urged, against my learning to read, only served to inspire me with a desire and determination to learn. . . .

I had resided but a short time in Baltimore before I observed a marked difference, in the treatment of slaves, from that which I had witnessed in the country. A city slave is almost a freeman, compared with a slave on the plantation. He is much better fed and clothed, and enjoys privileges altogether unknown to the slave on the plantation. There is a vestige of decency, a sense of shame, that does much to curb and check those outbreaks of atrocious cruelty so commonly enacted upon the plantation. He is a desperate slaveholder, who will shock the humanity of his non-slaveholding neighbors with the cries of his lacerated slave. Few are willing to incur the odium attaching to the reputation of being a cruel master; and above all things, they would not be known as not giving a slave enough to eat. Every city slaveholder is anxious to have it known of him, that he feeds his slaves well; and it is due to them to say, that most of them do give their slaves enough to eat. There are, however, some painful exceptions to this rule. Directly opposite to us, on Philpot Street, lived Mr. Thomas Hamilton. He owned two slaves. Their names were Henrietta and Mary. Henrietta was about twenty-two years of age, Mary was about fourteen; and of all the mangled and emaciated creatures I ever looked upon, these two were the most so. His heart must be harder than stone, that could look upon these unmoved. The head, neck, and shoulders of Mary were literally cut to pieces. I have frequently felt her head, and found it nearly covered with festering sores, caused by the lash of her cruel mistress. . . . Added to the cruel lashings to which these slaves were subjected, they were kept nearly half-starved. . . . I have seen Mary contending with the pigs for the offal thrown into the street. . . .

I lived in Master Hugh's family about seven years. During this time, I succeeded in learning to read and write. In accomplishing this, I was compelled to resort to various stratagems. I had no regular teacher. My mistress, who had kindly commenced to instruct me, had, in compliance with the advice and direction of her husband, not only ceased to instruct, but had set her face against my being instructed by any one else. . . .

My mistress was, as I have said, a kind and tender-hearted woman; and in the simplicity of her soul she commenced, when I first went to live with her, to treat me as she supposed one human being ought to treat another. In entering upon the duties of a slaveholder, she did not seem to perceive that I sustained to her the relation of a mere chattel, and that for her to treat me as a human being was not only wrong, but dangerously so. Slavery proved as injurious to her as it did to me. . . . Under its influence, the tender heart became stone, and the lamblike disposition gave way to one of tiger-like fierceness. The first step in her downward course was in her ceasing to instruct me. She now commenced to practice her husband's precepts. She finally became even more violent in her opposition than her husband himself. . . .

From this time I was most narrowly watched. If I was in a separate room any considerable length of time, I was sure to be suspected of having a book, and was at once called to give an account of myself. . . .

The plan which I adopted, and the one by which I was most successful, was that of making friends of all the little white boys whom I met in the street. As many of these as I could, I converted into teachers. With their kindly aid, obtained at different times and in different places, I finally succeeded in learning to read. When I was sent of errands, I always took my book with me, and by going one part of my errand quickly, I found time to get a lesson before my return. I used also to carry bread with me, enough of which was always in the house, and to which I was always welcome; for I was much better off in this regard than many of the poor white children in our neighborhood. This bread I used to bestow upon the hungry little urchins, who, in return, would give me that more valuable bread of knowledge. I am strongly tempted to give the names of two or three of those little boys, as a testimonial of the gratitude and affection I bear them; but prudence forbids;—not that it would injure me, but it might embarrass them; for it is almost an unpardonable offence to teach slaves to read in this Christian country. . . .

I was now about twelve years old, and the thought of being ~a slave for life~ began to bear heavily upon my heart. Just about this time, I got hold of a book entitled "The Columbian Orator." Every opportunity I got, I used to read this book. . . .

In the same book, I met with one of Sheridan's mighty speeches on and in behalf of Catholic emancipation. These were choice documents to me. I read them over and over again with unabated interest. They gave tongue to interesting thoughts of my own soul, which had frequently flashed through my mind, and died away for want of utterance. The moral which I gained from the dialogue was the power of truth over the conscience of even a slaveholder. What I got from Sheridan was a bold denunciation of slavery, and a powerful vindication of human rights. The reading of these documents enabled me to utter my thoughts, and to meet the arguments brought forward to sustain slavery; but while they relieved me of one difficulty, they brought on another even more painful than the one of which I was relieved. The more I read, the more I was led to abhor and detest my enslavers. . . . As I read and contemplated the subject, behold! that very discontentment which Master Hugh had predicted would follow my learning to read had already come, to torment and sting my soul to unutterable anguish. . . .

■ REFLECTIONS

This chapter asks you to compare European encounters with Native Americans and Africans. Why did Europeans enslave Africans and not, for the most part, American Indians? Because so many Africans were brought to the Americas to work on plantations, this topic is especially compelling.

Initially, of course, Indians *were* enslaved. Recall the letter of Columbus (Chapter 15, selection 4). Part of the reason this enslavement did not continue was the high mortality of Native Americans exposed to smallpox and other Old World diseases. In addition, Native Americans who survived the bacterial onslaught had the "local knowledge" and support needed to escape from slavery.

Above and beyond this were the humanitarian objections of Spanish priests like Bartolomeo de Las Casas and the concerns of the Spanish monarchy that slavery would increase the power of the conquistadors at the expense of the Crown. In 1542 the enslavement of Indians was outlawed in Spanish dominions of the New World. Clearly, these "New Laws" were not always obeyed by Spaniards in the Americas or by the Portuguese subjects of the unified Spanish-Portuguese crown between 1580 and 1640. Still, the different legal positions of Africans and Indians in the minds of Europeans require further explanation.

Some scholars have suggested that the difference in treatment lies in the differing needs of the main European powers involved in the encounter. The anthropologist Marvin Harris makes the argument this way:

> The most plausible explanation of the New Laws [of 1542] is that they represented the intersection of the interests of three power groups: the Church, the Crown, and the colonists. All three of these interests sought to maximize their respective control over the aboriginal populations. Outright enslavement of the Indians was the method preferred by the colonists. But neither the Crown nor the Church could permit this to happen without surrendering their own vested and potential interests in the greatest resource of the New World—its manpower.[1]

Why then did Europeans permit and even encourage the enslavement of Africans? In this matter all three power groups stood to gain. Africans who remained in Africa were of no use to anybody, since effective military and political domination of that continent by Europeans was not achieved until the middle of the nineteenth century. To make use of African manpower, Africans had to be removed from their homelands. The only way to accomplish this was to buy them as slaves from dealers on the coast. For both the Crown and the church, it was better to have Africans under the control of the New World colonists than to leave Africans under the control of Africans.

But of course the Atlantic world slave trade was just one of the lasting outcomes of Atlantic world encounters. Toward the end of his

---

[1] Marvin Harris, *Patterns of Race in the Americas* (New York: W. W. Norton, 1964), 17.

dramatic account of the Spanish conquest of Mexico (selection 1), Bernal Díaz describes a grizzly discovery made by the victorious conquistadors:

> I solemnly swear that all the houses and stockades in the lake were full of heads and corpses. I do not know how to describe it but it was the same in the streets and courts of Tlatelolco. We could not walk without treading on the bodies and heads of dead Indians. (Díaz, 1963, 405)

After two years of continual and heavy warfare, the fortunes of the Spanish turned in their favor and they seized a ravaged city where, according to Bernal Díaz, "the stench was so bad, no one could endure it." Díaz assumed that the Mexicans had been starved and denied fresh water, but we now know that at least part of the cause was the spread of smallpox, a disease that the Spanish carried from the Old World and for which the Native Americans had no immunities. Because of thousands of years of contact, Africans shared many of the same immunities as Europeans, but Native Americans, having inhabited a separate biological realm for over ten thousand years, were completely vulnerable to the new diseases and perished in droves.

Ultimately, slavery came to an end, even if in some cases — the work of Italians on Brazilian sugar plantations, Chinese rail workers, or free African day laborers — it was hard to see a difference in working conditions. In any case, the long-term impact of the "Columbian exchange" was more ecological than economic. The potatoes of South America and the corn of Mexico fed more families in Afro-Eurasia than had ever existed in the Americas. Conversely, the flora and fauna of the Americas were transformed through the introduction of the grasses, trees, fruits, grains, horses, cattle, pigs, and chickens that had nourished the ancestors of the conquistadors.

17

State and Religion

Asian, Islamic, and Christian States, 1500–1800

■ HISTORICAL CONTEXT

The relationship between state and religion is a matter of concern and debate almost everywhere in the modern world. In the United States, the issue of the separation of church and state engenders conflicts about the legality of abortion, prayer in the schools, government vouchers for religious schools, and the public display of religious symbols like the Ten Commandments, Nativity scenes, and Chanukah menorahs. Governments in countries as diverse as France and Turkey have recently debated the wearing of headscarves and the display of religious symbols in public schools and other public spaces.

Few states in the world today are dedicated to a single religion as are Saudi Arabia, Israel, and the Vatican. Yet even such places where religious devotion is extreme allow citizenship, residence, and rights in some measure for people of other religions. A few other states have official religions: Brazil is officially Roman Catholic, as was Italy until 1984; Iran is officially Muslim. But, with some notable exceptions, these types of designations often have little effect on what people believe or how they behave.

Although the role of religion in public life and the relationship between church and state are important current issues, from the long-term historical view, the state has become more important in peoples' lives while religion has become less influential. In the period before 1500, with the notable exception of China, many religious organizations were more important than political entities. But, in much of the world, the story of the last five hundred years has been the replacement of religious authority by that of the state. With the increased power of the state, secularism has become more pervasive, often triggering revivals of religious fundamentalism in reaction.

In this chapter, we look at religion and the state in various parts of the world two to five hundred years ago to see how different things were, but also to locate the roots of present church-state conflicts. We look first at China, where state formation began over two thousand years ago and official Confucianism supported the authority of the emperor. Japan, by contrast, emerged from feudalism to state formation after 1600. Both East Asian societies struggled with the claims of Buddhists, Christians, Muslims, and popular religious sects. Next we look at India, conquered by the Muslim Mughals after 1500, many of whom were remarkably tolerant of Hindus and Hinduism. Similarly, the Ottoman Empire protected a wide range of minority religions despite its Muslim majority. We conclude with the West (Europe and colonial America) to understand how Christian states struggled with some of the challenges posed by religion. Ultimately, we will be looking for the roots of religious toleration.

Kings and political leaders are almost all more comfortable with some kind of orthodoxy (conventional belief and practice) than with heterodoxy (dissident or heretical belief and practice). But one person's orthodox belief is another's heterodoxy. Most Islamic states, for instance, see Iran's Shi'ism as heterodox, but Shi'ism has been the orthodox norm for most Iranians for centuries. Orthodoxy frequently undermines religious toleration. In modern society, we often see toleration as a product of secularism. In fact, the history of church and state suggests something very different.

■ THINKING HISTORICALLY

Relating Past and Present

"The past," novelist L. P. Hartley famously wrote, "is a foreign country. They do things differently there." Understanding the past can be like learning a foreign language or exercising muscles gone slack from the daily grind of the commonplace and predictable. These are the muscles that help us imagine and tolerate differences, accept the strange as a possible norm, and allow us to hold conflicting ideas together without forcing agreement or rushing to judgment.

The issue of "state and religion" or "church and state" is a very modern one. We are invoking that modern concern in framing our study of the period between 1500 and 1800. But we should be wary of how past ideas of state and religion may differ from our own. Even the words we use reflect our modern vocabulary and understanding. For the most part, before the sixteenth century, the world's people did not make a distinction between state and religion.

In this chapter we ask questions about the history of religious toleration. This too is a modern question. Toleration is a modern idea, but, as we shall see, that does not mean that emperors or governments did not practice it. Various empires throughout history have allowed a variety of beliefs and practices among their subjects, not always because they believed it was morally the right thing to do, but because it made good practical political sense.

As you read the following selections, you will be asked to flex your imaginative muscles and reflect on how our modern conceptions of an apparently familiar topic are often different from those of our "foreign" predecessors. Then we can ask how those differences affect our ability to use the past to understand the present.

1

JONATHAN SPENCE
Emperor Kangxi on Religion

Kangxi[1] was emperor of China from 1661 to 1722. A descendant of conquering Manchu warriors, Kangxi overcame the last resistance of the previous Ming dynasty and, during his reign, which was the longest of any Chinese emperor, brought the Qing (or Manchu) dynasty to its greatest size and strength. In this selection, the modern historian Jonathan Spence presents the emperor in his own voice, drawn from innumerable primary sources and often the emperor's own words. How would you describe Kangxi's attitude toward religion? What do you think he would say if asked about the proper relationship between religion and the state? What characteristics of Chinese society might explain these ideas?

THINKING HISTORICALLY

Any historical expression or event inevitably carries some degree of familiarity, as well as some degree of remoteness from our own. Which ideas of Kangxi do you find most like those of our own present society? Which do you find most remote? What do you think accounts for the difference between these remote ideas and our own?

Every country must have some spirits that it reveres. This is true for our dynasty, as for Mongols or Mohammedans, Miao or Lolo, or other foreigners. Just as everyone fears something, some snakes but not toads,

[1] Cong SHE   Spelled K'ang Hsi in older Wade-Giles system of Romanization.

Source: Jonathan D. Spence, *Emperor of China: Self-Portrait of K'ang-Hsi* (New York: Vintage Books, 1975), 80–85.

some toads but not snakes; and as all countries have different pronunciations and different alphabets. But in this Catholic religion, the Society
of Peter quarrels with the Jesuits, Bouvet[2] quarrels with Mariani, and
among the Jesuits the Portuguese want only their own nationals in their
church while the French want only French in theirs. This violates the
principles of religion. Such dissension cannot be inspired by the Lord
of Heaven but by the Devil, who, I have heard the Westerners say, leads
men to do evil since he can't do otherwise. . . .

Since I discovered on the Southern Tour of 1703 that there were missionaries wandering at will over China, I had grown cautious and determined to control them more tightly: to bunch them in the larger cities and
in groups that included men from several different countries, to catalogue
their names and residences, and to permit no new establishments without
my express permission. For with so many Westerners coming to China it
has been hard to distinguish the real missionaries from other white men
pretending to be missionaries. As I clarified it for de Tournon[3]: "Hereafter we will permit residence in China to all those who come from the
West and will not return there. Residence permission will not be granted
to those who come one year expecting to go home the next—because
such people are like those who stand outside the main gate and discuss
what people are doing inside the house. Besides these meddlers there are
also those out for profit, greedy traders, who should not be allowed to
live here." After the arguments with de Tournon and Maigrot[4] I made
all missionaries who wanted to stay on in China sign a certificate, stat-
ing that they would remain here for life and follow Ricci on the Rites.[5]
Forty or fifty who refused were exiled to Canton; de Tournon was sent to
Macao, his secretary, Appiani, we kept in prison in Peking.

Despite these sterner restrictions, the Westerners continued to cause me
anxiety. Our ships were being sold overseas; reports came of ironwood for
keel blocks being shipped out of Kwangtung; Luzon and Batavia became
havens for Chinese outlaws; and the Dutch were strong in the Southern
Seas. I ordered a general inquiry among residents of Peking who had once

[2] Joachim Bouvet (1656–1730) was a French Jesuit who taught Kangxi astronomy and
mathematics and, according to the emperor, understood Chinese better than other Westerners.
As a leading "Figurist," Bouvet believed that all of Christianity could be found in the ancient
Chinese religious text, the *I Ching*. This idea was criticized by other missionaries who thought
it understated the importance of the Bible. [Ed.]

[3] Charles-Thomas Maillard de Tournon (1668–1710) was a papal legate to China to control missionaries and end the acceptance of some Chinese phrases and Confucian rites by
Chinese Christians; this led to his imprisonment by Kangxi. [Ed.]

[4] Charles Maigrot (1652–1730) was administrator of Christian missions in China after
1684. In 1692 Kangxi issued an Edict of Toleration that formally allowed Chinese to become
Christians. The following year Maigrot condemned the rites honoring Confucius and rituals
associated with ancestor worship. [Ed.]

[5] Refers to the position of Matteo Ricci (1552–1610), a founder of the Jesuit mission to
China, and later of Joachim Bouvet that the rites of Confucius were moral and civic rather than
religious and that therefore they could be practiced by Chinese Christians. [Ed.]

lived on the coast, and called a conference of the coastal governors-general. "I fear that some time in the future China is going to get into difficulties with these various Western countries," I said. "That is my prediction." Similarly I had warned earlier that China must be strong to forestall a possible threat from Russia. General Ch'en Mao insisted even more strongly on the dangers from Holland and France, Spain and England, and of missionaries and merchants conniving together. I did not agree with him that we should disarm all their ships, but I did agree to reiterate the 1669 edict that banned Westerners from preaching in the provinces.

Three of the Peking Jesuits—Suares, Parrenin, and Mourao—came to protest: "We learn that the Boards have pronounced a strict sentence and the Christian religion is proscribed."

I reassured them: "No. The sentence is not strict, and the Christian religion is not proscribed. Only Westerners without the certificate are forbidden to preach. This prohibition does not affect those who have the certificate."

"This distinction as made by the Emperor is not clearly expressed in the sentence."

"It is clearly expressed. I have read the sentence with care. If you were hoping that those without certificates might be permitted to preach your laws, then that hope is no longer possible."

"But at the beginning of the sentence the 1669 edict is cited."

"That is true, but the point of it is to prevent those without certificates from preaching."

"We are just afraid that the provincial officials will treat us all alike, and that they will not permit even those of us who have certificates to preach the holy law."

"If that occurs, those who have certificates have only to produce them. The officials will see that permission to preach your laws is granted. You can preach the law, and it's up to the Chinese to listen—if they so choose. As for those without a certificate, let them come here, and I will give them one." (I smiled during these last words.) "Anyway, even those with the certificate are only being permitted to preach for a time. Later on we'll see what decision to take in their case."

"But if they cause trouble to those with certificates, we will come to the Emperor for help."

"Take care to inform me if such is the case."

"There is one thing that causes us particular anguish—namely, that the Boards treat us as rebels."

"Don't worry about that. It's just a conventional formula that the Boards use."

"As soon as this edict is published, the officials will search out the missionaries and Christians and stir up trouble."

"As far as this searching out goes, it's essential. When I sent Li Ping-chung to Canton I gave him an order for the Governor-General, telling him to search out and to assemble in one place all those without certificates. And I've just given similar orders to Governor-General Yang Lin on his return to Canton, and am awaiting his reply."

The Westerners in China were only as drops of rain in the immensity of the ocean, said de Tournon in our audience, and I had to laugh. Yet some of their words were no different from the wild or improper teachings of Buddhists and Taoists, and why should they be treated differently? One of my censors wrote that the Western god fashioned a man with a human soul from the blood of a virgin, Mary; and they claimed that Jesus was born in the reign of Han Ai-ti [reigned 6 B.C.–A.D. 1], that he was killed on a cross for man's sins, and that they had meetings in which slaves and masters, men and women, mixed together and drank some holy substance. I had asked Verbiest[6] why God had not forgiven his son without making him die, but though he had tried to answer I had not understood him. Also, though in China there had been a flood at about the same time as that reported for Noah, those on the Chinese plains had been drowned, while those who escaped to the mountains were saved. And I told Fontaney[7] that I would gladly witness some of the miracles they talked about, but none was forthcoming.

In the past, both Buddhists and Taoists had been made to fill out certificates, and the superiors in the various temples have to register their monks—they are not allowed to chant or beg for alms or set out their sacred images in the streets of Peking, and may not act as exorcists for patients suffering from seizures without getting official permission. Certainly there are more Buddhists and Taoists—the census of 1667 listed 140,193 monks divided among 79,622 temples of various sizes—but there were many Christians also. When I asked Verbiest for exact figures in 1688 he said there were 15,758 Christians just in Peking. Even though I realized it was quite impractical to close down temples, and order people to return to secular life, there was no harm in following the principle of "preparing for trouble before trouble comes." So I strictly banned all the sects[8] such as the "non-action," "white lotus," "incense smelling," "origin of the dragon," and "all-submerging Yang," and stiffened the penalties for all officials who failed to report heterodox teachers in their localities. Also I banned the so-called "incense associations," where men and women mixed together and sold erotic works and special medicines; I ordered the printing blocks of certain mystical and magical books burned; and I continued to enforce the prohibitions against the private ownership of forbidden books—though I allowed exceptions for those working at home in astronomy and mathematics.

---

[6] Ferdinand Verbiest (1623–1688), Flemish Jesuit missionary in China; mathematician and astronomer. [Ed.]

[7] Baptist de Fontenay (1643–1710), missionary, mathematician, and astronomer. [Ed.]

[8] These were Daoist and Buddhist sects. [Ed.]

2

Japanese Edicts Regulating Religion

The history of the state in Japan was very different from that of China. Between 1200 and 1600 Japan went through a period in which the state was eclipsed by aristocratic, warrior, and religious groups. When the Tokugawa Shogunate reasserted the authority of a central state in 1600, the memory of monk-soldiers and numerous independent armies called for a series of measures directed at controlling religious institutions and other independent powers. In one measure, all farmers were forbidden to have swords. Another regulated all religious temples. Between 1633 and 1639 the Tokugawa government took the further step of closing the country to all foreign religions, a move directed mainly at the influence previously enjoyed by Portuguese Catholic missionaries.

The first of the two documents in this selection is a vow by which Japanese Christians renounced their faith in 1645. The second document is a government edict regulating temples, mainly Buddhist, in 1665. What do these documents tell you about the relationship between the state and religion in Tokugawa Japan?

THINKING HISTORICALLY

We tend to think of religions as fixed phenomena: eternal and unchanging. In fact, religious ideas and behavior change over time. Religious change is particularly striking when missionaries convert people from a foreign culture. Inevitably, the religion that the convert accepts is different from the religion the missionary preaches. Can you identify some of the changes Christianity underwent in Japan?

Similarly, the regulation of Buddhist temples by the new centralizing Tokugawa government brought changes in Buddhism. How would you expect the edict of 1665 to have changed Japanese Buddhism?

Much in these documents will strike the modern reader as very foreign, requiring an imaginative leap to understand how people might have thought. Choose one of these passages and explain how and why it is so strange to you. Try also to explain how you might understand it.

Source: Yosaburo Takekoshi, *The Economic Aspects of the History of the Civilization of Japan* (New York: Macmillan, 1930), 2:88–89. Reprinted in *Japan: A Documentary History,* ed. David J. Lu (Armonk, NY: M. E. Sharpe, 2005), 1:224–25.

Japan: A Documentary History, ed. David J. Lu (Armonk, NY: M. E. Sharpe, 2005), 1:219–20.

Renouncing the Kirishitan[1] Faith, 1645

Vow of Namban (Southern Barbarians): We have been Kirishitans for many years. But the more we learn of the Kirishitan doctrines the greater becomes our conviction that they are evil. In the first place, we who received instructions from the padre regarding the future life were threatened with excommunication which would keep us away from association with the rest of humanity in all things in the present world, and would cast us into hell in the next world. We were also taught that, unless a person committing a sin confesses it to the padre and secures his pardon, he shall not be saved in the world beyond. In that way the people were led into believing in the padres. All that was for the purpose of taking the lands of others.

When we learned of it, we "shifted" from Kirishitan and became adherents of Hokkekyō[2] while our wives became adherents of Ikkōshō.[3] We hereby present a statement in writing to you, worshipful Magistrate, as a testimony.

Hereafter we shall not harbor any thought of the Kirishitan in our heart. Should we entertain any thought of it at all, we shall be punished by Deus Paternus (God the Father), Jesus (His Son), Spirito Santo (the Holy Ghost), as well as by Santa Maria (St. Mary), various angels, and saints.

The grace of God will be lost altogether. Like Judas Iscariot, we shall be without hope, and shall be mere objects of ridicule to the people. We shall never rise. The foregoing is our Kirishitan vow.

Japanese Pledge: We have no thought of the Kirishitan in our hearts. We have certainly "shifted" our faith. If any falsehood be noted in our declaration now or in the future, we shall be subject to divine punishment by Bonten, Taishaku, the four deva kings, the great or little gods in all the sixty or more provinces of Japan, especially the Mishima Daimyōjin, the representatives of the god of Izu and Hakone, Hachiman Daibosatsu, Temman Daijizai Tenjin, especially our own family gods, Suwa Daimyōjin, the village people, and our relatives. This is to certify to the foregoing.

The second year of Shōhō [1645]
Endorsement.

---

[1] Christian. [Ed.]
[2] Buddhist sect based on the Lotus Sutra sermon of the Buddha. [Ed.]
[3] Pure Land Buddhism. [Ed.]

Regulations for Buddhist Temples, 1665

1. The doctrines and rituals established for different sects must not be mixed and disarranged. If there is anyone who does not behave in accordance with this injunction, an appropriate measure must be taken expeditiously.

2. No one who does not understand the basic doctrines or rituals of a given sect is permitted to become the chief priest of a temple. Addendum: If a new rite is established, it must not preach strange doctrines.

3. The regulations which govern relationships between the main temple and branch temples must not be violated. However, even the main temple cannot take measures against branch temples in an unreasonable manner.

4. Parishioners of the temples can choose to which temple they wish to belong and make contributions. Therefore priests must not compete against one another for parishioners.

5. Priests are enjoined from engaging in activities unbecoming of priests, such as forming groups or planning to fight one another.

6. If there is anyone who has violated the law of the land, and that fact is communicated to a temple, it must turn him away without question.

7. When making repairs to a temple or a monastery, do not make them ostentatiously. Addendum: Temples must be kept clean without fail.

8. The estate belonging to a temple is not subject to sale, nor can it be mortgaged.

9. Do not allow anyone who has expressed a desire to become a disciple but is not of good lineage to enter the priesthood freely. If there is a particular candidate who has an improper and questionable background, the judgment of the domanial lord or magistrate of his domicile must be sought and then act accordingly.

The above articles must be strictly observed by all the sects. . . .

Fifth year of Kanbun [1665], seventh month, 11th day.

3

BADA'UNI

Akbar and Religion

At the same time the Chinese and Japanese were confronting Christian missionaries, the descendants of Muslim Turkic and Mongol peoples of Central Asia were conquering the Hindu kingdoms of northern India. Babur (1483–1530), the first of these Mughal rulers, swept into India from Afghanistan in 1525. Successive Mughal emperors enlarged the empire, so that by the time of Akbar (r. 1556–1605) it included all of northern India. Like his contemporaries Philip II of Spain (r. 1556–1598) and Elizabeth of England (r. 1558–1603), Akbar created an elaborate and enduring administrative bureaucracy. But unlike Philip and Elizabeth, who waged religious wars against each other and forcibly converted their domestic subjects and newly conquered peoples, Akbar reached out to his Hindu subjects in ways that would have astonished his European contemporaries. In fact, he angered many of his own Muslim advisors, including Bada'uni, the author of the following memoir. What bothered Bada'uni about Akbar? What does this selection tell you about Akbar's rule? What factors might have motivated his toleration of heterodoxy?

THINKING HISTORICALLY

What strikes the modern reader here is Akbar's evident curiosity about religious ideas and his lack of doctrinal rigidity. These are not qualities most people expect from a Muslim ruler, perhaps especially a premodern one. Why are we modern readers surprised by this? How might our ideas about Islam and Hinduism in the modern world influence our understanding of these religious traditions in the past?

We know from other sources that Akbar made special efforts to include Hindus in his administration. About a third of his governing bureaucracy was Hindu, and he gave Hindu-governed territories a large degree of self-rule, allowing them to retain their own law and courts. Various taxes normally paid by non-Muslims were abolished. Among Akbar's five thousand wives, his favorite was the mother of his successor, Jahangir (r. 1605–1628). Akbar's policy of toleration continued under his son and grandson, Jahangir and Shah Jahan (r. 1628–1658), but was largely reversed by his great grandson, Aurangzeb (r. 1658–1707). How does this understanding of a particular past affect our ideas about the present? Does it make conflict seem less inevitable?

In the year nine hundred and eighty-three [1605] the buildings of the 'Ibādatkhāna¹ were completed. The cause was this. For many years previously the emperor had gained in succession remarkable and decisive

¹ Hall of Religious Discussions. [Ed.]

Source: 'Abdul Qadir Bada'uni, *Muntakhab ut-Tawarikh*, trans. G. S. A. Ranking and W. H. Lowe (Calcutta: Asiatic Society of Bengal, 1895–1925), 2:200–201, 255–61 *passim*, 324. Edited and reprinted in *Sources of Indian Tradition*, ed. Ainslie T. Embree (New York: Columbia University Press, 1988), 465–68.

victories. The empire had grown in extent from day to day; everything turned out well, and no opponent was left in the whole world. His Majesty had thus leisure to come into nearer contact with ascetics and the disciples of his reverence [the late] Mucīn, and passed much of his time in discussing the word of God and the word of the Prophet. Questions of Sufism,[2] scientific discussions, inquiries into philosophy and law, were the order of the day.

And later that day the emperor came to Fatehpur. There he used to spend much time in the Hall of Worship in the company of learned men and shaikhs and especially on Friday nights, when he would sit up there the whole night continually occupied in discussing questions of religion, whether fundamental or collateral. The learned men used to draw the sword of the tongue on the battlefield of mutual contradiction and opposition, and the antagonism of the sects reached such a pitch that they would call one another fools and heretics. The controversies used to pass beyond the differences of Sunni, and Shī'a, of Hanafī and Shā fi'ī, of lawyer and divine, and they would attack the very bases of belief. And Makhdūm-ul-Mulk wrote a treatise to the effect that Shaikh 'Abd-al-Nabī had unjustly killed Khizr Khān Sarwānī, who had been suspected of blaspheming the Prophet [peace be upon him!], and Mīr Habsh, who had been suspected of being a Shī'a, and saying that it was not right to repeat the prayers after him, because he was undutiful toward his father, and was himself afflicted with hemorrhoids. Shaikh 'Abd-al-Nabī replied to him that he was a fool and a heretic. Then the mullās [Muslim theologians] became divided into two parties, and one party took one side and one the other, and became very [much like] Jews and Egyptians for hatred of each other. And persons of novel and whimsical opinions, in accordance with their pernicious ideas and vain doubts, coming out of ambush, decked the false in the garb of the true, and wrong in the dress of right, and cast the emperor, who was possessed of an excellent disposition, and was an earnest searcher after truth, but very ignorant and a mere tyro,[3] and used to the company of infidels and base persons, into perplexity, till doubt was heaped upon doubt, and he lost all definite aim, and the straight wall of the clear law and of firm religion was broken down, so that after five or six years not a trace of Islam was left in him: and everything was turned topsy-turvy. . . .

And samanas [Hindu or Buddhist ascetics] and brāhmans (who as far as the matter of private interviews is concerned gained the advantage over everyone in attaining the honor of interviews with His Majesty, and in associating with him, and were in every way superior in reputation to

---

[2] Mystical, poetic Islamic tradition. [Ed.]
[3] Beginner. [Ed.]

all learned and trained men for their treatises on morals, and on physical and religious sciences, and in religious ecstasies, and stages of spiritual progress and human perfections) brought forward proofs, based on reason and traditional testimony, for the truth of their own, and the fallacy of our religion, and inculcated their doctrine with such firmness and assurance, that they affirmed mere imaginations as though they were self-evident facts, the truth of which the doubts of the sceptic could no more shake "Than the mountains crumble, and the heavens be cleft!" And the Resurrection, and Judgment, and other details and traditions, of which the Prophet was the repository, he laid all aside. And he made his courtiers continually listen to those revilings and attacks against our pure and easy, bright and holy faith. . . .

Some time before this a brāhman, named Puruk'hotam, who had written a commentary on the Book, *Increase of Wisdom* (Khirad-afzā), had had private interviews with him, and he had asked him to invent particular Sanskrit names for all things in existence. And at one time a brāhman, named Debi, who was one of the interpreters of the *Mahābhā rata*,[4] was pulled up the wall of the castle sitting on a bedstead till he arrived near a balcony, which the emperor had made his bedchamber. Whilst thus suspended he instructed His Majesty in the secrets and legends of Hinduism, in the manner of worshiping idols, the fire, the sun and stars, and of revering the chief gods of these unbelievers, such as Brahma, Mahadev [Shiva], Bishn [Vishnu], Kishn [Krishna], Ram, and Mahama (whose existence as sons of the human race is a supposition, but whose nonexistence is a certainty, though in their idle belief they look on some of them as gods, and some as angels). His Majesty, on hearing further how much the people of the country prized their institutions, began to look upon them with affection. . . .

Sometimes again it was Shaikh Tā j ud-dīn whom he sent for. This shaikh was son of Shaikh Zakarīya of Ajodhan. . . . He had been a pupil of Rashīd Shaikh Zamān of Panipat, author of a commentary on the *Paths* (*Lawā'ih*), and of other excellent works, was most excellent in Sufism, and in the knowledge of theology second only to Shaikh Ibn 'Arabī and had written a comprehensive commentary on the *Joy of the Souls* (*Nuzhat ul-Arwāh*). Like the preceding he was drawn up the wall of the castle in a blanket, and His Majesty listened the whole night to his Sufic obscenities and follies. The shaikh, since he did not in any great degree feel himself bound by the injunctions of the law, introduced arguments concerning the unity of existence, such as idle Sufis discuss, and which eventually lead to license and open heresy. . . .

Learned monks also from Europe, who are called *Padre*, and have an infallible head, called *Papa*,[5] who is able to change religious ordinances

---

[4] Classical Indian epic; source of Hinduism. See Volume 1, selection 5 in Chapter 3. [Ed.]
[5] The Roman Catholic pope. [Ed.]

as he may deem advisable for the moment, and to whose authority kings must submit, brought the Gospel, and advanced proofs for the Trinity. His Majesty firmly believed in the truth of the Christian religion, and wishing to spread the doctrines of Jesus, ordered Prince Murād to take a few lessons in Christianity under good auspices, and charged Abū'l Fazl to translate the Gospel. . . .

Fire worshipers also came from Nousarīin Gujarat, proclaimed the religion of Zardusht [Zarathustra] as the true one, and declared reverence to fire to be superior to every other kind of worship. They also attracted the emperor's regard, and taught him the peculiar terms, the ordinances, the rites and ceremonies of the Kaianians [a pre-Muslim Persian dynasty]. At last he ordered that the sacred fire should be made over to the charge of Abū'l Fazl, and that after the manner of the kings of Persia, in whose temples blazed perpetual fires, he should take care it was never extinguished night or day, for that it is one of the signs of God, and one light from His lights. . . .

His Majesty also called some of the yogis, and gave them at night private interviews, inquiring into abstract truths; their articles of faith; their occupation; the influence of pensiveness; their several practices and usages; the power of being absent from the body; or into alchemy, physiognomy, and the power of omnipresence of the soul.

4

IRA M. LEPIDUS

Ottoman State and Religion

The founders of the Ottoman Empire (1299–1922) were Turkic-speaking cousins of the Mughals. Both descended from nomadic horse-riding herdsmen and warriors from the grasslands of Central Asia. Both became Muslims and created large, wealthy, city-based empires with the help of huge cavalries and the new gunpowder technology. Both conquered peoples of other religions as well as fellow Muslims. The Ottoman Empire was an especially diverse empire, ethnically and religiously. At its height it included Roman and Orthodox Christians in the Balkans, Armenian Christians, Jewish refugees from Western Europe, Zoroastrians, and numerous Muslim in the Middle East and North Africa. Among the more influential of the Muslims were the Sufi orders, Muslim brotherhoods

Source: Ira M. Lepidus, *A History of Islamic Societies* (Cambridge: Cambridge University Press, 2002), 263–68.

of mystical thinkers, worshipers, and sometimes militant bands that both propelled Turkish expansion and challenged established authority.

Lepidus, a modern historian of Islam, describes a unique Turkish system of tolerance or government restraint about religion. How did the Ottoman system function? How was it different from the systems in China, Japan, and India? What factors in Ottoman society nourished a tradition of tolerance? What were the causes of a decline in tolerance in the sixteenth and seventeenth centuries?

THINKING HISTORICALLY

The relation of the past to the present has often been seen in two different ways: as prologue and as example. The idea of the past as prologue helps us understand how the past has become the present, as a trend from the past points to the future. But history does not always follow a straight line. It would be a mistake for us to see the Ottoman religious narrowing of the seventeenth century as a prelude to the present. In fact, Turkey today is the most tolerant (and secular) of Muslim societies because in 1922 the Ottoman state was replaced by the secular Republic of Turkey. A revolution broke the trend.

In addition to trends, history offers past examples of situations we face in the present. What might the example of Ottoman change, from tolerance in the fifteenth and early sixteenth centuries to intolerance in the seventeenth century, suggest about the effects of religion in politics? What lessons does this history offer for those who seek to make governments more religious today?

As a patrimonial, Islamic, and cosmopolitan regime, the Ottoman empire had a powerful effect on the fate of all Middle Eastern and Balkan peoples. To an unusual degree, the Ottoman regime dominated, controlled and shaped the society it governed. A central Ottoman concept was the distinction between *askeri* and *re'aya,* rulers and ruled, elites and subjects, warriors and producers, tax-collectors and tax-payers. The chief attribute of the ruling elite was the right to exploit the wealth of the subjects. In addition, to be a member of the ruling class one had to be cultivated in the distinctive language and manners called "the Ottoman way." One could become an Ottoman either by birth or by education in the imperial, military, or Muslim religious schools.

The distinction of rulers and ruled was not the same as between Muslims and non-Muslims. The ruling elites and the subject populations included both. Alongside of Turkish soldiers and Arab and Persian scribes and scholars, the ruling elite included Balkan Christian lords and scribes. The patrician Greek families of the Phanar district of Istanbul, who became prominent merchants, bankers, government functionaries, and provincial rulers in Rumania,[1] and the higher clergy of the Orthodox Church, may be considered part of the Ottoman elite. Jewish refugees from Spain also became important in Ottoman trade and banking in the fifteenth and sixteenth centuries. Joseph Nasi (1520–79), for example, a refugee descended from a Portuguese Jewish family which had moved to Antwerp and then to Italy after the expulsion of the Jews from Spain, came to Istanbul in 1554. Nasi had European business and diplomatic connections and soon became a close adviser to Sulayman,[2] played an influential role in French–Ottoman diplomatic relations, and in 1566 was made Duke of Naxos and given a monopoly on customs revenues and the export of wine. Nasi was also a patron of Jewish community life and of Jewish settlement in Palestine. In the course of the sixteenth and seventeenth centuries, however, the Ottoman elite became more uniformly Muslim. Only the Phanar Greek financial aristocracy maintained its position, owing to its administrative and economic role in Rumania.

The subjects, the re'aya, were organized into innumerable small communities. Ottoman society was an elaborate mosaic of territorial associations, religious fraternities, and corporate economic groups. From the Ottoman point of view, the religious communities organized to administer the educational, judicial, and charitable affairs of the subject population were fundamental. Most of the non-Muslim population were considered members of the Eastern Orthodox church which included Greek, Rumanian, Slavic, Bulgarian, and Arab believers. The Armenian church was an administrative body, which included monophysites in Syria and Egypt, Assyrians, Bogomils, and Gypsies. Maronites, Uniate Armenians, and Latin Catholics in Hungary, Croatia and Albania had their own churches; Sephardi and Ashkenazi Jews their own synagogues.

The Ottomans, like previous Muslim regimes, considered the non-Muslim subjects autonomous but dependent peoples whose internal social, religious, and communal life was regulated by their own religious organizations, but whose leaders were appointed by, and responsible to, a Muslim state. Non-Muslim communities were called by the generic terms of *dhimmi* (protected peoples), *ta'ifa* (group), or *jamat* (religious community). . . . Minority leaders, sometimes ecclesiastics, sometimes laymen, represented their communities to the authorities, and dealt with ecclesiastical matters, internal disputes, and fines and taxes on a local basis. . . .

The Muslim masses, as a subject or re'aya population, were organized in a parallel way. The Muslim population was subdivided into

---

[1] Modern Romania. [Ed.]
[2] Suleiman "the Magnificent" (r. 1520–1566), Ottoman sultan. [Ed.]

numerous schools of law and Sufi brotherhoods, which the Ottomans were keen to bring under state control. They did this by extending their patronage to the "ulama"[3] and Sufi elites. Ottoman patronage led to the organization of an elaborate system of madrasa[4] education. The first Ottoman madrasa was established in Iznik in 1331, when scholars were invited from Iran and Egypt to augment Muslim instruction in the new territories. Later Sultans founded colleges in Bursa, Edirne and Istanbul. In the late fifteenth century these were arranged in a hierarchy which defined the career path for the promotion of leading scholars. The college built by Sulayman between 1550 and 1559 eventually became the highest-ranking. Beneath it were ranked the colleges founded by previous Sultans, and beneath these the colleges founded by state officials and religious scholars. The madrasas were not only organized by rank but also were distinguished by their educational functions. The lowest-level madrasa taught Arabic grammar and syntax, logic, theology, astronomy, geometry and rhetoric. The second-level stressed literature and rhetoric. The higher-level colleges taught law and theology. . . .

Sufis were also important to the Ottoman state because of their large role in Turkish rural society. Sufi babas[5] mobilized bands of Turkish warriors and led them to holy war, protected travelers, mediated disputes, and otherwise helped to create social order in rural areas. Wandering dervishes,[6] called Malamatiya or Qalandariya, who openly disregarded the Shari'a and opposed contact with government authorities, were nonetheless venerated by rural people as bearers of God's blessings and of magical powers.

The rural Sufis were politically important because they could inspire resistance to the state. Eastern Anatolia, like northwestern Iran, was a breeding ground for Sufi revolts which espoused messianic beliefs and organized local opposition to state domination. For example, Bedreddin (d. 1416) denied the literal truth of heaven and hell, the day of judgment, the resurrection of the body, the creation of the world, and other basic tenets of Muslim belief. The Hurufiya (whose doctrine spread among both Muslims and Christians in Anatolia and Bulgaria at the end of the fourteenth century) preached that the only rightful income was that earned by manual work. Sufi-led rebellions also occurred in the late fifteenth century. In 1519 a preacher named Jelal took the name of Shah Isma'il, claimed to be the mahdi,[7] and attracted Turkish cultivator and pastoralist opposition to the imposition of taxes. The early

[3] Educated elite in Islamic society. [Ed.]

[4] Religious school. [Ed.]

[5] Holy men of the Sufi order; mystics. [Ed.]

[6] Sufi holy men or ascetics; some chant or dance in ecstatic ritual. [Ed.]

[7] Messiah, redeemer. [Ed.]

sixteenth-century wave of revolts was closely related to the Safavid[8] agitation and the opposition of eastern Anatolian peoples to the Ottoman-Sunni regime. . . .

Alongside the rural Sufis, urban religious orders also flourished in Anatolia and the Balkans. The Mevlevi leaders were spiritually descended from Mawlana Jalal al-Din Rumi (1207–73) and have become universally known for their ceremonial dancing as the whirling dervishes. . . .

In the course of the fifteenth and sixteenth centuries the Ottomans brought the Sufi orders under state control. The state coopted Sufi tekkes[9] by providing them with permanent endowments and gifts for charitable purposes. The Bektashis, in particular, were taken under the wing of the Ottomans as chaplains to the janissaries. They lived and marched with the soldiers and provided them with magical protection in battle. This enabled the order to spread throughout eastern Anatolia and among Turkish migrants in Macedonia and Albania. At the beginning of the sixteenth century the head of the order, Balim Sultan, was appointed by the Ottoman Sultan. The Mevlevis were similarly tied to the Ottoman state; they acquired the right to gird a Sultan with a holy sword upon his accession. Thus the Ottomans succeeded in domesticating the major Sufi brotherhoods without entirely eliminating the independent influence of Sufi teachers.

The absorption of the Ottoman "ulama" and the Sufi brotherhoods into the state bureaucracy made religious controversies matters of state concern. Ottoman scholars assimilated the Arabic and Persian classics, including the madrasa curriculum, theology, and science. The translation of Arabic and Persian classics, including important works on literature, history, politics, astrology, medicine, the life of the Prophet and Sufi treatises, made the corpus of Muslim religious literature available to Turkish elites. . . .

The narrow point of view progressively gained ground. As early as the 1540s theology and mathematics were losing popularity. In 1580 an observatory attached to the Sulaymaniya madrasa in Istanbul was destroyed. In the sixteenth and seventeenth centuries the more restrictive and puritanical forms of Islam asserted themselves against popular Sufi beliefs. Reform-minded religious scholars opposed popular ceremonies for the dead, Sufi dancing and singing, and the consumption of coffee and tobacco. Puritanical legalists, supported by madrasa students and tradesmen, won strong support for a more narrow definition of Islamic learning and practice. The supporters of Qadizade Mehmed Efendi (d. 1635) formed a party to control religious endowments and to persuade the authorities to enforce a Shari'a-oriented form of Islamic practice. Under the influence of this party tekkes were closed and Sufis were imprisoned.

---

[8] Persian Islamic regime. [Ed.]
[9] Lodges where Sufi mystics lived and taught. [Ed.]

Finally the quality of the religious elite declined. Intellectual discussion was suppressed. With the elaboration of a bureaucratic hierarchy, the biographies of scholars show that interest in careers outweighed genuine piety and learning. The influence of entrenched families enabled them to promote their children into the higher grades of the educational and judicial hierarchies without having reached the proper preliminary levels, while theological students who could not find patronage were excluded. In the course of the eighteenth century the "ulama," entrenched in their bureaucratic positions, became a powerful conservative pressure group.

The bureaucratization of the "ulama" gave them enormous social power as teachers, preachers, controllers of endowments, judges, and provincial officials. These powers, however, were acquired at high cost. As servants of the state the "ulama" could no longer represent the communal and religious interests of the mass of Muslim believers, and protect the people from the abuses of political power. The ideological consequences were equally heavy. Traditionally, the "ulama" had maintained an ambivalent position toward Muslim states, seeing them as indispensable adjuncts to Islamic communal life, but also as a major cause of harm to Muslim interests. In the Ottoman empire, however, the commitment of the "ulama" to the state regime was so complete that they could not effectively represent a transcendental Islamic ideal opposed to worldly corruption. Their dependency upon and integration into the Ottoman regime made them simply the spokesmen of Ottoman legitimacy.

5

BENJAMIN J. KAPLAN

European Faiths and States

In Europe, as in Ottoman Turkey, the state emerged as a major force after 1500. But the rise of the European state was accompanied by a cultural revolution that may not have occurred in the Ottoman Empire (outside of Sufi orders). That revolution was the creation of self-conscious faith-based communities, spurred by the Protestant Reformation and the Catholic response. In this selection, Benjamin J. Kaplan, a modern historian, shows the novelty and intolerance of this combination of confessional community and state power. Why was this combination so volatile? Did it make European society and European governments more intolerant than were other societies

Source: Benjamin J. Kaplan, *Divided by Faith: Religious Conflict and the Practice of Toleration in Early Modern Europe* (Cambridge: Harvard University Press, 2007), 28–32, 100–103.

like China, Japan, India, or the Ottoman Empire? How were these changes in Europe similar to, and different from, those in the Ottoman Empire during the same period?

THINKING HISTORICALLY

This selection, like the previous one, contrasts an early past (in both cases the thirteenth to early sixteenth centuries) with a later past (the later sixteenth to eighteenth centuries). The author's description of that early past seems very foreign to us today. It is difficult to imagine a world without religious belief or faith-based communities. Most people today even define religion as a belief system or faith. It is also difficult to imagine a world where states or governments do not play an important role. But this reading shows how both religion and the state, as we know them, are products of a later past, and that together they created a less tolerant society. Why is it disconcerting to think that religious intolerance may have actually increased from the earlier to the later period?

No religion is static, and over its two millennia of existence the Roman Catholic Church has transformed itself several times. The so-called Investiture Controversy[1] of the eleventh century precipitated one such transformation; in the 1960s, Vatican II[2] decreed another. So too in the sixteenth century, partly in response to the Protestant challenge, partly driven by internal impulses for renewal and reform, the Catholic Church initiated sweeping changes in everything from ecclesiastic administration and the training of priests to liturgy and forms of private devotion. Conventionally, the drive to enact these changes is referred to as either the Counter-Reformation or the Catholic Reformation, the first term emphasizing its reactive quality, the second its self-generation. Both terms, however, obscure a crucial fact: that changes in Catholicism resembled in some respects the reforms instituted by Protestants. That is, for all the differences and points of contention that bitterly divided them, in some respects the churches of early modern Europe were developing in parallel to one another. Christianity was changing, irrespective of church. The new type of Christianity that resulted from this process is known as "confessional." Its emergence, also called the "rise of confessionalism" or the "formation of confessions," can be charted beginning in the sixteenth century and continuing through the seventeenth.

[1] A struggle in Europe in the eleventh and twelfth centuries over whether kings or the pope had authority to appoint church officials. [Ed.]

[2] An important series of changes under Pope John XXIII said to modernize the Catholic church (1962–1965). [Ed.]

To dispel any confusion, it must be explained that the term *confession* and its derivatives do not refer in this context to the Catholic sacrament of penance. Rather they refer to a type of document, the "confession of faith," a declaration of the fundamental doctrines held by a church. Perhaps the most famous was the Augsburg Confession of 1530, which came to define Lutheran orthodoxy. All early modern churches issued such documents, which embodied three of the most basic trends then in Christianity: the internalization of church teaching, the drawing of sharp dichotomies, and the quest for "holy uniformity." Each fueled intolerance.

The timing and modalities of these trends varied greatly by church and by region, and in Ireland they had hardly affected the vast majority of peasants (who remained loyal to Catholicism) by the 1660s. According to Englishman Jeremy Taylor, the Irish peasantry could "give no account of their religion what it is: only they believe as their priest bids them and go to mass which they understand not, and reckon their beads to tell the number and the tale of their prayers, and abstain from eggs and flesh in Lent, and visit St. Patrick's well, and leave pins and ribbons, yarn or thread in their holy wells, and pray to God, S. Mary and S. Patrick, S. Columbanus and S. Bridget, and desire to be buried with S. Francis cord about them, and to fast on Saturdays in honour of our Lady."[3]

Granted that Taylor was a hostile outsider, his description not only matches what we know about seventeeth-century Ireland, it captures a state of affairs that was quite the norm across Europe prior to the Reformation. For medieval Christians, religion was as much a set of ritual practices as a set of beliefs. It entailed feasting and fasting on prescribed days; attending mass; reciting prayers in a language (Latin) they scarcely understood; making pilgrimages to holy places, where they offered sacrifices to wonder-working saints; and a wide array of other "works." These had merit, according to theologians, only if performed in a devout frame of mind. In practice, though, priests and laity attributed to them an efficacy as reliable as transubstantiation, the miracle of the mass whereby wafer and wine became Christ's body and blood. The more frequently they were performed, it was said, the more divine grace they conveyed and the better your chances of going to heaven. Many religious acts, in any event, were directed less toward attaining salvation after death than toward escaping misfortune in life. Making the sign of the cross, wearing an amulet containing the words from the Gospel of John, parading images of saints through parish streets: such acts were believed to ward off evil, offering protection from disease, accident, war, and famine.

In medieval Europe, ordinary laypeople knew little church doctrine. They received no formal religious instruction, and their pastors rarely

---

[3] Keith Thomas, *Religion and the Decline of Magic* (New York, 1971), pp. 76–77.

preached. Like Taylor's peasants, they could establish their orthodoxy simply by declaring they "believe as their priest bids them." Such ignorance did not matter greatly in a world where everyone was by default Catholic. It did after Europe split into competing "confessions," each propounding a rival truth. As each church began to define its identity in terms of its unique teachings, doctrine took on an unprecedented importance, and the expectation, echoed in Taylor's disdain, began to build that church members know what their church taught and how it differed from other churches. For Protestants, this expectation was built into the very definition of their religion, which taught that salvation is "by faith alone." All the Protestant churches accepted it as their mission to teach Christians what they needed to believe to be saved. At the same time, a more general dynamic operated: the very existence of alternatives created pressure for Christians to be better informed and more self-conscious in their commitments. Catholic reformers too began to demand that ordinary church members internalize the teachings of their church. Religion itself thus came increasingly to mean belief in a particular creed, and a life lived in accordance with it.

It was easy for churches to enunciate such dramatically raised standards. Implementing them required decades, in some regions as much as two centuries, of strenuous effort. The churches had to undertake massive pedagogic campaigns, which they conducted via preaching, education, printed propaganda, church discipline, and revamped rituals. In all these areas Protestant reformers broke new ground. They made the sermon the centerpiece of Protestant worship. They required that children receive elementary religious instruction, either at school or through special catechism[4] classes. They released torrents of printed propaganda and encouraged ordinary Christians to read scripture. They established new institutions and procedures to supervise parish life. . . .

Facing many of the same challenges as Protestant reformers, Catholic reformers had no qualms about adopting the former's pedagogic methods (and vice versa). The Jesuits in particular engaged in a range of activities that show striking parallels to those of their enemies. They became renowned preachers, wrote catechisms (that of Peter Canisius was the most popular in Catholic Europe), and founded hundreds of new schools, mostly at the secondary and college level. Using the *Spiritual Exercises* written by their founder, Ignatius of Loyola, they taught people how to examine their own consciences and achieve pious goals through a remarkable self-discipline. As confessors, chaplains, and organizers of a new type of club, the Marian sodality, they encouraged frequent confession and Communion. This disciplinary routine encouraged

---

[4] Indoctrination; memorizing doctrine. [Ed.]

the internalization of norms even as it provided an external mechanism for enforcing them. . . .

Just as the welfare of towns and villages depended on God's favor, Europeans believed, so did that of countries. . . . In 1663, when Ottoman armies launched an offensive into central Europe, prayers went up across the Continent. One pietist preacher warned his Dutch congregation that the Turks would conquer all unless lax, indifferent Christians put into practice the teachings they mouthed. Two decades later the Turks attacked again, this time reaching the walls of Vienna. At this critical juncture, Pope Innocent XI marshaled an international alliance to relieve the imperial capital. Protestant as well as Catholic princes of Germany sent troops to fight alongside Poles and Austrians. After the combined Christian army broke the Turks' siege, Innocent organized a "Holy League" whose forces drove the Turks once and for all back to the Balkans. This crusade was the last hurrah for the medieval concept of a united Christendom led by pope and emperor.

By then, two developments had made the concept almost completely anachronistic. One we have already examined: the division of Christendom into competing confessions. The other was the emergence of political units resembling modern nation-states. Particularism[5] did not disappear, either as a set of power relationships or as a mentality. Increasingly, though, Europe's rulers asserted an impersonal authority that can be called sovereignty, rather than (or, perhaps better, in addition to) the personal suzerainty[6] of the feudal Middle Ages. They codified laws, issued regulations, raised taxes, formalized institutions, and mobilized networks of officials, casting in this way a tighter net of control over society. One must not exaggerate the control rulers achieved, for early modern governments never had the tools of law enforcement modern ones take for granted. More than is often realized, their authority depended on the consent of the governed. Nevertheless, by the late seventeenth century some princes had achieved what at the time was called "absolute" authority: they could wage war, issue laws, and impose taxes without the approval of representative institutions, or with sure knowledge of their rubber stamp. "Absolutism" vested all sovereign power in a single individual, but even in polities that remained fragmented, like those of the Dutch and Swiss, there developed "a more encompassing, more systematic, and more literate articulation of power and authority."[7] The development took as many forms as there were

---

[5] Local, personal, and decentralized politics, as in medieval feudalism. [Ed.]

[6] Dependence. [Ed.]

[7] So characterized by Randolph C. Head in "Fragmented Dominion, Fragmented Churches: The Institutionalization of the *Landfrieden* in the Thurgau, 1531–1610," *Archiv für Reformationsgeschichte* 96 (205): 119.

forms of polity, but across Europe it was clear: the state grew stronger as an institution and more cohesive as a political community.

The fusion of these two developments, confessionalism and state formation, was explosive. The fictional Irishman Dooley, creation of modern humorist Finley Peter Dunne, once observed: "Rellijon is a quare thing. Be itself it's all right. But sprinkle a little pollyticks into it an' dinnymit is bran flour compared with it. Alone it prepares a man f'r a better life. Combined with polyticks it hurries him to it."[8] The observation has a special ring of truth in the mouth of an Irishman, for in modern Ireland, religious and political causes—Protestantism and Union with Britain, Catholicism and Irish Nationalism—have become inseparable. In the sixteenth century, religion and politics combined similarly across Europe. Religious enemies, their hatreds fanned by confessional ideology, became political enemies, and vice versa, as people at odds with one another for social or political reasons tended to choose opposing sides religiously as well. In this way, Europe's religious divisions not only created new conflicts, they threw ideological fuel on the fires of existing ones. Competitions for power, wealth, or land became cosmic struggles between the forces of God and Satan. Inversely, the bonds of a common confession brought people together in equally powerful ways. When they cut across social or political lines, they could make friends of strangers or even former enemies. On every level, from the local to the international, co-religionists felt an impulse to make common cause with one another.

To Europe's rulers, then, the rise of confessionalism held out both perils and promises. A difference in religion could alienate their subjects from them and undermine their authority. As the French Wars of Religion demonstrated, to the horror of contemporaries, it could set citizen against fellow citizen and tear states apart in civil war. A shared religion, on the other hand, could bolster rulers' authority, binding their subjects to them and to one another more firmly. Given these starkly contrasting possibilities, it is no wonder rulers tried to impose religious uniformity on their territories. Their personal piety impelled many to do the same. Since the thirteenth century, the Catholic Church had asked them to swear they would "strive in good faith and to the best of their ability to exterminate in the territories subject to their jurisdiction all heretics pointed out by the Church."[9] The division of Western Christendom gave them compelling new reasons to do so.

In its wake, Europe's rulers tried to make their personal choice of faith official for their state. Most succeeded, though, as we shall see, not all. Either way, the resulting confessional allegiance eventually became a

[8] Leonard W. Levy, *The Establishment Clause: Religion and the First Amendment* (New York, 1986), ix.

[9] Robert I. Moore, *The Formation of a Persecuting Society: Power and Deviance in Western Europe, 950–1250* (Oxford, 1987), 7.

defining aspect of political identity. Whether or not it initially had wide support, the allegiance was institutionalized and sank popular roots. In some essential and irreversible way, England became a Protestant country, Poland a Catholic one, Sweden Lutheran, the Dutch Republic Calvinist, and so forth. This fusion of religious and political identity, piety and patriotism, was (after confessionalism and the communal quest for holiness) the third great cause of religious intolerance in early modern Europe. Forged in the course of Europe's religious wars, it led both rulers and ordinary people to equate orthodoxy with loyalty and religious dissent with sedition. It gave national politics and even foreign affairs the power to spark waves of religious riots as well as official persecution.

6

MARTIN LUTHER

Law and the Gospel: Princes and Turks

Martin Luther (1483–1546) launched the Protestant Reformation when he published his "95 Theses" in 1517, challenging the domination of Christianity by Rome and the papacy. Luther's immediate complaint centered on the authority of the pope and his agents to sell indulgences, which promised lessened time in purgatory for deceased loved ones on receipt of a contribution to a building fund for St. Peter's Cathedral. As Luther's criticism of papal practices reached the point of a breach, Luther turned to the German princes to support churches independent of Rome.

The issue of religious and political authority has long been debated and negotiated in Christian Europe. Unlike Islam, which was founded by a prophet who also governed, Christianity was founded and grew in an anti-Roman and even antipolitical environment. Typically, Christianity settled on an ambiguous or dualistic relationship between government and God. "Render to Caesar the things that are Caesar's, and to God the things that are God's," Jesus declared according to Mark (12:17) and Matthew (22:21). St. Augustine distinguished between the two cities: the city of God and the city of man. In the Middle Ages, the doctrine of the two

Source: *The Table-Talk of Martin Luther*, trans. William Hazlitt, Esq. (Philadelphia: The Lutheran Publication Society, 1997). Center for Reformed Theology and Apologetics. www.reformed.org.

swords, temporal and spiritual, suggested a similar duality. Periodically one force asserted superiority over the other. In 800 Charlemagne took the coronation crown from the hands of the pope. In 1054 the Holy Roman Emperor was said to crawl through the snow on his hands and knees to beg forgiveness from the pope. The popes of the Italian Renaissance lived like kings, but in the sixteenth century secular princes increased the power of the state.

Martin Luther's initial break with Rome encouraged other protests against both secular and religious authorities. His stress on individual interpretation of scripture and the power of following one's own conscience inspired more radical groups like the German Anabaptists to defy all worldly authority. In the wake of a peasant's revolt throughout Germany in 1523–1525, Luther joined forces with the German princes and voiced approval of the authority of the state.

This selection is drawn from a collection of conversational statements by Luther that were recorded by his followers and published under the title *Table-Talk* in 1566, after Luther's death.

What was Luther's attitude toward law and the state? What role did he think princes or governments ought to have in enforcing religious doctrine or behavior? What did he think of the Ottoman Turks? In the selections on "Princes and Potentates" Luther turns his attention to the laws that would be enforced by his allies, the German princes. What vision of religion and politics is implied in these selections?

THINKING HISTORICALLY

Luther's ideas live on today in the minds of many, not just Lutherans and other Protestants. Even the words Luther used — *law, conscience, freedom, government* — are as familiar now as they were in the sixteenth century. But Luther's ideas are also the product of a sixteenth-century thinker in sixteenth-century circumstances. Consequently, we can never assume that when we use these words or express these ideas we mean what Luther meant.

Notice, for instance, how Martin Luther dealt with the laws of the state and the call of conscience or the Gospel in the selections on "Law and the Gospel." What did "law" mean for the first Protestant? How did "conscience" or "the Gospel" provide better footing for Luther's challenge of the church? How do people compare or contrast law and conscience today? Would Luther have understood a modern appeal to conscience that led to civil disobedience? Would we want to allow a greater freedom of conscience today? In what ways are Luther's ideas of the Ottoman Turks similar to some Westerners' ideas of Muslim countries today?

Of the Law and the Gospel

CCLXXI

We must reject those who so highly boast of Moses' laws, as to temporal affairs, for we have our written imperial and country laws, under which we live, and unto which we are sworn. Neither Naaman the Assyrian, nor Job, nor Joseph, nor Daniel, nor many other good and godly Jews, observed Moses' laws out of their country, but those of the Gentiles among whom they lived. Moses' law bound and obliged only the Jews in that place which God made choice of. Now they are free. If we should keep and observe the laws and rites of Moses, we must also be circumcised, and keep the mosaical ceremonies; for there is no difference; he that holds one to be necessary, must hold the rest so too. Therefore let us leave Moses to his laws, excepting only the *Moralia*,[1] which God has planted in nature, as the ten commandments, which concern God's true worshipping and service, and a civil life. . . .

CCLXXXVIII

In what darkness, unbelief, traditions, and ordinances of men have we lived, and in how many conflicts of the conscience we have been ensnared, confounded, and captivated under popedom, is testified by the books of the papists, and by many people now living. From all which snares and horrors we are now delivered and freed by Jesus Christ and his Gospel, and are called to the true righteousness of faith; insomuch that with good and peaceable consciences we now believe in God the Father, we trust in him, and have just cause to boast that we have sure and certain remission of our sins through the death of Christ Jesus, dearly bought and purchased. Who can sufficiently extol these treasures of the conscience, which everywhere are spread abroad, offered, and presented merely by grace? We are now conquerors of sin, of the law, of death, and of the devil; freed and delivered from all human traditions. If we would but consider the tyranny of auricular confession,[2] one of the least things we have escaped from, we could not show ourselves sufficiently thankful to God for loosing us out of that one snare. When popedom stood and flourished among us, then every king would willingly have given ten hundred thousand guilders, a prince one hundred thousand, a nobleman one thousand, a gentleman one hundred, a citizen or countryman twenty or ten, to have been freed from that tyranny. But now seeing that such freedom is obtained for nothing, by grace, it is not much regarded, neither give we thanks to God for it.

[1] Moral code. [Ed.]
[2] Catholic confession to a priest. [Ed.]

CCLXXXIX

. . . We must make a clear distinction; we must place the Gospel in heaven, and leave the law on earth; we must receive of the Gospel a heavenly and a divine righteousness; while we value the law as an earthly and human righteousness, and thus directly and diligently separate the righteousness of the gospel from the righteousness of the law, even as God has separated and distinguished heaven from earth, light from darkness, day from night, etc., so that the righteousness of the Gospel be the light and the day, but the righteousness of the law, darkness and night. Therefore all Christians should learn rightly to discern the law and grace in their hearts, and know how to keep one from the other, in deed and in truth, not merely in words, as the pope and other heretics do, who mingle them together, and, as it were, make thereout a cake not fit to eat. . . .

Of Princes and Potentates

DCCXI

Government is a sign of the divine grace, of the mercy of God, who has no pleasure in murdering, killing, and strangling. If God left all things to go where they would, as among the Turks and other nations, without good government, we should quickly dispatch one another out of this world.

DCCXII

Parents keep their children with greater diligence and care than rulers and governors keep their subjects. Fathers and mothers are masters naturally and willingly; it is a self-grown dominion; but rulers and magistrates have a compulsory mastery; they act by force, with a prepared dominion; when father and mother can rule no more, the public police must take the matter in hand. Rulers and magistrates must watch over the sixth commandment.

DCCXIII

The temporal magistrate is even like a fish net, set before the fish in a pond or a lake, but God is the plunger, who drives the fish into it. For when a thief, robber, adulterer, murderer, is ripe, he hunts him into the net, that is, causes him to be taken by the magistrate, and punished; for it is written: "God is judge upon earth." Therefore repent, or thou must be punished.

DCCXIV

Princes and rulers should maintain the laws and statutes, or they will be condemned. They should, above all, hold the Gospel in honor, and bear it ever in their hands, for it aids and preserves them, and ennobles the state and office of magistracy, so that they know where their vocation and calling is, and that with good and safe conscience they may execute the works of their office. At Rome, the executioner always craved pardon of the condemned malefactor, when he was to execute his office, as though he were doing wrong, or sinning in executing the criminal; whereas 'tis his proper office, which God has set.

St. Paul says: "He beareth not the sword in vain"; he is God's minister, a revenger, to execute wrath upon him that does evil. When the magistrate punishes, God himself punishes.

On the Turks

DCCCXXVII

The power of the Turk is very great; he keeps in his pay, all the year through, hundreds of thousands of soldiers. He must have more than two millions of florins annual revenue. We are far less strong in our bodies, and are divided out among different masters, all opposed the one to the other, yet we might conquer these infidels with only the Lord's prayer, if our own people did not spill so much blood in religious quarrels, and in persecuting the truths contained in that prayer. God will punish us as he punished Sodom and Gomorrah, but I would fain 'twere by the hand of some pious potentate, and not by that of the accursed Turk. . . .

DCCCXXX

News came from Torgau that the Turks had led out into the great square at Constantinople twenty-three Christian prisoners, who, on their refusing to apostatize, were beheaded. Dr. Luther said: Their blood will cry up to heaven against the Turks, as that of John Huss[3] did against the

---

[3] In Czech, known as Jan Hus. Hus (1369–1415) was a Czech forerunner for the Protestant Reformation. [Ed.]

papists. 'Tis certain, tyranny and persecution will not avail to stifle the Word of Jesus Christ. It flourishes and grows in blood. Where one Christian is slaughtered, a host of others arise. 'Tis not on our walls or our arquebusses[4] I rely for resisting the Turk, but upon the *Pater Noster*.[5] 'Tis that will triumph. The Decalogue[6] is not, of itself, sufficient. I said to the engineers at Wittenberg: Why strengthen your walls—they are trash; the walls with which a Christian should fortify himself are made, not of stone and mortar, but of prayer and faith. . . .

DCCCXXXV

. . . The Turks pretend, despite the Holy Scriptures, that they are the chosen people of God, as descendants of Ishmael. They say that Ishmael was the true son of the promise, for that when Issac was about to be sacrificed, he fled from his father, and from the slaughter knife, and, meanwhile, Ishmael came and truly offered himself to be sacrificed, whence he became the child of the promise; as gross a lie as that of the papists concerning one kind in the sacrament. The Turks make a boast of being very religious, and treat all other nations as idolaters. They slanderously accuse the Christians of worshipping three gods. They swear by one only God, creator of heaven and earth, by his angels, by the four evangelists, and by the eighty heaven-descended prophets, of whom Mohammed is the greatest. They reject all images and pictures, and render homage to God alone. They pay the most honorable testimony to Jesus Christ, saying that he was a prophet of preeminent sanctity, born of the Virgin Mary, and an envoy from God, but that Mohammed succeeded him, and that while Mohammed sits, in heaven, on the right hand of the Father, Jesus Christ is seated on his left. The Turks have retained many features of the law of Moses, but, inflated with the insolence of victory, they have adopted a new worship; for the glory of warlike triumphs is, in the opinion of the world, the greatest of all.

. . . 'Tis with the Turks as heretofore with the Romans, every subject is a soldier, as long as he is able to bear arms, so they have always a disciplined army ready for the field; whereas we gather together ephemeral bodies of vagabonds, untried wretches, upon whom is no dependence. My fear is, that the papists will unite with the Turks to exterminate us. Please God, my anticipation come not true, but certain it is, that the desperate creatures will do their best to deliver us over to the Turks.

---

[4] Primitive firearms used from the fifteenth to the seventeenth centuries. [Ed.]
[5] "Our Father," the Lord's Prayer. [Ed.]
[6] The Ten Commandments. [Ed.]

ROGER WILLIAMS

The Bloody Tenent of Persecution for Cause of Conscience

Roger Williams (1603–1683), a minister of the Church of England sympathetic to its Puritan reformist wing, sailed from England in 1630 to join the newly founded Massachusetts Bay Colony. But for Williams the colony remained too close to the Church of England, especially in its continuing legacies of Catholicism: bishops, infant baptism, ritual kneeling, and making the sign of the cross. Williams moved on to the more separatist Pilgrim colony in Plymouth and to a church in Salem in 1633. There he became engaged in a series of conflicts with the General Court of Massachusetts, which upheld Puritan orthodoxy, for defaming the churches and the civil authority of the colony. For his "dangerous opinions" he was given six weeks to leave. In the howling winter of 1635, he brought his small band of followers south to Narragansett Bay, where he bought a tract of land from the Indians that he called Providence and that would later become Rhode Island.

The Bloody Tenent, written sometime between 1636 and 1644, when it was finally published (and then burned) in London, summarized the disagreements that Williams had with the Massachusetts authorities, the Church of England, and, one might add, the long history of Catholicism. What did Williams mean by the "bloody tenent" (tenet or doctrine) of persecution for conscience? Why does he call this doctrine bloody? According to Williams, what should be the relationship between church and state? Why? How is Williams's idea of this relationship different from Luther's? How do you account for that difference?

THINKING HISTORICALLY

In Protestant America of the 1630s, the more fervent advocates of religious purity rallied around symbols and signs that more mainstream Protestants dismissed as unimportant. But the religious purists and the mainstreamers of the American seventeenth century argued the exact opposite of what we might expect to hear today. Roger Williams and his Separatist followers objected to the display of the most sacred Christian symbol, the cross, on the English flag. For them the

Source: Roger Williams, *The Bloody Tenent of Persecution for Cause of Conscience, Discussed in a Conference between Truth and Peace,* ed. Richard Groves (Macon, GA: Mercer University Press, 2001), 3–4.

cross on the flag was a sacrilegious confusion of nation and church, politics and faith. Some of the Separatists of Salem got into trouble with the Massachusetts government for desecrating the flag by cutting out the cross. Williams and the Separatists also objected to political officials saying "so help me God" when taking an oath of office. The judges and officials of the state should not presume to act for God, Williams argued, and nonbelievers should not be forced to take the name of "the Lord thy God" in vain. Nothing good could come from governments policing faith or from communities of the faithful mucking about in worldly affairs. What do you think Roger Williams would have thought of prayer in the public schools, the idea that America was a "Christian nation," or politicians saying "God Bless America"?

In this selection, Williams refers to a number of different historical periods. First he mentions the religious wars between Catholics and Protestants that had ravaged Europe. Like Luther, he also refers to two of the most important historical markers for Christians: ancient Israel of the Old Testament and the coming of Christ. Why does he say what he says about ancient Israel? What is his belief in the fate of Jews after the coming of Christ? Christian theology was (and is) highly historical. It envisions a timeline that stretches into the future as well. What future developments does Williams envision?

First, that the blood of so many hundred thousand souls of Protestants and papists, spilled in the wars of present and former ages for their respective consciences, is not required nor accepted by Jesus Christ the Prince of Peace.

Secondly, pregnant scriptures and arguments are throughout the work proposed against the doctrine of persecution for cause of conscience.

Thirdly, satisfactory answers are given to scriptures and objections produced by Mr. Calvin, Beza,[1] Mr. Cotton, and the ministers of the New English churches, and others former and later, tending to prove the doctrine of persecution for cause of conscience.

Fourthly, the doctrine of persecution for cause of conscience is proved guilty of all the blood of the souls crying for vengeance under the altar.

Fifthly, all civil states, with their officers of justice, in their respective constitutions and administrations, are proved essentially civil, and therefore not judges, governors, or defenders of the spiritual, or Christian, state and worship.

---

[1] Theodore Beza (1519–1605), John Calvin's successor. [Ed.]

Sixthly, it is the will and command of God that, since the coming of his Son the Lord Jesus, a permission of the most paganish, Jewish, Turkish, or anti-Christian consciences and worships be granted to all men in all nations and countries, and they are only to be fought against with that sword which is only, in soul matters, able to conquer, to wit, the sword of God's Spirit, the word of God.

Seventhly, the state of the land of Israel, the kings and people thereof, in peace and war, is proved figurative and ceremonial, and no pattern nor precedent for any kingdom or civil state in the world to follow.

Eighthly, God requires not a uniformity of religion to be enacted and enforced in any civil state; which enforced uniformity, sooner or later, is the greatest occasion of civil war, ravishing of conscience, persecution of Christ Jesus in his servants, and of the hypocrisy and destruction of millions of souls.

Ninthly, in holding an enforced uniformity of religion in a civil state, we must necessarily disclaim our desires and hopes of the Jews' conversion to Christ.

Tenthly, an enforced uniformity of religion throughout a nation or civil state confounds the civil and religious, denies the principles of Christianity and civility, and that Jesus Christ is come in the flesh.

Eleventhly, the permission of other consciences and worships that a state professes only can, according to God, procure a firm and lasting peace; good assurance being taken, according to the wisdom of the civil state, for uniformity of civil obedience from all sorts.

Twelfthly, lastly, true civility and Christianity may both flourish in a state or kingdom, notwithstanding the permission of divers and contrary consciences, either of Jew or Gentile.

■ REFLECTIONS

School prayer, abortion, the public display of religious symbols— what is the proper relationship of government and religion? Roger Williams reminds us that the principle of the separation of church and state, a pillar of modern civic society, originated in America not as a secular humanist denigration of religion but as an effort by the most fervent Protestant Separatists to preserve their religion's purity and independence.

Luther's discussion of government and religion strikes a more expected tone. The great reformer was able to dismiss thousands of years of law from ancient Israel and the Roman papacy, but he gave German princes far greater authority over religious matters than most Christians would allow today. How do we account for the differences between Martin Luther and Roger Williams on this issue? Is it simply a matter of each preaching the politics of his position — the privileged versus the persecuted?

If the Protestant Reformation led to the separation of church and state in America, this was not the intention of the early reformers. Luther, John Calvin, Henry VIII, and most early Protestants were vigorous proponents of state religions, the legislation of Christian morality, and the censorship and proscription of contrary beliefs and behavior. Benjamin Kaplan shows how both the Protestant Reformation and the similar Catholic Counter-Reformation created robustly intolerant religious communities. New kings and parliaments put religious doctrines into the service of national states as if they were badges of identity or flags to be saluted.

It is a modern conceit that tolerance must have gradually increased since the "dark ages," but Kaplan and Lepidus show us that both European and Ottoman societies went from tolerance to intolerance in the sixteenth century. There were different drivers of the change: government inclusion of religious dissidents in the Ottoman case, and the seizure or establishment of governments by the Europeans. In both cases, the religious fundamentalists made government less tolerant of diversity or heterodoxy. Fortunately for free expression, both Christian European and Islamic Ottoman societies changed direction. In the case of Christian society, the change came early and from within. The preservation of sectarianism required separation from the state. In Turkey, the end of state religion came with the end of the Ottoman regime itself and the creation of the modern secular republic under Ataturk in the 1920s (see selection 6 in Chapter 23).

The case of Mughal rule in India also shows a transition from generous toleration under Akbar, which continued despite interruption under his grandson Shah Jahan (r. 1628–1658), to far less toleration with Aurangzeb (r. 1658–1707). The religious leaders who suffered most under the Mughals were not Hindus but reformers who attempted to unite Hinduism and Islam under a new monotheism, the Sikhs. As often happens, the reformers close to home were found to be the most offensive.

Neither the Chinese nor Japanese traditions held religious orthodoxies, but both required proper observance of certain social and political proprieties. Strong governments, as in most of Chinese history, turned principles like Confucian filial piety into virtual religions, but they had the force of law and made little appeal to conscience or individual choice. Although Daoism and Buddhism appealed to the inner lives of Chinese and Japanese devotees, they normally posed no challenge to state power. Only in periods of unrest, feudalism, or the breakdown of the state did Buddhist or Daoist priests and monks exercise political power. Even then, however, they did not challenge the state as much as filled the vacuum left by its disappearance. In both Japan and

Europe, the postfeudal age was one in which the state's rise depended, in part, on the reclamation and monopolization of powers previously exercised by religious institutions.

There are many pasts, but increasingly one present. As cultural differences meld with the force of rockets and the speed of the Internet, one might well ask what separate histories matter to a common present. Increasingly principles of toleration are enshrined by international organizations in declarations of human rights and the proceedings of international tribunals. Whether we see the roots of modern principles of tolerance in Confucian secularism, Christian separation of church and state, or Muslim cosmopolitanism, we live in a world where intolerance is widely condemned and legitimately prosecuted.

And yet, fanaticism and intolerance have not disappeared. Religious fundamentalists of various stripes declare their missions to take over governments, convert populations, and bring about the rule of God. History has shown that tolerance need not be secular. Indeed, even the aggressively secular regimes of the twentieth and twenty-first centuries have demonstrated and continue to demonstrate a capacity for brutal persecution of dissidents, religious and otherwise.

The study of the past may be better at telling us what we want than how we can achieve it. But the knowledge of how to get there from here begins with the knowledge of where we are and where we have been. At the very least, the knowledge of how things have changed from the past to the present holds the key to unlocking the future.

18

Gender and Family

China, Southeast Asia, Europe, and "New Spain," 1600–1750

■ HISTORICAL CONTEXT

Women are half of humanity. The family is the oldest and most important social institution. Marriage is one of the most important passages in one's life. Yet up until the last few decades these subjects rarely registered as important topics in world history. There were at least two reasons for this: One was the tendency to think of history as the story of public events only—the actions of political officials, governments, and their representatives—instead of the private and domestic sphere. The second was the assumption that the private or domestic sphere had no history, that it had always been the same. As the documents in this chapter will show, nothing could be further from the truth.

Since the urban revolution five thousand years ago, most societies have been patriarchal. The laws, social codes, and dominant ideas have enshrined the power and prestige of men over women, husbands over wives, fathers over children, gods over goddesses, even brothers over sisters. Double standards for adultery, inheritance laws that favor sons, and laws that deny women property or political rights all attest to the power of patriarchal culture and norms. Almost everywhere patriarchies have limited women to the domestic sphere while granting men public and political power. Nevertheless, we will see in this chapter that not all patriarchies were alike. Some were less stringent than others, and in many societies during this period, women, individually, in families, and even in larger groups, discovered ways both large and small to assert their social, cultural, and economic independence. As you read about women in China, Southeast Asia, Europe, and the Americas, consider how women's lives varied from one patriarchal society to another and how women found openings to express themselves and create their own worlds.

■ THINKING HISTORICALLY

Making Comparisons

We learn by making comparisons. Every new piece of knowledge we acquire leads to a comparison with what we already know. For example, we arrive in a new town and we are struck by something that we have not seen before. The town has odd street lamps, flowerpots on the sidewalks, or lots of trucks on the street. We start to formulate a theory about the differences between what we observe in the new town and what we already know about our old town. We think we're on to something, but our theory falls apart when we make more observations by staying in the new town another day, or traveling on to the next town, or going halfway across the world. As we gain more experience and make more observations, our original theory explaining an observed difference is supplanted by a much more complex theory about *types* of towns.

History is very much like travel. We learn by comparison, one step at a time, and the journey is never ending. On this trip we begin in China and then move on to other regions of the world. We begin with primary sources but make comparisons based on secondary sources as well. In fact, we conclude with a secondary source that will allow us to draw upon our previous readings to make increasingly informed and complex comparisons. Welcome aboard. Next stop, China.

1

Family Instructions for the Miu Lineage

Chinese families in Ming times (1368–1644) often organized themselves into groups by male lineage. These groups often shared common land, built ancestral halls, published genealogies, honored their common ancestors, and ensured the success and well-being of future generations. To accomplish the last of these, lineage groups frequently compiled lists of family rules or instructions. This particular example, from the various lines of the Miu family of the Guangdong province in the south, shows how extensive these instructions could be. What values did these family instructions encourage? What activities did the Miu lineage regulate? What kind of families, and what kind of individuals, were these rules intended to produce? How would these rules have had a different impact on women and men?

Source: "Family Instructions for the Miu Lineage, Late Sixteenth Century," trans. Clara Yu, in *Chinese Civilization: A Sourcebook*, 2nd ed., ed. Patricia Ebrey (New York: Free Press, 1993), 238–40, 241–43.

It is difficult to read this selection without thinking of one's own family and of families in one's own society. How many of the Miu lineage's concerns are concerns of families you know? Family instructions and lineage organizations are not common features of modern American society, even among Chinese Americans who may have a sense of their lineage and family identity. What institutions in modern American society regulate the activities addressed by these family instructions? Or are these activities left for self-regulation or no regulation at all? From reading this document, what do you think are some of the differences between Ming-era Chinese families and modern American families?

Work Hard at One of the Principal Occupations

1. To be filial to one's parents, to be loving to one's brothers, to be diligent and frugal—these are the first tenets of a person of good character. They must be thoroughly understood and faithfully carried out.

One's conscience should be followed like a strict teacher and insight should be sought through introspection. One should study the words and deeds of the ancients to find out their ultimate meanings. One should always remember the principles followed by the ancients, and should not become overwhelmed by current customs. For if one gives in to cruelty, pride, or extravagance, all virtues will be undermined, and nothing will be achieved.

Parents have special responsibilities. *The Book of Changes*[1] says: "The members of a family have strict sovereigns." The "sovereigns" are the parents. Their position in a family is one of unique authority, and they should utilize their authority to dictate matters to maintain order, and to inspire respect, so that the members of the family will all be obedient. If the parents are lenient and indulgent, there will be many troubles which in turn will give rise to even more troubles. Who is to blame for all this? The elders in a family must demand discipline of themselves, following all rules and regulations to the letter, so that the younger members emulate their good behavior and exhort each other to abide by the teachings of the ancient sages. Only in this way can the family hope to last for generations. If, however, the elders of a family should find it difficult to abide by these regulations, the virtuous youngsters of the family should help them along. Because the purpose of my work is to make such work easier, I am not afraid of giving many small details. . . .

2. Those youngsters who have taken Confucian scholarship as their hereditary occupation should be sincere and hard-working, and try to

[1] The *I Ching*, a Chinese classic. [Ed.]

achieve learning naturally while studying under a teacher. Confucianism is the only thing to follow if they wish to bring glory to their family. Those who know how to keep what they have but do not study are as useless as puppets made of clay or wood. Those who study, even if they do not succeed in the examinations, can hope to become teachers or to gain personal benefit. However, there are people who study not for learning's sake, but as a vulgar means of gaining profit. These people are better off doing nothing.

Youngsters who are incapable of concentrating on studying should devote themselves to farming; they should personally grasp the ploughs and eat the fruit of their own labor. In this way they will be able to support their families. If they fold their hands and do nothing, they will soon have to worry about hunger and cold. If, however, they realize that their forefathers also worked hard and that farming is a difficult way of life, they will not be inferior to anyone. In earlier dynasties, officials were all selected because they were filial sons, loving brothers, and diligent farmers. This was to set an example for all people to devote themselves to their professions, and to ensure that the officials were familiar with the hardships of the common people, thereby preventing them from exploiting the commoners for their own profit.

3. Farmers should personally attend to the inspection, measurement, and management of the fields, noting the soil as well as the terrain. The early harvest as well as the grain taxes and the labor service obligations should be carefully calculated. Anyone who indulges in indolence and entrusts these matters to others will not be able to distinguish one kind of crop from another and will certainly be cheated by others. I do not believe such a person could escape bankruptcy.

4. The usual occupations of the people are farming and commerce. If one tries by every possible means to make a great profit from these occupations, it usually leads to loss of capital. Therefore it is more profitable to put one's energy into farming the land; only when the fields are too far away to be tilled by oneself should they be leased to others. One should solicit advice from old farmers as to one's own capacity in farming.

Those who do not follow the usual occupations of farming or business should be taught a skill. Being an artisan is a good way of life and will also shelter a person from hunger and cold. All in all, it is important to remember that one should work hard when young, for when youth expires one can no longer achieve anything. Many people learn this lesson only after it is too late. We should guard against this mistake.

5. Fish can be raised in ponds by supplying them with grass and manure. Vegetables need water. In empty plots one can plant fruit trees such as the pear, persimmon, peach, prune, and plum, and also beans, wheat, hemp, peas, potatoes, and melons. When harvested, these vegetables and fruits can sustain life. During their growth, one should give them constant care, nourishing them and weeding them. In this way, no

labor is wasted and no fertile land is left uncultivated. On the contrary, to purchase everything needed for the morning and evening meals means the members of the family will merely sit and eat. Is this the way things should be?

6. Housewives should take full charge of the kitchen. They should make sure that the store of firewood is sufficient, so that even if it rains several days in succession, they will not be forced to use silver or rice to pay for firewood, thereby impoverishing the family. Housewives should also closely calculate the daily grocery expenses, and make sure there is no undue extravagance. Those who simply sit and wait to be fed only are treating themselves like pigs and dogs, but also are leading their whole households to ruin. . . .

Exercise Restraint

1. Our young people should know their place and observe correct manners. They are not permitted to gamble, to fight, to engage in lawsuits, or to deal in salt[2] privately. Such unlawful acts will only lead to their own downfall.

2. If land or property is not obtained by righteous means, descendants will not be able to enjoy it. When the ancients invented characters, they put gold next to two spears to mean "money," indicating that the danger of plunder or robbery is associated with it. If money is not accumulated by good means, it will disperse like overflowing water; how could it be put to any good? The result is misfortune for oneself as well as for one's posterity. This is the meaning of the saying: "The way of Heaven detests fullness, and only the humble gain." Therefore, accumulation of great wealth inevitably leads to great loss. How true are the words of Laozi![3]

A person's fortune and rank are predestined. One can only do one's best according to propriety and one's own ability; the rest is up to Heaven. If one is easily contented, then a diet of vegetables and soups provides a lifetime of joy. If one does not know one's limitations and tries to accumulate wealth by immoral and dishonest means, how can one avoid disaster? To be able to support oneself through life and not leave one's sons and grandsons in hunger and cold is enough; why should one toil so much?

3. Pride is a dangerous trait. Those who pride themselves on wealth, rank, or learning are inviting evil consequences. Even if one's

---

[2] Get involved in the salt trade, a state monopoly. Salt was used as a preservative for fish, meat, and other foods. [Ed.]

[3] Lao Tzu, legendary Chinese philosopher and author of the *Dao de Jing*, the Daoist classic. [Ed.]

accomplishments are indeed unique, there is no need to press them on anyone else. "The way of Heaven detests fullness, and only the humble gain." I have seen the truth of this saying many times.

4. Taking concubines in order to beget heirs should be a last resort, for the sons of the legal wife and the sons of the concubine are never of one mind, causing innumerable conflicts between half brothers. If the parents are in the least partial, problems will multiply, creating misfortune in later generations. Since families have been ruined because of this, it should not be taken lightly.

5. Just as diseases are caused by what goes into one's mouth, misfortunes are caused by what comes out of one's mouth. Those who are immoderate in eating and unrestrained in speaking have no one else to blame for their own ruin.

6. Most men lack resolve and listen to what their women say. As a result, blood relatives become estranged and competitiveness, suspicion, and distance arise between them. Therefore, when a wife first comes into a family, it should be made clear to her that such things are prohibited. "Start teaching one's son when he is a baby; start teaching one's daughter-in-law when she first arrives." That is to say, preventive measures should be taken early.

7. "A family's fortune can be foretold from whether its members are early risers" is a maxim of our ancient sages. Everyone, male and female, should rise before dawn and should not go to bed until after the first drum. Never should they indulge themselves in a false sense of security and leisure, for such behavior will eventually lead them to poverty.

8. Young family members who deliberately violate family regulations should be taken to the family temple, have their offenses reported to the ancestors, and be severely punished. They should then be taught to improve themselves. Those who do not accept punishment or persist in their wrongdoings will bring harm to themselves.

9. As a preventive measure against the unpredictable, the gates should be closed at dusk, and no one should be allowed to go out. Even when there are visitors, dinner parties should end early, so that there will be no need for lighting lamps and candles. On very hot or very cold days, one should be especially considerate of the kitchen servants.

10. For generations this family had dwelt in the country, and everyone has had a set profession; therefore, our descendants should not be allowed to change their place of residence. After living in the city for three years, a person forgets everything about farming; after ten years, he does not even know his lineage. Extravagance and leisure transform people, and it is hard for anyone to remain unaffected. I once remarked that the only legitimate excuse to live in a city temporarily is to flee from bandits.

11. The inner and outer rooms, halls, doorways, and furniture should be swept and dusted every morning at dawn. Dirty doorways and courtyards and haphazardly placed furniture are sure signs of a

declining family. Therefore, a schedule should be followed for cleaning them, with no excuses allowed.

12. Those in charge of cooking and kitchen work should make sure that breakfast is served before nine o'clock in the morning and dinner before five o'clock in the afternoon. Every evening the iron wok and other utensils should be washed and put away, so that the next morning, after rising at dawn, one can expect tea and breakfast to be prepared immediately and served on time. In the kitchen no lamps are allowed in the morning or at night. This is not only to save the expense, but also to avoid harmful contamination of food. Although this is a small matter, it has a great effect on health. Furthermore, since all members of the family have their regular work to do, letting them toil all day without giving them meals at regular hours is no way to provide comfort and relief for them. If these rules are deliberately violated, the person in charge will be punished as an example to the rest.

13. On the tenth and twenty-fifth days of every month, all the members of this branch, from the honored aged members to the youngsters, should gather at dusk for a meeting. Each will give an account of what he has learned, by either calling attention to examples of good and evil, or encouraging diligence, or expounding his obligations, or pointing out tasks to be completed. Each member will take turns presenting his own opinions and listening attentively to others. He should examine himself in the matters being discussed and make efforts to improve himself. The purpose of these meetings is to encourage one another in virtue and to correct each other's mistakes.

The members of the family will take turns being the chairman of these meetings, according to schedule. If someone is unable to chair a meeting on a certain day, he should ask the next person in line to take his place. The chairman should provide tea, but never wine. The meetings may be canceled on days of ancestor worship, parties, or other such occasions, or if the weather is severe. Those who are absent from these meetings for no reason are only doing themselves harm.

There are no set rules for where the meeting should be held, but the place should be convenient for group discussions. The time of the meeting should always be early evening, for this is when people have free time. As a general precaution the meeting should never last until late at night.

14. Women from lower-class families who stop at our houses tend to gossip, create conflicts, peek into the kitchens, or induce our women to believe in prayer and fortune-telling, thereby cheating them out of their money and possessions. Consequently, one should question these women often and punish those who come for no reason, so as to put a stop to the traffic.

15. Blood relatives are as close as the branches of a tree, yet their relationships can still be differentiated according to importance and priority: Parents should be considered before brothers, and brothers should

be considered before wives and children. Each person should fulfill his own duties and share with others profit and loss, joy and sorrow, life and death. In this way, the family will get along well and be blessed by Heaven. Should family members fight over property or end up treating each other like enemies, then when death or misfortune strikes they will be of even less use than strangers. If our ancestors have consciousness, they will not tolerate these unprincipled descendants who are but animals in man's clothing. Heaven responds to human vices with punishments as surely as an echo follows a sound. I hope my sons and grandsons take my words seriously.

16. To get along with patrilineal relatives, fellow villages, and relatives through marriage, one should be gentle in speech and mild in manners. When one is opposed by others, one may remonstrate with them; but when others fall short because of their limitations, one should be tolerant. If one's youngsters or servants get into fights with others, one should look into oneself to find the blame. It is better to be wronged than to wrong others. Those who take affront and become enraged, who conceal their own shortcomings and seek to defeat others, are courting immediate misfortune. Even if the other party is unbearably unreasonable, one should contemplate the fact that the ancient sages had to endure much more. If one remains tolerant and forgiving, one will be able to curb the other party's violence.

2

MAO XIANG

How Dong Xiaowan Became My Concubine[1]

Mao Xiang* (1611–1693) was one of the great poets, artists, and calligraphers of the late Ming dynasty and, after its demise in 1644, a persistent critic of the succeeding Manchu or Ching dynasty. He was also known for his love of beautiful women, especially three famous courtesans who were also talented artists: Dong Xiaowan† (1625–1651), Cai Han (1647–1686),

* mow zhee ANG
† dong zhow AHN
[1] A concubine is a woman who lives with a man who supports her but does not marry her. In China, this was normally a relationship between a rich man, sometimes already married, and a poor woman.

Source: "How Dong Xiaowan Became My Concubine," in *Chinese Civilization: A Sourcebook*, 2nd ed., ed. Patricia Ebrey (New York: Free Press, 1993), 246–49.

and Qin Yue (c. 1660–1690). (Note what these dates reveal.) Whether or not this is a reliable account of how Dong Xiaowan became his concubine, what does this piece from Mao Xiang's memoir tell you about his society's attitudes toward women, marriage, and family?

THINKING HISTORICALLY

If comparisons originate in our recognition of institutions and ideas that are foreign to our own, certainly the acceptance of concubines in seventeenth-century Chinese society is a sharp contrast to modern American family values. Concubines were mainly an indulgence of upper-class Chinese men, but concubinage was an institution that touched all classes of Chinese society. Poor peasants knew that they could sell their daughters into the trade, if need be. And even middle-class wives worried that a concubine might be waiting in the wings should they prove to be infertile, unable to bear a son, or otherwise displeasing to their husband or mother-in-law.

We might also compare this selection with the previous one. How does the blatant acceptance of concubinage in this selection compare to the emphasis on family stability in the Miu lineage rules? Are these documents from two different Chinas, or are they compatible? Does this selection force you to modify the contrast you drew between Ming China and modern America from the previous selection?

I was rather depressed that evening, so I got a boat and went with a friend on an excursion to Tiger Hill. My plan was to send a messenger to Xiangyang the next morning and then set out for home. As our boat passed under a bridge, I saw a small building by the bank. When I asked who lived there, my friend told me that this was [the singing girl] Dong's home. I was wildly happy with memories of three years before. I insisted on the boat's stopping, wanting to see Xiaowan at once. My friend, however, restrained me, saying, "Xiaowan has been terrified by the threat of being kidnapped by a powerful man and has been seriously ill for eighteen days. Since her mother's death,[2] she is said to have locked her door and refrained from receiving any guests." I nevertheless insisted on going ashore.

Not until I had knocked two or three times did the door open. I found no light in the house and had to grope my way upstairs. There I discovered medicine all over the table and bed.

---

[2] The "mother" here may well be the woman who managed her, rather than her natural mother.

Xiaowan, moaning, asked where I had come from and I told her I was the man she once saw beside a winding balustrade, intoxicated.

"Well, Sir," she said, recalling the incident, "I remember years ago you called at my house several times. Even though she only saw you once, my mother often spoke highly of you and considered it a great pity that I never had the chance to wait on you. Three years have passed. Mother died recently, but on seeing you now, I can hear her words in my ears. Where are you coming from this time?"

With an effort, she rose to draw aside the curtains and inspected me closely. She moved the lamp and asked me to sit on her bed. After talking awhile, I said I would go, not wanting to tire her. She, however, begged me to remain, saying, "During the past eighteen days I have had no appetite for food, nor have I been able to sleep well. My soul has been restless, dreaming almost all the time. But on seeing you, I feel as if my spirit has revived and my vigor returned." She then had her servant serve wine and food at her bedside, and kept refilling my cup herself.

Several times I expressed my desire to leave, but each time she urged me to stay. . . . The following morning, I was eager to set off on the trip home, but my friend and my servant both asked me not to be ungrateful for Xiaowan's kindness as she had had only a brief chance to talk with me the previous night. Accordingly I went to say goodbye to her. I found her, fresh from her toilet, leaning against a window upstairs quite composed. On seeing my boat approaching the bank, she hurried aboard to greet me. I told her that I had to leave immediately, but she said that she had packed up her belongings and would accompany me. I felt unable to refuse her.

We went from Hushuguan to Wuxi, and from there to Changzhou, Yixing, and Jiangyin, finally arriving at Jinjiang. All this took twenty-seven days, and twenty-seven times I asked her to go back, but she was firm in her desire to follow me. On climbing Golden Hill, she pointed to the river and swore, "My body is as constant as the direction of the Yangzi River. I am determined never to go back to Suzhou!"

On hearing her words, I turned red and reiterated my refusal, "The provincial examination is coming up soon. Because my father's recent posts have been dangerous ones, I have failed to attend to family affairs and have not been able to look after my mother on a daily basis. This is my first chance to go back and take care of things. Moreover, you have so many creditors in Suzhou and it will take a lot to redeem your singing-girl's contract in Nanjing. So please go back to Suzhou for the time being. After I have taken the examination at the end of summer, I will send word and meet you in Nanjing. At any rate, I must await the result of the examination before I even think about these matters. Insisting on it now will do neither of us any good."

She, however, still hesitated. There were dice on the table, and one of my friends said to her jokingly, "If you are ever going to get your wish [to become his concubine], they will land with the same side up." She then bowed toward the window, said a prayer, and tossed the dice. They all landed on six. All on board expressed their amazement, and I said to her, "Should Heaven really be on our side, I'm afraid we might bungle the whole thing if we proceed too hurriedly. You had better leave me temporarily, and we'll see what we can do by and by." Thus against her wishes she said goodbye, concealing her tearstained face with her hands.

I had pity for her plight but at the same time once I was on my own felt relieved of a heavy burden. Upon arrival at Taizhou, I sat for the examination. When I got home in the sixth month, my wife said to me, "Xiaowan sent her father to bring word that since her return to Suzhou, she has kept to a vegetarian diet and confined herself to her home, waiting on tiptoe for you to bring her to Nanjing as you promised. I felt awkward and gave her father ten taels[3] of silver, asking him to tell her that I am in sympathy with her and consent to her request, but she must wait till you finish the examination."

I appreciated the way my wife had handled Xiaowan's request. I then directly proceeded to Nanjing without keeping my promise to send someone to fetch her, planning to write to her after I had finished the examination. However, scarcely had I come out of the examination hall on the morning of the 15th of the eighth month when she suddenly called at my lodgings at Peach Leaf Ferry. It turned out that after waiting in vain for news from me, she had hired a boat, setting out from Suzhou and proceeding along the river with an old woman as her companion. She met with robbers on the way, and her boat had to hide among reeds and rushes. With the rudder broken, the boat could not proceed, and she had had practically nothing to eat for three days. She arrived at Sanshan Gate of Nanjing on the 8th, but not wanting to disturb my thoughts during the examination, she delayed entering the city for two days.

Though delighted to see me, she looked and sounded rather sad as she vividly described what had happened during the hundred days of our separation, including her confinement at home on vegetarian fare, her encounter with robbers on the river, and her other experiences of a voyage fraught with danger. Now she was more insistent than ever on getting her wish. The men in my literary society from Kashan, Sungjiang, Fujian, and Henan all admired her farsightedness and sincerity and encouraged her with their verses and paintings.

When the examination was over, I thought I might pass it, so hoped I would soon be able to settle my affairs and gratify her desire to become my concubine. Unexpectedly, on the 17th I was informed that my father had arrived by boat. . . . I had not seen him for two years and was overjoyed that he had returned alive from the battlefront. Without delaying

[3] A tael is equivalent to about 1¼ ounce. [Ed.]

to tell Xiaowan, I immediately went to meet him. . . . Before long she set out by boat in pursuit of me from the lodging house at Peach Leaf Ferry. A storm at Swallow's Ledge nearly cost her her life. At Shierhui she came on board and stayed with me again for seven days.

When the results of the examination were announced, I found my name on the list of the not quite successful candidates. I then traveled day and night to get home, while she followed weeping, unwilling to part. I was, however, well aware that I could not by myself settle her affairs in Suzhou and that her creditors would, on discovering her departure, increase their demands. Moreover, my father's recent return and my disappointment in the exams had made it all the more difficult to gratify her desire at once. On arrival at Puchao on the outskirts of my native city, I had to put on a cold face and turn ironhearted to part from her, telling her to go back to Suzhou to set her creditors at ease and thus pave the way for our future plans.

In the tenth month, while passing Jinjiang, I went to visit Mr. Zheng, the man who had been my examiner. At that time, Liu Daxing of Fujian had arrived from the capital. During a drinking party in his boat with General Chen, my friend Prefect Liu, and myself, my servant returned from seeing Xiaowan home. He reported that on arrival at Suzhou she did not change out of her autumn clothing, saying that she intended to die of cold if I did not see my way to settle her affairs promptly. On hearing this, Liu Daxing pointed to me and said, "Pijiang, you are well known as a man of honor. Could you really betray a girl like this?"

"Surely scholars are not capable of the gallant deeds of Huang Shanke and Gu Yaya," I replied.

The prefect raised his cup, and with a gesture of excitement exclaimed, "Well, if I were given a thousand taels of silver to pay my expenses, I'd start right away today!"

General Chen at once lent me several hundred taels, and Liu Daxing helped with a present of several catties[4] of ginseng. But how could it have been anticipated that the prefect, on arrival at Suzhou, failed to carry out his mission, and that when the creditors had kicked up a row and the matter had been brought to a deadlock, he fled to Wujiang? I had no chance to make further inquiries, as I returned home shortly afterwards.

Xiaowan was left in an awkward position, with little she could do. On hearing of her trouble, Qian Qianyi of Changshu went to Bantang himself and brought her to his boat. He approached her creditors, from the gentry to the townsmen, and within three days managed to clear every single debt of hers, the bills redeemed piling up a foot in height. This done, he arranged a farewell banquet on a pleasure boat and entertained her at the foot of Tiger Hill. He then hired a boat and sent someone to see her to Rugao.

---

[4] One catty is equivalent to 16 taels, 20 ounces, or a British pound. [Ed.]

On the evening of the 15th of the eleventh month when I was drinking wine with my father in our Zhuocun Hall, I was suddenly informed that Xiaowan had arrived at the jetty. After reading Qian's long interesting letter, I learned how she had gotten here. I also learned that Qian had written to a pupil of his, Zhang of the ministry of rites, asking him to redeem her singing girl's contract at once. Her minor problems at Suzhou were later settled by Mr. Zhou of the bureau of ceremonies while Mr. Li, formerly attached to that bureau, had also rendered her great assistance in Nanjing.

Ten months thereafter, her desire was gratified [and she became my concubine]. After the endless tangle of troubles and emotional pain, we had what we wanted.

3

ANTHONY REID

Women and Men in Southeast Asia

The author of this selection is a modern historian of Southeast Asia who argues that women's roles in Southeast Asia were quite different from their roles in other parts of the world, including other parts of Asia. How were the lives of the women he examines in this essay different from the lives of women you read about in the selections on China? What might account for the differences? What impact did the following phenomena have on the roles of women in Southeast Asia: Christianity, Confucianism, Buddhism, Islam, European colonization?

THINKING HISTORICALLY

Making comparisons always involves some apples and oranges. Reid does not address the same topics as the earlier readings on China. Further, his essay is a secondary source and the selections on China are primary sources. What kinds of primary sources on gender roles in Southeast Asia would contrast with the primary sources you read from China? How were the roles of temporary wives in Southeast Asia similar to, and different from, the roles of wives and concubines in China? In which society did women have greater authority or respect?

Source: Anthony Reid, "Female Roles in Pre-colonial Southeast Asia," *Modern Asian Studies,* 22, no. 3 (1988): 629–45.

Relations between the sexes are one of the areas in which a distinctive Southeast Asian pattern exists. Even the gradual strengthening of the influence of Islam, Christianity, Buddhism and Confucianism in their respective spheres over the last four centuries has by no means eliminated this common pattern of relatively high female autonomy and economic importance. In the sixteenth and seventeenth centuries the region probably represented one extreme of human experience on these issues. It could not be said that women were *equal* to men, since there were very few areas in which they competed directly. Women had different functions from men, but these included transplanting and harvesting rice, weaving, and marketing. Their reproductive role gave them magical and ritual powers which it was difficult for men to match. These factors may explain why the value of daughters was never questioned in Southeast Asia as it was in China, India, and the Middle East; on the contrary, "the more daughters a man has, the richer he is."[1]

Marriage

The dominant marriage pattern was one of monogamy, with divorce relatively easy for both sides. Chirino[2] said that he "was in the Philippines almost ten years without knowing of a man married to several women." Although there were spectacular exceptions to this rule among rulers, the overwhelming majority of ordinary people had one marriage partner at a time, but readily dissolved an unsatisfactory union through divorce. In the Philippines, "marriages last only so long as harmony prevails, for at the slightest cause in the world they divorce one another."[3] In Siam, similarly, "Husband and Wife may part again at pleasure, dealing their goods and children without further circumstance, and may re-marry if they think good, without fear of shame or punishment."[4] It was noted at a later date of both the Chams of southern Vietnam and the Javanese that women were particularly inclined to initiate divorce. "A woman may at any time, when dissatisfied with her husband, demand a dissolution of the marriage contract, by paying him a sum established by custom."[5] Throughout the island world the rule appeared to be that the wife (or her parents) kept the bridewealth if the husband took the

---

[1] An old adage reported by two sixteenth-century European travelers: Antonio Galvão, *A Treatise on the Moluccas* (1544); and Miguel López de Legazpi's report on the Philippines (1569). [Ed.]

[2] Pedro Chirino, Spanish Jesuit missionary in the Philippines, *Relación de las Islas Filipinas* (1604).

[3] Chirino (1604) and Antonio de Morga, *Sucesos de las islas Filipinas* (1609).

[4] Joost Schouten, "A description . . . of the kingdom of Siam" (1636).

[5] Stamford Raffles, *History of Java* (1817).

initiative to end the marriage, but had to repay it if she was primarily responsible. At least in the Philippines and Siam the children of a marriage were divided at divorce, the first going to the mother, the second to the father, and so on. . . .

Christian Europe was until the eighteenth century a very "chaste" society in comparative terms, with exceptionally late age of marriage (in the twenties), high proportions never marrying and by later standards a low rate of extra-martial conceptions (the rate in England rose from only 12% in 1680 to 50% by 1800). Southeast Asia was in many respects the complete antithesis of that "chaste" pattern, and thus it seemed to European observers of the time that its inhabitants were preoccupied with sex. The Portuguese liked to say that the Malays were "fond of music and given to love," while Javanese, like Burmese, Thais and Filipinos, were characterized as "very lasciviously given, both men and women." What this meant was that pre-marital sexual relations were regarded indulgently, and virginity at marriage was not expected of either party. If pregnancy resulted from these pre-marital activities the couple were expected to marry, making illegitimacy uncommon. . . .

Sexual Partners for Itinerant Traders

The pattern of pre-marital sexual activity and easy divorce, together with the commercial element potentially involved in the paying of bridewealth, ensured that temporary marriage or concubinage rather than prostitution became the dominant means of coping with the vast annual influx of foreign traders of the major ports. As the system was described in Patani,

> when foreigners come there from other lands to do their business . . .
> men come and ask them whether they do not desire a woman; these
> young women and girls themselves also come and present them-
> selves, from whom they may choose the one most agreeable to
> them, provided they agree what he shall pay for certain months.
> Once they agree about the money (which does not amount to much
> for so great a convenience), she comes to his house, and serves him
> by day as his maidservant and by night as his wedded wife. He is
> then not able to consort with other women or he will be in grave
> trouble with his wife, while she is similarly wholly forbidden to
> converse with other men, but the marriage lasts as long as he keeps
> his residence there, in good peace and unity. When he wants to
> depart he gives her whatever is promised, and so they leave each
> other in friendship, and she may then look for another man as she
> wishes, in all propriety, without scandal.[6]

[6] Jacob Van Neck, *Journal* (1604).

Exactly the same pattern is described for Javanese traders in Banda for the nutmeg season, for Europeans and others in Vietnam, Cambodia, Siam and Burma. Hamilton described in loving detail how the system worked in Pegu, where an elaborate marriage ritual was held for these temporary relationships, to which both parties were bound by legal obligation. Like Chou Ta Kuan in Cambodia, he appreciated the double advantage of such local wives as not only bedmates but commercial partners—"if their Husbands have any goods to sell, they set up a shop and sell them by retail, to a much better account than they could be sold for by wholesale."[7]

The boundary between such temporary marriages and durable ones cannot have been clear, and interracial unions were a feature of all the commercial cities of Southeast Asia. Europeans found it strange and reprehensible that religion was also no bar to marriage: in Melaka "heathens marry with Moorish women and a Moor with a heathen woman"[8]; in Makassar "Christian Men kept Mahometan women, and Mahometan Men, Christian women."[9] Only when women close to the court sought to marry foreigners did it provoke strong opposition. . . .

In some of the Muslim ports of the Archipelago it may have become the practice to restrict such explicitly temporary marriages to slave women, who differed from the free in that they could be sold by one "husband" to another and had few rights over children. In Banten the practice of Chinese traders was described as "to buy women slaves . . . by whom they have manie children. And when they returne to their owne countrey . . . they sell their women, but their children they carrie with them."[10] The English in places may have had a similar practice if we can believe their great enemy Coen, who rejoiced that the English factors in Sukadana (West Borneo) were so empoverished that "they had to sell their whores" to pay for their victuals. . . .

Women in Trade

Since we have mentioned marketing as primarily a female domain, this is the place to start discussing the economic roles of women. Even today Southeast Asian countries top the comparative statistics assembled

---

[7] A. Hamilton, *A New Account of the East Indies* (1727), p. 28.

[8] T. Pires, *The Summa Oriental of Tome Pires* (1515), p. 268.

[9] D. F. Navarrete, *Tratados históricos, políticos, éticos y religiosos de la monarquia de China* (Madrid, 1676), pp. 122–23.

[10] E. Scott, *An exact discourse of the Subtleties . . . of the East Indians . . .* (1606) in *The Voyage of Henry Middleton to the Moluccas* (Hakluyt Society, 1943), p. 176.

by Ester Boserup for female participation in trade and marketing. Fifty-six per cent of those so listed in Thailand were women, 51% in the Philippines, 47% in Burma, and 46% in Cambodia. Although Indonesia had a lower rate at 31%, this still contrasted sharply with other Muslim countries, particularly in the Middle East (1%–5%). A famous Minangkabau poem first written down in the 1820s exhorts mothers to teach their daughters "to judge the rise and fall of prices." Even today Southeast Asian women are expected to show more commercially shrewd and thrifty attitudes than men, and Chinese and European traders are apt to be derided for having the mean spirit of a woman on such matters.

While the casual visitor to Southeast Asia today might not be aware of the female trading role now restricted to rural and small-scale markets, this was not always the case. Early European and Chinese traders were constantly surprised to find themselves dealing with women:

> In Cambodia it is the women who take charge of trade.[11]
>
> It is their [Siamese] custom that all affairs are managed by their wives . . . all trading transactions great and small.[12]
>
> The women of Siam are the only merchants in buying goods, and some of them trade very considerably.[13]
>
> Money-changing is a great profession here [Tongking]. It is managed by women, who are very dextrous and ripe in this employment.[14]
>
> In Cochin-China[15] every man is a soldier. The commercial operations are performed by women.[16]
>
> Women in the Birman country . . . manage the more important mercantile concerns of their husbands.[17]
>
> It is the women [of the Moluccas] who negotiate, do business, buy and sell.[18]
>
> Melaka has so much [tax revenue] per month from the women street sellers . . . because in Melaka they sell in every street.[19]
>
> [In Melaka] women hold a market at night.[20] . . .

---

[11] Chou Ta Kuan, *Memoire on the Customs of Cambodia* (1297).

[12] Ma Huan, *The Overall Survey of the Ocean's Shores* (1433).

[13] A. Hamilton, *A New Account of the East Indies* (1727).

[14] W. Dampier, *Voyages and Discoveries* (1699).

[15] The southern third of modern Vietnam. [Ed.]

[16] J. White, *A Voyage to Cochin-China* (1824).

[17] M. Symes, *An Account of an Embassy to the Kingdom of Ava in the Year 1795* (1827).

[18] Galvão, *A Treatise on the Moluccas* (1544).

[19] T. Pires, *The Summa Oriental of Tome Pires* (1515).

[20] Hwang Chung, "Words about the Sea" (1537).

Diplomacy

From trade it is not a major step to diplomacy, especially perhaps for those who had been both commercial and sexual partners of foreign traders. Such women frequently became fluent in the languages needed in commerce. Thus the first Dutch mission to Cochin-China found the King dealt with them through a Vietnamese woman who spoke excellent Portuguese and Malay and had long resided in Macao. She, along with another elderly woman who had had two Portuguese husbands as well as one Vietnamese, had been the principal translator for the Cochin-China court for 30 years. Similarly the elderly Burmese wife of the shahbandar[21] of Rangoon who had earlier been married to the French commander of the Burmese royal guard, was an indispensable intermediary between foreigners and that royal court in the eighteenth century. Later the Sultan of Deli, in Sumatra, ordered "a most extraordinary and eccentric old woman" named Che Laut to accompany John Anderson on his embassy to various Sumatran states. She was "a prodigy of learning," spoke Chinese, Thai, Chuliah, Bengali and Acehnese and knew the politics of all the Sumatran coastal states intimately.[22]

In some parts of the island world there appears to have been a positive preference for using women as envoys, particularly in the peacemaking process. . . . After describing the embassy of an old woman named Nyai Pombaya from the ruler of Demak to Banten while he was in the latter port in 1540, [Mendes] Pinto explained that the rulers of Java had always been accustomed

> to treat of the most important matters of their state by mediation of women, especially when it concerns peace . . . and all the reason they give for it is, "that God has given more gentleness and inclination to courtesie, yea and more authority to women than men, who are severe, as they say, and by consequent less agreeable to those unto whom they are sent."[23] . . .

Warriors

This peace-making role is difficult to reconcile with a tradition of female warriors. Since warfare is normally an exclusively male business, every culture is probably inclined to romanticize and celebrate those

[21] Ruler. [Ed.]
[22] J. Anderson, *Mission to the East Coast of Sumatra in 1823* (London: 1826, reprinted Kuala Lampur: 1971), pp. 44–45.
[23] M. Pinto, *The Voyages and Adventures of Ferdinand Mendez Pinto* (1614).

exceptional women who emerge to save a desperate situation. Vietnam has no heroes more renowned than the Trung sisters who rose up against the Chinese in A.D. 43. Thais remember two sisters who led the successful defence of Phuket in 1785, Queen Suriyothai who was killed defending Ayutthaya in 1564, and Lady Mo who rescued Khorat in 1826 after leading several hundred captive women to escape. Women were also said to have played a spirited part in the defence of Madura against Sultan Agung of Mataram in 1624. If such militant heroines played a larger role in Southeast Asia than elsewhere it is probably because status was more prominent than gender, and women were not excluded from taking the lead if the occasion required it.

More specific to the region was the habit of powerful rulers to surround themselves with large numbers of women, of whom some had the role of bodyguards. The King of Angkor was said to have had four to five thousand women in his palace, Iskandar Muda of Aceh three thousand and Sultan Agung of Mataram ten thousand. At least in the two latter cases these palace women included a corps trained in the use of arms, who mounted guard on the palace and took part in royal processions. A women's corps drilling regularly with rifles was still maintained in late eighteenth-century Java by the first Mangkunegaran ruler. Even as late as the 1880s the Siamese palace guard was supervised by the King's aunt, who determined access to the royal enclosure.

This pattern appears to have stemmed from the distrust which autocratic rulers felt towards any men close to them. As suggested above, in the island world at least men were expected to respond immediately, with the arms they always carried, to any slight to their honour. Indonesian history has many tragic examples of where this could lead. An unusually autocratic Aceh ruler, Sultan al Mukammil (1584–1604) evidently even had a woman as commander of his navy, "for he will trust no other." There appears to be no evidence that the confidence the rulers placed in these women was ever betrayed by a murder, as happened frequently at the hand of males. Nor is it established that the female corps took part in major battles. Their existence therefore tends to confirm the assumption that violence, the use of arms, and the defence of a touchy sense of honour were fundamentally men's business, and that women could be trusted not to use the arms they carried. Nevertheless such corps probably gave rise to exaggerated traveller's tales of amazon warriors in Southeast Asia.

Literature and the Arts

. . . Since most pre-modern Southeast Asian writers are anonymous, we cannot know what the share of women was either in composing verses for recitation or in writing them down. In the eighteenth century there were outstanding women poets in Hanoi (Ho Xuan Huong) and Surakarta, while the Malay woman who tutored John Anderson about Sumatran politics in the 1820s, Che Laut, was also a poet and historian. The best-known Thai epic romance of the Ayutthaya period, the *Lilit Phra Lo*, describes from a female viewpoint (whether or not that of a female author) how two court ladies lure the male hero into the palace for their amusement.

The association of learning with the formal religious systems probably increased literacy for men but reduced it for women. Already in the seventeenth century Thai boys in Ayutthaya went to the monasteries at about their sixth year to acquire a basic literacy, whereas girls "very seldom learn to write and read."[24] Islam provided less universally for boys, but had a similar effect on girls. There was, however, an older literate tradition for both sexes, which survived longer in some places than others. According to Zollinger,[25] for example, most Balinese women could still read in the nineteenth century. In sixteenth-century Luzon the Spanish friars claimed there was "scarcely a man, still less a woman, who cannot read and write" in the old Filipino script.[26] One source explained that Philippine women wrote not books and histories but "missives and notes to one another"[27] which provides a clue to the reason for this high literacy. The South Sumatran province of Lampung had the highest literacy for both sexes in Indonesia early this century. The 1930 Census recorded 45% of adult men and 34% of adult women could read, most of them in an ancient local script related to the Philippine one. The reason for this survival was that an essential part of Lampung courtship was the exchanging of poetic notes in the old script. Whatever the explanation, the existence of a more widespread female literacy in the sixteenth and seventeenth centuries makes it necessary to leave open the gender of the anonymous authors of many of the early classics.

---

[24] J. Van Vliet, *Description of the Kingdom of Siam* (1636).

[25] Heinrich Zollinger, Dutch naturalist, "The Island of Lombok" (1851).

[26] P. Chirino, *Relación de las Islas Filipinas, The Philippines in 1600* (1604), trans. Ramon Echevarria (Manila: Historical Conservation Society, 1969), p. 280.

[27] G. P. Dasmarinas, 1590, 'The manners, customs, and beliefs of the Philippine inhabitants of long ago, being chapters of "A Late Sixteenth Century Manuscript,"' trans. Carlos Quirino and Mauro Garcia, *The Philippine Journal of Science* 87, iv (1958), p. 424.

4

JOHN E. WILLS JR.
Sor Juana Inés de la Cruz

After the conquest of the Aztecs, the Spanish attempted to govern Mexico by converting the surviving Indians to Roman Catholicism and exploiting their labor. In addition, they encouraged fellow Spaniards to settle in the colony and imported African slaves, creating a mixed society of Europeans, Indians, and Africans. As in the rest of North America, the dividing line between slave and free was the most important social distinction. But unlike their English counterparts to the north, New Spain's colonists also distinguished between *Peninsulares*, colonists who were born in Spain, and Creoles, colonists who were born of Spanish parents in the Americas.[1]

In the following selection a modern historian evokes the life of Sor Juana Inés de la Cruz* (1651–1695), a poet, artist, and nun who lived in Mexico City in "New Spain." Sister Juana was a Creole woman, and the author argues she was distinctly a product of Mexican Creole society. In what ways was she Spanish? In what ways was she Mexican? How do you think the life of a Creole woman, born and raised in the colony, would be different from that of a woman born in Spain?

THINKING HISTORICALLY

The previous selection reminds us that some societies, like those in Southeast Asia, were less patriarchal than others. The arrival of Europeans sometimes enhanced the wealth and influence of women traders in Southeast Asia. The widows and daughters of mixed marriages often benefited from both worlds.

The daughters of Spanish settlers in the Americas had fewer opportunities for financial advancement than did the daughters of Dutch settlers in Java, and the Spanish patriarchy was as unyielding as any in Europe. Nevertheless, the culture that the Old World imported into the New provided alternatives for women that were absent in the East Indies. What alternatives for women does this selection reveal? Were they a product of Europe, America, or the intermixture of the two?

* sohr hoo AH nah   ee NEZ   day lah CROOZ

[1] This was the original meaning. Later *Creole* came to mean someone of mixed European and American ancestry.

Source: John E. Wills Jr., "Sor Juana Inés de la Cruz," in *1688: A Global History* (New York: W. W. Norton, 2001), 13–19.

On April 28, 1688, a long procession moved out of Mexico City, along the causeways that crossed the nearby lakes, and through the small towns and farms of the plateau, on its way toward the pass between the two volcanoes Iztaccihuatl* and Popocatépetl,† both more than sixteen thousand feet high, and down to the tropical port of Vera Cruz. The farmers in their villages and fields were used to a good deal of such coming and going, but this time they stopped their work to look and to call out to each other in Nahuatl,‡ the main indigenous language, for this was no ordinary procession. Cavalry outriders and a huge coach were followed by many baggage wagons and a long line of fine coaches. The marquis of Laguna had served as viceroy of New Spain from 1680 to 1686. With their wealth, powerful connections in Madrid, and a taste for elegance and the arts, he and his wife had given the viceregal court a few years of splendor and sophistication comparable, if not to Madrid, certainly to many of the lesser courts of Europe. Now their wealthy Spanish friends were riding in their coaches as far as the Villa de Guadalupe, seeing the marquis and marchioness off on their voyage home to Spain.

> A child born of a slave shall be received,
> according to our Law, as property
> of the owner to whom fealty
> is rendered by the mother who conceived.
>   The harvest from a grateful land retrieved,
> the finest fruit, offered obediently,
> is for the lord, for its fecundity
> is owing to the care it has received.
>   So too, Lysis divine, these my poor lines:
> as children of my soul, born of my heart,
> they must in justice be to you returned;
>   Let not their defects cause them to be spurned,
> for of your rightful due they are a part,
> as concepts of a soul to yours consigned.

These lines were written sometime later in 1688 and sent off from Mexico to the marchioness of Laguna in Spain. They make use of metaphors and classical conceits to express and conceal the feelings of the author, who had lost, with the marchioness's departure, the object of the nearest thing she had ever known to true love and, with the marquis's departure, her ultimate protection from those who found her opinions and her way of life scandalous. The trouble was not that the author was

---

* is tak SEE wat el
† poh poh kah TEH peh til
‡ NA wat ul

lesbian—although her feelings toward men and women were unusually complicated and unconventional, anything approaching a physical relation or even passion is most unlikely—but that she was a cloistered Hieronymite[2] nun, who read and studied a wide range of secular books, held long intellectual conversations with many friends, wrote constantly in a variety of religious and secular styles, and betrayed in her writings sympathy for Hermetic[3] and Neoplatonic[4] views that were on the edge of heresy if not beyond it. Her name in religion was Sor Juana Inés de la Cruz. She is recognized today as one of the great poets in the history of the Spanish language.

Mexico in the 1680s was a society of dramatic contradictions. The elegant viceregal court and the opulent ecclesiastical hierarchy looked toward Europe for style and ideas. The vast majority of the population sought to preserve as much as possible of the language, beliefs, and ways of life that had guided them before the coming of the Spaniards; the worship of the Virgin of Guadalupe, for example, owed much to the shrine of an Aztec goddess that had been the setting of the original appearance of the Virgin to a Mexican peasant. In between the "peninsular" elite and the "Indians," the native-born "creoles" of Spanish language and culture managed huge cattle ranches and sought constantly new veins of profitable silver ore and new techniques to exploit old ones. Neither "Spanish" nor "Indian," they experienced the full force of the contradictions of Mexican society and culture.

The literary world in which Sor Juana was such an anomalous eminence thrived on these contradictions of society and culture. This was a baroque culture. The word *baroque*, originating as a Portuguese term for the peculiar beauty of a deformed, uneven pearl, suggests a range of artistic styles in which the balance and harmony of the Renaissance styles are abandoned for imbalance, free elaboration of form, playful gesture, and surprising allusion, through which the most intense of emotions and the darkest of realities may be glimpsed, their power enhanced by the glittering surface that partially conceals them. Contradiction and its partial, playful reconciliation are the stuff of the baroque style. So is the layering of illusion on illusion, meaning upon meaning. And what more baroque conceit could be imagined than the literary eminence of a cloistered nun in a rough frontier society, with a church and state of the strongest and narrowest male supremacist prejudices? Look again at the poem quoted earlier: The chaste nun refers to her poem as her child or the harvest from a grateful land. She declares her love once again to the departed marchioness.

---

[2] An order of nuns particularly numerous in the Iberian Peninsula that followed the hermit life of St. Jerome. [Ed.]

[3] Occult; mystical. [Ed.]

[4] Following Plato; similar to occult and mystical. [Ed.]

Sor Juana was a product of Mexican creole society, born on a ranch on the shoulder of the great volcano Popocatépetl. Her mother was illiterate and very probably had not been married to her father. But some of the family branches lived in the city, with good books and advantageous connections. As soon as she discovered the books in her grandfather's library, she was consumed with a thirst for solitude and reading. Her extraordinary talents for literature and learning were recognized. When she was fifteen, in 1664, she was taken into the household of a newly arrived viceroy, as his wife's favorite and constant companion. She must have enjoyed the attention, the luxury, the admiration of her cleverness. She no doubt participated in the highly stylized exchange of "gallantries" between young men and young women. But she had no dowry. Solitude was her natural habitat. As a wife and mother, what chance would she have to read, to write, to be alone? In 1668 she took her vows in the Hieronymite convent of an order named after Saint Jerome, cloistered and meditative by rule.

This was a big decision, but less drastic than one might think. Certainly she was a believing Catholic. Her new status did not require total devotion to prayer and extinction of self. It did not imply that she was abandoning all the friendships and secular learning that meant so much to her. The nuns had a daily round of collective devotions; but many rules were not fully honored, and the regimen left her much free time for reading and writing. Each of the nuns had comfortable private quarters, with a kitchen, room for a bathtub, and sleeping space for a servant and a dependent or two; Sor Juana usually had one slave and one or two nieces or other junior dependents living in her quarters. The nuns visited back and forth in their quarters to the point that Sor Juana complained of the interruptions to her reading and writing, but outsiders spoke to the nuns only in the locutory especially provided for that purpose. From the beginning she turned the locutory into an elegant salon, as the viceroy and his lady and other fashionable people came to visit her and they passed hours in learned debate, literary improvisation, and gossip.

One of Sor Juana's most constant friends and supporters was Carlos de Sigüenza y Góngora, professor of mathematics at the University of Mexico, an eminently learned creole scholar whose position was almost as anomalous as hers. He had been educated by the Jesuits and had longed to be one of them but had been expelled from their college. He had managed to obtain his position, without a university degree, by demonstrating his superior knowledge of his subject. He had added Góngora to his name to emphasize his distant kinship, through his mother's family, with the most famous of Spain's baroque poets. But he always felt insecure among the European-born professors, churchmen, and high officials. He wrote a great deal, much of it about the history of Mexico. He was in no way Sor Juana's equal as a writer, but he probably was responsible for most of her smattering of knowledge of modern science and recent philosophy.

There was a rule of poverty among the Hieronymites, but it was generally ignored. Sor Juana received many gifts, some of them substantial enough to enable the former dowerless girl to invest money at interest. By gift and purchase she built up a library of about four thousand volumes and a small collection of scientific instruments, probably provided by Sigüenza. Her reading was broad but not very systematic, contributing to the stock of ideas and allusions she drew on constantly in her writings but giving her little sense of the intellectual tensions and transformations that were building up in Europe. She wrote constantly, in a wide variety of complex and exacting forms. Voluntarily or upon commission or request, she wrote occasional poems of all kinds for her friends and patrons. A celebration might call for a *loa*, a brief theatrical piece in praise of a dignitary. In one of hers, for example, a character "clad in sunrays" declares:

> I am a reflection
> of that blazing sun
> who, among shining rays
> numbers brilliant sons:
> when his illustrious rays
> strike a speculum,
> on it is portrayed
> the likeness of his form.

Sor Juana's standing in society reached a new height with the arrival in 1680 of the marquis and marchioness of Laguna. Even in the public festivities celebrating their arrival, she outdid herself in baroque elaborations of texts and conceits for a temporary triumphal arch erected at the cathedral. It was an allegory on Neptune, in which the deeds of the Greek god were compared to the real or imaginary deeds of the marquis. Much was made of the echoes among the marquis's title of Laguna, meaning *lake*, Neptune's reign over the oceans, and the origins of Mexico City as the Aztec city of Tenochtitlán* in the middle of its great lake: an elaborate union of sycophancy to a ruler, somewhat strained classical allusion, and a creole quest for a Mexican identity. In parts of the text the author even drew in Isis as an ancestor of Neptune, and in others of her works from this time she showed a great interest in Egyptian antiquity as it was then understood, including the belief that the god Hermes Trismegistus had revealed the most ancient and purest wisdom and anticipated the Mosaic and Christian revelations. These ideas, the accompanying quasi-Platonic separation

---

* teh NOCH teet LAHN

of soul and body, and her use of them to imply that a female or androgynous condition was closer to the divine wisdom than the male took her to the edge of heresy or beyond and was turned against her in later years.

Sor Juana soon established a close friendship with the marchioness of Laguna. Some of the poems she sent her are among her very finest, and they are unmistakably love poems. Some of them accompanied a portrait of the author. Several portraits in which a very handsome woman gazes boldly at us, her black-and-white habit simply setting off her own strength and elegance, have come down to us. [See Figure 18.1.]

> And if it is that you should rue
> the absence of a soul in me [the portrait],
> you can confer one, easily,
> from the many rendered you:
> and as my soul I [Sor Juana] tendered you,
> and though my being yours obeyed,
> and though you look on me amazed
> in this insentient apathy,
> you are the soul of this body,
> and are the body of this shade.

The marquis of Laguna stepped down as viceroy in 1686 but remained in Mexico until 1688. In that year Sor Juana was very busy. The marchioness was taking texts of her poems back to Spain, where they soon would be published. She added to them a play, *The Divine Narcissus*, interweaving the legend of Narcissus and the life of Jesus, which probably was performed in Madrid in 1689 or 1690. Her niece took her vows in the convent in 1688. Late in the year, after her noble friends had left, she wrote the poem quoted earlier as well as a romantic comedy, *Love Is the Greater Labyrinth*, which was performed in Mexico City early in 1689.

A large collection of her poetry was published in Madrid in 1689. The next year in Mexico she published a letter taking abstruse issue with a sermon preached decades before by the famous Portuguese Jesuit Antonio Vieira. Her casual way with the rules of the religious life, her flirtings with heresy, her many writings in secular forms with intimations of understanding of love inappropriate to her profession had made her many enemies, but they could do nothing while the marquis of Laguna and his lady were on hand to protect her. Now they closed in. In 1694 she was forced formally to renounce all writing and humane studies and to relinquish her library and collection of scientific instruments. In 1695 she devotedly cared for her sisters in the convent during an epidemic, caught the disease, and died.

Figure 18.1 Portrait of Sor Juana Inés de la Cruz, 1750.

This portrait of Sor Juana was done by one of Mexico's most famous painters, Miguel Cabrera (1695–1768), the official painter of the Archbishop of Mexico. The nun sits surrounded by the emblems of her literary life, including quill pens, inkwell, and an open volume from her enormous library. In the original portrait, the viewer can discern a host of classical authors lining the shelves, including Hippocrates, Virgil, and Cicero.

Source: Schalkwijk/Art Resource, N.Y.

5

ANNA BIJNS

"Unyoked Is Best! Happy the Woman without a Man"

Anna Bijns* (1494–1575) was a Flemish nun and poet who lived in Antwerp, taught in a Catholic school in that city, wrote biting criticism of Martin Luther and the Protestant Reformation, and in her many works helped shape the Dutch language. The impact of Luther, and Protestantism more generally, on the lives of women has been the subject of much debate. Luther opposed nunneries and monasticism, believing that it was the natural duty of all women to marry and bear children. At the same time, he encouraged a level of reciprocal love and respect in marriage that was less emphasized in Catholicism. The Protestant translations of the Bible from Latin also opened a pathway for individuals, including educated women, to participate in the religious life, though not as nuns. Whether or not the sentiments of this poem are more Catholic than Protestant, are they more European than Chinese? Why or why not?

THINKING HISTORICALLY

No one should imagine that the ideas conveyed in this poem were typical or representative of European thought in the sixteenth century. This was obviously an extreme view that ran counter to traditional and commonly accepted ideas. Note how some phrases of the poem convey the recognition that most people will disagree with the sentiments being expressed.

   When we are comparing documents from different cultures, we must always try to understand how representative they are of the views of the larger population. The Miu family document (selection 1) expresses the views of a single family, but lineage regulations were common in sixteenth-century China, and their ubiquity reflected an even greater consensus on the importance of the family. Anna Bijns's poem is a personal view that expresses a minority opinion. But in what sense is this a European, rather than Chinese, minority view? What sort of extreme minority views might Southeast Asian or

* bynz

Source: Anna Bijns, "Unyoked Is Best," trans. Kristiaan P. G. Aercke, in *Women and Writers of the Renaissance and Reformation*, ed. Katharina M. Wilson (Athens: The University of Georgia Press, 1987), 382–83.

European-American cultures produce? Do you think Anna Bijns's
view might appeal to more people today than it did in the sixteenth
century? If so, why?

How good to be a woman, how much better to be a man!
Maidens and wenches, remember the lesson you're about to hear.
Don't hurtle yourself into marriage far too soon.
The saying goes: "Where's your spouse? Where's your honor?"
But one who earns her board and clothes
Shouldn't scurry to suffer a man's rod.
So much for my advice, because I suspect—
Nay, see it sadly proven day by day—
'T happens all the time!
However rich in goods a girl might be,
Her marriage ring will shackle her for life.
If however she stays single
With purity and spotlessness foremost,
Then she is lord as well as lady, Fantastic, not?
Though wedlock I do not decry:
Unyoked is best! Happy the woman without a man.

Fine girls turning into loathly hags—
'Tis true! Poor sluts! Poor tramps! Cruel marriage!
Which makes me deaf to wedding bells.
Huh! First they marry the guy, luckless dears,
Thinking their love just too hot to cool.
Well, they're sorry and sad within a single year.
Wedlock's burden is far too heavy.
They know best whom it harnessed.
So often is a wife distressed, afraid.
When after troubles hither and thither he goes
In search of dice and liquor, night and day,
She'll curse herself for that initial "yes."
So, beware ere you begin.
Just listen, don't get yourself into it.
Unyoked is best! Happy the woman without a man.

A man oft comes home all drunk and pissed
Just when his wife had worked her fingers to the bone
(So many chores to keep a decent house!),
But if she wants to get in a word or two,
She gets to taste his fist—no more.
And that besotted keg she is supposed to obey?
Why, yelling and scolding is all she gets,
Such are his ways—and hapless his victim.

And if the nymphs of Venus he chooses to frequent,
What hearty welcome will await him home.
Maidens, young ladies: learn from another's doom,
Ere you, too, end up in fetters and chains,
Please don't argue with me on this,
No matter who contradicts, I stick to it:
Unyoked is best! Happy the woman without a man.

A single lady has a single income,
But likewise, isn't bothered by another's whims.
And I think: that freedom is worth a lot.
Who'll scoff at her, regardless what she does,
And though every penny she makes herself,
Just think of how much less she spends!
An independent lady is an extraordinary prize —
All right, of a man's boon she is deprived,
But she's lord and lady of her very own hearth.
To do one's business and no explaining sure is lots of fun!
Go to bed when she list,[1] rise when she list, all as she will,
And no one to comment! Grab tight your independence then.
Freedom is such a blessed thing.
To all girls: though the right Guy might come along:
Unyoked is best! Happy the woman without a man.

Regardless of the fortune a woman might bring,
Many men consider her a slave, that's all.
Don't let a honeyed tongue catch you off guard,
Refrain from gulping it all down. Let them rave,
For, I guess, decent men resemble white ravens.
Abandon the airy castles they will build for you.
Once their tongue has limed[2] a bird:
Bye bye love — and love just flies away.
To women marriage comes to mean betrayal
And the condemnation to a very awful fate.
All her own is spent, her lord impossible to bear.
It's *peine forte et dure*[3] instead of fun and games.
Oft it was the money, and not the man
Which goaded so many into their fate.
Unyoked is best! Happy the woman without a man.

---

[1] Wants. [Ed.]

[2] Caught. [Ed.]

[3] Long and forceful punishment; a form of torture whereby the victim was slowly crushed by heaping rocks on a board laid over his or her body. [Ed.]

MARY JO MAYNES AND ANN WALTNER

Women and Marriage in Europe and China

This article is the product of a rich collaboration between historians of China and Europe who show us how a study of women and marriage is anything but peripheral to a study of these areas. What is their thesis about European and Chinese marriage patterns? What do marriage patterns tell us about a society? How do the other readings in this chapter support or challenge their thesis?

THINKING HISTORICALLY

The authors begin by comparing the role of religion, the state, and the family in setting marriage patterns in both China and Europe. Did Christianity allow European women more independence than Confucianism allowed women in China? In which society was the patriarchal family more powerful, and what was the relative impact of patriarchy on women in both societies? How did the age and rate at which people married in each society compare? What was the importance of Chinese concubinage and Christian ideals of chastity?

The authors' questions about marriage in Europe and China lead finally to a consideration of one of the most frequently asked comparative questions: Why did Europe industrialize before China? Do the different European and Chinese marriage patterns answer this question? What other comparative questions would we have to ask to arrive at a full answer?

Comparing Marriage Cross-Culturally

... Beginning in the late 1500s, women in northern Italy began to appeal to legal courts run by the Catholic Church when they got into disputes with their families over arranged marriages. Within the early modern Italy family system the father held a great deal of authority over his children and it was usual for the parents to determine when and whom sons and daughters married. Women and children held little power in comparison with adult men. But the Catholic Church's insistence that both parties enter into the marriage willingly gave some women an

Source: Mary Jo Maynes and Ann Waltner, "Childhood, Youth, and the Female Life Cycle: Women's Life-Cycle Transitions in a World-Historical Perspective: Comparing Marriage in China and Europe," *Journal of Women's History* 12, no. 4 (Winter 2001): 11–19.

out—namely, an appeal to the Church court, claiming that the marriage their family wanted was being forced upon them without their consent. Surprisingly, these young women often won their cases against their fathers. In early modern China, by way of contrast, state, religion, and family were bound together under the veil of Confucianism. Paternal authority echoed and reinforced the political and the moral order. Religious institutions could rarely be called upon to intervene in family disputes. Therefore, young women (or young men, for that matter) had no clearly established institutional recourse in situations of unwanted marriage. So, despite the fact that paternal power was very strong in both early modern Italy and early modern China, specific institutional differences put young women at the moment of marriage in somewhat different positions.

We began with the presumption that however different the institution of "marriage" was in Italy and China, it nevertheless offered enough similarities that it made sense to speak comparatively about a category called "marriage." Parallels in the two cultures between the institution of marriage and the moment in the woman's life course that it represented make comparison useful. Nevertheless, this particular comparison also isolates some of the variable features of marriage systems that are especially significant in addressing gender relations in a world-historical context. In China, the rules of family formation and family governance were generally enforced within the bounds of each extended family group. State and religious influences were felt only indirectly through family leaders as mediators or enforcers of state and religious law. Throughout Europe, beginning in the Middle Ages, the institution of marriage was altered first by the effort of the Catholic Church to wrest some control over marriage from the family by defining it as a sacrament, and then eventually by the struggle between churches and state authorities to regulate families.

This contest among church, state, and family authorities over marriage decisions turns out to have been a particular feature of European history that had consequences for many aspects of social life. A focus on the moment of marriage presents special opportunities for understanding connections between the operation of gender relations in everyday life and in the realm of broader political developments. Marriage is a familial institution, of course, but, to varying degrees, political authorities also have a stake in it because of its implications for property transfer, reproduction, religion, and morality—in short, significant aspects of the social order. In this essay, we compare one dimension of marriage—its timing in a woman's life cycle—in two contexts, Europe and China. We argue that variations in marriage timing have world-historical implications. We examine how a woman's status and situation shifted at marriage and then suggest some implications of comparative differences in the timing and circumstances of this change of status.

The Moment of Marriage in European History

One striking peculiarity of Central and Western European history between 1600 and 1850 was the relatively late age at first marriage for men and women compared with other regions of the world. The so-called "Western European marriage pattern" was marked by relatively late marriage—that is, relative to other regions of the world where some form of marriage usually occurred around the time of puberty. In much of Europe, in contrast, men did not typically marry until their late twenties and women their mid-twenties. This practice of relatively late marriage was closely connected with the custom of delaying marriage until the couple commanded sufficient resources to raise a family. For artisans this traditionally meant having a shop and master status. For merchants it entailed saving capital to begin a business. In the case of peasant couples, this meant having a house and land and basic farming equipment. It was the responsibility of the family and the community to oversee courtship, betrothal, and marriage to assure that these conditions were met. This phenomenon was also rooted in the common practice of neo-locality—the expectation that a bride and groom would set up their own household at or soon after marriage. This "delayed" marriage has attracted the attention of European historical demographers. The delay of marriage meant, quite significantly, that most European women did not begin to have children until their twenties. But this marriage pattern also has significance in other realms as well. In particular, young people of both sexes experienced a relatively long hiatus between puberty and marriage.

Unmarried European youth played a distinctive role in economic, social, cultural, and political life through such institutions as guilds, village youth groups, and universities. For the most part, historians' attention to European youth has centered on young men. Major works on the history of youth in Europe, like theories of adolescent development, tend to center on the male experience as normative. Only when gender differences in youth are recognized and the history of young women is written will the broad historical significance of the European marriage pattern become clear. Contrast between European demographic history and that of other world regions suggests a comparative pattern of particular significance for girls: Delayed marriage and childbearing meant that teenage girls were available for employment outside the familial household (either natal or marital) to a degree uncommon elsewhere. Household divisions of labor according to age and gender created constant demand for servants on larger farms; typically, unmarried youth who could be hired in from neighboring farms as servants filled this role. A period of service in a farm household, as an apprentice, or as a domestic servant in an urban household characterized male and female European youth in the life-cycle phase preceding marriage. Historians have noted but never fully explored the role young women played in European economic development, and in particular their role in the early industrial labor force.

Late marriage had gender-specific cultural ramifications as well. Whereas it was considered normal and even appropriate for teenage men to be initiated into heterosexual intercourse at brothels, in most regions of Europe, young women were expected to remain chaste until marriage. Delay of marriage heightened anxiety over unmarried women's sexuality, especially the dangers to which young women were increasingly exposed as the locus of their labor shifted from home and village to factory and city. Premarital or extramarital sexuality was uncommon, and was rigorously policed especially in the period following the religious upheavals of the Reformation in the sixteenth century. In rural areas, church and community, in addition to the family, exerted control over sexuality. Moreover, the unmarried male youth cohort of many village communities often served, in effect, as "morals police," enforcing local customs. These young men regulated courtship rituals, organized dances that young people went to, and oversaw the formation of couples. Sometimes, judging and public shaming by the youth group was the fate of couples who were mismatched by age or wealth or who violated sexual taboos. Some customs, at least symbolically, punished young men from far away who married local women, removing them from the marriage pool. Often, such a bridegroom had to pay for drinks in each village that the bridal couple passed through as they moved from the bride's parish church to their new abode—the longer the distance, the more expensive his bill.

Once married, a couple would usually begin having children immediately. Demographic evidence suggests that for most of Central and Western Europe there was virtually no practice of contraception among lower classes prior to the middle of the nineteenth century. Women had babies about every two years (more or less frequently according to region and depending on such local customs as breast-feeding length and intercourse taboos). Even though completed family sizes could be large by modern standards, the number of children most women bore was still less than if they had married in their teens. And prevailing high mortality rates further reduced the number of children who survived to adulthood.

The Moment of Marriage in Chinese History

The Chinese marriage system was traditionally characterized by early age at marriage, nearly universal marriage for women, virilocal residence (a newly married couple resided with the groom's parents), concubinage for elite men, and norms that discouraged widow remarriage. From the sixteenth through twentieth centuries, Chinese men and women married much younger on average than did their European counterparts—late teens or early twenties for women and a bit later for men. A bride typically moved to her husband's family home, which was often in a different village from her own. The moment of marriage not only meant that a girl would leave her parents but that she would also leave her network of kin and friends, all that was familiar. Families chose marriage partners, and a matchmaker negotiated the arrangements. Nothing resembling courtship existed; the bride and groom would often first meet on their wedding day.

Because a newly married Chinese couple would typically reside in an already-existing household, it was not necessary for an artisan to become established, a merchant to accumulate capital, or a peasant to own a farm before marrying. Newly married couples participated in ongoing domestic and economic enterprises that already supported the groom's family. New households were eventually established by a process of household division, which typically happened at the death of the father rather than the moment of marriage (although it could happen at other points in the family cycle as well).

Daughters were groomed from birth for marriage. They were taught skills appropriate to their social class or the social class into which their parents aspired to marry them. (In the ideal Chinese marriage, the groom was in fact supposed to be of slightly higher social status than the bride.) The feet of upper-class girls (and some who were not upper class) were bound, since Chinese men found this erotic. Bound feet also symbolically, if not actually, restricted upper-class women's movement. Thus bound feet simultaneously enhanced the sexual desirability of upper-class women and served to contain their sexuality within domestic bounds.

Virtually all Chinese girls became brides, though not all of them married as principal wives. (This contrasts with the European pattern where a substantial minority of women in most regions never married.) Upper-class men might take one or more concubines in addition to a principal wife. The relationship between a man and his concubine was recognized legally and ritually, and children born of these unions were legitimate. A wife had very secure status: divorce was almost nonexistent. A concubine's status, in contrast, was much more tenuous. She could be expelled at the whim of her "husband"; her only real protection was community sentiment. Although only a small percentage of Chinese marriages (no more than 5 percent) involved concubines, the practice remained an important structural feature of the Chinese marriage system until the twentieth century. Concubinage also provides a partial explanation of why, despite the fact that marriage was nearly universal for women, a substantial proportion of men (perhaps as high as 10 percent) never married. Also contributing to this apparent anomaly was the practice of sex-selective infanticide, a common practice that discriminated against girl babies and, ultimately, reduced the number of potential brides.

Once married, Chinese couples began to have children almost immediately, generally spacing births at longer intervals than did European couples. The reasons for this are not yet completely understood, although infanticide, extended breast-feeding, and the fairly large number of days on which sexual intercourse was forbidden all seem to have played a role in lowering Chinese family size.

Early marriage in China meant that the category of "youth," which has been so significant for European social and economic history, has no precise counterpart in Chinese history. Young Chinese women labored, to be sure, but the location of their work was domestic—either in the household of their father or husband. Female servants existed in China, but their servitude was normally of longer duration than the life-cycle servitude common in Europe. The domestic location of young women's labor in the Chinese context also had implications for the particular ways in which Chinese industries were organized, as we suggest below.

Patterns of Marriage in Europe and China

To sum up, then, there are differences of both timing of and residency before and after marriage that are particularly germane to the comparative history of young women. As demographic historians James Z. Lee and Wang Feng also have argued, "in China, females have always married universally and early . . . in contrast to female marriage in Western Europe, which occurred late or not at all." Whereas, in the nineteenth century, all but 20 percent of young Chinese women were married by age twenty, among European populations, between 60 and 80 percent of young women remained single at this age. In traditional China, only 1 or 2 percent of women remained unmarried at age thirty, whereas between 15 and 25 percent of thirty-year-old Western European women were still single. (For men, the differences though in the same direction are far less stark.) As for residence, in the Western European neolocal pattern, norms and practices in many regions resulted in a pattern whereby newly married couples moved into a separate household at marriage; but concomitant with this was their delaying marriage until they could afford a new household. In China, newly married couples generally resided in the groom's father's household. In Western Europe, the majority of postpubescent young men and many young women left home in their teenage years for a period of employment. In the early modern era, such employment was often as a servant or apprentice in either a craft or a farm household, but, over time, that employment was increasingly likely to be in a nondomestic work setting, such as a factory, store, or other urban enterprise. "Youth" was a distinctive phase in the life course of young men and increasingly of young women in Europe, although there were important gender distinctions. Such a period of postpubescent semiautonomy from parental households did not exist for Chinese youth, especially not for young women in traditional China. Young men more typically remained in their father's household and young women moved at marriage in their late teens from their own father's household to that of their husband's father.

Comparing the Moment of Marriage: Implications and Cautions

We would now like to discuss some of the world-historical implications of this important (if crude) comparison in the marriage systems of China and Western Europe. There are obviously many possible realms for investigation. For example, these patterns imply differences in young women's education, intergenerational relationships among women (especially between mothers and daughters and mothers-in-law and daughters-in-law), and household power relations. Here, we restrict our discussion to two areas of undoubted world-historical significance, namely economic development, on the one hand, and sexuality and reproduction, on the other.

The question of why the Industrial Revolution, or, alternatively, the emergence of industrial capitalism, occurred first in Europe, has been and remains salient for both European and world historians. R. Bin Wong explores this question in his innovative comparative study of economic development in Europe and China. Wong argues that there were rough parallels in the dynamics linking demographic expansion and economic growth in China and Europe until the nineteenth century. Both economies were expanding on the basis of growth of rural industrial enterprises in which peasant families supplemented agricultural work and income with part-time industrial production. What the Chinese case demonstrates, Wong argues, is that this so-called protoindustrial form of development may be viewed as an alternative route to industrialization rather than merely a precursor of factory production. Indeed, Charles Tilly has suggested that a prescient contemporary observer of the European economy in 1750 would likely have predicted such a future—that is "a countryside with a growing proletariat working in both agriculture and manufacturing."

While Wong's study is devoted to comparative examination of the economic roots and implications of varying paths to industrial development, he also connects economic and demographic growth. In particular, Wong mentions the link between marriage and economic opportunity: "in both China and Europe, rural industry supported lower age at marriage and higher proportions of ever married than would have been plausible in its absence. This does not mean that ages at marriage dropped in Europe when rural industry appeared, but the possibility was present. For China, the development of rural industry may not have lowered ages at marriage or raised proportions married as much as it allowed previous practices of relatively low ages at marriage and high proportions of women ever married to continue." What Wong does not explore is the way in which these "previous practices" that connected the low age at marriage with both virilocality and a relatively high commitment to the domestic containment of daughters and wives also had implications for patterns of economic development. In a comparative account of why Chinese industrial development relied heavily on domestic production, the fact that the young female labor force in China was to an extent far greater than that of Europe both married and "tied" to the male-headed household needs to be part of the story. This pattern of female marriage and residency held implications for entrepreneurial choice that helped to determine the different paths toward industrialization in Europe and China. World-historical comparison, taking into account aspects of gender relations and marriage and kinship systems, highlights their possible significance for economic development, a significance that has not been given proper attention by economic historians. Indeed, it is arguable that the family and marital status of the young women who played so significant a role in the workforce (especially those employed in the textile industry, which was key to early industrial development in both Europe and China) were major factors in the varying paths to development followed in China and Europe in the centuries of protoindustrial growth and industrialization.

A second set of implications concerns sexuality and reproduction. Again, we are aided by another recent study, which, in a fashion parallel to Wong's, uses Chinese historical evidence to call into question generalizations about historical development based on a European model. In their book on Chinese demographic history, Lee and Wang argue against the hegemonic Malthusian (mis)understandings according to which the family and population history to China has been seen as an example of a society's failure to curb population growth by any means other than recurrent disaster (by "positive" rather than "preventive" checks in Malthusian terms). They note the important difference in marriage systems that we have just described, but they dispute conclusions too often drawn from the Chinese historical pattern concerning overpopulation. Instead, according to Lee and Wang "persistently high nuptiality . . . did not inflate Chinese fertility, because of . . . the low level of fertility within marriage."

This second example points to another important realm for which the age at which women marry has great consequences. But the findings reported by Lee and Wang also caution scholars against leaping to comparative conclusions about one society on the basis of models established in another, even while their claims still suggest the value of comparison. We should not presume that since Chinese women were married universally and young, they therefore had more children or devoted a greater proportion of their time and energy to childbearing and child rearing than did their later married counterparts in Europe. Although the evidence is far from definitive, it nevertheless indicates that total marital fertility may have been somewhat lower in China than in Europe until the late nineteenth or early twentieth centuries. The factors in China that produced this pattern included relatively high rates of infanticide, especially of female infants, as well as different beliefs and practices about child care and sexuality. For example, babies were apparently breast-fed longer in China than in Europe (a pattern in turn related to the domestic location of women's work), which would have both increased infants' chances of survival and also lengthened the intervals between births.[1] In the realm of sexuality, pertinent factors include both prescriptions for men against overly frequent intercourse, and coresidence with a parental generation whose vigilance included policing young couples' sexual behavior.

These two examples are meant to suggest how looking at women's life cycles comparatively both enhances our understanding of the implications of varying patterns for women's history and also suggests the very broad ramifications, indeed world-historical significance, of different ways of institutionalizing the female life cycle.

■ REFLECTIONS

Women's history has entered the mainstream during the last few decades. An older view, still pervasive in the academic world forty years ago, assumed that women's history was adequately covered by general history, which was largely the story of the exploits of men. Political, military, and diplomatic history took precedence over historical fields seen as less resolutely masculine, such as social and cultural history.

Today, women's history not only stands independently in college and university curriculums but has also helped open doors to a wide range of new fields in social history — gender, family, childhood, sexuality, domesticity, and health, to name but a few. These new research fields have contributed significantly to issues of general history, as the authors of the last reading show. In fact, the growth and development of new fields of research and teaching in social and cultural history have had the effect of relegating the study of presidents, wars, and treaties to the periphery of the profession. A recent meeting of the American Historical Association, where historians came together to

[1] Breastfeeding temporarily lowers female fertility. [Ed.]

talk about their work, had more sessions on women, gender, and sexuality than on politics, diplomacy, military, war, World War I, World War II, and the American Civil War combined.

Some more traditional historians complain that this is a fad, and that sooner or later the profession will get back to the more "important" topics. But others respond that it is hard to think of anything more important than the history of half of humanity. This debate leads to questions about the importance of particular individuals in history. Who had a greater impact, for instance, thirtieth U.S. president Calvin Coolidge (1872–1933) or Marie Curie (1867–1934), who won the Nobel Prize for isolating radium for therapeutic purposes?

What role do individuals play on the historical canvas anyway? A president or Nobel laureate works according to social norms, available resources, supporting institutions, and the work of hundreds or thousands of others, living and dead. Forty years ago, historians put greater stress on institutions, movements, and perceived forces than they do today. In recent years, historians have looked for the "agency" of individuals and groups, perhaps in an effort to see how people can have an impact on their world. The power of slavery and the impact of imperialism have been balanced with the tales of slave revolts, the stories of successful collaborators, adapters, and resisters, and the voices of slaves and indigenous and colonized peoples. We see this in the study of women's history as well.

We began this chapter with the observation that we live in a patriarchy. Even if we are dismantling it in the twenty-first century, it was a powerful force between 1500 and 1800: a historical force, not natural, but a product of the urban revolution, perhaps, beginning about five thousand years ago. It is useful to understand its causes, describe its workings, and relate its history. But does doing so only hamper our capacity for change? Does it ignore the stories of women who have made a difference? Conversely, are women empowered, humanity enriched, by knowing how individual women were able to work within the system, secure their needs, engage, negotiate, compromise? Do the stories of a Sor Juana or the poems of an Anna Bijns inspire us? Or do they misrepresent the past and, by consequence, delude us?

Perhaps there are no easy answers to those questions, but our exercise in comparison might come in handy. The rich and varied detail of the human past should warn us against absolute declarations. We may emphasize patriarchy or emphasize women's power, but we would be foolish to deny either. In consequence, it may be most useful to ask more specific questions and to compare. Can women own property here? Is there more restriction on women's movement in this society or that? Only then can we begin to understand why here and not there, why then and not now. And only then can we use our understanding of the past to improve the present.

19

The Scientific Revolution

Europe, the Ottoman Empire, China, Japan, and the Americas, 1600–1800

■ HISTORICAL CONTEXT

Modern life is unthinkable apart from science. We surround ourselves with its products, from cars and computers to telephones and televisions; we are dependent on its institutions—hospitals, universities, and research laboratories; and we have internalized the methods and procedures of science in every aspect of our daily lives, from balancing checkbooks to counting calories. Even on social and humanitarian questions, the scientific method has become almost the exclusive model of knowledge in modern society.

We can trace the scientific focus of modern society to what is often called the "scientific revolution" of the seventeenth century. The seventeenth-century scientific revolution was a European phenomenon, marked by the work of such notables as Nicolas Copernicus (1473–1543) in Poland, Galileo Galilei (1564–1642) in Tuscany, and Isaac Newton (1642–1727) in England. But it was also a global event, prompted initially by Europe's new knowledge from Asia, Africa, and the Americas, and ultimately spread as a universal method for understanding and manipulating the world.

What was the scientific revolution? How revolutionary was it? How similar, or different, was European science from that practiced elsewhere in the world? And how much did the European revolution affect scientific traditions elsewhere? These are some of the issues we will study in this chapter.

■ THINKING HISTORICALLY

Distinguishing Change from Revolution

The world is always changing; it always has been changing. Sometimes, however, the change seems so formidable, extensive, important, or quick that we use the term *revolution*. In fact, we will use the term in this and the next two chapters. In this chapter we will examine what historians call the scientific revolution. The next chapter will deal with political revolutions and the chapter following with the industrial revolution. In each of these cases there are some historians who object that the changes were not really revolutionary, that they were more gradual or limited. Thus, we ask the question, how do we distinguish between mere change and revolutionary change?

In this chapter you will be asked, how revolutionary were the changes that are often called the scientific revolution? The point, however, is not to get your vote, pro or con, but to get you to think about how you might answer such a question. Do we, for instance, compare "the before" with "the after" and then somehow divide by the time it took to get from one to the other? Do we look at what people said at the time about how things were changing? Are we gauging speed of change or extent of change? What makes things change at different speeds? What constitutes a revolution?

1

JACK GOLDSTONE

Why Europe?

This selection is drawn from a book by a modern historian who asks one of the enduring questions of modern history: Why was it that people in Europe pioneered the breakthroughs in modern scientific thought in the seventeenth century that led to an industrial revolution? This is a particularly intriguing question when you realize, as Goldstone points out, that between 1000 and 1500 China, India, and the Muslim world made far greater strides in science than Europe. What were the obstacles to advancement in scientific thought in most societies before 1500? What happened in Europe between 1500 and 1650 to change the way people thought about

---

Source: Jack Goldstone, *Why Europe? The Rise of the West in World History 1500–1850* (New York: McGraw-Hill, 2009), 144–53.

nature, and how did that thinking change? How did rationalism and empiricism change European science after 1650? How does a combination of rationalism and empiricism produce better science than either separately or than the other two sources of authority: tradition and religion?

THINKING HISTORICALLY

Goldstone does not use the term *scientific revolution* in this selection, but he discusses a number of changes in European society, politics, and beliefs that might be called revolutionary. What are these changes? What would make them revolutionary changes? Is it a matter of how fast they occurred, how widespread they were, what impact they had, or how unusual or uniquely European they were? Which of these measures makes them more revolutionary?

One must ask, given the glorious achievements of Islamic and other scientific traditions that were sustained over many centuries: Why did they not develop the same kind of advances leading to industrialization as did the modern European sciences?

Varieties of World Science and Different Approaches to Understanding Nature

Approaches to natural science varied across time and across different civilizations. Some traditions, such as that of China, made enormous advances in herbal medicine but remained weak in basic anatomy. Other traditions, like that of the Mayan Indians of Central America, were extremely accurate in observational astronomy but very weak in physics and chemistry.

Nonetheless, most premodern scientific traditions shared several common elements. First, their scientific understanding of nature was generally embedded in the framework for understanding the universe laid out in their society's major religious or philosophical traditions. Although there was potential for great conflict if scientific studies of nature should contradict elements of religion, this was usually avoided by making the religious views dominant, so that scientific findings would have to be reconciled with or subordinated to religious beliefs. This does *not* mean that religions were opposed to science — quite the opposite! Most political and religious leaders sponsored both scientific and religious studies, believing that each supported the other. Many distinguished Confucian scholars, Islamic judges, and Catholic priests were also outstanding mathematicians and scientists. For the most part, detailed observations of nature, including accurate measurements of planetary motions and natural phenomena, were considered valuable as privileged knowledge to political and religious elites or socially useful for improving architecture, farming, and medicine.

However, science generally remained intermingled with religious and philosophical beliefs, and any inconsistencies were generally resolved in favor of preserving the established religion. This meant that truly novel work risked being suppressed by political and religious authorities, especially during periods of religious conservatism or state enforcement of orthodox religious views.

Second, most premodern sciences maintained a separation between mathematics and natural philosophy (the study of nature). Mathematics was considered useful for exploring the properties of numbers (arithmetic) and relationships in space (geometry). It was also useful for a host of practical problems, such as surveying; compiling tables of planetary positions in the skies for navigation, calendars, and astrology; and accounting. But most premodern scientific traditions—including those of the ancient Greeks, medieval Europeans, Arabs, and the Chinese—held that mathematics was *not* useful for studying the basic constitution of the universe. This was the main subject matter of natural philosophy (the study of the natural world) and theology (the study of religious issues, including the relationship of humans and the natural world to the creator).

If one wanted to know the nature of God or the soul, or the relations between humankind and God, or the purpose of animals, or the nature of the stuff that composed the world—plants, stones, fire, air, liquids, gases, crystals—well, these were problems for reasoning based on experience and logic, not on mathematical equations. The task of philosophy was to comprehend the essential nature of things and their relationships. Measurement was a practical matter, useful but best left to surveyors, craftspeople, moneylenders, and other practical folks.

Thus the Chinese and Indian traditions believed in a basic hidden force of nature—*qi* in China and *prana* in India—that animated and infused the world. For Chinese scientists, the world was always changing, and these changes formed complex cycles and flows of opposing forces that operated to maintain an overall harmony. Thus despite their enormous skill and use of detailed mathematics and observation in areas from canals and irrigation works to astronomy and clocks, it never occurred to orthodox Chinese scientists to regard the universe as a mechanical clockwork or to apply mathematical equations to understand why natural processes occurred. What mattered was understanding signs of the ever-shifting flows of *qi* between opposing conditions—*yin* and *yang*—to avoid excesses and to maintain the harmony of the whole.

The Greeks too, since the time of Aristotle, similarly maintained a separation of mathematics from natural philosophy. Aristotle's philosophy of nature, which by the Middle Ages had become the dominant natural philosophy in Europe, analyzed nature by identifying the basic elements that composed all things. For Aristotle, there were four basic elements—earth, fire, air, and water—which were defined in terms of how they behaved. Things made of earth are solid and naturally tend to fall to the center of the universe, which is why the solid earth beneath us consists of a sphere, and all solid things fall toward it. Fire naturally rises, so things infused with fire rise. Air is transparent and moves across the surface of the Earth as winds; water flows and moves in currents and puddles and fills the seas and oceans. Since the Moon and Sun and stars and planets neither move up nor down but remain in the heavens, moving in circles in the skies, they must be composed of yet another, distinct element that was perfect and unchanging, which the Greeks called the "aether."

The way these principles were discovered and proved was through logic and argument based on experience, not through mathematics. Although mathematical forms and principles could help identify and measure relationships in nature, the true "essence" of reality was set by philosophy. For example, even though the planets actually move at varying speeds in elliptical orbits around the Sun, for over 1,000 years Islamic and European astronomers sought to describe their orbits solely in terms of combinations of uniform and circular motions, because Aristotle's natural philosophy had decreed that this was the only way that heavenly bodies could move.

In the Middle Ages, European scholars continued to treat mathematics as mainly a practical field, while focusing their attention on logic and argument as the keys to advancing knowledge. Although medieval scholars in Europe did make significant advances in the study of motion and absorbed much of the critical commentary on Greek science and philosophy from the Islamic world, they did not reject or replace the major tenets of classical Greek science or their own religious theology. Rather, much of the effort of European thought in the Middle Ages consisted of efforts to reconcile and synthesize the writings of the Greek authors on science and politics with the precepts of the Christian Bible and other religious texts, culminating in the work of St. Thomas Aquinas.

The Islamic scientific tradition went further than any other in using experiments and mathematical reasoning to challenge the arguments of Ptolemy, Galen, and others of the ancient Greeks, creating new advances in medicine, chemistry, physics, and astronomy. Yet within Islam, the discussion of the fundamental relationships and characteristics of nature was separated into the teachings of the Islamic sciences, based on classical religious texts, and the teachings of the foreign sciences, including all the works of Greek and Indian authors. After the writings of the philosophical critic Al-Ghazali in the eleventh century, who championed the value of the Islamic sciences on truly fundamental issues, this division was generally maintained, and even the most remarkable advances and findings with regard to revisions of Greek learning were not permitted to challenge the fundamental views of the universe as expressed in Islamic religious works.

Thus in all the major scientific traditions, whereas precise measurement and sophisticated mathematics were widely used, mathematical reasoning was not used to challenge the fundamental understanding of nature that was expressed in natural philosophy and religious thought.

Third, in most places, the dominant assumptions and traditions of science were so distinctive and so well established that they could hardly be shaken even by encounters with different notions and ideas. These scientific traditions tended to grow incrementally, with each successive generation modifying yet building on the works of their predecessors, so that over time a rich and longstanding tradition of scientific methods and findings grew up, intertwined with an established religious tradition. These structures of thought tended to resist wholesale change or replacement and to marginalize heterodox or conflicting views.

Thus by 1500, there were many different varieties of science in the world, each with their own strengths and distinctive characteristics. Most had developed precise observations of the Earth and heavens and had systematized a great number and variety of discoveries about nature. Most had developed a classification of essential relationships or characteristics of natural things. Most were linked in some fashion to one of the great axial age religions and over many centuries had worked to accumulate knowledge while building frameworks that were compatible with those religions. And in the next century or two, most scientific traditions would be driven to greater subordination to classical and religious orthodoxy by rulers who were responding to the political and social conflicts that struck over almost all of Europe and Asia.

How then was it possible that any culture could develop . . . technical innovations, based on new instruments and mathematical natural science . . . ? To understand this, we have to grasp the unusual events and discoveries that led to unexpected changes in Europe's approach to science.

Europe's Unusual Trajectory: From Embracing to Escaping Its Classical Tradition, 1500–1650

The study of ancient schools of thought was given a new direction by the realization, by the early 1500s, that the Spanish voyages to the west had discovered not just an alternate route to India, but in fact a whole new continent, a "New World" unknown to ancient geographers and scientists. Navigators came to realize that practically all of Greek geography was badly mistaken. Also in the early 1500s, the research of the Belgian anatomist Andreas Vesalius (who was building on the prior work of Arab scholars) demonstrated to Europeans that Galen's knowledge of human anatomy was, in many respects, inaccurate or deficient because it was based on deductions from animal dissections rather than on empirical study of human cadavers. Vesalius showed that many of Galen's (and Aristotle's) statements about the heart, the liver, the blood vessels, and the skeleton were wrong.

Then in 1543, Copernicus published his new methods for calculating the movements of the planets based on a solar system with a moving Earth circling the Sun. Although some supporters, trying to avoid conflict with the church, argued that his work should only be taken as a new method of predicting planetary positions, Copernicus argued quite forcefully that the structure and dynamics of the solar system made more sense, logically and aesthetically, if the Earth and all other planets revolved around the Sun. If so, then the system of Ptolemy and Aristotle, with the Earth as the center of all motion, was in error.

In 1573, the Danish astronomer Tycho Brahe published his account of the supernova that had suddenly appeared near the constellation of Cassiopeia in 1572. This was a phenomenon that had never been recorded in European astronomy. Indeed, since the time of Aristotle, it was assumed that the skies were unchanging and constant in their perfection. Comets and meteors were known, of course, but they were considered weather phenomena, like lightning that occurred close to the Earth rather than in the celestial heavens. But the supernova was not a comet or meteorite, because it showed no motion: It was a new body that behaved like a fixed star—something that was, according to Aristotle's philosophy, impossible.

Five years later, Brahe showed by careful observation of the movements of the great comet of 1577 that this comet must be farther away from the Earth than the Moon and thus was moving through the celestial heavens, not the atmosphere, striking yet another blow against Aristotle's cosmic system. Supernovae that can be observed from Earth by the naked eye are rare, but as chance would have it, in 1604, yet another supernova made its appearance, thus showing conclusively that the heavens were not unchanging after all.

By the late 1500s and early 1600s, therefore, the wisdom of Aristotle, Galen, and Ptolemy, which had been accepted for over 1,000 years, was coming under widespread attack. European scholars sought out new observations and new instruments for studying nature that could help determine who was correct, or incorrect, in their description of nature and the universe.

In 1609, Galileo used the new spyglass or telescope—invented by Dutch lens-grinders and then improved by Galileo himself—to observe the heavens. Looking at the Moon through a telescope rather than only the unaided eye, Galileo saw what looked like giant mountains and craters on the surface, which through the telescope looked positively Earthlike! Jupiter was found to have its own moons circling it, implying that the Earth could not be the center of all celestial motions. In every direction were previously unknown stars, and even the Milky Way was revealed to consist of thousands of tiny stars. Though many critics at first dismissed the views through the telescope as false magic, enough people acquired their own telescopes and confirmed Galileo's discoveries that they were widely accepted. People came to realize that the universe in which they lived was nothing like that described by the ancient Greek authorities.

Copernicus was not the first astronomer to suggest that the Earth revolved on its axis and moved around the Sun, instead of being the fixed center of the universe; a few ancient Greek and Islamic astronomers had also suggested that this was possible. However, until telescopic observations of the moons of Jupiter demonstrated the fact of motion around a body other than the Earth, there was no evidence on which to base a successful overthrow of Aristotle's views. It was only after 1600, with so many new observations that contradicted the ancient Greeks' knowledge—of geography, of anatomy, and of astronomy—piling up in all directions, that it became possible, even imperative, to adopt alternatives to Aristotle in particular and to Greek science and philosophy as a whole.

From 1600 to 1638, a series of books presenting new knowledge or proclaiming the need for a "new science" made a compelling case that the knowledge of the ancients was seriously flawed.

1600: William Gilbert, *On the Magnet*
1620: Francis Bacon, *The New Organon, or True Directions Concerning the Interpretation of Nature*
1620: Johannes Kepler, *The New Astronomy*
1626: Francis Bacon, *The New Atlantis*
1628: William Harvey, *On the Motion of the Heart and Blood*
1638: Galileo, *Discourses on Two New Sciences*

Gilbert argued that compass needles pointed north because the whole earth acted as a giant magnet. Francis Bacon argued that Aristotle's mainly deductive logic (collected under the title *Organon*—which means "instrument or tool") could not be trusted as a guide to understanding nature; instead Bacon argued for the use of inductive logic, based on a program of experiment and observation, as a superior method for discovering knowledge of the world. Kepler showed that the planets actually traveled in elliptical orbits around the sun, not in circles. And William Harvey showed that, contrary to Galen's teachings, the supposedly separate veins and arteries were in fact one system through which the blood was circulated by the beating of the heart.

By the mid-1600s, therefore, European philosophers and scientists found themselves in a world where the authority of ancient texts was clearly no longer a secure foundation for knowledge. Other major civilizations did not suffer such blows. For the Chinese, Indians, and Muslims—accustomed to operating in a vast intercontinental trade sphere from China to Europe and generally seeing themselves at the center of all that mattered—the discovery of new, lightly peopled lands far to the west made little difference. But for Europeans—who had long seen themselves on the literal edge of the civilized world with all that mattered lying to the east—the discovery of new and wholly unknown lands to the west changed their fundamental position in the world.

Similarly, Chinese and Indian astronomers had observed supernovae before (accurately recording observations of the heavens for thousands of years) and had long ago developed philosophies of nature that were built around ideas of continuous change as the normal course of things in the universe. Unlike the Greeks and Europeans, they had no rigid notions of perfect and unchanging heavens, separate from the Earth, that would cause their classical traditions to be fundamentally challenged by new observations of comets and stars.

Moreover, just when Europeans started their impassioned debates over these new observations and put forth their alternative ideas, the Ottoman, Mughal, and Chinese Empires were focused on internal concerns, seeking to recover from internal rebellions by closing off outside influences and strengthening traditional orthodox beliefs.

Thus the Europeans, more than any other major civilization, suddenly found that the classical tradition that they had sought to embrace now had to be escaped if they were going to understand the true nature of their world and their universe. This led Europeans to undertake a search for new systems of philosophy and new ways of studying and describing nature.

Searching for New Directions in European Science: Cartesian Reasoning and British Empiricism, 1650–1750

Prior to 1650, all major civilizations drew on four basic sources to justify knowledge and authority (which were generally closely connected). These were

1. Tradition—knowledge that was revered for its age and long use
2. Religion or revelation—knowledge that was based on sacred texts or the sayings of prophets, saints, and other spiritual leaders
3. Reason—knowledge that was obtained from logical demonstration, either in arithmetic and geometry or by deductive reasoning from basic premises

4. Repeated observation and experience—knowledge that was confirmed by widely shared and repeated observations and everyday experience, such as that day follows night, the sun rises in the east, objects fall, heat rises. This also includes various agricultural and manufacturing techniques that were proven in use.

We have noted that in Europe by the early 1600s new discoveries, observations, and concepts about the Earth and the universe had already started to chip away at tradition and religious belief as guides to knowledge about the natural world. In addition, the seventeenth century was a period of sharp religious schism and conflict in Europe, capped by the Thirty Years' War (1618–1648). During these years Catholics, Lutherans, Calvinists, and other sects all claimed to be correcting the errors of others' interpretation of Christian faith, and various religious groups rebelled and embroiled Europe in massive civil and international wars. The lack of accepted religious authority and of any way to choose between competing claims seemed to offer nothing but the prospect of endless conflict.

The same problems, as we have noted, led Asian empires to promote a return to their traditional orthodox beliefs to suppress these conflicts. Some European states tried to do the same thing. In Spain and Italy and part of Germany and Poland, the counter-Reformation led to the suppression of heresies and unorthodox views and enforcement of traditional Catholic beliefs. These states banned books that threatened Catholic orthodoxy and sought to curtail the actions of "dangerous" authors, such as Giordano Bruno and Galileo (Bruno was burned at the stake for his heresies; Galileo, more prudent and better connected, was allowed to live under house arrest). France and the Netherlands, though less severe, and Britain through 1640, also tried to restore uniform state religions and force dissenters underground or into exile. However, in a few states—including Britain after 1689, Denmark, and Prussia—religious tolerance remained, and throughout western Europe, there was a checkerboard of different states following different varieties of religion—Catholic, Calvinist, Lutheran. Throughout Europe, the result of the rise and spread of Protestantism in the sixteenth and seventeenth centuries was that the authority of the Catholic Church—and of the philosophical and scientific work that was closely associated with the church's teachings—was seriously weakened. This provided an additional reason for philosophers to struggle to find a new basis for more certain knowledge.

European thinkers therefore turned away from the first and second major sources of knowledge and authority—tradition and religion—to seek new systems of knowledge. After 1650, two major directions were proposed to deal with this dilemma—rationalism and empiricism.

One way to set aside traditional and revelation-based assumptions was to try to get down to bedrock conclusions by reasoning purely from logic. The critical figure leading this approach was the French philosopher and mathematician René Descartes, who resolved to begin by doubting everything—the teaching of the ancients, the teachings of the church, and even his own experience. He extended his doubt until only one thing remained certain—the fact of his own doubt! This fact could then be the basis for logical deductions. After all, if Descartes could not escape the fact of his own doubt, he—as a doubting, thinking entity—must exist! This conclusion was rendered in his famous statement "I think, therefore I am."

Descartes continued this argument further. If he doubted, he could not be perfect. But if was aware of his imperfection, this could only be because a perfect entity existed, thus there must be a perfect being, or God. And because we can only conceive of God as perfect, and hence perfectly logical, the universe constructed by God must also follow perfect logic. Descartes further argued that we can only logically perceive space if something is there, extending through space (empty space, Descartes argued, was a logical contradiction). What must fill space, then, are invisible particles whose motions and interactions must cause all that we see.

In this fashion, Descartes built up a logically consistent model of a mechanical universe in which all phenomena are to be explained by the movements and collisions of moving particles. This led Descartes to numerous valuable insights, such as the notion that we see things because invisible particles of light move from the objects we see to strike our eyes. But it also led him to deduce things that we now know are simply not true, such as the idea that the planets travel around the Sun because they are caught up in vortexes or whirlpools of swirling invisible particles.

This Cartesian rationalism provided a very attractive alternative to Aristotelian philosophy, which was now in disrepute. It seemed to have the power of purely logical demonstration behind its ideas. Also, because all phenomena were reduced to the motions of particles, it held the promise of applying mathematical principles—already worked out by Galileo for many kinds of particle motion—to all of nature. Finally, it allowed one to explain almost anything by coming up with some characteristics of particles. For example, one could suggest that spicy or sweet flavors were the respective results of sharp or smooth particles hitting the tongue or that different colors of light were produced by particles of light spinning at different speeds.

However, Cartesian rationalism also had its defects. In putting reason above experience, Cartesians disdained experiments. This limited what could be learned or discovered and often led to significant errors. Descartes' assumptions led him to misjudge the way bodies acted in collisions and turned his followers away from studying the properties of vacuums (since empty space could not exist, they must be tricks or errors by experimenters). Descartes also flatly ruled out the possibility of forces acting directly across space between objects, such as gravity. For all of its virtues, Cartesian rationalism therefore saddled its followers with a variety of errors and false explanations of the mechanics of motion in nature.

The motion of the Earth, the weight of the atmosphere, and the properties of vacuums were all discoveries whose proof rested on the use of scientific instruments (telescopes, barometers, vacuum pumps) to capture information not ordinarily available to the senses. The use of such instruments was a prime feature of the Baconian plan of developing scientific knowledge by experiments.

The experimental program reached its most systematic organization in the work of the Royal Society of London, led by Robert Boyle and later by Isaac Newton. The Royal Society based its research on experiments with scientific instruments and apparatus publicly performed at meetings of the society, and accounts of those experiments were widely published. The Royal Society used air pumps, telescopes, microscopes, electrostatic generators, prisms, lenses, and a variety of other tools to carry out its investigations. Indeed, the society came to rely on specially trained craftspeople to supply the growing demand for scientific instruments for its members.

The fame of the Royal Society in Britain skyrocketed with the achievements of Isaac Newton. Newton was the first to demonstrate that both motion on the Earth—whether the movement of falling apples, cannonballs, or the tides—and the motions of the planets through the heavens could *all* be explained by the action of a universal force of gravity. This force acted to attract objects to each other with a strength that increased with their mass but decreased with the inverse square of the distance between them. Newton's theory of gravity made it possible, for the first time, to explain the precise path and speed that the planets followed through the skies, as well as the movement of the Moon and the tides.

Newton also discovered the correct laws of mechanical force—that force was needed for all changes in the direction or speed of motion of an object, in proportion to the mass of the object and the magnitude of the change. Newton's laws of force made it possible to easily figure out the amount of work provided by, for example, a volume of falling water based on the height that it fell, or the amount of work it would take to raise a certain weight a desired distance. Newton further discovered the key principle of optics: that white light was composed of a number of different colors of light, each of which bent slightly differently when moving through water or a glass lens, thus creating rainbows in the sky and color patterns in prisms and lenses.

2

VESALIUS

Images of Anatomy

Andreas Vesalius (1514–1564), like generations of physicians before him, learned anatomy from the writings of Galen (129–216 c.e.), a Greek-born Roman. Because of Galen's authority, and subsequent Christian and Muslim strictures against conducting dissections, very little was learned about human anatomy for the next thousand years. Only gradually after 1200 were dissections performed again, and yet most physicians still read Galen while surgeons (formerly barbers) did the cutting. Vesalius himself began as a defender of Galen, until he moved from his native Belgium to teach at the University of Padua in Italy in 1537. There he was able to secure enough cadavers of executed criminals to perform multiple dissections and discover that Galen (who had only been able to dissect animals) had been wrong about elements of human anatomy. A facile artist himself, Vesalius engaged leading Italian draftsmen for the publication of his findings in *De humani corporis fabrica (On the Structure of the Human Body),* published in 1543.

Two images from the fourteenth century (Figures 19.1 and 19.2) are followed by two images from the *Fabrica,* one showing muscles (Figure 19.3) and another showing bones or the human skeleton (Figure 19.4). How would you describe the differences between the drawings in the *Fabrica* and those of the fourteenth century?

THINKING HISTORICALLY

The actual mistakes that Vesalius found in Galen might seem relatively trivial. For instance, Vesalius realized that the human jaw was one bone, not two as Galen claimed after dissecting monkeys. He also saw that the sternum (which protects the chest) is three bones instead of seven and that, also contrary to Galen, the fibula and tibula of the human leg were longer than the arm. In this regard we might think of his work as evolutionary rather than revolutionary. Yet when we compare the images of the fourteenth century with those of Vesalius, barely more than a hundred years later, the differences strike us as revolutionary. Why do you think that is? Was this a revolution? If so, in what?

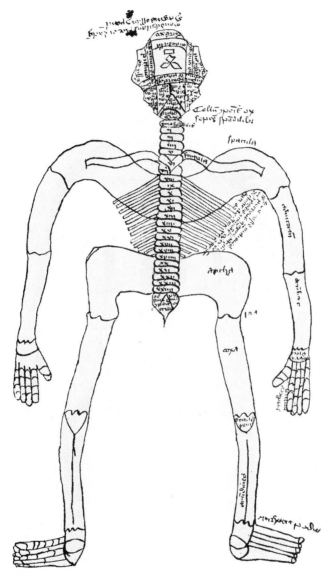

Figure 19.1 Skeleton Drawing, from the Latin Munich MS Codex, fourteenth century.

Source: Wellcome Library, London.

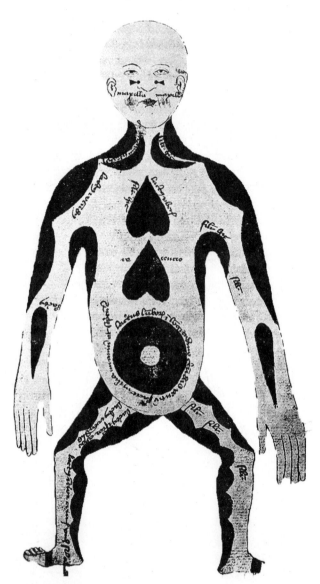

Figure 19.2 Muscular System of a Man, from the Rudnitz Five-Figure Series, 1399.

Source: Wellcome Library, London.

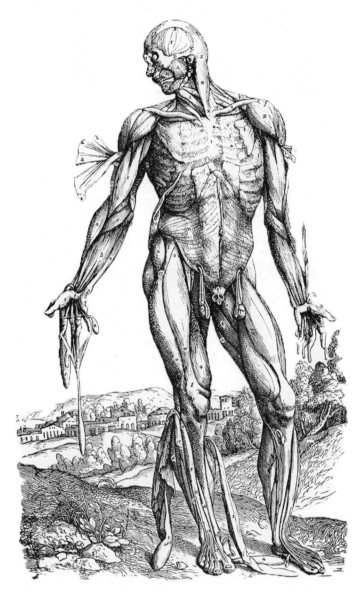

Figure 19.3 Woodcut of Muscles, from Vesalius, *De humani corporis fabrica*,1543.

Source: The Granger Collection, New York.

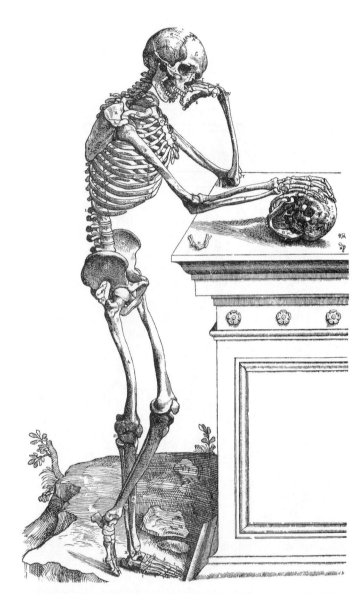

Figure 19.4 Woodcut of a Skeleton, from Vesalius, *De humani corporis fabrica*, 1543.

Source: The Granger Collection, New York.

3

ISAAC NEWTON

The Mathematical Principles of Natural Philosophy

Isaac Newton (1643–1727) was probably the most influential scientist in world history. His range was breathtaking, covering optics, astronomy, mathematics, and physics. He invented calculus, discovered the relationship between light and color, and devised laws of motion and gravity that provided the framework of modern science for the next two hundred years. *The Mathematical Principles of Natural Philosophy* (1687) was his most influential work. We include here only the four "Rules of Reasoning in Philosophy."[1] Try to put each one in your own words. Why do you think he called them general rules of reasoning rather than specific rules for science?

In the first selection, Jack Goldstone underlined the importance of the European method of applying mathematics to the study of nature and the British empirical or experimental method of creating knowledge. How do these passages in Newton's writing emphasize both of these approaches?

THINKING HISTORICALLY

When we look at *The Mathematical Principles of Natural Philosophy,* or the *Principia,* as it is called in abbreviated Latin form, and once we cut through the seventeenth-century language, we come upon ideas that seem fairly obvious to us today. That they were not obvious then is a measure of how revolutionary they were. Try to imagine what people believed before Newton established these principles. For example, before Newton established the law of gravity, people did not believe that objects flew around at will; so what exactly is new here? Give examples of thinking that ignores these rules of reasoning.

Rule I
We are to admit no more causes of natural things, than such as are both true and sufficient to explain their appearances.

To this purpose the philosophers say, that Nature does nothing in vain, and more is in vain, when less will serve; for Nature is pleased with simplicity, and affects not the pomp of superfluous causes.

[1] As they were revised in a later edition (1726).

Source: Isaac Newton, *The Mathematical Principles of Natural Philosophy,* trans. A. Motte (London, 1729). Available on the American Libraries website at http://www.archive.org/details/newtonspmathema00newtrich (accessed October 25, 2009).

Rule II

Therefore to the same natural effects we must, as far as possible, assign the same causes.

As to respiration in a man, and in a beast; the descent of stones in Europe and in America; the light of our culinary fire and of the sun; the reflection of light in the earth, and in the planets.

Rule III

The qualities of bodies, which admit neither intension nor remission of degrees,[2] and which are found to belong to all bodies within reach of our experiments, are to be esteemed the universal qualities of all bodies whatsoever.

For since the qualities of bodies are only known to us by experiments, we are to hold for universal, all such as universally agree with experiments; and such as are not liable to diminution, can never be quite taken away. We are certainly not to relinquish the evidence of experiments for the sake of dreams and vain fictions of our own devising; nor are we to recede from the analogy of Nature, which is wont to be simple, and always consonant to itself. We no other way know the extension of bodies, than by our senses, nor do these reach it in all bodies; but because we perceive extension in all that are sensible, therefore we ascribe it universally to all others, also. That abundance of bodies are hard we learn by experience. And because the hardness of the whole arises from the hardness of the parts, we therefore justly infer the hardness of the undivided particles not only of the bodies we feel but of all others. That all bodies are impenetrable we gather not from reason, but from sensation. The bodies which we handle we find impenetrable and thence conclude impenetrability to be a universal property of all bodies whatsoever. That all bodies are moveable, and endowed with certain powers (which we call the forces of inertia) or persevering in their motion or in their rest, we only infer from the like properties observed in the bodies which we have seen. The extension, hardness, impenetrability, mobility, and force of inertia of the whole result from the extension, hardness, impenetrability, mobility, and forces of inertia of the parts: and thence we conclude that the least particles of all bodies to be also all extended, and hard, and impenetrable, and moveable, and

---

[2] Qualities of bodies that do not get larger or smaller, harder or softer, etc. Refers to permanent qualities of bodies: their extension, hardness, movability. The point is that we can assume these qualities are universal, and that they will be found in similar bodies, even those that are in the heavens (and therefore not measurable). [Ed.]

endowed with their proper forces of inertia. And this is the foundation of all philosophy. Moreover, that the divided but contiguous particles of bodies may be separated from one another, is a matter of observation; and, in the particles that remain undivided, our minds are able to distinguish yet lesser parts, as is mathematically demonstrated. But whether the parts so distinguished, and not yet divided, may, by the powers of nature, be actually divided and separated from one another, we cannot certainly determine. Yet had we the proof of but one experiment, that any undivided particle, in breaking a hard and solid body, suffered a division, we might by virtue of this rule, conclude, that the undivided as well as the divided particles, may be divided and actually separated into infinity.

Lastly, if it universally appears, by experiments and astronomical observations, that all bodies about the earth, gravitate toward the earth; and that in proportion to the quantity of matter which they severally contain; that the moon likewise, according to the quantity of its matter, gravitates toward the earth; that on the other hand our sea gravitates toward the moon; and all the planets mutually one toward another; and the comets in like manner towards the sun; we must, in consequence of this rule, universally allow, that all bodies whatsoever are endowed with a principle of mutual gravitation. For the argument from the appearances concludes with more force for the universal gravitation of all bodies, than for their impenetrability, of which among those in the celestial regions, we have no experiments, nor any manner of observation. Not that I affirm gravity to be essential to all bodies. By their inherent force I mean nothing but their force of inertia. This is immutable. Their gravity is diminished as they recede from the earth.

Rule IV

In experimental philosophy we are to look upon propositions collected by general induction[3] from phenomena as accurately or very nearly true, notwithstanding any contrary hypotheses that may be imagined, till such time as other phenomena occur, by which they may either be made more accurate, or liable to exceptions.

This rule we must follow to ensure that the argument of induction may not be evaded by hypotheses.

---

[3] Induction is reasoning from the specific to the general: deriving a general principle from specific examples or instances. For example: This, that, and the other frog are gray, so frogs must be gray. [Ed.]

BONNIE S. ANDERSON AND
JUDITH P. ZINSSER

Women and Science

This selection from a history of European women shows how some
women, especially the better educated, could participate in the scientific
revolution of the seventeenth and eighteenth centuries. But Anderson
and Zinsser also demonstrate how much of the scientific revolution endowed male prejudices with false scientific respectability. What factors
seem to have enabled women to participate in the scientific revolution?
In what ways was the scientific revolution a new bondage for women?

THINKING HISTORICALLY

What do the authors mean when they say that for women "there was
no Scientific Revolution"? In what ways were women's lives different
after the scientific revolution? In what ways were they the same? Were
the differences caused by the scientific revolution?

Women Scientists

In the same way that women responded to and participated in
Humanism,[1] so they were drawn to the intellectual movement known
as the Scientific Revolution. The excitement of the new discoveries
of the seventeenth and eighteenth centuries, in particular, inspired a
few gifted women scientists to formulate their own theories about the
natural world, to perform their own experiments, and to publish their
findings. In contrast to those educated strictly and formally according to Humanist precepts, these women had little formal training, and
chose for themselves what they read and studied. Rather than encouraging them, their families at best left them to their excitement with
the wonders of the "Scientific Revolution"; at worst, parents criticized their daughters' absorption in such inappropriate, inelegant, and
unfeminine endeavors.

All across Europe from the sixteenth to the eighteenth centuries these
women found fascination in the natural sciences. They corresponded
and studied with the male scientists of their day. They observed, and

[1] A faith in the capacities of humans that reached religious dimensions in the sixteenth
century. Renaissance humanism valued reason, classical culture and literature, and civic
engagement. [Ed.]

Source: Bonnie S. Anderson and Judith P. Zinsser, *A History of Their Own: Women in Europe
from Prehistory to the Present* (New York: Harper & Row, 1988) 2:87–89, 96–99.

they formulated practical applications from their new knowledge of botany, horticulture, and chemistry. The Countess of Chinchon, wife of the Viceroy to Peru, brought quinine bark to Spain from Latin America because it had cured her malaria. Some noblewomen, like the German Anna of Saxony (1532–1582), found medical uses for the plants they studied. The most gifted of these early naturalists is remembered not as a scientist but as an artist. Maria Sibylla Merian (1647–1717) learned drawing and probably acquired her interest in plants and insects from her stepfather, a Flemish still-life artist. As a little girl she went with him into the fields to collect specimens. Though she married, bore two daughters, and ran a household, between 1679 and her death in 1717 she also managed to complete and have published six collections of engravings of European flowers and insects. These were more than art-ist's renderings. For example, her study of caterpillars was unique for the day. Unlike the still life done by her contemporaries, the drawings show the insect at every stage of development as observed from the specimens that she collected and nursed to maturity. She explained:

> From my youth I have been interested in insects, first I started with silkworms in my native Frankfurt-am-Main. After that . . . I started to collect all the caterpillars I could find to observe their changes.

Merian's enthusiasm, patience, and skill brought her to the atten-tion of the director of the Amsterdam Botanical Gardens and other male collectors. When her daughter married and moved to the Dutch colony of Surinam, their support was important when she wanted to raise the money for a new scientific project. In 1699, at the age of fifty-two, Maria Sibylla Merian set off on what became a two-year expedition into the interior of South America. She collected, made notations and sketches. Only yellow fever finally forced her to return to Amsterdam in 1701. The resulting book of sixty engravings established her contemporary reputation as a naturalist.

Mathematics, astronomy, and studies of the universe also inter-ested these self-taught women scientists. In 1566 in Paris Marie de Coste Blanche published *The Nature of the Sun and Earth*. Margaret Cavendish (1617–1673), the seventeenth-century Duchess of Newcastle, though haphazard in her approach to science, produced fourteen books on everything from natural history to atomic physics.

Even more exceptional in the eighteenth century was the French noblewoman and courtier, Emilie du Châtelet (1706–1749). She gained admission to the discussions of the foremost mathematicians and scien-tists of Paris, earned a reputation as a physicist and as an interpreter of the theories of Leibnitz and Newton. Emilie du Châtelet showed unusual intellectual abilities even as a child. By the age of ten she had read Cicero, studied mathematics and metaphysics. At twelve she could speak English, Italian, Spanish, and German and translated Greek and Latin texts like

Aristotle and Virgil. Presentation at court and life as a courtier changed none of her scientific interests and hardly modified her studious habits. She seemed to need no sleep, read incredibly fast, and was said to appear in public with ink stains on her fingers from her notetaking and writing. When she took up the study of Descartes, her father complained to her uncle: "I argued with her in vain; she would not understand that no great lord will marry a woman who is seen reading every day." Her mother despaired of a proper future for such a daughter who "flaunts her mind, and frightens away the suitors her other excesses have not driven off." It was her lover and lifelong friend, the Duke de Richelieu, who encouraged her to continue and to formalize her studies by hiring professors in mathematics and physics from the Sorbonne to tutor her. In 1733 she stormed her way into the Café Gradot, the Parisian coffee-house where the scientists, mathematicians, and philosophers regularly met. Barred because she was a woman, she simply had a suit of men's clothes made for herself and reappeared, her long legs now in breeches and hose, to the delight of cheering colleagues and the consternation of the management. . . .

Châtelet made her reputation as a scientist with her three-volume work on the German mathematician and philosopher Leibnitz, *The Institutions of Physics,* published in 1740. Contemporaries also knew of her work from her translation of Newton's *Principles of Mathematics,* her book on algebra, and her collaboration with Voltaire on his treatise about Newton.

From the fifteenth to the eighteenth centuries privileged women participated in the new intellectual movements. Like the men of their class, they became humanist scholars, naturalists, and scientists. Unfortunately, many of these women found themselves in conflict with their families and their society. A life devoted to scholarship conflicted with the roles that women, however learned, were still expected to fulfill.

Science Affirms Tradition

In the sixteenth and seventeenth centuries Europe's learned men questioned, altered, and dismissed some of the most hallowed precepts of Europe's inherited wisdom. The intellectual upheaval of the Scientific Revolution caused them to examine and describe anew the nature of the universe and its forces, the nature of the human body and its functions. Men used telescopes and rejected the traditional insistence on the smooth surface of the moon. Galileo, Leibnitz, and Newton studied and charted the movement of the planets, discovered gravity and the true relationship between the earth and the sun. Fallopio dissected the human body, Harvey discovered the circulation of the blood, and Leeuwenhoek found spermatozoa with his microscope.

For women, however, there was no Scientific Revolution. When men studied female anatomy, when they spoke of female physiology, of women's reproductive organs, of the female role in procreation, they ceased to be scientific. They suspended reason and did not accept the evidence of their senses. Tradition, prejudice, and imagination, not scientific observation, governed their conclusions about women. The writings of the classical authors like Aristotle and Galen continued to carry the same authority as they had when first written, long after they had been discarded in other areas. Men spoke in the name of the new "science" but mouthed words and phrases from the old misogyny. In the name of "science" they gave a supposed physiological basis to the traditional views of women's nature, function, and role. Science affirmed what men had always known, what custom, law, and religion had postulated and justified. With the authority of their "objective," "rational" inquiry they restated ancient premises and arrived at the same traditional conclusions: the innate superiority of the male and the justifiable subordination of the female.

In the face of such certainty, the challenges of women like Lucrezia Marinella and María de Zayas had little effect. As Marie de Gournay, the French essayist, had discovered at the beginning of the seventeenth century, those engaged in the scientific study of humanity viewed the female as if she were of a different species—less than human, at best; nature's mistake, fit only to "play the fool and serve [the male]."

The standard medical reference work, *Gynaecea,* reprinted throughout the last decades of the sixteenth century, included the old authorities like Aristotle and Galen, and thus the old premises about women's innate physical inferiority. A seventeenth-century examination for a doctor in Paris asked the rhetorical question "Is woman an imperfect work of nature?" All of the Aristotelian ideals about the different "humors" of the female and male survived in the popular press even after they had been rejected by the medical elite. The colder and moister humors of the female meant that women had a passive nature and thus took longer to develop in the womb. Once grown to maturity, they were better able to withstand the pain of childbirth.

Even without reference to the humors, medical and scientific texts supported the limited domestic role for women. Malebranche, a French seventeenth-century philosopher, noted that the delicate fibers of the woman's brain made her overly sensitive to all that came to it; thus she could not deal with ideas or form abstractions. Her body and mind were so relatively weak that she must stay within the protective confines of the home to be safe.

No amount of anatomical dissection dispelled old bits of misinformation or changed the old misconceptions about women's reproductive organs. Illustrations continued to show the uterus shaped like a flask with two horns, and guides for midwives gave the principal role in labor to the fetus. As in Greek and Roman medical texts these new "scientific" works assumed that women's bodies dictated their principal function, procreation. Yet even this role was devalued. All of the evidence of dissection and deductive reasoning reaffirmed the superiority of the male's role in reproduction. Men discovered the spermatazoon, but not the ovum. They believed that semen was the single active agent. Much as Aristotle had done almost two millennia earlier, seventeenth-century scientific study hypothesized that the female supplied the "matter," while the life and essence of the embryo came from the sperm alone.

These denigrating and erroneous conclusions were reaffirmed by the work of the seventeenth-century English scientist William Harvey. Having discovered the circulation of the blood, Harvey turned his considerable talents to the study of human reproduction and published his conclusions in 1651. He dissected female deer at all stages of their cycle, when pregnant and when not. He studied chickens and roosters. With all of this dissection and all of this observation he hypothesized an explanation for procreation and a rhapsody to male semen far more extreme than anything Aristotle had reasoned. The woman, like the hen with her unfertilized egg, supplies the matter, the man gives it form and life. The semen, he explained, had almost magical power to "elaborate, concoct"; it was "vivifying" . . . endowed with force and spirit and generative influence," coming as it did from "vessels so elaborate, and endowed with such vital energy." So powerful was this fluid that it did not even have to reach the woman's uterus or remain in the vagina. Rather he believed it gave off a "fecundating power," leaving the woman's body to play a passive, or secondary, role. Simple contact with this magical elixir of life worked like lightning, or—drawing on another set of his experiments—"in the same way as iron touched by the magnet is endowed with its powers and can attract other iron to it." The woman was but the receiver and the receptacle.

Anatomy and physiology confirmed the innate inferiority of woman and her limited reproductive function. They also proved as "scientific truth" all of the traditional negative images of the female nature. A sixteenth-century Italian anatomist accepted Galen's view and believed the ovaries to be internal testicles. He explained their strange placement so "as to keep her from perceiving and ascertaining her sufficient perfection," and to humble her "continual desire to dominate." An early-seventeenth-century French book on childbirth instructed the midwife to tie the umbilical cord far from the body to assure a long penis and a well-spoken young man for a male child and close to the body to give the female a straighter form and to ensure that she would talk less.

No one questioned the equally ancient and traditional connection between physiology and nature: the role of the uterus in determining a woman's behavior. The organ's potential influence confirmed the female's irrationality and her need to accept a subordinate role to the male. The sixteenth-century Italian anatomist Fallopio repeated Aristotle's idea that the womb lusted for the male in its desire to procreate. The French sixteenth-century doctor and writer Rabelais took Plato's view of the womb as insatiable, like an animal out of control when denied sexual intercourse, the cause of that singularly female ailment, "hysteria." Other sixteenth- and seventeenth-century writers on women and their health adopted all of the most misogynistic explanations of the traditional Greek and Roman authorities. No menstruation meant a diseased womb, an organ suffocating in a kind of female excrement. Only intercourse with a man could prevent or cure the condition. Left untreated the uterus would put pressure on other organs, cause convulsions, or drive the woman crazy. Thus, the male remained the key agent in the woman's life. She was innately inferior, potentially irrational, and lost to ill-health and madness without his timely intervention.

So much changed from the fifteenth to the eighteenth centuries in the ways in which women and men perceived their world, its institutions and attitudes. The Renaissance offered the exhilaration of a society in which the individual could be freed from traditional limitations. In the spirit of Humanistic and scientific inquiry men questioned and reformulated assumptions about the mind's capabilities and the description of the natural universe. New methods of reasoning and discourse, of observation and experimentation, evolved and led to the reorientation of the natural universe and more accurate descriptions of the physical world, including man's own body. Yet when it came to questions and assumptions about women's function and role and to descriptions of her nature and her body, no new answers were formulated. Instead, inspired by the intellectual excitement of the times and the increasing confidence in their own perceptions of the spiritual and material world, men argued even more strongly from traditional premises, embellishing and revitalizing the ancient beliefs. Instead of breaking with tradition, descriptions of the female accumulated traditions: the classical, the religious, the literary, the customary, and the legal—all stated afresh in the secular language of the new age. Instead of being freed, women were ringed with yet more binding and seemingly incontrovertible versions of the traditional attitudes about their inferior nature, their proper function and role, and their subordinate relationship to men.

With the advent of printing, men were able to disseminate these negative conclusions about women as they never could before. From the sixteenth century on the printing presses brought the new tracts, pamphlets, treatises, broadsides, and engravings to increasing numbers of Europeans: pictures of the sperm as a tiny, fully formed infant; works by scholars and jurists explaining the female's "natural" physical and legal incapacity; romances and ballads telling of unchaste damsels and vengeful wives set to plague man.

Although these misogynistic attitudes about women flourished and spread, the defense of women had also begun. In her *Book of the City of Ladies* Christine de Pizan, the fifteenth-century writer, asks why no one had spoken on their behalf before, why the "accusations and slanders" had gone uncontradicted for so long? Her allegorical mentor, "Rectitude," replies, "Let me tell you that in the long run, everything comes to a head at the right time."

The world of the courts had widened the perimeters of women's expectations and given some women increased opportunities. However, for the vast majority of women, still not conscious of their disadvantaged and subordinate status, changes in material circumstances had a far greater impact. From the seventeenth to the twentieth centuries more women were able to live the life restricted in previous ages to the few. In Europe's salons and parlors they found increased comfort, greater security, and new ways to value their traditional roles and functions. For these women, "the right time"—the moment for questioning and rejecting the ancient premises of European society—lay in the future.

5

LADY MARY WORTLEY MONTAGUE
Letter on Turkish Smallpox Inoculation

Lady Mary Wortley Montague, an English aristocrat, came down with smallpox in 1715. She survived, but was badly scarred by the rash that accompanied the often-fatal disease. Her younger brother died from smallpox, one of the tens of thousands who succumbed in epidemics across Europe and around the world in the eighteenth and nineteenth centuries. Two years after her recovery Montague traveled to Istanbul with her husband, who was the British ambassador to the Ottoman Empire. There, she witnessed a new approach to warding off smallpox infections, as she described in the following letter to a friend in England. What process does Montague describe in her letter? What was her response to the events she witnessed in Turkey?

Source: *Letters of Lady Mary Wortley Montague, written during her travels in Europe, Asia, and Africa, to which are added poems by the same author* (Bordeaux: J. Pinard, 1805). The UCLA Louis M. Darling Biomedical Library, History and Special Collections Division. Also available from Gutenberg E-Books at Lady Mary Wortley Montague, Her Life and Letters (1689–1762). Author: Lewis Melville. Release Date: January 4, 2004 [EBook #10590].

THINKING HISTORICALLY

This letter provides a clear example of how scientific observation can change the material world in which we live. After observing the Turkish smallpox inoculation, Montague had her son and daughter inoculated. In fact, she became an advocate for smallpox inoculation in England and played an important role in persuading the English medical profession to support the innovative procedure. Montague paved the way for a safer vaccine, developed by Edward Jenner in 1796, that would eventually eradicate the disease from the planet.

Despite her admirable efforts, it was difficult to convince Europeans to embrace smallpox inoculation, which had been practiced in Asia for centuries. Even though the effectiveness of this technology came to be recognized in England during Montague's lifetime, the French and other Europeans, according to Voltaire, thought that the English were "fools and madmen" for experimenting with inoculation. What does this suggest about the nature of scientific discovery? Besides lack of knowledge, what other obstacles need to be overcome? What does this resistance say about how revolutionary the "scientific revolution" was?

To Mrs. S. C., Adrianople, April 1, O.S.

A Propos of distempers, I am going to tell you a thing, that will make you wish yourself here. The small pox, so fatal, and so general amongst us, is here entirely harmless, by the invention of ingrafting, which is the term they give it. There is a set of old women, who make it their business to perform the operation, every autumn, in the month of September, when the great heat is abated. People send to one another to know if any of their family has a mind to have the small-pox; they make parties for this purpose, and when they are met (commonly fifteen or sixteen together) the old woman comes with a nut-shell full of the matter of the best sort of small pox, and asks what vein you please to have opened. She immediately rips open that you offer to her, with a large needle (which gives you no more pain than a common scratch), and puts into the vein as much matter as can lie upon the head of her needle, and after that, binds up the little wound with a hollow bit of shell, and in this manner opens four or five veins. The Grecians have commonly the superstition of opening one in the middle of the forehead, one in each arm, and one in the breast, to mark the sign of the cross; but this has a very ill effect, all these wounds leaving little scars, and is not done by those that are not superstitious, who choose to have them in the legs, or that part of the arm that is concealed. The children or young patients play together all the rest of the day, and are in perfect health to the eighth.

Then the fever begins to seize them, and they keep their beds two days, very seldom three. They have very rarely above twenty or thirty in their faces, which never mark, and in eight days time they are as well as before their illness. Where they are wounded, there remains running sores during the distemper, which I don't doubt is a great relief to it. Every year thousands undergo this operation, and the French ambassador says pleasantly that they take the small-pox here by way of diversion, as they take the waters in other countries. There is no example of any one that has died in it, and you may believe I am well satisfied of the safety of this experiment, since I intend to try it on my dear little son. I am patriot enough to take pains to bring this useful invention into fashion in England, and I should not fail to write to some of our doctors very particularly about it, if I knew any one of them that I thought had virtue enough to destroy such a considerable branch of their revenue, for the good of mankind. But that distemper is too beneficial to them, not to expose to all their resentment the hardy wight[1] that should undertake to put an end to it. Perhaps if I live to return, I may, however have the courage to war with them. Upon this occasion, admire the heroism in the heart of

Your friend, etc. etc.

[1] Creature. [Ed.]

6

LYNDA NORENE SHAFFER
China, Technology, and Change

In this essay an important contemporary world historian asks us to compare the revolutionary consequences of scientific and technological changes that occurred in China and Europe before the seventeenth century. What is Shaffer's argument? In what ways was the European scientific revolution different from the changes in China she describes here?

THINKING HISTORICALLY

What exactly was the impact of printing, the compass, and gunpowder in Europe? What was the "before" and "after" for each of these innovations? What, according to Shaffer, was the situation in China before and after each of these innovations? Were these innovations as revolutionary in China as they were in Europe?

Source: Lynda Norene Shaffer, "China, Technology, and Change," *World History Bulletin* 4, no. 1 (Fall/Winter 1986–1987): 1–6.

Francis Bacon (1561–1626), an early advocate of the empirical method, upon which the scientific revolution was based, attributed Western Europe's early modern take-off to three things in particular: printing, the compass, and gunpowder. Bacon had no idea where these things had come from, but historians now know that all three were invented in China. Since, unlike Europe, China did not take off onto a path leading from the scientific to the Industrial Revolution, some historians are now asking why these inventions were so revolutionary in Western Europe and, apparently, so unrevolutionary in China.

In fact, the question has been posed by none other than Joseph Needham, the foremost English-language scholar of Chinese science and technology. It is only because of Needham's work that the Western academic community has become aware that until Europe's take-off, China was the unrivaled world leader in technological development. That is why it is so disturbing that Needham himself has posed this apparent puzzle. The English-speaking academic world relies upon him and repeats him; soon this question and the vision of China that it implies will become dogma. Traditional China will take on supersociety qualities—able to contain the power of printing, to rein in the potential of the compass, even to muffle the blast of gunpowder.

The impact of these inventions on Western Europe is well known. Printing not only eliminated much of the opportunity for human copying errors, it also encouraged the production of more copies of old books and an increasing number of new books. As written material became both cheaper and more easily available, intellectual activity increased. Printing would eventually be held responsible, at least in part, for the spread of classical humanism and other ideas from the Renaissance. It is also said to have stimulated the Protestant Reformation, which urged a return to the Bible as the primary religious authority.

The introduction of gunpowder in Europe made castles and other medieval fortifications obsolete (since it could be used to blow holes in their walls) and thus helped to liberate Western Europe from feudal aristocratic power. As an aid to navigation the compass facilitated the Portuguese- and Spanish-sponsored voyages that led to Atlantic Europe's sole possession of the Western Hemisphere, as well as the Portuguese circumnavigation of Africa, which opened up the first all-sea route from Western Europe to the long-established ports of East Africa and Asia.

Needham's question can thus be understood to mean, Why didn't China use gunpowder to destroy feudal walls? Why didn't China use the compass to cross the Pacific and discover America, or to find an all-sea route to Western Europe? Why didn't China undergo a Renaissance or Reformation? The implication is that even though China possessed these technologies, it did not change much. Essentially Needham's question is asking, What was wrong with China?

Actually, there was nothing wrong with China. China was changed fundamentally by these inventions. But in order to see the changes, one must abandon the search for peculiarly European events in Chinese history, and look instead at China itself before and after these breakthroughs.

To begin, one should note that China possessed all three of these technologies by the latter part of the Tang dynasty (618–906)—between four and six hundred years before they appeared in Europe. And it was during just that time, from about 850, when the Tang dynasty began to falter, until 960, when the Song dynasty (960–1279) was established, that China underwent fundamental changes in all spheres. In fact, historians are now beginning to use the term *revolution* when referring to technological and commercial changes that culminated in the Song dynasty, in the same way that they refer to the changes in eighteenth- and nineteenth-century England as the Industrial Revolution. And the word might well be applied to other sorts of changes in China during this period.

For example, the Tang dynasty elite was aristocratic, but that of the Song was not. No one has ever considered whether the invention of gunpowder contributed to the demise of China's aristocrats, which occurred between 750 and 960, shortly after its invention. Gunpowder may, indeed, have been a factor although it is unlikely that its importance lay in blowing up feudal walls. Tang China enjoyed such internal peace that its aristocratic lineages did not engage in castle-building of the sort typical in Europe. Thus, China did not have many feudal fortifications to blow up.

The only wall of significance in this respect was the Great Wall, which was designed to keep steppe nomads from invading China. In fact, gunpowder may have played a role in blowing holes in this wall, for the Chinese could not monopolize the terrible new weapon, and their nomadic enemies to the north soon learned to use it against them. The Song dynasty ultimately fell to the Mongols, the most formidable force ever to emerge from the Eurasian steppe. Gunpowder may have had a profound effect on China—exposing a united empire to foreign invasion and terrible devastation—but an effect quite opposite to the one it had on Western Europe.

On the other hand, the impact of printing on China was in some ways very similar to its later impact on Europe. For example, printing contributed to a rebirth of classical (that is, preceding the third century A.D.) Confucian learning, helping to revive a fundamentally humanistic outlook that had been pushed aside for several centuries.

After the fall of the Han dynasty (206 B.C.–A.D. 220), Confucianism had lost much of its credibility as a world view, and it eventually lost its central place in the scholarly world. It was replaced by Buddhism, which had come from India. Buddhists believed that much human pain and confusion resulted from the pursuit of illusory pleasures and dubious ambitions: Enlightenment and, ultimately, salvation would come from a progressive disengagement from the real world, which they also believed to be illusory. This point of view dominated Chinese intellectual life until the ninth century. Thus the academic and intellectual comeback of classical Confucianism was in essence a return to a more optimistic literature that affirmed the world as humans had made it.

The resurgence of Confucianism within the scholarly community was due to many factors, but printing was certainly one of the most important. Although it was invented by Buddhist monks in China, and at first benefited Buddhism, by the middle of the tenth century, printers were turning out innumerable copies of the classical Confucian corpus. This return of scholars to classical learning was part of a more general movement that shared not only its humanistic features with the later Western European Renaissance, but certain artistic trends as well.

Furthermore, the Protestant Reformation in Western Europe was in some ways reminiscent of the emergence and eventual triumph of Neo-Confucian philosophy. Although the roots of Neo-Confucianism can be found in the ninth century, the man who created what would become its most orthodox synthesis was Zhu Xi (Chu Hsi, 1130–1200). Neo-Confucianism was significantly different from classical Confucianism, for it had undergone an intellectual (and political) confrontation with Buddhism and had emerged profoundly changed. It is of the utmost importance to understand that not only was Neo-Confucianism new, it was also heresy, even during Zhu Xi's lifetime. It did not triumph until the thirteenth century, and it was not until 1313 (when Mongol conquerors ruled China) that Zhu Xi's commentaries on the classics became the single authoritative text against which all academic opinion was judged.

In the same way that Protestantism emerged out of a confrontation with the Roman Catholic establishment and asserted the individual Christian's autonomy, Neo-Confucianism emerged as a critique of Buddhist ideas that had taken hold in China, and it asserted an individual moral capacity totally unrelated to the ascetic practices and prayers of the Buddhist priesthood. In the twelfth century Neo-Confucianists lifted the work of Mencius (Meng Zi, 370–290 B.C.) out of obscurity and assigned it a place in the corpus second only to that of the *Analects of Confucius*. Many facets of Mencius appealed to the Neo-Confucianists, but one of the most important was his argument that humans by nature are fundamentally good. Within the context of the Song dynasty, this was an assertion that morality could be pursued through an engagement in human affairs, and that the Buddhist monks' withdrawal from life's mainstream did not bestow upon them any special virtue.

The importance of these philosophical developments notwith-standing, printing probably had its greatest impact on the Chinese po-litical system. The origin of the civil service examination system in China can be traced back to the Han dynasty, but in the Song dynasty government-administered examinations became the most important route to political power in China. For almost a thousand years (except the early period of Mongol rule), China was governed by men who had come to power simply because they had done exceedingly well in examinations on the Neo-Confucian canon. At any one time thousands of students were studying for the exams, and thousands of inexpensive books were required. Without printing such a system would not have been possible.

The development of this alternative to aristocratic rule was one of the most radical changes in world history. Since the examinations were ultimately open to 98 percent of all males (actors were one of the few groups excluded), it was the most democratic system in the world prior to the development of representative democracy and popular suffrage in Western Europe in the eighteenth and nineteenth centuries. (There were some small-scale systems, such as the classical Greek city-states, which might be considered more democratic, but nothing comparable in size to Song China or even the modern nation-states of Europe.)

Finally we come to the compass. Suffice it to say that during the Song dynasty, China developed the world's largest and most technologi-cally sophisticated merchant marine and navy. By the fifteenth century its ships were sailing from the north Pacific to the east coast of Africa. They could have made the arduous journey around the tip of Africa and on into Portuguese ports; however, they had no reason to do so. Although the Western European economy was prospering, it offered nothing that China could not acquire much closer to home at much less cost. In particular, wool, Western Europe's most important export, could easily be obtained along China's northern frontier.

Certainly, the Portuguese and the Spanish did not make their un-precedented voyages out of idle curiosity. They were trying to go to the Spice Islands, in what is now Indonesia, in order to acquire the most valuable commercial items of the time. In the fifteenth century these islands were the world's sole suppliers of the fine spices, such as cloves, nutmeg, and mace, as well as a source for the more generally available pepper. It was this spice market that lured Columbus westward from Spain and drew Vasco Da Gama around Africa and across the Indian Ocean.

After the invention of the compass, China also wanted to go to the Spice Islands and, in fact, did go, regularly—but Chinese ships did not have to go around the world to get there. The Atlantic nations of Western Europe, on the other hand, had to buy spices from Venice (which con-trolled the Mediterranean trade routes) or from other Italian city-states;

or they had to find a new way to the Spice Islands. It was necessity that mothered those revolutionary routes that ultimately changed the world.

Gunpowder, printing, the compass—clearly these three inventions changed China as much as they changed Europe. And it should come as no surprise that changes wrought in China between the eighth and tenth centuries were different from changes wrought in Western Europe between the thirteenth and fifteenth centuries. It would, of course, be unfair and ahistorical to imply that something was wrong with Western Europe because the technologies appeared there later. It is equally unfair to ask why the Chinese did not accidentally bump into the Western Hemisphere while sailing east across the Pacific to find the wool markets of Spain.

7

SUGITA GEMPAKU

A Dutch Anatomy Lesson in Japan

Sugita Gempaku* (1733–1817) was a Japanese physician who, as he tells us here in his memoir, suddenly discovered the value of Western medical science when he chanced to witness a dissection shortly after he obtained a Dutch anatomy book.

What was it that Sugita Gempaku learned on that day in 1771? What were the differences between the treatments of anatomy in the Chinese *Book of Medicine* and the Dutch medical book? What accounts for these differences?

THINKING HISTORICALLY

How might the Dutch book have changed the way the author practiced medicine? How did it change his knowledge of the human body? How did it change the relevance of his knowledge of the human body to the medicine he practiced? How revolutionary was the new knowledge for Sugita Gempaku?

* SOO gee tah   gehm PAH koo

Source: Sugita Gempaku, *Ranto Kotohajime* (The Beginning of Dutch Studies in the East), in *Japan: A Documentary History*, ed. David J. Lu (Armonk, NY: M. E. Sharpe, 2005), 1:264–66. Iwanami Shoten, *Nihon Koten Bunka Taikei* (Major Compilation of Japanese Classics) (Tokyo: Iwanami Shoten, 1969), 95:487–93.

Whenever I met Hiraga Gennai (1729–1779), we talked to each other on this matter: "As we have learned, the Dutch method of scholarly investigation through field work and surveys is truly amazing. If we can directly understand books written by them, we will benefit greatly. However, it is pitiful that there has been no one who has set his mind on working in this field. Can we somehow blaze this trail? It is impossible to do it in Edo. Perhaps it is best if we ask translators in Nagasaki to make some translations. If one book can be completely translated, there will be an immeasurable benefit to the country." Every time we spoke in this manner, we deplored the impossibility of implementing our desires. However, we did not vainly lament the matter for long.

Somehow, miraculously I obtained a book on anatomy written in that country. It may well be that Dutch studies in this country began when I thought of comparing the illustrations in the book with real things. It was a strange and even miraculous happening that I was able to obtain that book in that particular spring of 1771. Then at the night of the third day of the third month, I received a letter from a man by the name of Tokuno Bambei, who was in the service of the then Town Commissioner, Magaribuchi Kai-no-kami. Tokuno stated in his letter that "A post-mortem examination of the body of a condemned criminal by a resident physician will be held tomorrow at Senjukotsukahara. You are welcome to witness it if you so desire." At one time my colleague by the name of Kosugi Genteki had an occasion to witness a post-mortem dissection of a body when he studied under Dr. Yamawaki Tōyō of Kyoto. After seeing the dissection firsthand, Kosugi remarked that what was said by the people of old was false and simply could not be trusted. "The people of old spoke of nine internal organs, and nowadays, people divide them into five viscera and six internal organs. That [perpetuates] inaccuracy," Kosugi once said. Around that time (1759) Dr. Tōyō published a book entitled *Zōshi* (*On Internal Organs*). Having read that book, I had hoped that some day I could witness a dissection. When I also acquired a Dutch book on anatomy, I wanted above all to compare the two to find out which one accurately described the truth. I rejoiced at this unusually fortunate circumstance, and my mind could not entertain any other thought. However, a thought occurred to me that I should not monopolize this good fortune, and decided to share it with those of my colleagues who were diligent in the pursuit of their medicine. . . . Among those I invited was one [Maeno] Ryōtaku (1723–1803). . . .

The next day, when we arrived at the location . . . Ryōtaku reached under his kimono to produce a Dutch book and showed it to us. "This is a Dutch book of anatomy called *Tabulae Anatomicae*. I bought this a few years ago when I went to Nagasaki, and kept it." As I examined it, it was the same book I had and was of the same edition. We held each other's hands and exclaimed: "What a coincidence!" Ryōtaku continued by saying: "When I went to Nagasaki, I learned and heard," and opened his book. "These are called *long* in Dutch, they are lungs," he taught us. "This is *hart*, or the heart. When it says *maag* it is the stomach, and when it says *milt* it is the spleen." However, they did not look like the heart given in the Chinese medical books, and none of us were sure until we could actually see the dissection.

Thereafter we went together to the place which was especially set for us to observe the dissection in Kotsukahara. . . . The regular man who performed the chore of dissection was ill, and his grandfather, who was ninety years of age, came in his place. He was a healthy old man. He had experienced many dissections since his youth, and boasted that he dissected a number of bodies. Those dissections were performed in those days by men of the *eta*[1] class. . . . That day, the old butcher pointed to this and that organ. After the heart, liver, gall bladder, and stomach were identified, he pointed to other parts for which there were no names. "I don't know their names. But I have dissected quite a few bodies from my youthful days. Inside of everyone's abdomen there were these parts and those parts." Later, after consulting the anatomy chart, it became clear to me that I saw an arterial tube, a vein, and the suprarenal gland. The old butcher again said, "Every time I had a dissection, I pointed out to those physicians many of these parts, but not a single one of them questioned 'what was this?' or 'what was that?'" We compared the body as dissected against the charts both Ryōtaku and I had, and could not find a single variance from the charts. The Chinese *Book of Medicine* (*Yi Jing*) says that the lungs are like the eight petals of the lotus flower, with three petals hanging in front, three in back, and two petals forming like two ears and that the liver has three petals to the left and four petals to the right. There were no such divisions, and the positions and shapes of intestines and gastric organs were all different from those taught by the old theories. The official physicians, Dr. Okada Yōsen and Dr. Fujimoto Rissen, have witnessed dissection seven or eight times. Whenever they witnessed the dissection, they found that the old theories contradicted reality. Each time they were perplexed and could not resolve their doubts. Every time they wrote

---

[1] The eta were an untouchable caste in Japan, defined by their restriction to certain occupations associated with death: tanning or working with hides, cremating the dead, butchering meat, and, thus, doing autopsies. They could not be physicians. [Ed.]

down what they thought was strange. They wrote in their books. "The more we think of it, there must be fundamental differences in the bodies of Chinese and of the eastern barbarians [i.e., Japanese]." I could see why they wrote this way.

That day, after the dissection was over, we decided that we also should examine the shape of the skeletons left exposed on the execution ground. We collected the bones, and examined a number of them. Again, we were struck by the fact that they all differed from the old theories while conforming to the Dutch charts.

The three of us, Ryōtaku, [Nakagawa] Junan (1739–1786), and I went home together. On the way home we spoke to each other and felt the same way. "How marvelous was our actual experience today. It is a shame that we were ignorant of these things until now. As physicians who serve their masters through medicine, we performed our duties in complete ignorance of the true form of the human body. How disgraceful it is. Somehow, through this experience, let us investigate further the truth about the human body. If we practice medicine with this knowledge behind us, we can make contributions for people under heaven and on this earth." Ryōtaku spoke to us. "Indeed, I agree with you wholeheartedly." Then I spoke to my two companions. "Somehow if we can translate anew this book called *Tabulae Anatomicae*, we can get a clear notion of the human body inside out. It will have great benefit in the treatment of our patients. Let us do our best to read it and understand it without the help of translators." Ryōtaku responded: "I have been wanting to read Dutch books for some time, but there has been no friend who would share my ambitions. I have spent days lamenting it. If both of you wish, I have been in Nagasaki before and have retained some Dutch. Let us use it as a beginning to tackle the book together." After hearing it, I answered, "This is simply wonderful. If we are to join our efforts, I shall also resolve to do my very best." . . .

The next day, we assembled at the house of Ryōtaku and recalled the happenings of the previous day. When we faced that *Tabulae Anatomicae*, we felt as if we were setting sail on a great ocean in a ship without oars or a rudder. With the magnitude of the work before us, we were dumbfounded by our own ignorance. However, Ryōtaku had been thinking of this for some time, and he had been in Nagasaki. He knew some Dutch through studying and hearing, and knew some sentence patterns and words. He was also ten years older than I, and we decided to make him head of our group and our teacher. At that time I did not know the twenty-five letters of the Dutch alphabet. I decided to study the language with firm determination, but I had to acquaint myself with letters and words gradually.

8

BENJAMIN FRANKLIN

Letter on a Balloon Experiment in 1783

Benjamin Franklin (1706–1790) was the preeminent statesman, diplomat, and spokesman for the British colonies that became the United States during his long lifetime. Trained as a candle maker and printer, he became a journalist, publisher, merchant, homespun philosopher, and inveterate inventor. He invented the lightning rod, the Franklin stove, bifocals, and the medical catheter, among other things. His inventions sprang from a gift of immense curiosity and an exhaustive reading in the science of his day.

Franklin, sometimes called "the first American," represented the fledging Republic in France during the Revolution, ensuring French participation against the British. In 1783 he signed the second Treaty of Paris, by which the British recognized the independence of the United States. Franklin was the only founding father to sign the Declaration of Independence (1776), the Treaty of Paris (1783), and the Constitution of the United States (1789). Throughout his life Franklin furthered his interest in scientific experiment and invention. In December of 1783, he wrote to a friend in England about a recent invention that he had witnessed in Paris: an early experiment in air travel in a balloon. What did Franklin see, and what did it mean to him?

THINKING HISTORICALLY

What evidence do you see in this letter that the scientific revolution was a genuinely revolutionary change? What was revolutionary about it? What evidence do you see that the people of the time thought they were living in a revolutionary age? How would you compare their attitudes with those of people today toward modern technological innovations?

To Sir Joseph Banks[1]

Passy, Dec. 1, 1783.

Dear Sir:—
In mine of yesterday I promised to give you an account of Messrs. Charles & Robert's experiment, which was to have been made this day, and at which I intended to be present. Being a little indisposed, and the

---

[1] Banks (1743–1820) was a leading British botanist and naturalist. He sailed to the South Pacific with Captain James Cook and served as president of the Royal Society, trustee of the British Museum, and advisor to George III, whom he encouraged to fund numerous scientific expeditions. (He was also an early British recipient of a smallpox vaccination, in 1760.) [Ed.]

Source: Nathan G. Goodman, ed., *The Ingenious Dr. Franklin, Selected Scientific Letters of Benjamin Franklin* (Philadelphia: University of Pennsylvania Press, 1931), 99–102.

air cool, and the ground damp, I declined going into the garden of the Tuileries, where the balloon was placed, not knowing how long I might be obliged to wait there before it was ready to depart, and chose to stay in my carriage near the statue of Louis XV, from whence I could well see it rise, and have an extensive view of the region of air through which, as the wind sat, it was likely to pass. The morning was foggy, but about one o'clock the air became tolerably clear, to the great satisfaction of the spectators, who were infinite, notice having been given of the intended experiment several days before in the papers, so that all Paris was out, either about the Tuileries, on the quays and bridges, in the fields, the streets, at the windows, or on the tops of houses, besides the inhabitants of all the towns and villages of the environs. Never before was a philosophical experiment so magnificently attended. Some guns were fired to give notice that the departure of the balloon was near, and a small one was discharged, which went to an amazing height, there being but little wind to make it deviate from its perpendicular course, and at length the sight of it was lost. Means were used, I am told, to prevent the great balloon's rising so high as might endanger its bursting. Several bags of sand were taken on board before the cord that held it down was cut, and the whole weight being then too much to be lifted, such a quantity was discharged as to permit its rising slowly. Thus it would sooner arrive at that region where it would be in equilibrio with the surrounding air, and by discharging more sand afterwards, it might go higher if desired. Between one and two o'clock, all eyes were gratified with seeing it rise majestically from among the trees, and ascend gradually above the buildings, a most beautiful spectacle. When it was about two hundred feet high, the brave adventurers held out and waved a little white pennant, on both sides [of] their car, to salute the spectators, who returned loud claps of applause. The wind was very little, so that the object though moving to the northward, continued long in view; and it was a great while before the admiring people began to disperse. The persons embarked were Mr. Charles, professor of experimental philosophy, and a zealous promoter of that science; and one of the Messieurs Robert, the very ingenious constructors of the machine. When it arrived at its height, which I suppose might be three or four hundred toises,[2] it appeared to have only horizontal motion. I had a pocket-glass, with which I followed it, till I lost sight first of the men, then of the car, and when I last saw the balloon, it appeared no bigger than a walnut. I write this at seven in the evening. What became of them is not yet known here. I hope they descended by daylight, so as to see and avoid falling among trees or on houses, and that the experiment was completed without any mischievous accident, which the novelty of it and the want of experience might well occasion.

---

[2] twaz A height rod equal to 1.949 meters (or about 2 yards). [Ed.]

I am the more anxious for the event, because I am not well informed of the means provided for letting themselves down, and the loss of these very ingenious men would not only be a discouragement to the progress of the art, but be a sensible loss to science and society.

I shall inclose one of the tickets of admission, on which the globe was represented, as originally intended, but is altered by the pen to show its real state when it went off. When the tickets were engraved the car was to have been hung to the neck of the globe, as represented by a little drawing I have made in the corner.

I suppose it may have been an apprehension of danger in straining too much the balloon or tearing the silk, that induced the constructors to throw a net over it, fixed to a hoop which went round its middle, and to hang the car to that hoop.

Tuesday morning, December 2d.—I am relieved from my anxiety by hearing that the adventurers descended well near L'Isle Adam before sunset. This place is near seven leagues from Paris. Had the wind blown fresh they might have gone much farther.

If I receive any further particulars of importance, I shall communicate them hereafter.

With great esteem, I am, dear sir, your most obedient and most humble servant,

FRANKLIN

P.S. *Tuesday evening.*—Since writing the above I have received the printed paper and the manuscript containing some particulars of the experiment, which I enclose. I hear further that the travellers had perfect command of their carriage, descending as they pleased by letting some of the inflammable air escape, and rising again by discharging some sand; that they descended over a field so low as to talk with the labourers in passing, and mounted again to pass a hill. The little balloon falling at Vincennes shows that mounting higher it met with a current of air in a contrary direction, an observation that may be of use to future aerial voyagers.

■ REFLECTIONS

Was there a scientific revolution in the seventeenth and eighteenth centuries? By most measures we would have to say "yes." There were new polished-glass instruments with which to observe and measure; books, theories, diagrams, debates, and discoveries emerged at a dizzying pace. Age-old authorities—Aristotle, Ptolemy, even the Bible—were called into question. The wisdom of the ages was interrogated for evidence and forced to submit to tests by experiment.

There was a revolution in the way Europeans looked at their surroundings. In the words of Shakespeare, the great English dramatist, the world became a stage, a spectacle apart that could be viewed and analyzed by objective observers. Nature no longer displayed its forces as omens or metaphors. The rainbow was no longer a sign of hope, the comet a harbinger of divine disapproval. Heavenly events might be explained in the same way as were events on Earth. Newton's rules underline the simplicity of assumptions that nature is uniform and not unnecessarily complex. We can assume that the fire in the fireplace has the same qualities as the fire of the sun, that unchanging qualities of hardness, mobility, or gravity would apply to objects too distant to measure as they do to those within our grasp. Nature follows laws that humans can derive by experiment and induction.

Goldstone reminds us that many of the scientific developments in Europe sprang from foreign innovations, and in some fields Europe was not as advanced as other societies. Lady Mary Montague provides a dramatic example of that fact. Yet the scientific revolution's unique combination of observation and generalization, experimentation and mathematics, induction and deduction established a body of knowledge and a method for research that proved lasting and irreversible.

Why was it that China, so scientifically and technologically adept during the Sung dynasty, pictured hearts and lungs as flower petals in the late-Ming and early-Qing seventeenth century? Was it that Chinese science lost momentum or changed direction? Or does such a question, as Lynda Shaffer warns, judge China unfairly by Western standards? Do the petal hearts reflect a different set of interests rather than a failure of Chinese science?

Chinese scientists excelled in acupuncture, massage, and herbal medicine, while European scientists excelled in surgery. It turned out that the inner workings of the human body were better revealed in surgical dissection than in muscle manipulation or pharmacology. And, as Sugita Gempaku reminds us, the Europeans not only cut and removed, but they also named what they found and tried to understand how it worked. Perhaps the major difference between science in Europe and that in India, China, and Japan in the seventeenth century was one of perspective: Europeans were beginning to imagine the human body as a machine and asking how it worked. In some respects, the metaphor of man as a machine proved more fruitful than organic metaphors of humans as plants or animals.

Asking probing questions and testing the answers also changed our understanding of the heavens. If mathematical calculations indicated that a star would appear at a particular spot in the heavens and it did not, Galileo might just as soon have questioned the observation as the math. From the seventeenth century on, scientists would check one or the other on the assumption that observation and mathematics could be brought together to understand the same event, that they would have to be in agreement, and that such agreement could lead to laws that could then be tested and proved or disproved.

It is this method of inquiry, not the discoveries, that was new. For the scientific method that emerged during this period constituted a systematic means of inquiry based on agreed-upon rules of hypothesis, experimentation, theory testing, law, and dissemination. This scientific inquiry was a social process in two important ways: First, any scientific discovery had to be reproducible and recognized by other scientists to gain credence. Second, a community of scientists was needed to question, dismiss, or validate the work of its members.

Europe in the seventeenth century saw the proliferation of numerous scientific associations, academies, institutes, and public experiments. These numerous organizations testified not only to a growing interest in science but also to a continuing public conversation. Science in Europe thus became a matter of public concern, a popular endeavor. Compare the masses of Parisians Ben Franklin described who turned out to view the balloon experiment with the few physicians gathered around Sugita Gempaku who could learn from the expertise of outcast butchers.

Ultimately, then, the difference between European science and that of India or China in the seventeenth century may have had more to do with society than with culture. The development of modern scientific methods relied on the numerous debates and discussions of a self-conscious class of gentlemen scientists in a Europe where news traveled quickly and ideas could be translated and tested with confidence across numerous borders. To what extent does science everywhere today demonstrate the hallmarks of the seventeenth-century scientific revolution?

20

Enlightenment and Revolution

Europe, the Americas, and India, 1650–1850

■ HISTORICAL CONTEXT

Much of the modern world puts its faith in science, reason, and democracy. The seventeenth-century scientific revolution established reason as the key to understanding nature. During the eighteenth century, philosophy, social organization, and government all came under the critical light of reason. Historians call this movement the "Enlightenment," and its consequences were revolutionary. Most—though, as we shall see, not all—people believed that reason would eventually lead to freedom. Freedom of thought, religion, and association, and political liberties and representative governments were hailed as hallmarks of the Age of Enlightenment.

For some, enlightened society meant a more controlled rather than a more democratic society. Philosophers like Immanuel Kant and Jean Jacques Rousseau wanted people to become free but thought most people were incapable of achieving such a state. Rulers who were called "enlightened despots" believed that the application of reason to society would make people happier, but not necessarily freer.

Ultimately, however, the Enlightenment's faith in reason led to calls for political revolution as well as for schemes of order. In England in the seventeenth century, in America and France at the end of the eighteenth century, and in Latin America shortly thereafter, revolutionary governments were created according to rational principles of liberty and equality that dispatched monarchs and enshrined the rule of the people. In this chapter we will concentrate on the heritage of the Enlightenment, examining competing tendencies toward order and revolution, stability and liberty, equality and freedom. We will also compare the American and the French Revolutions, and these with the later revolutions in Latin America. Finally, we will extend our understanding of the global nature of the Enlightenment by looking at similar developments in India.

■ THINKING HISTORICALLY

Close Reading and Interpretation of Texts

At the core of the Enlightenment was a trust in reasoned discussion, a belief that people could understand each other, even if they were not in agreement. Such understanding demanded clear and concise communication in a world where the masses were often swayed by fiery sermons and flamboyant rhetoric. But the Enlightenment also put its faith in the written word and a literate public. Ideas were debated face to face in the salons and coffeehouses of Europe and its colonies, but it was through letters, diaries, the new world of newspapers, and the burgeoning spread of printed books that the people of the Enlightenment learned what they and their neighbors thought.

It is appropriate, then, for us to read the selections in this chapter — most primary sources — in the spirit in which they were written. We will pay special attention to the words and language that the authors use and will attempt to understand exactly what they meant, even why they chose the words they did. Such explication is a twofold process; we must understand the words first and foremost; then we must strive to understand the words in their proper context, as they were intended by the author. To achieve our first goal, we will paraphrase, a difficult task because the eighteenth-century writing style differs greatly from our own: Sentences are longer and arguments are often complex. Vocabularies were broad during this period, and we may encounter words that are used in ways unknown to us and out of usage today. As to our latter goal, we must try to make the vocabulary and perspective of the authors our own. Grappling with what makes the least sense to us and trying to understand why it was said is the challenge.

1

DAVID HUME

On Miracles

The European Enlightenment of the eighteenth century was the expression of a new class of intellectuals, independent of the clergy but allied with the rising middle class. Their favorite words were *reason*, *nature*, and *progress*. They applied the systematic doubt of René Descartes (1596–1650) and the reasoning method of the scientific revolution to human affairs, including religion and politics. With caustic wit and

Source: *The Philosophical Works of David Hume* (Edinburgh: A. Black and W. Tait, 1826).

good humor, they asked new questions and popularized new points of view that would eventually revolutionize Western politics and culture. While the French *philosophes* and Voltaire (1694–1778) may be the best known, the Scottish philosopher David Hume (1711–1776) may have been the most brilliant. What does Hume argue in this selection? Does he prove his point to your satisfaction? How does he use reason and nature to make his case? Is reason incompatible with religion?

THINKING HISTORICALLY

The first step in understanding what Hume means in this essay must come from a careful reading — a sentence-by-sentence exploration. Try to paraphrase each sentence, putting it into your own words. For example, you might paraphrase the first sentence like this: "I've found a way to disprove superstition; this method should be useful as long as superstition exists, which may be forever." Notice the content of such words as *just* and *check*. What does Hume mean by these words and by *prodigies*?

The second sentence is a concise definition of the scientific method. How would you paraphrase it? The second and third sentences summarize the method Hume has discovered to counter superstition. What is the meaning of the third sentence?

In the rest of the essay, Hume offers four proofs, or reasons, why miracles do not exist. How would you paraphrase each of these? Do you find these more or less convincing than his more general opening and closing arguments? What does Hume mean by *miracles*?

I flatter myself that I have discovered an argument . . . , which, if just, will, with the wise and learned, be an everlasting check to all kinds of superstitious delusion, and consequently will be useful as long as the world endures; for so long, I presume, will the accounts of miracles and prodigies be found in all history, sacred and profane. . . .

A wise man proportions his belief to the evidence. . . .

A miracle is a violation of the laws of nature; and as a firm and unalterable experience has established these laws, the proof against a miracle, from the very nature of the fact, is as entire as any argument from experience can possibly be imagined. . . . Nothing is esteemed a miracle, if it ever happens in the common course of nature. It is no miracle that a man, seemingly in good health, should die on a sudden; because such a kind of death, though more unusual than any other, has yet been frequently observed to happen. But it is a miracle that a dead man should come to life; because that has never been observed in any age or country. There must, therefore, be an uniform experience against every miraculous event, otherwise the event would not merit that appellation. And as an uniform experience amounts to a proof, there is here a direct and full *proof*, from the nature of the fact, against the existence of any miracle. . . .

(Further) there is not to be found, in all history, any miracle attested by a sufficient number of men, of such unquestioned good sense, education, and learning, as to secure us against all delusion in themselves; of such undoubted integrity, as to place them beyond all suspicion of any design to deceive others; of such credit and reputation in the eyes of mankind, as to have a great deal to lose in case of their being detected in any falsehood. . . .

Secondly, We may observe in human nature a principle which, if strictly examined, will be found to diminish extremely the assurance, which we might, from human testimony, have in any kind of prodigy. . . . The passion of *surprise* and *wonder*, arising from miracles, being an agreeable emotion, gives a sensible tendency towards the belief of those events from which it is derived. . . .

With what greediness are the miraculous accounts of travellers received, their descriptions of sea and land monsters, their relations of wonderful adventures, strange men, and uncouth manners? But if the spirit of religion join itself to the love of wonder, there is an end of common sense; and human testimony, in these circumstances, loses all pretensions to authority. A religionist may be an enthusiast, and imagine he sees what has no reality: He may know his narrative to be false, and yet persevere in it, with the best intentions in the world, for the sake of promoting so holy a cause: Or even where this delusion has not place, vanity, excited by so strong a temptation, operates on him more powerfully than on the rest of mankind in any other circumstances; and self-interest with equal force. . . .

The many instances of forged miracles and prophecies and supernatural events, which, in all ages, have either been detected by contrary evidence, or which detect themselves by their absurdity, prove sufficiently the strong propensity of mankind to the extraordinary and marvellous, and ought reasonably to beget a suspicion against all relations of this kind.[1] . . .

Thirdly, It forms a strong presumption against all supernatural and miraculous relations, that they are observed chiefly to abound among ignorant and barbarous nations; or if a civilized people has ever given admission to any of them, that people will be found to have received them from ignorant and barbarous ancestors, who transmitted them with that inviolable sanction and authority which always attend received opinions. . . .

I may add, as a *fourth* reason, which diminishes the authority of prodigies, that there is no testimony for any, even those which have not been expressly detected, that is not opposed by any infinite number of witnesses; so that not only the miracle destroys the credit of testimony, but the testimony destroys itself. To make this the better understood, let

[1] Accounts of miracles. [Ed.]

us consider, that in matters of religion, whatever is different is contrary; and that it is impossible the religions of ancient Rome, of Turkey, of Siam, and of China, should all of them be established on any solid foundation. Every miracle, therefore, pretended to have been wrought in any of these religions (and all of them abound in miracles), as its direct scope is to establish the particular system to which it is attributed; so has it the same force, though more indirectly, to overthrow every other system. In destroying a rival system, it likewise destroys the credit of those miracles on which that system was established, so that all the prodigies of different religions are to be regarded as contrary facts, and the evidences of these prodigies, whether weak or strong, as opposite to each other. . . .

Upon the whole, then, it appears, that no testimony for any kind of miracle has ever amounted to a probability, much less to a proof; and that, even supposing it amounted to proof, it would be opposed by another proof, derived from the very nature of the fact which it would endeavour to establish. It is experience only which gives authority to human testimony; and it is the same experience which assures us of the laws of nature. When, therefore, these two kinds of experience are contrary, we have nothing to do but to subtract the one from the other, and embrace an opinion either on one side or the other, with that assurance which arises from the remainder. But according to the principle here explained, this subtraction with regard to all popular religions amounts to an entire annihilation; and therefore we may establish it as a maxim, that no human testimony can have such force as to prove a miracle, and make it a just foundation for any such system of religion.

2

JEAN JACQUES ROUSSEAU

The Social Contract

Jean Jacques Rousseau (1712–1778) was one of the leading thinkers of the Enlightenment, whose ideas were as central as those of Diderot (with whom he studied and quarreled), Voltaire (next to whom he is buried in the Pantheon), and Hume (who sheltered him in England toward the end of his life). Rousseau's indifference to formal religion both reflected and influenced French Enlightenment thought, and his

Source: Jean Jacques Rousseau, *The Social Contract, Or Principles of Political Right*, trans. G. D. H. Cole. Rendered into HTML and text by Jon Roland of the Constitution Society. Available at www. constitution.org/jjr/socon.htm.

political ideas affected the radicals of the French Revolution, though he died eleven years before its outbreak. In both his native Geneva and France, where he spent most of his life, Rousseau's work was often banned. In fact, most of his work was not published until after his death.

The Social Contract, Or Principles of Political Right (1762) challenged the monarchy and called for a government of the people, a force Rousseau saw not in individuals or the competing classes of a society of unequals, but in a "general will" that was greater than any institution or the sum of the people. Which ideas expressed here would be a threat to the French monarchy or establishment? Why would Rousseau's writing appeal to people who wanted to overthrow the regime?

THINKING HISTORICALLY

The power of Enlightenment thought was its radical willingness to ask, and try to answer, fundamental questions. What are some of the fundamental questions this selection grapples with? What does Rousseau mean by such phrases as the "state of nature," the "social compact," and the "general will"?

Book I

I mean to inquire if, in the civil order,[1] there can be any sure and legitimate rule of administration, men being taken as they are and laws as they might be. In this inquiry I shall endeavor always to unite what right sanctions with what is prescribed by interest, in order that justice and utility may in no case be divided.

I enter upon my task without proving the importance of the subject. I shall be asked if I am a prince or a legislator, to write on politics. I answer that I am neither, and that is why I do so. If I were a prince or a legislator, I should not waste time in saying what wants doing; I should do it, or hold my peace.

As I was born a citizen of a free State, and a member of the Sovereign,[2] I feel that, however feeble the influence my voice can have on public affairs, the right of voting on them makes it my duty to study them: and I am happy, when I reflect upon governments, to find my inquiries always furnish me with new reasons for loving that of my own country.

---

[1] Civil order: opposed to the state of nature; civic society, the world of citizens. [Ed.]
[2] The ultimate authority, which Rousseau says should be the General Will. [Ed.]

1. Subject of the First Book

Man is born free; and everywhere he is in chains. One thinks himself the master of others, and still remains a greater slave than they. How did this change come about? I do not know. What can make it legitimate? That question I think I can answer.

If I took into account only force, and the effects derived from it, I should say: "As long as a people is compelled to obey, and obeys, it does well; as soon as it can shake off the yoke, and shakes it off, it does still better; for, regaining its liberty by the same right as took it away, either it is justified in resuming it, or there was no justification for those who took it away." But the social order is a sacred right which is the basis of all other rights. Nevertheless, this right does not come from nature, and must therefore be founded on conventions. . . .

4. Slavery

Since no man has a natural authority over his fellow, and force creates no right, we must conclude that conventions[3] form the basis of all legitimate authority among men. . . .

So, from whatever aspect we regard the question, the right of slavery is null and void, not only as being illegitimate, but also because it is absurd and meaningless. The words *slave* and *right* contradict each other, and are mutually exclusive. It will always be equally foolish for a man to say to a man or to a people: "I make with you a convention wholly at your expense and wholly to my advantage; I shall keep it as long as I like, and you will keep it as long as I like."

6. The Social Compact

I suppose men to have reached the point at which the obstacles in the way of their preservation in the state of nature[4] show their power of resistance to be greater than the resources at the disposal of each individual for his maintenance in that state. That primitive condition can then subsist no longer; and the human race would perish unless it changed its manner of existence.

But, as men cannot engender new forces, but only unite and direct existing ones, they have no other means of preserving themselves than the formation, by aggregation, of a sum of forces great enough to overcome the resistance. These they have to bring into play by means of a single motive power, and cause to act in concert.

---

[3] Agreements, compacts. [Ed.]

[4] A hypothetical or primitive existence before government; a frequent starting point in Enlightenment thinking about government. [Ed.]

This sum of forces can arise only where several persons come together: but, as the force and liberty of each man are the chief instruments of his self-preservation, how can he pledge them without harming his own interests, and neglecting the care he owes to himself? This difficulty, in its bearing on my present subject, may be stated in the following terms:

"*The problem is to find a form of association which will defend and protect with the whole common force the person and goods of each associate, and in which each, while uniting himself with all, may still obey himself alone, and remain as free as before.*" This is the fundamental problem of which the *Social Contract* provides the solution. . . .

. . . [F]or, in the first place, as each gives himself absolutely, the conditions are the same for all; and, this being so, no one has any interest in making them burdensome to others. Moreover, the alienation being without reserve,[5] the union is as perfect as it can be, and no associate has anything more to demand: for, if the individuals retained certain rights, as there would be no common superior to decide between them and the public, each, being on one point his own judge, would ask to be so on all; the state of nature would thus continue, and the association would necessarily become inoperative or tyrannical.

Finally, each man, in giving himself to all, gives himself to nobody; and as there is no associate over whom he does not acquire the same right as he yields others over himself, he gains an equivalent for everything he loses, and an increase of force for the preservation of what he has.

If then we discard from the social compact what is not of its essence, we shall find that it reduces itself to the following terms:

"*Each of us puts his person and all his power in common under the supreme direction of the general will, and, in our corporate capacity, we receive each member as an indivisible part of the whole.*"

[5] Each gives his freedom to the whole freely and completely. [Ed.]

3

The American Declaration of Independence

If anyone had taken a poll of Americans in the thirteen colonies as late as 1775, independence would not have won a majority vote anywhere. Massachusetts might have come close, perhaps, but nowhere in the land was there a definitive urge to separate from the British Empire. Still, three thousand miles was a long way for news,

Source: *A Documentary History of the United States*, ed. Richard D. Heffner (New York: Penguin Books, 1991), 15–18.

views, appointees, and petitions to travel, and tensions between the colonies and Britain had been growing.

Of course, each side looked at the cost of colonial administration differently. The British believed that they had carried a large part of the costs of migration, administration of trade, and control of the sea, while the colonists resented the humiliation resulting from their lack of political representation and the often inept royal officials and punitive legislation imposed on them from afar by the Parliament and the king.

By the spring of 1775, events were rapidly pushing the colonies toward independence. In April, British troops engaged colonial forces at Lexington and Concord, instigating a land war that was to last until 1781. In the midst of other urgent business, most notably raising an army, the Continental Congress asked a committee that included Thomas Jefferson, Benjamin Franklin, and John Adams to compose a statement outlining these and other reasons for separation from Britain. Jefferson wrote the first draft, the bulk of which became the final version accepted by the Continental Congress on July 4, 1776.

The Declaration of Independence was preeminently a document of the Enlightenment. Its principal author, Thomas Jefferson, exemplified the Enlightenment intellectual. Conversant in European literature, law, and political thought, he made significant contributions to eighteenth-century knowledge in natural science and architecture. Benjamin Franklin and other delegates to the Congress in Philadelphia were similarly accomplished.

It is no wonder, then, that the Declaration and the establishment of an independent United States of America should strike the world as the realization of the Enlightenment's basic tenets. That a wholly new country could be created by people with intelligence and foresight, according to principles of reason, and to realize human liberty, was heady stuff.

What were the goals of the authors of this document? In what ways was the Declaration a call for democracy? In what ways was it not?

THINKING HISTORICALLY

Before interpreting any document, we must read it carefully and put it into context—that is, determine the what, where, and why. Some of this information may be available in the text itself. For instance, to whom is the Declaration addressed? What is the reason given for writing it?

The urgency and immediate purpose of the Declaration of Independence separate it from the more theoretical *Social Contract* by Rousseau. But the age of Enlightenment enshrined similar concerns, and therefore similar ideas and language. What words or phrases are similar in both documents? How is their meaning similar or different?

Consider also the disparity between the lofty sentiments of liberty
and independence and the existence of slavery in the Americas. How
is Rousseau's treatment of slavery different from Jefferson's? How is
it possible that Jefferson and some of the signers of the Declaration
could own slaves while declaring it "self-evident that all men are created equal"? To whom did this statement apply?

In Congress, July 4, 1776, the Unanimous Declaration of the Thirteen United States of America

When in the course of human events, it becomes necessary for one people
to dissolve the political bands which have connected them with another,
and to assume among the powers of the earth, the separate and equal
station to which the Laws of Nature and of Nature's God entitle them,
a decent respect to the opinions of mankind requires that they should
declare the causes which impel them to the separation.

We hold these truths to be self-evident, that all men are created
equal, that they are endowed by their Creator with certain unalien-
able rights, that among these are life, liberty, and the pursuit of happiness. That to secure these rights, governments are instituted among
men, deriving their just powers from the consent of the governed. That
whenever any form of government becomes destructive of these ends,
it is the right of the people to alter or to abolish it, and to institute new
government, laying its foundation on such principles and organizing
its powers in such form, as to them shall seem most likely to effect their
safety and happiness. Prudence, indeed, will dictate that governments
long established should not be changed for light and transient causes;
and accordingly all experience hath shown, that mankind are more disposed to suffer, while evils are sufferable, than to right themselves by
abolishing the forms to which they are accustomed. But when a long
train of abuses and usurpations, pursuing invariably the same object
evinces a design to reduce them under absolute despotism, it is their
right, it is their duty, to throw off such government, and to provide
new guards for their future security. Such has been the patient sufferance of these Colonies; and such is now the necessity which constrains
them to alter their former systems of government. The history of the
present King of Great Britain is a history of repeated injuries and usurpations, all having in direct object the establishment of an absolute
tyranny over these States. To prove this, let facts be submitted to a
candid world.

He has refused his assent to laws, the most wholesome and necessary for the public good.

He has forbidden his Governors to pass laws of immediate and
pressing importance, unless suspended in their operation till his assent

should be obtained; and when so suspended, he has utterly neglected to attend to them.

He has refused to pass other laws for the accommodation of large districts of people, unless those people would relinquish the right of representation in the Legislature, a right inestimable to them and formidable to tyrants only.

He has called together legislative bodies at places unusual, uncomfortable, and distant from the depository of their public records, for the sole purpose of fatiguing them into compliance with his measures.

He has dissolved representative houses repeatedly, for opposing with manly firmness his invasions on the rights of the people.

He has refused for a long time, after such dissolutions, to cause others to be elected; whereby the legislative powers, incapable of annihilation, have returned to the people at large for their exercise; the State remaining in the meantime exposed to all the dangers of invasion from without and convulsions within.

He has endeavoured to prevent the population of these states; for that purpose obstructing the laws of naturalization of foreigners; refusing to pass others to encourage their migration hither, and raising the conditions of new appropriations of lands.

He has obstructed the administration of justice, by refusing his assent to laws for establishing judiciary powers.

He has made judges dependent on his will alone, for the tenure of their offices, and the amount and payment of their salaries.

He has erected a multitude of new offices, and sent hither swarms of officers to harass our people, and eat out their substance.

He has kept among us, in times of peace, standing armies without the consent of our legislatures.

He has affected to render the military independent of and superior to the civil power.

He has combined with others to subject us to a jurisdiction foreign to our constitution, and unacknowledged by our laws; giving his assent to their acts of pretended legislation:

For quartering large bodies of armed troops among us:

For protecting them, by a mock trial, from punishment for any murders which they should commit on the inhabitants of these States:

For cutting off our trade with all parts of the world:

For imposing taxes on us without our consent:

For depriving us in many cases, of the benefits of trial by jury:

For transporting us beyond seas to be tried for pretended offences:

For abolishing the free system of English laws in a neighbouring Province, establishing therein an arbitrary government, and enlarging its boundaries so as to render it at once an example and fit instrument for introducing the same absolute rule into these Colonies:

For taking away our Charters, abolishing our most valuable laws, and altering fundamentally the forms of our governments:

For suspending our own Legislatures, and declaring themselves invested with power to legislate for us in all cases whatsoever.

He has abdicated government here, by declaring us out of his protection and waging war against us.

He has plundered our seas, ravaged our coasts, burnt our towns, and destroyed the lives of our people.

He is at this time transporting large armies of foreign mercenaries to complete the works of death, desolation, and tyranny, already begun with circumstances of cruelty and perfidy scarcely paralleled in the most barbarous ages, and totally unworthy the head of a civilized nation.

He has constrained our fellow citizens taken captive on the high seas to bear arms against their country, to become the executioners of their friends and brethren, or to fall themselves by their hands.

He has excited domestic insurrections amongst us, and has endeavoured to bring on the inhabitants of our frontiers, the merciless Indian savages, whose known rule of warfare, is an undistinguished destruction of all ages, sexes, and conditions.

In every state of these oppressions we have petitioned for redress in the most humble terms: our repeated petitions have been answered only by repeated injury. A prince whose character is thus marked by every act which may define a tyrant is unfit to be the ruler of a free people.

Nor have we been wanting in attention to our British brethren. We have warned them from time to time of attempts by their legislature to extend an unwarrantable jurisdiction over us. We have reminded them of the circumstances of our emigration and settlement here. We have appealed to their native justice and magnanimity, and we have conjured them by the ties of our common kindred to disavow these usurpations, which would inevitably interrupt our connections and correspondence. They too have been deaf to the voice of justice and of consanguinity. We must, therefore, acquiesce in the necessity, which denounces our separation, and hold them, as we hold the rest of mankind, enemies in war, in peace friends.

We, therefore, the Representatives of the United States of America, in General Congress assembled, appealing to the Supreme Judge of the world for the rectitude of our intentions, do, in the name, and by authority of the good people of these Colonies, solemnly publish and declare, That these United Colonies are, and of right ought to be Free and Independent States; that they are absolved from all allegiance to the British Crown, and that all political connection between them and the State of Great Britain, is and ought to be totally dissolved; and that as Free and Independent States, they have full power to levy war, conclude peace, contract alliances, establish commerce, and to do all other acts and things which Independent States may of right do. And for the support of this declaration, with a firm reliance on the protection of Divine Province, we mutually pledge to each other our lives, our fortunes, and our sacred honor.

4

ABIGAIL ADAMS AND JOHN ADAMS

Remember the Ladies

As a delegate to the Second Continental Congress, future American president John Adams was in Philadelphia in the spring of 1776, collaborating on writing the Declaration of Independence. In the meantime his wife, Abigail, assumed the role of the head of the household, caring for their children and managing the family farm in Braintree, Massachusetts. Their relationship had always been characterized by robust intellectual debate, and John even referred to his wife as "Sister Delegate." In their famous correspondence during this period, Abigail urged her husband to "remember the ladies" as he and his fellow revolutionaries constructed the basis for the new American government. What did she mean by this? How did her husband respond? What did she think of his response?

THINKING HISTORICALLY

Enlightenment thinkers often employed grand abstractions like "all men are created equal" for both their rational simplicity and their dramatic revolutionary claim. As a consequence, such abstractions were often more sweeping in their implications than even the revolutionaries of the era intended. For example, John and Abigail Adams, both of whom opposed slavery, did not intend for "all men" to include blacks, either enslaved or free. But men like Adams might not have seriously considered how women would respond to the proclamation of universal equality. What in Adams's response to his wife reveals that he did not intend to extend universal equality to women? Does his response somehow undermine the Declaration of Independence?

Source: Letters from Abigail Adams to John Adams, 31 March–5 April 1776, John Adams to Abigail Adams, 14 April 1776, Abigail Adams to John Adams, 7–9 May 1776 [electronic editions]. *Adams Family Papers: An Electronic Archive* (Boston: Massachusetts Historical Society, 2002), http://www.masshist.org/digitaladams/.

Letter from Abigail Adams to John Adams, 31 March–5 April 1776

. . . I long to hear that you have declared an independency—and by the way in the new Code of Laws which I suppose it will be necessary for you to make I desire you would Remember the Ladies, and be more generous and favourable to them than your ancestors. Do not put such unlimited power into the hands of the Husbands. Remember all Men would be tyrants if they could. If perticuliar care and attention is not paid to the Ladies we are determined to foment a Rebellion, and will not hold ourselves bound by any Laws in which we have no voice, or Representation.

That your Sex Naturally Tyrannical is a Truth so thoroughly established as to admit of no dispute, but such of you as wish to be happy willingly give up the harsh title of Master for the more tender and endearing one of Friend. Why then, not put it out of the power of the vicious and the Lawless to use us with cruelty and indignity [with impunity]. Men of Sense in all Ages abhor those customs which treat us only as the vassals of your Sex. Regard us then as Beings placed by providence under your protection and in imitation of the Supreme Being make use of the power only for our happiness.

Letter from John Adams to Abigail Adams, 14 April 1776

. . . As to Declarations of Independency, be patient. Read our Privateering Laws, and our Commercial Laws. What signifies a Word.

As to your extraordinary Code of Laws, I cannot but laugh. We have been told that our Struggle has loosened the bands of Government every where. That Children and Apprentices were disobedient—that schools and Colleges were grown turbulent—that Indians slighted their Guardians and Negroes grew insolent to their Masters.

But your Letter was the first Intimation that another Tribe more numerous and powerfull than all the rest were grown discontented.—This is rather too coarse a Compliment but you are so saucy, I wont blot it out.

Depend upon it, We know better than to repeal our Masculine systems. Altho they are in full Force, you know they are little more than Theory. We dare not exert our Power in its full Latitude. We are obliged to go fair, and softly, and in Practice you know We are the subjects. We have only the Name of Masters, and rather than give up this, which would compleatly subject Us to the Despotism of the Peticoat, I hope General Washington, and all our brave Heroes would fight. I am sure every good Politician would plot, as long as he would against Despotism, Empire, Monarchy, Aristocracy, Oligarchy, or Ochlocracy. . . .

Letter from Abigail Adams to John Adams, 7–9 May 1776

. . . I can not say that I think you very generous to the Ladies, for whilst you are proclaiming peace and good will to Men, Emancipating all Nations, you insist upon retaining an absolute power over Wives. But you must remember that Arbitary power is like most other things which are very hard, very liable to be broken—and notwithstanding all your wise Laws and Maxims we have it in our power not only to free ourselves but to subdue our Masters, and without violence throw both your natural and legal authority at our feet. . . .

5

The French Declaration of the Rights of Man and Citizen

The founding of the Republic of the United States of America provided a model for other peoples chafing under oppressive rule to emulate. Not surprisingly then, when the French movement to end political injustices turned to revolution in 1789 and the revolutionaries convened at the National Assembly, the Marquis de Lafayette (1757–1834), hero of the American Revolution, proposed a Declaration of the Rights of Man and Citizen. Lafayette had the American Declaration in mind, and he had the assistance of Thomas Jefferson, present in Paris as the first United States ambassador to France.

While the resulting document appealed to the French revolutionaries, the French were not able to start afresh as the Americans had done. In 1789 Louis XVI was still king of France: He could not be made to leave by a turn of phrase. Nor were men created equal in France in 1789. Those born into the nobility led lives different from those born into the Third Estate (the 99 percent of the population who were not nobility or clergy), and they had different legal rights as well. This disparity was precisely what the revolutionaries and the Declaration sought to change. Inevitably, though, such change would prove to be a more violent and revolutionary proposition than it had been in the American colonies.

In what ways did the Declaration of the Rights of Man and Citizen resemble the American Declaration of Independence? In what ways was it different? Which was more democratic?

Source: *A Documentary History of the French Revolution*, ed. John Hall Stewart (London: Macmillan, 1979), 113–15.

THINKING HISTORICALLY

Compare the language of the Declaration of the Rights of Man and Citizen with that of Rousseau and that of Jefferson. In what ways does it borrow from each? Like both prior documents, the French Declaration is full of abstract, universal principles. But notice how such abstractions can claim our consent by their rationality without informing us as to how they will be implemented. What is meant by the first right, for instance? What does it mean to say that men are "born free"? Why is it necessary to distinguish between "born" and "remain"? What is meant by the phrase "general usefulness"? Do statements like these increase people's liberties, or are they intentionally vague so they can be interpreted at will?

The slogan of the French Revolution was "Liberty, Equality, Fraternity." Which of the rights in the French Declaration emphasize liberty, which equality? Can these two goals be opposed to each other? Explain how.

The representatives of the French people, organized in National Assembly, considering that ignorance, forgetfulness, or contempt of the rights of man are the sole causes of public misfortunes and of the corruption of governments, have resolved to set forth in a solemn declaration the natural, inalienable, and sacred rights of man, in order that such declaration, continually before all members of the social body, may be a perpetual reminder of their rights and duties; in order that the acts of the legislative power and those of the executive power may constantly be compared with the aim of every political institution and may accordingly be more respected; in order that the demands of the citizens, founded henceforth upon simple and incontestable principles, may always be directed towards the maintenance of the Constitution and the welfare of all.

Accordingly, the National Assembly recognizes and proclaims, in the presence and under the auspices of the Supreme Being, the following rights of man and citizen.

1. Men are born and remain free and equal in rights; social distinctions may be based only upon general usefulness.

2. The aim of every political association is the preservation of the natural and inalienable rights of man; these rights are liberty, property, security, and resistance to oppression.

3. The source of all sovereignty resides essentially in the nation; no group, no individual may exercise authority not emanating expressly therefrom.

4. Liberty consists of the power to do whatever is not injurious to others; thus the enjoyment of the natural rights of every man has for its limits only those that assure other members of society the enjoyment of those same rights; such limits may be determined only by law.

5. The law has the right to forbid only actions which are injurious to society. Whatever is not forbidden by law may not be prevented, and no one may be constrained to do what it does not prescribe.

6. Law is the expression of the general will; all citizens have the right to concur personally, or through their representatives, in its formation; it must be the same for all, whether it protects or punishes. All citizens, being equal before it, are equally admissible to all public offices, positions, and employments, according to their capacity, and without other distinction than that of virtues and talents.

7. No man may be accused, arrested, or detained except in the cases determined by law, and according to the forms prescribed thereby. Whoever solicit, expedite, or execute arbitrary orders, or have them executed, must be punished; but every citizen summoned or apprehended in pursuance of the law must obey immediately; he renders himself culpable by resistance.

8. The law is to establish only penalties that are absolutely and obviously necessary; and no one may be punished except by virtue of a law established and promulgated prior to the offence and legally applied.

9. Since every man is presumed innocent until declared guilty, if arrest be deemed indispensable, all unnecessary severity for securing the person of the accused must be severely repressed by law.

10. No one is to be disquieted because of his opinions, even religious, provided their manifestation does not disturb the public order established by law.

11. Free communication of ideas and opinions is one of the most precious of the rights of man. Consequently, every citizen may speak, write, and print freely, subject to responsibility for the abuse of such liberty in the cases determined by law.

12. The guarantee of the rights of man and citizen necessitates a public force; therefore, is instituted for the advantage of all and not for the particular benefit of those to whom it is entrusted.

13. For the maintenance of the public force and for the expenses of administration a common tax is indispensable; it must be assessed equally on all citizens in proportion to their means.

14. Citizens have the right to ascertain, by themselves or through their representatives, the necessity of the public tax, to consent to it freely, to supervise its use, and to determine its quota, assessment, payment, and duration.

15. Society has the right to require of every public agent an accounting of his administration.

16. Every society in which the guarantee of rights is not assured or the separation of powers not determined has no constitution at all.

17. Since property is a sacred and inviolate right, no one may be deprived thereof unless a legally established public necessity obviously requires it, and upon condition of a just and previous indemnity.

6

TOUSSAINT L'OUVERTURE
Letter to the Directory

When the French revolutionaries proclaimed the Declaration of the Rights of Man and Citizen in 1789, the French colony of Saint-Domingue[1] (now Haiti) contained a half million African slaves, most of whom worked on the sugar plantations that made France one of the richest countries in the world. Thus, the French were confronted with the difficult problem of reconciling their enlightened principles with the extremely profitable, but fundamentally unequal, institution of slavery.

French revolutionaries remained locked in debate about this issue when in 1791, the slaves of Saint-Domingue organized a revolt that culminated in establishing Haiti's national independence twelve years later. François Dominique Toussaint L'Ouverture,* a self-educated Haitian slave, led the revolt and the subsequent battles against the French planter class and French armies, as well as the Spanish forces of neighboring Santo Domingo—the eastern side of the island now known as the Dominican Republic—and the antirevolutionary forces of Britain, all of whom vied for control of the island at the end of the eighteenth century.

At first Toussaint enjoyed the support of the revolutionary government in Paris; in the Decree of 16 Pluviôse[2] (1794) the National Convention abolished slavery in the colonies. But after 1795 the revolution turned on itself, and Toussaint feared that the new conservative government, called the Directory, might send troops to restore slavery on the island.

In 1797 he wrote the Directory the letter that follows. Notice how Toussaint negotiated a difficult situation. How did he try to reassure the government of his allegiance to France? At the same time, how did he attempt to convince the Directory that a return to slavery was unthinkable?

* too SAN loo vehr TUR
[1] san doh MANG *Santo Domingo* was the Spanish name for the eastern half of Hispaniola (now the Dominican Republic). *Saint-Domingue* was the French name for the western half of the island, now Haiti. *San Domingo*, which is used in the text, is a nineteenth-century abbreviation for *Saint-Domingue*. To further complicate matters, both the Spanish and French sometimes used their term for the whole island of Hispaniola. Spain controlled the entire island until 1697, when the Spanish recognized French control of the west.
[2] PLOO vee ohs Rainy; the name of the second winter month according to the revolutionary calendar.

Source: Toussaint L'Ouverture, "Letter to the Directory, November 5, 1797," in *The Black Jacobins*, ed. C. L. R. James (New York: Vintage Books, 1989), 195–97.

THINKING HISTORICALLY

Notice how Toussaint defines different groups of people. What does he mean, for instance, by "the proprietors of San Domingo" as opposed to "the people of San Domingo"? What does he mean by "the colonists" and "our common enemies"? How does the use of these terms aid his cause?

. . . The impolitic and incendiary discourse of Vaublanc[3] has not affected the blacks nearly so much as their certainty of the projects which the proprietors of San Domingo are planning: insidious declarations should not have any effect in the eyes of wise legislators who have decreed liberty for the nations. But the attempts on that liberty which the colonists propose are all the more to be feared because it is with the veil of patriotism that they cover their detestable plans. We know that they seek to impose some of them on you by illusory and specious promises, in order to see renewed in this colony its former scenes of horror. Already perfidious emissaries have stepped in among us to ferment the destructive leaven prepared by the hands of liberticides. But they will not succeed. I swear it by all that liberty holds most sacred. My attachment to France, my knowledge of the blacks, make it my duty not to leave you ignorant either of the crimes which they meditate or the oath that we renew, to bury ourselves under the ruins of a country revived by liberty rather than suffer the return of slavery.

It is for you, Citizens Directors, to turn from over our heads the storm which the eternal enemies of our liberty are preparing in the shades of silence. It is for you to enlighten the legislature, it is for you to prevent the enemies of the present system from spreading themselves on our unfortunate shores to sully it with new crimes. Do not allow our brothers, our friends, to be sacrificed to men who wish to reign over the ruins of the human species. But no, your wisdom will enable you to avoid the dangerous snares which our common enemies hold out for you. . . .

I send you with this letter a declaration which will acquaint you with the unity that exists between the proprietors of San Domingo who are in France, those in the United States, and those who serve under the English banner. You will see there a resolution, unequivocal and carefully constructed, for the restoration of slavery; you will see there that their determination to succeed has led them to envelop themselves in

---

[3] Vincent-Marie Viénot, Count of Vaublanc (1756–1845). Born into an aristocratic family in San Domingo, he was a French royalist politician. In Paris in September 1797, he gave a speech intended to impeach republican Directors and trigger a royalist coup. [Ed.]

the mantle of liberty in order to strike it more deadly blows. You will see that they are counting heavily on my complacency in lending myself to their perfidious views by my fear for my children. It is not astonishing that these men who sacrifice their country to their interests are unable to conceive how many sacrifices a true love of country can support in a better father than they, since I unhesitatingly base the happiness of my children on that of my country, which they and they alone wish to destroy.

I shall never hesitate between the safety of San Domingo and my personal happiness; but I have nothing to fear. It is to the solicitude of the French Government that I have confided my children. . . . I would tremble with horror if it was into the hands of the colonists that I had sent them as hostages; but even if it were so, let them know that in punishing them for the fidelity of their father, they would only add one degree more to their barbarism, without any hope of ever making me fail in my duty. . . . Blind as they are! They cannot see how this odious conduct on their part can become the signal of new disasters and irreparable misfortunes, and that far from making them regain what in their eyes liberty for all has made them lose, they expose themselves to a total ruin and the colony to its inevitable destruction. Do they think that men who have been able to enjoy the blessing of liberty will calmly see it snatched away? They supported their chains only so long as they did not know any condition of life more happy than that of slavery. But to-day when they have left it, if they had a thousand lives they would sacrifice them all rather than be forced into slavery again. But no, the same hand which has broken our chains will not enslave us anew. France will not revoke her principles, she will not withdraw from us the greatest of her benefits. She will protect us against all our enemies; she will not permit her sublime morality to be perverted, those principles which do her most honour to be destroyed, her most beautiful achievement to be degraded, and her Decree of 16 Pluviôse which so honours humanity to be revoked. *But if, to re-establish slavery in San Domingo, this was done, then I declare to you it would be to attempt the impossible: we have known how to face dangers to obtain our liberty, we shall know how to brave death to maintain it.*

This, Citizens Directors, is the morale of the people of San Domingo, those are the principles that they transmit to you by me.

My own you know. It is sufficient to renew, my hand in yours, the oath that I have made, to cease to live before gratitude dies in my heart, before I cease to be faithful to France and to my duty, before the god of liberty is profaned and sullied by the liberticides, before they can snatch from my hands that sword, those arms, which France confided to me for the defence of its rights and those of humanity, for the triumph of liberty and equality.

SIMÓN BOLÍVAR

A Constitution for Venezuela

As we have seen, the Enlightenment principles of reason, human rights, and equality ignited revolutions on both sides of the Atlantic. In Europe, these revolutions overturned kings and tyrannies, marshaling national citizen armies and creating parliamentary democracies. In the American colonies, the revolutions took shape as anticolonial struggles for independence. Sometimes the effort to create an independent nation was at odds with the struggle for democracy.

Simón Bolívar* (1783–1830), called "the Liberator," successfully led the Latin American revolution for independence from Spain between 1810 and 1824. (See Map 20.1.) In 1819 he became president of a short-lived Republic of Colombia[1] that included what is today Venezuela, Ecuador, Panama, and Colombia, and he gave the speech on the Constitution of Venezuela that follows.

What does Bolívar see as the difference between Spanish-American and English-American colonies? What does he see as the advantages of the Roman and British constitutions for Spanish America? Would you call Bolívar a "democrat"? Is he more or less democratic than the French or North American revolutionaries?

THINKING HISTORICALLY

Notice how Bolívar uses the words *liberty* and *tyranny*. What does he mean when he says at the end of the second paragraph: "we, having been placed in a state lower than slavery, had been robbed not only of our freedom but also of the right to exercise an active domestic tyranny"? What does he mean in the last paragraph by a "neutral power" that would weaken "two eternally rival powers"? What might Jefferson or Rousseau think of such an idea?

Let us review the past to discover the base upon which the Republic of Venezuela is founded.

America, in separating from the Spanish monarchy, found herself in a situation similar to that of the Roman Empire when its enormous framework fell to pieces in the midst of the ancient world. Each Roman

---

* see MOHN boh LEE vahr
[1] Called Gran Colombia by later historians, 1819–1831. [Ed.]

Source: *Selected Writings of Bolívar*, comp. Vincent Lecuna, ed. Harold A. Bierck Jr. (New York: Colonial Press, 1951), 1:175–77, 179–80, 183, 184–87.

Map 20.1 Latin American Independence, 1804–1830.

division then formed an independent nation in keeping with its location or interests; but this situation differed from America's in that those members proceeded to reestablish their former associations. We, on the contrary, do not even retain the vestiges of our original being. We are not Europeans; we are not Indians; we are but a mixed species of aborigines and Spaniards. Americans by birth and Europeans by law, we find ourselves engaged in a dual conflict: We are disputing with the natives for titles of ownership, and at the same time we are struggling to maintain ourselves in the country that gave us birth against the opposition of the invaders. Thus our position is most extraordinary and complicated. But there is more. As our role has always been strictly passive and political existence nil, we find that our quest for liberty is now even more difficult of accomplishment; for we, having been placed in a state lower than slavery, had been robbed not only of our freedom but also of the right to exercise an active domestic tyranny. Permit me to explain this paradox.

In absolute systems, the central power is unlimited. The will of the despot is the supreme law, arbitrarily enforced by subordinates who take part in the organized oppression in proportion to the authority that they wield. They are charged with civil, political, military, and religious functions; but, in the final analysis, the satraps of Persia are Persian, the pashas of the Grand Turk are Turks, and the sultans of Tartary are Tartars. China does not seek her mandarins in the homeland of Genghis Khan, her conqueror. America, on the contrary, received everything from Spain, who, in effect, deprived her of the experience that she would have gained from the exercise of an active tyranny by not allowing her to take part in her own domestic affairs and administration. This exclusion made it impossible for us to acquaint ourselves with the management of public affairs; nor did we enjoy that personal consideration, of such great value in major revolutions, that the brilliance of power inspires in the eyes of the multitude. In brief, Gentlemen, we were deliberately kept in ignorance and cut off from the world in all matters relating to the science of government.

Subject to the three-fold yoke of ignorance, tyranny, and vice, the American people have been unable to acquire knowledge, power, or [civic] virtue. The lessons we received and the models we studied, as pupils of such pernicious teachers, were most destructive. We have been ruled more by deceit than by force, and we have been degraded more by vice than by superstition. Slavery is the daughter of darkness: An ignorant people is a blind instrument of its own destruction. Ambition and intrigue abuse the credulity and experience of men lacking all political, economic, and civic knowledge; they adopt pure illusion as reality; they take license for liberty, treachery for patriotism, and vengeance for justice. This situation is similar to that of the robust blind man who, beguiled by his strength, strides forward with all the assurance of one who can see, but, upon hitting every variety of obstacle, finds himself unable to retrace his steps.

If a people, perverted by their training, succeed in achieving their liberty, they will soon lose it, for it would be of no avail to endeavor to explain to them that happiness consists in the practice of virtue; that the rule of law is more powerful than the rule of tyrants, because, as the laws are more inflexible, every one should submit to their beneficent austerity; that proper morals, and not force, are the bases of law; and that to practice justice is to practice liberty. Therefore, Legislators, your work is so much the more arduous, inasmuch as you have to reeducate men who have been corrupted by erroneous illusions and false incentives. Liberty, says Rousseau, is a succulent morsel, but one difficult to digest. Our weak fellow-citizens will have to strengthen their spirit greatly before they can digest the wholesome nutriment of freedom. Their limbs benumbed by chains, their sight dimmed by the darkness of dungeons, and their strength sapped by the pestilence of servitude, are they capable of marching toward the august temple of Liberty without faltering? Can they come near enough to bask in its brilliant rays and to breathe freely the pure air which reigns therein? . . .

The more I admire the excellence of the federal Constitution of Venezuela,[2] the more I am convinced of the impossibility of its application to our state. And to my way of thinking, it is a marvel that its prototype in North America[3] endures so successfully and has not been overthrown at the first sign of adversity or danger. Although the people of North America are a singular model of political virtue and moral rectitude; although the nation was cradled in liberty, reared on freedom, and maintained by liberty alone; and—I must reveal everything—although those people, so lacking in many respects, are unique in the history of mankind, it is a marvel, I repeat, that so weak and complicated a government as the federal system has managed to govern them in the difficult and trying circumstances of their past. But, regardless of the effectiveness of this form of government with respect to North America, I must say that it has never for a moment entered my mind to compare the position and character of two states as dissimilar as the English-American and the Spanish-American. Would it not be most difficult to apply to Spain the English system of political, civil, and religious liberty? Hence, it would be even more difficult to adapt to Venezuela the laws of North America. Does not *L'Esprit des Lois*[4] state that laws should be suited to the people for whom they are made; that it would be a major coincidence if those of one nation could be adapted to another; that laws must take into account the physical conditions of the country, climate, character of the land, location, size, and mode of living of the people; that they should be in keeping with the degree of liberty that the Constitution can sanction respecting the religion of the inhabitants, their inclinations, resources, number, commerce, habits, and customs? This is the code we must consult, not the code of Washington! . . .

Venezuela had, has, and should have a republican government. Its principles should be the sovereignty of the people, division of powers, civil liberty, proscription of slavery, and the abolition of monarchy and privileges. We need equality to recast, so to speak, into a unified nation, the classes of men, political opinions, and public customs. . . .

Among the ancient and modern nations, Rome and Great Britain are the most outstanding. Both were born to govern and to be free and both were built not on ostentatious forms of freedom, but upon solid institutions. Thus I recommend to you, Representatives, the study of the British Constitution, for that body of laws appears destined to bring about the greatest possible good for the peoples that adopt it; but, however perfect it may be, I am by no means proposing that you imitate it slavishly. When I speak of the

---

[2] The first constitution of Venezuela (1811), which had a weak central government and executive. [Ed.]

[3] The U.S. Constitution (1789), which was actually less "federal" or decentralized than the earlier Articles of Confederation. [Ed.]

[4] *The Spirit of the Laws* by Montesquieu (1748): a major Enlightenment text that argued for the rule of law, separation of powers, and the need for government to fit the geography and society. [Ed.]

British government, I only refer to its republican features; and, indeed, can a political system be labelled a monarchy when it recognizes popular sovereignty, division and balance of powers, civil liberty, freedom of conscience and of press, and all that is politically sublime? Can there be more liberty in any other type of republic? Can more be asked of any society? I commend this Constitution to you as that most worthy of serving as model for those who aspire to the enjoyment of the rights of man and who seek all the political happiness which is compatible with the frailty of human nature.

Nothing in our fundamental laws would have to be altered were we to adopt a legislative power similar to that held by the British Parliament. Like the North Americans, we have divided national representation into two chambers; that of Representatives and the Senate. The first is very wisely constituted. It enjoys all its proper functions, and it requires no essential revision, because the Constitution, in creating it, gave it the form and powers which the people deemed necessary in order that they might be legally and properly represented. If the Senate were hereditary rather than elective, it would, in my opinion, be the basis, the tie, the very soul of our republic. In political storms this body would arrest the thunderbolts of the government and would repel any violent popular reaction. Devoted to the government because of a natural interest in its own preservation, a hereditary senate would always oppose any attempt on the part of the people to infringe upon the jurisdiction and authority of their magistrates. It must be confessed that most men are unaware of their best interests, and that they constantly endeavor to assail them in the hands of their custodians—the individual clashes with the mass, and the mass with authority. It is necessary, therefore, that in all governments there be a neutral body to protect the injured and disarm the offender. To be neutral, this body must not owe its origin to appointment by the government or to election by the people, if it is to enjoy a full measure of independence which neither fears nor expects anything from these two sources of authority. The hereditary senate, as a part of the people, shares its interests, its sentiments, and its spirit. For this reason it should not be presumed that a hereditary senate would ignore the interests of the people or forget its legislative duties. The senators in Rome and in the House of Lords in London have been the strongest pillars upon which the edifice of political and civil liberty has rested.

At the outset, these senators should be elected by Congress. The successors to this Senate must command the initial attention of the government, which should educate them in a *colegio* designed especially to train these guardians and future legislators of the nation. They ought to learn the arts, sciences, and letters that enrich the mind of a public figure. From childhood they should understand the career for which they have been destined by Providence, and from earliest youth they should prepare their minds for the dignity that awaits them.

The creation of a hereditary senate would in no way be a violation of political equality. I do not solicit the establishment of a nobility, for as a celebrated republican has said, that would simultaneously destroy equality and liberty. What I propose is an office for which the candidates must prepare themselves, an office that demands great knowledge and the ability to acquire such knowledge. All should not be left to chance and the outcome of elections. The people are more easily deceived than is Nature perfected by art; and, although these senators, it is true, would not be bred in an environment that is all virtue, it is equally true that they would be raised in an atmosphere of enlightened education. Furthermore, the liberators of Venezuela are entitled to occupy forever a high rank in the Republic that they have brought into existence. I believe that posterity would view with regret the effacement of the illustrious names of its first benefactors. I say, moreover, that it is a matter of public interest and national honor, of gratitude on Venezuela's part, to honor gloriously, until the end of time, a race of virtuous, prudent, and persevering men who, overcoming every obstacle, have founded the Republic at the price of the most heroic sacrifices. And if the people of Venezuela do not applaud the elevation of their benefactors, then they are unworthy to be free, and they will never be free.

A hereditary senate, I repeat, will be the fundamental basis of the legislative power, and therefore the foundation of the entire government. It will also serve as a counterweight to both government and people; and as a neutral power it will weaken the mutual attacks of these two eternally rival powers. In all conflicts the calm reasoning of a third party will serve as the means of reconciliation. Thus the Venezuelan senate will give strength to this delicate political structure, so sensitive to violent repercussions; it will be the mediator that will lull the storms and it will maintain harmony between the head and the other parts of the political body.

8

DIPESH CHAKRABARTY

Compassion and the Enlightenment

In this essay, a modern historian argues that the Enlightenment was not confined to Europe and was more profound than is often thought. Here Chakrabarty demonstrates an Indian Enlightenment in the northeastern region of Bengal. He further reveals the profound way in which the Enlightenment changed not only peoples' ideas but also their feelings, signaling the beginning of the modern self. What

Source: Dipesh Chakrabarty, *Provincializing Europe: Postcolonial Thought and Historical Difference*, Princeton Studies in Culture/Power/History (Princeton: Princeton University Press, 2000), 119–24.

does he mean by "the modern self"? What, according to the author, is the role of reason and compassion in creating the modern self? How did the Enlightenment change human feelings?

Compare the ideas noted in this essay of the Bengali Indian authors, Rammohun Roy and Iswarchandra Vidyasagar, with the ideas of European Enlightenment thinkers that you have read in this chapter. How is Roy's compassion for women similar to, or different from, that of Abigail Adams? How is it like the compassion of Toussaint?

THINKING HISTORICALLY

Chakrabarty underscores the use of some key Enlightenment concepts by these Bengali authors. What does he mean by "compassion in general"? What are the connections, according to Chakrabarty, among such concepts as suffering, compassion, reason, natural sentiments, universality, and custom?

The capacity to notice and document suffering (even if it be one's own suffering) from the position of a generalized and necessarily disembodied observer is what marks the beginnings of the modern self. This self has to be generalizable in principle; in other words, it should be such that it signifies a position available for occupation by anybody with proper training. If it were said, for instance, that only a particular type of person—such as a Budhha or a Christ—was capable of noticing suffering and of being moved by it, one would not be talking of a generalized subject position. To be a Budhha or Christ is not within the reach of everybody through simple education and training. So the capacity for sympathy must be seen as a potential inherent in the nature of man in general and not in the uniqueness of a particular person. Such a "natural theory of sentiments," as we shall see, was indeed argued by Enlightenment philosophers such as David Hume and Adam Smith.

A critical distinction also has to be made between the act of displaying suffering and that of observing or facing the sufferer. To display suffering in order to elicit sympathy and assistance is a very old—and perhaps universal and still current—practice. The deformed beggars of medieval Europe or of contemporary Indian or U.S. cities are subjects of suffering, but they are not disembodied subjects. The sufferer here is an embodied self, which is always a particular self, grounded in this or that body. Nor would the sympathy felt for only a particular sufferer (such as a kin or a friend) be "modern" in my sense. The person who is not an immediate sufferer but who has the capacity to become a secondary sufferer through sympathy for a generalized picture of suffering, and who documents this suffering in the interest of eventual social intervention—such a person occupies the position of the modern subject. In other words, the moment of the modern observation of suffering is a certain moment of self-recognition on the part of an abstract, general human being. It is as though a person who is able to see in himself or herself the general human also recognizes the same figure in the particular sufferer, so that the moment of recognition is a moment when the general human splits into the two mutually recognizing and mutually constitutive figures of the sufferer and the observer of suffering. It was argued, however, in the early part of the nineteenth century that this could not happen without the aid of reason, for habit and custom—unopposed by reason—could blunt the natural human capacity for sympathy. Reason, that is, education in rational argumentation, was seen as a critical factor in helping to realize in the modern person this capacity for seeing the general.

Something like such a natural theory of sentiments was argued, in effect, by the two most important nineteenth-century Bengali social reformers who exerted themselves on questions concerning the plight of widows: Rammohun Roy (1772/4–1833) and Iswarchandra Vidyasagar (1820–1901). Roy was instrumental in the passing of the act that made *sati* illegal in 1829, and Vidyasagar successfully agitated for widows to have the legal right to remarry, a right enshrined in the Act for the Remarriage of Hindu Widows, 1856. These legal interventions also allow us to make a further distinction between suffering as viewed by religions such as Buddhism and suffering as a subject of modern social thought. In religious thought, suffering is existential. It shadows man in his life. In social thought, however, suffering is not an existential category. It is specific and hence open to secular interventions.

Rammohun Roy's well-known tract entitled *Brief Remarks Regarding Modern Encroachments on the Ancient Right of Females*, was one of the first written arguments in modern India in favor of women's right to property. This document on property rights also discusses the place of sentiments such as cruelty, distress, wounding feelings, misery, and so on, in human relations. Both strands—rights and sentiments—were intertwined in Roy's argument connecting the question of property with the issue of sentiments, and both saw suffering as an historical and eradicable problem in society:

> In short a widow, according to the [current] exposition of the law, can receive nothing . . . [unless her husband dies] leaving two or more sons, and all of them survive and be inclined to allot a share to their mother. . . . The consequence is, that a woman who is looked upon as the sole mistress of a family one day, on the next

becomes dependent on her sons, and subject to the slights of her daughters-in-law. . . . Cruel sons often wound the feelings of their dependent mothers. . . . Step-mothers, who are often numerous on account of polygamy, are still more shamefully neglected in general by their step-sons, and sometimes dreadfully treated by their sisters-in-law. . . . [The] restraints on female inheritance encourage, in a great degree, polygamy, a frequent source of the greatest misery in native families.[1]

There are two interesting features of this document that make it the work of a modern observer of suffering. First, in observing this cruelty to widows and women, Roy put himself in the transcendental position of the modern subject. This becomes clear if we look closely at the following sentence of his text: "How distressing it must be to the female community and to those who interest themselves in their behalf, to observe daily that several daughters in a rich family can prefer no claim to any portion of the property . . . left by their deceased father . . . ; while they . . . are exposed to be given in marriage to individuals who already have several wives and have no means of maintaining them."[2] Roy presents himself here both as a subject experiencing affect—"distress"—as well as a representative subject, one who "interests [himself] in their [women's] behalf." The capacity for sympathy is what unites the representative person with those who are represented; they share the same "distress." The second clause in the sentence refers to a new type of representation: people who took an interest in women's condition on behalf of women. But who were these women? They were not particular, specific women marked by their belonging to particular families or particular networks of kinship. Women here are a collective subject; the expression "female community" connotes a general community. It is this "general community" that shares the distress of a Rammohun Roy, the observer who observes on behalf of this collective community. And therefore the feeling of "distress" that Rammohun Roy speaks of refers to a new kind of compassion, something one could feel for suffering beyond one's immediate family. Compassion in general, we could call it.

But from where would such compassion or sympathy spring? What made it possible for a Rammohun or Vidyasagar to feel this "compassion in general" that most members of their community (presumably) did not yet feel? How would society train itself to make this compassion

---

[1] Rammohun Roy, "Brief Remarks Regarding Modern Encroachments on the Ancient Rights of Females," in Ajitkumar Ghosh, ed., *Rammohan rachanabali* (Calcutta: Haraf Prakashani, 1973), pp. 496–497.
[2] Ibid., pp. 496–497, 500–501.

a part of the comportment of every person, so that compassion became a generally present sentiment in society? It is on this point that both Rammohun and Vidyasagar gave an answer remarkable for its affiliation to the European Enlightenment. Reason, they argued in effect, was what could release the flow of the compassion that was naturally present in all human beings, for only reason could dispel the blindness induced by custom and habit. Reasonable human beings would see suffering and that would put to work the natural human capacity for sympathy, compassion, and pity.

Rammohun raised the question of compassion in a pointed manner in his 1819 answer to Kashinath Tarkabagish's polemical tract *Bidhayak nishedhak shombad* directed against his own position on *sati*. "What is a matter of regret," he said, "is that the fact of witnessing with your own eyes women who have thus suffered much sadness and domination, does not arouse even a small amount of compassion in you so that the forcible burning [of widows] may be stopped."[3] Why was this so? Why did the act of seeing not result in sympathy? Rammohun's answer is clearly given in his 1818 tract called *Views on Burning Widows Alive*, which targeted the advocates of the practice. Here Rammohun refers to the forcible way in which widows were "fastened" to the funeral pyre in the course of the performance of *sati*, and directly raises the question of mercy or compassion (*daya*): "you are unmercifully resolved to commit the sin of female murder." His opponent, the "advocate" of *sati*, replies: "You have repeatedly asserted that from want of feeling we promote female destruction. This is incorrect. For it is declared in our Veda and codes of law, that mercy is the root of virtue, and from our practice of hospitality, &c., our compassionate dispositions are well known."[4]

Rammohun's response to this introduces an argument for which he presents no scriptural authority and which went largely unanswered in the debates of the time. This is the argument about "habits of insensibility." Much like the Enlightenment thinkers of Europe, and perhaps influenced by them, Rammohun argued that it was because the practice of *sati* had become a custom—a matter of blind repetition—that people were prevented from experiencing sympathy even when they watched somebody being forced to become a *sati*. The natural connection between their vision and feelings of pity was blocked by habit. If this habit could be corrected or removed, the

---

[3] "Prabartak o nibartaker dvitiyo shombad," in *Rammohun rachanabali*, p. 203.

[4] *Rammohan rachanabali*, p. 575. This is Rammohun's own translation of his 1818 text "sahamaran bishaye prabartak o nibartaker shombad," ibid., p. 175.

sheer act of seeing a woman being forced to die would evoke compassion. Roy said:

> That in other cases you show charitable dispositions is acknowledged. But by witnessing from your youth the voluntary burning of women amongst your elder relatives, your neighbours and the inhabitants of the surrounding villages, and by observing the indifference at the time when the women are writhing under the torture of the flames, habits of insensibility are produced. For the same reason, when men or women are suffering the pains of death, you feel for them no sense of compassion, like worshippers of female deities who, witnessing from their infancy the slaughter of kids and buffaloes, feel no compassion for them in the time of their suffering death.[5]

We encounter the same argument about the relationship between sight and compassion in the writings of Iswarchandra Vidyasagar, the Bengali reformer responsible for the act that in 1856 permitted Hindu widows to remarry. Vidyasagar's fundamental reasoning as to the solution of widows' problems had some critical differences from the position of Rammohun Roy but like the latter, he too argued that it was custom and habit that stymied the otherwise natural relationship between the sight and compassion:[6]

> People of India! . . . Habit has so darkened and overwhelmed your intellect and good sense that it is hard for the juice of compassion to flow in the ever-dry hearts of yours even when you see the plight of hapless widows. . . . Let no woman be born in a country where men have no compassion, no feelings of duty and justice, no sense of good and bad, no consideration, where only the preservation of custom is the main and supreme religion—let the ill-fated women not take birth in such a country.
>
> Women! I cannot tell what sins [of past lives] cause you to be born in India![7]

---

[5] Ibid. Distinguishing between "custom" and "reason," Hume equated the former with "habit." David Hume, *Enquiries Concerning Human Understanding and Concerning the Principles of Morals* (1777), introduction by L. A. Sigby-Bigge (Oxford: Clarendon Press, 1990), p. 43. In his *Treatise*, he argues that it is "custom or repetition" that can convert "pain into pleasure." See idem, *A Treatise of Human Nature* (1739–1740), edited by L. A. Selby-Bigge, revised by P. H. Nidditch (Oxford: Clarendon, 1978), p. 422.

[6] Vidyasagar's intellectual positions are discussed with insight and critical sympathy in Asok Sen, *Iswarchandra Vidyasagar and His Elusive Milestones* (Calcutta: Ridhhi, 1975).

[7] I have followed and modified the translation provided in Isvarchandra Vidyasagar, *Marriage of Hindu Widows*, edited by Arabindo Poddar (Calcutta, 1976), pp. 107–108.

Both Rammohun and Vidyasagar thus espoused a natural theory of compassion, the idea that compassion was a sentiment universally present in something called "human nature," however blocked its expression might be in a particular situation. This recalls Adam Smith, explaining his theory of sympathy: "How selfish soever man may be supposed, there are some principles in his nature which interest him in the fortune of others. . . . Of this kind is pity or compassion, the emotion we feel for the misery of others."[8] Hume also defined "pity" as a general sentiment, as "a concern for . . . the misery of others, without any friendship . . . to occasion this concern," and connected it to the general human capacity for sympathy. He wrote: "No quality of human nature is more remarkable . . . than that propensity we have to sympathize with others."[9] It is only on the basis of this kind of an understanding that Roy and Vidyasagar assigned to reason a critical role in fighting the effects of custom. Reason did not produce the sentiment of compassion; it simply helped in letting sentiments take their natural course by removing the obstacle of mindless custom. Needless to say, the underlying vision of the human being was truly a universal one.

■ REFLECTIONS

The Enlightenment and its political legacies—secular order and revolutionary republicanism—were European in origin but global in impact. In this chapter, we have touched on just a few of the crosscurrents of what some historians call an "Atlantic Revolution." A tide of revolutionary fervor swept through France, the United States, and Latin America, found sympathy in Russia in 1825, and echoed in the Muslim heartland, resulting in secular, modernizing regimes in Turkey and Egypt in the next century. Chakrabarty helps us ask if there may have been independent roots of reasoned compassion in India as well.

The political appeal of the Enlightenment, of rationally ordered society, and of democratic government continues. Some elements of this eighteenth-century revolution—the rule of law; regular, popular elections of representatives; the separation of church and state, of government and politics, and of civil and military authority—are widely recognized ideals and emerging global realities. Like science, the principles of the Enlightenment are universal in their claims and often seem

---

[8] Adam Smith, *The Theory of Moral Setiments*, edited by D. D. Raphael and A. L. Macfie (Indianapolis: Liberty Fund, 1984), p. 9. See also p. 22. Raphael and Macfie explain (p. 14n) that Smith's theories were in part a refutation of Hobbes's and Mandeville's contention that all sentiments arose from self-love.

[9] Hume, *Treatise*, pp. 316, 369.

universal in their appeal. Nothing is simpler, more rational, or easier to follow than a call to reason, law, liberty, justice, or equality. And yet every society has evolved its own guidelines under different circumstances, often with lasting results. France had its king and still has a relatively centralized state. The United States began with slavery and still suffers from racism. South American states became free of Europe only to dominate Native Americans, and they continue to do so. None of the enlightened or revolutionary societies of the eighteenth century extended the "rights of man" to women. One democratic society had a king, another a House of Lords, another a national church. Are these different adaptations of the Enlightenment ideal? Or are these examples of incomplete revolution, cases of special interests allowing their governments to fall short of principle?

The debate continues today as more societies seek to realize responsive, representative government and the rule of law while oftentimes respecting conflicting traditions. Muslim countries and Israel struggle with the competing demands of secular law and religion, citizenship and communalism. Former communist countries adopt market economies and struggle with traditions of collective support and the appeal of individual liberty.

Perhaps these are conflicts within the Enlightenment tradition itself. How is it possible to have both liberty and equality? How can we claim inalienable rights on the basis of a secular, scientific creed? How does a faith in human reason lead to revolution? And how can ideas of order or justice avoid the consequences of history and human nature?

The great revolutionary declarations of the Enlightenment embarrass the modern skeptic with their naïve faith in natural laws, their universal prescriptions to cure all ills, and their hypocritical avoidance of slaves, women, and the colonized. The selections by Toussaint and Abigail Adams, however, remind us that Enlightenment universalism was based not only on cool reason and calculation and the blind arrogance of the powerful. At least some of the great Enlightenment thinkers based their global prescription on the *felt* needs, even the sufferings, of others. For Toussaint, Adams, and Rammohun Roy, the recognition of human commonality began with a reasoned capacity for empathy that the Enlightenment may have bequeathed to the modern world, even shaping modern sensibility.

21

Capitalism and the Industrial Revolution

Europe and the World, 1750–1900

■ HISTORICAL CONTEXT

Two principal forces have shaped the modern world: capitalism and the industrial revolution. As influential as the transformations discussed in Chapters 19 and 20 (the rise of science and the democratic revolution), these two forces are sometimes considered to be one and the same, because the industrial revolution occurred first in capitalist countries such as England, Belgium, and the United States. In fact, the rise of capitalism preceded the industrial revolution by centuries.

Capitalism denotes a particular economic organization of a society, whereas *industrial revolution* refers to a particular transformation of technology. Specifically, in capitalism market forces (supply and demand) set money prices that determine how goods are distributed. Before 1500, most economic behavior was regulated by family, religion, tradition, and political authority rather than by markets. Increasingly after 1500 in Europe, feudal dues were converted into money rents, periodic fairs became institutionalized, banks were established, modern bookkeeping procedures were developed, and older systems of inherited economic status were loosened. After 1800, new populations of urban workers had to work for money to buy food and shelter; after 1850 in urban areas even clothing was usually purchased in the new "department stores." By 1900, the market had become the operating metaphor of society: One sold oneself; everything had its price. Viewed positively, a capitalist society is one in which buyers and sellers, who together compose the market, make most decisions about the production and distribution of resources. Viewed less favorably, it is the capitalists—those who own the "capital" (resources, stores, factories, and money)—who make the decisions about production and distribution.

The industrial revolution made mass production possible with the use of power-driven machines. Mills driven by waterwheels existed in ancient times, but the construction of identical, replaceable machinery—the machine production of machines—revolutionized industry and enabled the coordination of production on a vast scale, occurring first in England's cotton textile mills at the end of the eighteenth century. The market for such textiles was capitalist, though the demand for many early mass-produced goods, such as muskets and uniforms, was government-driven.

The origins of capitalism are hotly debated among historians. Because the world's first cities, five thousand years ago, created markets, merchants, money, and private ownership of capital, some historians refer to an ancient capitalism. In this text, *capitalism* refers to those societies whose markets, merchants, money, and private ownership became central to the way society operated. As such, ancient Mesopotamia, Rome, and Sung dynasty China, which had extensive markets and paper money a thousand years ago, were not among the first capitalist societies. Smaller societies in which commercial interests and merchant classes took hold to direct political and economic matters were the capitalist forerunners. Venice, Florence, Holland, and England, the mercantile states of the fifteenth to seventeenth centuries, exemplify *commercial capitalism* or mercantile capitalism. Thus, the shift to industrial capitalism was more than a change in scale; it was also a transition from a trade-based economy to a manufacturing-based economy, a difference that meant an enormous increase in productivity, profits, and prosperity.

■ THINKING HISTORICALLY

Distinguishing Historical Processes

When two distinct historical processes occur simultaneously and in mutually reinforcing ways, like the spread of agriculture and languages—or capitalism and industrialization—we might confuse one process of change with the other. This confusion makes it difficult to see exactly what causes what. Here you will be encouraged to distinguish between the latter two historical processes. As you read these selections, keep in mind that capitalism is an economic system that spreads markets, commerce, and the interests of private capital; the industrial revolution was a transformation in technology. How did these two very different processes coincide in the nineteenth century? In what ways were they moving toward different ends, causing different effects, or benefiting different interests?

1

ARNOLD PACEY

Asia and the Industrial Revolution

Here a modern historian of technology demonstrates how Indian and East Asian manufacturing techniques were assimilated by Europeans, particularly by the English successors of the Mughal Empire, providing a boost to the industrial revolution in Britain. In what ways was Indian technology considered superior prior to the industrial revolution? How did European products gain greater markets than those of India?

THINKING HISTORICALLY

Notice how the author distinguishes between capitalism and the industrial revolution. Was India more industrially advanced than capitalistic? Did the British conquest of India benefit more from capitalism, industry, or something else?

Deindustrialization

During the eighteenth century, India participated in the European industrial revolution through the influence of its textile trade, and through the investments in shipping made by Indian bankers and merchants. Developments in textiles and shipbuilding constituted a significant industrial movement, but it would be wrong to suggest that India was on the verge of its own industrial revolution. There was no steam engine in India, no coal mines, and few machines. . . . [E]xpanding industries were mostly in coastal areas. Much of the interior was in economic decline, with irrigation works damaged and neglected as a result of the breakup of the Mughal Empire and the disruption of war. Though political weakness in the empire had been evident since 1707, and a Persian army heavily defeated Mughal forces at Delhi in 1739, it was the British who most fully took advantage of the collapse of the empire. Between 1757 and 1803, they took control of most of India except the Northwest. The result was that the East India Company now administered major sectors of the economy, and quickly reduced the role of the big Indian bankers by changes in taxes and methods of collecting them.

Meanwhile, India's markets in Europe were being eroded by competition from machine-spun yarns and printed calicoes made in Lancashire, and high customs duties were directed against Indian imports into

Source: Arnold Pacey, *Technology in World Civilization* (Cambridge: MIT Press, 1990), 128–35.

Britain. Restrictions were also placed on the use of Indian-built ships for voyages to England. From 1812, there were extra duties on any imports they delivered, and that must be one factor in the decline in shipbuilding. A few Indian ships continued to make the voyage to Britain, however, and there was one in Liverpool Docks in 1839 when Herman Melville arrived from America. It was the *Irrawaddy* from Bombay and Melville commented: "Forty years ago, these merchantmen were nearly the largest in the world; and they still exceed the generality." They were "wholly built by the native shipwrights of India, who . . . surpassed the European artisans." . . .

Attitudes to India changed markedly after the subcontinent had fallen into British hands. Before this, travellers found much to admire in technologies ranging from agriculture to metallurgy. After 1803, however, the arrogance of conquest was reinforced by the rapid development of British industry. This meant that Indian techniques which a few years earlier seemed remarkable could now be equalled at much lower cost by British factories. India was then made to appear rather primitive, and the idea grew that its proper role was to provide raw materials for western industry, including raw cotton and indigo dye, and to function as a market for British goods. This policy was reflected in 1813 by a relaxation of the East India Company's monopoly of trade so that other British companies could now bring in manufactured goods freely for sale in India. Thus the textile industry, iron production, and shipbuilding were all eroded by cheap imports from Britain, and by handicaps placed on Indian merchants.

By 1830, the situation had become so bad that even some of the British in India began to protest. One exclaimed, "We have destroyed the manufactures of India," pleading that there should be some protection for silk weaving, "the last of the expiring manufactures of India." Another observer was alarmed by a "commercial revolution" which produced "so much present suffering to numerous classes in India."

The question that remains is the speculative one of what might have happened if a strong Mughal government had survived. Fernand Braudel argues that although there was no lack of "capitalism" in India, the economy was not moving in the direction of home-grown industrialization. The historian of technology inevitably notes the lack of development of machines, even though there had been some increase in the use of water-wheels during the eighteenth century both in the iron industry and at gunpowder mills. However, it is impossible not to be struck by the achievements of the shipbuilding industry, which produced skilled carpenters and a model of large-scale organizations. It also trained up draughtsmen and people with mechanical interests. It is striking that one of the Wadia shipbuilders installed gas lighting in his home in 1834 and built a small foundry in which he made parts for steam engines. Given an independent and more prosperous India, it is difficult not to believe that a response to British industrialization might well have taken the form of a spread of skill and innovation from the shipyards into other industries.

As it was, such developments were delayed until the 1850s and later, when the first mechanized cotton mill opened. It is significant that some of the entrepreneurs who backed the development of this industry were from the same Parsi families as had built ships in Bombay and invested in overseas trade in the eighteenth century.

Guns and Rails: Asia, Britain, and America

Asian Stimulus

Britain's "conquest" of India cannot be attributed to superior armaments. Indian armies were also well equipped. More significant was the prior breakdown of Mughal government and the collaboration of many Indians. Some victories were also the result of good discipline and bold strategy, especially when Arthur Wellesley, the future Duke of Wellington, was in command. Wellesley's contribution also illustrates the distinctive western approach to the organizational aspect of technology. Indian armies might have had good armament, but because their guns were made in a great variety of different sizes, precise weapons drill was impossible and the supply of shot to the battlefield was unnecessarily complicated. By contrast, Wellesley's forces standardized on just three sizes of field gun, and the commander himself paid close attention to the design of gun carriages and to the bullocks which hauled them, so that his artillery could move as fast as his infantry, and without delays due to wheel breakages.

Significantly, the one major criticism regularly made of Indian artillery concerned the poor design of gun carriages. Many, particularly before 1760, were little better than four-wheeled trolleys. But the guns themselves were often of excellent design and workmanship. Whilst some were imported and others were made with the assistance of foreign craftworkers, there was many a brass cannon and mortar of Indian design, as well as heavy muskets for camel-mounted troops. Captured field guns were often taken over for use by the British, and after capturing ninety guns in one crucial battle, Wellesley wrote that seventy were "the finest brass ordnance I have ever seen." They were probably made in northern India, perhaps at the great Mughal arsenal at Agra.

Whilst Indians had been making guns from brass since the sixteenth century, Europeans could at first only produce this alloy in relatively small quantities because they had no technique for smelting zinc. By the eighteenth century, however, brass was being produced in large quantities in Europe, and brass cannon were being cast at Woolwich Arsenal near London. Several European countries were importing metallic zinc from China for this purpose. However, from 1743 there was a smelter near Bristol in England producing zinc, using coke[1] as fuel, and zinc smelters were also developed in Germany. At the end of the century, Britain's imports of zinc from the Far East were only about forty tons per year. Nevertheless, a British party which visited China in 1797 took particular note of zinc smelting methods. These were similar to the process used in India, which involved vaporizing the metal and then condensing it. There is a suspicion that the Bristol smelting works of 1743 was based on Indian practice, although the possibility of independent invention cannot be excluded.

A much clearer example of the transfer of technology from India occurred when British armies on the subcontinent encountered rockets, a type of weapon of which they had no previous experience. The basic technology had come from the Ottoman Turks or from Syria before 1500, although the Chinese had invented rockets even earlier. In the 1790s, some Indian armies included very large infantry units equipped with rockets. French mercenaries in Mysore had learned to make them, and the British Ordnance Office was enquiring for somebody with expertise on the subject. In response, William Congreve, whose father was head of the laboratory at Woolwich Arsenal, undertook to design a rocket on Indian lines. After a successful demonstration, about two hundred of his rockets were used by the British in an attack on Boulogne in 1806. Fired from over a kilometre away, they set fire to the town. After this success, rockets were adopted quite widely by European armies, though some commanders, notably the Duke of Wellington, frowned on such imprecise weapons, and they tended to drop out of use later in the century. What happened next, however, was typical of the whole British relationship with India. William Congreve set up a factory to manufacture the weapons in 1817, and part of its output was exported to India to equip rocket troops operating there under British command.

Yet another aspect of Asian technology in which eighteenth-century Europeans were interested was the design of farm implements. Reports on seed drills and ploughs were sent to the British Board of Agriculture from India in 1795. A century earlier the Dutch had found much of interest in ploughs and winnowing machines of a Chinese type which they saw in Java. Then a Swedish party visiting Guangzhou (Canton)

---

[1] Fuel from soft coal. [Ed.]

took a winnowing machine back home with them. Indeed, several of these machines were imported into different parts of Europe, and similar devices for cleaning threshed grain were soon being made there. The inventor of one of them, Jonas Norberg, admitted that he got "the initial idea" from three machines "brought here from China," but had to create a new type because the Chinese machines "do not suit our kinds of grain." Similarly, the Dutch saw that the Chinese plough did not suit their type of soil, but it stimulated them to produce new designs with curved metal mould-boards in contrast to the less efficient flat wooden boards used in Europe hitherto.

In most of these cases, and especially with zinc smelting, rockets, and winnowing machines, we have clear evidence of Europeans studying Asian technology in detail. With rockets and winnowers, though perhaps not with zinc, there was an element of imitation in the European inventions which followed. In other instances, however, the more usual course of technological dialogue between Europe and Asia was that European innovation was challenged by the quality or scale of Asian output, but took a different direction, as we have seen in many aspects of the textile industry. Sometimes, the dialogue was even more limited, and served mainly to give confidence in a technique that was already known. Such was the case with occasional references to China in the writings of engineers designing suspension bridges in Britain. The Chinese had a reputation for bridge construction, and before 1700 Peter the Great had asked for bridge-builders to be sent from China to work in Russia. Later, several books published in Europe described a variety of Chinese bridges, notably a long-span suspension bridge made with iron chains.

Among those who developed the suspension bridge in the West were James Finley in America, beginning in 1801, and Samuel Brown and Thomas Telford in Britain. About 1814, Brown devised a flat, wrought-iron chain link which Telford later used to form the main structural chains in his suspension bridges. But beyond borrowing this specific technique, what Telford needed was evidence that the suspension principle was applicable to the problem he was then tackling. Finley's two longest bridges had spanned seventy-four and ninety-three metres, over the Merrimac and Schuylkill Rivers in the eastern United States. Telford was aiming to span almost twice the larger distance with his 176-metre Menai Bridge. Experiments at a Shropshire ironworks gave confidence in the strength of the chains. But Telford may have looked for reassurance even further afield. One of his notebooks contains the reminder, "Examine Chinese bridges." It is clear from the wording which follows that he had seen a recent booklet advocating a "bridge of chains," partly based on a Chinese example, to cross the Firth of Forth in Scotland.

2

ADAM SMITH
The Wealth of Nations

An Inquiry into the Nature and Causes of the Wealth of Nations might justly be called the bible of free-market capitalism. Written in 1776 in the context of the British (and European) debate over the proper role of government in the economy, Smith's work takes aim at *mercantilism,* or government supervision of the economy. Mercantilists believed that national economies required government assistance and direction to prosper.

Smith argues that free trade will produce greater wealth than mercantilist trade and that free markets allocate resources more efficiently than the government. His notion of *laissez-faire* (literally "let do") capitalism assumes neither that capitalists are virtuous nor that governments should absent themselves entirely from the economy. However, Smith does believe that the greed of capitalists generally negates itself and produces results that are advantageous to, but unimagined by, the individual. "It is not from the benevolence of the butcher, the brewer, or the baker, that we expect our dinner," Smith writes, "but from their regard of their own interest. We address ourselves not to their humanity, but to their self-love, and never talk to them of our own necessities, but of their advantage."[1] Each person seeks to maximize his or her own gain, thereby creating an efficient market in which the cost of goods is instantly adjusted to exploit changes in supply and demand, while the market provides what is needed at the price people are willing to pay "as if by an invisible hand."

According to Smith, what is the relationship between money and industry, and which is more important? What would Smith say to a farmer or manufacturer who wanted to institute tariffs or quotas to limit the number of cheaper imports entering the country and to minimize competition? What would he say to a government official who wanted to protect an important domestic industry? What would he say to a worker who complained about low wages or boring work? What would Smith think about a "postindustrial" or "service" economy in which few workers actually make products? What would he think of a prosperous country that imported more than it exported?

THINKING HISTORICALLY

The Wealth of Nations was written in defense of free capitalism at a moment when the industrial revolution was just beginning. Some elements

[1] Book I, chapter 2.

Source: Adam Smith, *An Inquiry into the Nature and Causes of the Wealth of Nations* (Indianapolis: Liberty Fund, 1981, a reprint of the Oxford University Press edition of 1976), 1:13–15, 31, 47, 73–74, 449–50, 455–57.

of Smith's writing suggest a preindustrial world, as in the quotation about the butcher, brewer, and baker mentioned earlier. Still, Smith was aware how new industrial methods were transforming age-old labor relations and manufacturing processes. In some respects, Smith recognized that capitalism could create wealth, not just redistribute it, because he appreciated the potential of industrial technology.

As you read this selection, note when Smith is discussing capitalism, the economic system, and the power of the new industrial technology. In his discussion of the division of labor, what relationship does Smith see between the development of a capitalistic market and the rise of industrial technology? To what extent could the benefits that Smith attributes to a free market be attributed to the new system of industrial production?

Book I
Of the Causes of Improvement in the Productive Powers of Labour, and of the Order According to Which Its Produce Is Naturally Distributed among the Different Ranks of the People

Chapter 1: Of the Division of Labour

The greatest improvement in the productive powers of labour, and the greater part of the skill, dexterity, and judgment with which it is anywhere directed, or applied, seem to have been the effects of the division of labour.

The effects of the division of labour, in the general business of society, will be more easily understood by considering in what manner it operates in some particular manufactures. . . .

To take an example, therefore, from a very trifling manufacture; but one in which the division of labour has been very often taken notice of, the trade of the pin-maker; a workman not educated to this business (which the division of labour has rendered a distinct trade), nor acquainted with the use of the machinery employed in it (to the invention of which the same division of labour has probably given occasion), could scarce, perhaps, with his utmost industry, make one pin in a day, and certainly could not make twenty. But in the way in which this business is now carried on, not only the whole work is a peculiar trade, but it is divided into a number of branches, of which the greater part are likewise peculiar trades. One man draws out the wire, another straights it, a third cuts it, a fourth points it, a fifth grinds it at the top for receiving the head; to make the head requires two or three distinct operations; to put it on is a peculiar business, to whiten the pins is another; it is even a trade by itself to put them into the paper; and the important business of making a pin is, in this manner, divided into about eighteen distinct operations, which, in some manufactories, are all performed by distinct hands, though in others the same man will sometimes perform two or three of them. I have seen a small manufactory of this kind where ten men only were employed, and where some of them consequently performed two or three distinct operations. But though they were very poor, and therefore but indifferently accommodated with the necessary machinery, they could, when they exerted themselves, make among them about twelve pounds of pins in a day. There are in a pound upwards of four thousand pins of a middling size. Those ten persons, therefore, could make among them upwards of forty-eight thousand pins in a day. Each person, therefore, making a tenth part of forty-eight thousand pins, might be considered as making four thousand eight hundred pins in a day. But if they had all wrought separately and independently, and without any of them having been educated to this peculiar business, they certainly could not each of them have made twenty, perhaps not one pin in a day; that is, certainly, not the two hundred and fortieth, perhaps not the four thousand eight hundredth part of what they are at present capable of performing, in consequence of a proper division and combination of their different operations.

In every other art and manufacture, the effects of the division of labour are similar to what they are in this very trifling one; though, in many of them, the labour can neither be so much subdivided, nor reduced to so great a simplicity of operation. . . .

Chapter 3: That the Division of Labour Is Limited by the Extent of the Market

As it is the power of exchanging that gives occasion to the division of labour, so the extent of this division must always be limited by the extent of that power, or, in other words, by the extent of the market. When the market is very small, no person can have any encouragement to dedicate himself entirely to one employment, for want of the power to exchange all that surplus part of the produce of his own labour, which is over and above his own consumption, for such parts of the produce of other men's labour as he has occasion for.

There are some sorts of industry, even of the lowest kind, which can be carried on nowhere but in a great town. A porter, for example, can find employment and subsistence in no other place. A village is by much too narrow a sphere for him. . . .

Chapter 5: Of the Real and Nominal Price of Commodities, or Their Price in Labour, and Their Price in Money

Every man is rich or poor according to the degree in which he can afford to enjoy the necessaries, conveniences, and amusements of human life. But after the division of labour has once thoroughly taken place, it is but a very small part of these with which a man's own labour can supply him. The far greater part of them he must derive from the labour of other people, and he must be rich or poor according to the quantity of that labour which he can command, or which he can afford to purchase. The value of any commodity, therefore, to the person who possesses it, and who means not to use or consume it himself, but to exchange it for other commodities, is equal to the quantity of labour which it enables him to purchase or command. Labour, therefore, is the real measure of the exchangeable value of all commodities. . . .

Chapter 7: Of the Natural and Market Price of Commodities

. . . When the quantity of any commodity which is brought to market falls short of the effectual demand, all those who are willing to pay the whole value of the rent, wages, and profit, which must be paid in order to bring it thither, cannot be supplied with the quantity which they want. Rather than want[2] it altogether, some of them will be willing to give more. A competition will immediately begin among them, and the market price will rise more or less above the natural price, according as either the greatness of the deficiency, or the wealth and wanton luxury of the competitors, happen to animate more or less the eagerness of the competition. Among competitors of equal wealth and luxury the same deficiency will generally occasion a more or less eager competition, according as the acquisition of the commodity happens to be of more or less importance to them. Hence the exorbitant price of the necessaries of life during the blockade of a town or in a famine.

When the quantity brought to market exceeds the effectual demand, it cannot be all sold to those who are willing to pay the whole value of the rent, wages, and profit, which must be paid in order to bring it thither. Some part must be sold to those who are willing to pay less, and the low price which they give for it must reduce the price of the whole. The market price will sink more or less below the natural price, according as the greatness of the excess increases more or less the competition of the sellers, or according as it happens to be more or less important to them to get immediately rid of the commodity. The same excess in the importation of perishables will occasion a much greater competition than in that of durable commodities; in the importation of oranges, for example, than in that of old iron.

When the quantity brought to market is just sufficient to supply the effectual demand, and no more, the market price naturally comes to be either exactly, or as nearly as can be judged of, the same with the natural price. The whole quantity upon hand can be disposed of for this price,

---

[2] Be without it. [Ed.]

and cannot be disposed of for more. The competition of the different dealers obliges them all to accept of this price, but does not oblige them to accept of less.

The quantity of every commodity brought to market naturally suits itself to the effectual demand. It is the interest of all those who employ their land, labour, or stock, in bringing any commodity to market, that the quantity never should exceed the effectual demand; and it is the interest of all other people that it never should fall short of that demand.

Book IV
Of Systems of Political Economy

Chapter 1: Of the Principle of the Commercial or Mercantile System

. . . I thought it necessary, though at the hazard of being tedious, to examine at full length this popular notion that wealth consists in money, or in gold and silver. Money in common language, as I have already observed, frequently signifies wealth, and this ambiguity of expression has rendered this popular notion so familiar to us that even they who are convinced of its absurdity are very apt to forget their own principles, and in the course of their reasonings to take it for granted as a certain and undeniable truth. Some of the best English writers upon commerce set out with observing that the wealth of a country consists, not in its gold and silver only, but in its lands, houses, and consumable goods of all different kinds. In the course of their reasonings, however, the lands, houses, and consumable goods seem to slip out of their memory, and the strain of their argument frequently supposes that all wealth consists in gold and silver, and that to multiply those metals is the great object of national industry and commerce. . . .

Chapter 2: Of Restraints upon the Importation from Foreign Countries of Such Goods as Can Be Produced at Home

. . . The produce of industry is what it adds to the subject or materials upon which it is employed. In proportion as the value of this produce is great or small, so will likewise be the profits of the employer. But it is only for the sake of profit that any man employs a capital in the support of industry; and he will always, therefore, endeavour to employ it in the support of that industry of which the produce is likely to be of the greatest value, or to exchange for the greatest quantity either of money or of other goods.

But the annual revenue of every society is always precisely equal to the exchangeable value of the whole annual produce of its industry, or rather is precisely the same thing with that exchangeable value. As every individual, therefore, endeavours as much as he can both to employ his capital in the support of domestic industry, and so to direct that industry that its produce may be of the greatest value; every individual necessarily labours to render the annual revenue of the society as great as he can. He generally, indeed, neither intends to promote the public interest, nor knows how much he is promoting it. By preferring the support of domestic to that of foreign industry, he intends only his own security; and by directing that industry in such a manner as its produce may be of the greatest value, he intends only his own gain, and he is in this, as in many other cases, led by an invisible hand to promote an end which was no part of his intention. Nor is it always the worse for the society that it was no part of it. By pursuing his own interest he frequently promotes that of the society more effectually than when he really intends to promote it. I have never known much good done by those who affected to trade for the public good. It is an affectation, indeed, not very common among merchants, and very few words need be employed in dissuading them from it.

What is the species of domestic industry which his capital can employ, and of which the produce is likely to be of the greatest value, every individual, it is evident, can, in his local situation, judge much better than any statesman or lawgiver can do for him. The statesman who should attempt to direct private people in what manner they ought to employ their capitals would not only load himself with a most unnecessary attention, but assume an authority which could safely be trusted, not only to no single person, but to no council or senate whatever, and which would nowhere be so dangerous as in the hands of a man who had folly and presumption enough to fancy himself fit to exercise it.

To give the monopoly of the home market to the produce of domestic industry, in any particular art or manufacture, is in some measure to direct private people in what manner they ought to employ their capitals, and must, in almost all cases, be either a useless or a hurtful regulation. If the produce of domestic can be brought there as cheap as that of foreign industry, the regulation is evidently useless. If it cannot, it must generally be hurtful. It is the maxim of every prudent master of a family never to attempt to make at home what it will cost him more to make than to buy. The tailor does not attempt to make his own shoes, but buys them of the shoemaker. The shoemaker does not attempt to make his own clothes, but employs a tailor. The farmer attempts to make neither the one nor the other, but employs those different artificers. All of them find it for their interest to employ their whole industry in a way in which they have some advantage over their neighbours, and to purchase with a part of its produce, or what is the same thing, with the price of a part of it, whatever else they have occasion for.

What is prudence in the conduct of every private family can scarce be folly in that of a great kingdom. If a foreign country can supply us with a commodity cheaper than we ourselves can make it, better buy it of them with some part of the produce of our own industry employed in a way in which we have some advantage. The general industry of the country, being always in proportion to the capital which employs it, will not thereby be diminished, no more than that of the abovementioned artificers; but only left to find out the way in which it can be employed with the greatest advantage. It is certainly not employed to the greatest advantage when it is thus directed towards an object which it can buy cheaper than it can make. . . .

3

The Sadler Report of the House of Commons

Although, for many factory owners, children were among the ideal workers in the factories of the industrial revolution, increasingly their exploitation became a concern of the British Parliament. One important parliamentary investigation, chaired by Michael Sadler, took volumes of testimony from child workers and older people who had worked as children in the mines and factories. The following is a sample of that testimony: an interview with a former child worker named Matthew Crabtree who had worked in a textile factory. The Sadler Commission report led to child-labor reform in the Factory Act of 1833.

What seem to be the causes of Crabtree's distress? How could it have been alleviated? If the owner were asked why he didn't pay more, shorten the workday, provide more time for meals, or provide medical assistance when it was needed, how do you think he would have responded? Do you think Crabtree would have been in favor of reduced hours if it meant reduced wages?

THINKING HISTORICALLY

To what extent are the problems faced by Crabtree the inevitable results of machine production? To what extent are his problems caused by capitalism? How might the owner of this factory have addressed these issues?

Source: From *The Sadler Report: Report from the Committee on the Bill to Regulate the Labour of Children in the Mills and Factories of the United Kingdom* (London: The House of Commons, Parliamentary Papers, 1831–1832), 15:95–97.

Friday, 18 May 1832 — Michael Thomas Sadler, Esquire, in the Chair

Mr. Matthew Crabtree, *called in; and Examined.*

What age are you? — Twenty-two.

What is your occupation? — A blanket manufacturer.

Have you ever been employed in a factory? — Yes.

At what age did you first go to work in one? — Eight.

How long did you continue in that occupation? — Four years.

Will you state the hours of labour at the period when you first went to the factory, in ordinary times? — From 6 in the morning to 8 at night.

Fourteen hours? — Yes.

With what intervals for refreshment and rest? — An hour at noon.

Then you had no resting time allowed in which to take your breakfast, or what is in Yorkshire called your "drinking"? — No.

When trade was brisk what were your hours? — From 5 in the morning to 9 in the evening.

Sixteen hours? — Yes.

With what intervals at dinner[1]? — An hour.

How far did you live from the mill? — About two miles.

Was there any time allowed for you to get your breakfast in the mill? — No.

Did you take it before you left your home? — Generally.

During those long hours of labour could you be punctual; how did you awake? — I seldom did awake spontaneously; I was most generally awoke or lifted out of bed, sometimes asleep, by my parents.

Were you always in time? — No.

What was the consequence if you had been too late? — I was most commonly beaten.

Severely? — Very severely, I thought.

In whose factory was this? — Messrs. Hague & Cook's, of Dewsbury.

Will you state the effect that those long hours had upon the state of your health and feelings? — I was, when working those long hours, commonly very much fatigued at night, when I left my work; so much so that I sometimes should have slept as I walked if I had not stumbled and started awake again; and so sick often that I could not eat, and what I did eat I vomited.

Did this labour destroy your appetite? — It did.

In what situation were you in that mill? — I was a piecener.

Will you state to this Committee whether piecening is a very laborious employment for children, or not? — It is a very laborious employment. Pieceners are continually running to and fro, and on their feet the whole day.

[1] The main meal, in the afternoon. Not the evening supper. [Ed.]

The duty of the piecener is to take the cardings from one part of the machinery, and to place them on another? — Yes.

So that the labour is not only continual, but it is unabated to the last? — It is unabated to the last.

Do you not think, from your own experience, that the speed of the machinery is so calculated as to demand the utmost exertions of a child supposing the hours were moderate? — It is as much as they could do at the best; they are always upon the stretch, and it is commonly very difficult to keep up with their work.

State the condition of the children toward the latter part of the day, who have thus to keep up with the machinery. — It is as much as they can do when they are not very much fatigued to keep up with their work, and toward the close of the day, when they come to be more fatigued, they cannot keep up with it very well, and the consequence is that they are beaten to spur them on.

Were you beaten under those circumstances? — Yes.

Frequently? — Very frequently.

And principally at the latter end of the day? — Yes.

And is it your belief that if you had not been so beaten, you should not have got through the work? — I should not if I had not been kept up to it by some means.

Does beating then principally occur at the latter end of the day, when the children are exceedingly fatigued? — It does at the latter end of the day, and in the morning sometimes, when they are very drowsy, and have not got rid of the fatigue of the day before.

What were you beaten with principally? — A strap.

Anything else? — Yes, a stick sometimes; and there is a kind of roller which runs on the top of the machine called a billy, perhaps two or three yards in length, and perhaps an inch and a half, or more in diameter; the circumference would be four or five inches; I cannot speak exactly.

Were you beaten with that instrument? — Yes.

Have you yourself been beaten, and have you seen other children struck severely with that roller? — I have been struck very severely with it myself, so much so as to knock me down, and I have seen other children have their heads broken with it.

You think that it is a general practice to beat the children with the roller? — It is.

You do not think then that you were worse treated than other children in the mill? — No, I was not, perhaps not so bad as some were.

In those mills is chastisement towards the latter part of the day going on perpetually? — Perpetually.

So that you can hardly be in a mill without hearing constant crying? — Never an hour, I believe.

Do you think that if the overlooker were naturally a humane person it would be still found necessary for him to beat the children, in order to keep up their attention and vigilance at the termination of those extraordinary days of labour? — Yes, the machine turns off a regular quantity of cardings, and of course they must keep as regularly to their work the whole of the day; they must keep with the machine, and therefore however humane the slubber may be, as he must keep up with the machine or be found fault with, he spurs the children to keep up also by various means but that which he commonly resorts to is to strap them when they become drowsy.

At the time when you were beaten for not keeping up with your work, were you anxious to have done it if you possibly could? — Yes; the dread of being beaten if we could not keep up with our work was a sufficient impulse to keep us to it if we could.

When you got home at night after this labour, did you feel much fatigued? — Very much so.

Had you any time to be with your parents, and to receive instruction from them? — No.

What did you do? — All that we did when we got home was to get the little bit of supper that was provided for us and go to bed immediately. If the supper had not been ready directly, we should have gone to sleep while it was preparing.

Did you not, as a child, feel it a very grievous hardship to be roused so soon in the morning? — I did.

Were the rest of the children similarly circumstanced? — Yes, all of them; but they were not all of them so far from their work as I was.

And if you had been too late you were under the apprehension of being cruelly beaten? — I generally was beaten when I happened to be too late; and when I got up in the morning the apprehension of that was so great, that I used to run, and cry all the way as I went to the mill.

That was the way by which your punctual attendance was secured? — Yes.

And you do not think it could have been secured by any other means? — No.

Then it is your impression from what you have seen, and from your own experience, that those long hours of labour have the effect of rendering young persons who are subject to them exceedingly unhappy? — Yes.

You have already said it had a considerable effect upon your health? — Yes.

Do you conceive that it diminished your growth? — I did not pay much attention to that; but I have been examined by some persons who said they thought I was rather stunted, and that I should have been taller if I had not worked at the mill.

What were your wages at that time? — Three shillings (per week).

And how much a day had you for overwork when you were worked so exceedingly long? — A halfpenny a day.

Did you frequently forfeit that if you were not always there to a moment? — Yes; I most frequently forfeited what was allowed for those long hours.

You took your food to the mill; was it in your mill, as is the case in cotton mills, much spoiled by being laid aside? — It was very frequently covered by flues from the wool; and in that case they had to be blown off with the mouth, and picked off with the fingers before it could be eaten.

So that not giving you a little leisure for eating your food, but obliging you to take it at the mill, spoiled your food when you did get it? — Yes, very commonly.

And that at the same time that this over-labour injured your appetite? — Yes.

Could you eat when you got home? — Not always.

What is the effect of this piecening upon the hands? — It makes them bleed; the skin is completely rubbed off, and in that case they bleed in perhaps a dozen parts.

The prominent parts of the hand? — Yes, all the prominent parts of the hand are rubbed down till they bleed; every day they are rubbed in that way.

All the time you continue at work? — All the time we are working. The hands never can be hardened in that work, for the grease keeps them soft in the first instance, and long and continual rubbing is always wearing them down, so that if they were hard they would be sure to bleed.

It is attended with much pain? — Very much.

Do they allow you to make use of the back of the hand? — No; the work cannot be so well done with the back of the hand, or I should have made use of that.

4

KARL MARX AND FRIEDRICH ENGELS

The Communist Manifesto

The Communist Manifesto was written in 1848 in the midst of European upheaval, a time when capitalist industrialization had spread from England to France and Germany. Marx and Engels were Germans who studied and worked in France and England. In the *Manifesto*, they

Source: Karl Marx and Friedrich Engels, *The Communist Manifesto* (1888; Boston: Bedford/ St. Martin's, 1999), 65–72.

imagine a revolution that will transform all of Europe. What do they see as the inevitable causes of this revolution? How, according to their analysis, is the crisis of "modern" society different from previous crises? Were Marx and Engels correct?

THINKING HISTORICALLY

Notice how Marx and Engels describe the notions of capitalism and industrialization without using those words. The term *capitalism* developed later from Marx's classic *Das Kapital* (1859), but the term *bourgeoisie,** as Engels notes in this selection, stands for the capitalist class. For Marx and Engels, the industrial revolution (another later phrase) is the product of a particular stage of capitalist development. Thus, if Marx and Engels were asked whether capitalism or industry was the principal force that created the modern world, what would their answer be?

The Communist Manifesto is widely known as the classic critique of capitalism, but a careful reading reveals a list of achievements of capitalist or "bourgeois civilization." What are these achievements? Did Marx and Engels consider them to be achievements? How could Marx and Engels both praise and criticize capitalism?

Bourgeois and Proletarians[1]

The history of all hitherto existing society is the history of class struggles.

Freeman and slave, patrician and plebeian, lord and serf, guild-master and journeyman, in a word, oppressor and oppressed, stood in constant opposition to one another, carried on an uninterrupted, now hidden, now open fight, a fight that each time ended, either in a revolutionary reconstitution of society at large, or in the common ruin of the contending classes.

In the earlier epochs of history, we find almost everywhere a complicated arrangement of society into various orders, a manifold gradation of social rank. In ancient Rome we have patricians, knights, plebeians, slaves; in the Middle Ages, feudal lords, vassals, guildmasters, journeymen, apprentices, serfs; in almost all of these classes, again, subordinate gradations.

---

* bohr zhwah ZEE

[1] In French *bourgeois* means a town-dweller. *Proletarian* comes from the Latin *proletarius*, which meant a person whose sole wealth was his offspring (*proles*). [Ed.] [Note by Engels] By "bourgeoisie" is meant the class of modern capitalists, owners of the means of social production and employers of wage labor; by "proletariat," the class of modern wage-laborers who, having no means of production of their own, are reduced to selling their labor power in order to live.

The modern bourgeois society that has sprouted from the ruins of feudal society, has not done away with class antagonisms. It has but established new classes, new conditions of oppression, new forms of struggle in place of the old ones.

Our epoch, the epoch of the bourgeoisie, possesses, however, this distinctive feature: It has simplified the class antagonisms. Society as a whole is more and more splitting up into the two great hostile camps, into two great classes directly facing each other—bourgeoisie and proletariat.

From the serfs of the Middle Ages sprang the chartered burghers of the earliest towns. From these burgesses the first elements of the bourgeoisie were developed.

The discovery of America, the rounding of the Cape, opened up fresh ground for the rising bourgeoisie. The East-Indian and Chinese markets, the colonization of America, trade with the colonies, the increase in the means of exchange and in commodities generally, gave to commerce, to navigation, to industry, an impulse never before known, and thereby, to the revolutionary element in the tottering feudal society, a rapid development.

The feudal system of industry, in which industrial production was monopolized by closed guilds, now no longer sufficed for the growing wants of the new markets. The manufacturing system took its place. The guildmasters were pushed aside by the manufacturing middle class; division of labor between the different corporate guilds vanished in the face of division of labor in each single workshop.

Meantime the markets kept ever growing, the demand ever rising. Even manufacture[2] no longer sufficed. Thereupon, steam and machinery revolutionized industrial production. The place of manufacture was taken by the giant, modern industry, the place of the industrial middle class, by industrial millionaires—the leaders of whole industrial armies, the modern bourgeois.

Modern industry has established the world market, for which the discovery of America paved the way. This market has given an immense development to commerce, to navigation, to communication by land. This development has, in its turn, reacted on the extension of industry; and in proportion as industry, commerce, navigation, railways extended, in the same proportion the bourgeoisie developed, increased its capital, and pushed into the background every class handed down from the Middle Ages.

We see, therefore, how the modern bourgeoisie is itself the product of a long course of development, of a series of revolutions in the modes of production and of exchange.

---

[2] By *manufacture* Marx meant the system of production that succeeded the guild system but that still relied mainly on direct human labor for power. He distinguished it from modern industry, which arose when machinery driven by water and steam was introduced. [Ed.]

Each step in the development of the bourgeoisie was accompanied by a corresponding political advance of that class. An oppressed class under the sway of the feudal nobility, it became an armed and self-governing association in the medieval commune; here independent urban republic (as in Italy and Germany), there taxable "third estate" of the monarchy (as in France); afterwards, in the period of manufacture proper, serving either the semifeudal or the absolute monarchy as a counterpoise against the nobility, and, in fact, cornerstone of the great monarchies in general—the bourgeoisie has at last, since the establishment of modern industry and of the world market, conquered for itself, in the modern representative state, exclusive political sway. The executive of the modern state is but a committee for managing the common affairs of the whole bourgeoisie.

The bourgeoisie has played a most revolutionary role in history.

The bourgeoisie, wherever it has got the upper hand, has put an end to all feudal, patriarchal, idyllic relations. It has pitilessly torn asunder the motley feudal ties that bound man to his "natural superiors," and has left no other bond between man and man than naked self-interest, than callous "cash payment." It has drowned the most heavenly ecstasies of religious fervor, of chivalrous enthusiasm, of philistine sentimentalism, in the icy water of egotistical calculation. It has resolved personal worth into exchange value, and in place of the numberless indefensible chartered freedoms, has set up that single, unconscionable freedom—Free Trade. In one word, for exploitation, veiled by religious and political illusions, it has substituted naked, shameless, direct, brutal exploitation.

The bourgeoisie has stripped of its halo every occupation hitherto honored and looked up to with reverent awe. It has converted the physician, the lawyer, the priest, the poet, the man of science, into its paid wage-laborers.

The bourgeoisie has torn away from the family its sentimental veil, and has reduced the family relation to a mere money relation.

The bourgeoisie has disclosed how it came to pass that the brutal display of vigor in the Middle Ages, which reactionaries so much admire, found its fitting complement in the most slothful indolence. It has been the first to show what man's activity can bring about. It has accomplished wonders far surpassing Egyptian pyramids, Roman aqueducts, and Gothic cathedrals; it has conducted expeditions that put in the shade all former migrations of nations and crusades.

The bourgeoisie cannot exist without constantly revolutionizing the instruments of production, and thereby the relations of production, and with them the whole relations of society. Conservation of the old modes of production in unaltered form, was, on the contrary, the first condition of existence for all earlier industrial classes. Constant revolutionizing of production, uninterrupted disturbance of all social conditions, everlasting uncertainty and agitation distinguished the bourgeois epoch from all earlier ones. All fixed, fast-frozen relations, with their train of ancient and venerable prejudices and opinions, are swept away, all new-formed ones become antiquated before they can ossify. All that is solid melts into air, all that is holy is profaned, and man is at last compelled to face with sober senses his real conditions of life and his relations with his kind.

The need of a constantly expanding market for its products chases the bourgeoisie over the whole surface of the globe. It must nestle everywhere, settle everywhere, establish connections everywhere.

The bourgeoisie has through its exploitation of the world market given a cosmopolitan character to production and consumption in every country. To the great chagrin of reactionaries, it has drawn from under the feet of industry the national ground on which it stood. All old-established national industries have been destroyed or are daily being destroyed. They are dislodged by new industries, whose introduction becomes a life and death question for all civilized nations, by industries that no longer work up indigenous raw material, but raw material drawn from the remotest zones; industries whose products are consumed, not only at home, but in every quarter of the globe. In place of the old wants, satisfied by the production of the country, we find new wants, requiring for their satisfaction the products of distant lands and climes. In place of the old local and national seclusion and self-sufficiency, we have intercourse in every direction, universal interdependence of nations. And as in material, so also in intellectual production. The intellectual creations of individual nations become common property. National one-sidedness and narrow-mindedness become more and more impossible, and from the numerous national and local literatures there arises a world literature.

The bourgeoisie, by the rapid improvement of all instruments of production, by the immensely facilitated means of communication, draws all nations, even the most barbarian, into civilization. The cheap prices of its commodities are the heavy artillery with which it batters down all Chinese walls, with which it forces the barbarians' intensely obstinate hatred for foreigners to capitulate. It compels all nations, on pain of extinction, to adopt the bourgeois mode of production; it compels them to introduce what it calls civilization into their midst, i.e., to become bourgeois themselves. In a word, it creates a world after its own image.

The bourgeoisie has subjected the country to the rule of the towns. It has created enormous cities, has greatly increased the urban population as compared with the rural, and has thus rescued a considerable part of the population from the idiocy of rural life. Just as it has made the country dependent on the towns, so it has made barbarian and semi-barbarian countries dependent on the civilized ones, nations of peasants on nations of bourgeois, the East on the West.

More and more the bourgeoisie keeps doing away with the scattered state of the population, of the means of production, and of property. It has agglomerated population, centralized means of production, and has concentrated property in a few hands. The necessary consequence of this was political centralization. Independent, or but loosely connected provinces, with separate interests, laws, governments and systems of taxation, became lumped together into one nation, with one government, one code of laws, one national class interest, one frontier and one customs tariff.

The bourgeoisie, during its rule of scarce one hundred years, has created more massive and more colossal productive forces than have all preceding generations together. Subjection of nature's forces to man, machinery, application of chemistry to industry and agriculture, steam-navigation, railways, electric telegraphs, clearing of whole continents for cultivation, canalization of rivers, whole populations conjured out of the ground—what earlier century had even a presentiment that such productive forces slumbered in the lap of social labor?

We see then that the means of production and of exchange, which served as the foundation for the growth of the bourgeoisie, were generated in feudal society. At a certain stage in the development of these means of production and of exchange, the conditions under which feudal society produced and exchanged, the feudal organization of agriculture and manufacturing industry, in a word, the feudal relations of property became no longer compatible with the already developed productive forces; they became so many fetters. They had to be burst asunder; they were burst asunder.

Into their place stepped free competition, accompanied by a social and political constitution adapted to it, and by the economic and political sway of the bourgeois class.

A similar movement is going on before our own eyes. Modern bourgeois society with its relations of production, of exchange and of property, a society that has conjured up such gigantic means of production and exchange, is like the sorcerer who is no longer able to control the powers of the nether world whom he has called up by his spells. For many a decade past the history of industry and commerce is but the history of the revolt of modern productive forces against modern conditions of production, against the property relations that are the conditions for the existence of the bourgeoisie and of its rule. It is enough to mention the commercial crises that by their periodical return put the existence of the entire bourgeoisie society on trial, each time more threateningly. In these crises a great part not only of the existing products, but also of the previously created productive forces, are periodically destroyed. In these crises there breaks out an epidemic that, in all earlier epochs, would have seemed an absurdity—the epidemic of overproduction.

Society suddenly finds itself put back into a state of momentary barbarism; it appears as if a famine, a universal war of devastation had cut off the supply of every means of subsistence; industry and commerce seem to be destroyed. And why? Because there is too much civilization, too much means of subsistence, too much industry, too much commerce. The productive forces at the disposal of society no longer tend to further the development of the conditions of bourgeois property; on the contrary, they have become too powerful for these conditions, by which they are fettered, and no sooner do they overcome these fetters than they bring disorder into the whole of bourgeois society, endanger the existence of bourgeois property. The conditions of bourgeois society are too narrow to comprise the wealth created by them. And how does the bourgeoisie get over these crises? On the one hand by enforced destruction of a mass of productive forces; on the other, by the conquest of new markets, and by the more thorough exploitation of the old ones. That is to say, by paving the way for more extensive and more destructive crises, and by diminishing the means whereby crises are prevented.

The weapons with which the bourgeoisie felled feudalism to the ground are now turned against the bourgeoisie itself.

But not only has the bourgeoisie forged the weapons that bring death to itself; it has also called into existence the men who are to wield those weapons—the modern working class—the proletarians.

In proportion as the bourgeoisie, i.e., capital, is developed, in the same proportion is the proletariat, the modern working class, developed—a class of labourers, who live only so long as they find work, and who find work only so long as their labour increases capital. These labourers, who must sell themselves piece-meal, are a commodity, like every other article of commerce, and are consequently exposed to all the vicissitudes of competition, to all the fluctuations of the market.

Owing to the extensive use of machinery and to division of labour, the work of the proletarians has lost all individual character, and consequently, all charm for the workman. He becomes an appendage of the machine, and it is only the most simple, most monotonous, and most easily acquired knack, that is required of him. Hence, the cost of production of a workman is restricted, almost entirely, to the means of subsistence that he requires for his maintenance, and for the propagation of his race. But the price of a commodity, and therefore also of labour, is equal to its cost of production. In proportion therefore, as the repulsiveness of the work increases, the wage decreases. Nay more, in proportion as the use of machinery and division of labour increases, in the same proportion the burden of toil also increases, whether by prolongation of the working hours, by increase of the work exacted in a given time or by increased speed of the machinery, etc.

Modern industry has converted the little workshop of the patriarchal master into the great factory of the industrial capitalist. Masses of labourers, crowded into the factory, are organised like soldiers. As privates of the industrial army they are placed under the command of a perfect hierarchy of officers and sergeants. Not only are they slaves of the bourgeois class, and of the bourgeois State; they are daily and hourly enslaved by the machine, by the over-looker, and, above all, by the individual bourgeois manufacturer himself. The more openly this despotism proclaims gain to be its end and aim, the more petty, the more hateful and the more embittering it is.

The less the skill and exertion of strength implied in manual labour, in other words, the more modern industry becomes developed, the more is the labour of men superseded by that of women. Differences of age and sex have no longer any distinctive social validity for the working class. All are instruments of labour, more or less expensive to use, according to their age and sex.

No sooner is the exploitation of the labourer by the manufacturer, so far, at an end, that he receives his wages in cash, than he is set upon by the other portions of the bourgeoisie, the landlord, the shopkeeper, the pawnbroker, etc.

The lower strata of the middle class—the small tradespeople, shopkeepers, retired tradesmen generally, the handicraftsmen and peasants—all these sink gradually into the proletariat, partly because their diminutive capital does not suffice for the scale on which Modern Industry is carried on, and is swamped in the competition with the large capitalists, partly because their specialized skill is rendered worthless by the new methods of production. Thus the proletariat is recruited from all classes of the population.

5

PETER N. STEARNS

The Industrial Revolution outside the West

Stearns, a modern historian, discusses the export of industrial machinery and techniques outside the West (Europe and North America) in the nineteenth century. Again and again, he finds that initial attempts at industrialization—in Russia, India, Egypt, and South America—led to increased production of export crops and resources but failed to stimulate true industrial revolutions. Consequently, as producers of raw materials, these countries became more deeply dependent on

Source: Peter N. Stearns, *The Industrial Revolution in World History* (Boulder, CO: Westview Press, 1993), 71–79.

Western markets for their products, while at the same time importing from the West more valuable manufactured products like machinery. What common reasons can you find for these failures?

THINKING HISTORICALLY

Did nineteenth-century efforts to ignite industrial revolutions outside the West fail because these societies neglected to develop capitalism, or did they fail because their local needs were subordinated to those of Western capitalists? Explain.

Before the 1870s no industrial revolution occurred outside Western society. The spread of industrialization within western Europe, while by no means automatic, followed from a host of shared economic, cultural, and political features. The quick ascension of the United States was somewhat more surprising—the area was not European and had been far less developed economically during the eighteenth century. Nevertheless, extensive commercial experience in the northern states and the close mercantile and cultural ties with Britain gave the new nation advantages for its rapid imitation of the British lead. Abundant natural resources and extensive investments from Europe kept the process going, joining the United States to the wider dynamic of industrialization in the nineteenth-century West.

Elsewhere, conditions did not permit an industrial revolution, an issue that must be explored in dealing with the international context for this first phase of the world's industrial experience. Yet the West's industrial revolution did have substantial impact. It led to a number of pilot projects whereby initial machinery and factories were established under Western guidance. More important, it led to new Western demands on the world's economies that instigated significant change without industrialization; indeed, these demands in several cases made industrialization more difficult.

Pilot Projects

Russia's contact with the West's industrial revolution before the 1870s offers an important case study that explains why many societies could not follow the lead of nations like France or the United States in imitating Britain. Yet Russia did introduce some new equipment for economic and military-political reasons, and these initiatives did generate change—they were not mere window dressing.

More than most societies not directly part of Western civilization, Russia had special advantages in reacting to the West's industrial lead and special motivation for paying attention to this lead. Russia had been part of Europe's diplomatic network since about 1700. It saw itself as one of Europe's great powers, a participant in international conferences and military alliances. The country also had close cultural ties with western Europe, sharing in artistic styles and scientific developments — though Russian leadership had stepped back from cultural alignment because of the shock of the French Revolution in 1789 and subsequent political disorders in the West. Russian aristocrats and intellectuals routinely visited western Europe. Finally, Russia had prior experience in imitating Western technology and manufacturing: importation of Western metallurgy and shipbuilding had formed a major part of Peter the Great's reform program in the early eighteenth century.

Contacts of this sort explain why Russia began to receive an industrial outreach from the West within a few decades of the advent of the industrial revolution. British textile machinery was imported beginning in 1843. Ernst Knoop, a German immigrant to Britain who had clerked in a Manchester cotton factory, set himself up as export agent to the Russians. He also sponsored British workers who installed the machinery in Russia and told any Russian entrepreneur brash enough to ask not simply for British models but for alterations or adaptations: "That is not your affair; in England they know better than you." Despite the snobbism, a number of Russian entrepreneurs set up small factories to produce cotton, aware that even in Russia's small urban market they could make a substantial profit by underselling traditional manufactured cloth. Other factories were established directly by Britons.

Europeans and Americans were particularly active in responding to calls by the tsar's government for assistance in establishing railway and steamship lines. The first steamship appeared in Russia in 1815, and by 1820 a regular service ran on the Volga River. The first public railroad, joining St. Petersburg to the imperial residence in the suburbs, opened in 1837. In 1851 the first major line connected St. Petersburg and Moscow, along a remarkably straight route desired by Tsar Nicholas I himself. American engineers were brought in, again by the government, to set up a railroad industry so that Russians could build their own locomotives and cars. George Whistler, the father of the painter James McNeill Whistler (and thus husband of Whistler's mother), played an important role in the effort. He and some American workers helped train Russians in the needed crafts, frequently complaining about their slovenly habits but appreciating their willingness to learn.

Russian imports of machinery increased rapidly; they were over thirty times as great in 1860 as they had been in 1825. While in 1851 the nation manufactured only about half as many machines as it imported, by 1860 the equation was reversed, and the number of machine-building factories had quintupled (from nineteen to ninety-nine). The new cotton industry surged forward with most production organized in factories using wage labor.

These were important changes. They revealed that some Russians were alert to the business advantages of Western methods and that some Westerners saw the great profits to be made by setting up shop in a huge but largely agricultural country. The role of the government was vital: The tsars used tax money to offer substantial premiums to Western entrepreneurs, who liked the adventure of dealing with the Russians but liked their superior profit margins even more.

But Russia did not then industrialize. Modern industrial operations did not sufficiently dent established economic practices. The nation remained overwhelmingly agricultural. High percentage increases in manufacturing proceeded from such a low base that they had little general impact. Several structural barriers impeded a genuine industrial revolution. Russia's cities had never boasted a manufacturing tradition; there were few artisans skilled even in preindustrial methods. Only by the 1860s and 1870s had cities grown enough for an artisan core to take shape—in printing, for example—and even then large numbers of foreigners (particularly Germans) had to be imported. Even more serious was the system of serfdom that kept most Russians bound to agricultural estates. While some free laborers could be found, most rural Russians could not legally leave their land, and their obligation to devote extensive work service to their lords' estates reduced their incentive even for agricultural production. Peter the Great had managed to adapt serfdom to a preindustrial metallurgical industry by allowing landlords to sell villages and the labor therein for expansion of ironworks. But this mongrel system was not suitable for change on a grander scale, which is precisely what the industrial revolution entailed.

Furthermore, the West's industrial revolution, while it provided tangible examples for Russia to imitate, also produced pressures to develop more traditional sectors in lieu of structural change. The West's growing cities and rising prosperity claimed rising levels of Russian timber, hemp, tallow, and, increasingly, grain. These were export goods that could be produced without new technology and without altering the existing labor system. Indeed, many landlords boosted the work-service obligations of the serfs in order to generate more grain production for sale to the West. The obvious temptation was to lock in an older economy—to respond to new opportunity by incremental changes within the traditional system and to maintain serfdom and the rural preponderance rather than to risk fundamental internal transformation.

The proof of Russia's lag showed in foreign trade. It rose but rather modestly, posting a threefold increase between 1800 and 1860. Exports of raw materials approximately paid for the imports of some machinery, factory-made goods from abroad, and a substantial volume of luxury products for the aristocracy. And the regions that participated most in the growing trade were not the tiny industrial enclaves (in St. Petersburg, Moscow, and the iron-rich Urals) but the wheat-growing areas of southern Russia where even industrial pilot projects had yet to surface. Russian manufacturing exported nothing at all to the West, though it did find a few customers in Turkey, central Asia, and China.

The proof of Russia's lag showed even more dramatically in Russia's new military disadvantage. Peter the Great's main goal had been to keep Russian military production near enough to Western levels to remain competitive, with the huge Russian population added into the equation. This strategy now failed, for the West's industrial revolution changed the rules of the game. A war in 1854 pitting Russia against Britain and France led to Russia's defeat in its own backyard. The British and French objected to new Russian territorial gains (won at the expense of Turkey's Ottoman Empire) that brought Russia greater access to the Black Sea. The battleground was the Crimea. Yet British and French steamships connected their armies more reliably with supplies and reinforcements from home than did Russia's ground transportation system with its few railroads and mere three thousand miles of first-class roads. And British and French industry could pour out more and higher-quality uniforms, guns, and munitions than traditional Russian manufacturing could hope to match. The Russians lost the Crimean War, surrendering their gains and swallowing their pride in 1856. Patchwork change had clearly proved insufficient to match the military, much less the economic, power the industrial revolution had generated in the West.

After a brief interlude, the Russians digested the implications of their defeat and launched a period of basic structural reforms. The linchpin was the abolition of serfdom in 1861. Peasants were not entirely freed, and rural discontent persisted, but many workers could now leave the land; the basis for a wage labor force was established. Other reforms focused on improving basic education and health, and while change in these areas was slow, it too set the basis for a genuine commitment to industrialization. A real industrial revolution lay in the future, however. By the 1870s Russia's contact with industrialization had deepened its economic gap vis-à-vis the West but had yielded a few interesting experiments with new methods and a growing realization of the need for further change.

Societies elsewhere in the world—those more removed from traditional ties to the West or more severely disadvantaged in the ties that did exist—saw even more tentative industrial pilot projects during the West's industrialization period. The Middle East and India tried some industrial imitation early on but largely failed—though not without generating some important economic change. Latin America also launched some revealingly limited technological change. Only eastern Asia and sub-Saharan Africa were largely untouched by any explicit industrial imitations until the late 1860s or beyond; they were too distant from European culture to venture a response so quickly.

Prior links with the West formed the key variable, as Russia's experience abundantly demonstrated. Societies that had some familiarity with Western merchants and some preindustrial awareness of the West's steady commercial gains mounted some early experiments in industrialization. Whether they benefited as a result compared with areas that did nothing before the late nineteenth century might be debated.

One industrial initiative in India developed around Calcutta, where British colonial rule had centered since the East India Company founded the city in 1690. A Hindu Brahman family, the Tagores, established close ties with many British administrators. Without becoming British, they sponsored a number of efforts to revivify India, including new colleges and research centers. Dwarkanath Tagore controlled tax collection in part of Bengal, and early in the nineteenth century he used part of his profit to found a bank. He also bought up a variety of commercial landholdings and traditional manufacturing operations. In 1834 he joined with British capitalists to establish a diversified company that boasted holdings in mines (including the first Indian coal mine), sugar refineries, and some new textile factories; the equipment was imported from Britain. Tagore's dominant idea was a British-Indian economic and cultural collaboration that would revitalize his country. He enjoyed a high reputation in Europe and for a short time made a success of his economic initiatives. Tagore died on a trip abroad, and his financial empire declined soon after.

This first taste of Indian industrialization was significant, but it brought few immediate results. The big news in India, even as Tagore launched his companies, was the rapid decline of traditional textiles under the bombardment of British factory competition; millions of Indian villagers were thrown out of work. Furthermore, relations between Britain and the Indian elite worsened after the mid-1830s as British officials sought a more active economic role and became more intolerant of Indian culture. One British official, admitting no knowledge of Indian scholarship, wrote that "all the historical information" and science available in Sanskrit was "less valuable than what may be found in the most paltry abridgements used at preparatory schools in England." With these attitudes, the kind of collaboration that might have aided Indian appropriation of British industry became impossible.

The next step in India's contact with the industrial revolution did not occur until the 1850s when the colonial government began to build a significant railroad network. The first passenger line opened in 1853. Some officials feared that Hindus might object to traveling on such smoke-filled monsters, but trains proved very popular and there ensued a period of rapid economic and social change. The principal result, however, was not industrial development but further extension of commercial agriculture (production of cotton and other goods for export) and intensification of British sales to India's interior. Coal mining did expand, but manufacturing continued to shrink. There was no hint of an industrial revolution in India.

Imitation in the Middle East was somewhat more elaborate, in part because most of this region, including parts of North Africa, retained independence from European colonialism. Muslims had long disdained Western culture and Christianity, and Muslim leaders, including the rulers of the great Ottoman Empire, had been very slow to recognize the West's growing dynamism after the fifteenth century. Some Western medicine was imported, but technology was ignored. Only in the eighteenth century did this attitude begin, haltingly, to change. The Ottoman government imported a printing press from Europe and began discussing Western-style technical training, primarily in relationship to the military.

In 1798 a French force briefly seized Egypt, providing a vivid symbol of Europe's growing technical superiority. Later an Ottoman governor, Muhammed Ali, seized Egypt from the imperial government and pursued an ambitious agenda of expansionism and modernization. Muhammed Ali sponsored many changes in Egyptian society in imitation of Western patterns, including a new tax system and new kinds of schooling. He also destroyed the traditional Egyptian elite. The government encouraged agricultural production by sponsoring major irrigation projects and began to import elements of the industrial revolution from the West in the 1830s. English machinery and technicians were brought in to build textile factories, sugar refineries, paper mills, and weapons shops. Muhammed Ali clearly contemplated a sweeping reform program in which industrialization would play a central role in making Egypt a powerhouse in the Middle East and an equal to the European powers. Many of his plans worked well, but the industrialization effort failed. Egyptian factories could not in the main compete with European imports, and the initial experiments either failed or stagnated. More durable changes involved the encouragement to the production of cash crops like sugar and cotton, which the government required in order to earn tax revenues to support its armies and its industrial imports. Growing concentration on cash crops also enriched a new group of Egyptian landlords and merchants. But the shift actually formalized Egypt's dependent position in the world economy, as European businesses and governments increasingly interfered with the internal economy. The Egyptian reaction to the West's industrial revolution, even more than the Russian response, was to generate massive economic redefinition without industrialization, a strategy that locked peasants into landlord control and made a manufacturing transformation at best a remote prospect.

Spurred by the West's example and by Muhammed Ali, the Ottoman government itself set up some factories after 1839, importing equipment from Europe to manufacture textiles, paper, and guns. Coal and iron mining were encouraged. The government established a postal system in 1834, a telegraph system in 1855, and steamships and the beginning of railway construction from 1866 onward. These changes increased the role of European traders and investors in the Ottoman economy and produced no overall industrial revolution. Again, the clearest result of improved transport and communication was a growing emphasis on the export of cash crops and minerals to pay for necessary manufactured imports from Europe. An industrial example had been set, and, as in Egypt, a growing though still tiny minority of Middle Easterners gained some factory experience, but no fundamental transformation occurred. . . .

Developments of preliminary industrial trappings — a few factories, a few railroads — nowhere outside Europe converted whole economies to an industrialization process until late in the nineteenth century, though they provided some relevant experience on which later (mainly after 1870) and more intensive efforts could build. A few workers became factory hands and experienced some of the same upheaval as their Western counterparts in terms of new routines and pressures on work pace. Many sought to limit their factory experience, leaving for other work or for the countryside after a short time; transience was a problem for much the same reasons as in the West: the clash with traditional work and leisure values. Some technical and business expertise also developed. Governments took the lead in most attempts to imitate the West, which was another portent for the future; with some exceptions, local merchant groups had neither the capital nor the motivation to undertake such ambitious and uncertain projects. By the 1850s a number of governments were clearly beginning to realize that some policy response to the industrial revolution was absolutely essential, lest Western influence become still more overwhelming. On balance, however, the principal results of very limited imitation tended to heighten the economic imbalance with western Europe, a disparity that made it easier to focus on nonindustrial exports. This too was a heritage for the future. . . .

6

Italians in Two Worlds: An Immigrant's Letters from Argentina

One of the distinctive features of the capitalist industrial revolution was the globalization of capital and labor. The capital for the British industrial revolution, beginning toward the end of the eighteenth century, filtered in from the treasures of the Indies — East and West — and owed much to the labor of slaves and legally free workers

Source: *One Family, Two Worlds: An Italian Family's Correspondence across the Atlantic,* ed. Samuel L. Baily and Franco Ramella, trans. John Lenaghan (New Brunswick: Rutgers University Press, 1988), 34–42.

who were shipped from one end of the world to the other.
By the second half of the nineteenth century, the owners of farms, factories, mines, and railroads called for many more laborers.

Millions of these workers came from Italy alone. From 1860 to 1885, most traveled from northern Italy to South America, mainly Argentina. Between 1890 and 1915, Italian immigration to Argentina continued, but even more came from southern Italy to the United States. By the beginning of the twentieth century, New York City and Buenos Aires each had larger Italian populations than many Italian cities.

This selection contains the first few letters sent back home by one of those Italian immigrants, Oreste Sola, who arrived in Buenos Aires in 1901 from northern Italy. What do these letters tell you about this immigrant's expectations? What sort of work did he do? How did he manage to navigate his new world? What are his challenges? How would you describe his strengths? Based on the few hints of events in Italy, how was his life in Argentina different from what it would have likely been in Italy?

THINKING HISTORICALLY

What signs do you see in these letters of industrialization in Argentina? What signs do you see of a capitalist economic system? How is the life of Oreste shaped by the needs of capitalists? How is it shaped by a capitalist economic system? How is his life shaped by industrialization?

Letter 1

Buenos Ayres, 17 August 1901

Dearest parents,

I have been here since the 5th of this month; I am in the best of health as are my two companions. As soon as we got here, we went to the address of Godfather Zocco, who then introduced us to several people from Valdengo who have been in America for some years and all are doing well more or less. The language here is Castilian, quite similar to Spanish, but you don't hear anyone speaking it. Wherever you go, whether in the hotel or at work, everyone speaks either Piedmontese or Italian, even those from other countries, and the Argentines themselves speak Italian.[1]

[1] He does not speak or understand Spanish and therefore does not realize that Spanish and Castilian are the same thing. Although 25 percent of the total population and an even higher percentage of the adult population of Buenos Aires was Italian-born, and therefore the Italian language was indeed spoken in many places, Oreste obviously exaggerates when he claims that everyone speaks it.

This city is very beautiful. There is an enormous amount of luxury. All the streets—they call them *calle* [sic] here—are paved either with hard wood or in cement as smooth as marble, even too smooth since the horses, tram horses as well as carriage horses, which run here, keep slipping constantly. It is not unusual to see twenty or more of them fall in one day. . . .

The piazza Victoria (Plaza de Mayo) is also beautiful, where all around on two sides there are only banks. They are of all nations: English, French, Italian, Spanish, North American, etc., etc. On another side is the government building where the president of the Argentine Republic resides. He is Italian, Rocca by name, the third Italian president in a row who sits on the Argentine throne.[2] There is also the railway station of the south, which is something colossal. With workshops, offices, and the station itself it will cover one million square meters. Now they are at work on a government building for the Congress (Parliament). The architect was an Italian, as is the chief contractor, who is supervising all the work. It is a job which in the end will cost more than 700 million lire. It will occupy an area of a block which is 10,000 square meters and will be surrounded by a square, which, along with the building, will constitute an area of about 100,000 square meters. This work will be better than the first [the railway station], but perhaps I shall not be able to see it finished.

All of this is inside the city, but if you should go outside for a few hours, it's worse than a desert. You only find houses made solely out of mortar, with only a ground floor and a door you have to enter on all fours. Outside you don't see a plant; everything is desert. The plains stretch as far as the eye can see; it takes hours on the train before you come to the mountains. There are a few tracts of land, sort of green, where they may let a few horses loose to graze. Here they let the animals go out no matter what the weather might be. Here you can't find a rock, though you pay its weight in gold for it. All the ground is black like manure, thick and muddy. When it doesn't rain, it gets hard, and if you try to dig, it shoots out as if it were rock.

The food here is pretty good, but it doesn't have much flavor. This is true for all Argentina.

All the guys here are jolly as crazy men. In the evening when we get together before going to bed we split our sides laughing. They would all like to go back to Italy, but they don't ever budge. Perhaps I will do

---

[2] Oreste is in error here. The president to whom he refers, Julio Roca, was Argentine not Italian. The preceding president, José Uriburu, also was not Italian. However, Carlos Pellegrini, president from 1890 to 1892, was the son of a French-Italian father from Savoy.

the same. Here we eat, drink, and laugh and enjoy ourselves; we are in America. . . .

> Take one last loving kiss and hug
> from your always loving son,
> Oreste

Letter 2

Mendoza, 18 September 1901

Dearest parents,

I am still in good spirits and happy that I am in America. I am now at Mendoza instead of Buenos Ayres. I didn't like Buenos Ayres too much because you don't get good wine there; and then every day the temperature changes twenty times, and I was always chilly. Otherwise it was fine.

One day I got the idea, knowing that Secondino's brother-in-law and sister were in Mendoza. Since the boss advanced me the money for the trip,[3] I made up my mind to come here, where you see nothing but hills and mountains in the distance, like at home. You drink very well here; the wine costs half what it does in Buenos Ayres and is pure and delicious. I am living here with Carlo and his wife and a man by the name of Luigi Ferraro from Chiavazza, who has been here for seven years traveling around in America. There are few people here from Biella, but there is no shortage of Italians. I still haven't learned a word of Castilian because, everywhere you go, they speak Italian or Piedmontese.

I am better off here than in Buenos Ayres. I am only sorry to be so far from my friends—they didn't want to come—and from Godfather and the rest.

This city is ugly; it never rains even though it is close to the mountains. I have written a friend to send me the address of my schoolmate Berretta, and I might just go and see him in Peru; it takes four days or more on the train. From Buenos Ayres to Mendoza takes two nights and a day on the railroad without ever changing trains or getting off. The longest stop is a half hour. In the entire journey you don't see a plant. [There are] two or three rivers about 400 meters wide. They are all in the plain, so calm that you can't tell which way the water is going, and yet they flow on in an imperceptible way.

---

[3] The government of the province of Mendoza and many individual employers made a major effort to attract European immigrants during the two decades preceding World War I. It was not unusual for an employer to advance money to pay for the trip from Buenos Aires to Mendoza.

Throughout the journey one meets only horses, cows, and goats, none of which have stables. On the rail line you don't see a house for three hours or more, and everything is like that. . . .

Everyone, Carlo, Cichina, and Luigi, give their regards to you. Tell Secondino to come and see America, to drink and eat and travel.

Time is pressing since I have to work every evening until ten. I work at home after work.

You should write me at:

El Taller del Ferro Carril G.O.A.
Mendoza

Goodbye everybody. Kisses to Abele and Narcisa. Tell Abele to study hard and to learn to work. Send him to the technical schools; I imagine he has been promoted. Goodbye, Mom and Dad. Be in good spirits as I am.

Yours always,
Orestes

Letter 3

Mendoza, 13 November 1901
Dearest Father, Mother, brother, and sister,

This morning Secondino arrived as you had already indicated he would in your letter of 14 October. He had a very good trip, and he made everyone happy to see him healthy and cheerful—as we are, Carlo, Cichina, and Luigi. He gave me the trousers which you gave him to bring me and the letter written by Dad and Narcisa.

I have been here in Mendoza for about three months, and I am happy that Secondino is here now too. But I don't plan to stay fixed here. I would like to go to Peru with Berretta or to Cuba, where dear Cousin Edvino is staying, since I know that those who are there are doing well now. It wouldn't be bad here except you aren't sure about employment or about anything, especially for the type of work I do. So you can't even be sure of staying in one place. Before leaving I am waiting to get the address of Berretta.

I thought that I could send something, instead I had to make some purchases. Be patient. I think of our family conditions too often to be able to think of anything else. Excuse me if I have been slow in writing. It's because I hoped to get a particular job, and I wanted to let you know. I was waiting for the decision of the company. The job went to another, also Italian, with whom nobody could compete. But let's leave the subject of work because here there are so many professions and so many trades that you can't say what you are doing. Today it's this and tomorrow it's that. I tried to go into the construction business for myself, but it didn't work out. So much effort and expense. Now I am doing something else, and I shall change again soon.

My friends as well as Godfather are still in Buenos Aires. They are fine and want to be remembered to you. I receive news (from Buenos Aires) almost every week.

Pardon me, dear parents, brother, and sister, if I am sometimes slow in writing. It is not that I forget, quite the contrary. Only please don't reproach me the way Narcisa does because, if you knew how painful these reproaches are to us here, especially when they come from the family, you would not believe it. I shall try to write more often.

Narcisa asks me for postcards, Abele for stamps. I cannot satisfy anyone since they don't sell illustrated postcards here even though there would be many beautiful things [to show], like, for example, the ruins of Mendoza of 1860 caused by the earthquake, which often happens here six or seven times a year.[4] If it is a special earthquake, you seem to be in a boat, rocking like at sea. But if it gets a bit strong, you have to lie down so as not to fall. Some attribute it to the various volcanoes, mostly extinct however, which are in the mountains here. Others say it is because of the huge storms of the Pacific meeting the winds that come from the Atlantic. However, no one can verify it.

From what I make out from Dad's letter, he says that he was planning to send me some clothes when I get established here. Excuse me, dear parents, your sacrifices are already excessive. Now it is my job to pay them back at least in part, and I shall do everything possible to that end. But excuse me, I am old enough now to earn my bread. I beg you not to be offended about this. If later I shall be in a position to, I shall send you money and everything. But for now, first of all, I have clothes to wear. I have already purchased here two suits and four pairs of trousers. So don't be upset then. Rather, I repeat, as soon as I am able, I'll see that you get something. Now I cannot; it has gone badly for me before I got started. When I shall again be the way I was in the beginning—but I don't know when because here [in] America [things] can change from one day to the next—you will have some repayment.

I have received your newspapers and bulletins, letters and all, because the telegraph and postal service here is something very precise. I was very pleased to get them. I read also in the bulletin of the professional school that they are asking for the address of members who are living outside the country. If I should send it and then, before publication, I should move, I would be in the same situation I was before. Also they want you to indicate the kind of work you are doing for publication in the bulletin because it will be, I believe, an issue with all the graduates of the professional school, and I can't tell them that. I change from one day to

---

[4] The earthquake to which he refers occurred on March 20, 1861. It destroyed the entire city of Mendoza and killed much of its population.

the next. At that moment I was a draftsman second grade in the workshop of the Trans Andes railway. It is a direct railway to Chile now under construction. But I am not doing it anymore because the section that the four of us were assigned to work on has been finished.

Now I am working as a smith and various things for the Great Western Railway of Argentina. But since they don't pay me as I want and I have to be first a blacksmith, then work as a planer, then at the lathe, I don't like it. At the first other job that comes along, I'm off. When I find something better, I don't want to work as a laborer for low wages anymore. . . .

Your most loving son and
brother,
Oreste Sola

Letter 4

Mendoza, 25 November 1901

Dearest ones,

A few days before this letter you will have received another written on the day of Secondino's arrival; a few days later he received some newspapers which indicated that you were on strike.[5] I understand that in this season such a big strike will be very distressing. I, however, right now absolutely cannot, for the moment, help you in any way. If I had been able to get that damned construction job, I assure you I would have "hit the jackpot." From one day to the next another bit of bad luck could come my way; but everything is in doubt, there is then no certainty nor prospect.

Now they are coming here every day on the emigration train, about 600 persons a week. They are then sent out of the city in great numbers; but many remain, and we are beginning to see some unemployment but only in a small way. It's just that working in such conditions you only earn a bare living and with difficulty at that. If I have bad luck, I'm not staying here any longer. I want to go to Cuba with Boffa and the rest since Berretta doesn't answer. Nothing is certain however. The ideas come in crowds, but the execution is just miserable. Still I am not losing heart ever. I have been through a good period at first, then an excellent one, and now I am in a third one that is very tough. But I'll get back on my feet. We are in America.

Be patient then. I too am aware that Mom is working at night, that you are working on Sundays, etc. — things that don't happen here. Here

---

[5] Oreste is referring to the major strike at the Biella textile factory in which [his parents] Luigi and Margherita worked. The strike, which ended in defeat for the workers, was provoked when the owners increased the work load without increasing salaries.

in every profession and everywhere you work nine hours a day and only 'til noon on Saturday. You don't work on Sunday nor after midday meal on Saturday, and you get more respect. When you ask for some improvement in pay, the owners don't say that they will show up with a rifle and fire at the first one who makes trouble, as the famous Giovanni Rivetti used to say.[6] Here, if they don't want to give it to you, they look into it, they review it; but generally they give it to you, and all this without unions or anything. They are capitalists who are more aware; that's all there is to it.

Think always of your loving son who is in America, always in good spirits, even when things are going badly for him.

Oreste Sola

Secondino, like me, is always in good spirits, and we are always together. He sends you his warmest greetings and so does Carlo's family. Secondino would like you to say hello to his wife if it is not too much trouble.

[6] Giovanni Rivetti was one of the owners of the Biella textile factory in which Luigi and Margherita worked. Given the size and importance of the factory, Rivetti's conduct greatly influenced that of the other owners in the entire area.

■ REFLECTIONS

It was because of certain traits in private capitalism that the machine—which was a neutral agent—has often seemed, and in fact has sometimes been, a malicious element in society, careless of human life, indifferent to human interests. The machine has suffered for the sins of capitalism; contrariwise, capitalism has often taken credit for the virtues of the machine.[1]

Our chapter turns the above proposition by writer Lewis Mumford into a series of questions: What has been the impact of capitalism? Is the machine only neutral, or does it have its own effects? How can we distinguish between the economic and the technological chains of cause and effect?

Capitalism and industrialization are difficult concepts to distinguish. Adam Smith illustrated the power of the market and the division of labor by imagining their impact not on a shop or trading firm but on a pin factory, an early industrial enterprise. Karl Marx summarized the achievements of the capitalist age by enumerating "wonders far surpassing Egyptian pyramids," which included chemical industries, steam navigation, railroads, and electric telegraphs. Neither Smith nor Marx used the terms *capitalism* or *industrial revolution*, although

[1] Lewis Mumford, *Technics and Civilization* (New York: Harcourt Brace, 1963), 27.

such variants as *capitalist* and *industrial* were already in circulation. Modern historians fought over their meaning and relevance as explanations of change through most of the last century. To understand the great transformation into modernity, some emphasized the expansion of market capitalism; others emphasized the power of the machine. The rise of state-capitalist and communist industrial societies politicized the debate, but even after the fall of communism, the historical questions remained. Peter Stearns looks for the forces that spread or retarded industrialization. The letters of Oreste Sola support the argument of some historians of Latin America that the continent was modernized more by trade and capital than by industrialization.

After 1900 the industrial revolution spread throughout the world, but its pace was not always revolutionary. Even today some societies are still largely rural, with a majority of workers engaged in subsistence farming or small-scale manufacturing by hand. But over the long course of history people have always tried to replace human labor with machines and increase the production of machine-made goods. In some cases, the transformation has been dramatic. Malaysia, once a languid land of tropical tea and rubber plantations, sprouted enough microchip and electronics factories after 1950 to account for 60 percent of its exports by the year 2000. By the 1990s an already highly industrialized country like Japan could produce luxury cars in factories that needed only a handful of humans to monitor the work of computer-driven robots. Despite occasional announcements of the arrival of a "postindustrial" society, the pressure to mechanize continues unabated in the twenty-first century.

The fate of capitalism in the twentieth century was more varied. The second wave of industrial revolutions—beginning with Germany after 1850 and Japan after 1880—was directed by governments as much as capitalists. Socialist parties won large support in industrial countries in the first half of the twentieth century, creating welfare states in some after World War II. In Russia after 1917, the Communist Party pioneered a model of state-controlled industrialization that attracted imitators from China to Chile and funded anticapitalist movements throughout the world.

The Cold War (1947–1991) between the United States and the Soviet Union, though largely a power struggle between two superpowers, was widely seen as an ideological contest between capitalism and socialism. Thus the demise of the Soviet Union and its Communist Party in 1991 was heralded as the victory of capitalism over socialism. As Russia, China, and other previously communist states embraced market economies, socialism was declared dead.

But could proclaiming the death of socialism be as premature as heralding the end of industrial society? *The Communist Manifesto* of 1848 long predates the Russian Revolution of 1917. Karl Marx died in 1883. Socialists like Rosa Luxembourg criticized Lenin and the Russian communists for misinterpreting Marxism in their impatience to transform Russian society. Socialists, even Marxists, continue to write, advise, and govern today, often urging restraints on the spread of global capital markets and the threat of unregulated capitalism for the global environment. Rarely are they willing to relinquish the advantages of industrial technology; rather, they seek to release the "virtues of the machine."

22

Colonized and Colonizers

Europeans in Africa and Asia, 1850–1930

■ HISTORICAL CONTEXT

The first stage of European colonialism, beginning with Columbus, was a period in which Europeans—led by the Spanish and Portuguese—settled in the Western Hemisphere and created plantations with African labor. From 1492 to 1776, European settlement in Asia was limited to a few coastal port cities where merchants and missionaries operated. The second stage—the years between 1776, when Britain lost most of its American colonies, and 1880, when the European scramble for African territory began—has sometimes been called a period of *free-trade imperialism*. This term refers to the desire by European countries in general and by Britain in particular to expand their zones of free trade. It also refers to a widespread opposition to the expense of colonization, a conviction held especially among the British, who garnered all of the advantages of political empire without the costs of occupation and outright ownership.

The British used to quip that their second global empire was created in the nineteenth century "in a fit of absentmindedness." But colonial policy in Britain and the rest of Europe was more planned and continuous than that comment might suggest. British control of India (including Burma) increased throughout the nineteenth century, as did British control of South Africa, Australia, the Pacific, and parts of the Americas. At the same time, France, having lost most of India to the British, began building an empire that included parts of North Africa, Southeast Asia, and the Pacific.

Thus, a third stage of colonialism, beginning in the mid-nineteenth century, reached a fever pitch with the partition of Africa after 1880. The period between 1888 and 1914 spawned renewed settlement and massive population transfers, with most European migrants settling in the older colonies of the Americas (as well as in South Africa and Australia), where indigenous populations had been reduced. Even where settlement remained light, however, Europeans took political control of large areas of the Earth's surface (see Map 22.1).

■ THINKING HISTORICALLY

Using Literature in History

This chapter also explores how literature can be used in the quest to better understand history. We examine a number of fictional accounts of colonialism, some written by the colonizers, others by the colonized or their descendants, in addition to a critical study of a historical novel and a poem. How do these pieces of literature add to, or detract from, a historical understanding of colonialism? We explore this question because the European colonial experience produced a rich, evocative literature, which, used carefully, can offer a wide range of detail and insight about the period and colonialism.

Historical novels are particularly tricky. The structure of a novel bears certain similarities to history—a description of a place, proper names and biographies, descriptions of human interactions, an accounting of change, and a story. There are also structural differences in a novel—a lot of dialogue, greater attention to physical appearance and character, and a more prominent narrative. These fictional elements are often unattainable for historians. Dialogue, a person's actual words, especially thoughts, are often absent from the historical sources. A good novelist creates these elements based on historical research and familiarity with the time and place. Such details provide a great sense of verisimilitude (resemblance to reality). We feel as if we are there, a feeling that further reinforces our sense of the novel's truth. But in this regard we are captives of the novelist, caught in the web of his or her imagination. In good hands we may see what would otherwise be invisible. In bad hands, we may vividly see what was never there.

A good novel, like a good history, shows us something we did not know, something unexpected, even surprising. But the problem is that we are most easily seduced by what is most familiar to us. Thus, in the hands of the uninformed, we are most likely to believe we have seen the historical truth when we have only projected our own world onto the past. How successfully do the authors of these fictional pieces show you something about the past that is likely true?

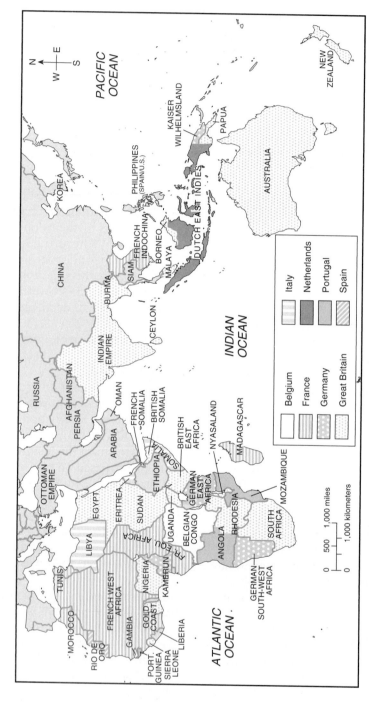

Map 22.1 European Colonialism in Africa and Asia, 1880–1914.

GEORGE ORWELL

Burmese Days

George Orwell, the pen name of Eric Arthur Blair (1903–1950), is best known for such novels as *Animal Farm* (1945) and *Nineteen Eighty-Four* (1949), from which the term *Orwellian* has come to define totalitarianism. *Burmese Days* (1934) was Orwell's first novel, based on his experience in the British police in Burma from 1922 to 1927.

This selection from the novel captures the life of the British colonial class in a remote "upcountry" town in Burma in the 1920s, a hundred years after British conquest and settlement had begun and fifty years after all of Burma had been integrated into the British Indian empire.

The central character is Flory, the only Englishman at all sympathetic to the Burmese. Though he has befriended the Indian physician, Dr. Veraswami, Flory is too weak to propose him as the first "native" member of the club. The other main characters are Westfield, district superintendent of police; Ellis, local company manager and the most racist of the group; Lackersteen, local manager of a timber company who is usually drunk; Maxwell, a forest officer; and Macgregor, deputy commissioner and secretary of the club.

Why does the club loom so large in the lives of these Englishmen? If they complain so much, why are they in Burma? How do you account for the virulent racism of these men? Why does Ellis "correct" the butler's English? What does this story suggest about women in the colonial world?

THINKING HISTORICALLY

Orwell knew Burma quite well. He was born in India in 1903, and his father worked in the Opium Department of the Indian Civil Service. After attending school at Eton in England, Orwell spent five years as a member of the Indian Imperial Police in Burma. Orwell's mother had grown up in Burma, and his grandmother continued to live there in the 1920s. In his various postings, Orwell no doubt spent time in British social clubs like the one that serves as the setting for this chapter. Orwell, therefore, had a broad knowledge of Burma on which to base his story. Is there any way to determine what Orwell invented and what he merely described in this account?

Orwell was politically engaged throughout his life. Would political ideas make him better or worse as a historian or novelist? How so?

Source: George Orwell, *Burmese Days* (1934; reprint, San Diego: Harcourt Brace, 1962), 17–27.

Flory's house was at the top of the maidan,[1] close to the edge of the jungle. From the gate the maidan sloped sharply down, scorched and khaki-coloured, with half a dozen dazzling white bungalows scattered round it. All quaked, shivered in the hot air. There was an English cemetery within a white wall half-way down the hill, and nearby a tiny tin-roofed church. Beyond that was the European Club, and when one looked at the Club—a dumpy one-storey wooden building—one looked at the real centre of the town. In any town in India the European Club is the spiritual citadel, the real seat of the British power, the Nirvana for which native officials and millionaires pine in vain. It was doubly so in this case, for it was the proud boast of Kyauktada Club that, almost alone of Clubs in Burma, it had never admitted an Oriental[2] to membership. Beyond the Club, the Irrawaddy flowed huge and ochreous, glittering like diamonds in the patches that caught the sun; and beyond the river stretched great wastes of paddy fields, ending at the horizon in a range of blackish hills.

The native town, and the courts and the jail, were over to the right, mostly hidden in green groves of peepul trees. The spire of the pagoda rose from the trees like a slender spear tipped with gold. Kyauktada[3] was a fairly typical Upper Burma town, that had not changed greatly between the days of Marco Polo and 1910, and might have slept in the Middle Ages for a century more if it had not proved a convenient spot for a railway terminus. In 1910 the Government[4] made it the headquarters of a district and a seat of Progress—interpretable as a block of law courts, with their army of fat but ravenous pleaders, a hospital, a school, and one of those huge, durable jails which the English have built everywhere between Gibraltar and Hong Kong. The population was about four thousand, including a couple of hundred Indians, a few score Chinese and seven Europeans. There were also two Eurasians named Mr. Francis and Mr. Samuel, the sons of an American Baptist missionary and a Roman Catholic missionary respectively. The town contained no curiosities of any kind, except an Indian fakir[5] who had lived for twenty years in a tree near the bazaar, drawing his food up in a basket every morning.

---

[1] Parade-ground. [Ed.]

[2] The term *Oriental* included all Asians or people of the "East" as opposed to Occidentals or Westerners, as in Rudyard Kipling's *Barrack-room Ballads*: "East is East and West is West, and never the twain [two] shall meet" (1892). But in this case, Orwell means Indians and Burmese as well as the few Chinese. [Ed.]

[3] Fictional name for Katha or Kathar, a town on the Irrawaddy (or Ayeyarwady) River and the railroad, in northern Burma, where Orwell lived 1926–1927. [Ed.]

[4] The British government eliminated the Burmese monarchy, exiling the king to India, and abolished the traditional role of the Buddhist monks, imposing instead the kind of bureaucracy they used to rule India. [Ed.]

[5] Originally a term for a Muslim Sufi mystic, here used to mean any ascetic, Hindu or Muslim, or even a beggar. [Ed.]

Flory yawned as he came out of the gate. He had been half drunk the night before, and the glare made him feel liverish. "Bloody, bloody hole!" he thought, looking down the hill. And, no one except the dog being near, he began to sing aloud, "Bloody, bloody, bloody, oh, how thou art bloody" to the tune of "Holy, holy, holy, oh how Thou art holy," as he walked down the hot red road, switching at the dried-up grasses with his stick. It was nearly nine o'clock and the sun was fiercer every minute. The heat throbbed down on one's head with a steady, rhythmic thumping, like blows from an enormous bolster. Flory stopped at the Club gate, wondering whether to go in or to go farther down the road and see Dr. Veraswami. Then he remembered that it was "English mail day" and the newspapers would have arrived. He went in, past the big tennis screen, which was overgrown by a creeper with starlike mauve flowers.

In the borders beside the path swathes of English flowers, phlox and larkspur, hollyhock and petunia, not yet slain by the sun, rioted in vast size and richness. The petunias were huge, like trees almost. There was no lawn, but instead a shrubbery of native trees and bushes—gold mohur trees like vast umbrellas of blood-red bloom, frangipanis with creamy, stalkless flowers, purple bougainvillea, scarlet hibiscus, and the pink, Chinese rose, bilious-green crotons, feathery fronds of tamarind. The clash of colours hurt one's eyes in the glare. A nearly naked *mali*,[6] watering-can in hand, was moving in the jungle of flowers like some large nectar-sucking bird.

On the Club steps a sandy-haired Englishman, with a prickly moustache, pale grey eyes too far apart, and abnormally thin calves to his legs, was standing with his hands in the pockets of his shorts. This was Mr. Westfield, the District Superintendent of Police. With a very bored air he was rocking himself backwards and forwards on his heels and pouting his upper lip so that his moustache tickled his nose. He greeted Flory with a slight sideways movement of his head. His way of speaking was clipped and soldierly, missing out every word that well could be missed out. Nearly everything he said was intended for a joke, but the tone of his voice was hollow and melancholy.

"Hullo, Flory me lad. Bloody awful morning, what?"

"We must expect it at this time of year, I suppose," Flory said. He had turned himself a little sideways, so that his birthmarked cheek was away from Westfield.

"Yes, dammit. Couple of months of this coming. Last year we didn't have a spot of rain till June. Look at that bloody sky, not a cloud in it. Like one of those damned great blue enamel saucepans. God! What'd you give to be in Piccadilly now, eh?"

"Have the English papers come?"

[6] Gardener. [Ed.]

"Yes. Dear old *Punch, Pink'un,* and *Vie Parisienne.* Makes you homesick to read 'em, what? Let's come in and have a drink before the ice all goes. Old Lackersteen's been fairly bathing in it. Half pickled already."

They went in, Westfield remarking in his gloomy voice, "Lead on, Macduff." Inside, the Club was a teak-walled place smelling of earth-oil, and consisting of only four rooms, one of which contained a for-lorn "library" of five hundred mildewed novels, and another an old and mangy billiard-table—this, however, seldom used, for during most of the year hordes of flying beetles came buzzing round the lamps and littered themselves over the cloth. There were also a card-room and a "lounge" which looked towards the river, over a wide veranda; but at this time of day all the verandas were curtained with green bamboo chicks. The lounge was an unhomelike room, with coco-nut matting on the floor, and wicker chairs and tables which were littered with shiny illustrated papers. For ornament there were a number of "Bonzo" pictures,[7] and the dusty skulls of sambhur.[8] A punkah,[9] lazily flapping, shook dust into the tepid air.

There were three men in the room. Under the punkah a florid, fine-looking, slightly bloated man of forty was sprawling across the table with his head in his hands, groaning in pain. This was Mr. Lackersteen, the local manager of a timber firm. He had been badly drunk the night before, and he was suffering for it. Ellis, local manager of yet another company, was standing before the notice board studying some notice with a look of bitter concentration. He was a tiny wiry-haired fellow with a pale, sharp-featured face and restless movements. Maxwell, the acting Divisional Forest Officer, was lying in one of the long chairs read-ing the *Field,* and invisible except for two large-boned legs and thick downy forearms.

"Look at this naughty old man," said Westfield, taking Mr. Lackersteen half affectionately by the shoulders and shaking him. "Example to the young, what? There, but for the grace of God and all that. Gives you an idea what you'll be like at forty."

Mr. Lackersteen gave a groan which sounded like "brandy."

"Poor old chap," said Westfield; "regular martyr to booze, eh? Look at it oozing out of his pores. Reminds me of the old colonel who used to sleep without a mosquito net. They asked his servant why and the ser-vant said: 'At night, master too drunk to notice mosquitoes; in the morn-ing, mosquitoes too drunk to notice master.' Look at him—boozed last

---

[7] Bulldog puppy cartoons created by G. E. Studdy in the 1920s for magazines like *Punch.* [Ed.]

[8] Large South Asian deer, like elk. [Ed.]

[9] Large cloth panel fan hanging from the ceiling, usually pulled by a rope to move the air. [Ed.]

night and then asking for more. Got a little niece coming to stay with him, too. Due tonight, isn't she, Lackersteen?"

"Oh, leave that drunken sot alone," said Ellis without turning round. He had a spiteful cockney voice. Mr. Lackersteen groaned again, "—the niece! Get me some brandy, for Christ's sake."

"Good education for the niece, eh? Seeing uncle under the table seven times a week.—Hey, butler! Bringing brandy for Lackersteen master!"

The butler, a dark, stout Dravidian[10] with liquid, yellow-irised eyes like those of a dog, brought the brandy on a brass tray. Flory and West-field ordered gin. Mr. Lackersteen swallowed a few spoonfuls of brandy and sat back in his chair, groaning in a more resigned way. He had a beefy, ingenuous face, with a toothbrush moustache. He was really a very simple-minded man, with no ambitions beyond having what he called "a good time." His wife governed him by the only possible method, namely, by never letting him out of her sight for more than an hour or two. Only once, a year after they were married, she had left him for a fortnight, and had returned unexpectedly a day before her time, to find Mr. Lackersteen, drunk, supported on either side by a naked Burmese girl, while a third up-ended a whisky bottle into his mouth. Since then she had watched him, as he used to complain, "like a cat over a bloody mousehole." However, he managed to enjoy quite a number of "good times," though they were usually rather hurried ones.

"My Christ, what a head I've got on me this morning," he said. "Call that butler again, Westfield. I've got to have another brandy before my missus gets here. She says she's going to cut my booze down to four pegs a day when our niece gets here. God rot them both!" he added gloomily.

"Stop playing the fool, all of you, and listen to this," said Ellis sourly. He had a queer wounding way of speaking, hardly ever opening his mouth without insulting somebody. He deliberately exaggerated his cockney accent, because of the sardonic tone it gave to his words. "Have you seen this notice of old Macgregor's? A little nosegay for everyone. Maxwell, wake up and listen!"

Maxwell lowered the *Field*. He was a fresh-coloured blond youth of not more than twenty-five or six—very young for the post he held. With his heavy limbs and thick white eyelashes he reminded one of a carthorse colt. Ellis nipped the notice from the board with a neat, spite-ful little movement and began reading it aloud. It had been posted by Mr. Macgregor, who, besides being Deputy Commissioner, was secretary of the Club.

"Just listen to this. 'It has been suggested that as there are as yet no Oriental members of this club, and as it is now usual to admit officials of gazetted rank, whether native or European, to membership of most

---

[10] Dated racial term used to refer to darker-skinned inhabitants of southern India. [Ed.]

European Clubs, we should consider the question of following this practice in Kyauktada. The matter will be open for discussion at the next general meeting. On the one hand it may be pointed out'—oh, well, no need to wade through the rest of it. He can't even write out a notice without an attack of literary diarrhoea. Anyway, the point's this. He's asking us to break all our rules and take a dear little nigger-boy into this Club. *Dear* Dr. Veraswami, for instance. Dr. Very-slimy, I call him. That *would* be a treat, wouldn't it? Little pot-bellied niggers breathing garlic in your face over the bridge-table. Christ, to think of it! We've got to hang together and put our foot down on this at once. What do you say, Westfield? Flory?"

Westfield shrugged his thin shoulders philosophically. He had sat down at the table and lighted a black, stinking Burma cheroot.

"Got to put up with it, I suppose," he said. "B_____s of natives are getting into all the Clubs nowadays. Even the Pegu Club, I'm told. Way this country's going, you know. We're about the last Club in Burma to hold out against 'em."

"We are; and what's more, we're damn well going to go on holding out. I'll die in the ditch before I'll see a nigger in here." Ellis had produced a stump of pencil. With the curious air of spite that some men can put into their tiniest action, he re-pinned the notice on the board and pencilled a tiny, neat "B. F." against Mr. Macgregor's signature—"There, that's what I think of his idea. I'll tell him so when he comes down. What do *you* say, Flory?"

Flory had not spoken all this time. Though by nature anything but a silent man, he seldom found much to say in Club conversations. He had sat down at the table and was reading G. K. Chesterton's article in the *London News*, at the same time caressing [his dog] Flo's head with his left hand. Ellis, however, was one of those people who constantly nag others to echo their own opinions. He repeated his question, and Flory looked up, and their eyes met. The skin round Ellis's nose suddenly turned so pale that it was almost grey. In him it was a sign of anger. Without any prelude he burst into a stream of abuse that would have been startling, if the others had not been used to hearing something like it every morning.

"My God, I should have thought in a case like this, when it's a question of keeping those black, stinking swine out of the only place where we can enjoy ourselves, you'd have the decency to back me up. Even if that pot-bellied, greasy little sod of a nigger doctor *is* your best pal. *I* don't care if you choose to pal up with the scum of the bazaar. If it pleases you to go to Veraswami's house and drink whisky with all his nigger pals, that's your look-out. Do what you like outside the Club. But, by God, it's a different matter when you talk of bringing niggers in here. I suppose you'd like little Veraswami for a Club member, eh? Chipping into our conversation and pawing everyone with his sweaty hands and breathing his filthy garlic breath in our faces. By God, he'd go out with my boot behind him if ever I saw his black snout inside that door. Greasy, pot-bellied little———!" etc.

This went on for several minutes. It was curiously impressive, because it was so completely sincere. Ellis really did hate Orientals—hated them with a bitter, restless loathing as of something evil or unclean. Living and working, as the assistant of a timber firm must, in perpetual contact with the Burmese, he had never grown used to the sight of a black face. Any hint of friendly feeling towards an Oriental seemed to him a horrible perversity. He was an intelligent man and an able servant of his firm, but he was one of those Englishmen—common, unfortunately—who should never be allowed to set foot in the East.

Flory sat nursing Flo's head in his lap, unable to meet Ellis's eyes. At the best of times his birthmark made it difficult for him to look people straight in the face. And when he made ready to speak, he could feel his voice trembling—for it had a way of trembling when it should have been firm; his features, too, sometimes twitched uncontrollably.

"Steady on," he said at last, sullenly and rather feebly. "Steady on. There's no need to get so excited. *I* never suggested having any native members in here."

"Oh, didn't you? We all know bloody well you'd like to, though. Why else do you go to that oily little babu's house every morning, then? Sitting down at table with him as though he was a white man, and drinking out of glasses his filthy black lips have slobbered over—it makes me spew to think of it."

"Sit down, old chap, sit down," Westfield said. "Forget it. Have a drink on it. Not worth while quarrelling. Too hot."

"My God," said Ellis a little more calmly, taking a pace or two up and down, "my God, I don't understand you chaps. I simply don't. Here's that old fool Macgregor wanting to bring a nigger into this Club for no reason whatever, and you all sit down under it without a word. Good God, what are we supposed to be doing in this country? If we aren't going to rule, why the devil don't we clear out? Here we are, supposed to be governing a set of damn black swine who've been slaves since the beginning of history, and instead of ruling them in the only way they understand, we go and treat them as equals. And all you silly b———s take it for granted. There's Flory, makes his best pal of a black babu who calls himself a doctor because he's done two years at an Indian so-called university. And you, Westfield, proud as Punch of your knock-kneed, bribe-taking cowards of policemen. And there's Maxwell, spends his time running after Eurasian tarts. Yes, you do, Maxwell; I heard about your goings-on in Mandalay with some smelly little bitch called Molly Pereira. I supposed you'd have gone and married her if they hadn't transferred you up here? You all seem to *like* the dirty black brutes. Christ, I don't know what's come over us all. I really don't."

"Come on, have another drink," said Westfield. "Hey, butler! Spot of beer before the ice goes, eh? Beer, butler!"

The butler brought some bottles of Munich beer. Ellis presently sat down at the table with the others, and he nursed one of the cool bottles between his small hands. His forehead was sweating. He was sulky, but not in a rage any longer. At all times he was spiteful and perverse, but his violent fits of rage were soon over, and were never apologised for. Quarrels were a regular part of the routine of Club life. Mr. Lackersteen was feeling better and was studying the illustrations in *La Vie Parisienne*. It was after nine now, and the room, scented with the acrid smoke of Westfield's cheroot, was stifling hot. Everyone's shirt stuck to his back with the first sweat of the day. The invisible *chokra*[11] who pulled the punkah rope outside was falling asleep in the glare.

"Butler!" yelled Ellis, and as the butler appeared, "go and wake that bloody *chokra* up!"

"Yes, master."

"And butler!"

"Yes, master?"

"How much ice have we got left?"

"'Bout twenty pounds, master. Will only last to-day, I think. I find it very difficult to keep ice cool now."

"Don't talk like that, damn you—'I find it very difficult!' Have you swallowed a dictionary? 'Please, master, can't keeping ice cool'—that's how you ought to talk. We shall have to sack this fellow if he gets to talk English too well. I can't stick servants who talk English. D'you hear, butler?"

"Yes, master," said the butler, and retired.

"God! No ice till Monday," Westfield said. "You going back to the jungle, Flory?"

"Yes. I ought to be there now. I only came in because of the English mail."

"Go on tour myself, I think. Knock up a spot of Travelling Allowance. I can't stick my bloody office at this time of year. Sitting there under the damned punkah, signing one chit after another. Paperchewing. God, how I wish the war was on again!"

"I'm going out the day after to-morrow," Ellis said. "Isn't that damned padre coming to hold his service this Sunday? I'll take care not to be in for that, anyway. Bloody knee-drill."

"Next Sunday," said Westfield. "Promised to be in for it myself. So's Macgregor. Bit hard on the poor devil of a padre, I must say. Only gets here once in six weeks. Might as well get up a congregation when he does come."

---

[11] Person who pulls the punkah rope that moves a large panel to let in a breeze. [Ed.]

"Oh, hell! I'd snivel psalms to oblige the padre, but I can't stick the way these damned native Christians come shoving into our church. A pack of Madrassi servants and Karen[12] school-teachers. And then those two yellow-bellies, Francis and Samuel—they call themselves Christians too. Last time the padre was here they had the nerve to come up and sit on the front pews with the white men. Someone ought to speak to the padre about that. What bloody fools we were ever to let those missionaries loose in this country! Teaching bazaar sweepers they're as good as we are. 'Please, sir, me Christian same like master.' Damned cheek."

[12] An ethnic minority group in Burma. [Ed.]

2

JOSEPH CONRAD

Heart of Darkness

Although his native tongue was Polish (and French his second language), Joseph Conrad (1857-1924) became one of the leading English novelists of the era of British imperialism. Drawing on his experience as a mariner and ship captain, he secured a post as an officer on river steamboats on the Congo River in 1890. Nine years later he published *Heart of Darkness*, a novel that has introduced generations since to Africa, the Congo, the era of colonialism, and European ideas of "the other."

In this selection from the novel, Conrad's narrator, Marlow, tells of his voyage up the Congo to meet the enigmatic European Kurtz, who has secured prodigious amounts of ivory for his Belgian employer but (we learn at the end of the novel) has lost his mind in the process.

What impression does *Heart of Darkness* give of Africa and Africans? What does it suggest were the motives or intentions of European explorers and traders in Africa? What feeling does this selection convey about European colonization of Africa?

THINKING HISTORICALLY

Like many novels, *Heart of Darkness* is based on the actual experiences of the author. Despite the basis in fact, however, it is very different from historical writing. Imagine Conrad writing a history of the events described in this selection. How would it be different? Would one account be truer, or merely reveal different truths?

Source: Joseph Conrad, *Heart of Darkness*, A Norton Critical Edition (New York: Norton, 1988), 35–39. Originally published by *Blackwood's Magazine* (London, 1899, 1902).

Going up that river was like travelling back to the earliest beginnings of the world, when vegetation rioted on the earth and the big trees were kings. An empty stream, a great silence, an impenetrable forest. The air was warm, thick, heavy, sluggish. There was no joy in the brilliance of sunshine. The long stretches of the waterway ran on, deserted, into the gloom of overshadowed distances. On silvery sandbanks hippos and alligators sunned themselves side by side. The broadening waters flowed through a mob of wooded islands. You lost your way on that river as you would in a desert and butted all day long against shoals trying to find the channel till you thought yourself bewitched and cut off for ever from everything you had known once—somewhere—far away—in another existence perhaps. There were moments when one's past came back to one, as it will sometimes when you have not a moment to spare to yourself; but it came in the shape of an unrestful and noisy dream remembered with wonder amongst the overwhelming realities of this strange world of plants and water and silence. And this stillness of life did not in the least resemble a peace. It was the stillness of an implacable force brooding over an inscrutable intention. It looked at you with a vengeful aspect. I got used to it afterwards. I did not see it any more. I had no time. I had to keep guessing at the channel; I had to discern, mostly by inspiration, the signs of hidden banks; I watched for sunken stones; I was learning to clap my teeth smartly before my heart flew out when I shaved by a fluke some infernal sly old snag that would have ripped the life out of the tin-pot steamboat and drowned all the pilgrims; I had to keep a look-out for the signs of dead wood we could cut up in the night for next day's steaming. When you have to attend to things of that sort, to the mere incidents of the surface, the reality—the reality I tell you—fades. The inner truth is hidden—luckily, luckily. But I felt it all the same; I felt often its mysterious stillness watching me at my monkey tricks. . . .

I managed not to sink that steamboat on my first trip. It's a wonder to me yet. Imagine a blindfolded man set to drive a van over a bad road. I sweated and shivered over that business considerably, I can tell you. After all, for a seaman, to scrape the bottom of the thing that's supposed to float all the time under his care is the unpardonable sin. No one may know of it, but you never forget the thump—eh? A blow on the very heart. You remember it, you dream of it, you wake up at night and think of it—years after—and go hot and cold all over. I don't pretend to say that steamboat floated all the time. More than once she had to wade for a bit, with twenty cannibals splashing around and pushing. We had enlisted some of these chaps on the way for a crew. Fine fellows—cannibals—in their place. They were men one could work with, and I am grateful to them. And, after all, they did not eat each other before my face: they had brought along a provision of hippo-meat which went rotten and made the mystery of the wilderness stink in my nostrils. Phoo! I can sniff it now. I had the Manager on board and three or four pilgrims with their staves — all complete. Sometimes we came upon a station close by the bank clinging to the skirts of the unknown, and the white men rushing out of a tumbledown hovel with great gestures of joy and surprise and welcome seemed very strange, had the appearance of being held there captive by a spell. The word "ivory" would ring in the air for a while — and on we went again into the silence, along empty reaches, round the still bends, between the high walls of our winding way, reverberating in hollow claps the ponderous beat of the stern-wheel. Trees, trees, millions of trees, massive, immense, running up high, and at their foot, hugging the bank against the stream, crept the little begrimed steamboat like a sluggish beetle crawling on the floor of a lofty portico. It made you feel very small, very lost, and yet it was not altogether depressing, that feeling. After all, if you were small, the grimy beetle crawled on — which was just what you wanted it to do. Where the pilgrims imagined it crawled to I don't know. To some place where they expected to get something, I bet! For me it crawled towards Kurtz — exclusively; but when the steam-pipes started leaking we crawled very slow. The reaches opened before us and closed behind, as if the forest had stepped leisurely across the water to bar the way for our return. We penetrated deeper and deeper into the heart of darkness. It was very quiet there. At night sometimes the roll of drums behind the curtain of trees would run up the river and remain sustained faintly, as if hovering in the air high over our heads till the first break of day. Whether it meant war, peace, or prayer we could not tell. The dawns were heralded by the descent of a chill stillness. The woodcutters slept, their fires burned low, the snapping of a twig would make you start. We were wanderers on a prehistoric earth, on an earth that wore the aspect of an unknown planet. We could have fancied ourselves the first of men taking possession of an accursed inheritance, to be subdued at the cost of profound anguish and of excessive toil. But suddenly as we struggled round a bend there would be a glimpse of rush walls, of peaked grass-roofs, a burst of yells, a whirl of black limbs, a mass of hands clapping, of feet stamping, of bodies swaying, of eyes rolling under the droop of heavy and motionless foliage. The steamer toiled along slowly on the edge of a black and incomprehensible frenzy. The prehistoric man was cursing us, praying to us, welcoming us — who could tell? We were cut off from the comprehension of our surroundings; we glided past like phantoms, wondering and secretly appalled, as sane men would be before an enthusiastic outbreak in a madhouse. We could not understand because we were too far and could not remember because we were travelling in the night of first ages, of those ages that are gone, leaving hardly a sign—and no memories.

The earth seemed unearthly. We are accustomed to look upon the shackled form of a conquered monster, but there—there you could look at a thing monstrous and free. It was unearthly and the men were. . . . No they were not inhuman. Well, you know that was the worst of it—this suspicion of their not being inhuman. It would come slowly to one. They howled and leaped and spun and made horrid faces, but what thrilled you was just the thought of their humanity—like yours—the thought of your remote kinship with this wild and passionate uproar. Ugly. Yes, it was ugly enough, but if you were man enough you would admit to yourself that there was in you just the faintest trace of a response to the terrible frankness of that noise, a dim suspicion of there being a meaning in it which you—you so remote from the night of first ages—could comprehend. And why not? The mind of man is capable of anything—because everything is in it, all the past as well as all the future. What was there after all? Joy, fear, sorrow, devotion, valour, rage—who can tell?—but truth—truth stripped of its cloak of time. Let the fool gape and shudder—the man knows and can look on without a wink. But he must at least be as much of a man as these on the shore. He must meet that truth with his own true stuff—with his own inborn strength. Principles? Principles won't do. Acquisitions, clothes, pretty rags—rags that would fly off at the first good shake. No. You want a deliberate belief. An appeal to me in this fiendish row—is there? Very well. I hear, I admit, but I have a voice too, and for good or evil mine is the speech that cannot be silenced. Of course, a fool, what with sheer fright and fine sentiments, is always safe. Who's that grunting? You wonder I didn't go ashore for a howl and a dance? Well, no—I didn't. Fine sentiments, you say? Fine sentiments be hanged! I had no time. I had to mess about with whitelead and strips of woollen blanket helping to put bandages on those leaky steam-pipes—tell you. I had to watch the steering and circumvent those snags and get the tin-pot along by hook or by crook. There was surface-truth enough in these things to save a wiser man. And between whiles I had to look after the savage who was fireman. He was an improved specimen; he could fire up a vertical boiler. He was there below me and, upon my word, to look at him was as edifying as seeing a dog in a parody of breeches and a feather hat walking on his hind legs. A few months of training had done for that really fine chap. He squinted at the steam-gauge and at the water-gauge with an evident effort of intrepidity—and he had filed teeth too, the poor devil, and the wool of his pate shaved into queer patterns, and three ornamental scars on each of his cheeks. He ought to have been clapping his hands and stamping his feet on the bank, instead of which he was hard at work, a thrall to strange witchcraft, full of improving knowledge. He was useful because he had been instructed;

and what he knew was this—that should the water in that transparent thing disappear the evil spirit inside the boiler would get angry through the greatness of his thirst and take a terrible vengeance. So he sweated and fired up and watched the glass fearfully (with an impromptu charm, made of rags, tied to his arm and a piece of polished bone as big as a watch stuck flatways through his lower lip) while the wooded banks slipped past us slowly, the shore noise was left behind, the interminable miles of silence—and we crept on, towards Kurtz.

3

CHINUA ACHEBE

An Image of Africa: Racism in Conrad's *Heart of Darkness*

Chinua Achebe* is modern Africa's most read novelist. His *Things Fall Apart,* about the impact of European missionaries in his native Nigeria at the end of the nineteenth century, is a classic that is as widely read as *Heart of Darkness.* In this selection, which first took form as an address to an American college audience in 1975, Achebe tackles *Heart of Darkness.* What is his argument? Are you persuaded?

THINKING HISTORICALLY

Achebe is a novelist criticizing another novelist for distorting history. Could any of Achebe's criticisms be directed at Orwell? What are the responsibilities of a novelist to historical accuracy? How does a critique of literature like this add to our understanding of the past?

Heart of Darkness projects the image of Africa as "the other world," the antithesis of Europe and therefore of civilization, a place where man's vaunted intelligence and refinement are finally mocked by triumphant bestiality. The book opens on the River Thames, tranquil, resting,

---

* chih NOO ah ah CHEH bay

Source: Chinua Achebe, "An Image of Africa: Racism in Conrad's *Heart of Darkness*," an emended version (1987) of the second Chancellor's Lecture at the University of Massachusetts, Amherst, February 18, 1975; later published in the *Massachusetts Review* 18 (1977): 782–94. Reprinted in *Heart of Darkness*, A Norton Critical Edition (New York: Norton, 1988), 252–54, 257–60.

peacefully "at the decline of day after ages of good service done to the race that peopled its banks." But the actual story will take place on the River Congo, the very antithesis of the Thames. The River Congo is quite decidedly not a River Emeritus. It has rendered no service and enjoys no old-age pension. We are told that "Going up that river was like travelling back to the earliest beginnings of the world."

Is Conrad saying then that these two rivers are very different, one good, the other bad? Yes, but that is not the real point. It is not the differentness that worries Conrad but the lurking hint of kinship, of common ancestry. For the Thames too "has been one of the dark places of the earth." It conquered its darkness, of course, and is now in daylight and at peace. But if it were to visit its primordial relative, the Congo, it would run the terrible risk of hearing grotesque echoes of its own forgotten darkness, and falling victim to an avenging recrudescence of the mindless frenzy of the first beginnings.

These suggestive echoes comprise Conrad's famed evocation of the African atmosphere in *Heart of Darkness*. In the final consideration his method amounts to no more than a steady, ponderous, fake-ritualistic repetition of two antithetical sentences, one about silence and the other about frenzy. We can inspect samples of this on pages 36 and 37[1] of the present edition: a) *It was the stillness of an implacable force brooding over an inscrutable intention* and b) *The steamer toiled along slowly on the edge of a black and incomprehensible frenzy.* Of course there is a judicious change of adjective from time to time, so that instead of *inscrutable,* for example, you might have *unspeakable,* even plain *mysterious,* etc., etc.

The eagle-eyed English critic F. R. Leavis drew attention long ago to Conrad's "adjectival insistence upon inexpressible and incomprehensible mystery." That insistence must not be dismissed lightly, as many Conrad critics have tended to do, as a mere stylistic flaw; for it raises serious questions of artistic good faith. When a writer while pretending to record scenes, incidents, and their impact is in reality engaged in inducing hypnotic stupor in his readers through a bombardment of emotive words and other forms of trickery much more has to be at stake than stylistic felicity. Generally normal readers are well armed to detect and resist such underhand activity. But Conrad chose his subject well—one which was guaranteed not to put him in conflict with the psychological pre-disposition of his readers or raise the need for him to contend with their resistance. He chose the role of purveyor of comforting myths.

The most interesting and revealing passages in *Heart of Darkness* are, however, about people. I must crave the indulgence of my reader

---

[1] See pp. 838 and 839. [Ed.]

to quote almost a whole page from about the middle of the story when representatives of Europe in a steamer going down the Congo encounter the denizens of Africa.

> We were wanderers on a prehistoric earth, on an earth that wore the aspect of an unknown planet. We could have fancied ourselves the first of men taking possession of an accursed inheritance, to be subdued at the cost of profound anguish and of excessive toil. But suddenly as we struggled round a bend there would be a glimpse of rush walls, of peaked grass-roofs, a burst of yells, a whirl of black limbs, a mass of hands clapping, of feet stamping, of bodies sway-ing, of eyes rolling under the droop of heavy and motionless foliage. The steamer toiled along slowly on the edge of a black and incom-prehensible frenzy. The prehistoric man was cursing us, praying to us, welcoming us—who could tell? We were cut off from the com-prehension of our surroundings; we glided past like phantoms, wondering and secretly appalled, as sane men would be before an enthusiastic outbreak in a madhouse. We could not understand be-cause we were too far and could not remember, because we were travelling in the night of first ages, of those ages that are gone, leav-ing hardly a sign—and no memories.

> The earth seemed unearthly. We are accustomed to look upon the shackled form of a conquered monster, but there—there you could look at a thing monstrous and free. It was unearthly and the men were. . . . No they were not inhuman. Well, you know that was the worst of it—this suspicion of their not being inhuman. It would come slowly to one. They howled and leaped and spun and made horrid faces, but what thrilled you was just the thought of their humanity—like yours—the thought of your remote kinship with this wild and passionate uproar. Ugly. Yes, it was ugly enough, but if you were man enough you would admit to yourself that there was in you just the faintest trace of a response to the terrible frank-ness of that noise, a dim suspicion of there being a meaning in it which you—you so remote from the night of first ages—could comprehend.

Herein lies the meaning of *Heart of Darkness* and the fascination it holds over the Western mind: "What thrilled you was just the thought of their humanity—like yours. . . . Ugly."

Having shown us Africa in the mass, Conrad then zeros in, half a page later, on a specific example, giving us one of his rare descriptions of an African who is not just limbs or rolling eyes:

> And between whiles I had to look after the savage who was fire-man. He was an improved specimen; he could fire up a vertical

boiler. He was there below me and, upon my word, to look at him was as edifying as seeing a dog in a parody of breeches and a feather hat walking on his hind legs. A few months of training had done for that really fine chap. He squinted at the steam-gauge and at the water-gauge with an evident effort of intrepidity—and he had filed his teeth too, the poor devil, and the wool of his pate shaved into queer patterns, and three ornamental scars on each of his cheeks. He ought to have been clapping his hands and stamping his feet on the bank, instead of which he was hard at work, a thrall to strange witchcraft, full of improving knowledge.

As everybody knows, Conrad is a romantic on the side. He might not exactly admire savages clapping their hands and stamping their feet but they have at least the merit of being in their place, unlike this dog in a parody of breeches. For Conrad things being in their place is of the utmost importance.

"Fine fellows—cannibals—in their place," he tells us pointedly. Tragedy begins when things leave their accustomed place, like Europe leaving its safe stronghold between the policeman and the baker to take a peep into the heart of darkness. . . .

The point of my observations should be quite clear by now, namely that Joseph Conrad was a thoroughgoing racist. That this simple truth is glossed over in criticisms of his work is due to the fact that white racism against Africa is such a normal way of thinking that its manifestations go completely unremarked. Students of *Heart of Darkness* will often tell you that Conrad is concerned not so much with Africa as with the deterioration of one European mind caused by solitude and sickness. They will point out to you that Conrad is, if anything, less charitable to the Europeans in the story than he is to the natives, that the point of the story is to ridicule Europe's civilizing mission in Africa. A Conrad student informed me in Scotland that Africa is merely a setting for the disintegration of the mind of Mr. Kurtz.

Which is partly the point. Africa as setting and backdrop which eliminates the African as human factor. Africa as a metaphysical battlefield devoid of all recognizable humanity, into which the wandering European enters at his peril. Can nobody see the preposterous and perverse arrogance in thus reducing Africa to the role of props for the break-up of one petty European mind? But that is not even the point. The real question is the dehumanization of Africa and Africans which this age-long attitude has fostered and continues to foster in the world. And the question is whether a novel which celebrates this dehumanization, which depersonalizes a portion of the human race, can be called a great work of art. My answer is: No, it cannot. I do not doubt Conrad's great talents. Even *Heart of Darkness* has its memorably good passages and moments:

> The reaches opened before us and closed behind, as if the forest had stepped leisurely across the water to bar the way for our return.

Its exploration of the minds of the European characters is often penetrating and full of insight. But all that has been more than fully discussed in the last fifty years. His obvious racism has, however, not been addressed. And it is high time it was!

Conrad was born in 1857, the very year in which the first Anglican missionaries were arriving among my own people in Nigeria. It was certainly not his fault that he lived his life at a time when the reputation of the black man was at a particularly low level. But even after due allowances have been made for all the influences of contemporary prejudice on his sensibility there remains still in Conrad's attitude a residue of antipathy to black people which his peculiar psychology alone can explain. His own account of his first encounter with a black man is very revealing:

> A certain enormous buck nigger encountered in Haiti fixed my conception of blind, furious, unreasoning rage, as manifested in the human animal to the end of my days. Of the nigger I used to dream for years afterwards.

Certainly Conrad had a problem with niggers. His inordinate love of that word itself should be of interest to psychoanalysts. Sometimes his fixation on blackness is equally interesting as when he gives us this brief description:

> A black figure stood up, strode on long black legs, waving long black arms. . . . as though we might expect a black figure striding along on black legs to wave white arms! But so unrelenting is Conrad's obsession. . . .

Whatever Conrad's problems were, you might say he is now safely dead. Quite true. Unfortunately his heart of darkness plagues us still. Which is why an offensive and deplorable book can be described by a serious scholar as "among the half dozen greatest short novels in the English language." And why it is today perhaps the most commonly prescribed novel in twentieth-century literature courses in English Departments of American universities.

There are two probable grounds on which what I have said so far may be contested. The first is that it is no concern of fiction to please people about whom it is written. I will go along with that. But I am not talking about pleasing people. I am talking about a book which parades in the most vulgar fashion prejudices and insults from which a section of mankind has suffered untold agonies and atrocities in the past and continues to do so in many ways and many places today. I am talking about a story in which the very humanity of black people is called in question.

Secondly, I may be challenged on the grounds of actuality. Conrad, after all, did sail down the Congo in 1890 when my own father was still a babe in arms. How could I stand up more than fifty years after his death and purport to contradict him? My answer is that as a sensible man I will not accept just any traveller's tales solely on the grounds that I have not made the journey myself. I will not trust the evidence even of a man's very eyes when I suspect them to be as jaundiced as Conrad's. And we also happen to know that Conrad was, in the words of his biographer, Bernard C. Meyer, "notoriously inaccurate in the rendering of his own history."

But more important by far is the abundant testimony about Conrad's savages which we could gather if we were so inclined from other sources and which might lead us to think that these people must have had other occupations besides merging into the evil forest or materializing out of it simply to plague Marlow and his dispirited band. For as it happened, soon after Conrad had written his book an event of far greater consequence was taking place in the art world of Europe. This is how Frank Willett, a British art historian, describes it:

> Gaugin had gone to Tahiti, the most extravagant individual act of turning to a non-European culture in the decades immediately before and after 1900, when European artists were avid for new artistic experiences, but it was only about 1904–5 that African art began to make its distinctive impact. One piece is still identifiable; it is a mask that had been given to Maurice Vlaminck in 1905. He records that Derain was "speechless" and "stunned" when he saw it, bought it from Vlaminck and in turn showed it to Picasso and Matisse, who were also greatly affected by it. Ambroise Vollard then borrowed it and had it cast in bronze. . . . The revolution of twentieth century art was under way!

The mask in question was made by other savages living just north of Conrad's River Congo. They have a name too: the Fang people, and are without a doubt among the world's greatest masters of the sculptured form. The event Frank Willett is referring to marked the beginning of cubism and the infusion of new life into European art, which had run completely out of strength.

The point of all this is to suggest that Conrad's picture of the peoples of the Congo seems grossly inadequate even at the height of their subjection to the ravages of King Leopold's International Association for the Civilization of Central Africa.[2]

[2] King Leopold II of Belgium established the International Association for the Exploration and Civilization of Central Africa in 1876, with himself as president. The expeditions of the association, particularly those of the explorer Henry Stanley (1880–1884), led to the claim by the association of sovereignty over the Congo basin. The territory of what was then known as the International African Association was reorganized by Leopold as the Congo Free State in 1885. [Ed.]

4

JOYCE CARY
Mister Johnson

Joyce Cary (1888–1957) was an English novelist. Born in Ireland, he lived most of his life in England, except for a series of postings between 1914 and 1920 with the British colonial police and administration in Nigeria, including service in World War I in German Cameroon, where he was wounded. This colonial experience led to the publication of a number of novels set in Nigeria, *Mister Johnson* (1939) being the most successful. In this brief selection from the novel we meet Rudbeck, a junior officer, recently assigned to the town of Fadeh, Nigeria, under the command of Blore. What does the dispute between Rudbeck and Blore about roads suggest about colonial administration?

The rest of the selection introduces Mr. Johnson, the young African assistant of Rudbeck. The plot is complicated by the introduction of Rudbeck's wife. What complications did the arrival of a European spouse add?

Compare Cary's European colonialists with those of Orwell and Conrad. How does his treatment of Africans compare with that of Conrad?

THINKING HISTORICALLY

Cary employs two strategies in telling his story that are rarely used in history writing. One is the use of the present tense, and the other is the spelling to capture dialect, in this case the Nigerian Pidgin English of Mr. Johnson. How does each of these strategies add to, or detract from, the sense of historical reality in the novel? What other aspects of this selection increase or diminish your sense of being there? How might a novel's sense of "being there" actually lessen your historical knowledge?

Source: Joyce Cary, *Mister Johnson* (New York: New Direction Books, 1989), 46–47, 87–94. Originally published in Great Britain by Gollanzl, 1939.

Rudbeck has a passion for roads.

Just as Blore is particular about tax assessment and is always collecting statistics, so Rudbeck, even as a junior, as soon as he comes to a station, sends for the chief and complains about the roads. He spends his afternoons riding or driving about the country inspecting bridges; and he loves to make maps and draw on them, in dotted lines of red ink, new trade routes.

In this he has no sympathy from Blore, who considers motor roads to be the ruin of Africa, bringing swindlers, thieves and whores, disease, vice and corruption, and the vulgarities of trade, among decent, unspoilt tribesmen.

It was the same, he says, with the railways, when he was a junior. They spoilt the old Nigeria wherever they went.

In fact, Blore and Rudbeck have already had a slight quarrel about the Dorua road which Rudbeck is now going to inspect. When Rudbeck has suggested, the night before, that a certain curve needs straightening, Blore has smiled and said, "Still on the road game?"

Rudbeck has looked haughty and wooden, like a small boy being chaffed. Although he is modest and respectful, he has a strong will of his own. He doesn't change his mind easily, after he, or somebody else, has made it up for him. He says now in a cool and defiant voice, "Don't you think it's about time we had a few motor roads?"

"The voice of old Sturdee—I heard him declare—"

Rudbeck turns red and looks still more obstinate. He says coldly. "I didn't get the idea from Sturdee—it's obvious."

Old Sturdee is a resident well known for his enthusiasm in road-building, and Blore is fond of suggesting that Rudbeck caught it from Sturdee, with whom he spent his first six months in the service. This is quite true. Rudbeck, like other juniors, had no idea when he joined of what would be expected of him. If he had come to Blore first, no doubt he would have fallen into a routine of office, drinks and an evening walk; prided himself on his assessment and considered census much the most important duty of a political officer. But from Sturdee he has caught the belief that to build a road, any road anywhere is the noblest work a man can do. He has also found it enjoyable. As Sturdee is fond of saying, "When you make a road you know you've done something—you can see it."

But by now, two years after his last contact with Sturdee, Rudbeck honestly believes that he has always advocated roads. He admits to a warm admiration for Sturdee's work, but doesn't acknowledge that his own creations in Fada owe their being to anyone else's inspiration. . . .

Rudbeck is now camping at road head thirty miles away and visits the office only on alternate days. One morning, he comes in unexpectedly, wanders about the office with a perplexed expression and finally stops before Johnson. "Johnson, I'll be leaving here to-morrow. I have to go and meet Mrs. Rudbeck at railhead. That means four days altogether. Do you think you can go up to road head and keep an eye on Tasuki and Audu?" He gives long and elaborate instructions about the road work, to all of which Johnson says, "Yes, sah—I do 'em, sah."

"I'm depending on you, Johnson."

"Oh, sah, you depend on me for my life's worth. I hope Missus Rudbeck like dis Africa country."

"She is looking forward to it very much. Why shouldn't she like it?"

Johnson can't refer him to his wife's own letters, from which Johnson has discovered that she is longing to come to Africa, whereas Rudbeck is afraid that she may be bored there. He says therefore, "Oh, I'm sure she like it very much. P'raps I go build her a new grass house up road."

"Yes, that might be a good idea."

"With a nice little lady latrine."

"What d'you mean, a lady latrine."

"Dose latrine for white lady so dey go in all by herself—nobody see 'um."

"That's a good idea."

"I make um, sah—he ready so soon as Missus Rudbeck come here."

"Yes, I expect you'll have to look after Mrs. Rudbeck a bit, Johnson—if I have to be moved down the road. I want to get this bad stretch finished before the rains."

"Oh, yes, sah. I like dat very much. I like to make Missus Rudbeck too happy in Africa."

"Show her round a bit, you understand."

"I show her everyting—prison, market, all tings ladies like—I keep her too happy for you, sah."

"Thanks. By the way, what about that roof of yours—has anything been done to it?"

Nothing has been done to the roof, but Johnson feels a delicacy in mentioning it. He says therefore, "Very good roof, sah, now, only jes' one little small hole," as if the hole were growing smaller by itself.

"I must come and see the clerk's quarters. They were condemned three years ago. It's quite time that they were pulled down."

Johnson goes and tells the whole town that Rudbeck has charged him with the care of his wife. Naturally, this greatly increases his prestige in Fada, where the Emir does not even trust his chief eunuch with his wives. Saleh demands half a crown and the Waziri gives him ten shillings and a bottle of gin. Only Ajali and Benjamin, who understand

white manners, are not impressed. Benjamin shakes his head and fore-
sees trouble; Ajali goes to Johnson and cries hopefully, "I hear Missus
Rudbeck come soon."

"She come in two day now."

"I tink she give you plenty trouble, Mister Johnson."

"Oh, no, Ajali. She very nice kind woman—she ma frien'."

"What, she you frien' now. How she see you?"

"She don't see me, but she tink of me. She say many times to her
husband, 'Mister Rudbeck, I feel very kind to dat Mister Johnson. I con-
gratulate you with him. I hope to see him very much.'"

"What, Mister Johnson, when she say so?" Ajali pokes out his neck
and opens his little eyes as bright as half-sucked brandy balls.

"She say plenty more, Ajali." Johnson's imagination is now at work
upon the theme. "She say she like me better than anyone. She very pleased
I make her new house—she mos' glad to hear I make a lady latrine for
herself; she say nobody ever thought of that good idea except Mister
Johnson. Did you hear, Mister Benjamin, dat Missus Rudbeck de mos'
beautiful woman in England; she dance with Prince—I tink she will surprise dese savage people in Fada. Dey never see any government lady so
beautiful—she got hair like corn, her eyes are so blue dey burn you right
up with blueness like de sky. She six feet high, higher than Rudbeck, and
her arm is so white as elephant tusk and more big than ma leg. She big as
two men and her teeth so white as de moon. Her mouth so red as henna
and she sing and laugh all day, she like dis country too much."

The next day Rudbeck drives up in his old roaring Bentley to road
head, bringing a pale dark little woman with very black eyes. She jumps
out of the car in front of Johnson's new grass house and cries, "How
perfectly lovely."

Rudbeck presents Johnson to her. "Celia, this is Mr. Johnson."

She shakes hands warmly, then looks at Rudbeck as if to say, "I did
that right, didn't I?"

"Mr. Johnson is my right-hand man in the office."

"Oh, but I expect he's the real boss."

Johnson, overcome, bows, grins, wriggles and exclaims. "Oh, mam,
you make fun for me."

Celia gives his hand another shake and says, "I have to thank you
for looking after him till I came, Mr. Johnson—he needs a lot of looking
after, doesn't he?"

"Oh, mam, but he look after me—he too good."

She drops the hand and looks round her with the same affectionate
curiosity, smiling at the gaping labourers, the drummers bowing sideways with their drums under their arms, Audu curtseying to the ground,
at a broken hoe left lying by the roadside and at the trees behind.

"How marvellous," she murmurs. "You couldn't believe it, could
you? Oh, Harry, you will show me everything, won't you?"

Rudbeck, assuming his most stolid air, takes out his pipe and growls, "There's not much to see."

"Oh, mam, I will show you," Johnson exclaims.

"Thank you—you must take me round."

"Oh, yes, mam. What you like to see?"

"Everything. It won't be a nuisance for you, will it?"

"Oh, no, mam."

"Where shall we go first?"

Johnson looks round and sees the house. "I show you you house mam—de new house."

Rudbeck takes out his pipe. "Johnson made it for you." His tone means, "So be careful to admire it."

"Oh, I asked you not to make any difference—but how perfectly palatial—"

They are in the big *rumfa,* a square room of woven mats about twenty feet each way. The new mats are bright gold. The bars of sun, falling through the gaps of leaves, sparkle between the straws like hundreds of small suns.

"What a marvellous house—and what's this door?"

"Dat's you own latrine, mam—you own lady latrine."

"Oh, I see—a kind of drawing-room."

"Yes, mam—latrine, mam." Johnson leads the way into a narrow passage of mats roofed over and points to a hole in the ground, neatly shaped to the broken neck of a large water-pot. In front of this hole two short, forked branches carry for perch another round stick almost straight and carefully peeled of its bark.

Johnson catches up a straw pot cover from the floor and puts it over the hole. "You see, mam—he catch cover you no fit put you foot der in de dark." He rubs his hand along the peeled stick. "I scrape you seat he no fit scratch you legs."

Celia bursts out laughing and says between peals of laughter, "Oh, thanks, Mr. Johnson—I see, it's a beautiful arrangement."

Johnson also laughs. He does not see the joke. He has taken much trouble with the latrine, especially to make the perch firm and give it a smooth stick. He has suffered, like all Nigerians, from rickety perches which collapse at the wrong moment and top bars with bark like sandpaper, splinters like needles, twig ends sharp as chisels. He has set out to compose a masterpiece of sanitary engineering and he is extremely proud of it. But, since Missus Rudbeck laughs, he also laughs. He is delighted by her good humour.

Celia, afraid that she has hurt his feelings, puts her hand on his arm and makes solemn eyes at him. "Thank you so much, Mr. Johnson—it is a beautiful latrine."

"I tink you like him—I make stick smoot." He pats his favourite stick again.

"I'm sure I shall. Oh, what a lovely tune. What are they singing? It's like a shanty."

She hurries out to see the road work, tries to learn the tune by ear, asks for instruction in playing the hour-glass drum, tests the weight of a Fada hoe, and tries to swing an axe.

She works at axe-swinging till she has blisters on both her hands. She shows these proudly to Johnson and Rudbeck, who stands always in the background, gripping a cold pipe in his teeth. He does not take the pipe out of his mouth in case he should grin or otherwise betray his delight in Celia's brilliant qualities of heart and head. As soon as he does take out his pipe, as they go in to breakfast, he smiles, rolls in his walk and says, "Nice of you to be nice to Johnson."

"Oh, but he's a darling—anyone could see."

"Yes, but then you're a good sort."

"Oh, no, darling—not really."

Celia does not know whether she is a good sort. Sometimes she thinks so; sometimes she thinks that she is a fraud, that she is acting a part; that all her life is acting. She is determined, however, not to be a fraud as Rudbeck's wife. She is going to be useful to him, an encouragement and an inspiration. She means to enjoy Africa, to admire his friends and his staff, to understand his work. Above all, she refuses to be a nuisance to him. When, therefore, she wants to see the survey gang at work, she insists that he shall not leave his labourers; Johnson will take her. The next day Johnson takes her to a village to see a village assembly. Every day there is a new excursion, to see women making water-pots without a wheel, to see a house being built, mats being plaited, cotton woven on the native loom.

Everywhere Celia is curious, attentive and charmed by the African people, and tells Rudbeck in the evening how much she has enjoyed herself, how marvellous Africa is.

Rudbeck is extremely busy. While Johnson is away with Celia, he has to do his own office work and type his own letters. Office work in a bush camp is always troublesome, because the files, kept in a tin case, are not easily consulted, mail-runners are erratic, and wires take three days to get an answer. At the same time he is planning the most difficult section of the road, where it runs through high jungle among lakes and swamps. Swamp road is expensive and he has to pick the driest route, in spite of deviations. He thanks goodness very often while he wades through half-dried swamps, from dawn to dark, in clouds of tsetse, that Celia is happy with Johnson, visiting the sights. Rudbeck adores his young wife, but is still, like other young married men, the essential bachelor. He cannot do with a woman except for amusement.

Celia doesn't notice this while she is enjoying Africa with the delightful Johnson, with whom, as she says, she is quite in love. She calls him privately, "Mr. Wog." Rudbeck hears her laughing at six in the morning and asks, "What's the joke, darling?"

"Only Mr. Wog."

"He's a comic, isn't he?"

"A perfect quaint."

"Where are you going to-day?"

"I don't really know. Mr. Wog said something about weaving."

"You've seen that, haven't you?"

"Oh, yes, but we must do weaving again for Wog's sake."

In fact Johnson now finds Celia difficult to amuse. Instead of ecstatic exclamations, she utters a sigh, gazes blankly and says, "Oh, yes, they're making pots," or "It's a fish trap, isn't it?" She knows Africa.

Johnson can't understand this. He has seen pot-making all his life, but he is always interested to hear the life history of each pot, to criticize its form, to argue with the potter about its quality, or to discuss the general state of the pot trade at that moment. To him Africa is simply perpetual experience, exciting, amusing, alarming or delightful, which he soaks into himself through all his five senses at once, and produces again in the form of reflections, comments, songs, jokes, all in the pure Johnsonian form. Like a horse or a rose tree, he can turn the crudest and simplest form of fodder into beauty and power of his own quality.

But to Celia Africa is simply a number of disconnected events which have no meaning for her at all. She gazes at the pot-maker without seeing that she has one leg shorter than the other, that she is in the first stages of leprosy, that her pot is bulging on one side. She doesn't really see either woman or pot, but only a scene in Africa. Even Mr. Wog is to her a scene in Africa, and one morning when he suggests going to see a fish-hunt in a river pool, she yawns in his face without even knowing her rudeness. Yet she is a most kind and considerate girl.

Now she begins to notice that Rudbeck doesn't seek her company at road head. She cannot decide whether this is a slight or injustice, or whether it is just what a sensible girl would expect and a silly one resent. She says nothing, but she is sometimes a little stiff and uninterested when Rudbeck climbs into her bed at night. She begins to be critical of his broken nails, his too long hair, his bad shaving, his stoop, his monkey jaw, his rolling walk, his affected bluntness of speech. She remembers that he prefers Edgar Wallace to Jane Austen and cannot distinguish "God Save the King" from the "Marriage of Figaro." She thinks calmly that he is rather stupid, obstinate, clumsy and greedy. She sets him apart for the first time as a distinct and real person and examines him with critical judgment. She is astonished above all by his sensitiveness.

One day she ventures to hint that he ought not to grunt and puff smoke in her face when she asks him a civil question. He takes out his pipe, turns crimson and exclaims, "You think I'm an ape, don't you—a ring-tail baboon? Well, I'm sorry, Celia—it seems we've made a mistake."

Celia, amazed and furious, answers, "If that's the way you take a simple remark, it obviously is."

"It isn't what you say, it's what you think."

"If you must invent a grievance, why not choose something a little more plausible?"

"You've been thinking me a hog for about six weeks—and a fool for the rest of the time."

"Do you always read thoughts that aren't there?"

"I'm not blaming you—I know I'm a blockhead, I haven't got an eye and an ear. I wish I had. Everybody wonders why you married me, and you know it knocked me over a bit myself—it was too good to be true. Well, it was, that's all."

"If you think like that about me, of course—"

"Thank goodness there's no baby—we can split up evens."

"As soon as you like—I'm not so terribly amused in this god-forsaken hole to stay on sufferance."

"I must apologize for the hole."

"I must apologize for being so much in the way."

For the next twenty-four hours they meet only for meals and converse only in the presence of the servants, with extraordinary politeness. But they are full of such hatred for each other that everybody in the camp feels it, and Mr. Johnson looks and behaves so nearly like an imbecile, when either speaks to him, that Rudbeck damns him for a fool and Celia suspects him of robbing her bag. She has missed money and Johnson cannot look her in the face, because she is angry and full of hatred.

At the same time, each is obsessed by the other. Rudbeck hates Celia with such continuous passion that he cannot even think of his work, writes letters at random, and allows the road to go two miles into a cul-de-sac of bluffs; Celia cannot eat, sleep or read or sit still out of pure spite. She loses weight, her cheeks are chalk blue, her eyes are red and sunken. She looks like a debauchee, a Messalina after some long, frenzied orgy.

On the third night, when both have created for themselves, out of a chance remark, a romantic epic of despair and revenge, Rudbeck is found, at one o'clock in the morning, tugging at Celia's mosquito net.

"Wha-at is it?" she says in a voice trembling with astonishment.

He clambers over her, planting his bony knees on her tenderest spots, and crushes her in his arms.

"Go away!" she screams.

"Bill, darling—forgive me."

"Oh, Harry, what a perfect beast I am."

"I was simply mad."

"We always said that the honeymoon would be difficult—thank goodness it's over."

"Dearest."

"What's this damn thing?" Rudbeck mutters in a fearful rage.

"What? Oh, wait—you're on the wrong side of the sheet—yes, darling, tear the beastly thing."

5

FRANCIS BEBEY

King Albert

Francis Bebey (1929–2001) was an African writer, artist, and musician from Cameroon. In this novel, he carries the reader to a village called Effidi in the twilight of European imperialism after World War II but before the late 1950s and early 1960s, when Cameroon and other former colonies became independent states. In this brief selection from the novel, the young Bikounou, whom everyone calls Vespasian because he rides a Vespa Motor Scooter, has returned to Effidi to speak with Chief Ndengué. What is his message? What do his message and his manner of delivery tell you about the chief, the village, and the larger world of which it is a part at this time?

THINKING HISTORICALLY

The dialogue between Bikounou and the chief tells a story about how parts of Africa changed in the period leading up to independence. What are these changes? Where and how did they occur? In a few paragraphs, write a brief history that summarizes these changes. How is your history different from the section in the novel?

The next day, a Sunday, Bikounou went to see Chief Ndengué while the other villagers were at Mass.

"I have come to thank you for the welcome which you permitted the people of Effidi to extend to us, myself and my friend Féfé."

"My son, I permitted nothing. The village spoke for itself. As you could see yourself, nobody bears you any grudge. On the contrary,

Source: Francis Bebey, *King Albert*, trans. Joyce A. Hutchinson (Westport, CT: Lawrence Hill & Co., 1981), 109–18.

everybody is very fond of you. But, as a matter of interest, where is your friend Féfé?"

"I wanted to see you alone, Chief Ndengué, to talk to you while the others are not around."

"And what is so important that you need this secrecy?"

"You are the Chief of us all, and you have a right to hear the news first. The others will hear it later if they don't know it already."

"Bikounou, I think I have understood. You are going to get married. That's good, my son, but you know our procedure."

"I'm in a good position to know, Chief Ndengué. But that is not the news I have for you."

"Ah? What do you mean?"

"I mean I want to talk to you about something quite different from my marriage. Besides, as you have just reminded yourself; would you expect me to think of marriage again without consulting all the elders of our community? One should not make the same mistakes more than once in one's life."

"I see, my son. I see that your experience has widened, and you know, I am absolutely delighted. Now I know that you have come back to live among us as we live ourselves, following the laws laid down by our tradition, and not the examples given by people who are not our own people, whether their skin is black or white."

"Chief Ndengué, may all my links with our community be severed if I am not determined to follow the advice of my elders, which is dictated by the experience of generations and generations who lived before our own generation came into the world."

"You speak well, my son."

"But please, let me tell you what brings me here this morning."

"I am listening."

"Now, Chief Ndengué, there is going to be an election."

"What?"

"I am saying there is going to be an election."

"My son, please explain: what does that mean?"

"It means that the whites are going to ask us to choose a person to represent us."

"A person to represent us? But, my son, why do we have to choose someone to represent us? Am I not, myself, the man whom tradition has placed at the head of our community to represent everybody? Am I not the Chief of this community, the person to whom you turn to obtain this or that? The person who says yes, or maybe no, according to whether he sees in his answer some means of benefiting the whole community? Tell me, my son, what is this story you've brought back from the town?"

"Chief Ndengué, I knew you wouldn't understand me straightaway. You are the Chief of our community. You will remain our Chief until the day—when—until the time when—"

"Until my death, my son. Do not be afraid to say so. We are all destined to live for a period and then to die. You know, man is like a flower. He smiles at life as it smiles at the sunlight. Then at the end of his life he closes his eyes just as it droops its head and wilts. There is nothing to be afraid of, Bikounou. I should be lying if I told you that Chief Ndengué would never die. In any case, you would't believe me."

"I am saying, Chief Ndengué, that you will remain at the head of our community until the day when you are no longer with us. So it's not a question of choosing someone to replace you among us."

"Then what is it about?"

"I will explain. You know that our country is governed by the whites?"

"I know, I know. But what have they done now, these whites?"

"Nothing, except that they now realize the need to let us govern our country ourselves."

"What? What country are you talking about, my son?"

"This one, where we live, the country which takes in Effidi, Zaabat, Nkool, Palmtree Village, and even Ngala, as well as other towns."

"My son, what you have just told me is perhaps important, but you can't make me believe that Effidi, Nkool, Zaabat, Palmtree Village, and even Ngala are part of one and the same country and that they will let themselves be governed by one man, one single great Chief! For if you tell me that I shall remain at the head of the community of Effidi, then another chief will be needed to be responsible for governing the whole country, isn't that so?"

"Chief Ndengué, for a long time the whites have occupied our country and governed it in their own way. We, the educated men, have told them that we've had enough and that we wish to govern ourselves, since we are now capable of doing so."

"And the whites agreed?"

"Yes, they have agreed . . . yes . . . that is to say that—"

"My son, tell me the exact truth."

"That is to say that they don't believe we are capable of governing ourselves all alone."

"That is exactly what I think, too."

"But, Chief Ndengué, don't take their side! They think we can't govern ourselves alone, but *we* want to prove the opposite. We want to show them that we can live without them and govern ourselves."

"And so?"

"So they have decided to put us to the test."

"By doing what?"

"Precisely, by organizing elections. That's what I wanted—"

"Bikounou, you're mixing everything up—the country, the whites, ourselves, elections. How do you expect me to understand anything in all that?"

"Let me explain it to you, Chief Ndengué. The whites have a way of governing a country which is different from ours. With us, there is a Chief—that's to say, somebody like you—to govern the whole community. But *they* put several people at the head of the country. It is those people who make decisions for the good of the whole country because they have been chosen by the whole country to represent them. It is this new way of governing the country that the whites wish to teach us, and that is why there is going to be an election."

"Now it's becoming clearer," said Chief Ndengué.

He remained plunged in thought for several minutes, during which Bikounou realized that he should say nothing.

"Now, it's becoming clearer," he added. "If I understand correctly, each community like ours will have to choose someone to represent it—"

"In an assembly which will therefore represent the whole country," Bikounou continued.

"Yes, yes, I see."

He thought for a few more moments, then suggested:

"Naturally, if Effidi is asked to choose, I don't see who our brothers will elect to represent them other than myself, do you?"

A logical argument on the part of a village chief incapable of understanding the evolution of a whole of the society of which his community is a part, and only a small part, when all's said and done. Bikounou would not have replied immediately if the Chief had not insisted:

"That is how things will turn out, isn't it?"

"Chief, when you talk about elections, you must not say in advance which man or woman is going to win."

"Which man or woman?" What do you mean? Are the women also invited to stand for election? And to represent whom? The men?"

"Chief Ndengué, you must not get carried away. There may well not be a woman presumptuous enough to stand as a candidate in the election. But in the new system that the whites wish to teach us, the women have the right to stand, just like the men."

"What, what are you saying? Is that the kind of thing they wish to introduce here, and for what purpose?"

"Chief Ndengué, times change. Even in this village, which lives in closer proximity to the town than others on account of the road passing through it, people are not sufficiently informed about the evolution of the country."

"Our country is here!" Chief Ndengué shouted. "If you young people and those others educated by the whites wish to sell it, that's different. But, my son, I warn you that there are still enough people at Effidi to oppose such an idea should it ever cross your mind one day. The evolution of the country . . . the evolution of what country? Do you think you know better than old Ndengué what is our country and what it means?"

"Chief Ndengué," said Bikounou, trying to appease him, "you are right. Our country exists inasmuch as you exist as our Chief. All that is built on the tradition of our ancestors."

"Then why have you come back to the village to tell me what other people want, people who have nothing to do with what our ancestors wished this country to be? Why do you all obey these foreigners?"

"Chief Ndengué, you must not give way to sudden anger and refuse to hear the other reasons which bring me here. I can understand your wish to exclude women from any competition concerning the government of the country. The women are in the village to bear children for their husbands and perpetuate the community with boys and girls who will follow traditional ways. I accept it myself, and I shall oppose any person who might seek to give to women the opportunity, the slightest opportunity, of interfering in men's affairs, such as, for example, the government of our society. But, you know, times change. In any case, they have changed a lot since, at the wish of our ancestors, you yourself became our Chief. You have to admit that, these days, you need the support of the whites to make everybody obey you."

"You're lying! You're lying, Bikounou, you're lying! What had the whites to do with your return to the village? Was it not because you felt the ancestral power commanding you to return to your own people that you came back? And this ancestral power, who else but me represents it here?"

"It's true. It's true that what I said was not quite fair. It is not the whites who order all the members of the community to come to you to settle their differences, or to organize tactics about a possible marriage, or to talk about future sowings or the distribution of the harvest to come. But today there is nevertheless something changed about a village chief like yourself. I'm thinking particularly of the allowance paid you by the government."

"Allowance! Look at it! I am compensated because I have the unpleasant task of raising taxes among my people, and you dare call that an allowance? My son, you are too young for me to tell you all I think. But don't force me to believe that you have adopted the mentality of the foreigners who come and make us work for them, in our own country, and afterwards boast that they are doing it for our own good! For, tell me, what happens to all these taxes that I collect each year? Who uses the money that I am responsible for collecting? And after that, you come and defend your bosses and remind me that I am paid by them."

Bikounou wondered what answer he could possibly give to all that. He had come with the firm intention of being submissive, and you, too, must have noticed how diplomatic he was being in order not to shock Chief Ndengué. That is understandable, for it must be realized that, however innocent he might seem, on this Sunday morning when the other inhabitants of Effidi had gone to sing Mass in Latin—too bad for Father Bonsot if he hears about it—the Vespasian had the difficult job of explaining to the old chief that his period of glory and prestige based on tradition was over, and worse still, that new leaders would take his place, chosen with no reference to the law of bygone days. The young man knew what this would mean for this old man accustomed to considering as his personal property what some people would pompously call "power." He therefore decided to introduce into the conversation as much subtlety as was desirable or indeed necessary to lead Chief Ndengué gradually to accept the very principle of an election during which the people of Effidi would be free to choose him or to elect some other candidate.

"If I mentioned an allowance, Chief Ndengué, you must forgive me. You know the village people are not always aware what an unpleasant task the Administration expects you to carry out, and we have all come more or less to believe that you are paid for doing it. I confess that I personally should know something about it, since I work in a government office. In any case, I was joking when I said that, but I'm already at fault for joking with my elder. You must forgive me, Chief Ndengué. I came to see you as an obedient son comes to see his father and not to presume to make you angry."

"Now you're talking sense, my son. So, you inform me there is going to be an election. But tell me, if *I* am not elected, then who will be?"

"I have no idea, Chief Ndengué. What matters now is to know who else at Effidi might intend to stand at this election when you consider all the qualities and the knowledge a person needs to have to represent our community successfully."

"What do you mean?"

"Well, how can I explain it? It must first be understood that the elected representative will have to go to Ngala."

"Each village will have to send someone to Ngala?"

"That is where all the representatives will meet to discuss the measures to be taken concerning the country."

"Then I shall have to go to Ngala?"

"If you are elected by our community, yes."

"That's true. It's true that the community, according to your system, could very well decide that it didn't want me to represent them at Ngala. In any case, I must tell you from the start that, if things really turn out as you have just explained, I am not interested in your story of an election. I have no intention of going to sit at the side of the road every morning and wait for a truck to be kind enough to stop and take me to the town."

Bikounou gave an almost imperceptible sigh of relief. But Chief Ndengué was a crafty old man, who missed no detail of the attitude of those speaking with him. He noticed the suppressed satisfaction of the young man.

"What's the matter? Did I say something unpleasant?"

"No, Chief Ndengué, it's not that. I was in fact wondering whether you realized how difficult it would be for you to make frequent visits to the town if you were elected to represent Effidi."

"I realize it perfectly well. I also realize that in future—if your system works as you have said—it will be someone else who will go to the town to bring back orders to be passed on to the community. Yes, my son, I understand what you were saying just now: times change."

The pathos of these last words was perfectly clear to Bikounou. Nevertheless, he kept his poise, trying to allay the old man's fears:

"Oh, Chief Ndengué, don't take it like that. It's possible that someone else will go to the town to represent our community in the assembly which will meet there, but not to bring back orders, as long as you remain our Chief."

"My son, you are trying to calm me down, but since you began talking to me, I have a feeling that there is to be a change much greater than that suffered by our fathers when the whites arrived."

"There can't be any change more important for our country than when the whites arrived."

"You mean it's a continuation of the same change?"

"Yes and no, Chief Ndengué. Yes, because if the whites had not come, we should perhaps never have felt the need to prove that we are capable of governing ourselves. As a result, there would have been no need to talk of elections. But, on the other hand, we now have to choose from among us people to whom we shall entrust the conduct of our affairs."

"And you believe that, my son? You believe that one day the whites will leave us to manage our own affairs?"

"That is what the younger generation is asking them more and more urgently. They will simply be forced to leave us alone one day."

"Forced? Forced? Who can force them to do anything? These people who manufacture guns and arms who would kill us all if we refused to obey them, who can force them?"

"Chief Ndengué, these people are doubtless very intelligent. They manufacture guns, arms, motor cars, airplanes, the good Lord gives them all they desire. But they overlooked one thing."

"What thing, my son?"

"They overlooked that they shouldn't have taught us to read and write."

"I don't understand what you mean by that."

"You see, by teaching us to read, they gave us the key to their own knowledge, and there we discovered that they spoke of liberty, equality and fraternity."

"So?"

"So they are obliged to give us liberty, equality and fraternity. That's what we're asking for, Chief Ndengué."

"And that is really why there is going to be an election?"

"Actually, this election will not give us liberty, but the assembly which will be established will pave the way for the independence of the whole country."

"My son, I tell you that our country is Effidi!" the Chief growled again.

"You are right, Chief Ndengué, but I tell you that times change. And since times began to change, our country has grown bigger."

"You mean that those savages of Palmtree Village are going to send a representative to the town just like us?"

"They will have the right to do so."

"Like us? With no difference?"

"Like us. But they may be obliged to choose a representative elsewhere than among themselves."

"Why?"

"Well, Chief, because the fact that the elected representative can get to the town fairly often won't be the end of the matter. The representative will also have to be someone educated, someone who understands politics and who—"

"What? What did you say?"

"Politics."

"And poli—, poli—. This thing, what is it?"

"To be exact, it is politics that the representatives will be engaged in when they meet."

"So they won't be speaking?"

"Yes, they will, Chief Ndengué. They will probably speak a great deal. That's what politics is all about. They talk, they talk, they talk. And then they say, good, we will build a road to Nkool, or to Palmtree Village."

Chief Ndengué burst out laughing, and at once, a shaft of sunlight coming through a little hole in the wall and falling on the beaten earth floor in a small luminous circle also began to laugh, with all the particles of fine colored dust dancing in the rainbow that penetrated the half-light. Bikounou wondered what on earth he had said or done that was so amusing.

"My son," said Chief Ndengué at last, "don't be surprised to hear me laugh like this. The fact is that for some time I had been worrying for no reason and it's only now that I've realized my error."

"I don't understand," the Vespasian confessed.

"I will explain," replied the Chief, reverting to his normal serious manner. "This is why I am laughing. Since you began talking to me about your elections, I had become convinced that you were preparing to see someone else take my place at the head of our community, with the help, obviously, of your friends, the white Administrators. And now I see that I was stupid to imagine that. For if the poli—, poli—Oh, what did you say just now the representatives would do in the town?"

"Politics."

"Yes, that's it. If poli—, poli—. If whatever it is consists of talking and saying you're going to build a road, then it will have no effect on Effidi, seeing that we already have our road. Is that not true, my son?"

The serious tone showed that the man wished to be reassured.

"That is to say—I mean, Chief Ndengué—yes, you are right, partly," the Vespasian replied, in a somewhat embarrassed tone. "But I spoke of building a road just as an example. In fact, politics means doing lots and lots of other things."

"Ah?"

"Yes, yes, and that's why I was telling you that we must elect representatives who understand these things. And as I cannot see in Palmtree Village anybody who can claim to understand them, then I think those people will be obliged to choose a representative from outside their own community."

"How shameful for them!"

"I suppose, in fact, that they will not be very proud when they have to come to Effidi to ask if we can provide somebody to represent them in the assembly in the town."

"And if they come, my son, you who understand these things, tell me: what answer do we give these idiots ?"

"I don't yet exactly know how these things will work out. But I think we shall be obliged to represent them because, in any case, there will not be a separate representative from each village."

"This business of yours is complicated, my son. I hope that you at least will be able to understand it, so that we don't make a laughing-stock of ourselves in the eyes of our neighbors. You know that they will seize on the slightest opportunity—"

"I'll take care of it, Chief."

The conversation went on into details until the time when the other villagers returned from Mass. It was the Chief's job to announce the news of the coming election, as it had been given him by Bikounou. He did this solemnly, during an evening meeting. The news was received and commented upon in almost as many ways as there were men present at the meeting, for the people of Effidi, outstandingly intelligent, at least in their own opinion, were keen to show that they had understood what they had just been told, and that they would be perfectly capable of playing the new game which was being wished on them by the town.

Naturally, many chests swelled with pride at the idea that, once again, the neighboring villagers would remain in the background of the regional scene, since their sons were unable to compete with those of Effidi.

6

RUDYARD KIPLING

The White Man's Burden

This poem, written by Rudyard Kipling (1865–1936), is often presented as the epitome of colonialist sentiment, though some readers see in it a critical, satirical attitude toward colonialism. Do you find the poem to be for or against colonialism? Can it be both?

THINKING HISTORICALLY

"The White Man's Burden" is a phrase normally associated with European colonialism in Africa. In fact, however, Kipling wrote the poem in response to the annexation of the Philippines by the United States. How does this historical context change the meaning of the poem for you? Does the meaning of a literary work depend on the motives of the writer, the historical context in which it is written, or both?

Take up the White Man's burden—
Send forth the best ye breed—
Go, bind your sons to exile
To serve your captives' need;
To wait, in heavy harness,
On fluttered folk and wild—
Your new-caught sullen peoples,
Half devil and half child.

Take up the White Man's burden—
In patience to abide,
To veil the threat of terror
And check the show of pride;
By open speech and simple,

Source: Rudyard Kipling, "The White Man's Burden," *McClure's Magazine* 12, no. 4 (February 1899): 290–91.

An hundred times made plain,
To seek another's profit
And work another's gain.

Take up the White Man's burden—
The savage wars of peace—
Fill full the mouth of Famine,
And bid the sickness cease;
And when your goal is nearest
(The end for others sought)
Watch sloth and heathen folly
Bring all your hope to nought.

Take up the White Man's burden—
No iron rule of kings,
But toil of serf and sweeper—
The tale of common things.
The ports ye shall not enter,
The roads ye shall not tread,
Go, make them with your living
And mark them with your dead.

Take up the White Man's burden,
And reap his own reward—
The blame of those ye better
The hate of those ye guard—
The cry of hosts ye humour
(Ah, slowly!) toward the light:—
"Why brought ye us from bondage,
Our loved Egyptian night?"

Take up the White Man's burden—
Ye dare not stoop to less—
Nor call too loud on Freedom
To cloke your weariness.
By all ye will or whisper,
By all ye leave or do,
The silent sullen peoples
Shall weigh your God and you.

Take up the White Man's burden!
Have done with childish days—
The lightly-proffered laurel,
The easy ungrudged praise:
Comes now, to search your manhood

Through all the thankless years,
Cold, edged with dear-bought wisdom,
The judgment of your peers.

■ REFLECTIONS

Many of the selections within this chapter as well as its title point to
the dual character of colonial society. There are the colonized and the
colonizers, the "natives" and the Europeans, and, as racial categories
hardened in the second half of the nineteenth century, the blacks and
the whites. Colonialism centered on the construction of an accepted
inequality. The dominant Europeans invested enormous energy in keeping the double standards, dual pay schedules, and separate rules and
residential areas—the two castes.

One problem with maintaining a neat division between the colonized and the colonizers is that the Europeans were massively outnumbered by the indigenous people. Thus, the colonizers needed a vast
class of middle-status people to staff the army, police, and bureaucracy.
These people might be educated in Paris or London, raised in European
culture, and encouraged to develop a sense of pride in their similarity
to the Europeans ("me Christian, same like master") and their differences from the other "natives." Often, like the Indian Dr. Veraswami,
they were chosen for their ethnic or religious differences from the rest
of the colonized population.

In short, colonialism created a whole class of people who were
neither fully colonized nor colonizers. They were in between. To the
extent that the colonial enterprise was an extension of European social
class differences, these in-between people could be British as well as
"native." Orwell's Flory is only one of the characters in *Burmese Days*
caught between two worlds. One of the most notorious of this class of
Europeans "gone native" is the Mr. Kurtz that Conrad's crew will meet
upriver. Achebe's point that Africa becomes a setting for the breakup
of a European mind might be generalized to apply to the European
perception of the colonial experience. It is certainly one of the dominant themes of the European colonial novel. Even the great ones often
center on the real or imagined rape, ravishing, or corruption of the
European by the seething foreign unknown. This attitude also helps
us understand how Kipling could be both anti-imperialist and racist.
Imperialism could seem like a thankless act to those who tried to carry
civilization to "sullen peoples, half devil and half child."

All the novels and poetry excerpted in this chapter are well worth
reading in their entirety, and many other excellent colonial novels can
be chosen from this period as well as from the 1930s and 1940s.

E. M. Forster's *A Passage to India* and Paul Scott's *The Raj Quartet* stand out as fictional introductions to British colonialism in India. (Both have also received excellent adaptations to film, the latter as the series for television called *The Jewel in the Crown*.) In addition to Chinua Achebe, Amos Tutuola and Wole Soyinka have written extensively on Nigeria. Besides Francis Bebey, Ferdinand Oyono and Mongo Beti address French colonialism in Cameroon. On South Africa, the work of Alan Payton, Andre Brink, J. M. Coetzee, Peter Abrams, and James McClure, among many others, stands out.

The advantage of becoming engrossed in a novel is that we feel part of the story and have a sense that we are learning something first-hand. Of course, we are reading a work of fiction, not gaining first-hand experience or reading an accurate historical account of events. A well-made film poses an even greater problem. Its visual and aural impact imparts a psychological reality that becomes part of our experience. If it is about a subject of which we know little, the film quickly becomes our "knowledge" of the subject, and this knowledge may be incomplete or inaccurate.

On the other hand, a well-written novel or film can whet our appetite and inspire us to learn more. Choose and read a novel about colonialism or some other historical subject. Then read a biography of the author or research his or her background to determine how much the author knew about the subject. Next, read a historical account of the subject. How much attention does the historian give to the novelist's subject? How does the novel add depth to the historical account? How does the historical account place the novel in perspective? Finally, how does the author's background place the novel in historical context?

23

Westernization and Nationalism

Japan, India, Turkey, and Egypt, 1860–1950

■ HISTORICAL CONTEXT

By the second half of the nineteenth century, the West (meaning Europe and North America) had industrialized, created more representative governments and open societies than the world had known before, and demonstrated the power of its science, technology, and military might by colonizing much of the rest of the world. For those who looked on from outside, the West was a force to be reckoned with.

Some of those observers knew the impact of the West firsthand. The Japanese had experienced Western traders and missionaries since 1543 but had controlled their numbers and influence. The Act of Seclusion in 1636 limited European contact in Japan to a small colony of Dutch traders for the next two hundred years. Not until the appearance of Admiral Perry's steam fleet in 1853 did a new policy toward the West seem necessary.

India had experienced Western colonization and trade since the early 1600s, losing coastal trading cities to various European powers until the English consolidated their hold in the eighteenth century. By 1880 all but a few princely states had come under the rule of the British Indian Empire.

Ottoman Turkey and Ottoman Egypt escaped European colonialism until Napoleon conquered Egypt in 1798. From 1805 until 1882 Egypt was independent of both Ottoman and European rule until, overwhelmed by debts to European banks, the country became a British protectorate (1882–1922). Egypt gained full independence from British troops incrementally from 1922 until 1956.

Ottoman Turkey lost control of its European territory in Greece and the Balkans in the nineteenth century and its control of what was to become Palestine, Syria, Jordan, Lebanon, and Iraq in World War I. At its founding in 1923, the Republic of Turkey extended to its present boundaries.

We have then, in these four examples, different degrees of Western influence and penetration. Nevertheless, all of these societies were forced to confront the power of the West during the period from 1860 to 1950. In all cases, the effort to become independent of the West meant considering what might be imitated or borrowed. Broadly speaking, this meant some degree of Westernization.

How did the people of Japan, India, Turkey, and Egypt answer the challenge of the West? What motivated some to seek to Westernize? What led others to reject Westernization entirely? And what role did nationalism play in the struggle over Westernization?

Nationalism had been a potent force in Europe since the French Revolution, with its national draft army, National Assembly, nationalization of church lands, national flag, national anthem, and celebration of French citizenship. Napoleon's armies inadvertently spread national consciousness among his enemies. Poets and politicians from Vienna to Madrid sought to create and establish the elements of their own national cultures and nation states. European colonization ignited the same spark of national identity in Asia and Africa. Nationalism was itself a Western movement, but nationalism could be built from any indigenous or traditional culture. Extreme Westernizers might be willing to dispense with traditional ways entirely. Extreme anti-Westernizers could invoke nationalism alone. But most thoughtful subjects of Western influence between the mid-nineteenth and mid-twentieth centuries recognized the need to draw on old strengths while borrowing what worked. How did the authors of these selections face the challenge?

■ THINKING HISTORICALLY

Appreciating Contradictions

The process of Westernization, like the experience of conquest and colonization that often preceded it, was fraught with conflict and led to frequent contradictions. Often, the struggle for national independence meant the borrowing of Western practices and ideologies, both Marxist and liberal. Indeed, the idea of national self-determination was a product of the French and American revolutions, as we have seen. Even the words and languages employed in the debate reflected Western origins, as English or French was often the only common language of educated colonized peoples. Therefore, it is not surprising that contradictory behavior and ambivalent relationships were endemic in the postcolonial world, just as they had been under colonialism. These contradictions usually manifested themselves in an individual's cultural identity. How do colonized persons adopt Western ways, embrace traditional culture, and not feel as though their identity has been divided between the two? Such individuals may not fit entirely into either world and so may be torn between who they were and who they have become. The somewhat anguished experiences of these colonized people are difficult to understand. We typically want to accept one view or another, to praise or to blame. But as we have learned, the history of peoples and nations is rarely that clear. In examining some of the fundamental contradictions in the history of Westernization, we might better understand how people were variously affected.

The historical thinking skill one learns in reading documents from people torn between different ideals is the appreciation of contradictions. This operates on a number of levels. We learn that people can hold two contradictory ideas in their minds at the same time; and, in consequence, we learn to do it ourselves. This prevents us from jumping to conclusions or oversimplifying the historical process. In addition, we learn how the struggle over contradictory goals, whether internalized or expressed in group conflict, moves history forward.

1

FUKUZAWA YUKICHI

Good-bye Asia

Fukuzawa* Yukichi (1835–1901) was one of the most important Japanese Westernizers during Japan's late-nineteenth-century rush to catch up with the West. The son of a lower samurai (military) family, his pursuit of Western knowledge took him to a Dutch school in Osaka, where he studied everything from the Dutch language to chemistry, physics, and anatomy, and to Yedo, where he studied English. Due to his privileged background and Western schooling, he was naturally included in the first Japanese mission to the United States in 1860 as well as in the first diplomatic mission to Europe in 1862. After he returned to Japan, he spent many years teaching and writing the books that would make him famous. The best known of these was *Seiyo Jijo (Things Western)*, which in 1866 introduced Japanese readers to the daily life and typical institutions of Western society. According to Fukuzawa Yukichi, the main obstacle that prevented Japanese society from catching up with the West was a long heritage of Chinese Confucianism, which stifled educational independence.

In the years after the Meiji Restoration of 1868, in which feudalism was abolished and power was restored to the emperor, Fukuzawa Yukichi became the most popular spokesman for the Westernizing policies of the new government. In this essay, "Good-bye Asia," written in 1885, he describes the spread of Western civilization in Japan.

* foo koo ZAH wah

Why does he believe that it is both inevitable and desirable? What do you make of his attitude toward Chinese and Korean civilizations?

THINKING HISTORICALLY

Fukuzawa Yukichi is an unapologetic Westernizer. How does his attitude resemble that of a religious convert? Despite his lack of doubt about the advantages of Western ways, however, he does not criticize Japanese culture. He shows how a Westernizer could at the same time be nationalistic. In what ways is his attitude also nationalistic?

Transportation has become so convenient these days that once the wind of Western civilization blows to the East, every blade of grass and every tree in the East follow what the Western wind brings. Ancient Westerners and present-day Westerners are from the same stock and are not much different from one another. The ancient ones moved slowly, but their contemporary counterparts move vivaciously at a fast pace. This is possible because present-day Westerners take advantage of the means of transportation available to them. For those of us who live in the Orient, unless we want to prevent the coming of Western civilization with a firm resolve, it is best that we cast our lot with them. If one observes carefully what is going on in today's world, one knows the futility of trying to prevent the onslaught of Western civilization. Why not float with them in the same ocean of civilization, sail the same waves, and enjoy the fruits and endeavors of civilization?

The movement of a civilization is like the spread of measles. Measles in Tokyo start in Nagasaki and come eastward with the spring thaw. We may hate the spread of this communicable disease, but is there any effective way of preventing it? I can prove that it is not possible. In a communicable disease, people receive only damages. In a civilization, damages may accompany benefits, but benefits always far outweigh them, and their force cannot be stopped. This being the case, there is no point in trying to prevent their spread. A wise man encourages the spread and allows our people to get used to its ways.

The opening to the modern civilization of the West began in the reign of Kaei (1848–58).[1] Our people began to discover its utility and

---

[1] Refers to the Kaei era of the emperor Kōmei (r. 1846–1867). The emperor opposed Western influences but was forced to allow Dutch vaccination in 1849, admit Admiral Perry's U.S. fleet in 1853, permit coaling rights to U.S. ships in 1854, and accept the Treaty of Amity and Commerce in 1859. [Ed.]

Source: Fukuzawa Yukichi, "Datsu-a Ron" ("On Saying Good-bye to Asia"), in *Japan: A Documentary History*, ed. David J. Lu (Armonk, NY: M. E. Sharpe, 1997), 2:351–53. From Takeuchi Yoshimi, ed., *Azia Shugi (Asianism) Gendai Nihon Shisō Taikei (Great Compilation of Modern Japanese Thought)* (Tokyo: Chikuma Shobō, 1963), 8:38–40.

gradually and yet actively moved toward its acceptance. However, there was an old-fashioned and bloated government that stood in the way of progress. It was a problem impossible to solve. If the government were allowed to continue, the new civilization could not enter. The modern civilization and Japan's old conventions were mutually exclusive. If we were to discard our old conventions, that government also had to be abolished. We could have prevented the entry of this civilization, but it would have meant loss of our national independence. The struggles taking place in the world civilization were such that they would not allow an Eastern island nation to slumber in isolation. At that point, dedicated men (*shijin*) recognized the principle of "the country is more important than the government," relied on the dignity of the Imperial Household, and toppled the old government to establish a new one.[2] With this, public and the private sectors alike, everyone in our country accepted the modern Western civilization. Not only were we able to cast aside Japan's old conventions, but we also succeeded in creating a new axle toward progress in Asia. Our basic assumptions could be summarized in two words: "Good-bye Asia (*Datsu-a*)."

Japan is located in the eastern extremities of Asia, but the spirit of her people have already moved away from the old conventions of Asia to the Western civilization. Unfortunately for Japan, there are two neighboring countries. One is called China and another Korea. These two peoples, like the Japanese people, have been nurtured by Asiatic political thoughts and mores. It may be that we are different races of people, or it may be due to the differences in our heredity or education; significant differences mark the three peoples. The Chinese and Koreans are more like each other and together they do not show as much similarity to the Japanese. These two peoples do not know how to progress either personally or as a nation. In this day and age with transportation becoming so convenient, they cannot be blind to the manifestations of Western civilization. But they say that what is seen or heard cannot influence the disposition of their minds. Their love affairs with ancient ways and old customs remain as strong as they were centuries ago. In this new and vibrant theater of civilization when we speak of education, they only refer back to Confucianism. As for school education, they can only cite [Chinese philosopher Mencius's] precepts of humanity, righteousness, decorum, and knowledge. While professing their abhorrence to ostentation, in reality they show their ignorance of truth and principles. As for their morality, one only has to observe their unspeakable acts of cruelty and shamelessness. Yet they remain arrogant and show no sign of self-examination.

[2] The Meiji Restoration (1868). Meiji was a son of Kōmei (who died of smallpox in 1867). Meiji restored the power of the emperor over the Tokugawa Shogunate, a feudal council that had ruled since 1603. Meiji eagerly sought contacts with the West so that Japan would not fall behind. [Ed.]

In my view, these two countries cannot survive as independent nations with the onslaught of Western civilization to the East.[3] Their concerned citizens might yet find a way to engage in a massive reform, on the scale of our Meiji Restoration, and they could change their governments and bring about a renewal of spirit among their peoples. If that could happen they would indeed be fortunate. However, it is more likely that would never happen, and within a few short years they will be wiped out from the world with their lands divided among the civilized nations. Why is this so? Simply at a time when the spread of civilization and enlightenment (*bummei kaika*) has a force akin to that of measles, China and Korea violate the natural law of its spread. They forcibly try to avoid it by shutting off air from their rooms. Without air, they suffocate to death. It is said that neighbors must extend helping hands to one another because their relations are inseparable. Today's China and Korea have not done a thing for Japan. From the perspectives of civilized Westerners, they may see what is happening in China and Korea and judge Japan accordingly, because of the three countries' geographical proximity. The governments of China and Korea still retain their autocratic manners and do not abide by the rule of law. Westerners may consider Japan likewise a lawless society. Natives of China and Korea are deep in their hocus pocus of nonscientific behavior. Western scholars may think that Japan still remains a country dedicated to the *yin* and *yang* and five elements.[4] Chinese are meanspirited and shameless, and the chivalry of the Japanese people is lost to the Westerners. Koreans punish their convicts in an atrocious manner, and that is imputed to the Japanese as heartless people. There are many more examples I can cite. It is not different from the case of a righteous man living in a neighborhood of a town known for foolishness, lawlessness, atrocity, and heartlessness. His action is so rare that it is always buried under the ugliness of his neighbors' activities. When these incidents are multiplied, that can affect our normal conduct of diplomatic affairs. How unfortunate it is for Japan.

What must we do today? We do not have time to wait for the enlightenment of our neighbors so that we can work together toward the development of Asia. It is better for us to leave the ranks of Asian nations and cast our lot with civilized nations of the West. As for the way of dealing with China and Korea, no special treatment is necessary just because they happen to be our neighbors. We simply follow the manner of the Westerners in knowing how to treat them. Any person who cherishes a bad friend cannot escape his bad notoriety. We simply erase from our minds our bad friends in Asia.

---

[3] By 1885 China been "opened" by Western powers in two opium wars (1839–1842, 1856–1860). Korea had been invaded by France (1866) and the United States (1871). Its isolation ended in 1885 by treaty with the United States. [Ed.]

[4] *Yin* and *yang* is a traditional Chinese duality (cold/hot, passive/active, female/male) illustrated by a circle divided by an "s" to show unity within duality. The five elements suggest another traditional, prescientific idea that everything is made of five basic ingredients. [Ed.]

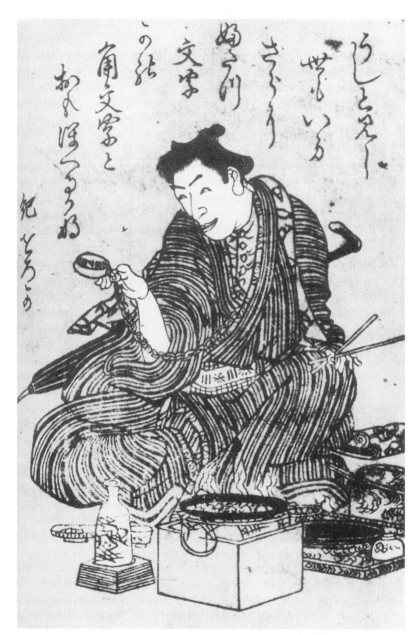

Figure 23.1   Beef Eater.

Source: *Beef Eater*, from Kanagaki Robun, *Aguranabe* (1871) in G. B. Sansom, *The Western World and Japan* (Tokyo: Charles E. Tuttle Co., 1977).

2

Images from Japan: Views of Westernization

This selection consists of three prints by Japanese artists from the Meiji period of Westernization. The first print, Figure 23.1 (on facing page), called *Beef Eater* (1871), illustrates a character in Kanagaki Robun's *Aguranabe* (1871). The author, a popular newspaper humorist, parodies a new class of urban Westernized Japanese who carry watches and umbrellas and eat beef (banned by Buddhist law for centuries but added to the Japanese diet by Westerners). What response in the viewer does the artist seek to evoke?

The second piece, Figure 23.2, is called *Monkey Show Dressing Room* (1879), by Honda Kinkachiro. What is this print's message? What is the artist's attitude toward Westernization?

The third piece, Figure 23.3, *The Exotic White Man*, shows a child born to a Western man and a Japanese woman. What is the artist's message? Does the artist favor such unions? What does the artist think of Westerners?

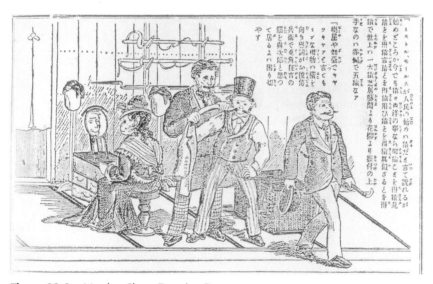

Figure 23.2 Monkey Show Dressing Room.

Source: Honda Kinkachiro, *Monkey Show Dressing Room*, in Julia Meech-Pekarik, *The World of the Meiji Print* (New York: John Weatherhill, 1986).

Figure 23.3   The Exotic White Man.

Source: Japanese color print, late 19th c., Dutch private collection, in C. A. Burland, *The Exotic White Man* (New York: McGraw-Hill, 1969), fig. 38. Werner Forman/Art Resource, NY.

THINKING HISTORICALLY

Compare the attitudes of these artists with that of Fukuzawa Yukichi. Prints, like cartoons, are a shorthand that must capture an easily recognizable trait. What, evidently, were the widely understood Japanese images of the West? Where do you think these stereotypes of the West came from? Do you see any signs in these prints of ambivalence on the part of the artist?

JUN'ICHIRŌ TANIZAKI

In Praise of Shadows

Jun'ichirō Tanizaki (1886–1965) was a J̲...
and screenwriter. A student at the end...
in which Japan opened to the W̲est an...
era of the Emperor Taisho (...
Tanizaki helped spread the...
Westernization, a faith apr...
among the victors of Worl...
however, he became critical...
astating earthquake of 1923, the rise of We...
munist parties, and the economic and political...
global depression in the late 1920s and 1930s.

In Praise of Shadows was published in 1933. What disadvantages does he see in Western culture? How does he contrast the ways of the West with the traditions of Asia? How would you compare his attitude with that of Fukuzawa Yukichi or the artists in the previous selection?

THINKING HISTORICALLY

The life of Jun'ichirō Tanizaki forces us to ask how it was possible for an ardent advocate of Westernization to become such a nationalist. How might aging or historical circumstances account for the change? How is his critique of the West extremely radical (in the core sense of cutting to the roots)? How is his critique merely wistful or nostalgic rather than confidently revolutionary? Try to imagine how it feels to believe that something is radically wrong but hopelessly likely to remain (perhaps by drawing on some incident in your own life). How does holding those contrary ideas make one feel and behave?

The recent vogue for electric lamps in the style of the old standing lanterns comes, I think, from a new awareness of the softness and warmth of paper, qualities which for a time we had forgotten; it stands as evidence of our recognition that this material is far better suited than glass to the Japanese house. But no toilet fixtures or stoves that are at all tasteful have yet come on the market. A heating system like my own, an electric brazier in a sunken hearth, seems to me ideal; yet no one ventures to produce even so simple a device as this (there are, of course,

Source: Jun'ichirō Tanizaki, *In Praise of Shadows*, trans. Thomas J. Harper and Edward G. Seidensticker (Sedgwick, ME: Leete's Islands Books, 1977), 6–11.

hey provide no more heat than an or-
n be had ready-made are those ugly

t to quibble over matters of taste in the
ravagance, that as long as a house keeps
d keeps off starvation, it matters little
or even the sternest ascetic the fact re-
there is no denying the impulse to
ppens to be there in front of one, no
ay shatter the spell of the day. But it
ways think how different everything
d developed our own science. Suppose
veloped our own physics and chemistry:
s and industries based on them have taken a dif-
ot our myriads of everyday gadgets, our medicines,
the products of our industrial art—would they not have suited our national temper better than they do? In fact our conception of physics itself, and even the principles of chemistry, would probably differ from
that of Westerners; and the facts we are now taught concerning the nature and function of light, electricity, and atoms might well have presented themselves in different form.

Of course I am only indulging in idle speculation; of scientific matters I know nothing. But had we devised independently at least the more
practical sorts of inventions, this could not but have had profound influence upon the conduct of our everyday lives, and even upon government, religion, art, and business. The Orient quite conceivably could
have opened up a world of technology entirely its own.

To take a trivial example near at hand: I wrote a magazine article
recently comparing the writing brush with the fountain pen, and in the
course of it I remarked that if the device had been invented by the ancient Chinese or Japanese it would surely have had a tufted end like our
writing brush. The ink would not have been this bluish color but rather
black, something like India ink, and it would have been made to seep
down from the handle into the brush. And since we would have then
found it inconvenient to write on Western paper, something near
Japanese paper—even under mass production, if you will—would have
been most in demand. Foreign ink and pen would not be as popular as
they are; the talk of discarding our system of writing for Roman letters
would be less noisy; people would still feel an affection for the old system. But more than that: our thought and our literature might not be
imitating the West as they are, but might have pushed forward into new
regions quite on their own. An insignificant little piece of writing equipment, when one thinks of it, has had a vast, almost boundless, influence
on our culture.

But I know as well as anyone that these are the empty dreams of a novelist, and that having come this far we cannot turn back. I know that I am only grumbling to myself and demanding the impossible. If my complaints are taken for what they are, however, there can be no harm in considering how unlucky we have been, what losses we have suffered, in comparison with the Westerner. The Westerner has been able to move forward in ordered steps, while we have met superior civilization and have had to surrender to it, and we have had to leave a road we have followed for thousands of years. The missteps and inconveniences this has caused have, I think, been many. If we had been left alone we might not be much further now in a material way than we were five hundred years ago. Even now in the Indian and Chinese countryside life no doubt goes on much as it did when Buddha and Confucius were alive. But we would have gone only in a direction that suited us. We would have gone ahead very slowly, and yet it is not impossible that we would one day have discovered our own substitute for the trolley, the radio, the airplane of today. They would have been no borrowed gadgets, they would have been the tools of our own culture, suited to us.

One need only compare American, French, and German films to see how greatly nuances of shading and coloration can vary in motion pictures. In the photographic image itself, to say nothing of the acting and the script, there somehow emerge differences in national character. If this is true even when identical equipment, chemicals, and film are used, how much better our own photographic technology might have suited our complexion, our facial features, our climate, our land. And had we invented the phonograph and the radio, how much more faithfully they would reproduce the special character of our voices and our music. Japanese music is above all a music of reticence, of atmosphere. When recorded, or amplified by a loudspeaker, the greater part of its charm is lost. In conversation, too, we prefer the soft voice, the understatement. Most important of all are the pauses. Yet the phonograph and radio render these moments of silence utterly lifeless. And so we distort the arts themselves to curry favor for them with the machines. These machines are the inventions of Westerners, and are, as we might expect, well suited to the Western arts. But precisely on this account they put our own arts at a great disadvantage.

Paper, I understand, was invented by the Chinese; but Western paper is to us no more than something to be used, while the texture of Chinese paper and Japanese paper gives us a certain feeling of warmth, of calm and repose. Even the same white could as well be one color for Western paper and another for our own. Western paper turns away the light, while our paper seems to take it in, to envelop it gently, like the soft surface of a first snowfall. It gives off no sound when it is crumpled or folded, it is quiet and pliant to the touch as the leaf of a tree.

As a general matter we find it hard to be really at home with things that shine and glitter. The Westerner uses silver and steel and nickel tableware, and polishes it to a fine brilliance, but we object to the practice. While we do sometimes indeed use silver for teakettles, decanters, or saké cups, we prefer not to polish it. On the contrary, we begin to enjoy it only when the luster has worn off, when it has begun to take on a dark, smoky patina. Almost every householder has had to scold an insensitive maid who has polished away the tarnish so patiently waited for.

Chinese food is now most often served on tableware made of tin, a material the Chinese could only admire for the patina it acquires. When new it resembles aluminum and is not particularly attractive; only after long use brings some of the elegance of age is it at all acceptable. Then, as the surface darkens, the line of verse etched upon it gives a final touch of perfection. In the hands of the Chinese this flimsy, glittering metal takes on a profound and somber dignity akin to that of their red unglazed pottery.

The Chinese also love jade. That strange lump of stone with its faintly muddy light, like the crystallized air of the centuries, melting dimly, dully back, deeper and deeper — are not we Orientals the only ones who know its charms? We cannot say ourselves what it is that we find in this stone. It quite lacks the brightness of a ruby or an emerald or the glitter of a diamond. But this much we can say: when we see that shadowy surface, we think how Chinese it is, we seem to find in its cloudiness the accumulation of the long Chinese past, we think how appropriate it is that the Chinese should admire that surface and that shadow.

It is the same with crystals. Crystals have recently been imported in large quantities from Chile, but Chilean crystals are too bright, too clear. We have long had crystals of our own, their clearness always moderated, made graver by a certain cloudiness. Indeed, we much prefer the "impure" varieties of crystal with opaque veins crossing their depths. Even of glass this is true; for is not fine Chinese glass closer to jade or agate than to Western glass? Glassmaking has long been known in the Orient, but the craft never developed as in the West. Great progress has been made, however, in the manufacture of pottery. Surely this has something to do with our national character. We do not dislike everything that shines, but we do prefer a pensive luster to a shallow brilliance, a murky light that, whether in a stone or an artifact, bespeaks a sheen of antiquity.

Of course this "sheen of antiquity" of which we hear so much is in fact the glow of grime. In both Chinese and Japanese the words denoting this glow describe a polish that comes of being touched over and over again, a sheen produced by the oils that naturally permeate an object over long years of handling — which is to say grime. If indeed "elegance is frigid," it can as well be described as filthy. There is no denying, at any rate, that among the elements of the elegance in which we take such delight is a measure of the unclean, the unsanitary. I suppose I shall sound terribly defensive if I say that Westerners attempt to expose every speck of grime and eradicate it, while we Orientals carefully preserve and even idealize it.

4

MOHANDAS K. GANDHI

Hind Swaraj

Mohandas K. Gandhi (1869–1948), the father of Indian independence, combined the education of an English lawyer with the temperament of an Indian ascetic to lead a national resistance movement against the British. In the century that followed British-supported reforms to the Indian education system (in the early nineteenth century), British rule had become far more pervasive and increasingly hostile toward Indian culture. Unlike Indian educational reformers, who had embraced Western culture as a means to uplift Indians, Gandhi became extremely critical of Western culture as he witnessed the havoc British rule wreaked on his country.

Gandhi began to develop his ideas of *Hind Swaraj,** or Indian Home Rule, in 1909 while he sailed from England to South Africa, where he served as a lawyer for fellow Indians. An early version of this essay, published then, was reissued in its present form in 1921, two years after he returned to his birthplace, India, and again in 1938, in the last years of struggle against British rule.

After Gandhi's introduction, the essay takes the form of questions and answers. The questions are posed by a presumed "reader" of Gandhi's pamphlet. As "editor," Gandhi explains what he means. How does Gandhi compare life in Europe and India? What does he think of the possibility of Hindus and Muslims living together? What does he mean by passive resistance or soul-force (Satyagraha)? Why does he think it is preferable to violence, or body-force? Gandhi was assassinated by a Hindu extremist in 1948 before he had a chance to shape the new nation. What kind of India would Gandhi have tried to

---

* hihnd swah RAHJ

Source: M. K. Gandhi, *Hind Swaraj* (Ahmedabad, India: Navajivan, 1938), 31–33, 44–45, 58–59, 69–71.

create had he lived? Compare Gandhi's response to the West with that of Jun'ichirō Tanizaki in the previous selection.

THINKING HISTORICALLY

Some historians have argued that Gandhi's contradictory roles — Hindu philosopher espousing secular nationalism and anti-modernist revolutionary — were ultimately unbridgeable. Notice how Gandhi makes a lawyer's case for traditional Indian values. How does he combine both religious and secular goals for India? How does he combine Hindu religious ideas with respect for Muslims? Were Gandhi's contradictions a fatal flaw, or could they have been his strength?

Civilization

READER   Now you will have to explain what you mean by civilization.

EDITOR   Let us first consider what state of things is described by the word "civilization." Its true test lies in the fact that people living in it make bodily welfare the object of life. We will take some examples. The people of Europe today live in better-built houses than they did a hundred years ago. This is considered an emblem of civilization, and this is also a matter to promote bodily happiness. Formerly, they wore skins, and used spears as their weapons. Now, they wear long trousers, and, for embellishing their bodies, they wear a variety of clothing, and, instead of spears, they carry with them revolvers containing five or more chambers. If people of a certain country, who have hitherto not been in the habit of wearing much clothing, boots, etc., adopt European clothing, they are supposed to have become civilized out of savagery. Formerly, in Europe, people ploughed their lands mainly by manual labour. Now, one man can plough a vast tract by means of steam engines and can thus amass great wealth. This is called a sign of civilization. Formerly, only a few men wrote valuable books. Now, anybody writes and prints anything he likes and poisons people's minds. Formerly, men travelled in waggons. Now, they fly through the air in trains at the rate of four hundred and more miles per day. This is considered the height of civilization. It has been stated that, as men progress, they shall be able to travel in airship and reach any part of the world in a few hours. Men will not need the use of their hands and feet. They will press a button, and they will have their clothing at their side. They will press another button, and they will have their newspaper. A third, and motor-car will be in waiting for them. They will have a variety of delicately dished up food. Everything will be done by machinery. Formerly, when people wanted to fight with one another, they measured between them their bodily strength; now it is possible to take away thousands of lives by one man working behind a gun from a hill. This is civilization. Formerly, men worked in the open air only as much as they liked. Now thousands of workmen meet together and for the sake of maintenance work in factories or mines. Their condition is worse than that of beasts. They are obliged to work, at the risk of their lives, at most dangerous occupations, for the sake of millionaires. Formerly, men were made slaves under physical compulsion. Now they are enslaved by temptation of money and of the luxuries that money can buy. There are now diseases of which people never dreamt before, and an army of doctors is engaged in finding out their cures, and so hospitals have increased. This is a test of civilization. Formerly, special messengers were required and much expense was incurred in order to send letters; today, anyone can abuse his fellow by means of a letter for one penny. True, at the same cost, one can send one's thanks also. Formerly, people had two or three meals consisting of home-made bread and vegetables; now, they require something to eat every two hours so that they have hardly leisure for anything else. What more need I say? . . . Even a child can understand that in all I have described above there can be no inducement to morality.

The Hindus and the Mahomedans

READER   Has the introduction to Mahomedanism [Islam] not unmade the nation?

EDITOR   India cannot cease to be one nation because people belonging to different religions live in it. The introduction of foreigners does not necessarily destroy the nation; they merge in it. A country is one nation only when such a condition obtains in it. That country must have a faculty for assimilation. India has ever been such a country. In reality there are as many religions as there are individuals; but those who are conscious of the spirit of nationality do not interfere with one another's religion. If they do, they are not fit to be considered a nation. If the Hindus believe that India should be peopled only by Hindus, they are living in dreamland. The Hindus, the Mahomedans, the Parsis and the Christians who have made India their country are fellow-countrymen, and they will have to live in unity, if only for their own interest. In no part of the world are one nationality and one religion synonymous terms; nor has it ever been so in India.

READER   But what about the inborn enmity between Hindus and Mahomedans?

EDITOR   That phrase has been invented by our mutual enemy. When the Hindus and Mahomedans fought against one another, they certainly spoke in that strain. They have long since ceased to fight. How, then, can there be any inborn enmity? Pray remember this too, that we did not cease to fight only after British occupation. The Hindus flourished under Moslem sovereigns and Moslems under the Hindu. Each party recognized that mutual fighting was suicidal, and that neither party would abandon its religion by force of arms. Both parties, therefore, decided to live in peace. With the English advent quarrels recommenced. . . .

How Can India Become Free?

READER   If Indian civilization is, as you say, the best of all, how do you account for India's slavery?

EDITOR   This civilization is unquestionably the best, but it is to be observed that all civilizations have been on their trial. That civilization which is permanent outlives it. Because the sons of India were found wanting, its civilization has been placed in jeopardy. But its strength is to be seen in its ability to survive the shock. Moreover, the whole of India is not touched. Those alone who have been affected by Western civilization have become enslaved. We measure the universe by our own miserable foot-rule. When we are slaves, we think that the whole universe is enslaved. Because we are in an abject condition, we think that the whole of India is in that condition. As a matter of fact, it is not so, yet it is as well to impute our slavery to the whole of India. But if we bear in mind the above fact, we can see that if we become free, India is free. And in this thought you have a definition of Swaraj. It is Swaraj when we learn to rule ourselves. It is, therefore, in the palm of our hands. Do not consider this Swaraj to be like a dream. There is no idea of sitting still. The Swaraj that I wish to picture is such that, after we have once realized it, we shall endeavour to the end of our life-time to persuade others to do likewise. But such Swaraj has to be experienced, by each one for himself. One drowning man will never save another. Slaves ourselves, it would be a mere pretension to think of freeing others. Now you will have seen that it is not necessary for us to have as our goal the expulsion of the English. If the English become Indianized, we can accommodate them. If they wish to remain in India along with their civilization, there is no room for them. It lies with us to bring about such a state of things. . . .

Passive Resistance

READER   Is there any historical evidence as to the success of what you have called soul-force or truth-force? No instance seems to have happened of any nation having risen through soul-force. I still think that the evil-doers will not cease doing evil without physical punishment.

EDITOR   The [Hindu] poet Tulsidas [1532–1623] has said: "Of religion, pity, or love, is the root, as egotism of the body. Therefore, we should not abandon pity so long as we are alive." This appears to me to be a scientific truth. We have evidence of its working at every step. The universe would disappear without the existence of that force. . . .

   The fact that there are so many men still alive in the world shows that it is based not on the force of arms but on the force of truth or love. Therefore, the greatest and most unimpeachable evidence of the success of this force is to be found in the fact that, in spite of the wars of the world, it still lives on.

   Thousands, indeed tens of thousands, depend for their existence on a very active working of this force. Little quarrels of millions of families in their daily lives disappear before the exercise of this force. Hundreds of nations live in peace. History does not and cannot take note of this fact. History is really a record of every interruption of the even working of the force of love or of the soul. Two brothers quarrel; one of them repents and re-awakens the love that was lying dormant in him; the two again begin to live in peace; nobody takes note of this. But if the two brothers, through the intervention of solicitors or some other reason take up arms or go to law—which is another form of the exhibition of brute force,—their doings would be immediately noticed in the press, they would be the talk of their neighbours and would probably go down to history. And what is true of families and communities is true of nations. There is no reason to believe that there is one law for families and another for nations. History, then, is a record of an interruption of the course of nature. Soul-force, being natural, is not noted in history.

READER   According to what you say, it is plain that instances of this kind of passive resistance are not to be found in history. It is necessary to understand this passive resistance more fully. It will be better, therefore, if you enlarge upon it.

EDITOR   Passive resistance is a method of securing rights by personal suffering; it is the reverse of resistance by arms. When I refuse to do a thing that is repugnant to my conscience, I use soul-force. For instance, the Government of the day has passed a law which is applicable to me. I do not like it. If by using violence I force the Government to repeal the law, I am employing what may be termed body-force. If I do not obey the law and accept the penalty for its breach, I use soul-force. It involves sacrifice of self.

5

JAWAHARLAL NEHRU

Gandhi

Mohandas K. Gandhi and Jawaharlal Nehru* were the two most important leaders of India's national independence movement. In 1942 Nehru published his autobiography, excerpted here, in which he had much to say about the importance of Gandhi in his life. Though they worked together and Nehru was Gandhi's choice as the first Indian prime minister, they expressed in their personalities and ideas two very different Indias. How would you describe these two Indias? Was it Gandhi's or Nehru's vision of the future that was realized? Who do you think was a better guide for India?

THINKING HISTORICALLY

Think of Gandhi and Nehru as the two sides of the Indian struggle for independence. Did India benefit from having both of these sides represented? What would have happened if there had been only Gandhi's view or only Nehru's?

How was the debate in India about the influence of the West different from the debate in Japan?

I imagine that Gandhiji[1] is not so vague about the objective as he sometimes appears to be. He is passionately desirous of going in a certain direction, but this is wholly at variance with modern ideas and conditions, and he has so far been unable to fit the two, or to chalk out all the

---

* jah wah HAHR lahl   NAY roo
[1] Term of endearment for Gandhi. [Ed.]

Source: Jawaharlal Nehru, *An Autobiography* (New Delhi: Allied Publishers, 1942–1962), 510–11.

intermediate steps leading to his goal. Hence the appearance of vague-
ness and avoidance of clarity. But his general inclination has been clear
enough for a quarter of a century, ever since he started formulating his
philosophy in South Africa. I do not know if those early writings still
represent his views. I doubt if they do so in their entirety, but they do
help us to understand the background of his thought.

"India's salvation consists," he wrote in 1909, "in unlearning what
she has learned during the last fifty years. The railways, telegraphs, hospitals, lawyers, doctors, and suchlike have all to go; and the so-called
upper classes have to learn consciously, religiously, and deliberately the
simple peasant life, knowing it to be a life giving true happiness." And
again: "Every time I get into a railway car or use a motor bus I know
that I am doing violence to my sense of what is right"; "to attempt to
reform the world by means of highly artificial and speedy locomotion is
to attempt the impossible."

All this seems to me utterly wrong and harmful doctrine, and impossible of achievement. Behind it lies Gandhiji's love and praise of poverty
and suffering and the ascetic life. For him progress and civilization consist not in the multiplication of wants, of higher standards of living, "but
in the deliberate and voluntary restriction of wants, which promotes real
happiness and contentment, and increases the capacity for service." If
these premises are once accepted, it becomes easy to follow the rest of
Gandhiji's thought and to have a better understanding of his activities.
But most of us do not accept those premises, and yet we complain later
on when we find that his activities are not to our liking.

Personally I dislike the praise of poverty and suffering. I do not think
they are at all desirable, and they ought to be abolished. Nor do I appreciate the ascetic life as a social ideal, though it may suit individuals.
I understand and appreciate simplicity, equality, self-control; but not the
mortification of the flesh. Just as an athlete requires to train his body,
I believe that the mind and habits have also to be trained and brought
under control. It would be absurd to expect that a person who is given
to too much self-indulgence can endure much suffering or show unusual
self-control or behave like a hero when the crisis comes. To be in good
moral condition requires at least as much training as to be in good
physical condition. But that certainly does not mean asceticism or
self-mortification.

Nor do I appreciate in the least the idealization of the "simple peasant life." I have almost a horror of it, and instead of submitting to it
myself I want to drag out even the peasantry from it, not to urbanization, but to the spread of urban cultural facilities to rural areas. Far from
his life's giving me true happiness, it would be almost as bad as imprisonment for me. What is there in "The Man with the Hoe" to idealize
over? Crushed and exploited for innumerable generations, he is only
little removed from the animals who keep him company.

Who made him dead to rapture and despair,
A thing that grieves not and that never hopes,
Stolid and stunned, a brother to the ox?[2]

This desire to get away from the mind of man to primitive conditions where mind does not count, seems to me quite incomprehensible.
The very thing that is the glory and triumph of man is decried and discouraged, and a physical environment which will oppress the mind and
prevent its growth is considered desirable. Present-day civilization is full
of evils, but it is also full of good; and it has the capacity in it to rid itself
of those evils. To destroy it root and branch is to remove that capacity
from it and revert to a dull, sunless, and miserable existence. But even if
that were desirable it is an impossible undertaking. We cannot stop the
river of change or cut ourselves adrift from it, and psychologically we
who have eaten of the apple of Eden cannot forget that taste and go back
to primitiveness.

[2] From poem by Edwin Markam, "The Man with the Hoe" (1899), which was a response
to the painting of the same title by Jean Millet. [Ed.]

6

MUSTAFA KEMAL ATATURK

A Turkish Republic for the Civilized World

Modern Turkey's life as an independent state follows an arc closer
to that of Japan than India. Like Japan, and unlike India, Turkey was
never colonized. But like Japan, its independence was seriously
threatened by European colonial powers at a critical moment — in
this case the moment of its birth from the ashes of the Ottoman
Empire in 1919. Since the fourteenth century, the formative Ottoman Empire had been the center of the Islamic faith and the power
of the eastern Mediterranean. But by the beginning of the twentieth
century, the Ottoman Empire was in rapid decline, beset by nationalist movements in the Balkans and the ambitions of European
powers, including Russia, France, and England. The World War I
alliance with Germany and the Austro-Hungarian Empire offered
only a temporary delay of its inevitable collapse. But the Ottoman

Source: Ghazi Mustapha Kemal, *A Speech Delivered by Ghazi Mustapha Kemal, President of the Turkish Republic, October 1927* (Leipzig: K. F. Koehler, Publisher, 1929), 9, 16–18, 684–85, 721–23.

defeat gave new life to the nationalist, progressive, antimonarchist movement that had been the legacy of the "Young Turks" of the early twentieth century. The leader of that movement in 1919 was Mustafa Kemal Ataturk.

Mustafa Kemal (1881–1938) was given the surname Ataturk (father of Turks) by the National Assembly of Turkey in 1934. The young Kemal chose a military career and joined the Young Turk reform movement within the army, participating in the Young Turk revolution of 1908 that revived constitutional parliamentary government. During World War I, he successfully commanded Ottoman forces at Gallipoli in 1915, along the Russian front in 1917, and in Jordan and Syria in 1918. In 1919 he returned to Istanbul, which was occupied by foreign troops and an Ottoman government beholden to British direction. Ordered to disband the Ottoman army, Kemal instead resigned, called a Grand National Assembly of Turkey, and raised a Turkish army to fight for independence. Between 1920 and 1923, Kemal fought British designs to carve up the Ottoman Empire by waging wars against Greece in the west, Armenia in the east, and England and France in Mesopotamia. Victorious in 1923, Kemal established the Turkish Republic and became its first president, thus ending the Ottoman Empire.

The first years of the new republic were tumultuous, especially for those who expected a return to Ottoman ways. Kemal set out to transform an empire of Muslim subjects into a modern, secular, and democratic republic of citizens. In addition to abolishing the sultanate, Kemal abolished the caliphate, the institution of religious authority over the Muslim world that had enjoyed its own army as well as competing political power. He made the clergy subject to the state ministry of religious affairs, banned polygamy, and added a state-wide system of civil courts to take over most responsibilities from religious courts, including marriage. He also closed Sufi orders like that of the famous Mevlana "whirling dirvishes." But the modernization of education was the central plank in the Kemalist platform for a modern Turkey. Kemal enlisted public intellectual and educational reformer John Dewey to design a system of education and common curriculum for public schools through which civic culture would be taught to girls as well as boys. Even clothing was to be modernized: Western suits and hats instead of robes and fez for men; and Western dress instead of veils for women.

As early as 1924, a reaction had set in. That year a tribal sheik declared the government anti-Islamic and led a rebellion, seizing government offices in a few cities. In response, the government passed a "Law for the Maintenance of Public Order" that banned a wide variety of groups as subversive. (The law was not repealed until 1929.) In 1926 a plot to assassinate Kemal was uncovered in the city of Izmir. An investigation led to the conviction and execution of some of the plotters.

The speech that is excerpted in this selection was a response to the rebellion against the government. Kemal delivered the speech to the National Assembly during a period of over thirty-six hours from October 15 to October 20, 1927. He recounted events from 1919 until 1927 in chronological order and encyclopedic detail. Then he explained his goals for the continued development of the Turkish Republic. This selection contains excerpts from the beginning and end of that speech. From the evidence of this selection, what were his goals? What sort of country was he trying to create? In what ways did he want Turkey to be independent? In what ways did he want Turkey to follow the Western model of modernity? Compare Kemal with Gandhi.

THINKING HISTORICALLY

Make a note of the occasions in this speech where Kemal seeks to resolve a contradiction between two ideals or types of behavior. How does he resolve these? Notice how Kemal was both a Turkish nationalist and an admirer of Western civilization. How does he see the relationship between these two ideals? How does he envision the relationship between Turkey and the West?

I

Gentlemen,

I landed at Samsoon on the 19th May, 1919. This was the position at that time:

The group of Powers which included the Ottoman Government had been defeated in the Great War. The Ottoman Army had been crushed on every front. An armistice had been signed under severe conditions. The prolongation of the Great War had left the people exhausted and empoverished. Those who had driven the people and the country into the general conflict had fled and now cared for nothing but their own safety. Wahideddin, the degenerate occupant of the throne and the Caliphate, was seeking for some despicable way to save his person and his throne, the only objects of his anxiety. The Cabinet, of which Damad Ferid Pasha was the head, was weak and lacked dignity and courage. It was subservient to the will of the Sultan alone and agreed to every proposal that could protect its members and their sovereign.

The Army had been deprived of their arms and ammunition, and this state of affairs continued.

The Entente Powers did not consider it necessary to respect the terms of the armistice. On various pretexts, their men-of-war and troops remained at Constantinople. The Vilayet of Adana was occupied by the French; Urfah, Marash, Aintab, by the English. In Adalia and Konia were the Italians, whilst at Merifun and Samsoon were English troops. Foreign officers and officials and their special agents were very active in all directions. At last, on the 15th May, that is to say, four days before the following account of events begins, the Greek Army, with the consent of the Entente Powers, had landed at Smyrna. Christian elements were also at work all over the country, either openly or in secret, trying to realise their own particular ambitions and thereby hasten the breakdown of the Empire. . . .

I must mention another point here. In seeking how to save the situation it was considered to be specially important to avoid irritating the Great Powers—England, France and Italy. The idea that it was impossible to fight even one of these Powers had taken root in the mind of nearly everybody. Consequently, to think of doing so and thus bring on another war after the Ottoman Empire, all-powerful Germany and Austria-Hungary together had been defeated and crushed would have been looked upon as sheer madness.

Not only the mass of the people thought in this strain, but those also who must be regarded as their chosen leaders shared the same opinion. Therefore, in seeking a way out of the difficulty, two questions had to be eliminated from discussion. First of all, no hostility was to be shown towards the Entente Powers; secondly, the most important thing of all was to remain, heart and soul, loyal to the Padishah-Caliph.

Now, Gentlemen, I will ask you what decision I ought to have arrived at in such circumstances to save the Empire?

As I have already explained, there were three propositions that had been put forward:

1. To demand protection from England;
2. To accept the United States of America as a mandatory Power.

The originators of these two proposals had as their aim the preservation of the Ottoman Empire in its complete integrity and preferred to place it as a whole under the protection of a single Power, rather than allow it to be divided among several States.

3. The third proposal was to deliver the country by allowing each district to act in its own way and according to its own capability. Thus, for instance, certain districts, in opposition to the theory of separation, would have to see that they remained an integral part of the Empire. Others holding a different opinion already appeared to regard the dismemberment of the Empire as an accomplished fact and sought only their own safety.

You will remember that I have already referred to these three points.

None of these three proposals could be accepted as the correct one, because the arguments and considerations on which they were based were groundless. In reality, the foundations of the Ottoman Empire were themselves shattered at that time. Its existence was threatened with extermination. All the Ottoman districts were practically dismembered. Only one important part of the country, affording protection to a mere handful of Turks, still remained, and it was now suggested also to divide this.

Such expressions as: the Ottoman Empire, Independence, Padishah-Caliph, Government—all of them were mere meaningless words.

Therefore, whose existence was it essential to save? and with whose help? and how? But how could these questions be solved at such a time as this?

In these circumstances, one resolution alone was possible, namely, to create a New Turkish State, the sovereignty and independence of which would be unreservedly recognised by the whole world.

This was the resolution we adopted before we left Constantinople and which we began to put into execution immediately after we set foot on Anatolian soil at Samsoon.

These were the most logical and most powerful arguments in support of this resolution:

The main point was that the Turkish nation should be free to lead a worthy and glorious existence. Such a condition could only be attained by complete independence. Vital as considerations of wealth and prosperity might be to a nation, if it is deprived of its independence it no longer deserves to be regarded otherwise than as a slave in the eyes of civilised humanity.

To accept the protectorate of a foreign Power would signify that we acknowledge that we lack all human qualities; it would mean that we admit our own weakness and incapacity. Indeed, how could we make people understand that we can accept a foreign master if we have not descended to this degree of abject servitude?

But the Turk is both dignified and proud; he is also capable and talented. Such a nation would prefer to perish rather than subject itself to the life of a slave. Therefore, Independence or Death!

This was the rallying cry of all those who honestly desired to save their country.

Let us suppose for a moment that in trying to accomplish this we had failed. What would have been the result?—why, slavery!

In that case, would not the consequence have been the same if we had submitted to the other proposal? Undoubtedly, it would; but with this difference, that a nation that defies death in its struggle for independence derives comfort from the thought that it had resolved to make every sacrifice compatible with human dignity. There is no doubt whatever that in the eyes of both friend and foe throughout the world its position is more respected than would be that of a craven and degraded nation capable of surrendering itself to the yoke of slavery.

Moreover, to labour for the maintenance of the Ottoman dynasty and its sovereign would have been to inflict the greatest injustice upon the Turkish nation; for, if its independence could have been secured at the price of every possible sacrifice, it could not have been regarded as secure so long as the Sultanate existed. How could it be admitted that a crowd of madmen, united by neither a moral nor a spiritual bond to the country or the nation as a whole, could still be trusted to protect the independence and the dignity of the nation and the State?

As for the Caliphate, it could only have been a laughing-stock in the eyes of the really civilised and cultured people of the world.

As you see, in order to carry out our resolution, questions had to be dealt with about which the nation had hitherto known practically nothing. It was imperative that questions should be brought forward that could not be discussed in public without giving rise to serious dissentions.

We were compelled to rebel against the Ottoman Government, against the Padishah, against the Caliph of all the Mohamedans, and we had to bring the whole nation and the army into a state of rebellion. . . .

[1924]

. . . In the speech which I delivered on the 1st March, the fifth anniversary of the opening of the Assembly, I especially emphasised the three following points:

1. The nation demands that now, in the future, for ever and unconditionally the Republic shall be protected from every attack. The wish of the nation can be expressed through the fact that the Republic will be founded a moment earlier and completely on the whole of the positive principles which have been put to the test.

2. We declare that it is necessary without loss of time to apply the principle of unity of instruction and education which has been decided by the vote of the nation.

3. We also recognise that it is indispensable in order to secure the revival of the Islamic Faith, to disengage it from the condition of being a political instrument, which it has been for centuries through habit. . . .

. . . The discussion lasted for nearly five hours. When the discussion closed at 6.45 p.m. the Grand National Assembly had promulgated the Laws No. 429, 430 and 431.

In virtue of these laws the "Grand National Assembly of Turkey and the Government formed by it is authorised to give legal form to the stipulations which are in force in the Turkish Republic with reference to public affairs and to carry through their application," "The Ministry for Religious Affairs and the Evkaf have been suppressed."

All scientific and educational institutions in Turkish territory . . . , all ecclesiastical schools, are transferred to the Ministry of Public Instruction.

The Caliph is declared deposed and the dignity abolished. All members of the deposed Ottoman dynasty are for ever forbidden to reside within the frontiers of the territory of the Turkish Republic.

Certain persons who wrongly believed that it was necessary, for religious and political reasons to maintain the Caliphate, proposed at the last moment when the decisions were to be taken, that I should assume the office of the Caliphate.

I immediately gave a negative reply to these men. . . .

[1926]

Honourable Gentlemen, when, in consequence of serious necessity we became convinced for the first time that it would be useful for the Government to take extraordinary measures, there were people who disapproved of our action.

There were persons who disseminated and sought to gain credence to the thought that we were making use of the law for Restoration of Order and the Courts of Independence as tools of dictatorship or despotism.

There is no doubt that time and events will show to those who disseminated this opinion how mistaken they were, and put them to shame.

We never used the exceptional measures, which all the same were legal, to set ourselves in any way above the law.

On the contrary, we applied them to restore peace and quietness in the country. We made use of them to insure the existence and independence of the country. We made use of them with the object of contributing to the social development of the nation.

Gentlemen, as soon as the necessity for the application of the exceptional measures to which we had turned no longer existed, we did not hesitate to renounce them. Thus, for instance, the Courts of Independence ceased their activity at the given moment, just as the law regarding the Restoration of Order was re-submitted to the Assembly for examination as soon as its legislative term had elapsed. If the Assembly considered it necessary to prolong its application for some time this certainly happened because it saw therein the higher interest of the nation and of the Republic.

Can anyone be of the opinion that this decision of the High Assembly was intended to hand over to us the means for the carrying on of a dictatorship?

Gentlemen, it was necessary to abolish the fez, which sat on our heads as a sign of ignorance, of fanaticism, of hatred to progress and civilisation, and to adopt in its place the hat, the customary headdress of the whole civilised world, thus showing, among other things, that no difference existed in the manner of thought between the Turkish nation and the whole family of civilised mankind. We did that while the law for the Restoration of Order was still in force. If it had not been in force we should have done so all the same; but one can say with complete truth that the existence of this law made the thing much easier for us. As a matter of fact the application of the law for the Restoration of Order prevented the morale of the nation being poisoned to a great extent by reactionaries. . . .

Gentlemen, while the law regarding the Restoration of Order was in force there took place also the closing of the Tekkes,[1] of the convents, and of the mausoleums, as well as the abolition of all sects and all kinds of titles such as Sheikh, Dervish, "Junger," Tschelebi, Occultist, Magician, Mausoleum Guard, etc.

One will be able to imagine how necessary the carrying through of these measures was, in order to prove that our nation as a whole was no primitive nation, filled with superstitions and prejudices.

Could a civilised nation tolerate a mass of people who let themselves be led by the nose by a herd of Sheikhs, Dedes, Seids, Tschelebis, Babas and Emirs; who entrusted their destiny and their lives to chiromancers, magicians, dice-throwers and amulet sellers? Ought one to conserve in the Turkish State, in the Turkish Republic, elements and institutions such as those which had for centuries given the nation the appearance of being other than it really was? Would one not therewith have committed the greatest, most irreparable error to the cause of progress and reawakening?

If we made use of the law for the Restoration of Order in this manner, it was in order to avoid such a historic error; to show the nation's brow pure and luminous, as it is; to prove that our people think neither in a fanatical nor a reactionary manner.

Gentlemen, at the same time the new laws were worked out and decreed which promise the most fruitful results for the nation on the social and economic plane, and in general in all the forms of the expression of human activity . . . the Citizens' Law-book, which ensures the liberty of women and stabilises the existence of the family.

Accordingly we made use of all circumstances only from one point of view, which consisted therein: to raise the nation on to that step on which it is justified in standing in the civilised world, to stabilise the Turkish Republic more and more on steadfast foundations . . . and in addition to destroy the spirit of despotism for ever.

These detailed descriptions, which have occupied you for so many days, are, after all, merely a report of a period of time, which will henceforth belong to the past.

I shall consider myself very happy if I have succeeded in the course of this report in expressing some truths which are calculated to rivet the interest and attention of my nation and of future generations.

---

[1] Buildings designed for gatherings of the Sufi brotherhood. [Ed.]

Gentlemen, I have taken trouble to show, in these accounts, how a great people, whose national course was considered as ended, reconquered its independence; how it created a national and modern State founded on the latest results of science.

The result we have attained to day is the fruit of teachings which arose from centuries of suffering, and the price of streams of blood which have drenched every foot of the ground of our beloved Fatherland.

This holy treasure I lay in the hands of the youth of Turkey.

Turkish Youth! your primary duty is ever to preserve and defend the National independence, the Turkish Republic.

7

HASSAN AL-BANA

The Tyranny of Materialism over the Lands of Islam

Hassan al-Bana (1906–1949) was an Egyptian social critic who came to believe that the cure to political corruption, foreign influence, and materialistic culture could be found in a social transformation based on the original tenets of Islam. To that effect, in 1928 he launched the Society of Muslim Brothers, an organization in which members met in cells, which were called "families," to bring about social, cultural, and political change. While actively engaged in organizing prayer groups and providing aid to the poor, the Brotherhood was seen by the Egyptian monarchy and (after 1953) the republic as a dangerous threat to the state. Members recruited volunteers to fight in Palestine and, in the wake of the war against the establishment of Israel, the Brotherhood became a powerful force in Egypt. In 1948 the organization was banned. Hassan al-Bana was assassinated in 1949 after one of the Brotherhood members assassinated the prime minister. The Muslim Brotherhood has continued to be popular and influential in Egypt and other Muslim countries despite its illegal status.

What did al-Bana see as the impact of Europe in Egypt? What seems to have offended him most about European influence? How did he hope to counter this influence?

Source: "Six Tracts of Hasan al-Bana," from the *Majmu'at Rasa'il al-Iman al-Shahid Hasan al-Banna* (1906–1949), International Islamic Federation of Student Organizations, Kuwait & Africa, for Publishing & Distribution, Accra Ghana (2006), 42–48.

THINKING HISTORICALLY

Compare al-Bana's nationalism with that of the other anticolonialists in this chapter. Some of these proponents of independence were more personally conflicted than others. Where would you place al-Bana on a continuum from those who were completely certain to those who were torn between the appeals of opposing values? In this respect, who in the chapter does al-Bana most resemble? Who is he most unlike?

VIII. The Tyranny of Materialism over the Lands of Islam

The Europeans worked assiduously to enable the tide of this materialistic life, with its corrupting traits and its murderous germs, to overwhelm all the Islamic lands toward which their hands were outstretched. An ill destiny overtook these under their domination, for they were avid to appropriate for themselves the elements of power and prosperity through science, knowledge, industry, and good organization, while barring these very nations from them. They laid their plans for this social aggression in masterly fashion, invoking the aid of their political acumen and their military predominance until they had accomplished their desire. They deluded the Muslim leaders by granting them loans and entering into financial dealings with them, making all of this easy and effortless for them, and thus they were able to obtain the right to infiltrate the economy and to flood the countries with their capital, their banks, and their companies; to take over the workings of the economic machinery as they wished; and to monopolize, to the exclusion of the inhabitants, enormous profits and immense wealth. After that, they were able to alter the basic principles of government, justice, and education, and to imbue political, juridical, and cultural systems with their own peculiar character in even the most powerful Islamic countries. They imported their half-naked women into these regions, together with their liquors, their theatres, their dance halls, their amusements, their stories, their newspapers, their novels, their whims, their silly games, and their vices. Here they countenanced crimes they did not tolerate in their own countries, and decked out this frivolous, strident world, reeking with sin and redolent with vice, to the eyes of deluded, unsophisticated Muslims of wealth and prestige, and to those of rank and authority. This being insufficient for them, they founded schools and scientific and cultural institutes in the very heart of the Islamic domain, which cast doubt and heresy into the souls of its sons and taught them how to demean themselves, disparage their religion and their fatherland, divest themselves of their traditions and beliefs, and to regard as sacred anything Western, in the belief that only that which had a European source could serve as a model to be emulated in this life. These schools took in the sons of the upper class alone, and became a preserve restricted to them. The sons of this class consisted of the mighty and ruling group, and those who would shortly hold within their grasp the keys to all important matters that concerned these nations and peoples. Those who did not complete their finishing in these local institutes found all that would guarantee them this finishing in the continuing series of student missions.[1] This drastic, well-organized social compaign had a tremendous success, since it was rendered most attractive to the mind, and would continue to exert a strong intellectual influence on individuals over a long period of time. For this reason, it was more dangerous than the political and military campaigns by far, and some Islamic countries went overboard in their admiration for this European civilization and in their dissatisfaction with their own Islamic character, to the point that Turkey declared itself a non-Islamic state and imitated the Europeans with the utmost rigor in everything they did. Aman Allah khan,[2] King of Afghanistan, tried this, but the attempt swept away his throne, and in Egypt the manifestations of this mimicry increased and became so serious that one of her intellectual leaders could say openly that the only path to progress was to adopt this civilization with all it contained of good and evil, sweet and bitter, the appealing and the hateful, the praiseworthy and the reprehensible. From Egypt it began to spread rapidly and vigorously into neighboring countries, until it reached Morocco and circumambulated the very shrines in the purlieus of the Hijaz.[3] We may subdivide the Islamic countries, according to the degrees to which they were affected by this materialistic civilization and the domination of its materialism over them, into three groups:

1. Countries in which this influence has reached serious proportions, penetrating even the mind and the feelings, apart from outward forms and conventions. Among these countries are Turkey and Egypt, where even the slightest trace of Islamic ideology has disappeared from all social situations, and has been driven off to take up quarters inside the mosques and Sufi establishments and retreats.

2. Countries which have been influenced by this civilization in their official observances and conventions, but in which it has not triumphed over their inward sensibilities. Such are Iran and the countries of North Africa.

---

[1] These were the famous student missions inaugurated by Muhammad Ali Pasha in Egypt. Groups of promising Egyptian students would be sent to Europe to learn modern Western languages and sciences, so that they might be able to translate works dealing with these disciplines into Arabic and Turkish on the completion of their studies. Many also taught in the new government schools on their return to Egypt. See J. Heyworth-Dunne, *An Introduction to the History of Education in Modern Egypt.*

[2] Ruler of Afghanistan from 1919. His premature attempt to emulate Egypt and Turkey by instituting modernist reforms in his country led to open revolt and his forced abdication and exile.

[3] The region of Mecca and Medina. [Ed.]

3. Countries which have not been influenced by this civilization, except for a particular class consisting of the well-educated and the ruling group, to the exclusion of the common people and the masses. Such are Syria, Iraq, the Hijaz, many sections of the Arabian Peninsula, and the remainder of the Islamic countries.

Nevertheless, this wave is spreading out with the speed of lightning to reach into minds, social classes, and mores that it has not yet penetrated. Enemies of Islam can deceive Muslim intellectuals and draw a thick veil over the eyes of the zealous by depicting Islam itself as being defective in various aspects of doctrine, ritual observance, and morality, besides accommodating a host of rites, superstitions, and inane formalities. What helps them to carry out this deception is the Muslims' ignorance of the true meaning of their religion, so that many of them are satisfied with this presentation, rest content with it, and accept it. For so long a time has this been true of them that it is difficult for us to make any of them understand that Islam is a perfect system of social organization which encompasses all the affairs of life. As a result, it is possible for us to say that Western civilization, with its materialistic ideology, has triumphed in this social struggle over Islamic civilization, with its sound ideology comprising both spirit and matter, in the very territories of Islam, and in a ruthless war whose battlefield has been the spirits and souls of Muslims as well as their beliefs and intellects, exactly as it has triumphed on the political and military battlefields. It is no wonder, for the phenomena of life are not fragmented: what is strong is wholly strong, and what is weak is wholly weak: "These are the days which we apportion to mankind in turn" [Q.3:140]. And even if the ideology and teachings of Islam have gone astray, it is powerful in its essential nature, abundantly fertile and vital, attractive and enchanting in its splendor and beauty, and it will remain so because it is the truth, and human existence will never achieve perfection and virtue through any other means. And because it is of God's creation and under His care: "Lo, We have sent down the Reminder, and lo, We are its Protector" [Q.15:9]; "God refuses aught but that He should perfect His light, though the unbelievers feel aversion" [Q.9:32].

Awakening: Just as political aggression had its effect in arousing nationalist feelings, so has social aggression had its effect in reviving the Islamic ideology. Voices have been raised on every hand, demanding a return to Islam, an understanding of its precepts, and an application of its rules. The day must soon come when the castles of this materialistic civilization will be laid low upon the heads of their inhabitants. Then they will feel the burning of a spiritual hunger in which their hearts and souls will go up in flames, and they will find no sustenance, no healing, no remedy, save in the teachings of this Noble Book: "O man, an admonition from your Lord has come to you, and a healing for what is in your hearts, a guidance and a mercy for the believers. Say: 'In God's bounty, and in His mercy: let them rejoice in that.' It is better than what they hoard" [Q.10:58–59].

IX. Our Mission is One of Reawakening and Deliverance

A. A Weighty Heritage: So, Brethren, did Allah will that we inherit this heritage weighty with consequence, that the light of your mission glow amidst this darkness, and that Allah prepare you to exalt His Word and reveal His Sacred Law and reestablish His state: "Allah will surely aid one who helps Him. Allah is Mighty, Glorious;" [Q.22:40].

B. Our General Aims: What do we want, Brethren? Do we want to hoard up wealth, which is an evanescent shadow? Or do we want abundance of fame, which is a transient accident? Or do we went dominion over the earth? — "The earth is Allah's: He gives to inherit it those whom He will of His servants" [Q.7:127]—even as we read the Speech of Allah (Blessed and Almighty is He!): "That is the Abode of the Hereafter which We assign to those who do not want exaltation in the earth, nor any corruption. The final consequence is to the pious" [Q.28:83]. May Allah witness that we do not want any of these, that our work is not toward these ends, and that our mission is not on their behalf. Rather always bear in mind that you have two fundamental goals:

1. That the Islamic fatherland be freed from all foreign domination, for this is a natural right belonging to every human being which only the unjust oppressor or the conquering exploiter will deny.
2. That a free Islamic state may arise in this free fatherland, acting according to the precepts of Islam, applying its social regulations, proclaiming its sound principles, and broadcasting its sage mission to all mankind. For as long as this state does not emerge, the Muslims in their totality are committing sin, and are responsible before Allah the Lofty, the Great for their failure to establish it and for their slackness in creating it. In these bewildering circumstances, it is counter to humanity that a state should arise, extolling an ideology of injustice and proclaiming a propaganda of oppression, while there should be no one among all mankind working for the advent of a state founded on truth, justice, and peace. We want to realize these two goals in the Nile Valley and the Arab domain, and in every land which Allah has made fortunate through the Islamic creed: a religion, a nationality, and a creed uniting all Muslims.

C. Our Special Aims: Following these two aims, we have some special aims without the realization of which our society cannot become completely Islamic. Brethren, recall that more than 60 percent of the Egyptians live at a subhuman level, that they get enough to eat only through the most arduous toil, and Egypt is threatened by murderous famines and exposed to many economic problems of which only Allah can know the outcome. Recall too that there are more than 320 foreign companies in Egypt, monopolizing all public utilities and all important facilities in every part of the country; that the wheels of commerce, industry, and all economic institutions are in the hands of profiteering foreigners; and that our wealth in land is being transferred with lightning speed from the possession of our compatriots to that of these others. Recall also that Egypt, out of the entire civilized world, is the most subject to diseases, plagues, and illnesses; that over 90 percent of the Egyptian people are threatened by physical infirmity, the loss of some sensory perception, and a variety of sicknesses and ailments; and that Egypt is still backward, with no more than one-fifth of the population possessing any education, and of these more than 100,000 have never gone farther than the elementary school level. Recall that crime has doubled in Egypt, and that it is increasing at an alarming rate to the point that the prisons are putting out more graduates than the schools; that up to the present time Egypt has been unable to outfit a single army division with its full complement of material; and that these symptoms and phenomena may be observed in any Islamic country. Among your aims are to work for the reform of education; to war against poverty, ignorance, disease, and crime; and to create an exemplary society which will deserve to be associated with the Islamic Sacred Law.

■ REFLECTIONS

We have looked at the conflict between Westernization and nationalism through windows on four different societies: Japan, India, and two Muslim societies—Turkey and Egypt. For the Japanese, the borrowing of Western institutions and ideas provided an escape from colonization. By the time India gained political independence in 1947, it had become partially Westernized by three hundred years of colonialism. Yet in both countries, as in the Islamic world, there were those who resisted Western ways, those who embraced them, and others still who developed ambivalent feelings toward the West.

This last response—often accepting the contradictions: treasuring the traditional while trying the new—may have been the most difficult, but ultimately the most useful. It must have been far easier to cast off everything Asian, as Fukuzawa Yukichi urged, or make fun of any contact with the West as buffoonery, monkeying around, or frightful miscegenation, as the Japanese cartoons suggested. Japan may have made the most successful non-Western transition to industrial modernity because it steered a path between Fukuzawa Yukichi's prescription for wholesale cultural capitulation and the cartoonists' blanket rejection of anything new and foreign. By the 1930s, Jun'ichirō Tanizaki recognized that there was no turning back from a world in which bright electric lights and gold-flecked lacquerware had replaced lamplight and soft wood. According to a story told later by the author's wife, when Jun'ichirō Tanizaki decided to build a new house, the architect said proudly that he had read *In Praise of Shadows* and so he knew exactly what the author wanted. "But no," Jun'ichirō Tanizaki replied. "I could never *live* in a house like that."[1]

India, with older indigenous traditions than Japan but also a longer period confronting the influence of Western culture, approached independence in 1947 with a political elite trained in English law, liberal and Marxist political parties, a literate English-speaking middle class, and a long-suppressed hunger for economic freedom and material well-being. Gandhi feared violence, anticolonial in 1909 and anti-Muslim in 1947, more than the repressions of the old society. While he sought a new social cohesion in traditional religious spiritualism, Nehru hoped to forge a new solidarity along the Western industrial socialist model.

Like India and Japan, the Islamic world has also had its Westernizers and anti-Westernizers. In fact, Turkey and Egypt have known both, and many in between. Kemal could represent a more hopeful age of Western liberalism, and al-Bana might be seen in the context of failed alternatives from liberalism to socialism to Arab nationalism. But Kemal's optimism about the West stands in stark contrast to his contemporaries like Gandhi and Lenin, and his democratic secularism is still the guiding principle of Turkey. The Muslim Brotherhood is still a powerful force in Egypt, and today it speaks for only a small part of fundamentalist Islam. But on the infinite channels of satellite radio and television there are many other voices. One recently heard in Cairo is the liberal voice of Gamal al-Banna, the eighty-eight-year-old brother of the founder of the Muslim Brotherhood. He has been a spokesman for religious toleration throughout his life but finds a greater variety of outlets for his views today. "Everything has its time,"[2] Mr. Banna has said.

---

[1] Story told by Thomas J. Harper in "Afterword" to *In Praise of Shadows*, p. 48.

[2] Michael Slackman, "Hints of Pluralism in Egyptian Religious Debates," *New York Times*, August 30, 2009.

24

World War I and Its Consequences

Europe and the Soviet Union, 1914–1920

■ HISTORICAL CONTEXT

The Europe that so many non-European intellectuals sought to imitate or reject between 1880 and 1920 came very close to self-destructing between 1914 and 1918, and bringing many of the world's peoples from Asia, Africa, and the Americas down with it. The orgy of bloodletting, then known as the "Great War," put seventy million men in uniform, of whom ten million were killed and twenty million were wounded. Most of the soldiers were Western European, though Russia contributed more soldiers than France or Germany, while Japan enlisted as many as the Austro-Hungarian Empire that began the war. Enlisted men also came from the United States, Canada, Australia, New Zealand, South Africa, and the colonies: India, French West Africa, and German East Africa, among others. The majority of soldiers were killed in Europe, especially along the German Western Front—four hundred miles of trenches that spanned from Switzerland to the English Channel, across northeastern France. But battles were also fought along the borders of German, French, and English colonies in Africa, and there were high Australian casualties on the coast of Gallipoli in Ottoman Turkey.

The selections in this chapter focus on the lives and deaths of the soldiers, as well as the efforts of some of their political leaders to redefine the world around them. We examine the experiences of soldiers and how the war changed the lives of those who survived its devastating toll. We compare the accounts of those who fought on both sides of the great divide. Germany and the Austro-Hungarian Empire, joined by the Ottoman Empire, formed an alliance called the Central Powers (see Map 24.1).

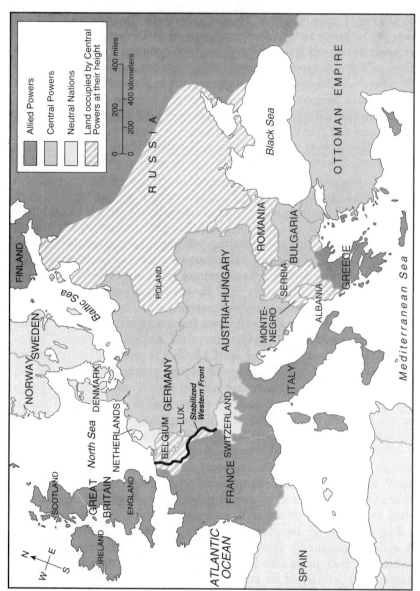

Map 24.1 Allied Powers and Central Powers in World War I.

In opposition, England, France, and Russia, the Allied Powers, were later joined by Italy, Greece, Japan, and the United States. We compare views across the generational divide as well as from the trenches and government offices.

■ THINKING HISTORICALLY

Understanding Causes and Consequences

From 1914 to 1920, the greatest divide was the war itself. It marked the end of one era and the beginning of another. Few events have left the participants with such a profound sense of fundamental change. And so our study of the war is an appropriate place to ask two of the universal questions of major historical change: What caused it? What were the consequences?

The *causes* are those events or forces that came before; the *consequences* are the results, what the war itself prompted to occur. Thus, causes and consequences are part of the same continuum. Still, we must remember that not everything that happened before the war was a cause of the war. Similarly, not everything that happened afterward was a result of the war.

In this chapter we explore specific ideas about cause and consequence. Our goal is not to compile a definitive list of either but, rather, to explore some of the ways that historians and thoughtful readers can make sense of the past.

1

STEPHEN O'SHEA

Back to the Front

The author of this selection is a journalist who recently decided to walk along the site of the famous trenches of World War I, the "Western Front" (west of Germany) that ran through France and Belgium and separated the troops of Belgium, France and its colonies, England and the British Empire, Russia (until 1918), and the United States (beginning in 1917) from those of Germany and the Austro-Hungarian Empire for most of 1914–1918, claiming over two million

Source: Stephen O'Shea, *Back to the Front: An Accidental Historian Walks the Trenches of World War I* (New York: Walker & Company, 1997), 21–30.

lives on each side. As an introduction to the account of his walk, he recalls the opening events of the war. How would you summarize his view of the causes of the war?

THINKING HISTORICALLY

When historians discuss causes, especially of anything as important as a war, they approach the question from many angles, among them the role of particular individuals, the chain of events, the existence of long-term conflicts, government policies, economic interests, communication breakdowns and accidents, mass movements, the viability or frailty of alliances, national interests or international commitments, military preparedness, and the ideas and interests of various domestic parties. From which of these perspectives does O'Shea explain the origin of World War I in this selection? What might be the advantages and disadvantages of some of these different approaches to the question of causes?

Pfft! Pfft!

Two shots were fired at 10:34 A.M., on June 28, 1914, in front of Schiller's Delicatessen in Sarajevo. Gavrilo Princip, the nineteen-year-old Bosnian Serb holding the gun, mortally wounded Franz Ferdinand, the Habsburg heir to the imperial throne of Austria-Hungary, and his wife, Sophie. When they died, about half an hour after Princip had blasted away at point-blank range, the nineteenth century entered its death throes. The event was a fluke: The archduke's driver made a wrong turn onto Appel Quay and had to back up, right into the sights of the scrawny Serb student with the world-historical mission. But for the chauffeur's inept driving, the continent-wide car wreck of the next four years might have been avoided.

Earlier in the morning of that June 28, the victims had been celebrating their fourteenth wedding anniversary. Since Sophie's soon-to-be-spilt blood was not blue enough—she did not have the requisite degrees, or *quartiers*, of nobility—to be accorded formal honors at the Viennese court, her doting archduke of a husband made a point of going to places where she could be given royal treatment. Sarajevo was just such a city. As every protocol martinet in central Europe knew, when Franz Ferdinand acted in a military capacity, in this instance as Inspector General of the Austro-Hungarian army on a tour of the Bosnian capital's garrison, he—and his wife—had to be given the full panoply of feathered deference, decorous bowing, and stylized scraping that Habsburg vanity required. Franz loved his wife, and the cream-puff perquisites of his office.

Princip loved his cause. June 28, 1914, was also the 525th anniversary of the Battle of Kosovo, the resounding defeat that Serbs still perversely celebrate as their nation's brush with greatness and respectability. Today they might mark the occasion by gunning down demonstrators—as they did in Sarajevo, to open the latest bout of barbarity in Bosnia;[1] in Princip's day the anniversary usually called for beetle-browed acts of sedition against foreign overlords. In this the Bosnian Serbs were helped, surreptitiously, by their brethren in Belgrade, who had enjoyed independence in a sovereign Serbia (or "Servia," as it was often called) ever since an earlier conflict had wrested their territory from the control of the Ottoman Turks. And everyone in Europe, then as now, got excited when real estate changed hands.

In fact, all five of the Great Powers—Britain, France, Russia, Austro-Hungary, Germany—were talking Turkey. The Divan, as the Ottoman court was known, had once controlled the Balkans, but Turkey was now the so-called "Sick Man of Europe," a tottering empire no longer able to restrain its restive peoples. As outsiders greedily looked on, insiders weakened the Ottoman presence in Europe. A vocal, dissident faction, impatient with the dotty despots in the Topkapi Palace, agitated for modernization under the name of the Young Turks, a term that entered turn-of-the-century English to describe any collection of lean and hungry hotheads.

This Balkan cocktail of Young Turks (many of whom were Bosnian Muslims), angry Serbs, and smitten Habsburgs was the brew that sent the Old World on its self-destructive bender of 1914–18. Even though Prussian Chancellor Otto von Bismarck had famously adjudged the Balkans undeserving of "the bones of a single Pomeranian grenadier," and every political commentator worth his postprandial cigar had pointed out that, *pace* the English humorist Saki, the benighted region produced more politics than could be consumed locally, it was indeed the mountainous, hidebound, backward Balkans that ushered in—and would later usher out—the twentieth century.

To review: Austria was Hungary, so it took a piece of Turkey. The piece was Bosnia-Herzegovina, annexed in 1908. The powers-that-reclined in Istanbul, enfeebled by recent wars and undermined by the Young Turks, could do nothing to prevent their former possession from slipping away. Serb nationalists in the region were not so listless—they, like most Europeans, knew that Bosnia's latest landlord was far from robust. Istanbul's empire might be a frail old man, but Vienna's was no youngster either, the government of its eighty-four-year-old Emperor Franz Josef renowned for comic opera intrigues and mind-numbing bureaucracy. Serb nationalists in Belgrade and Sarajevo, like their descendants Slobodan Milošević and Radovan Karadžić, saw a power vacuum and dreamed of filling it with Greater Serbia. The most radical

---

[1] Refers to war in Bosnia (1992–1995), especially the massacre of (mainly Muslim) Bosnians by Serbs, in the aftermath of the breakup of Yugoslavia. Slobodan Milošević was Yugoslav president, and Radovan Karadžić became president of the declared independent Serbian state of Bosnia in 1992. Karadžić pursued a policy of "ethnic cleansing" of Bosnian Muslims. Both were tried for war genocide by the International Court at the Hague. Milošević died in custody. [Ed.]

of them formed *Ujedinjeje ili Smrt* (Union or Death), a terrorist group also known as the Black Hand. Run by Colonel Dragutin Dimitrijevic, a loose cannon in the Belgrade government, the organization abetted would-be assassins wherever they served the cause of Serbian nationhood. Dimitrijevic, a bald colossus who today would not look out of place wrestling on TV, went by the name of Apis, the potent bull in the pantheon of ancient Egypt. Apis supplied Princip and his fellow conspirators with the guns to do the dirty deed in Sarajevo. Thus it was Apis and his bloody-minded Black Hand, the template for all the semi-official dirty tricks squads to have enlivened recent history, that delivered the ultimate insult to the spluttering autocrats of Austria. . . .

When the authorities in Vienna learned of Franz Ferdinand's murder, they saw a golden opportunity to squelch the upstart on their southern border. Foreign Minister Leopold von Berchtold, the man most at fault for the ensuing debacle, issued the Serbian government a blisteringly severe ultimatum, the terms of which were tantamount to surrendering sovereignty. The advisers of Serbia's King Peter, suitably cowed by the Habsburg tantrum, agreed to comply with all of the demands contained in von Berchtold's ultimatum save one—the order giving Austrian police a free hand on Serbian soil. Rather like an old man buying a red sports car, the Austro-Hungarian empire then declared war on Serbia. By telegram, in French. It was 1:00 P.M., July 28, 1914.

The story now leaves the precincts of south-central Europe to involve the rest of the continent. Over the years a system of alliances had developed to transform international affairs into a shifting, intrigue-ridden round of diplomatic skirmishing that gave a civilized veneer to the cutthroat commercial rivalries of the time. Crises in Morocco and the Balkans came and went in the first decade of the century, causing mustaches to moisten and horses to snort, but large-scale wars had always been averted. The game of diplomacy was wonderful and glamorous and cosmopolitan and aristocratic, but in the summer of 1914 it fell apart. The well-bred grandees in the chancelleries and foreign offices drafted their customary cables and issued their usual exquisitely worded warnings, all to no avail. In its final, prewar stages, diplomacy slipped out of civilian control to fall in step with the implacable logic of military timetables. When that happened, the traditional ruling classes of Europe became history, in the Boomer sense of the word. They had delivered their citizenry into the maw of the industrial battlefield. At war's end, they would not be forgiven.

The road to the Western Front began in the east. Austria's bullying of Serbia induced Russia to order the mobilization of its troops. Pan-Slavic nationalists in Petrograd (as St. Petersburg was then called) viewed the Slavs of the Balkans as their protégés. The armies of Czar Nicholas II headed by the millions toward the western borders of Russia. Germany, the industrial and military powerhouse under the somewhat loopy leadership of Kaiser Wilhelm II, was aghast. The government in Berlin had foolishly given its ally Austria a "blank check"—that is, a guarantee of assistance no matter what the outcome of its saber-rattling policy toward the Serbs. Now, panic-stricken at the results, Germany demanded that Russia stop its mobilization.

This was easier demanded than done. Mobilization was a machine years in the planning that required massive resources to effect quickly, so you couldn't just stop it halfway and run all the troop trains backward—unless you were willing to leave yourself defenseless in the ensuing chaos. Naturally, Russia refused to do this.

Not that getting your army up to strength and poised on your borders necessarily meant you were going to war. When France, an ally of Russia at the time, began mobilizing in the last days of July, it was preparing for hostilities, not starting them. Likewise Austria-Hungary, Russia, Serbia, Great Britain, and Turkey. This may seem like hairsplitting, but it's not—there's a big difference between pointing a pistol at someone and actually shooting him. In only one country was this distinction not made: Germany.

In the 1890s a Prussian military planner, Count Alfred von Schlieffen, had rightly surmised that Germany might one day have to face hostile armies in both the east and the west. He, like all German policy makers, feared *Einkreisung*, or encirclement. Positing that his country could not wage a victorious war on two fronts at once, Schlieffen masterminded a scheme whereby the Kaiser's armies would deliver a knockout blow to France, then race over the rails to deal with the Russians. Speed was of the essence for the Schlieffen Plan. When German fighting forces mobilized they would automatically blast their way into France. And, to get there, they would surprise everyone by marching through neutral Belgium. So what if this bald violation of treaties brought in Britain against them? As a German military planner had once said of the prospect of the British sending their small professional army to the Continent: "If the British land, we'll arrest them." . . .

The Schlieffen Plan laid out the route of attack. The bulk of the German army—its right wing—would swing through Belgium, skirt the Atlantic coast, pass west and then south of Paris. By doing this it could eventually encircle the French armies that, Schlieffen had once again correctly surmised, would be busy throwing themselves at well-fortified defensive lines to regain Alsace and Lorraine. Indeed, since the debacle of the Franco-Prussian War of 1870, in which France had lost Alsace and Lorraine, the general staff of its army had thought of little else but recovering the two provinces from the Germans. Out of this keen sense of injured pride came a military doctrine that elevated the attack to an almost quasi-mystical status. Attacking *a outrance* (to the utmost), no matter what the terrain or the strength of the opposition, entailed wearing the dashing but conspicuous red trousers and blue coat of the infantryman and running directly at enemy machine-gun fire, presumably protected from injury by one's warrior insouciance, or *élan*. Such were the pitifully inadequate tactics taught at elite French military academies. Their strategic thinking, which had been dignified by the name of "Plan XVII," called for remorseless, predictable, frontal attacks into Alsace and Lorraine. As in 1870 and 1940, in August 1914 the French were hopelessly outsmarted by the Germans.

Under the command of Joseph Jacques Césaire Joffre, an avuncular officer with a seemingly boundless appetite for casualties, the French army went to the slaughter, launching attack after attack à outrance until entire battalions were annihilated. In the summer and fall of 1914, France lost as many men on the battlefield as the American army would in all of the twentieth century. Their conscript army was thrown away by incompetent generalship. In the month of August alone, more than 210,000 Frenchmen died in the headlong offensives of Plan XVII. The bloodbath was more than appalling, it was absurd.

Joffre blamed his subordinates. He demoted dozens of generals and sent them to the city of Limoges for reassignment: whence the French verb *limoger* for any high-profile firing. According to many accounts, Joffre's imperturbable demeanor in the face of horrific losses sometimes reassured but more often repelled. The sacredness of the general's stomach—Joffre always had two well-cooked, uninterrupted feasts a day, no matter how dire the military situation—contrasted dramatically with his callow disregard for the lives of his soldiers.

While Joffre minded his digestion and sent tens of thousands to their doom in the east, 750,000 Germans were walking toward France from the north. As the Kaiser's armies advanced through Belgium, they carried out a highly publicized policy of *Schrecklichkeit*, or "Frightfulness," meant to discourage any attempts at civilian resistance. Hostages were taken and shot, and cities were burned, a brutal overture for the total war to come. The Belgians became a nation of refugees, crowding the roads south to France and the boats over to England. Of the hundred thousand or so who reached Britain, the most famous of the lot never really landed there at all because he was, in point of fact, fictional. Like his unfortunate compatriots, Hercule Poirot, Agatha Christie's sleuth, was chased from his homeland by Schrecklichkeit. (Why else would a Belgian detective be living in London?)

The Belgian refugees were welcomed as heroes. In Britain enthusiasm for the war ran high. Shopkeepers with German surnames had their businesses patriotically looted, and, in just the first month of a recruiting drive for a volunteer army, half a million young Britons rushed to sign up to avenge what was called "poor little Belgium." It is difficult to imagine the naïveté of expectations, the trust in one's country, the excitement of being young in that summer of 1914. . . .

On August 23, 1914, a small force of the British army fought the advancing Germans at Mons, Belgium. It was the first time the British had fought in Europe since defeating Napoleon at nearby Waterloo, ninety-nine years previously. Although ludicrously outnumbered, since neither the French nor the British command had yet figured out that the main German offensive was coming through Belgium, they held off their attackers for a full day before beating a tactical retreat. The engagement, minor in comparison to the suicidal French maneuvers in Lorraine, nonetheless loomed large in the collective imagination of the British Isles. . . .

The British and the French fell back in desperation as the size of the German onslaught coming from the north dawned at last on the dim minds sharing dinner with Joffre. The French commander, unflappable as ever, ordered a full-scale retreat so that his shattered armies could regroup and finally do something other than die in futile assaults in the east of the country. In the meantime, the Germans continued their march south and came closer and closer to Paris. When Alexander von Kluck, the commander of the now tired 350,000-man corps on the extreme right of the German lines, elected to go east rather than west of the French capital and cross the River Marne, the reinforced Allied legions wheeled about and attacked. The Battle of the Marne raged from September 6 to 9, and involved more than two million men. The Kaiser's armies, overextended and far from their supply lines, blinked first.

The giant German attacking force then retreated northward, to the heights overlooking the next major river: the Aisne, in Champagne. There they dug trenches, set up machine-gun nests, and mowed down waves of infantrymen foolishly ordered to take a run at the German lines. They could not be budged. It was late September 1914. Realizing, temporarily, that the best way to defeat a dug-in army was not to attack it head-on, the Allied generals had their exhausted troops attempt flanking movements—that is, they tried to swing around and attack their opponents from the side. This led to a series of fierce battles up through northern France and eventually back into Belgium, as each adversary frantically tried to encircle the other. It came to be known as "the Race to the Sea," but was more akin to a zipper closing. With each failed flanking movement, the armies dug in, extended the miles of trenches, and moved farther north to attack again.

In Flanders they hit the sea. It was the end of October. The German high command sensed that, at Ypres,* the ragged British lines that were just forming could be easily smashed. It was their last chance to thwart *Stellungskrieg*, or the war of position that the framer of the Schlieffen Plan had so single-mindedly striven to avoid. The Kaiser came to watch. His officers, anticipating the Aryan prose of a German army a generation later, issued the following message to their troops on October 30, 1914:

> The breakthrough will be of decisive importance. We must and therefore will conquer, settle forever the centuries-long struggle, end the war, and strike the decisive blow against our most detested

---

* EEE pruh

enemy. We will finish the British, Indians, Canadians, Moroccans, and other trash, feeble adversaries, who surrender in great numbers if they are attacked with vigor.

They did not succeed, but only by a hair-breadth. In one particularly dramatic moment during the murderous melee, a British commander rounded up a squadron of cooks to plug a gaping hole in the lines to the east of Ypres; in another, a major launched a foolhardy counterattack because he had not enough men left alive to mount a credible defense. Both tactics worked, stalling the German assaults at a critical juncture and thus thwarting their plans for a rout. There would be no breakthrough, ever.

It was late November 1914. The digging started in earnest from Nieuport to Switzerland. The Western Front went underground,[2] as did an unimaginable number of young men killed in the three-month-old war. British propagandists, stunned by the near extermination of the 100,000-man force sent across the Channel in August, searched for a symbol to keep civilian enthusiasm at a fever pitch. They found one in Ypres. It would have to pass for the infantry's apotheosis, a sort of Anglo Alamo in the muddy slough of Flanders. Only here the fort would not be overrun, the enemy would not get through the gates. No matter what the cost, Ypres would not be surrendered.

Thus was born the Salient,[3] the death trap into which the English general staff would place its citizen army. A German officer remarked that British soldiers were "lions led by donkeys."

[2] In trenches. [Ed.]
[3] Area around Ypres surrounded by German troops on three sides. [Ed.]

2

ERICH MARIA REMARQUE

All Quiet on the Western Front

All Quiet on the Western Front, one of the most famous war novels ever written, follows the daily routines of the German army on the "Western Front," the long line of trenches that stretched across northern France from Switzerland to the English Channel for most of the war between 1914 and 1918. In this selection from the beginning of the novel, the narrator recalls how his teacher, Kantorek, induced him and his friends to enlist. Now one of them, Franz Kemmerich, has

Source: Erich Maria Remarque, *All Quiet on the Western Front*, trans. A. W. Wheen (New York: Fawcett Books, 1929), 1–18.

been seriously wounded and the group of friends visit him. What does this selection suggest about the types of people recruited to serve in the army? How do they experience the war, and how does it change them? Do you imagine these German soldiers behaved very differently from French or English soldiers?

THINKING HISTORICALLY

Remarque's novel is not intended as an explanation of the causes of war, but this excerpt sheds light on what caused men to support the war and enlist. How might you use material from this novel, assuming that it is based on fact, to propose at least one cause of World War I?

In this brief selection, the author also suggests something about the consequences of the war. What are the war's likely outcomes projected here?

Kantorek had been our schoolmaster, a stern little man in a grey tail-coat, with a face like a shrew mouse. He was about the same size as Corporal Himmelstoss, the "terror of Klosterberg." It is very queer that the unhappiness of the world is so often brought on by small men. They are so much more energetic and uncompromising than the big fellows. I have always taken good care to keep out of sections with small company commanders. They are mostly confounded little martinets.

During drill-time Kantorek gave us long lectures until the whole of our class went, under his shepherding, to the District Commandant and volunteered. I can see him now, as he used to glare at us through his spectacles and say in a moving voice: "Won't you join up, Comrades?"

These teachers always carry their feelings ready in their waistcoat pockets, and trot them out by the hour. But we didn't think of that then.

There was, indeed, one of us who hesitated and did not want to fall into line. That was Joseph Behm, a plump, homely fellow. But he did allow himself to be persuaded, otherwise he would have been ostracized. And perhaps more of us thought as he did, but no one could very well stand out, because at that time even one's parents were ready with the word "coward"; no one had the vaguest idea what we were in for. The wisest were just the poor and simple people. They knew the war to be a misfortune, whereas those who were better off, and should have been able to see more clearly what the consequences would be, were beside themselves with joy.

Katczinsky said that was a result of their upbringing. It made them stupid. And what Kat said, he had thought about.

Strange to say, Behm was one of the first to fall. He got hit in the eye during an attack, and we left him lying for dead. We couldn't bring him with us, because we had to come back helter-skelter. In the afternoon suddenly we heard him call, and saw him crawling about in No Man's Land. He had only been knocked unconscious. Because he could not see, and was mad with pain, he failed to keep under cover, and so was shot down before anyone could go and fetch him in.

Naturally we couldn't blame Kantorek for this. Where would the world be if one brought every man to book? There were thousands of Kantoreks, all of whom were convinced that they were acting for the best — in a way that cost them nothing.

And that is why they let us down so badly.

For us lads of eighteen they ought to have been mediators and guides to the world of maturity, the world of work, of duty, of culture, of progress — to the future. We often made fun of them and played jokes on them, but in our hearts we trusted them. The idea of authority, which they represented, was associated in our minds with a greater insight and a more humane wisdom. But the first death we saw shattered this belief. We had to recognize that our generation was more to be trusted than theirs. They surpassed us only in phrases and in cleverness. The first bombardment showed us our mistake, and under it the world as they had taught it to us broke in pieces.

While they continued to write and talk, we saw the wounded and dying. While they taught that duty to one's country is the greatest thing, we already knew that death-throes are stronger. But for all that we were no mutineers, no deserters, no cowards — they were very free with all these expressions. We loved our country as much as they; we went courageously into every action; but also we distinguished the false from true, we had suddenly learned to see. And we saw that there was nothing of their world left. We were all at once terribly alone; and alone we must see it through.

Before going over to see Kemmerich we pack up his things: He will need them on the way back.

In the dressing station there is great activity: It reeks as ever of carbolic, pus, and sweat. We are accustomed to a good deal in the billets, but this makes us feel faint. We ask for Kemmerich. He lies in a large room and receives us with feeble expressions of joy and helpless agitation. While he was unconscious someone had stolen his watch.

Müller shakes his head: "I always told you that nobody should carry as good a watch as that."

Müller is rather crude and tactless, otherwise he would hold his tongue, for anybody can see that Kemmerich will never come out of this place again. Whether he finds his watch or not will make no difference, at the most one will only be able to send it to his people.

"How goes it, Franz?" asks Kropp.

Kemmerich's head sinks.

"Not so bad . . . but I have such a damned pain in my foot."

We look at his bed covering. His leg lies under a wire basket. The bed covering arches over it. I kick Müller on the shin, for he is just about to tell Kemmerich what the orderlies told us outside: that Kemmerich has lost his foot. The leg is amputated. He looks ghastly, yellow and wan. In his face there are already the strained lines that we know so well, we have seen them now hundreds of times. They are not so much lines as marks. Under the skin the life no longer pulses, it has already pressed out the boundaries of the body. Death is working through from within. It already has command in the eyes. Here lies our comrade, Kemmerich, who a little while ago was roasting horse flesh with us and squatting in the shellholes. He it is still and yet it is not he any longer. His features have become uncertain and faint, like a photographic plate from which two pictures have been taken. Even his voice sounds like ashes.

I think of the time when we went away. His mother, a good plump matron, brought him to the station. She wept continually, her face was bloated and swollen. Kemmerich felt embarrassed, for she was the least composed of all; she simply dissolved into fat and water. Then she caught sight of me and took hold of my arm again and again, and implored me to look after Franz out there. Indeed he did have a face like a child, and such frail bones that after four weeks' pack-carrying he already had flat feet. But how can a man look after anyone in the field!

"Now you will soon be going home," says Kropp. "You would have had to wait at least three or four months for your leave."

Kemmerich nods. I cannot bear to look at his hands, they are like wax. Under the nails is the dirt of the trenches, it shows through blue-black like poison. It strikes me that these nails will continue to grow like lean fantastic cellar-plants long after Kemmerich breathes no more. I see the picture before me. They twist themselves into corkscrews and grow and grow, and with them the hair on the decaying skull, just like grass in a good soil, just like grass, how can it be possible———

Müller leans over. "We have brought your things, Franz."

Kemmerich signs with his hands. "Put them under the bed."

Müller does so. Kemmerich starts on again about the watch. How can one calm him without making him suspicious?

Müller reappears with a pair of airman's boots. They are fine English boots of soft, yellow leather which reach to the knees and lace up all the way—they are things to be coveted.

Müller is delighted at the sight of them. He matches their soles against his own clumsy boots and says: "Will you be taking them with you then, Franz?"

We all three have the same thought; even if he should get better, he would be able to use only one—they are no use to him. But as things are now it is a pity that they should stay here; the orderlies will of course grab them as soon as he is dead.

"Won't you leave them with us?" Müller repeats.

Kemmerich doesn't want to. They are his most prized possessions.

"Well, we could exchange," suggests Müller again. "Out here one can make some use of them." Still Kemmerich is not to be moved.

I tread on Müller's foot; reluctantly he puts the fine boots back again under the bed.

We talk a little more and then take our leave.

"Cheerio, Franz."

I promise him to come back in the morning. Müller talks of doing so, too. He is thinking of the lace-up boots and means to be on the spot.

Kemmerich groans. He is feverish. We get hold of an orderly outside and ask him to give Kemmerich a dose of morphia.

He refuses. "If we were to give morphia to everyone we would have to have tubs full——— "

"You only attend to officers properly," says Kropp viciously.

I hastily intervene and give him a cigarette. He takes it.

"Are you usually allowed to give it, then?" I ask him.

He is annoyed. "If you don't think so, then why do you ask?"

I press a few more cigarettes into his hand. "Do us the favour——— "

"Well, all right," he says.

Kropp goes in with him. He doesn't trust him and wants to see. We wait outside.

Müller returns to the subject of the boots. "They would fit me perfectly. In these boots I get blister after blister. Do you think he will last till tomorrow after drill? If he passes out in the night, we know where the boots——— "

Kropp returns. "Do you think———?" he asks.

"Done for," said Müller emphatically.

We go back to the huts. I think of the letter that I must write tomorrow to Kemmerich's mother. I am freezing. I could do with a tot of rum. Müller pulls up some grass and chews it. Suddenly little Kropp throws his cigarette away, stamps on it savagely, and looking around him with a broken and distracted face, stammers "Damned shit, the damned shit!"

We walk on for a long time. Kropp has calmed himself; we understand, he saw red; out there every man gets like that sometime.

"What has Kantorek written to you?" Müller asks him.

He laughs. "We are the Iron Youth."

We all three smile bitterly, Kropp rails: He is glad that he can speak.

Yes, that's the way they think, these hundred thousand Kantoreks! Iron Youth! Youth! We are none of us more than twenty years old. But young? Youth? That is long ago. We are old folk.

3

World War I Propaganda Posters

Posters were the communication medium of the First World War. In an age when governments had still not taught most people how to read but increasingly needed their consent or compliance, images often spoke louder than words, but those images had to be *persuasive.*

The American poster from 1917 and the German poster from 1915–1916 (Figures 24.1 and 24.3) implore men to enlist in the

Figure 24.1   Recruiting Poster for U.S. Army.

Figure 24.2　Italian Poster for National War Loan, 1917.
Source: Snark/Art Resource, NY.

army; the Italian poster from 1917 (Figure 24.2) encourages people to buy war bonds. What do you think accounts for the similar graphic style used in these three posters? How effective do you think they were, and why?

Another strategy for promoting loyalty, patriotism, and support for a war that was lasting far longer than anyone had anticipated was to demonize or ridicule the enemy. What feelings does the U.S.

Figure 24.3   Recruiting Poster for German Army, 1915–1916.

anti-German poster from 1916 (Figure 24.4) attempt to provoke in viewers, and how does the scene shown achieve this?

Women contributed to the war in various ways. Figure 24.5 asks German women to contribute their gold. Figure 24.6 urges women in London to come to work in the munitions industry. What images of women do these posters portray? Finally, Figure 24.7 asks Americans to support Armenian refugees from the Ottoman Empire in newly proclaimed independent Armenia and Syria. What response is the image of woman and child supposed to evoke?

THINKING HISTORICALLY

When war broke out overseas in 1914, President Woodrow Wilson declared it a European matter that had nothing to do with the United States, and most Americans agreed. Indeed, the United States did

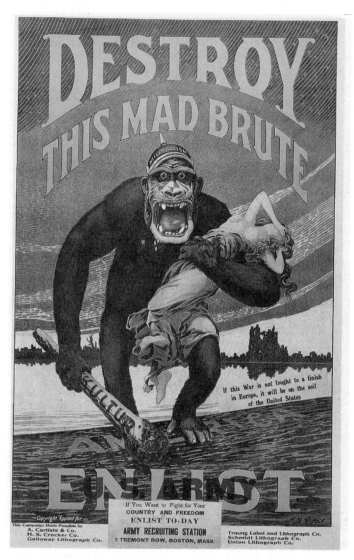

Figure 24.4   Propaganda Poster, United States, 1916.

not join the war and throw its crucial weight behind the Allied Powers until April 1917. What role do you think propaganda such as Figure 24.4 played in swaying public opinion? This and the other posters illustrate both sides' efforts to promote and sustain the cause of war. What do they tell you about the causes of the war? What do they tell you about the consequences?

Figure 24.5 German Appeal to Women: Gold for the War.
Source: Library of Congress.

Figure 24.6   English Appeal to Women: Munitions Work.

Source: World War Poster Collection, Manuscripts Division, University of Minnesota Libraries, Minneapolis, MN.

YOU CAN'T LET US STARVE

2½ million women and children now starving to death.

YOUR BIT SAVES A LIFE

Send Money to

ARMENIAN and SYRIAN RELIEF

1 Madison Ave. N.Y. City

Figure 24.7 "Your Bit Saves a Life."

Source: World War Poster Collection, Manuscripts Division, University of Minnesota Libraries, Minneapolis, MN.

4

WILFRED OWEN

Dulce et Decorum Est

Wilfred Owen (1893–1918) enlisted in the British Army in 1915, was wounded in 1917, and was hospitalized, released, and sent back to the front, where he died on November 4, 1918, one week before the end of the war. In this poem, he describes a poison gas attack. Like the machine gun and the airplane, gas was a common element of the new mechanized mass warfare. Owen describes how physically debilitating the effects of gas were. Why was gas such an effective and deadly weapon? How, according to Owen, had the nature of war changed?

THINKING HISTORICALLY

The concluding phrase, which means "Sweet and proper it is to die for one's country," was a Latin declaration of patriotic duty that English students repeated as a lesson, not only in Latin classes but, more importantly, in their political education as subjects of the British Empire. How does Owen portray this lesson as a cause of the war? What does he imagine to be the consequences of fighting a war with such patriotic slogans in mind? How does Owen's attitude toward patriotism compare with that of Remarque?

Dulce et Decorum Est

Bent double, like old beggars under sacks,
Knock-kneed, coughing like hags, we cursed through sludge,
Till on the haunting flares we turned our backs
And towards our distant rest began the trudge.
Men marched asleep. Many had lost their boots
But limped on, blood-shod. All went lame; all blind;
Drunk with fatigue; deaf even to the hoots
Of tired, outstripped Five-Nines[1] that dropped behind.

Gas! GAS! Quick, boys!—An ecstasy of fumbling,
Fitting the clumsy helmets just in time;
But someone still was yelling out and stumbling,
And flound'ring like a man in fire or lime. . . .

[1] German artillery shells. [Ed.]

Source: Wilfred Owen, *Poems*, ed. Siegfried Sassoon (London: Chatto and Windus, 1920).

Dim, through the misty panes and thick green light,
As under a green sea, I saw him drowning.

In all my dreams, before my helpless sight,
He plunges at me, guttering, choking, drowning.

If in some smothering dreams you too could pace
Behind the wagon that we flung him in,
And watch the white eyes writhing in his face,
His hanging face, like a devil's sick of sin;
If you could hear, at every jolt, the blood
Come gargling from the froth-corrupted lungs,
Obscene as cancer, bitter as the cud
Of vile, incurable sores on innocent tongues,
My friend, you would not tell with such high zest,
To children ardent for some desperate glory.
The old Lie: Dulce et decorum est
Pro patria mori.

5

Memories of Senegalese Soldiers

Not only did the roots of the First World War lie in competing imperial claims, but some of the fighting took place along imperial divides of colonies as well. Africans in French and English colonies were mobilized to fight Africans in neighboring German colonies, and vice versa. In addition, many Africans were mobilized to fight in Europe, especially after European troops suffered heavy losses along the Western Front. Over 140,000 West Africans were recruited into the French Army between 1914 and 1918 to serve in Europe. Some 45,000 never returned. Senegal mobilized more than other colonies: 29,000, probably more than one-third of the men of military age.

The historian Joe Lunn interviewed eighty-five of these Senegalese veterans for his book *Memoirs of the Maelstrom: A Senegalese Oral History of the First World War*, from which these selections are drawn. What do these various Senegalese voices tell you about the African experience in the First World War? How was their

Source: Joe Lunn, *Memoirs of the Maelstrom: A Senegalese Oral History of the First World War* (Portsmouth, NH: Heinemann, 1999), 40, 42, 78–79, 97–98, 102–3, 110, 137, 165–66, 172–73, 174, 108–9, 190, 230, 232–33. Headings added, individual names and footnotes deleted.

experience of the war different from that of European soldiers? How were Senegalese soldiers recruited, and why did they enlist? What were their expectations?

THINKING HISTORICALLY

These memories provide greater insight into the consequences than the causes of World War I. How did the war change the lives of those African troops who survived? How did it change the way the Senegalese and French thought of themselves and each other?

[Recruitment]

Many of the young men fled from the village [when the *chef de canton* came to take soldiers]. [But] they used to arrest their fathers [if] they [did not] come back. [And] often their mothers used to say to their sons [when they returned from the countryside for food]: "You know that your name has been written [down by the *che de canton*] and [yet] you ran away. And now your father has been arrested and he will be taken [to] prison. So go and enter the army." And often they used to go and enter the army [so that] their fathers [would be] released.

In each family they only took one young man, never two. And my father decided that I should go and enter the army instead of my elder brother. Because, he told me: "If I die, your elder brother could care for the family, but you are too young for that." That's why he sent me into the army. I was not happy to go, [but] because I was very close to my father . . . I felt obliged to.

I was in Bamako [on leave] when Blaise Diagne and Galandou Diouf[1] came to recruit soldiers. [And my friend and I] attended the meeting he called for recruitment. [And] Blaise Diagne's propaganda [at] this meeting [was very effective]. Because, before he came, he had made the son of the *chef de quartier* in Bamako a lieutenant. [So] almost all the town was there, because the chief had called everybody, and there were a lot, a lot, a lot of people! The fact that Blaise Diagne had made his son a lieutenant was a very important thing for him personally, because . . . for the Bambara becoming an officer in the army was a very great honor. [And Diagne came] with many, many people—August Brunet [the lieutenant

---

[1] Blaise Diagne (1872–1934), from Senegal, became in 1914 the first black African elected to the French national parliament where he fought for and won the right of urban Senegalese to be citizens and soldiers. He was appointed by French prime minister George Clemenceau to head the recruitment drive in French West Africa during the war. Galandou Diouf (1875–1941), the first black African elected (in 1909) to the Senegalese assembly, was Diagne's assistant. They argued that military service was a vehicle to full and equal citizenship for Africans. [Ed.]

governor of Haut-Sénégal et Niger] and [other] French administrators. [And] he was [accompanied by] some Bambara soldiers too. But they were not simple soldiers; all of them had *"grades."*[2] [And after speeches by Galandou Diouf, the *chef de quartier*, and his son, Diagne spoke.] [And although] I have forgotten almost all his speech, I remember that he told them that he was sent by the President of the Republic of France who needed [more] soldiers to go on fighting. And after [he finished], he introduced the son of the *chef de quartier* to [all] the other parents that were at the meeting. [And he told them:] "I want some other soldiers to enter the army, so perhaps they too can become lieutenants." So as soon as he said that, everybody gave him the name of his son. And the secretary was writing down their names. [And] that's why he succeeded with his recruitment mission [among the Bambara]—[because] everybody was expecting his son to become an officer one day.

[Becoming Soldiers]

We all joined the same army—the French army. . . . So we did not think about our [previous] way of living, our behavior, our [former] kingdoms. We were bound to follow the French regulations and their way of thinking about all these things. [And although] little arguments sometimes [occurred] between soldiers from the same country, [the status of a man's family] wasn't stressed. . . . There wasn't any [social] differentiation [with regard to slaves] because we were following another system—another [way of] life—which was the French one.

[Departures]

We [sailed from Dakar] on a boat called *l'Afrique* on May 9, 1916. There was a French officer with us—[a lieutenant called Oeuvre]—[who] was a very very bad man. We spent [the first] three days [being allowed to go on deck] in the boat . . . and we had a good journey. [But] when we arrived at a place called "the Gulf" [Golfe de Gascogne] . . . this French officer said that all the soldiers had to go downstairs—deep inside the ship. And he put [a guard] at the door [to prevent] any of us from going out. . . . And we [were confined for] the [next] six days in the bottom [of the boat near] the keel. [And] we suffered a lot in the bottom of the ship because there was no air. From time to time they opened the [portholes] to let some air [in, but] after that they closed them [again]. And even during meals, we were eating in the bottom of the ship. And it was very hot [there] and it was very tight.

[2] Ranks. [Ed.]

[In France]

When we went [to the camps in France,] Diagne joined us [there] to see about our conditions. Whenever you had problems, he came and solved them. Sometimes the food was bad or insufficient, for example. [So] when Diagne came, if we said the food was not good, he called the officers together and asked [them] why. He said, "I brought soldiers to fight for you and to help you. And I don't see why you treat them like this!" So he would tear off the ranks [of insignia] of the officers and put them on the table.

We felt very proud after the attack because the French had tried many times to retake the fort, but finally, we [were the ones] that took it. . . . And when we were leaving the fort, our officers told us not to wash our uniforms even though they were very dirty and covered with mud. But we were told: "Don't wash your uniforms. Cross the country as you are so that everyone who meets you will know that you made the attack on Fort Douaumont." And we took the train [and traveled] for three days between Douaumont and St. Raphäel. And in every town we crossed, the French were clapping their hands and shouting: "*Vive les tirailleurs sénégalais!*" . . . And afterwards, whenever we were walking in the country—everywhere we used to go—if we told people that we made the attack on Fort Douaumont, the French were looking at us with much admiration.

One day I was in the [mess hall] in the camp [where] we used to eat. And often after eating, we used to drink coffee in cups. But before drinking it, we used to make "cheers" with the other soldiers. So on this day, I took my cup and I wanted to make "cheers" with a French soldier who was sitting next to me. So I made the "cheers," [but] the soldier said to me, "don't touch my cup, you are too dirty!" And [this made] me very angry. [So] I punched him and we began to fight. And when they went to get the captain, the captain told me that I was right, and he told the French soldier that he would be punished. But afterwards, I became very friendly with this same soldier.

I had a very good [French] friend—his name was Perout—[and we] were in the same unit. . . . I was his only African friend, [but] we spent a lot of time together. [And] I often went to his house [when on leave]. He invited me [there] for lunch, or dinner, and sometimes I spent the night. . . . And when his [family] came to visit him, they kissed me before they kissed him—his father, his mother, and his sisters.

"*Marraine de guerre*" . . . was the term used by the soldiers to say "my girlfriend"; instead of saying "my girlfriend," they said "my *marraine de guerre.*" [And] the African soldiers in France had their *marraines de guerre* too. They were not prostitutes. They were girls of good families who saw us and knew that we were [far from] our countries. [And they realized] we needed some affection and some money . . . to buy cigarettes with, to go to the movies, and so on.

[And we met them] on the street or in cafés. A French girl saw you and felt very pleased by [your appearance]. And she said to you that she wanted to take you to her house to present you to her parents. And you got [an adopted] French family in that way. [But] it wasn't necessary to have love affairs [with them]. From time to time some *marraines de guerre* fell in love with the soldiers they invited home. But generally, they were only friendly relations.

Some of the French who had never seen a "black" man used to pay to come and see us. [And the European soldiers] were making money selling tickets. [They] used to take us to a hidden place and told us: "Stay here. We are going to bring some Frenchmen who have never seen 'black' people before." [But] we didn't know they were making money in that way.

[And after they] got the money, they used to bring the *Tubabs*[3] to look at us. And [they] said: "This one is a Senegalese, this one is a Somalian, [and so forth]." And the *Tubabs* were touching us, and peeking, creeping very close to us because we [looked so different].

[Return]

One day [we were on] the ship that brought us back to Senegal from Bordeaux. . . . There were [many] Senegalese soldiers [aboard, and sometimes] they got into arguments with some of the "white" men who treated them like "dirty niggers." . . . And one of these soldiers—a citizen from Goree—was [called] a "*sale nègre*" by a "white" man. . . . I think maybe the [French]man was not well educated, or perhaps he was drunk. [And the soldier hit] him hard . . . and [they] started fighting. [And] we all [joined in] and started to give our friend some help. And we beat [the Frenchman] badly until he asked to be forgiven. He was crying and said that he would never do it again.

So what happened [afterwards]? Nothing! We were within our rights, because discrimination between people [was no longer tolerated] at that time, [and] we were French citizens like anybody else. [If] the "white" man wanted to start acting like that, we [could retaliate] and nothing happened. [But] if the same thing had happened before the war, [we] would not have done the same thing. Because we had

[3] Europeans. [Ed.]

less power then, and [we] were treated badly like this [by the French] all the time.

[The parents of those who had been killed] knew the number of soldiers who went to the war together, and they [also] knew the number of soldiers who came back. So no one [had to tell] them that their sons were dead; they guessed it [on their own]. [But afterward], we told them how they died. Those [of us who] knew their sons had died explained to their families [what had happened to them]. . . . [I had to do this once.] . . . A son [from my grandfather's family] was lost in Champagne. . . . And [they] knew that we went [to the war] together. But when I came back, they didn't see him. And after a while, they began to ask me where he was. And I told them: "He is dead; you have to make the sacrifices."

[After the War]

We went to France, we fought for France, and the French took us by force to fight for them. [But] we learned nothing [there]—[not] even the French language. They only taught us some rudimentary [commands], [in order] to use us in the war. But they didn't care about teaching us the structure and the sound of their language. So [although we] went to the war, [we] came back here without any real knowledge of the French language.

I received many lasting things from the war. I demonstrated my dignity and courage, and [I] won the respect of the people and the [colonial] government. And whenever the people of the village had something to contest [with the French]—and they didn't dare do it [themselves] because they were afraid of them—I used to do it for them. And many times when people had problems with the government, I used to go with my decorations and arrange the situation for [them]. Because whenever the *Tubabs* saw your decorations, they knew that they [were dealing with] a very important person. . . . And I gained this ability—of obtaining justice over a *Tubab*—from the war.

The war changed many, many things. At first, when we joined the army, when you had an argument or a problem with a "white" man, what happened? You were wrong; you were [always] wrong. But later, those things changed. [Then] they looked into the matter and determined who was wrong or right. [But] before that time, the "black" man didn't mean anything. So that [change] was something [very important]. [And] the respect we gained [from] the war [continued] increasing; it never [diminished]. [And this] respect [continued] increasing day to day—up until [it culminated in] the Independence Day.

6

V. I. LENIN

War and Revolution

One of the great casualties of the First World War was the Russian Empire, including the czar, his family, many of the members of their class, and its centuries-old autocratic system. The burden of war was simply too much for Russian society to bear. The disillusionment in the army and civilian society, along with the overwhelming costs of war, fueled uprisings among civilians and the army, and Czar Nicholas II was forced to abdicate in February of 1917. The government that emerged, under Alexander Kerensky, proved unable to satisfy the growing demands of peasants, veterans, and urban workers for "land, peace, and bread," a slogan that V. I. Lenin (1870–1924) and the communists exploited, successfully seizing power from the moderate parliamentarians in October of that year.

As a Marxist, Lenin believed that he could establish a socialist society in Russia, but he argued that Russian conditions (such as economic underdevelopment; the devastation of war; the opposition of Europe, the United States, and Russian nobles to the revolution) made a democratic transition impossible. According to Lenin, a self-appointed government acting in the interests of the working class was the only way to a socialist Soviet Union. Lenin called this government "the dictatorship of the proletariat." Lenin delivered his "War and Revolution" address in May of 1917, during the fateful summer that followed the liberal February revolution and preceded the Bolshevik revolution in October. How did Lenin view the First World War and Russia's continued participation in it? What did he hope to accomplish in the summer of 1917? How did he hope to accomplish it? The most important news for Russia's allies, England and France, in the summer of 1917 was the United States' entry into the war on their behalf. What was Lenin's reaction to this development?

THINKING HISTORICALLY

According to Lenin, what were the causes of the First World War? What did he believe to be the main cause of the Russian revolution that occurred in February? What were the consequences of that revolution? What did he think would be the causes of a new revolution in Russia?

Source: V. I. Lenin, *Collected Works*, 4th English ed. (Moscow: Progress Publishers, 1964), 24:398–421.

What we have at present is primarily two leagues, two groups of capitalist powers. We have before us all the world's greatest capitalist powers—Britain, France, America, and Germany—who for decades have doggedly pursued a policy of incessant economic rivalry aimed at achieving world supremacy, subjugating the small nations, and making threefold and tenfold profits on banking capital, which has caught the whole world in the net of its influence. That is what Britain's and Germany's policies really amount to. . . .

These policies show us just one thing—continuous economic rivalry between the world's two greatest giants, capitalist economies. On the one hand we have Britain, a country which owns the greater part of the globe, a country which ranks first in wealth, which has created this wealth not so much by the labour of its workers as by the exploitation of innumerable colonies, by the vast power of its banks which have developed at the head of all the others into an insignificantly small group of some four or five super-banks handling billions of rubles, and handling them in such a way that it can be said without exaggeration that there is not a patch of land in the world today on which this capital has not laid its heavy hand, not a patch of land which British capital has not enmeshed by a thousand threads. . . .

On the other hand, opposed to this, mainly Anglo-French group, we have another group of capitalists, an even more rapacious, even more predatory one, a group who came to the capitalist banqueting table when all the seats were occupied, but who introduced into the struggle new methods for developing capitalist production, improved techniques, and superior organization, which turned the old capitalism, the capitalism of the free-competition age, into the capitalism of giant trusts, syndicates, and cartels. This group introduced the beginnings of state-controlled capitalist production, combining the colossal power of capitalism with the colossal power of the state into a single mechanism and bringing tens of millions of people within the single organization of state capitalism. Here is economic history, here is diplomatic history, covering several decades, from which no one can get away. It is the one and only guide-post to a proper solution of the problem of war; it leads you to the conclusion that the present war, too, is the outcome of the policies of the classes who have come to grips in it, of the two supreme giants, who, long before the war, had caught the whole world, all countries, in the net of financial exploitation and economically divided the globe up among themselves. They were bound to clash, because a redivision of this supremacy, from the point of view of capitalism, had become inevitable. . . .

The present war is a continuation of the policy of conquest, of the shooting down of whole nationalities, of unbelievable atrocities committed by the Germans and the British in Africa, and by the British and the Russians in Persia—which of them committed most it is difficult to say. It was for this reason that the German capitalists looked upon them as their enemies. Ah, they said, you are strong because you are rich? But we are stronger, therefore we have the same "sacred" right to plunder. That is what the real history of British and German finance capital in the course of several decades preceding the war amounts to. That is what the history of Russo-German, Russo-British, and German-British relations amounts to. There you have the clue to an understanding of what the war is about. That is why the story that is current about the cause of the war is sheer duplicity and humbug. Forgetting the history of finance capital, the history of how this war had been brewing over the issue of redivision, they present the matter like this: Two nations were living at peace, then one attacked the other, and the other fought back. All science, all banks are forgotten, and the peoples are told to take up arms, and so are the peasants, who know nothing about politics. . . .

What revolution did we make? We overthrew Nicholas. The revolution was not so very difficult compared with one that would have overthrown the whole class of landowners and capitalists. Who did the revolution put in power? The landowners and capitalists—the very same classes who have long been in power in Europe. . . . The [February] Russian revolution has not altered the war, but it has created organizations which exist in no other country and were seldom found in revolutions in the West. . . . We have all over Russia a network of Soviets of Workers', Soldiers', and Peasants' Deputies. Here is a revolution which has not said its last word yet. . . .

In the two months following the revolution the industrialists have robbed the whole of Russia. Capitalists have made staggering profits; every financial report tells you that. And when the workers, two months after the revolution, had the "audacity" to say they wanted to live like human beings, the whole capitalist press throughout the country set up a howl.

On the question of America entering the war I shall say this. People argue that America is a democracy, America has the White House. I say: Slavery was abolished there half a century ago. The anti-slave war ended in 1865. Since then multimillionaires have mushroomed. They have the whole of America in their financial grip. They are making ready to subdue Mexico and will inevitably come to war with Japan over a carve-up of the Pacific. This war has been brewing for several decades. All literature speaks about it. America's real aim in entering the war is to prepare for this future war with Japan. The American people do enjoy considerable freedom and it is difficult to conceive them standing for compulsory military service, for the setting up of an army pursuing any aims of conquest—a struggle with Japan, for instance. The Americans have the example of Europe to show them what this leads to. The American capitalists have stepped into this war in order to have an excuse, behind a smoke-screen of lofty ideals championing the rights of small nations, for building up a strong standing army. . . .

Tens of millions of people are facing disaster and death; safeguarding the interests of the capitalists is the last thing that should bother us. The only way out is for all power to be transferred to the Soviets, which represent the majority of the population. Possibly mistakes may be made in the process. No one claims that such a difficult task can be disposed of offhand. We do not say anything of the sort. We are told that we want the power to be in the hands of the Soviets, but they don't want it. We say that life's experience will suggest this solution to them, and the whole nation will see that there is no other way out. We do not want a "seizure" of power, because the entire experience of past revolutions teaches us that the only stable power is the one that has the backing of the majority of the population. "Seizure" of power, therefore, would be adventurism, and our Party will not have it. . . .

Nothing but a workers' revolution in several countries can defeat this war. The war is not a game, it is an appalling thing taking a toll of millions of lives, and it is not to be ended easily.

. . . The war has been brought about by the ruling classes and only a revolution of the working class can end it. Whether you will get a speedy peace or not depends on how the revolution will develop.

Whatever sentimental things may be said, however much we may be told: Let us end the war immediately—this cannot be done without the development of the revolution. When power passes to the Soviets the capitalists will come out against us. Japan, France, Britain—the governments of all countries will be against us. The capitalists will be against, but the workers will be for us. That will be the end of the war which the capitalists started. There you have the answer to the question of how to end the war.

7

WOODROW WILSON

Fourteen Points

Woodrow Wilson (1856–1924) was president of the United States during the First World War. He presented these "Fourteen Points" to Congress in January 1918, several months before the war ended, as a basis for a just peace treaty to end the war and to try to break the will of the Central Powers.

You may wish to compare Wilson's proposals with the actual peace settlement that emerged from the Paris Peace Conference

Source: Woodrow Wilson, *War and Peace: Presidential Messages, Addresses, and Public Papers (1917–1924)*, vol. 1, ed. Ray Stannard Baker and William E. Dodd (New York: Harper Brothers, 1927).

and the five treaties that followed. Only points VII, VIII, X, and XIV were realized. Point IV was applied only to the defeated nations. The Versailles Treaty, which the defeated Germans were forced to sign on June 28, 1919, contained much harsher terms, including the famous "war guilt" clause (Article 231):

> The Allied and Associated Governments affirm and Germany accepts the responsibility of Germany and her allies for causing all the loss and damage to which the Allied and Associated Governments and their nationals have been subjected as a consequence of the war imposed upon them by the aggression of Germany and her allies.

Why do you think there was such a gap between Wilson's ideals and the actual treaty? How might Wilson have improved on these Fourteen Points? Could he reasonably expect all of them to be accepted?

THINKING HISTORICALLY

What does the first paragraph suggest about what Wilson thought was one cause of the war? What does the beginning of the second paragraph suggest about the cause for U.S. entry into the war? What would have been the consequences of a peace fashioned along the lines Wilson envisioned in his Fourteen Points?

It will be our wish and purpose that the processes of peace, when they are begun, shall be absolutely open, and that they shall involve and permit henceforth no secret understandings of any kind. The day of conquest and aggrandizement is gone by; so is also the day of secret covenants entered into in the interest of particular Governments and likely at some unlooked-for moment to upset the peace of the world. It is this happy fact, now clear to the view of every public man whose thoughts do not still linger in an age that is dead and gone, which makes it possible for every nation whose purposes are consistent with justice and the peace of the world to avow now or at any other time the objects it has in view.

We entered this war because violations of right had occurred which touched us to the quick and made the life of our own people impossible unless they were corrected and the world secured once for all against their recurrence. What we demand in this war, therefore, is nothing peculiar to ourselves. It is that the world be made fit and safe to live in; and particularly that it be made safe for every peace-loving nation which, like our own, wishes to live its own life, determine its own institutions, be assured of justice and fair dealing by the other peoples of the world as against force and selfish aggression. All the peoples of the world are in effect partners in this interest, and for our own part we see very clearly that unless justice be done to others it will not be done to us.

The program of the world's peace, therefore, is our program; and that program, the only possible program, as we see it, is this:

I. Open covenants of peace, openly arrived at, after which there shall be no private international understandings of any kind but diplomacy shall proceed always frankly and in the public view.

II. Absolute freedom of navigation upon the seas, outside territorial waters, alike in peace and in war, except as the seas may be closed in whole or in part by international action. . . .

III. The removal, so far as possible, of all economic barriers and the establishment of an equality of trade conditions among all the nations consenting to the peace and associating themselves for its maintenance.

IV. Adequate guarantees given and taken that national armaments will be reduced to the lowest point consistent with domestic safety.

V. A free, open-minded, and absolutely impartial adjustment of all colonial claims, based upon a strict observance of the principle that in determining all such questions of sovereignty the interests of the populations concerned must have equal weight with the equitable claims of the government whose title is to be determined.

VI. The evacuation of all Russian territory and such a settlement of all questions affecting Russia as will secure the best and freest co-operation of the other nations of the world in obtaining for her an unhampered and unembarrassed opportunity for the independent determination of her own political development and national policy and assure her of a sincere welcome into the society of free nations under institutions of her own choosing; and, more than a welcome, assistance also of every kind that she may need and may herself desire. The treatment accorded Russia by her sister nations in the months to come will be the acid test of their good will, of their comprehension of her needs as distinguished from their own interests, and of their intelligent and unselfish sympathy.

VII. Belgium, the whole world will agree, must be evacuated and restored, without any attempt to limit the sovereignty which she enjoys in common with all other free nations. No other single act will serve to restore confidence among the nations in the laws which they have themselves set and determined for the government of their relations with one another. Without this healing act the whole structure and validity of international law is forever impaired.

VIII. All French territory should be freed and the invaded portions restored, and the wrong done to France by Prussia in 1871 in the matter of Alsace-Lorraine, which has unsettled the peace of the world for nearly fifty years, should be righted, in order that peace may once more be made secure in the interest of all.

IX. A readjustment of the frontiers of Italy should be effected along clearly recognizable lines of nationality.

X. The peoples of Austria-Hungary, whose place among the nations we wish to see safeguarded and assured, should be accorded the freest opportunity of autonomous development.

XI. Rumania, Serbia, and Montenegro should be evacuated; occupied territories restored; Serbia accorded free and secure access to the sea; and the relations of the several Balkan states to one another determined by friendly counsel along historically established lines of allegiance and nationality; and international guarantees of the political and economic independence and territorial integrity of the several Balkan states should be entered into.

XII. The Turkish portions of the present Ottoman Empire should be assured a secure sovereignty, but the other nationalities which are now under Turkish rule should be assured an undoubted security of life and an absolutely unmolested opportunity of autonomous development, and the Dardanelles should be permanently opened as a free passage to the ships and commerce of all nations under international guarantees.

XIII. An independent Polish state should be erected which should include the territories inhabited by indisputably Polish populations, which should be assured a free and secure access to the sea, and whose political and economic independence and territorial integrity should be guaranteed by international covenant.

XIV. A general association of nations must be formed under specific covenants for the purpose of affording mutual guarantees of political independence and territorial integrity to great and small states alike.

In regard to these essential rectifications of wrong and assertions of right we feel ourselves to be intimate partners of all the governments and peoples associated together against the Imperialists. We cannot be separated in interest or divided in purpose. We stand together until the end.

For such arrangements and covenants we are willing to fight and to continue to fight until they are achieved; but only because we wish the right to prevail and desire a just and stable peace such as can be secured only by removing the chief provocations to war, which this program does remove. We have no jealousy of German greatness, and there is nothing in this program that impairs it. We grudge her no achievement or distinction of learning or of pacific enterprise such as have made her record very bright and very enviable. We do not wish to injure her or to block in any way her legitimate influence or power. We do not wish to fight her either with arms or with hostile arrangements of trade if she is willing to associate herself with us and the other peace-loving nations of the world in covenants of justice and law and fair dealing. We wish her only to accept a place of equality among the peoples of the world, — the new world in which we now live — instead of a place of mastery.

. . . An evident principle runs through the whole program I have outlined. It is the principle of justice to all peoples and nationalities, and their right to live on equal terms of liberty and safety with one another, whether they be strong or weak. Unless this principle be made its foundation no part of the structure of international justice can stand. The people of the United States could act upon no other principle; and to the vindication of this principle they are ready to devote their lives, their honor, and everything that they possess. The moral climax of this the culminating and final war for human liberty has come, and they are ready to put their own strength, their own highest purpose, their own integrity and devotion to the test.

8

Syrian Congress Memorandum

Point XII in Wilson's Fourteen Points began: "The Turkish portions of the present Ottoman Empire should be assured a secure sovereignty, but the other nationalities which are now under Turkish rule should be assured an undoubted security of life and an absolutely unmolested opportunity of autonomous development." The Arabs of the Middle East constituted at least one of these "other nationalities," and many of them expected their independence after the war. Instead the Paris Peace Conference instituted a system of "mandates" by which the victorious European powers maintained control over enemy colonies, including the Ottoman Arab territories, until the Europeans determined the colonies were prepared for independence.

This selection details the Syrians' objections to this arrangement, sent as a memorandum to the King-Crane Commission, the body responsible for overseeing the transfer of Ottoman territory. What were their objections? What evidence did they give to support their position? What did they want?

THINKING HISTORICALLY

Do you think this conflict could have been an expected consequence of the First World War? Do you think Wilson's Fourteen Points made the Syrian demands more likely? Do you think the European powers expected this response?

We the undersigned members of the General Syrian Congress, meeting in Damascus on Wednesday, July 2nd 1919, . . . provided with credentials and

---

Source: "The King-Crane Commission Report," in *Papers Relating to the Foreign Relations of the United States: Paris Peace Conference, 1919* (Washington, DC: GPO, 1947), 12:780–81.

authorizations by the inhabitants of our various districts, Muslims, Christians, and Jews, have agreed upon the following statement of the desires of the people of the country who have elected us to present them to the American Section of the International Commission; the fifth article was passed by a very large majority; all the other articles were accepted unanimously.

1. We ask absolutely complete political independence for Syria within these boundaries. The Taurus System on the North; Rafah and a line running from Al Jauf to the south of the Syrian and the Hejazian line to Akaba on the south; the Euphrates and Khabur Rivers and a line extending east of Abu Kamal to the east of Al Jauf on the east; and the Mediterranean on the west.

2. We ask that the Government of this Syrian country should be a democratic civil constitutional Monarchy on broad decentralization principles, safeguarding the rights of minorities, and that the King be the Emir Feisal, who carried on a glorious struggle in the cause of our liberation and merited our full confidence and entire reliance.

3. Considering the fact that the Arabs inhabiting the Syrian area are not naturally less than other more advanced races and that they are by no means less developed than the Bulgarians, Serbians, Greeks, and Romanians at the beginning of their independence, we protest against Article 22 of the Covenant of the League of Nations, placing us among the nations in their middle stage of development which stand in need of a mandatory power.

4. In the event of the rejection by the Peace Conference of this just protest for certain considerations that we may not understand, we, relying on the declarations of President Wilson that his object in waging war was to put an end to the ambition of conquest and colonization, can only regard the mandate mentioned in the Covenant of the League of Nations as equivalent to the rendering of economical and technical assistance that does not prejudice our complete independence. And desiring that our country should not fall a prey to colonization and believing that the American Nation is furthest from any thought of colonization and has no political ambition in our country, we will seek the technical and economical assistance from the United States of America, provided that such assistance does not exceed 20 years.

5. In the event of America not finding herself in a position to accept our desire for assistance, we will seek this assistance from Great Britain, also provided that such assistance does not infringe the complete independence and unity of our country and that the duration of such assistance does not exceed that mentioned in the previous article.

6. We do not acknowledge any right claimed by the French Government in any part whatever of our Syrian country and refuse that she should assist us or have a hand in our country under any circumstances and in any place.

7. We oppose the pretensions of the Zionists to create a Jewish commonwealth in the southern part of Syria, known as Palestine, and oppose

Zionist migration to any part of our country; for we do not acknowledge their title but consider them a grave peril to our people from the national, economical, and political points of view. Our Jewish compatriots shall enjoy our common rights and assume the common responsibilities.

8. We ask that there should be no separation of the southern part of Syria, known as Palestine, nor of the littoral western zone, which includes Lebanon, from the Syrian country. We desire that the unity of the country should be guaranteed against partition under whatever circumstances.

9. We ask complete independence for emancipated Mesopotamia and that there should be no economic barriers between the two countries.

10. The fundamental principles laid down by President Wilson in condemnation of secret treaties impel us to protest most emphatically against any treaty that stipulates the partition of our Syrian country and against any private engagement aiming at the establishment of Zionism in the southern part of Syria; therefore we ask the complete annulment of these conventions and agreements.

The noble principles enunciated by President Wilson strengthen our confidence that our desires emanating from the depths of our hearts, shall be the decisive factor in determining our future; and that President Wilson and the free American people will be our supporters for the realization of our hopes, thereby proving their sincerity and noble sympathy with the aspiration of the weaker nations in general and our Arab people in particular.

We also have the fullest confidence that the Peace Conference will realize that we would not have risen against the Turks, with whom we had participated in all civil, political, and representative privileges, but for their violation of our national rights, and so will grant us our desires in full in order that our political rights may not be less after the war than they were before, since we have shed so much blood in the cause of our liberty and independence.

We request to be allowed to send a delegation to represent us at the Peace Conference to defend our rights and secure the realization of our aspirations.

■ REFLECTIONS

By studying causes and consequences of world events, we learn how things change; more importantly, we learn how to avoid repeating past mistakes. History is full of lessons that breed humility as well as confidence. In *The Origins of the First World War*,[1] historian James Joll points out how unprepared people were for the war as late as the summer of 1914. Even after the Austrian ultimatum to Serbia was issued on July 23 (almost a month after the assassination of the Archduke Franz Ferdinand on June 28), diplomats across Europe left for their

---

[1] James Joll, *The Origins of the First World War* (London: Longman, 1992), 200.

summer holidays. By August, all of Europe was at war, though the expectation was that it would be over in a month.

We could make a good case for diplomatic blundering as an important cause of the First World War. It is safe to say that few statesmen had any inkling of the consequences of their actions in 1914. And yet, if we concentrate on the daily decisions of diplomats that summer, we may pay attention only to the tossing of lit matches by people sitting on powder kegs rather than on the origins of the powder kegs themselves.

President Wilson blamed secret diplomacy, the international system of alliances, and imperialism as the chief causes of the war. On the importance of imperialism, Wilson's conclusion was the same as that of Lenin, though he certainly did not share Lenin's conviction that capitalism was the root cause of imperialism, and in 1919 neither alliances nor imperialism was regarded as un-American or likely to end anytime soon. Still, Wilson's radical moral aversion to reviving Old World empires might have prevented a new stage of imperialism, as it developed in the mandate system. One of the consequences of a Wilsonian peace might have been the creation of independent states in the Middle East and Africa a generation earlier.

The principle of the "self-determination of nations" that Wilson espoused, however, was a double-edged sword. The fact that the war had been "caused" by a Bosnian Serb nationalist assassin in 1914 might have been a warning that national self-determination could become an infinite regress in which smaller and smaller units sought to separate themselves from "foreign" domination.

The rise of nationalist movements and the rise of international organizations were only two consequences of the First World War. Historians have attributed many other aspects of the twentieth century to the war. Stephen O'Shea offers a striking list of cultural changes:

> It is generally accepted that the Great War and its fifty-two months of senseless slaughter encouraged, or amplified, among other things: the loss of a belief in progress, a mistrust of technology, the loss of religious faith, the loss of a belief in Western cultural superiority, the rejection of class distinctions, the rejection of traditional sexual roles, the birth of the Modern [in art], the rejection of the past, the elevation of irony to a standard mode of apprehending the world, the unbuttoning of moral codes, and the conscious embrace of the irrational.[2]

Evidence of any of these consequences is only barely visible in the accounts of a chapter that ends in 1919, but many of the developments described in the next few chapters were consequences of World War I as well.

---

[2] Stephen O'Shea, *Back to the Front: An Accidental Historian Walks the Trenches of World War I* (New York: Avon Books, 1996), 9.

25

World War II and Mass Killing

Germany, the Soviet Union, Japan, and the United States, 1931–1945

■ HISTORICAL CONTEXT

In some ways World War II resembled World War I. At the European core, England and France again fought Germany and Austria. As in World War I, the United States eventually came to the aid of England and France, playing a decisive role. In both conflicts Russia also fought against Germany, only until the Soviet revolution in 1917, but fiercely and at great cost as the Soviet Union from 1941 to 1945. By contrast, Japan, an enemy of Germany in World War I, became an important German ally in World War II, and the pro-German Ottoman Empire of World War I was an independent, neutral Turkey in World War II.

While the main combatants were aligned on the same sides, and both wars ended in the defeat of Germany and its allies, the causes and consequences of the two wars were significantly different. The causes of World War II are clearer than those of World War I. German aggression was a factor in both wars, but in the buildup to World War I, there was much blame to go around. World War II, on the other hand, followed the aggressive conquests of Japan and Germany. Both countries had been militarized by extreme nationalist regimes. Similar "fascist" movements took power in Italy and Eastern Europe, partly in response to the economic hardship of the Great Depression of the 1930s. These movements, like the German Nazi Party, were led by demagogues — Hitler in Germany, Mussolini in Italy — who called for dictatorial power, the expulsion or conquest of foreigners, colonial expansion, and aggressive, violent solutions to social and economic problems. Similarly, the military party that took power in Japan sought an empire in China and Southeast Asia to ensure its economic prosperity.

The aggressions of Germany and Japan unleashed forces of violence that also distinguished World War II from World War I. New technologies of warfare (machine guns, biplanes, and gas in World War I) that had been directed almost entirely at soldiers in trenches were transformed by World War II into missiles and warheads that rained down on civilian populations. Even the victorious Allies directed previously unheard of violence against civilian populations in the fire-bombing of cities like Dresden and Tokyo and the use of nuclear bombs on Hiroshima and Nagasaki.

Despite the pounding barbarity of the Western Front, the era of World War I still contained features of earlier gentlemanly conflict. Like chivalric jousters, aristocratic World War I pilots displayed colorful scarves and saluted their falling rivals. But the extreme nationalist and racist movements of the interwar years instilled a hatred of the enemy that eviscerated any possibility of compassion or fellow feeling. Totalitarian governments indoctrinated mass citizen armies with a hatred that sometimes made the new technologies of violence redundant. Millions of newly designated enemies — neighbors as well as foreigners — were murdered by hand.

This chapter begins with selections on Nazi Germany: a modern historian's account of the rise of Hitler, a Nazi speech on the extermination of Jews, and a description of the workings of one death camp, Treblinka. Then a recent historical essay places the holocaust of German Jews in a larger perspective. An even larger global view of the war and genocide brings us to the late Iris Chang's expose of Japanese atrocities in China. We conclude this chapter on the war that killed so many millions by reflecting on its ending in mass death by a new weapon of far greater magnitude. We ask how, amidst the greatest technological progress the world had ever seen, the lives of ordinary people became so cheap.

■ THINKING HISTORICALLY

Thinking about the Unthinkable

To be able to think about the unthinkable is to be able to understand without excusing. Occasionally when we learn of something horrendous, we simply say, "I don't believe it." Our disbelief harbors two feelings: first, our sense of outrage and anger, a rejection of what was done; second, our unwillingness to believe that such a thing could happen or did happen. Our choice of words expresses the difficulty we have making sense of the senseless.

We must try, however, to understand such catastrophes so that we can help to prevent similar horrors in our own time. Understanding reprehensible acts requires a level of empathy that is often difficult to arouse. As you read these selections, you will be encouraged to understand and explain events that are easier to not think about. To understand what is offensive is not to excuse it, but to be better prepared to avoid it in the future.

1

JOACHIM C. FEST

The Rise of Hitler

World War II had its origins in World War I. The peace terms imposed by the victors demanded the removal of the kaiser, the demilitarization of Germany, the transfer of Germany's industrial heartland to France, and the payment of enormous sums in reparation for the war. In addition, the revolutionary establishment of a republic by the German Socialist Party was followed by the unsuccessful uprising by the far more radical Spartacus League, which had raised the specter of a Bolshevik coup that would later turn Germany into a communist state.

In this essay, historian Joachim Fest explores the response of German conservative, nationalist, and middle-class groups to these developments. The National Socialists (the Nazi Party) was just one of many fascist groups in Germany. Initiated by Mussolini in Italy in 1922, fascism was a movement that spread throughout Europe. As defined by Mussolini, in fascism the state dominates everything else:

> For the Fascist the state is all-embracing; outside it no human or spiritual values exist, much less have worth. In this sense Fascism is totalitarian, and the Fascist State — a synthesis and a unity of all values — interprets, develops, and gives power to the whole life of the people.[1]

According to Fest, why did fascism appeal more to the middle class than to the working class? Was Hitler typical of those who were

[1] *Enciclopedia Italiana* (1932), s.v. "fascism" (signed by Mussolini but actually written by the philosopher Giovanni Gentile).

Source: Joachim C. Fest, *Hitler*, trans. Clara and Richard Winston (New York: Harcourt Brace and Co., 1974), 89–91, 92–93, 99–102, 104–5.

attracted to fascism? Was Hitler out of touch with reality, or was he tuned in to the feelings of many?

THINKING HISTORICALLY

Fest helps us understand some of the appeal of fascism by putting it into the context of Germany's defeat in World War I and the real or imagined threat of a Bolshevik revolution. Can you imagine empathizing with antirevolutionary fears if you lived then? Imagine how you might have responded to some of the other fascist appeals: fewer politicians, more police; the nobility of sacrificing for higher purposes; challenging the gray ordinariness of modern life; following instinct rather than reason; and war as authentic experience.

At the end of the First World War the victory of the democratic idea seemed beyond question. Whatever its weaknesses might be, it rose above the turmoil of the times, the uprisings, the dislocations, and the continual quarrels among nations as the unifying principle of the new age. For the war had not only decided a claim to power. It had at the same time altered a conception of government. After the collapse of virtually all the governmental structures of Central and Eastern Europe, many new political entities had emerged out of turmoil and revolution. And these for the most part were organized on democratic principles. In 1914 there had been only three republics alongside of seventeen monarchies in Europe. Four years later there were as many republics as monarchies. The spirit of the age seemed to be pointing unequivocally toward various forms of popular rule.

Only Germany seemed to be opposing this mood of the times, after having been temporarily gripped and carried along by it. Those who would not acknowledge the reality created by the war organized into a fantastic swarm of *völkisch* (racist-nationalist) parties, clubs, and free corps. To these groups the revolution had been an act of treason; parliamentary democracy was something foreign and imposed from without, merely a synonym for "everything contrary to the German political will," or else an "institution for pillaging created by Allied capitalism."

Germany's former enemies regarded the multifarious symptoms of nationalistic protest as the response of an inveterately authoritarian people to democracy and civic responsibility. To be sure, the Germans were staggering beneath terrible political and psychological burdens: There was the shock of defeat, the moral censure of the Versailles Treaty, the loss of territory and the demand for reparations, the impoverishment and spiritual undermining of much of the population. Nevertheless, the conviction remained that a great moral gap existed between the Germans and most of their neighbours. Full of resentment, refusing to learn a lesson, this incomprehensible country had withdrawn into its reactionary doctrines, made of them a special virtue, abjured Western rationality and humanity, and in general set itself against the universal trend of the age. For decades this picture of Germany dominated the discussion of the reasons for the rise of National Socialism.

But the image of democracy victorious was also deceptive. The moment in which democracy seemed to be achieving historic fulfillment simultaneously marked the beginning of its crisis. Only a few years later the idea of democracy was challenged in principle as it had never been before. Only a few years after it had celebrated its triumph it was overwhelmed or at least direly threatened by a new movement that had sprung to life in almost all European countries.

This movement recorded its most lasting successes in countries in which the war had aroused considerable discontent or made it conscious of existing discontent, and especially in countries in which the war had been followed by leftist revolutionary uprisings. In some places these movements were conservative, harking back to better times when men were more honorable, the valleys more peaceable, and money had more worth; in others these movements were revolutionary and vied with one another in their contempt for the existing order of things. Some attracted chiefly the petty bourgeois elements, others the peasants, others portions of the working class. Whatever their strange compound of classes, interests, and principles, all seemed to be drawing their dynamic force from the less conscious and more vital lower strata of society. National Socialism was merely one variant of this widespread European movement of protest and opposition aimed at overturning the general order of things.

National Socialism rose from provincial beginnings, from philistine clubs, as Hitler scornfully described them, which met in Munich bars over a few rounds of beer to talk over national and family troubles. No one would have dreamed that they could ever challenge, let alone outdo, the powerful, highly organized Marxist parties. But the following years proved that in these clubs of nationalistic beer drinkers, soon swelled by disillusioned homecoming soldiers and proletarianized members of the middle class, a tremendous force was waiting to be awakened, consolidated, and applied.

In Munich alone there existed, in 1919, nearly fifty more or less political associations, whose membership consisted chiefly of confused remnants of the prewar parties that had been broken up by war and revolution. . . . What united them all and drew them together theoretically and in reality was nothing but an overwhelming feeling of anxiety.

First of all, and most immediate, there was the fear of revolution, that *grande peur*[2] which after the French Revolution had haunted the European-bourgeoisie throughout the nineteenth century. The notion that revolutions were like forces of nature, elemental mechanisms operating without reference to the will of the actors in them, following their own logic and leading perforce to reigns of terror, destruction, killing, and chaos—that notion was seared into the public mind. That was the unforgettable experience, not [German philosopher Immanuel] Kant's belief that the French Revolution had also shown the potentiality for betterment inherent in human nature. For generations, particularly in Germany, this fear stood in the way of any practical revolutionary strivings and produced a mania for keeping things quiet, with the result that every revolutionary proclamation up to 1918 was countered by the standard appeal to law and order.

This old fear was revived by the pseudorevolutionary events in Germany and by the menace of the October Revolution in Russia. Diabolical traits were ascribed to the Reds. The refugees pouring into Munich described bloodthirsty barbarians on a rampage of killing. Such imagery had instant appeal to the nationalists. . . .

This threat dominated Hitler's speeches of the early years. In garish colors he depicted the ravages of the "Red squads of butchers," the "murderous communists," the "bloody morass of Bolshevism." In Russia, he told his audiences, more than thirty million persons had been murdered, "partly on the scaffold, partly by machine guns and similar means, partly in veritable slaughterhouses, partly, millions upon millions, by hunger; and we all know that this wave of hunger is creeping on . . . and see that this scourge is approaching, that it is also coming upon Germany." The intelligentsia of the Soviet Union, he declared, had been exterminated by mass murder, the economy utterly smashed. Thousands of German prisoners-of-war had been drowned in the Neva or sold as slaves. Meanwhile, in Germany the enemy was boring away at the foundations of society "in unremitting, ever unchanging undermining work." The fate of Russia, he said again and again, would soon be ours! . . .

National Socialism owed a considerable part of its emotional appeal, its militancy, and its cohesion to this defensive attitude toward the threat of Marxist revolution. The aim of the National Socialist Party, Hitler repeatedly declared, "is very brief: Annihilation and extermination of the Marxist world view." This was to be accomplished by an "incomparable, brilliantly orchestrated propaganda and information organization" side by side with a movement "of the most ruthless force and most brutal resolution, prepared to oppose all terrorism on the part of the Marxists with tenfold greater terrorism." At about the same time, for similar reasons, Mussolini was founding his Fasci di combattimento

[2] Great fear. [Ed.]

[battle group]. Henceforth, the new movements were to be identified by the general name of "Fascism."

But the fear of revolution would not have been enough to endow the movement with that fierce energy, which for a time seemed to stem the universal trend toward democracy. After all, for many people revolution meant hope. A stronger and more elemental motivation had to be added. And in fact Marxism was feared as the precursor of a far more comprehensive assault upon all traditional ideas. It was viewed as the contemporary political aspect of a metaphysical upheaval, as a "declaration of war upon the European . . . idea of culture." Marxism itself was only the metaphor for something dreaded that escaped definition. . . .

This first phase of the postwar era was characterized both by fear of revolution and anticivilizational resentments; these together, curiously intertwined and reciprocally stimulating each other, produced a syndrome of extraordinary force. Into the brew went the hate and defense complexes of a society shaken to its foundations. German society had lost its imperial glory, its civil order, its national confidence, its prosperity, and its familiar authorities. The whole system had been turned topsy-turvy, and now many Germans blindly and bitterly wanted back what they thought had been unjustly taken from them. These general feelings of unhappiness were intensified and further radicalized by a variety of unsatisfied group interests. The class of white-collar workers, continuing to grow apace, proved especially susceptible to the grand gesture of total criticism. For the industrial revolution had just begun to affect office workers and was reducing the former "non-commissioned officers of capitalism" to the status of last victims of "modern slavery." It was all the worse for them because unlike the proletarians they had never developed a class pride of their own or imagined that the breakdown of the existing order was going to lead to their own apotheosis. Small businessmen were equally susceptible because of their fear of being crushed by corporations, department stores, and rationalized competition. Another unhappy group consisted of farmers who, slow to change and lacking capital, were fettered to backward modes of production. Another group were the academics and formerly solid bourgeois who felt themselves caught in the tremendous suction of proletarianization.[3] Without outside support you found yourself "at once despised, declassed; to be unemployed is the same as being a communist," one victim stated in a questionnaire of the period. No statistics, no figures on rates of inflation, bankruptcies, and suicides can describe the feelings of those threatened by unemployment or poverty, or can express the anxieties of those others who still possessed some property and feared the consequences of so much accumulated discontent. . . .

[3] Becoming like wage laborers. [Ed.]

The vigilante groups and the free corps that were being organized in great numbers, partly on private initiative, partly with covert government support, chiefly to meet the threat of Communist revolution, formed centers of bewildered but determined resistance to the *status quo*. The members of these paramilitary groups were vaguely looking around for someone to lead them into a new system. At first there was another reservoir of militant energies alongside the parliamentary groups: the mass of homecoming soldiers. Many of these stayed in the barracks dragging out a pointless military life, baffled and unable to say good-bye to the warrior dreams of their recent youth. In the frontline trenches they had glimpsed the outlines of a new meaning to life; in the sluggishly resuming normality of the postwar period they tried in vain to find that meaning again. They had not fought and suffered for years for the sake of this weakened regime with its borrowed ideals which, as they saw it, could be pushed around by the most contemptible of their former enemies. And they also feared, after the exalting sense of life the war had given them, the ignobility of the commonplace bourgeois world.

It remained for Hitler to bring together these feelings and to appoint himself their spearhead. Indeed, Hitler regarded as a phenomenon seems like the synthetic product of all the anxiety, pessimism, nostalgia, and defensiveness we have discussed. For him, too, the war had been education and liberation. If there is a "Fascistic" type, it was embodied in him. More than any of his followers he expressed the underlying psychological, social, and ideological motives of the movement. He was never just its leader; he was also its exponent.

His early years had contributed their share to that experience of overwhelming anxiety which dominated his intellectual and emotional constitution. That lurking anxiety can be seen at the root of almost all his statements and reactions. It had everyday as well as cosmic dimensions. Many who knew him in his youth have described his pallid, "timorous" nature, which provided the fertile soil for his lush fantasies. His "constant fear" of contact with strangers was another aspect of that anxiety, as was his extreme distrust and his compulsion to wash frequently, which became more and more pronounced in later life. The same complex is apparent in his oft-expressed fear of venereal disease and his fear of contagion in general. He knew that "microbes are rushing at me." He was ridden by the Austrian Pan-German's fear of being overwhelmed by alien races, by fear of the "locust-like immigration of Russian and Polish Jews," by fear of "the niggerizing of the Germans," by fear of the Germans' "expulsion from Germany," and finally by fear that the Germans would be "exterminated." He had the *Völkischer Boebachter*[4] print an alleged French soldier's song whose refrain was: "Germans, we will possess your daughters!" Among his phobias were American technology, the birth rate of the Slavs, big cities, "industrialization as

---

[4] *Völkischer Boebachter* was the Nazi Party newspaper from 1920. [Ed.]

unrestricted as it is harmful," the "economization of the nation," corporations, the "morass of metropolitan amusement culture," and modern art, which sought "to kill the soul of the people" by painting meadows blue and skies green. Wherever he looked he discovered the "signs of decay of a slowly ebbing world." Not an element of pessimistic anticivilizational criticism was missing from his imagination.

What linked Hitler with the leading Fascists of other countries was the resolve to halt this process of degeneration. What set him apart from them, however, was the manic single-mindedness with which he traced all the anxieties he had ever felt back to a single source. For at the heart of the towering structure of anxiety, black and hairy, stood the figure of the Jew: evil-smelling, smacking his lips, lusting after blonde girls, eternal contaminator of the blood, but "racially harder" than the Aryan, as Hitler uneasily declared as late as the summer of 1942. A prey to his psychosis, he saw Germany as the object of a worldwide conspiracy, pressed on all sides by Bolshevists, Freemasons, capitalists, Jesuits, all hand in glove with each other and directed in their nefarious projects by the "bloodthirsty and avaricious Jewish tyrant." The Jew had 75 per cent of world capital at his disposal. He dominated the stock exchanges and the Marxist parties, the Gold and Red Internationals. He was the "advocate of birth control and the idea of emigration." He undermined governments, bastardized races, glorified fratricide, fomented civil war, justified baseness, and poisoned nobility: "the wirepuller of the destinies of mankind." The whole world was in danger, Hitler cried imploringly; it had fallen "into the embrace of this octopus." He groped for images in which to make his horror tangible, saw "creeping venom," "belly-worms," and "adders devouring the nation's body." . . .

The appearance of Hitler signaled a union of those forces that in crisis conditions had great political potential. The Fascistic movements all centered on the charismatic appeal of a unique leader. The leader was to be the resolute voice of order controlling chaos. He would have looked further and thought deeper, would know the despairs but also the means of salvation. This looming giant had already been given established form in a prophetic literature that went back to German folklore. Like the mythology of many other nations unfortunate in their history, that of the Germans has its sleeping leaders dreaming away the centuries in the bowels of a mountain, but destined some day to return to rally their people and punish the guilty world. . . .

The success of Fascism in contrast to many of its rivals was in large part due to its perceiving the essence of the crisis, of which it was itself the symptom. All the other parties affirmed the process of industrialization and emancipation, whereas the Fascists, evidently sharing the universal anxiety, tried to deal with it by translating it into violent action and histrionics. . . .

2

HEINRICH HIMMLER
Speech to the SS

Heinrich Himmler (1900–1945) was one of the most powerful leaders of Nazi Germany. He was the head of the SS, or *Schutzstaffel,* an
elite army that was responsible for, among other things, running the
many concentration camps. Hitler gave Himmler the task of implementing the "final solution of the Jewish question": attempted genocide of the Jewish population of Germany and the other countries the
Nazis occupied. The horror that resulted is today often referred to by
the word *holocaust* (literally, holy burnt offering).

The following reading is an excerpt from a speech Himmler gave to
SS leaders on October 4, 1943. What was Himmler's concern in this
speech? What kind of general support for the extermination of the
Jews does this excerpt suggest existed?

THINKING HISTORICALLY

Psychiatrists say that people use various strategies to cope when they
must do something distasteful. We might summarize these strategies as
denial, distancing, compartmentalizing, ennobling, rationalizing, and
scapegoating. *Denial* is pretending that something has not happened.
Distancing removes the idea, memory, or reality from the mind, placing it
at a distance. *Compartmentalizing* separates one action, memory, or idea
from others, allowing one to "put away" certain feelings. *Ennobling* makes
the distasteful act a matter of pride rather than guilt, nobility rather than
disgrace. *Rationalizing* creates "good" reasons for doing something, while
scapegoating puts blame on someone else.

What evidence do you see of these strategies in Himmler's speech?
Judging from the speech, which of these strategies do you think his
listeners used to justify their actions?

I also want to make reference before you here, in complete frankness,
to a really grave matter. Among ourselves, this once, it shall be uttered
quite frankly; but in public we will never speak of it. Just as we did
not hesitate on June 30, 1934, to do our duty as ordered, to stand up
against the wall comrades who had transgressed,[1] and shoot them, so

---

[1] A reference to the "Night of the Long Knives," when Hitler ordered the SS to murder the
leaders of the SA, a Nazi group he wished to suppress. [Ed.]

Source: Heinrich Himmler, "Secret Speech at Posen," in *A Holocaust Reader*, ed. Lucy S.
Dawidowicz (New York: Behrman House, 1976), 132–33.

we have never talked about this and never will. It was the tact which I am glad to say is a matter of course to us that made us never discuss it among ourselves, never talk about it. Each of us shuddered, and yet each one knew that he would do it again if it were ordered and if it were necessary.

I am referring to the evacuation of the Jews, the annihilation of the Jewish people. This is one of those things that are easily said. "The Jewish people is going to be annihilated," says every party member. "Sure, it's in our program, elimination of the Jews, annihilation — we'll take care of it." And then they all come trudging, 80 million worthy Germans, and each one has his one decent Jew. Sure, the others are swine, but this one is an A-1 Jew. Of all those who talk this way, not one has seen it happen, not one has been through it. Most of you must know what it means to see a hundred corpses lie side by side, or five hundred, or a thousand. To have stuck this out — excepting cases of human weakness — to have kept our integrity, that is what has made us hard. In our history, this is an unwritten and never-to-be-written page of glory, for we know how difficult we would have made it for ourselves if today — amid the bombing raids, the hardships, and the deprivations of war — we still had the Jews in every city as secret saboteurs, agitators, and demagogues. If the Jews were still ensconced in the body of the German nation, we probably would have reached the 1916–17 stage by now.[2]

The wealth they had we have taken from them. I have issued a strict order, carried out by SS-Obergruppenfuhrer Pohl, that this wealth in its entirety is to be turned over to the Reich as a matter of course. We have taken none of it for ourselves. Individuals who transgress will be punished in accordance with an order I issued at the beginning, threatening that whoever takes so much as a mark of it for himself is a dead man. A number of SS men — not very many — have transgressed, and they will die, without mercy. We had the moral right, we had the duty toward our people, to kill this people which wanted to kill us. But we do not have the right to enrich ourselves with so much as a fur, a watch, a mark, or a cigarette, or anything else. Having exterminated a germ, we do not want, in the end, to be infected by the germ, and die of it. I will not stand by and let even a small rotten spot develop or take hold. Wherever it may form, we together will cauterize it. All in all, however, we can say that we have carried out this heaviest of our tasks in a spirit of love for our people. And our inward being, our soul, our character has not suffered injury from it.

---

[2] Here Himmler is apparently referring to the stalemate on Germany's Western Front in World War I. [Ed.]

3

JEAN-FRANÇOIS STEINER

Treblinka

Treblinka, in Poland, was one of several Nazi extermination camps (see Map 25.1). In these "death factories," the Nazis murdered millions of Jews as well as Roma and Sinti, communists, socialists, Poles, Soviet prisoners of war, and other people. Extermination of Jews became official Nazi policy in 1942. Extermination camps were built to supplement earlier concentration camps used to contain political prisoners, Jews, and other forced laborers (many of whom also died there). In this selection, Steiner describes some of the elaborate study and preparation that went into the design of an extermination camp, focusing on the work of Kurt Franz, whom the prisoners called Lalka. What were the problems the Nazis faced in building an extermination camp? How did they solve them? What does this level of efficiency and scientific planning tell you about the Nazi regime or the people involved?

THINKING HISTORICALLY

Try to imagine what went through the mind of Lalka as he designed the extermination process at Treblinka. How did concerns for efficiency and humanity enter into his deliberations? Do you think he found his work distasteful? If so, which of the strategies mentioned in the previous selection did he adopt?

   What would it have been like to be a sign-painter, guard, or hair-cutter at Treblinka? What do you imagine went through the minds of the victims?

Each poorly organized debarkation [of deportees from trains arriving at Treblinka] gave rise to unpleasant scenes—uncertainties and confusion for the deportees, who did not know where they were going and were sometimes seized with panic.

   So, the first problem was to restore a minimum of hope. Lalka had many faults, but he did not lack a certain creative imagination. After a few days of reflection he hit upon the idea of transforming the platform where the convoys [trains] arrived into a false station. He had the ground filled in to the level of the doors of the cars in order to give the appearance of a train platform and to make it easier to get off the trains. . . . On [a] wall Lalka had . . . doors and windows painted in gay and pleasing colors. The windows were decorated with cheerful curtains

Source: Jean-François Steiner, *Treblinka* (New York: Simon & Schuster, 1967), 153–54, 155–58, 159–60.

Map 25.1 Major Nazi Concentration Camps in World War II.

and framed by green blinds which were just as false as the rest. Each door was given a special name, stencilled at eye level: "Stationmaster," "Toilet," "Infirmary" (a red cross was painted on this door). Lalka carried his concern for detail so far as to have his men paint two doors leading to the waiting rooms, first and second class. The ticket window, which was barred with a horizontal sign reading, "Closed," was a little masterpiece with its ledge and false perspective and its grill, painted line for line. Next to the ticket window a large timetable announced the departure times of trains for Warsaw, Bialystok, Wolkowysk, etc. . . . Two doors were cut into the [wall]. The first led to the "hospital," bearing a wooden arrow on which "Wolkowysk" was painted. The second led to the place where the Jews were undressed; that arrow said "Bialystok." Lalka also had some flower beds designed, which gave the whole area a neat and cheery look. . . .

Lalka also decided that better organization could save much time in the operations of undressing and recovery of the [deportees'] baggage. To do this you had only to rationalize the different operations, that is, to organize the undressing like an assembly line. But the rhythm of this assembly line was at the mercy of the sick, the old, and the wounded, who, since they were unable to keep the pace, threatened to bog down the operation and make it proceed even more slowly than before. . . . Individuals of both sexes over the age of ten, and children under ten, at a maximum rate of two children per adult, were judged fit to follow the complete circuit,[1] as long as they did not show serious wounds or marked disability. Victims who did not correspond to the norms were to be conducted to the "hospital" by members of the blue commando and turned over to the Ukrainians [guards] for special treatment. A bench was built all around the ditch of the "hospital" so that the victims would fall of their own weight after receiving the bullet in the back of the head. This bench was to be used only when Kurland[2] was swamped with work. On the platform, the door which these victims took was surmounted by the Wolkowysk arrow. In the Sibylline language of Treblinka, "Wolkowysk" meant the bullet in the back of the neck or the injection. "Bialystok" meant the gas chamber.

Beside the "Bialystok" door stood a tall Jew whose role was to shout endlessly, "Large bundles here, large bundles here!" He had been nicknamed "Groysse Pack." As soon as the victims had gone through, Groysse Pack and his men from the red commando carried the bundles

---

[1] The "complete" circuit was getting off the train, walking along the platform through the door to the men's or women's barracks, undressing, and being led to the gas chamber "showers." [Ed.]

[2] Kurland was a Jew assigned to the "hospital," where he gave injections of poison to those who were too ill or crippled to make the complete circuit. [Ed.]

at a run to the sorting square, where the sorting commandos immediately took possession of them. As soon as they had gone through the door came the order, "Women to the left, men to the right." This moment generally gave rise to painful scenes.

While the women were being led to the left-hand barracks to undress and go to the hairdresser,[3] the men, who were lined up double file, slowly entered the production line. This production line included five stations. At each of these a group of "reds" shouted at the top of their lungs the name of the piece of clothing that it was in charge of receiving. At the first station the victim handed over his coat and hat. At the second, his jacket. (In exchange, he received a piece of string.) At the third he sat down, took off his shoes, and tied them together with the string he had just received. Until then the shoes were not tied together in pairs, and since the yield was at least fifteen thousand pairs of shoes per day, they were all lost, since they could not be matched up again.) At the fourth station the victim left his trousers, and at the fifth his shirt and underwear.

After they had been stripped, the victims were conducted, as they came off the assembly line, to the right-hand barracks and penned in until the women had finished: ladies first. However, a small number, chosen from among the most able-bodied, were singled out at the door to carry the clothing to the sorting square. They did this while running naked between two rows of Ukrainian guards. Without stopping once they threw their bundles onto the pile, turned around, and went back for another.

Meanwhile the women had been conducted to the barracks on the left. This barracks was divided into two parts: a dressing room and a beauty salon. "Put your clothes in a pile so you will be able to find them after the shower," they were ordered in the first room. The "beauty salon" was a room furnished with six benches, each of which could seat twenty women at a time. Behind each bench twenty prisoners of the red commando, wearing white tunics and armed with scissors, waited at attention until all the women were seated. Between haircutting sessions they sat down on the benches and, under the direction of a *kapo* [prisoner guard] who was transformed into a conductor, they had to sing old Yiddish melodies.

Lalka, who had insisted on taking personal responsibility for every detail, had perfected the technique of what he called the "Treblinka cut." With five well-placed slashes the whole head of hair was transferred to a sack placed beside each hairdresser for this purpose. It was simple and efficient. How many dramas did this "beauty salon" see? From the very beautiful young woman who wept when her hair was cut off, because she would be ugly, to the mother who grabbed a pair of scissors from

[3] Haircutter. [Ed.]

one of the "hairdressers" and literally severed a Ukrainian's arm; from the sister who recognized one of the "hairdressers" as her brother to the young girl, Ruth Dorfman, who, suddenly understanding and fighting back her tears, asked whether it was difficult to die and admitted in a small brave voice that she was a little afraid and wished it were all over.

When they had been shorn the women left the "beauty salon" double file. Outside the door, they had to squat in a particular way also specified by Lalka, in order to be intimately searched. Up to this point, doubt had been carefully maintained. Of course, a discriminating eye might have observed that . . . the smell was the smell of rotting bodies. A thousand details proved that Treblinka was not a transient camp, and some realized this, but the majority had believed in the impossible for too long to begin to doubt at the last moment. The door of the barracks, which opened directly onto the "road to heaven," represented the turning point. Up to here the prisoners had been given a minimum of hope, from here on this policy was abandoned.

This was one of Lalka's great innovations. After what point was it no longer necessary to delude the victims? This detail had been the subject of rather heated controversy among the Technicians. At the Nuremberg trials, Rudolf Höss, Commandant of Auschwitz, criticized Treblinka where, according to him, the victims knew that they were going to be killed. Höss was an advocate of the towel distributed at the door to the gas chamber. He claimed that this system not only avoided disorder, but was more humane, and he was proud of it. But Höss did not invent this "towel technique"; it was in all the manuals, and it was utilized at Treblinka until Lalka's great reform.

Lalka's studies had led to what might be called the "principle of the cutoff." His reasoning was simple: Since sooner or later the victims must realize that they were going to be killed, to postpone this moment was only false humanity. The principle "the later the better" did not apply here. Lalka had been led to make an intensive study of this problem upon observing one day completely by chance, that winded victims died much more rapidly than the rest. The discovery had led him to make a clean sweep of accepted principles. Let us follow his industrialist's logic, keeping well in mind that his great preoccupation was the saving of time. A winded victim dies faster. Hence, a saving of time. The best way to wind a man is to make him run—another saving of time. Thus Lalka arrived at the conclusion that you must make the victims run. A new question had then arisen: At what point must you make the victims run and thus create panic (a further aid to breathlessness)? The question had answered itself: As soon as you have nothing more to make them do. Franz located the exact point, the point of no return: the door of the barracks.

The rest was merely a matter of working out the details. Along the "road to heaven" and in front of the gas chambers he stationed a cordon of guards armed with whips, whose function was to make the victims run, to make them rush into the gas chambers of their own accord in search of refuge. One can see that this system is more daring than the classic system, but one can also see the danger it represents. Suddenly abandoned to their despair, realizing that they no longer had anything to lose, the victims might attack the guards. Lalka was aware of this risk, but he maintained that everything depended on the pace. "It's close work," he said, "but if you maintain a very rapid pace and do not allow a single moment of hesitation, the method is absolutely without danger." There were still further elaborations later on, but from the first day, Lalka had only to pride himself on his innovation: It took no more than three quarters of an hour, by the clock, to put the victims through their last voyage, from the moment the doors of the cattle cars were unbolted to the moment the great trap doors of the gas chamber were opened to take out the bodies. . . .

But let us return to the men. The timing was worked out so that by the time the last woman had emerged from the left-hand barracks, all the clothes had been transported to the sorting square. The men were immediately taken out of the right-hand barracks and driven after the women into the "road to heaven," which they reached by way of a special side path. By the time they arrived at the gas chambers the toughest, who had begun to run before the others to carry the bundles, were just as winded as the weakest. Everyone died in perfect unison for the greater satisfaction of that great Technician Kurt Franz, the Stakhanovite [model worker] of extermination.

4

TIMOTHY SNYDER

Holocaust: The Ignored Reality

As the first selection shows, the mass killing of Jews was a policy of the Nazis fueled by long-standing anti-Semitism, aggravated by German economic collapse and propaganda that linked Jews to both communist laborer agitation and the bankers at the upper levels of finance capitalism. This anti-Semitism was not limited to Germany, however. It was especially pervasive throughout Eastern Europe, where most Jews lived. Thus, it would be a mistake, according to the

Source: Timothy Snyder, "Holocaust: The Ignored Reality," *New York Review of Books 56*, no. 12 (July 16, 2009), http://www.nybooks.com/articles/22875.

author of this selection, to think of the Holocaust solely in terms of Germany and German Jews. What are the broader dimensions of the Holocaust that the author describes? Further, if the Holocaust refers only to the killing of Jews, how might a focus on this genocide alone minimize the scale of civilian casualties in World War II?

THINKING HISTORICALLY

The process of understanding without excusing is a struggle between the intellect and the emotions. No historical study can be entirely divorced from the emotions, but subjects like mass slaughter make it harder than many other subjects to be objective. Other factors might inhibit the historian's ability to get to the truth. One difficulty, for instance, lies with sources. What limitations does Snyder see in the sources that have been available to understand the Holocaust? How representative are survivors? What can we learn from the perpetrators? How do statistics help and hinder our understanding? What is gained, and lost, by distinguishing between such events as holocaust, genocide, war crimes, massacres, civilian casualties, and "collateral damage"?

Though Europe thrives, its writers and politicians are preoccupied with death. The mass killings of European civilians during the 1930s and 1940s [see Map 25.2] are the reference of today's confused discussions of memory, and the touchstone of whatever common ethics Europeans may share. The bureaucracies of Nazi Germany and the Soviet Union turned individual lives into mass death, particular humans into quotas of those to be killed. The Soviets hid their mass shootings in dark woods and falsified the records of regions in which they had starved people to death; the Germans had slave laborers dig up the bodies of their Jewish victims and burn them on giant grates. Historians must, as best we can, cast light into these shadows and account for these people. This we have not done. Auschwitz, generally taken to be an adequate or even a final symbol of the evil of mass killing, is in fact only the beginning of knowledge, a hint of the true reckoning with the past still to come.

The very reasons that we know something about Auschwitz warp our understanding of the Holocaust: we know about Auschwitz because there were survivors, and there were survivors because Auschwitz was a labor camp as well as a death factory. These survivors were largely West European Jews, because Auschwitz is where West European Jews were usually sent. After World War II, West European Jewish survivors were free to write and publish as they liked, whereas East European Jewish survivors, if caught behind the iron curtain, could not. In the West, memoirs of the Holocaust could (although very slowly) enter into historical writing and public consciousness.

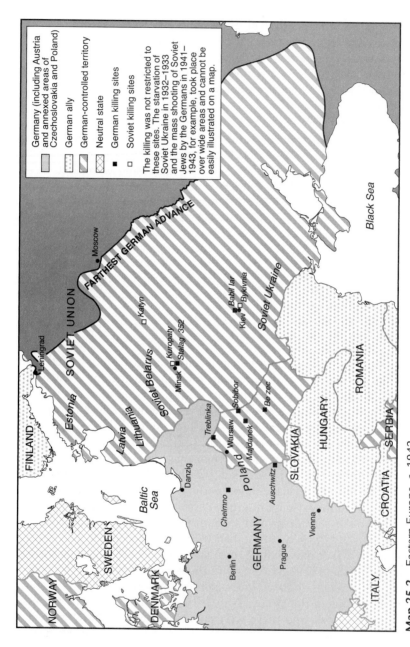

Map 25.2 Eastern Europe, c. 1942.

Source: Courtesy of the New York Review of Books.

This form of survivors' history, of which the works of Primo Levi[1] are the most famous example, only inadequately captures the reality of the mass killing. *The Diary of Anne Frank* concerns assimilated European Jewish communities, the Dutch and German, whose tragedy, though horrible, was a very small part of the Holocaust. By 1943 and 1944, when most of the killing of West European Jews took place, the Holocaust was in considerable measure complete. Two thirds of the Jews who would be killed during the war were already dead by the end of 1942. The main victims, the Polish and Soviet Jews, had been killed by bullets fired over death pits or by carbon monoxide from internal combustion engines pumped into gas chambers at Treblinka, Be zec,[2] and Sobibor in occupied Poland.

Auschwitz as symbol of the Holocaust excludes those who were at the center of the historical event. The largest group of Holocaust victims—religiously Orthodox and Yiddish-speaking Jews of Poland, or, in the slightly contemptuous German term, *Ostjuden*[3]—were culturally alien from West Europeans, including West European Jews. To some degree, they continue to be marginalized from the memory of the Holocaust. The death facility Auschwitz-Birkenau was constructed on territories that are today in Poland, although at the time they were part of the German Reich. Auschwitz is thus associated with today's Poland by anyone who visits, yet relatively few Polish Jews and almost no Soviet Jews died there. The two largest groups of victims are nearly missing from the memorial symbol.

An adequate vision of the Holocaust would place Operation Reinhardt, the murder of the Polish Jews in 1942, at the center of its history. Polish Jews were the largest Jewish community in the world, Warsaw the most important Jewish city. This community was exterminated at Treblinka, Be zec, and Sobibor. Some 1.5 million Jews were killed at those three facilities, about 780,863 at Treblinka alone. Only a few dozen people survived these three death facilities. Be zec, though the third most important killing site of the Holocaust, after Auschwitz and Treblinka, is hardly known. Some 434,508 Jews perished at that death factory, and only two or three survived. About a million more Polish Jews were killed in other ways, some at Chelmno, Majdanek, or Auschwitz, many more shot in actions in the eastern half of the country.

All in all, as many if not more Jews were killed by bullets as by gas, but they were killed by bullets in easterly locations that are blurred in painful remembrance. The second most important part of the Holocaust is the mass murder by bullets in eastern Poland and the Soviet Union.

[1] Primo Levi (1919–1987), Italian chemist, poet, essayist, novelist. Author of memoir *Survival in Auschwitz*. [Ed.]

[2] Also rendered as Belzec. [Ed.]

[3] Eastern Jews (from Eastern Europe). [Ed.]

It began with SS Einsatzgruppen shootings of Jewish men in June 1941, expanded to the murder of Jewish women and children in July, and extended to the extermination of entire Jewish communities that August and September. By the end of 1941, the Germans (along with local auxiliaries and Romanian troops) had killed a million Jews in the Soviet Union and the Baltics. That is the equivalent of the total number of Jews killed at Auschwitz during the entire war. By the end of 1942, the Germans (again, with a great deal of local assistance) had shot another 700,000 Jews, and the Soviet Jewish populations under their control had ceased to exist.

There were articulate Soviet Jewish witnesses and chroniclers, such as Vassily Grossman. But he and others were forbidden from presenting the Holocaust as a distinctly Jewish event. Grossman discovered Treblinka as a journalist with the Red Army in September 1944. Perhaps because he knew what the Germans had done to Jews in his native Ukraine, he was able to guess what had happened there, and wrote a short book about it. He called Treblinka "hell," and placed it at the center of the war and of the century. Yet for Stalin, the mass murder of Jews had to be seen as the suffering of "citizens." Grossman helped to compile a *Black Book* of German crimes against Soviet Jews, which Soviet authorities later suppressed. If any group suffered especially under the Germans, Stalin maintained wrongly, it was the Russians. In this way Stalinism has prevented us from seeing Hitler's mass killings in proper perspective.

In shorthand, then, the Holocaust was, in order: Operation Reinhardt, Shoah[4] by bullets, Auschwitz; or Poland, the Soviet Union, the rest. Of the 5.7 million or so Jews killed, roughly 3 million were pre-war Polish citizens, and another 1 million or so pre-war Soviet citizens: taken together, 70 percent of the total. (After the Polish and Soviet Jews, the next-largest groups of Jews killed were Romanian, Hungarian, and Czechoslovak. If these people are considered, the East European character of the Holocaust becomes even clearer.)

Yet even this corrected image of the Holocaust conveys an unacceptably incomplete sense of the scope of German mass killing policies in Europe. The Final Solution, as the Nazis called it, was originally only one of the exterminatory projects to be implemented after a victorious war against the Soviet Union. Had things gone the way that Hitler, Himmler, and Göring expected, German forces would have implemented a Hunger Plan in the Soviet Union in the winter of 1941–1942. As Ukrainian and south Russian agricultural products were diverted to Germany, some 30 million people in Belarus, northern Russia, and Soviet cities were to be starved to death. The Hunger Plan was only a prelude to Generalplan Ost, the colonization plan for the western Soviet Union, which foresaw the elimination of some 50 million people.

---

[4] Mass murder. [Ed.]

The Germans did manage to carry out policies that bore some resemblance to these plans. They expelled half a million non-Jewish Poles from lands annexed to the Reich. An impatient Himmler ordered a first stage of Generalplan Ost implemented in eastern Poland: ten thousand Polish children were killed and a hundred thousand adults expelled. The Wehrmacht[5] purposefully starved about one million people in the siege of Leningrad, and about a hundred thousand more in planned famines in Ukrainian cities. Some three million captured Soviet soldiers died of starvation or disease in German prisoner-of-war camps. These people were purposefully killed: as with the siege of Leningrad, the knowledge and intention to starve people to death was present. Had the Holocaust not taken place, this would be recalled as the worst war crime in modern history.

In the guise of anti-partisan actions, the Germans killed perhaps three quarters of a million people, about 350,000 in Belarus alone, and lower but comparable numbers in Poland and Yugoslavia. The Germans killed more than a hundred thousand Poles when suppressing the Warsaw Uprising of 1944. Had the Holocaust not happened, these "reprisals" too would be regarded as some of the greatest war crimes in history. In fact they, like the starvation of Soviet prisoners of war, are scarcely recalled at all beyond the countries directly concerned. German occupation policies killed non-Jewish civilians in other ways as well, for example by hard labor in prison camps. Again: these were chiefly people from Poland or the Soviet Union.

The Germans killed somewhat more than ten million civilians in the major mass killing actions, about half of them Jews, about half of them non-Jews. The Jews and the non-Jews mostly came from the same part of Europe. The project to kill all Jews was substantially realized; the project to destroy Slavic populations was only very partially implemented.

Auschwitz is only an introduction to the Holocaust, the Holocaust only a suggestion of Hitler's final aims. Grossman's novels *Forever Flowing* and *Life and Fate* daringly recount both Nazi and Soviet terror, and remind us that even a full characterization of German policies of mass killing is incomplete as a history of atrocity in mid-century Europe. It omits the state that Hitler was chiefly concerned to destroy, the other state that killed Europeans en masse in the middle of the century: the Soviet Union. In the entire Stalinist period, between 1928 and 1953, Soviet policies killed, in a conservative estimate, well over five million Europeans. Thus when one considers the total number of European civilians killed by totalitarian powers in the middle of the twentieth century, one should have in mind three groups of roughly equal size: Jews killed by Germans, non-Jews killed by Germans, and Soviet citizens killed by the Soviet state. As a general rule, the German regime killed civilians

---

[5] German Army. [Ed.]

who were not German citizens, whereas the Soviet regime chiefly killed civilians who were Soviet citizens. Soviet repressions are identified with the Gulag, much as Nazi repressions are identified with Auschwitz. The Gulag,[6] for all of the horrors of slave labor, was not a system of mass killing. If we accept that mass killing of civilians is at the center of political, ethical, and legal concerns, the same historical point applies to the Gulag as to Auschwitz. We know about the Gulag because it was a system of labor camps, but not a set of killing facilities. The Gulag held about 30 million people and shortened some three million lives. But a vast majority of those people who were sent to the camps returned alive. Precisely because we have a literature of the Gulag, most famously Aleksandr Solzhenitsyn's *Gulag Archipelago*, we can try to imagine its horrors — much as we can try to imagine the horrors of Auschwitz.

Yet as Auschwitz draws attention away from the still greater horrors of Treblinka, the Gulag distracts us from the Soviet policies that killed people directly and purposefully, by starvation and bullets. Of the Stalinist killing policies, two were the most significant: the collectivization famines of 1930–1933 and the Great Terror of 1937–1938. It remains unclear whether the Kazakh famine of 1930–1932 was intentional, although it is clear that over a million Kazakhs died of starvation. It is established beyond reasonable doubt that Stalin intentionally starved to death Soviet Ukrainians in the winter of 1932–1933. Soviet documents reveal a series of orders of October–December 1932 with evident malice and intention to kill. By the end, more than three million inhabitants of Soviet Ukraine had died.

What we read of the Great Terror[7] also distracts us from its true nature. The great novel and the great memoir are Arthur Koestler's *Darkness at Noon* and Alexander Weissberg's *The Accused*. Both focus our attention on a small group of Stalin's victims, urban Communist leaders, educated people, sometimes known in the West. This image dominates our understanding of the Great Terror, but it is incorrect. Taken together, purges of Communist Party elites, the security police, and military officers claimed not more than 47,737 lives.

The largest action of the Great Terror, Operation 00447, was aimed chiefly at "kulaks," which is to say peasants who had already been oppressed during collectivization.[8] It claimed 386,798 lives. A few national minorities, representing together less than 2 percent of the Soviet

---

[6] A system of Soviet labor camps, many in remote locations, where political prisoners were sent and sometimes disappeared. [Ed.]

[7] Period in 1930s of Stalin's purges of political rivals and anyone who voiced criticism. [Ed.]

[8] Soviet policy from 1928 to 1940 to end private property in farmland and create large farming communes. Forced collectivization of peasant kulaks led to mass starvation. [Ed.]

population, yielded more than a third of the fatalities of the Great Terror. In an operation aimed at ethnic Poles who were Soviet citizens, for example, 111,091 people were shot. Of the 681,692 executions carried out for alleged political crimes in 1937 and 1938, the kulak operation and the national operations accounted for 633,955, more than 90 percent of the total. These people were shot in secret, buried in pits, and forgotten.

The emphasis on Auschwitz and the Gulag understates the numbers of Europeans killed, and shifts the geographical focus of the killing to the German Reich and the Russian East. Like Auschwitz, which draws our attention to the Western European victims of the Nazi empire, the Gulag, with its notorious Siberian camps, also distracts us from the geographical center of Soviet killing policies. If we concentrate on Auschwitz and the Gulag, we fail to notice that over a period of twelve years, between 1933 and 1944, some 12 million victims of Nazi and Soviet mass killing policies perished in a particular region of Europe, one defined more or less by today's Belarus, Ukraine, Poland, Lithuania, and Latvia. More generally, when we contemplate Auschwitz and the Gulag, we tend to think of the states that built them as systems, as modern tyrannies, or totalitarian states. Yet such considerations of thought and politics in Berlin and Moscow tend to overlook the fact that mass killing happened, predominantly, in the parts of Europe between Germany and Russia, not in Germany and Russia themselves.

The geographic, moral, and political center of the Europe of mass killing is the Europe of the East, above all Belarus, Ukraine, Poland, and the Baltic States, lands that were subject to sustained policies of atrocity by both regimes. The peoples of Ukraine and Belarus, Jews above all but not only, suffered the most, since these lands were both part of the Soviet Union during the terrible 1930s and subject to the worst of the German repressions in the 1940s. If Europe was, as Mark Mazower[9] put it, a dark continent, Ukraine and Belarus were the heart of darkness.

Historical reckonings that can be seen as objective, such as the counting of victims of mass killing actions, might help to restore a certain lost historical balance. German suffering under Hitler and during the war, though dreadful in scale, does not figure at the center of the history of mass killing. Even if the ethnic Germans killed during flight from the Red Army, expulsion from Poland and Czechoslovakia in 1945–1947, and the firebombings in Germany are included, the total number of German civilians killed by state power remains comparatively small. . . .

The main victims of direct killing policies among German citizens were the 70,000 "euthanasia" patients and the 165,000 German Jews. The main German victims of Stalin remain the women raped by the Red Army and the prisoners of war held in the Soviet Union. Some

[9] Historian, author of *The Dark Continent: Europe's Twentieth Century* (2000). [Ed.]

363,000 German prisoners died of starvation and disease in Soviet captivity, as did perhaps 200,000 Hungarians. At a time when German resistance to Hitler receives attention in the mass media, it is worth recalling that some participants in the July 1944 plot to kill Hitler were right at the center of mass killing policies: Arthur Nebe, for example, who commanded Einsatzgruppe B in the killing fields of Belarus during the first wave of the Holocaust in 1941; or Eduard Wagner, the quartermaster general of the Wehrmacht, who wrote a cheery letter to his wife about the need to deny food to the starving millions of Leningrad.

It is hard to forget Anna Akhmatova: "It loves blood, the Russian earth." Yet Russian martyrdom and heroism, now loudly proclaimed in Putin's Russia, must be placed against the larger historical background. Soviet Russians, like other Soviet citizens, were indeed victims of Stalinist policy: but they were much less likely to be killed than Soviet Ukrainians or Soviet Poles, or members of other national minorities. During World War II several terror actions were extended to eastern Poland and the Baltic states, territories absorbed by the Soviet Union. In the most famous case, 22,000 Polish citizens were shot in 1940 at Katyn and four other sites; tens of thousands more Poles and Balts died during or shortly after deportations to Kazakhstan and Siberia. During the war, many Soviet Russians were killed by the Germans, but far fewer proportionately than Belarusians and Ukrainians, not to mention Jews. Soviet civilian deaths are estimated at about 15 million. About one in twenty-five civilians in Russia was killed by the Germans during the war, as opposed to about one in ten in Ukraine (or Poland) or about one in five in Belarus.

Belarus and Ukraine were occupied for much of the war, with both German and Soviet armies passing through their entire territory twice, in attack and retreat. German armies never occupied more than a small portion of Russia proper, and that for shorter periods. Even taking into account the siege of Leningrad and the destruction of Stalingrad, the toll taken on Russian civilians was much less than that on Belarusians, Ukrainians, and Jews. Exaggerated Russian claims about numbers of deaths treat Belarus and Ukraine as Russia, and Jews, Belarusians, and Ukrainians as Russians: this amounts to an imperialism of martyrdom, implicitly claiming territory by explicitly claiming victims. This will likely be the line propounded by the new historical committee appointed by President Dmitri Medvedev to prevent "falsifications" of the Russian past. Under legislation currently debated in Russia, statements such as those contained in this paragraph would be a criminal offense.

Ukrainian politicians counter Russia's monopolization of common suffering, and respond to Western European stereotypes of Ukrainians as Holocaust collaborators, by putting forward a narrative of suffering of their own: that millions of Ukrainians were deliberately starved by Stalin. President Viktor Yushchenko does his country a grave disservice by claiming ten million deaths, thus exaggerating the number of

Ukrainians killed by a factor of three; but it is true that the famine in Ukraine of 1932–1933 was a result of purposeful political decisions, and killed about three million people. With the exception of the Holocaust, the collectivization famines were the greatest political disaster of the European twentieth century. Collectivization nevertheless remained the central element of the Soviet model of development, and was copied later by the Chinese Communist regime, with the predictable consequence: tens of millions dead by starvation in Mao's Great Leap Forward.[10]

The preoccupation with Ukraine as a source of food was shared by Hitler and Stalin. Both wished to control and exploit the Ukrainian breadbasket, and both caused political famines: Stalin in the country as a whole, Hitler in the cities and the prisoner-of-war camps. Some of the Ukrainian prisoners who endured starvation in those camps in 1941 had survived the famine in 1933. German policies of starvation, incidentally, are partially responsible for the notion that Ukrainians were willing collaborators in the Holocaust. The most notorious Ukrainian collaborators were the guards at the death facilities at Treblinka, Be zec, and Sobibor. What is rarely recalled is that the Germans recruited the first cadres of such men, captured Soviet soldiers, from their own prisoner-of-war camps. They rescued some people from mass starvation, one great crime in the east, in order to make them collaborators in another, the Holocaust.

Poland's history is the source of endless confusion. Poland was attacked and occupied not by one but by both totalitarian states between 1939 and 1941, as Nazi Germany and the Soviet Union, then allies, exploited its territories and exterminated much of its intelligentsia at that time. Poland's capital was the site of not one but two of the major uprisings against German power during World War II: the ghetto[11] uprising of Warsaw Jews in 1943,[12] after which the ghetto was leveled; and the Warsaw Uprising of the Polish Home Army in 1944, after which the rest of the city was destroyed. These two central examples of resistance and mass killing were confused in the German mass media in August 1994, 1999, and 2004, on all the recent five-year anniversaries of the Warsaw Uprising of 1944, and will be again in August 2009.

If any European country seems out of place in today's Europe, stranded in another historical moment, it is Belarus under the dictatorship of Aleksandr Lukashenko. Yet while Lukashenko prefers to ignore the Soviet killing fields in his country, wishing to build a highway over

---

[10] Chinese communist collectivization (1958–1961) under Mao Zedong, which failed. [Ed.]

[11] Ghettos were urban areas in which Jews were forced to live, apart from the rest of the society. [Ed.]

[12] Revolt of Polish Jews in April 1943 in opposition to removal to Treblinka. Crushed by German troops in May. [Ed.]

the death pits at Kuropaty, in some respects Lukashenko remembers European history better than his critics. By starving Soviet prisoners of war, shooting and gassing Jews, and shooting civilians in anti-partisan actions, German forces made Belarus the deadliest place in the world between 1941 and 1944. Half of the population of Soviet Belarus was either killed or forcibly displaced during World War II: nothing of the kind can be said of any other European country.

Belarusian memories of this experience, cultivated by the current dictatorial regime, help to explain suspicions of initiatives coming from the West. Yet West Europeans would generally be surprised to learn that Belarus was both the epicenter of European mass killing and the base of operations of anti-Nazi partisans who actually contributed to the victory of the Allies. It is striking that such a country can be entirely displaced from European remembrance. The absence of Belarus from discussions of the past is the clearest sign of the difference between memory and history.

Just as disturbing is the absence of economics. Although the history of mass killing has much to do with economic calculation, memory shuns anything that might seem to make murder appear rational. Both Nazi Germany and the Soviet Union followed a path to economic self-sufficiency, Germany wishing to balance industry with an agrarian utopia in the East, the USSR wishing to overcome its agrarian backwardness with rapid industrialization and urbanization. Both regimes were aiming for economic autarky in a large empire, in which both sought to control Eastern Europe. Both of them saw the Polish state as a historical aberration;[13] both saw Ukraine and its rich soil as indispensable. They defined different groups as the enemies of their designs, although the German plan to kill every Jew is unmatched by any Soviet policy in the totality of its aims. What is crucial is that the ideology that legitimated mass death was also a vision of economic development. In a world of scarcity, particularly of food supplies, both regimes integrated mass murder with economic planning.

They did so in ways that seem appalling and obscene to us today, but which were sufficiently plausible to motivate large numbers of believers at the time. Food is no longer scarce, at least in the West; but other resources are, or will be soon. In the twenty-first century, we will face shortages of potable water, clean air, and affordable energy. Climate change may bring a renewed threat of hunger.

If there is a general political lesson of the history of mass killing, it is the need to be wary of what might be called privileged development: attempts by states to realize a form of economic expansion that designates victims, that motivates prosperity by mortality. The possibility

[13] Polish territory had often been part of one or more larger states. [Ed.]

cannot be excluded that the murder of one group can benefit another, or at least can be seen to do so. That is a version of politics that Europe has in fact witnessed and may witness again. The only sufficient answer is an ethical commitment to the individual, such that the individual counts in life rather than in death, and schemes of this sort become unthinkable.

The Europe of today is remarkable precisely in its unity of prosperity with social justice and human rights. Probably more than any other part of the world, it is immune, at least for the time being, to such heartlessly instrumental pursuits of economic growth. Yet memory has made some odd departures from history, at a time when history is needed more than ever. The recent European past may resemble the near future of the rest of the world. This is one more reason for getting the reckonings right.

5

IRIS CHANG

The Rape of Nanking

Nazi genocide and Soviet atrocities were not the only systematic slaughter of civilian populations during World War II. The military government of Japan, a German ally during the war, engaged in some of the same tactics of brutal and indiscriminate mass murder of civilians. In fact, atrocities in Japan preceded those in Germany.

While for Europeans World War II began with the German invasion of Poland on September 1, 1939, and for Americans with the Japanese attack at Pearl Harbor, Hawaii, on December 7, 1941, for the Chinese it began ten years earlier with the Japanese invasion of Manchuria in 1931. By 1937, Japanese troops occupied Peking and Shanghai as well as the old imperial capital of Nanking. It is estimated that more than twenty-five thousand civilians were killed by Japanese soldiers in the months after the fall of Nanking on December 13, 1937. But it was the appalling brutality of Japanese troops that foreign residents remembered, even those who could recall the brutality of the Chinese nationalist troops who captured the city in 1927. In the Introduction to *The Rape of Nanking* (p. 6), Iris Chang writes:

Source: Iris Chang, *The Rape of Nanking* (New York: Basic Books, 1997), 55–59.

The Rape of Nanking should be remembered not only for the number of people slaughtered but for the cruel manner in which many met their deaths. Chinese men were used for bayonet practice and in decapitation contests. An estimated 20,000 to 80,000 Chinese women were raped. Many soldiers went beyond rape to disembowel women, slice off their breasts, nail them alive to walls. Fathers were forced to rape their daughters, and sons their mothers, as other family members watched. Not only did live burials, castration, the carving of organs, and the roasting of people become routine, but more diabolical tortures were practiced, such as hanging people by their tongues on iron hooks or burying people to their waist and watching them get torn apart by German shepherds. So sickening was the spectacle that even the Nazis in the city were horrified, one declaring the massacre to be the work of "bestial machinery."

In the selection that follows, the author asks how Japanese soldiers were capable of such offenses. What is her answer?

THINKING HISTORICALLY

What would have happened to these recruits if they had refused an order to kill a prisoner or noncombatant? Once they had killed one prisoner, why did they find it easier to kill another? Did they eventually enjoy it, feel pride, or think it insignificant? The last informant, Nagatomi, says he had been a "devil." Had he been possessed? By whom?

How then do we explain the raw brutality carried out day after day after day in the city of Nanking? Unlike their Nazi counterparts, who have mostly perished in prisons and before execution squads or, if alive, are spending their remaining days as fugitives from the law, many of the Japanese war criminals are still alive, living in peace and comfort, protected by the Japanese government. They are therefore some of the few people on this planet who, without concern for retaliation in a court of international law, can give authors and journalists a glimpse of their thoughts and feelings while committing World War II atrocities.

Here is what we learn. The Japanese soldier was not simply hardened for battle in China; he was hardened for the task of murdering Chinese combatants and noncombatants alike. Indeed, various games and exercises were set up by the Japanese military to numb its men to the human instinct against killing people who are not attacking.

For example, on their way to the capital, Japanese soldiers were made to participate in killing competitions, which were avidly covered by the Japanese media like sporting events. The most notorious one appeared in the December 7 issue of the *Japan Advertiser* under the headline "Sub-Lieutenants in Race to Fell 100 Chinese Running Close Contest."

> Sub-Lieutenant Mukai Toshiaki and Sub-Lieutenant Noda Takeshi, both of the Katagiri unit at Kuyung, in a friendly contest to see which of them will first fell 100 Chinese in individual sword combat before the Japanese forces completely occupy Nanking, are well in the final phase of their race, running almost neck to neck. On Sunday [December 5] . . . the "score," according to the Asahi, was: Sub-Lieutenant Mukai, 89, and Sub-Lieutenant Noda, 78.

A week later the paper reported that neither man could decide who had passed the 100 mark first, so they upped the goal to 150. "Mukai's blade was slightly damaged in the competition," the *Japan Advertiser* reported. "He explained that this was the result of cutting a Chinese in half, helmet and all. The contest was 'fun' he declared." . . .

For new soldiers, horror was a natural impulse. One Japanese wartime memoir describes how a group of green Japanese recruits failed to conceal their shock when they witnessed seasoned soldiers torture a group of civilians to death. Their commander expected this reaction and wrote in his diary: "All new recruits are like this, but soon they will be doing the same things themselves."

But new officers also required desensitization. A veteran officer named Tominaga Shozo recalled vividly his own transformation from innocent youth to killing machine. Tominaga had been a fresh second lieutenant from a military academy when assigned to the 232nd Regiment of the 39th Division from Hiroshima. When he was introduced to the men under his command, Tominaga was stunned. "They had evil eyes," he remembered. "They weren't human eyes, but the eyes of leopards or tigers."

On the front Tominaga and other new candidate officers underwent intensive training to stiffen their endurance for war. In the program an instructor had pointed to a thin, emaciated Chinese in a detention center and told the officers: "These are the raw materials for your trial of courage." Day after day the instructor taught them how to cut off heads and bayonet living prisoners.

> On the final day, we were taken out to the site of our trial. Twenty-four prisoners were squatting there with their hands tied behind their backs. They were blindfolded. A big hole had been dug — ten meters long, two meters wide, and more than three meters deep. The regimental commander, the battalion commanders, and the company commanders all took the seats arranged for them. Second Lieutenant Tanaka bowed to the regimental commander and reported, "We shall now begin." He ordered a soldier on fatigue duty

to haul one of the prisoners to the edge of the pit; the prisoner was kicked when he resisted. The soldiers finally dragged him over and forced him to his knees. Tanaka turned toward us and looked into each of our faces in turn. "Heads should be cut off like this," he said, unsheathing his army sword. He scooped water from a bucket with a dipper, then poured it over both sides of the blade. Swishing off the water, he raised his sword in a long arc. Standing behind the prisoner, Tanaka steadied himself, legs spread apart, and cut off the man's head with a shout, "Yo!" The head flew more than a meter away. Blood spurted up in two fountains from the body and sprayed into the hole.

The scene was so appalling that I felt I couldn't breathe.

But gradually, Tominaga Shozo learned to kill. And as he grew more adept at it, he no longer felt that his men's eyes were evil. For him, atrocities became routine, almost banal. Looking back on his experience, he wrote: "We made them like this. Good sons, good daddies, good elder brothers at home were brought to the front to kill each other. Human beings turned into murdering demons. Everyone became a demon within three months."

Some Japanese soldiers admitted it was easy for them to kill because they had been taught that next to the emperor, all individual life—even their own—was valueless. Azuma Shiro, the Japanese soldier who witnessed a series of atrocities in Nanking, made an excellent point about his comrades' behavior in his letter to me. During his two years of military training in the 20th Infantry Regiment of Kyoto-fu Fukuchi-yama, he was taught that "loyalty is heavier than a mountain, and our life is lighter than a feather." He recalled that the highest honor a soldier could achieve during war was to come back dead: To die for the emperor was the greatest glory, to be caught alive by the enemy the greatest shame. "If my life was not important," Azuma wrote to me, "an enemy's life became inevitably much less important. . . . This philosophy led us to look down on the enemy and eventually to the mass murder and ill treatment of the captives."

In interview after interview, Japanese veterans from the Nanking massacre reported honestly that they experienced a complete lack of remorse or sense of wrongdoing, even when torturing helpless civilians. Nagatomi Hakudo spoke candidly about his emotions in the fallen capital:

I remember being driven in a truck along a path that had been cleared through piles of thousands and thousands of slaughtered bodies. Wild dogs were gnawing at the dead flesh as we stopped and pulled a group of Chinese prisoners out of the back. Then the Japanese officer proposed a test of my courage. He unsheathed his sword, spat on it, and with a sudden mighty swing he brought it down on the neck of a Chinese boy cowering before us. The head was cut clean off and tumbled away on the group as the body slumped forward, blood spurting in two great gushing fountains from the neck. The officer suggested I take the head home as a souvenir. I remember smiling proudly as I took his sword and began killing people.

After almost sixty years of soul-searching, Nagatomi is a changed man. A doctor in Japan, he has built a shrine of remorse in his waiting room. Patients can watch videotapes of his trial in Nanking and a full confession of his crimes. The gentle and hospitable demeanor of the doctor belies the horror of his past, making it almost impossible for one to imagine that he had once been a ruthless murderer.

"Few know that soldiers impaled babies on bayonets and tossed them still alive into pots of boiling water," Nagatomi said. "They gang-raped women from the ages of twelve to eighty and then killed them when they could no longer satisfy sexual requirements. I beheaded people, starved them to death, burned them, and buried them alive, over two hundred in all. It is terrible that I could turn into an animal and do these things. There are really no words to explain what I was doing. I was truly a devil."

6

President Truman's Announcement of the Dropping of an Atom Bomb on Hiroshima

In World War II the aerial bombing of civilian populations became increasingly common. A war that began for the British in a Nazi blitzkrieg of bombs and missiles on London, and that began for the United States in a Japanese air attack on the naval base at Pearl Harbor, came to a conclusion with an increased intensity of allied aerial attacks on the populated cities of Germany and Japan. In February of 1945, 1,300 U.S. and British bombers dropped 3,900 pounds of explosives on the medieval German city of Dresden, unleashing a firestorm that claimed tens of thousands of lives. Tokyo was bombed throughout the war, but in March of 1945, a single bombing run of 179 new long-range B-29s took well over a hundred thousand lives. By the end of the war 50 percent of Tokyo, the most densely populated city in the world, had been leveled, an area that had once

Source: "Statement by the President Announcing the Use of the A-Bomb at Hiroshima," Truman Library, http://www.trumanlibrary.org/calendar/viewpapers.php?pid=100.

housed one and a half million people. By the summer of 1945, a new kind of weapon was about to harness the atom for even greater destruction.

The U.S. effort to make an atomic bomb had been a secret wartime project, begun initially by President Franklin D. Roosevelt out of fear that Germany was already developing one. Work continued in 1945, despite the death of Roosevelt in April and the surrender of Germany in May, as the United States and its allies turned their attention to defeating the Japanese in the Pacific. President Truman was also interested in the propaganda value of the bomb to ward off possible Soviet intentions in China and Japan. On August 6, 1945, the United States dropped the world's first atomic bomb on the city of Hiroshima, Japan. Three days later, a second atomic bomb was dropped on the Japanese city of Nagasaki. On August 15, Japan surrendered.

This selection is President Truman's address after the bombing of Hiroshima. What reasons does he give for the use of such a weapon? How does he relate the atomic bomb to the use of other weapons of war? How does he relate it to the issue of peace?

THINKING HISTORICALLY

President Truman was aware there would be controversy about the use of an atomic bomb. He had received a petition from atomic scientists urging him to first demonstrate the power of the weapon to the Japanese by exploding it in an uninhabited area. He heard his secretary of war Stimson compare the army's imprecise bombing and high civilian causalities to Nazi atrocities. On the very day he gave the order to drop the bomb, July 25, 1945, he wrote in his diary: "I have told the Sec. of War, Mr. Stimson, to use it so that military objectives and soldiers and sailors are the target and not women and children. . . . The target will be a purely military one."[1] However, the order contained no such language.

What signs do you see in this announcement of an effort to counter some of these concerns? How might Truman have shielded himself from recognizing some of the consequences of his decision?

Sixteen hours ago an American airplane dropped one bomb on Hiroshima, an important Japanese Army base. That bomb had more power than 20,000 tons of T.N.T. It had more than two thousand times the blast power of the British "Grand Slam" which is the largest bomb ever yet used in the history of warfare.

[1] Truman quoted in Robert H. Ferrell, *Off the Record: The Private Papers of Harry S. Truman* (New York: Harper and Row, 1980), 55–56.

The Japanese began the war from the air at Pearl Harbor. They have been repaid many fold. And the end is not yet. With this bomb we have now added a new and revolutionary increase in destruction to supplement the growing power of our armed forces. In their present form these bombs are now in production and even more powerful forms are in development.

It is an atomic bomb. It is a harnessing of the basic power of the universe. The force from which the sun draws its power has been loosed against those who brought war to the Far East.

Before 1939, it was the accepted belief of scientists that it was theoretically possible to release atomic energy. But no one knew any practical method of doing it. By 1942, however, we knew that the Germans were working feverishly to find a way to add atomic energy to the other engines of war with which they hoped to enslave the world. But they failed. We may be grateful to Providence that the Germans got the V-1's and the V-2's late and in limited quantities and even more grateful that they did not get the atomic bomb at all.

The battle of the laboratories held fateful risks for us as well as the battles of the air, land and sea, and we have now won the battle of the laboratories as we have won the other battles.

Beginning in 1940, before Pearl Harbor, scientific knowledge useful in war was pooled between the United States and Great Britain, and many priceless helps to our victories have come from that arrangement. Under that general policy the research on the atomic bomb was begun. With American and British scientists working together we entered the race of discovery against the Germans.

The United States had available the large number of scientists of distinction in the many needed areas of knowledge. It had the tremendous industrial and financial resources necessary for the project and they could be devoted to it without undue impairment of other vital war work. In the United States the laboratory work and the production plants, on which a substantial start had already been made, would be out of reach of enemy bombing, while at that time Britain was exposed to constant air attack and was still threatened with the possibility of invasion. For these reasons Prime Minister Churchill and President Roosevelt agreed that it was wise to carry on the project here. We now have two great plants and many lesser works devoted to the production of atomic power. Employment during peak construction numbered 125,000 and over 65,000 individuals are even now engaged in operating the plants. Many have worked there for two and a half years. Few know what they have been producing. They see great quantities of material going in and they see nothing coming out of these plants, for the physical size of the explosive charge is exceedingly small. We have spent two billion dollars on the greatest scientific gamble in history—we won.

But the greatest marvel is not the size of the enterprise, its secrecy, nor its cost, but the achievement of scientific brains in putting together infinitely complex pieces of knowledge held by many men in different fields of science into a workable plan. And hardly less marvelous has been the capacity of industry to design, and of labor to operate, the machines and methods to do things never done before so that the brain child of many minds came forth in physical shape and performed as it was supposed to do. Both science and industry worked under the direction of the United States Army, which achieved a unique success in managing so diverse a problem in the advancement of knowledge in an amazingly short time. It is doubtful if such another combination could be got together in the world. What has been done is the greatest achievement of organized science in history. It was done under high pressure and without failure.

We are now prepared to obliterate more rapidly and completely every productive enterprise the Japanese have above ground in any city. We shall destroy their docks, their factories, and their communications. Let there be no mistake; we shall completely destroy Japan's power to make war.

It was to spare the Japanese people from utter destruction that the ultimatum of July 26 was issued at Potsdam.[2] Their leaders promptly rejected that ultimatum.[3] If they do not now accept our terms they may expect a rain of ruin from the air, the like of which has never been seen on this earth. Behind this air attack will follow sea and land forces in such numbers and power as they have not yet seen and with the fighting skill of which they are already well aware.

The Secretary of War, who has kept in personal touch with all phases of this project, will immediately make public a statement giving further details.

His statement will give facts concerning the sites of Oak Ridge near Knoxville, Tennessee, and at Richland near Pasco, Washington, and an installation near Santa Fe, New Mexico. Although the workers at the sites have been making materials to be used in producing the greatest destructive force in history they have not themselves been in danger beyond that of many other occupations, for the utmost care has been taken of their safety.

The fact that we can release atomic energy ushers in a new era in man's understanding of nature's forces. Atomic energy may in the future supplement the power that now comes from coal, oil, and falling water, but at present it cannot be produced on a basis to compete with them commercially. Before that comes there must be a long period of intensive research.

[2] Potsdam proclamation called for immediate unconditional surrender or "complete and utter destruction." [Ed.]

[3] Japan wanted the condition that it could keep the emperor (which the Allies later allowed). [Ed.]

It has never been the habit of the scientists of this country or the policy of the Government to withhold from the world scientific knowledge. Normally, therefore, everything about the work with atomic energy would be made public.

But under present circumstances it is not intended to divulge the technical processes of production or all the military applications, pending further examination of possible methods of protecting us and the rest of the world from the danger of sudden destruction. I shall recommend that the Congress of the United States consider promptly the establishment of an appropriate commission to control the production and use of atomic power within the United States. I shall give further consideration and make further recommendations to the Congress as to how atomic power can become a powerful and forceful influence towards the maintenance of world peace.

7

AKIHIRO TAKAHASHI

Memory of Hiroshima

The author of this selection, Akihiro Takahashi, was fourteen years old on August 6, 1945, when the United States bombed Hiroshima. He was standing in line with other students in the courtyard of the Hiroshima Municipal Junior High School. His and other survivors' recollections of that day and its aftermath were recorded, transcribed, and translated some forty years later by a Japanese peace project called "The Voice of Hibakusha."[1] How do you weigh the experience of Akihiro Takahashi against the reasons given by President Truman for dropping the bomb?

THINKING HISTORICALLY

One of the difficulties in thinking about the unthinkable is remembering the details we want to forget. Trauma victims often repress memories that are too painful to bear. In some cases time revives memories as well as heals. Akihiro Takahashi's recollections display both a prodigious and courageous memory. How might this process of remembering and telling be helpful to him? How might it be helpful to others?

---

[1] Japanese term for the victims of Hiroshima and Nagasaki: literally, the "explosion-affected people."

Source: "The Voice of Hibakusha," Testimony of Akihiro Takahashi in Atomic Archive, http://www.atomicarchive.com/Docs/Hibakusha/Akihiro.shtml.

. . . [W]e saw a B-29 approaching and about fly over us. All of us were looking up the sky, pointing out the aircraft. Then the teachers came out from the school building and the class leaders gave the command to fall in. Our faces were all shifted from the direction of the sky to that of the platform. That was the moment when the blast came. And then the tremendous noise came and we were left in the dark. I couldn't see anything at the moment of explosion just like in this picture. We had been blown by the blast. Of course, I couldn't realize this until the darkness disappeared. I was actually blown about 10 m. My friends were all marked down on the ground by the blast just like this. Everything collapsed for as far as I could see. I felt the city of Hiroshima had disappeared all of a sudden. Then I looked at myself and found my clothes had turned into rags due to the heat. I was probably burned at the back of the head, on my back, on both arms and both legs. My skin was peeling and hanging like this. Automatically I began to walk heading west because that was the direction of my home. After a while, I noticed somebody calling my name. I looked around and found a friend of mine who lived in my town and was studying at the same school. His name was Yamamoto. He was badly burnt just like myself. We walked toward the river. And on the way we saw many victims. I saw a man whose skin was completely peeled off the upper half of his body and a woman whose eye balls were sticking out. Her whole body was bleeding. A mother and her baby were lying with a skin completely peeled off. We desperately made away crawling. And finally we reached the river bank. At the same moment, a fire broke out. We made a narrow escape from the fire. If we had been slower by even one second, we would have been killed by the fire. Fire was blowing into the sky, becoming 4 or even 5 m high. There was a small wooden bridge left, which had not been destroyed by the blast. I went over to the other side of the river using that bridge. But Yamamoto was not with me any more. He was lost somewhere. I remember I crossed the river by myself and on the other side, I purged myself into the water three times. The heat was tremendous. And I felt like my body was burning all over. For my burning body the cold water of the river was as precious as a treasure. Then I left the river, and I walked along the railroad tracks in the direction of my home. On the way, I ran into another friend of mine, Tokujiro Hatta. I wondered why the soles of his feet were badly burnt. It was unthinkable to get burned there. But it was an undeniable fact that the soles were peeling and red muscle was exposed. Even though I myself was terribly burnt, I could not go home ignoring him. I made him crawl using his arms and knees. Next, I made him stand on his heels and I supported him. We walked heading toward my home repeating the two methods. When we were resting because we were so exhausted, I found my grandfather's brother and his wife, in other words, great uncle and great aunt, coming toward us. That was quite a coincidence. As you know, we have a proverb about meeting Buddha in Hell. My encounter with my relatives at that time was just like that. They seemed to be the Buddha to me wandering in the living hell.

Afterwards I was under medical treatment for one year and half and I miraculously recovered. Out of sixty of junior high school classmates, only ten of us are alive today. Yamamoto and Hatta soon died from the acute radiation disease. The radiation corroded their bodies and killed them. I myself am still alive on this earth suffering after-effects of the bomb. I have to see regularly an ear doctor, an eye doctor, a dermatologist and a surgeon. I feel uneasy about my health every day. Further, on both of my hands, I have keloids.[2] My injury was most serious on my right hand and I used to have terrible keloids right here. I had them removed by surgery in 1954, which enabled me to move my wrist a little bit like this. For my four fingers are fixed just like this, and my elbow is fixed at one hundred twenty degrees and doesn't move. The muscle and bones are attached [to] each other. Also the fourth finger of my right hand doesn't have a normal nail. It has a black nail. A piece of glass which was blown by the blast stuck here and destroyed the cells of the base of the finger. That is why a black nail continues to grow and from now on, too, it will continue to be black and never become normal. Anyway I'm alive today together with nine of my classmates for this forty years. I've been living believing that we can never waste the deaths of the victims. I've been living on, dragging my body full of sickness, and from time to time I question myself; I wonder if it is worth living in such hardship and pain and I become desperate. But it's time I manage to pull myself together and I tell myself once my life was saved, I should fulfill my mission as a survivor; in other words, it has been and it is my belief that those who survived must continue to talk about our experiences. To hand down the awful memories to future generations representing the silent voices of those who had to die in misery. Throughout my life, I would like to fulfill this mission by talking about my experience both here in Japan and overseas.

■ REFLECTIONS

Short of war, the world community has adopted three strategies to counter genocide and the mass killing of civilians. The first is the trial of war criminals. At the conclusion of World War II, the victorious Allies conducted war-crime trials of leading Nazi and Japanese officials. Twelve high Nazi officials and seven Japanese leaders were sentenced to death. Many others served prison sentences. Critics argued that

[2] Scars. [Ed.]

some of the alleged crimes ("wars of aggression" and "crimes against peace") were vague and that the victorious Allies might be guilty of these as well. Other charges — specifically "war crimes" and "crimes against humanity" — were devised as a response to the trials, an ex post facto (after the fact) violation of standard procedure where prosecution must be based on criminal statutes.

The problem was that the technology and practice of warfare had largely outrun international agreements. The first Geneva Conventions, dating from 1864, were mainly concerned with the treatment of the wounded and prisoners. Therefore, the second strategy was developing and refining international laws regarding human rights and the protection of civilians. In 1948, the "Universal Declaration of Human Rights" passed by the United Nations, itself a shaper and guardian of international law, offered a recognized standard and continuing process for defining and preventing genocide, mass murder, and "crimes against humanity." A fourth Geneva Convention in 1949 added the destruction of civilian populations in time of war to the list of war crimes for which a country would be held responsible. In addition, the precedent of the "International Military Tribunal" that tried Nazi and Japanese officials led to the creation of international laws and courts for the prosecution of war crimes and mass murder. The legacy continues. In 2002, the United Nations' International Court of Criminal Justice in the Hague, Netherlands, brought President Milošević of Yugoslavia to trial for the "ethnic cleansing" of Muslims in Kosovo and Bosnia, and (at this writing) the court continues with the prosecution of others. An International Tribunal for Genocide in Rwanda is similarly trying Hutu Rwandans charged with the mass murder of Tutsi fellow citizens in 1994.

A third strategy has emerged in recent years, largely where human rights abuses or civilian casualties have occurred within a national population. Often without the benefit of international courts or agencies, governments seeking to put past grievances aside, rather than prosecute offenders, have created "truth and reconciliation" commissions. In 1995, after decades of racist violence, the new South African government under Nelson Mandela established such a commission. Former white officials were guaranteed immunity from prosecution in return for complete and remorseful testimony of their crimes. Similarly, in El Salvador after a decade of violence in the 1980s, a new government established a Truth Commission in 1992 with United Nations assistance.

Finding the truth is the beginning of any strategy toward renewal. To promote understanding, archives must be opened, press and Internet censorship must be challenged, and laws such as the Freedom of Information Act must be used aggressively. But in addition, we must develop sensitivity to the plight of victims, knowledge of the victimizers' motives, and understanding about the ways that the horrendous can happen.

26

The Cold War and the Third World

China, Vietnam, Cuba, and Afghanistan, 1945–1989

■ HISTORICAL CONTEXT

The United States and the Union of Soviet Socialist Republics (USSR or Soviet Union) were allies during World War II. Meetings between the heads of state could be strained, but the Allies cooperated in the war and reached many agreements on the peace that followed, including the division of Europe and the creation of the United Nations and other international organizations. The Cold War developed within these agreements about postwar Europe and in the debates of the new international organizations, but it also festered from prewar ideological differences and antagonisms. U.S. troops were sent to fight "communist" Latin American regimes throughout the first half of the century; the Soviets never forgot Western efforts to reverse the Russian Revolution of 1917, and they never imagined that capitalism would outlast socialism.

World War II ended with the devastation of Germany and Japan and the exhaustion of England and France. One of the casualties turned out to be the colonial system that had fed and served the imperial powers. Some German colonies in Africa and Japanese colonies in Asia were turned over to the Allies after the war, but the postwar decades eventually brought an end to English and French colonies as well: British India as early as 1947, French Vietnam (Indochina) in 1954, and most of Africa by the early 1960s.

Although the Soviet Union had suffered enormous losses, it emerged with the United States as one of the two great "superpowers" of the postwar world. Both countries hoped to build a new world in which they would play a dominant role. Both professed opposition to imperialism, by which the Soviets meant the capitalist commercial and military expansion that they believed caused two world wars and by which the Americans meant the expansion of Soviet military power in Eastern Europe and communist governments in China and beyond. Both the United States and the Soviet Union championed the emergence of new independent nations from the ashes of colonialism, but neither wanted these new states to ally with the other power. In response, leaders of some of these new states declared themselves "noncommitted" to communism or capitalism—they were members of a "Third World" caught between the first two. Many Third World leaders were nationalists who sought help where they could find it, and some found the road to independence blockaded at either end. The Cold War, the author of our first selection argues, had much to do with the effort by the United States and the Soviet Union to woo these new nations to capitalism or communism and into American or Soviet spheres of influence.

■ THINKING HISTORICALLY

Finding a Point of View in Word Selection

> The great enemy of clear language is insincerity. When there is a gap between one's real and one's declared aims, one turns as it were instinctively to long words and exhausted idioms, like a cuttlefish spurting out ink. In our age there is no such thing as "keeping out of politics." All issues are political issues, and politics itself is a mass of lies, evasions, folly, hatred, and schizophrenia.
>
> —George Orwell, "Politics and the English Language"

In his 1946 essay, George Orwell flagged the Big Lies of Hitler, Stalin, and fascist dictatorships, but he also ruminated on the ways that all political language disguised intentions and manipulated meaning. When reality does not conform to beliefs or wishes, the words that are chosen distort the truth and delude the speaker as well as the audience.

Since Orwell confronted the political distortions of language in the period of the developing Cold War, we will use our study of the Cold War as an opportunity to examine how words were often chosen in political argument. It was an era of new mass media like television; government efforts to control public opinion through pollsters, advertisers, and public relations; and a competitive struggle between superpowers to win the "hearts and minds" of the world. Thus, many of the efforts of political writers were devoted to propaganda. But propagandists were not the only ones to choose their words for political purposes. Political practitioners did so as well, and often without realizing that the words they chose trapped them in dogma, fantasy, or fog.

1

ODD ARNE WESTAD
The Global Cold War

The author of this selection, Odd Arne Westad, is a modern historian of the Cold War. In this excerpt from his recent book, he argues that the Cold War was a global struggle between the United States and the Soviet Union for the "hearts and minds" of the peoples of the Third World. How, according to the author, was the Cold War different from earlier periods of Western imperialism? He says that the two superpowers had different ideas of modernity. What were these different ideas? What role did "Third World elites" play in the conflict between Washington and Moscow? How did peasants respond to the modernizing ideas of Washington or Moscow and the pressures of their own governments?

THINKING HISTORICALLY

Westad says the leaders and representatives of both the United States and the Soviet Union were motivated by ideology: They deeply believed that their view of the world — capitalism and freedom for the Americans versus communism and justice for the Soviets — was the only proper course of action for the Third World. How might that ideology color the way they understood and described what they saw? Westad also says that both powers believed in modernization (by which they both meant more industrialization and fewer peasants). How might that view shape their thinking? How, according to Westad, did these beliefs lead Americans or Soviets to delude themselves or others?

. . . The United States and the Soviet Union were driven to intervene in the Third World by the ideologies inherent in their politics. Locked in conflict over the very concept of European modernity — to which both states regarded themselves as successors — Washington and Moscow

---

Source: Odd Arne Westad, *The Global Cold War: Third World Interventions and the Making of Our Times* (Cambridge: Cambridge University Press, 2007), 4–5, 396–400.

needed to change the world in order to prove the universal applicability of their ideologies, and the elites of the newly independent states proved fertile ground for their competition. By helping to expand the domains of freedom or of social justice, both powers saw themselves as assisting natural trends in world history and as defending their own security at the same time. Both saw a specific mission in and for the Third World that only their own state could carry out and which without their involvement would flounder in local hands.

It is easy, therefore, to see the Cold War in the South as a continuation of European colonial interventions and of European attempts at controlling Third World peoples. I have little doubt that this is how historians of the future will regard the epoch—as one of the final stages of European global control. The means and the immediate motivations of Cold War interventions were remarkably similar to those of the "new imperialism" of the late colonial era, when European administrators set out to save the natives from ignorance, filth, and the consequences of their own actions. In both the early and the late twentieth century the European ideological rationale was that the path toward the future had been discovered by them and that they had a duty to help Third World peoples along that road. Throughout my research I have been astonished at the sense of duty and sacrifice that advisers on both sides showed in aiding friends or opposing foes in, for them, faraway places. The Cold War ethos—for those who accepted it—was at least as alluring and evocative as the imperialist ethos that it replaced, both for Europeans and for their collaborators. (While interviewing leaders of long-forgotten Third World people's republics, I have often been reminded of the Indian writer Nirad Chaudhury's dedication of his autobiography to the memory of the British empire, by which "all that was good and living within us was made, shaped, and quickened."[1])

One crucial comparative distinction needs to be made, however. It is to me less meaningful to talk about patterns of US or Soviet domination as "empires" than to describe them in a specific temporal sense. Different from the European expansion that started in the early modern period, Moscow's and Washington's objectives were not exploitation or subjection, but control and improvement. While this distinction may be rather ethereal seen from the receiving end, it is crucial for understanding the Cold War discourse itself: while imperialism got its social consciousness almost as an afterthought, in the Cold War it was inherent from the very beginning. Both US and Soviet criticisms of early twentieth-century European imperialist practices were genuine and deeply held ideological views. Indeed, some of the extraordinary brutality of Cold War interventions—such as those in Vietnam or Afghanistan—can only

---

[1] Nirad Chaudhury, *Autobiography of an Unknown Indian* (London: Macmillan, 1951).

be explained by Soviet and American identification with the people they sought to defend. Cold War interventions were most often extensions of ideological civil wars, fought with the ferocity that only civil wars can bring forth.

Conclusion: Revolutions, Interventions, and Great Power Collapse

The Cold War is still generally assumed to have been a contest between two superpowers over military power and strategic control, mostly centered on Europe. This book, on the contrary, claims that the most important aspects of the Cold War were neither military nor strategic, nor Europe-centered, but connected to political and social development in the Third World. . . . While the dual processes of decolonization and Third World radicalization were not in themselves products of the Cold War, they were influenced by it in ways that became critically important and that formed a large part of the world as we know it today. Some of these influences were coincidental, while others were brought about through direct interventions. Together they formed a pattern that had disastrous consequences for today's relationship between the pan-European states and other parts of the world.

In an historical sense — and especially as seen from the South — the Cold War was a continuation of colonialism through slightly different means. As a process of conflict, it centered on control and domination, primarily in ideological terms. The methods of the superpowers and of their local allies were remarkably similar to those honed during the last phase of European colonialism: giant social and economic projects, bringing promises of modernity to their supporters and mostly death to their opponents or those who happened to get in the way of progress. For the Third World, the continuum of which the Cold War forms a part did not start in 1945, or even 1917, but in 1878 — with the Conference of Berlin that divided Africa between European imperialist powers — or perhaps in 1415, when the Portuguese conquered their first African colony. Not even the conflict between the superpowers, or its ideological dimension, was a new element in this *longue durée*[2] of attempted European domination. The powers that had intervened before had often been in conflict with each other, sometimes as a result of competing ideas. As Joseph Conrad put it in 1902 in *Heart of Darkness* — the most searing critique of colonialism ever published:

> The conquest of the earth, which mostly means taking it away from those who have a different complexion or slightly flatter noses than

[2] Long period. [Ed.]

ourselves, is not a pretty thing when you look into it too much. What redeems it is the idea only. An idea at the back of it; not a sentimental pretence but an idea; and an unselfish belief in the idea — something you can set up, and bow down before, and offer a sacrifice to.[3]

The tragedy of Cold War history, both as far as the Third World and the superpowers themselves were concerned, was that two historical projects that were genuinely anticolonial in their origins became part of a much older pattern of domination because of the intensity of their conflict, the stakes they believed were involved, and the almost apocalyptic fear of the consequences if the opponent won. Even though both Washington and Moscow remained opposed to formal colonialism throughout the Cold War, the methods they used in imposing their version of modernity on Third World countries were very similar to those of the European empires that had gone before them, especially their immediate predecessors, the British and French colonial projects of the late nineteenth and early twentieth centuries. These methods were centered on inducing cultural, demographic, and ecological change in Third World societies, while using military power to defeat those who resisted. With their founding concepts of social justice or individual liberty long atrophied into self-referential ideologies, the starting point was what the anthropologist James C. Scott, following David Harvey, has called *high modernism*, defined, in Harvey's terms, as

the belief in linear progress, absolute truths, and rational planning of ideal social orders under standardized conditions of knowledge and production. . . . The modernism that resulted was . . . positivistic, technocratic, and rationalistic at the same time as it was imposed as the work of an elite avant-garde of planners, artists, architects, critics. . . . The "modernization" of European economies proceeded apace, while the whole thrust of international politics and trade was justified as bringing a benevolent and progressive "modernization process" to a backward Third World.[4]

As parts of the Third World rebelled against colonial control around the mid-third of the twentieth century, the revolutions that followed were often inspired by either the Soviet or the American form of high modernism. In a period of extreme global instability, it is not surprising that highly ideologized regimes such as the United States and the Soviet Union opted for intervention in what seemed to be a zero-sum game,[5]

[3] Joseph Conrad, *Heart of Darkness* (1902; Harmondsworth: Penguin, 1994).
[4] James C. Scott, *Seeing Like a State* (New Haven, CT: Yale University Press, 1988), p. 377, quoting David Harvey, *The Condition of Post-Modernity: An Inquiry into the Origins of Social Change* (Oxford: Basil Blackwell, 1989), p. 35.
[5] A situation in which one person's gain is another's loss. [Ed.]

unless there were strong domestic reasons against it. What is more surprising is the key role local elites played in abetting and facilitating these superpower interventions. Marrying their own domestic purposes to a faith in a common, international ideology, many aimed at some form of superpower involvement from the revolutionary stage onwards. A few of them set agendas—economic, political, military—that they knew could only be fulfilled through American or Soviet intervention. A large number waged war on their own peasant populations, attempting to force them—sometimes in conjunction with foreign interveners—to accept centralized plans for their improvement. Perhaps even more than the Cold War superpowers to which they were allied, these Third World elites viewed the modernization and ultimate abolition of the peasantry as a supreme aim, the pursuit of which justified the most extreme forms of violence.

Cold War ideologies and superpower interventions therefore helped put a number of Third World countries in a state of semipermanent civil war. In some cases there is likely to have been violent conflict at the end of the colonial period anyhow, but the existence of two ideologically opposed superpowers often perpetuated such clashes and made them much harder to settle. There were two main reasons for the perpetuation of war. One was the conviction among local elites that their aims were necessary and moral. Seeing the gulf that separated the lives of their populations from the lives led by those in the pan-European world, their agendas were fueled by the certainty that change was not just possible but necessary, and that almost any price was reasonable for defeating hunger, disease, ignorance, and injustice. Moreover, the moral imperative of progress that they appealed to was one that both superpowers shared, while the specifics for how to implement it were often inspired by one of them. It was not difficult, in other words, to find confirmation for agendas of change.[6]

Confronting the conditions under which the majority of the peasant population lived gave little room for moral equivalence between revolution and its opponents. As Che Guevara[7] put it in his speech to the Afro-Asian Solidarity Conference in Algiers in 1965, entitled "The Death of Imperialism and the Birth of a Moral World,"

> The struggle against imperialism—to be rid of colonial or neocolonial bondage—that is being carried on by means of political weapons or weapons of war . . . is not unconnected with the struggle

---

[6] For attempt at understanding the destruction wrought by anti-government forces, see Thandika Mkandawire, "The Terrible Toll of Post-Colonial 'Rebel Movements' in Africa: Towards an Explanation of the Violence against the Peasantry," *Journal of African Studies*, 40:2 (2002): 181–215.

[7] Che Guevara (1928–1987), Argentine physician who became a leader of the Cuban revolution, Marxist theorist, and revolutionary leader in Latin America. He died in Bolivia. [Ed.]

against backwardness and poverty. Both are stages in a single journey toward the creation of a new society that is rich and just at the same time. . . . We must win the battle of development by using the most advanced technology possible. We cannot start at the bottom of humanity's long ascent from feudalism to the atomic age of automation. . . . There must be a great technological leap forward . . . in the great factories and also in a suitably developed agriculture.[8]

The Westernized elites generally engineered Cold War plans for progress—and the ensuing military interventions—for what they saw as the best of purposes. In its first major declaration, the Communist regime in Afghanistan told the population that its aims were land reform, "abolition of old feudal and prefeudal relations," "ensuring the equality of rights of women and men in all social, economic, political, cultural, and civil aspects," universal education, free health services, and the elimination of illiteracy and unemployment.[9] To believe in this as a realistic agenda for change in what was Asia's poorest country, with a literacy rate of 24 percent and an average life expectancy of 42 years, took a rather extreme effort of will.[10] But, as the Communist leader Hafizullah Amin put it in his first message as president,

People are the makers of history and it is the people who bring about the most important phenomenon of social evolution through victorious social revolutions. It is here that the Great Leader[11] of the world's workers has said: revolutions are the festivals of the oppressed and exploited. In no other time except the time of revolution, are the masses in a position to actively go ahead as creators of a new social regime. In such times people can make miracles.[12]

Because of the bipolarity of the Cold War international system, Third World regimes and movements always stood a fair chance of gaining a superpower ally, however foolish their domestic plans were. Sometimes such alliances came about almost by default—in the style of "my enemy's enemy is my friend"; in other cases they were inspired by strategic considerations or by economic need. Most often, however, they were created by some sense of ideological cohesion, brought about by a

---

[8] Speech delivered 26 February 1965, quoted from John Gerassi, ed., *Venceremos! The Speeches and Writings of Ernesto Che Guevara* (New York: Macmillan, 1968), pp. 378–385.

[9] A. M. Baryalai, ed., *Democratic Republic of Afghanistan Annual: 1979* (Kabul: Kabul Times Publishing Agency, 1979), pp. 62–70.

[10] UNDP, Human Development Report, 1990, on http://hdr.undp.org/reports/global/1990/en/pdf/hdr_1990_ch2.pdf.

[11] Lenin. [Ed.]

[12] Speech delivered 17 September 1979, quoted from Emine Engin, ed., *The Revolution in Afghanistan* (London: İşçinin Sesi, 1982). The reference is to Lenin's "Two Tactics of Social-Democracy in the Democratic Revolution," in *Collected Works* (4th English edn; Moscow: Progress, 1972), vol. IX, pp. 15–140.

reading of your ally's ideas and purposes as matching your own. In some cases such projections could lead to the most extraordinary meetings of minds, as when the authoritarian developmentalism of South Vietnamese elites found US modernization theory in a joint battle against Communism. The instruments they created, such as the strategic hamlet program (very similar, by the way, to the program used by Soviets and Communists against their peasant enemies in Ethiopia) were ecstatically modern. As one of Walt Rostow's[13] young aides explained in 1961,

> Over the years each of the . . . villages could create its own subsidiary clusters. In the meantime a new agro-center could be constructed in the center of the "community compound." It would have a market place, bus terminal, stores, meeting hall, mid school, vocational training institute, landing strip, chopper pad [and] fair grounds. The agro-center would be completely modern—it would "futurize" village life without killing the old village.[14]

In a surprising number of cases peasants chose to fight back. Their resistance took different shapes and seldom conformed to the ideological patterns preferred by the high modernists. In most cases peasants were fighting for their villages, their beliefs, and their families. In a few cases, such as Vietnam or Algeria, large numbers opted for the form of modernity that seemed willing to give them some dignity and respect, while defending them from attack. But generally their battles were against centralized power, even when that power claimed to be representing "communal" values, such as in Ethiopia or Afghanistan. While their leaders sometimes chose to represent one imported ideology or another, there is little sign that the peasants themselves fought against anything other than a state—the "imported state," in Bertrand Badie's parlance—that was extending its grip toward their villages. Their battles were defensive, just as they had been in the colonial era, and just as they would be after their rebellions had helped to topple states of one ideological persuasion or another.

The wars fought in the Third World during the Cold War were despairingly destructive. Since they were, mostly, wars against the peasantry, the best way of winning them was through hunger and thirst rather than through battles and bombing. The methods of these wars were to destroy lives rather than to destroy property. In country after country—Kurdistan, Guatemala, Vietnam, Angola, Ethiopia—peasants were taken off their land and out of their villages, and given the choice

---

[13] Walt Rostow (1916–2003), American security advisor to Presidents Kennedy and Johnson, staunch anticommunist and architect of Vietnam War. Professional economist and author of *The Stages of Economic Growth: A Non-communist Manifesto* (1960). [Ed.]

[14] Memorandum from Kenneth Young to Walt Rostow, 17 February 1961, NSF, Box 325, John F. Kennedy Presidential Library, quoted from David Milne, "America's Mission Civilisatrice: The Strategic Hamlet Program for South Vietnam," unpublished paper.

between submission and starvation. Even after the battles were declared over, governments continued to wage war on parts of their peasant populations: much of what the IMF and the World Bank—in their twenty-twenty wisdom of the late 1980s—called mismanagement and indifference was in fact warfare intended to break the will of recalcitrant peasant communities through destroying water resources, irrigation systems, and pastures. The *cultural* violence was sometimes as bad as the physical: millions were forced to change their religion, their language, their family structure, and even their names in order to fit in with progress.

2

X [GEORGE F. KENNAN]
The Sources of Soviet Conduct

This is a selection from a document that was most influential in setting U.S. policy toward the Soviet Union after World War II. It appeared in *Foreign Affairs* magazine, a periodical read by many State Department professionals and diplomats. The author, who signed the article "X," was known to be George F. Kennan, the deputy chief of mission of the United States to the USSR from 1944 to 1946 under Ambassador W. Averell Harriman. The article's analysis of "Soviet conduct" and recommendations for U.S. policy elaborated on a secret long telegram Kennan had sent to the U.S. secretary of state the previous year. What U.S. policies does Kennan recommend? How does this article support or contradict the interpretation of the Cold War offered in the preceding selection?

THINKING HISTORICALLY

The word most identified with Kennan's recommendations is *containment*. For most of the Cold War period, the United States saw its mission as containing the expansion of Soviet influence in the world. Often this "containment" policy took military form: wars fought on the periphery of the Soviet Union in Korea, Vietnam, and Afghanistan, as well as skirmishes and conflicts by surrogates in

Source: X, "The Sources of Soviet Conduct" *Foreign Affairs*, July 1947, Part IV of four.

other parts of the world. The word is ambiguous, however, and later in life Kennan said he intended mainly economic and diplomatic pressure. Whatever Kennan's meaning, containment of Soviet military power remained the centerpiece of U.S. policy. Why might the Soviet Union see containment as a war-mongering or imperialist policy? What words or ideas in this document seem to be based more on the author's hopes or ideology than on a disinterested or neutral view?

It is clear that the United States cannot expect in the foreseeable future to enjoy political intimacy with the Soviet regime. It must continue to regard the Soviet Union as a rival, not a partner, in the political arena. It must continue to expect that Soviet policies will reflect no abstract love of peace and stability, no real faith in the possibility of a permanent happy coexistence of the Socialist and capitalist worlds, but rather a cautious, persistent pressure toward the disruption and weakening of all rival influence and rival power.

Balanced against this are the facts that Russia, as opposed to the western world in general, is still by far the weaker party, that Soviet policy is highly flexible, and that Soviet society may well contain deficiencies which will eventually weaken its own total potential. This would of itself warrant the United States entering with reasonable confidence upon a policy of firm containment, designed to confront the Russians with unalterable counter-force at every point where they show signs of encroaching upon the interests of a peaceful and stable world.

But in actuality the possibilities for American policy are by no means limited to holding the line and hoping for the best. It is entirely possible for the United States to influence by its actions the internal developments, both within Russia and throughout the international Communist movement, by which Russian policy is largely determined. This is not only a question of the modest measure of informational activity which this government can conduct in the Soviet Union and elsewhere, although that, too, is important. It is rather a question of the degree to which the United States can create among the peoples of the world generally the impression of a country which knows what it wants, which is coping successfully with the problem of its internal life and with the responsibilities of a World Power, and which has a spiritual vitality capable of holding its own among the major ideological currents of the time. To the extent that such an impression can be created and maintained, the aims of Russian Communism must appear sterile and quixotic, the hopes and enthusiasm of Moscow's supporters must wane, and added strain must be imposed on the Kremlin's foreign policies.

For the palsied decrepitude of the capitalist world is the keystone of Communist philosophy. Even the failure of the United States to experience the early economic depression which the ravens of the Red Square have been predicting with such complacent confidence since hostilities ceased would have deep and important repercussions throughout the Communist world.

By the same token, exhibitions of indecision, disunity and internal disintegration within this country have an exhilarating effect on the whole Communist movement. At each evidence of these tendencies, a thrill of hope and excitement goes through the Communist world; a new jauntiness can be noted in the Moscow tread; new groups of foreign supporters climb on to what they can only view as the band wagon of international politics; and Russian pressure increases all along the line in international affairs.

It would be an exaggeration to say that American behavior unassisted and alone could exercise a power of life and death over the Communist movement and bring about the early fall of Soviet power in Russia. But the United States has it in its power to increase enormously the strains under which Soviet policy must operate, to force upon the Kremlin a far greater degree of moderation and circumspection than it has had to observe in recent years, and in this way to promote tendencies which must eventually find their outlet in either the breakup or the gradual mellowing of Soviet power. For no mystical, Messianic movement—and particularly not that of the Kremlin—can face frustration indefinitely without eventually adjusting itself in one way or another to the logic of that state of affairs.

Thus the decision will really fall in large measure in this country itself. The issue of Soviet-American relations is in essence a test of the overall worth of the United States as a nation among nations. To avoid destruction the United States need only measure up to its own best traditions and prove itself worthy of preservation as a great nation.

Surely, there was never a fairer test of national quality than this. In the light of these circumstances, the thoughtful observer of Russian-American relations will find no cause for complaint in the Kremlin's challenge to American society. He will rather experience a certain gratitude to a Providence which, by providing the American people with this implacable challenge, has made their entire security as a nation dependent on their pulling themselves together and accepting the responsibilities of moral and political leadership that history plainly intended them to bear.

3

The Vietnamese Declaration of Independence

Although this document may predate the Cold War, it demonstrates the importance of the anticolonial struggle to create new states at the end of World War II. Vietnam had been part of French Indochina from 1887 until World War II, when it was occupied by Japan. This Declaration of Independence represented an effort by Vietnamese nationalists to prevent the French from retaking the country from the defeated Japanese.

The author of the declaration, Ho Chi Minh (1890–1969), is a prime example of the kind of new national leader torn between the appeals of Washington and Moscow. A founder of the French Communist Party in 1921 as well as the Vietnamese Communist Party in 1930, he was also the leader of the Vietminh, the Vietnamese nationalist movement, even enjoying the secret help of the United States during World War II in the battle against Japan.

What, according to Ho Chi Minh, were the effects of French colonialism in Vietnam? What reasons does he give for Vietnamese independence?

THINKING HISTORICALLY

Since this document was intended as a declaration of Vietnamese nationalism, delivered in Vietnamese to the Vietnamese people, one is struck by the use of language from both the U.S. Declaration of Independence and the French Declaration of the Rights of Man and Citizen. What other signs do you see that Ho Chi Minh may have been interested in attracting the favor of a U.S. or French audience? What purpose would such a strategy serve?

"All men are created equal. They are endowed by their Creator with certain inalienable rights, among these are Life, Liberty, and the pursuit of Happiness."

This immortal statement was made in the *Declaration of Independence* of the United States of America in *1776*. In a broader sense, this means: All the peoples on the Earth are equal from birth, all the peoples have a right to live, to be happy and to be free.

The Declaration of the *French Revolution* made in *1791* on *the Rights of Man and the Citizen* also states: "All men are born free and with equal rights, and must always remain free and have equal rights."

Source: *Ho Chi Minh, Selected Works* (Hanoi, 1960–1962), 3:17–21.

Those are undeniable truths.

Nevertheless, for more than eighty years, the French imperialists, abusing the standard of *Liberty, Equality, and Fraternity*,[1] have violated our Motherland and oppressed our fellow-citizens. They have acted contrary to the ideals of humanity and justice. In the field of politics, they have deprived our people of every democratic liberty.

They have enforced inhuman laws; they have set up three distinct political regimes in the North, the Center and the South of Vietnam in order to wreck our national unity and prevent our people from being united.

They have built more prisons than schools. They have mercilessly slain our patriots—they have drowned our uprisings in rivers of blood. They have fettered public opinion; they have practised obscurantism against our people. To weaken our race they have forced us to use opium and alcohol.

In the fields of economics, they have fleeced us to the backbone, impoverished our people, and devastated our land.

They have robbed us of our rice fields, our mines, our forests, and our raw materials. They have monopolised the issuing of bank-notes and the export trade. They have invented numerous unjustifiable taxes and reduced our people, especially our peasantry, to a state of extreme poverty.

They have hampered the prospering of our national bourgeoisie; they have mercilessly exploited our workers.

In the autumn of 1940, when the Japanese Fascists violated Indochina's territory to establish new bases in their fight against the Allies, the French imperialists went down on their bended knees and handed over our country to them.

Thus, from that date, our people were subjected to the double yoke of the French and the Japanese. Their sufferings and miseries increased. The result was that from the end of last year to the beginning of this year, from Quang Tri province to the North of Vietnam, more than two million of our fellow-citizens died from starvation. On March 9, the French troops were disarmed by the Japanese. The French colonialists either fled or surrendered, showing that not only were they incapable of "protecting" us, but that, in the span of five years, they had twice sold our country to the Japanese.

On several occasions before March 9, the Vietminh League urged the French to ally themselves with it against the Japanese. Instead of agreeing to this proposal, the French colonialists so intensified their terrorist activities against the Vietminh members that before fleeing they massacred a great number of our political prisoners detained at Yen Bai and Cao Bang.

---

[1] This was the rallying cry of the French Revolution of 1789. (*Fraternity* means brotherhood.) [Ed.]

Notwithstanding all this, our fellow-citizens have always manifested toward the French a tolerant and humane attitude. Even after the Japanese putsch of March 1945, the Vietminh League helped many Frenchmen to cross the frontier, rescued some of them from Japanese jails, and protected French lives and property.

From the autumn of 1940, our country had in fact ceased to be a French colony and had become a Japanese possession.

After the Japanese had surrendered to the Allies, our whole people rose to regain our national sovereignty and to found the Democratic Republic of Vietnam.

The truth is that we have wrested our independence from the Japanese and not from the French.

The French have fled, the Japanese have capitulated, Emperor Bao Dai has abdicated. Our people have broken the chains which for nearly a century have fettered them and have won independence for the Fatherland. Our people at the same time have overthrown the monarchic regime that has reigned supreme for dozens of centuries. In its place has been established the present Democratic Republic.

For these reasons, we, members of the Provisional Government, representing the whole Vietnamese people, declare that from now on we break off all relations of a colonial character with France; we repeal all the international obligation that France has so far subscribed to on behalf of Vietnam and we abolish all the special rights the French have unlawfully acquired in our Fatherland.

The whole Vietnamese people, animated by a common purpose, are determined to fight to the bitter end against any attempt by the French colonialists to reconquer their country.

We are convinced that the Allied nations which at Tehran and San Francisco have acknowledged the principles of self-determination and equality of nations, will not refuse to acknowledge the independence of Vietnam.

A people who have courageously opposed French domination for more than eighty years, a people who have fought side by side with the Allies against the Fascists during these last years, such a people must be free and independent.

For these reasons, we, members of the Provisional Government of the Democratic Republic of Vietnam, solemnly declare to the world that Vietnam has the right to be a free and independent country and in fact it already has been so. The entire Vietnamese people are determined to mobilise all their physical and mental strength, to sacrifice their lives and property in order to safeguard their independence and liberty.

4

EDWARD LANSDALE

Report on CIA Operations in Vietnam, 1954–1955

France did not cede independence to Vietnam in 1945; nor did the United States support the Viet Minh against the French. The newly declared Democratic Republic of Vietnam controlled only the north while French forces controlled the south. Ho Chi Minh and the Viet Minh forces continued their struggle against the French, finally defeating them at the battle of Dien Bien Phu in 1954. An international peace conference at Geneva called for a temporary division of northern and southern Vietnam to be followed in two years by a national election for a unified government. However, in the wake of the Chinese communist victory in China in 1949 and the American fear of its further spread in the Korean War (1950–1953), the United States increasingly saw Ho Chi Minh and the Viet Minh as part of the expansion of communism rather than a national independence movement. In 1954 President Eisenhower voiced belief in a "falling domino" theory in which the loss of Vietnam would lead to communist victories throughout Southeast Asia and beyond. Fearing that Ho Chi Minh would win 80 percent of the vote in a general Vietnamese election, Eisenhower created a separate South Vietnamese government and army in violation of the Geneva Accords, and he sent U.S. advisors and resources to make this division along the 17th parallel permanent. But one of the problems was that many pro-French Catholics lived in the north where the Viet Minh were strongest, and many Viet Minh lived and operated in the south. Thus, the creation of a southern Republic of Vietnam required large-scale population transfers as well as efforts to bolster the resources and legitimacy of an untried southern government and army.

In this selection, Edward Lansdale informs his CIA superiors of some of the activities of one of the teams of advisors sent by the United States to accomplish these tasks. Lansdale was a legendary early CIA operative, known for his work in defeating a similar communist and nationalist movement in the Philippines. What did Lansdale's team attempt to do in the north? What was the purpose of the first rumor campaign? How would you judge the tactics and success of the Saigon Military Mission (SMM) team in the north? What did the CIA do in the south? How successful were its efforts?

Source: Edward Lansdale, "Report on CIA Operations in Vietnam, 1954–55," in *The Pentagon Papers*, abr. ed., ed. George C. Herring (New York: McGraw-Hill, 1993), 23–36.

THINKING HISTORICALLY

What do you make of Lansdale's quotation marks around "cold war"? What does Lansdale's use of the word *team* suggest to you? What does Lansdale mean by "the Geneva Agreements . . . imposed restrictive rules on all official Americans?" Notice how Lansdale uses the terms *Vietminh* and *Vietnamese*. How might others use these terms? What do you think of Lansdale's praise of American reporters for giving "the U.S. an objective account of events in Vietnam"? How does Lansdale describe the differences between the Vietminh and the "Vietnamese national army"? What conclusions does he draw from the differences between those two armies? What different conclusions could one draw?

I. Foreword

This is the condensed account of one year in the operations of a "cold war" combat team, written by the team itself in the field, little by little in moments taken as the members could. The team is known as the Saigon Military Mission. The field is Vietnam. There are other teams in the field, American, French, British, Chinese, Vietnamese, Vietminh, and others. Each has its own story to tell. This is ours. . . .

It was often a frustrating and perplexing year, up close. The Geneva Agreements signed on 21 July 1954 imposed restrictive rules upon all official Americans, including the Saigon Military Mission. An active and intelligent enemy made full use of legal rights to screen his activities in establishing his stay-behind organizations south of the 17th Parallel and in obtaining quick security north of that Parallel. The nation's economy and communications system were crippled by eight years of open war. The government, including its Army and other security forces, was in a painful transition from colonial to self rule, making it a year of hot-tempered incidents. Internal problems arose quickly to points where armed conflict was sought as the only solution. The enemy was frequently forgotten in the heavy atmosphere of suspicion, hatred and jealousy.

The Saigon Military Mission received some blows from allies and the enemy in this atmosphere, as we worked to help stabilize the government and to beat the Geneva time-table of Communist takeover in the north. However, we did beat the time-table. The government did become stabilized. The Free Vietnamese are now becoming unified and learning how to cope with the Communist enemy. We are thankful that we had a chance to help in this work in a critical area of the world, to be positive and constructive in a year of doubt.

II. Mission

The Saigon Military Mission (SMM) was born in a Washington policy meeting in early 1954, when Dien Bien Phu was still holding out against the encircling Vietminh. The SMM was to enter into Vietnam quietly and assist the Vietnamese, rather than the French, in unconventional warfare. The French were to be kept as friendly allies in the process, as far as possible.

The broad mission for the team was to undertake paramilitary operations against the enemy and to wage political-psychological warfare. Later, after Geneva, the mission was modified to prepare the means for undertaking paramilitary operations in Communist areas rather than to wage unconventional warfare. . . .

III. Highlights of the Year

a. Early Days

. . . Working in close cooperation with George Hellyer, USIS[1] Chief, a new psychological warfare campaign was devised for the Vietnamese Army and for the government in Hanoi. Shortly after, a refresher course in combat psywar was constructed and Vietnamese Army personnel were rushed through it. A similar course was initiated for the Ministry of Information. Rumor campaigns were added to the tactics and tried out in Hanoi. It was almost too late.

The first rumor campaign was to be a carefully planted story of a Chinese Communist regiment in Tonkin taking reprisals against a Vietminh village whose girls the Chinese had raped, recalling Chinese Nationalist troop behavior in 1945 and confirming Vietnamese fears of Chinese occupation under Vietminh rule; the story was to be planted by soldiers of the Vietnamese Armed Psywar Company in Hanoi dressed in civilian clothes. The troops received their instructions silently, dressed in civilian clothes, went on the mission, and failed to return. They had deserted to the Vietminh. . . .

Ngo Dinh Diem[2] arrived on 7 July, and within hours was in despair as the French forces withdrew from the Catholic provinces of

---

[1] United States Information Service, the overseas offices of the United States Information Agency (USIA), which was created by President Eisenhower in 1953 to project a positive image of the United States in the world. [Ed.]

[2] Ngo Dinh Diem (1901–1963), a Catholic, became a favorite of the United States while in exile. He returned to Vietnam in 1954 and became first president of South Vietnam as the French withdrew; was deposed and killed in a coup in 1963. [Ed.]

Phat Diem and Nam Dinh in Tonkin.[3] Catholic militia streamed north to Hanoi and Haiphong, their hearts filled with anger at French abandonment. The two SMM officers stopped a planned grenade attack by militia girls against French troops guarding a warehouse; the girls stated they had not eaten for three days; arrangements were made for Chinese merchants in Haiphong to feed them. Other militia attacks were stopped, including one against a withdrawing French artillery unit; the militia wanted the guns to stand and fight the Vietminh. The Tonkinese had hopes of American friendship and listened to the advice given them. Governor [name illegible] died, reportedly by poison. Tonkin's government changed as despair grew. On 21 July, the Geneva Agreement was signed. Tonkin was given to the Communists. Anti-Communists turned to SMM for help in establishing a resistance movement and several tentative initial arrangements were made. . . .

b. August 1954

An agreement had been reached that the personnel ceiling of U.S. military personnel with MAAG[4] would be frozen at the number present in Vietnam on the date of the cease-fire, under the terms of the Geneva Agreement. In South Vietnam this deadline was to be 11 August. It meant that SMM might have only two members present, unless action were taken. General O'Daniel agreed to the addition of ten SMM men under MAAG cover, plus any others in the Defense pipeline who arrived before the deadline. A call for help went out. Ten officers in Korea, Japan, and Okinawa were selected and rushed to Vietnam.

SMM had one small MAAG house. Negotiations were started for other housing, but the new members of the team arrived before housing was ready and were crammed three and four to a hotel room for the first days. Meetings were held to assess the new members' abilities. None had had political-psychological warfare experience. Most were experienced in paramilitary and clandestine intelligence operations. Plans were made quickly, for time was running out in the north; already the Vietminh had started taking over secret control of Hanoi and other areas of Tonkin still held by French forces.

Major Conein was given responsibility for developing a paramilitary organization in the north, to be in position when the Vietminh took over. . . . [His] . . . team was moved north immediately as part

[3] Area of northern Vietnam. French Indochina consisted of Cambodia, Laos, and three areas now making up Vietnam: Tonkin in the north, Annam in the center, and Cochinchina in what is now southernmost Vietnam. [Ed.]

[4] Military Assistance Advisory Group: military advisors sent to Vietnam by President Truman beginning in 1950 to train a Vietnamese national army for South Vietnam. [Ed.]

of the MAAG staff working on the refugee problem. The team had headquarters in Hanoi, with a branch in Haiphong. Among cover duties, this team supervised the refugee flow for the Hanoi airlift,[5] organized by the French. One day, as a CAT C-46[6] finished loading, they saw a small child standing on the ground below the loading door. They shouted for the pilot to wait, picked the child up and shoved him onto the aircraft, which they promptly taxied out for its takeoff in the constant air shuffle. A Vietnamese man and woman ran up to the team, asking what they had done with their small boy, whom they'd brought to say goodbye to relatives. The chagrined team explained, finally talked the parents into going south to Free Vietnam, put them in the next aircraft to catch up with their son in Saigon. . . .

c. September 1954

. . . Towards the end of the month, it was learned that the largest printing establishment in the north intended to remain in Hanoi and do business with the Vietminh. An attempt was made by SMM to destroy the modern presses, but Vietminh security agents already had moved into the plant and frustrated the attempt. This operation was under a Vietnamese patriot whom we shall call Trieu; his case officer was Capt. Arundel. Earlier in the month they had engineered a black psywar strike in Hanoi: leaflets signed by the Vietminh instructing Tonkinese on how to behave for the Vietminh takeover of the Hanoi region in early October, including items about property, money reform, and a three-day holiday of workers upon takeover. The day following the distribution of these leaflets, refugee registration tripled. Two days later Vietminh currency was worth half the value prior to the leaflets. The Vietminh took to the radio to denounce the leaflets; the leaflets were so authentic in appearance that even most of the rank and file Vietminh were sure that the radio denunciations were a French trick.

The Hanoi psywar strike had other consequences. Binh had enlisted a high police official of Hanoi as part of his team, to effect the release from jail of any team members if arrested. The official at the last moment decided to assist in the leaflet distribution personally. Police officers spotted him, chased his vehicle through the empty Hanoi streets of early morning, finally opened fire on him and caught him. He was the only member of the group caught. He was held in prison as a Vietminh agent.

---

[5] To fly Catholics from the northern city of Hanoi to South Vietnam. [Ed.]

[6] A plane; Civil Air Transport was established in Shanghai in 1946 as a Chinese airline and was owned and used by the CIA after 1950. The C-46 was a military transport and cargo plane made by the Curtiss-Wright Company. [Ed.]

d. October 1954

Hanoi was evacuated on 9 October. The northern SMM team left with the last French troops, disturbed by what they had seen of the grim efficiency of the Vietminh in their takeover, the contrast between the silent march of the victorious Vietminh troops in their tennis shoes and the clanking armor of the well-equipped French whose Western tactics and equipment had failed against the Communist military-political-economic campaign.

The northern team had spent the last days of Hanoi in contaminating the oil supply of the bus company for a gradual wreckage of the engines in the buses, in taking the first actions for delayed sabotage of the railroad (which required teamwork with a CIA special technical team in Japan who performed their part brilliantly), and in writing detailed notes of potential targets for future paramilitary operations. (U.S. adherence to the Geneva Agreement prevented SMM from carrying out the active sabotage it desired to do against the power plant, water facilities, harbor, and bridge.) The team had a bad moment when contaminating the oil. They had to work quickly at night, in an enclosed storage room. Fumes from the contaminant came close to knocking them out. Dizzy and weak-kneed, they masked their faces with handkerchiefs and completed the job.

Meanwhile, Polish and Russian ships had arrived in the south to transport southern Vietminh to Tonkin under the Geneva Agreement. This offered the opportunity for another black psywar strike. A leaflet was developed by Binh with the help of Capt. Arundel, attributed to the Vietminh Resistance Committee. Among other items, it reassured the Vietminh they would be kept safe below decks from imperialist air and submarine attacks, and requested that warm clothing be brought; the warm clothing item would be coupled with a verbal rumor campaign that Vietminh were being sent into China as railroad laborers. . . .

f. December 1954

. . . Till and Peg Durdin of the N.Y. Times, Hank Lieberman of the N.Y. Times, Homer Bigart of the N.Y. Herald-Tribune, John Mecklin of Life-Time and John Roderick of Associated Press, have been warm friends of SMM and worked hard to penetrate the fabric of French propaganda and give the U.S. an objective account of events in Vietnam. The group met with us at times to analyze objectives and motives of propaganda known to them, meeting at their own request as U.S. citizens. These mature and responsible news correspondents performed a valuable service for their country. . . .

g. January 1955

The Vietminh long ago had adopted the Chinese Communist thought that the people are the water and the army is the fish. Vietminh relations with the mass of the population during the fighting had been exemplary, with a few exceptions; in contrast, the Vietnamese National Army had been like too many Asian armies, adept at cowing a population into feeding them, providing them with girls. SMM had been working on this problem from the beginning. Since the National Army was the only unit of government with a strong organization through the country and with good communications, it was the key to stabilizing the situation quickly on a nation-wide basis. If Army and people could be brought together into a team, the first strong weapon against Communism could be forged. . . .

President Diem had continued requesting SMM help with the guard battalion for the Presidential Palace. We made arrangements with President Magsaysay in the Philippines and borrowed his senior aide and military advisor, Col. Napoleon Valeriano, who had a fine combat record against the Communist Huks[7] and also had reorganized the Presidential Guard Battalion for Magsaysay. Valeriano, with three junior officers, arrived in January and went to work on Diem's guard battalion. Later, selected Vietnamese officers were trained with the Presidential Guards in Manila. An efficient unit gradually emerged. Diem was warmly grateful for this help by Filipinos who also continuously taught our concept of loyalty and freedom.

The patriot we've named Trieu Dinh had been working on an almanac for popular sale, particularly in the northern cities and towns we could still reach. Noted Vietnamese astrologers were hired to write predictions about coming disasters to certain Vietminh leaders and undertakings, and to predict unity in the south. The work was carried out under the direction of Lt. Phillips, based on our concept of the use of astrology for psywar in Southeast Asia. Copies of the almanac were shipped by air to Haiphong and then smuggled into Vietminh territory.

Dinh also had produced a Thomas Paine[8] type series of essays on Vietnamese patriotism against the Communist Vietminh, under the guidance of Capt. Arundel. These essays were circulated among influential groups in Vietnam, earned front-page editorials in the leading daily newspapers in Saigon. Circulation increased with the publication of these essays. The publisher is known to SMM as the Dragon Lady and is a fine Vietnamese girl who has been the mistress of an anti-American French civilian. Despite anti-American remarks by her boy friend, we had helped her keep her paper from being closed by the government . . . and she found it profitable to heed our advice on the editorial content of her paper. . . .

---

[7] Nationalist movement in the Philippines that fought against the Japanese during World War II and then against the pro-American government. Lansdale had helped defeat them. [Ed.]

[8] Thomas Paine (1737–1809), British immigrant and supporter of the American Revolution and author of *Common Sense* (1776). [Ed.]

TIME MAGAZINE

Nikita Khrushchev: "We Will Bury You"

The first years of the Cold War pitted former World War II allies Soviet Premier Joseph Stalin and Presidents Roosevelt, Truman, and Eisenhower against each other. Stalin died in 1953, to be followed by two inconsequential leaders[1] and then longtime Communist Party leader Nikita Khrushchev, premier from 1955 to 1964. Khrushchev initiated the Soviet space and missile program, but he attempted to reduce the size of the army and strengthen the consumer sector of the economy. In February 1956, Khrushchev startled party members with a speech denouncing Stalin as a brutal dictator. The speech expressed long suppressed grievances, especially in the dependent Soviet satellite states of Poland, East Germany, Romania, and Hungary.

Hungarians opposed to continued Soviet rule saw an opportunity in the new climate and took to the streets in protest in October 1956. On November 1 their leader Imre Nagy declared an independent Hungarian government and asked for UN recognition. On November 4 Soviet troops invaded Hungary, crushing the revolution by November 10. This selection is a *Time* magazine report of a routine event the following week.

On November 17 Khrushchev hosted a reception for visiting Polish communist leader Wladyslaw Gomulka, inviting representatives of Western countries. At the reception, Khrushchev compared Soviet troops in Hungary and Eastern Europe with Western troops in two areas. What are these areas? What do you think of these comparisons? What was Khrushchev's attitude toward the United States and Western capitalist countries? What was his attitude toward colonialism?

THINKING HISTORICALLY

No four words better raised the fear of a Soviet threat for Americans during the Cold War than Khrushchev's "We will bury you." Numerous American political leaders, commentators, and citizens referred to that quote in the following years to underscore Soviet aggressive intentions. With those four words, the reformist premier who de-Stalinized Kremlin policy and later traveled through the United States arguing for nuclear disarmament and peaceful coexistence could be pictured as a dangerous belligerent.

[1] Georgy Malenkov and Nikolai Bulganin.

Source: "We Will Bury You!" *Time*, November 26, 1956.

But who said, "We will bury you"? Was it Khrushchev or *Time* magazine? The *New York Times* carried two reports of the same reception on November 18, the day after it occurred. Neither of these news accounts contains the phrase "We will bury you" or anything like it. Did other reporters not hear it, not translate Russian the same way, interpret it metaphorically, or not think it significant? We do not know. How does this and other language in the *Time* magazine article insinuate certain things or guide the reader toward a particular viewpoint? What is that viewpoint?

At the final reception for Poland's visiting Gomulka, stubby Nikita Khrushchev planted himself firmly with the Kremlin's whole hierarchy at his back, and faced the diplomats of the West, and the satellites, with an intemperate speech that betrayed as much as it threatened.

"We are Bolsheviks!" he declared pugnaciously. "We stick firmly to the Lenin precept—don't be stubborn if you see you are wrong, but don't give in if you are right." "When are you right?" interjected First Deputy Premier Mikoyan—and the crowd laughed. Nikita plunged on, turning to the Western diplomats. "About the capitalist states, it doesn't depend on you whether or not we exist. If you don't like us, don't accept our invitations, and don't invite us to come to see you. Whether you like it or not, history is on our side. We will bury you!"

Just the day before, ambassadors of twelve NATO nations had walked out on a Khrushchev tirade that lumped Britain, France and Israel as bandits. Now Khrushchev was off again.

The Kremlin men cheered. Gomulka laughed. Red-faced and gesticulating, Nikita rolled on: "The situation is favorable to us. If God existed, we would thank him for this. On Hungary—we had Hungary thrust upon us. We are very sorry that such a situation exists there, but the most important thing is that the counterrevolution must be shattered. They accuse us of interfering in Hungary's internal affairs. They find the most fearful words to accuse us. But when the British, French and Israelis cut the throats of the Egyptians,[2] that is only a police action aimed at restoring order! The Western powers are trying to denigrate Nasser,[3] although Nasser is not a Communist. Politically, he is closer to those who are waging war on him, and he has even put Communists in jail."

---

[2] On November 5, 1956, combined British and French forces invaded Egypt in retaliation for Egyptian nationalization of the Suez Canal, while Israel occupied the Egyptian Sinai Peninsula. [Ed.]

[3] Gamal Abdel Nasser (1918–1970), nationalist leader and president of Egypt, 1956–1970. Nasser was a socialist, a leader of neutral "nonaligned nations," and sought help from the United States, Soviet Union, and China. [Ed.]

"He had to," offered Soviet President Kliment Voroshilov.[4] Khrushchev turned on him and said: "Don't try to help me."

"Nasser is the hero of his nation, and our sympathies are on his side. We sent sharp letters to Britain, France and Israel — well, Israel, that was just for form, because, as you know, Israel carries no weight in the world, and if it plays any role, it was just to start a fight. If Israel hadn't felt the support of Britain, France and others, the Arabs would have been able to box her ears and she would have remained at peace. I think the British and French will be wise enough to withdraw their forces, and then Egypt will emerge stronger than ever."

Turning again to the Westerners, Khrushchev declared: "You say we want war, but you have now got yourselves into a position I would call idiotic" ("Let's say delicate," offered Mikoyan) "but we don't want to profit by it. If you withdraw your troops from Germany, France and Britain — I'm speaking of American troops — we will not stay one day in Poland, Hungary and Rumania." His voice was scornful as he added: "But we, Mister Capitalists, we are beginning to understand your methods."

By this time, the diplomats — who, in turn, have come to understand Mister Khrushchev's methods — had already left the room.

---

[4] Chairman of the Presidium of the Supreme Soviet, the head of state but a largely symbolic office compared to the premier or the head of the Communist Party, both of which positions Khrushchev held. [Ed.]

6

Soviet Telegram on Cuba

On January 1, 1959, Cuban revolutionaries under Fidel Castro overthrew the government of U.S.-backed dictator Fulgencio Batista. The Castro government increasingly faced opposition from the United States and relied on the support of the Soviet Union. U.S. efforts to depose Castro included a failed CIA-sponsored invasion by Cuban exiles at the Cuban Bay of Pigs, April 17–19, 1961, three

---

Source: Telegram of Soviet Ambassador to Cuba A. I. Alekseev to the USSR Ministry of Foreign Affairs (MFA), 7 September 1962 at Woodrow Wilson International Center for Scholars, Cold War International History Project, Virtual Archive: http://www.wilsoncenter. org/index.cfm?topic_id=1409&fuseaction=va2.document&identifier=5034DA8F-96B6-175C-97D258B27DC3A0E6&sort=Collection&item=Cuban%20Missile%20Crisis. [Source: Archive of Foreign Policy of the Russian Federation (AVP RF), Moscow, copy courtesy of National Security Archive (NSA), Washington, DC; translation by Mark H. Doctoroff.]

months after John F. Kennedy came into office. Expecting further
U.S. attempts at toppling the regime, the Castro government received from the Soviet Union midrange nuclear missiles. President
Kennedy learned of their existence on October 14, 1962. He demanded they be withdrawn and ordered a naval blockade of Cuban
ports. The confrontation, known as the Cuban Missile Crisis,
October 18–29, came dangerously close to erupting into a nuclear
war. The crisis ended with Khrushchev withdrawing the missiles and
the U.S. pledging not to invade Cuba and to withdraw American
missiles from Turkey.

This document reveals Cuban and Soviet attitudes shortly after the
Cuban receipt of the missiles but a month before the crisis. The document is a telegram, dated September 7, 1962, from the Soviet
ambassador in Cuba to the Soviet Foreign Ministry in Moscow. In it
he informs Moscow about recent events on the island. What seems
to be happening? What conclusions does the Soviet ambassador
draw? What does the ambassador want the Soviet government to
do? How well informed does the ambassador seem to be about
events in Cuba, the United States, and Latin America? Do you think
President Kennedy would have been less alarmed if he had read this
telegram?

THINKING HISTORICALLY

How are the words that the Soviet ambassador uses to describe the
situation in Cuba different from the way Americans would understand it? How significant were the Soviet missiles for the ambassador? Why are the charges of aggressive activity by the United States
against Cuba more believable in this document than they would be in
a magazine article or a public speech?

Recently, the ruling circles of the USA have noticeably activated a policy
of provocation against Cuba;[1] military preparations and its political
isolation. Nearly every day, the air space and territorial waters of Cuba
are violated by American airplanes, submarines and ships trying to
establish permanent control over the territory of Cuba and diverting
passenger and transport ships bound for Cuba. The landing of counter-
revolutionary bands of spies and arms has been increased.

[1] In November 1961, President Kennedy initiated Operation Mongoose, a secret plan to
stimulate a rebellion in Cuba, bring Cuban exiles into the U.S. army for training, undermine
the regime, and assassinate Castro. General Edward Lansdale was put in charge of operations.
The program was stepped up in the spring of 1962. The CIA also continued to support internal
resistance to Castro and engaged the assistance of organized crime figures who had interests in
Cuba to assassinate Castro. [Ed.]

The constant acts of provocation are carried out from the territory of the USA base at Guantanamo, most often in the form of shooting at Cuban patrols. Especially noteworthy among all these provocations are far reaching acts like the August 24 shelling of the hotel in which mainly live Soviet specialists, and also the lies published by the Kennedy Administration about the alleged August 30 attack, in international waters, on an American airplane from two small Cuban ships. In the USA government's announcement, it is noted that in the event of a repeat of "an incident of this type," the armed forces of the United States "will take all necessary retaliatory measures." It is entirely evident that this carries a great danger for Cuba, since it gives the most reactionary anti-Cuban authorities in the USA an opening at any moment to organize a provocation and unleash aggressive actions against Cuba.

In regard to the above two last actions undertaken by the USA, the government of Cuba came forward with corresponding official declarations signed by Fidel Castro. Both of these declarations were circulated as official documents to the UN. The goal of these declarations is to attract the attention of the appropriate international organizations and all of world public opinion to the provocative and far-reaching acts of the USA, to unmask the aggressive schemes of the United States in relation to Cuba, and to ward them off. In these declarations the government of Cuba precisely makes the point that the anti-Cuban actions and schemes of the USA present a threat not only to Cuba, but to the whole world.

The series of provocations is now accompanied by a whipped up, broad anti-Cuba campaign in the USA press, striving with all its might to convince the population of the United States of the alleged presence in Cuba of large contingents of Soviet troops and of the fact that Cuba has turned into a military base of "world Communism" which presents a grave threat to the USA and all Latin American countries. Under this pretext, the press, certain American senators and other public figures demand of the Kennedy administration the revival of the Monroe Doctrine,[2] establishment of a sea and air blockade of Cuba, the bringing into force of the Treaty of Rio de Janeiro,[3] and the military occupation of Cuba.

Following the signing in Moscow of the Soviet-Cuban communiqué in which the agreement of the Soviet government to provide assistance in strengthening its armed forces is noted, Kennedy in a public statement on September 4 pointed to the defensive nature of Cuba's military preparations and noted that Soviet military specialists are in Cuba to teach the Cubans how to use defensive equipment presented by the Soviet Union.

---

[2] The Monroe Doctrine (1823) warned European nations that any efforts by them to interfere in affairs of the Americas would be viewed as aggression requiring U.S. intervention. [Ed.]

[3] The Inter-American Treaty of Reciprocal Assistance (1947) held that any attack on one nation of the Americas would be viewed as an attack on them all. [Ed.]

Several USA press agencies, commenting on that part of Kennedy's statement, underline the evidence of the fact that the president of the USA obviously preferred an attempt to calm down those circles in the USA which are supporting quick, decisive actions against Cuba. Along with this, in Kennedy's statement there are contained insinuations of purported aggressive Cuban schemes regarding influence on the American continent and a threat to use "all necessary means" to "defend" the continent.

According to certain information, the USA State Department through its ambassadors notified the governments of Latin American countries that they can expect changes in the situation in the Caribbean basin "if Castro's government does not come to its senses." More probably, in the near future the USA, using the pretext of an allegedly growing threat to the Western hemisphere, will embark on a long process of increasing the pressure on governments of the Latin-American countries and will probably convene a meeting of foreign ministers of the member-countries of the OAS[4] to work out supplementary sanctions against Cuba. One can also assume that the most wildly aggressive powers in the USA (the Pentagon, the Cuban external counter-revolution,[5] and others) will continue to exert pressure on Kennedy in order to realize the most decisive actions against Cuba.

The campaign of anti-Cuban hysteria has been conveyed via American propaganda to Latin American countries too. There the publication of articles and transmissions of radio programs of anti-Cuban and anti-Soviet content is constantly encouraged, while the external Cuban counter-revolution and local reaction put constant pressure on the governments of those countries, conduct loud demonstrations and terrorize individuals and organizations which speak out in defense of the Cuban revolution, and by means of bribery and blackmail get a range of people who have visited Cuba to make anti-Cuban statements, and so forth.

Simultaneously, the USA continues actively to conduct purely military preparations,[6] aimed at repressing possible centers of the national-liberation movement in Latin America, and, given the appropriate circumstances, the Cuban revolution itself. This is shown by such facts as the organization by the United States of schools for instruction in methods of street-fighting and anti-partisan struggle in many Latin

[4] Organization of American States. A State Department memo dated May 17, 1962, lists Operation Mongoose "Task 1" as "obtain some special and significant action within the OAS organization against the Castro-Communist regime." For this and following U.S. security memos, see http://www.globalsecurity.org/intell/library/reports. [Ed.]

[5] "External counter-revolution" refers to Cuban exiles in the United States and elsewhere, including veterans of the Bay of Pigs, who were still organized to topple Castro. [Ed.]

[6] Whether President Kennedy was willing to mount another military operation is uncertain, but active preparations were made to train exiles, prepare a blockade, and consider all options, including military. [Ed.]

American countries (in Panama, Peru, Colombia, Equador, Bolivia, and others); continuing intensive instruction of Cuban counter-revolutionaries in camps located on the territory of the USA, in Puerto Rico and in several Central American countries; many inspection trips to these bases, schools, and camps by responsible American military officials and the heads of the Cuban counter-revolution, including Miro Cardona;[7] unflagging efforts of the USA aimed at strengthening the unity of the external Cuban counter-revolution and unity in the action of counter-revolutionary organizations active in Cuba itself, etc.

At the same time, the USA is actively continuing to conduct its efforts towards the political isolation of Cuba, particularly in Latin America. The USA is concentrating on putting pressure on the governments of Mexico and Brazil,[8] which continue to express their support for the principle of non-interference and self-determination of peoples. This pressure is applied through economic means, and also by exploiting the domestic reaction. The realization of Kennedy's visit to Mexico, following which he was to have quickly visited Brazil too (this visit was put off to the last months of the year), served the goals of determining the likelihood of attracting these two countries to the anti-Cuban plans of the USA.

Until now none of the attempts of the USA to attract Brazil and Mexico to its anti-Cuban adventures has had any success.

Under pressure from the USA, in a majority of Latin American countries the local authorities are applying the harshest measures aimed at forbidding or tightly limiting visits of any groups or individuals to Cuba, and also their contacts with Cuban delegations in third countries. People who visit Cuba or make contact with Cuban delegations in third countries are subject to arrest, repression, investigations upon return to their homeland. The USA does not lack means for organizing broad and loud provocations against Cuban delegations taking part in international quorums, as took place recently in Finland[9] and Jamaica.

Referring to the decision taken at the meeting at Punta-del-Este about the exclusion of Cuba from the OAS, the USA is undertaking all measures to deny Cuba participation in any organizations connected with the inter-American system. In particular, they recently undertook an attempt to secure the exclusion of Cuba from the Pan American Health Organization (PAHO). The unlawful denial of Cuba's application to join the

[7] Jose Miro Cardona (1902–1974): briefly prime minister of Cuba in 1959; went into exile and led anti-Castro Cubans in the United States. Was to be president if Bay of Pigs invasion succeeded. [Ed.]

[8] Mexico and Brazil were thought particularly important propaganda targets by the United States. [Ed.]

[9] U.S. State Department memo, June 27, 1962: "it is important to work with the forthcoming youth festival in Helsinki (where there will be 2,000 Latin American students) to take the festival away from the Communists and ensure a good amount of anti-Communist propaganda emanating from this support." [Ed.]

so-called Latin American Free Trade Association is another example.[10] In response to the American policy towards Cuba of provocation, military threats, and political isolation, the Cuban government is intensifying its efforts on strengthening its own armed forces, struggling with the internal counter-revolution, unmasking before world public opinion the aggressive designs of the USA, and broadening its anti-American propaganda in Latin America. At the end of August, taking into account the activization of provocative actions by the USA and the possible increase in the unleashing of counter-revolutionary bands and manifestations of domestic counter-revolution, preventive arrests were carried out in the country and strengthened control was established over many registered [known] counter-revolutionary elements and the places where they gather.

The Cuban leaders are paying serious attention to the question of strengthening the devotion to the revolution of the cadres of its diplomatic missions, particularly in Latin American countries; they are taking every opportunity, as was the case with their presentation at the Latin American Free Trade Association, to widen the sphere of their activity in Latin America; they are strengthening their connections with the Latin American peoples by inviting to Cuba society delegations and individual Latin American officials; in timely fashion and aggressively, they speak at international organizations, unmasking the aggressive schemes and actions of the USA; they are striving to take part in any international forums at which there is a possibility to expose the aggressive character of American imperialism; they are strengthening Cuba's ties with African and Asian countries, etc.

The Cuban leadership believes, however, that the main guarantee of the development of the Cuban Revolution under conditions of possible direct American aggression is the readiness of the Soviet government to provide military assistance to Cuba and simultaneously to warn the USA of that fact. From this position, the joint Soviet-Cuban communiqué about [Ernesto "Che"] Guevara's visit to Moscow was greeted by the Cuban leaders and the vast majority of the Cuban people with great enthusiasm and gratitude. The Cuban leadership and Fidel Castro himself suggest that these warnings will help to prevail against those forces in the USA that are warning of the outbreak now of a world conflict, and are staving off a direct American attack on Cuba in the near future.

In our opinion, in the near future the ruling circles of the USA will continue to expand the attacks on Cuba by all the above-mentioned means: provocations, the propaganda campaign, military preparations,

---

[10] Memo from Lansdale on Operation Mongoose, July 5, 1962: "State reports that diplomatic efforts are being made to block Cuba's application for accreditation to the European Economic Community. Similarly, efforts are being made to exclude Cuba from the proposed Latin American Free Trade area." [Ed.]

and actions of the domestic counter-revolution, political isolation, and so forth. Their success in drawing the Latin American countries into their aggressive actions will most depend on the positions of the governments of Mexico and Brazil.

We also suggest that the question of direct American actions against Cuba will be decided by the correlation of forces in American ruling circles which have differing approaches to questions of war and peace in the present period, and the struggle between them on these issues.

The mood of the overwhelming majority of the Cuban people is defiant, and regardless of the reality of the threat of intervention, no panic or fear before the threat which is hanging over Cuba is observed in the masses of the people. The American provocations make possible an ever-tighter unity of the Cuban workers and raise the political consciousness of the masses.

Regarding the provocations, the influence of the Soviet Union in Cuba has grown as never before, and our cooperation with the Cuban leaders has been strengthened even more.

In the interest of future productive work with our Cuban friends it would be desirable to receive from you for dispatch to the Cuban leaders information which we have about the plans of the USA government toward Cuba.

7

MAO TSE TUNG

Imperialism and All Reactionaries Are Paper Tigers

Mao Tse Tung (or Mao Zedong) (1893–1976) was the primary leader of the communist revolution in China (1949), the first president of the People's Republic of China (1954–1958), and the chairman of the Chinese Communist Party from 1943 until his death in 1976. Mao Tse Tung's version of Marxism-Leninism fit the circumstances of China, with its powerful landowning class, by emphasizing the importance of the peasants. He fought both the Japanese occupation army and the army of warlord-supported Chinese leader Chiang Kai-shek

Source: *Quotations from Chairman Mao Tsetung* (Peking: Foreign Language Press, 1972), 75–81; also available at http://www.marxists.org/reference/archive/mao/works/red-book/ch06.htm.

with a "People's Army" known for its discipline and lack of corruption. After 1949 Mao Tse Tung governed the People's Republic with increasing fervor and decreasing humanity. In the 1960s, fearing the emergence of a new social class, he led a "cultural revolution" in which millions of young devotees chanted the "Quotations from Chairman Mao," some of which are reprinted here, while urban professionals were sent to work in the countryside, landlords were dispossessed, and many Chinese lost their lives in the upheaval.

How would you compare Mao Tse Tung's attitude toward the United States with that of Khrushchev? In what ways was Mao Tse Tung's approach similar to the U.S. policy of containment? Would you call his foreign policy offensive or defensive?

THINKING HISTORICALLY

Mao Tse Tung's use of words like *imperialism*, *reactionaries*, and *paper tigers* is an example of what Orwell meant by empty abstractions that gloss over ideas instead of giving them meaning. Orwell argued that such abstractions not only misled their intended audience but also were a disability for those who used them because they led to sloppy thinking. What do you think of this criticism in relation to these quotations?

I have said that all the reputedly powerful reactionaries are merely paper tigers. The reason is that they are divorced from the people. Look! Was not Hitler a paper tiger? Was Hitler not overthrown? I also said that the tsar of Russia, the emperor of China and Japanese imperialism were all paper tigers. As we know, they were all overthrown. U.S. imperialism has not yet been overthrown and it has the atom bomb. I believe it also will be overthrown. It, too, is a paper tiger.

—Speech at the Moscow Meeting of Communist and Workers' Parties (November 18, 1957).

"Lifting a rock only to drop it on one's own feet" is a Chinese folk saying to describe the behavior of certain fools. The reactionaries in all countries are fools of this kind. In the final analysis, their persecution of the revolutionary people only serves to accelerate the people's revolutions on a broader and more intense scale. Did not the persecution of the revolutionary people by the tsar of Russia and by Chiang Kai-shek perform this function in the great Russian and Chinese revolutions?

—Speech at the Meeting of the Supreme Soviet of the USSR in Celebration of the 40th Anniversary of the Great October Socialist Revolution (November 6, 1957).

U.S. imperialism invaded China's territory of Taiwan[1] and has occupied it for the past nine years. A short while ago it sent its armed forces to invade and occupy Lebanon.[2] The United States has set up hundreds of military bases in many countries all over the world. China's territory of Taiwan, Lebanon and all military bases of the United States on foreign soil are so many nooses round the neck of U.S. imperialism. The nooses have been fashioned by the Americans themselves and by nobody else, and it is they themselves who have put these nooses round their own necks, handing the ends of the ropes to the Chinese people, the peoples of the Arab countries and all the peoples of the world who love peace and oppose aggression. The longer the U.S. aggressors remain in those places, the tighter the nooses round their necks will become.

—Speech at the Supreme State Conference (September 8, 1958).

Imperialism will not last long because it always does evil things. It persists in grooming and supporting reactionaries in all countries who are against the people, it has forcibly seized many colonies and semi-colonies and many military bases, and it threatens the peace with atomic war. Thus, forced by imperialism to do so, more than 90 per cent of the people of the world are rising or will rise in struggle against it. Yet, imperialism is still alive, still running amuck in Asia, Africa and Latin America. In the West imperialism is still oppressing the people at home. This situation must change. It is the task of the people of the whole world to put an end to the aggression and oppression perpetrated by imperialism, and chiefly by U.S. imperialism.

—Interview with a Hsinhua News Agency correspondent
(September 29, 1958).

Riding roughshod everywhere, U.S. imperialism has made itself the enemy of the people of the world and has increasingly isolated itself. The atom bombs and hydrogen bombs in the hands of the U.S. imperialists will never cow those who refuse to be enslaved. The raging tide of the people of the world against the U.S. aggressors is irresistible. Their struggle against U.S. imperialism and its lackeys will assuredly win still greater victories.

—"Statement Supporting the Panamanian People's Just Patriotic Struggle
Against U.S. Imperialism" (January 12, 1964), People of the World,
Unite and Defeat the U.S. Aggressors and All Their Lackeys, 2nd ed., pp. 9–10.

---

[1] The defeated army of Chiang Kai-shek and its supporters retreated to the island of Taiwan when they were defeated by the communists. There they established the government of the Republic of China, which still remains in delicate opposition to the much larger People's Republic on the mainland. [Ed.]

[2] President Eisenhower sent U.S. forces to Lebanon in July 1958 to support the pro-Western Christian government against socialist opposition (which Eisenhower determined to be communist). [Ed.]

If the U.S. monopoly capitalist groups persist in pushing their policies of aggression and war, the day is bound to come when the people of the whole world will hang them. The same fate awaits the accomplices of the United States.

—Speech at the Supreme State Conference (September 8, 1958).

Over a long period, we have developed this concept for the struggle against the enemy: strategically we should despise all our enemies, but tactically we should take them all seriously. This also means that we must despise the enemy with respect to the whole, but that we must take him seriously with respect to each concrete question. If we do not despise the enemy with respect to the whole, we shall be committing the error of opportunism. Marx and Engels were only two individuals, and yet in those early days they already declared that capitalism would be overthrown throughout the world. However, in dealing with concrete problems and particular enemies we shall be committing the error of adventurism unless we take them seriously. In war, battles can only be fought one by one and the enemy forces can only be destroyed one by one. Factories can only be built one by one. The peasants can only plough the land plot by plot. The same is even true of eating a meal. Strategically, we take the eating of a meal lightly—we know we can finish it. Actually, we eat it mouthful by mouthful. It is impossible to swallow an entire banquet in one gulp. This is known as a piecemeal solution. In military parlance, it is called wiping out the enemy forces one by one.

—Speech at the Moscow Meeting of Communist and Workers' Parties (November 18, 1957).

It is my opinion that the international situation has now reached a new turning point. There are two winds in the world today, the East Wind and the West Wind. There is a Chinese saying, "Either the East Wind prevails over the West Wind or the West Wind prevails over the East Wind." I believe it is characteristic of the situation today that the East Wind is prevailing over the West Wind. That is to say, the forces of socialism have become overwhelmingly superior to the forces of imperialism.

—Ibid.

8

Telephone Transcript: Soviet Premier and Afghan Prime Minister

The Soviet war in Afghanistan (1979–1989), which eventually contributed to the dissolution of the Soviet Union itself, began, like the American war in Vietnam, with seemingly small steps on behalf of a client who lacked widespread support. This document reveals one of the first of those steps. The Soviet client was Nur Mohammed Taraki, a leader of the communist movement in Afghanistan who came to the Afghan presidency as a result of a military coup in April 1978. His ambitious program of radical social reform alienated tribal and religious leaders. After only a year of an Afghan communist experiment, he was seeking aid from Moscow—an effort captured in this document. It is a transcript of a telephone conversation between the Soviet premier Alexei Kosygin and the Afghan prime minister Nur Mohammed Taraki on March 18, 1979, about six months before the Soviets sent troops into Afghanistan. Alexei Kosygin succeeded Khrushchev as Soviet premier, serving from 1964 to 1980.

It was common in the Cold War period to speak of clients of the big powers, like Taraki, as "puppets," but historians have since recognized that such collaborators had considerable power. What are the different powers that Kosygin and Taraki exert in this conversation? How are their differences expressed and resolved?

THINKING HISTORICALLY

Notice that Kosygin uses different words than Taraki to describe the Afghan people. What are these differences, and how do you explain them? How significant is this difference in word use?

KOSYGIN   Ask Comrade Taraki, perhaps he will outline the situation in Afghanistan.

TARAKI   The situation is bad and getting worse.

KOSYGIN   Do you have support among the workers, city dwellers, the petty bourgoisie, and the white collar workers in Herat? Is there still anyone on your side?

Source: Transcript of telephone conversation between Soviet premier Alexei Kosygin and Afghan prime minister Nur Mohammed Taraki, March 18, 1979. Cold War International History Project Bulletin, Issues 8–9, Winter 1996/1997, 145–46. Available at http://wilsoncenter.org/topics/pubs/ACF193.pdf.

TARAKI There is no active support on the part of the population. It is almost wholly under the influence of Shiite slogans—follow not the heathens, but follow us. The propaganda is underpinned by this.

KOSYGIN Are there many workers there?

TARAKI Very few—between 1,000 and 2,000 people in all.

KOSYGIN What are the prospects?

TARAKI We are convinced that the enemy will form new units and will develop an offensive.

KOSYGIN Do you not have the forces to rout them?

TARAKI I wish it were the case.

KOSYGIN What, then, are your proposals on this issue?

TARAKI We ask that you extend practical and technical assistance, involving people and arms.

KOSYGIN It is a very complex matter.

TARAKI Iran and Pakistan are working against us, accordingly to the same plan. Hence, if you now launch a decisive attack on Herat, it will be possible to save the revolution.

KOSYGIN The whole world will immediately get to know this. The rebels have portable radio transmitters and will report it directly.

TARAKI I ask that you extend assistance.

KOSYGIN We must hold consultations on this issue. Do you not have connections with Iran's progressives? Can't you tell them that it is currently the United States that is your and their chief enemy? The Iranians are very hostile toward the United States and evidently this can be put to use as propaganda. What foreign policy activities or statements would you like to see coming from us? Do you have any ideas on this question, propaganda-wise?

TARAKI Propaganda help must be combined with practical assistance. I suggest that you place Afghan markings on your tanks and aircraft and no one will be any the wiser. Your troops could advance from the direction of Kushka and from the direction of Kabul. In our view, no one will be any the wiser. They will think these are Government troops.

KOSYGIN I do not want to disappoint you, but it will not be possible to conceal this. Two hours later the whole world will know about this. Everyone will begin to shout that the Soviet Union's intervention in Afghanistan has begun. If we quickly airlift tanks, the necessary ammunition and make mortars available to you, will you find specialists who can use these weapons?

TARAKI I am unable to answer this question. The Soviet advisers can answer that.

KOSYGIN Hundreds of Afghan officers were trained in the Soviet Union. Where are they all now?

TARAKI Most of them are Moslem reactionaries. We are unable to rely on them, we have no confidence in them.

Kosygin   Can't you recruit a further 50,000 soldiers if we quickly air-lift arms to you? How many people can you recruit?

Taraki   The core can only be formed by older secondary school pupils, students, and a few workers. The working class in Afghanistan is very small, but it is a long affair to train them. But we will take any measures, if necessary.

Kosygin   We have decided to quickly deliver military equipment and property to you and to repair helicopters and aircraft. All this is for free. We have also decided to deliver to you 100,000 tons of grain and to raise gas prices from $21 per cubic meter to $37.

Taraki   That is very good, but let us talk of Herat. Why can't the Soviet Union send Uzbeks, Tajiks, and Turkmens in civilian clothing? No one will recognize them. We want you to send them. They could drive tanks, because we have all these nationalities in Afghanistan. Let them don Afghan costume and wear Afghan badges and no one will recognize them. It is very easy work, in our view. If Iran's and Pakistan's experience is anything to go by, it is clear that it is easy to do this work, they have already shown how it can be done.

Kosygin   You are, of course, oversimplifying the issue. It is a complex political and international issue, but, irrespective of this, we will hold consultations again and will get back to you.

Taraki   Send us infantry fighting vehicles by air.

Kosygin   Do you have anyone to drive them?

Taraki   We will find drivers for between 30 and 35 vehicles.

Kosygin   Are they reliable? Won't they flee to the enemy, together with their vehicles? After all, our drivers do not speak the language.

Taraki   Send vehicles together with drivers who speak our language— Tajiks and Uzbeks.

Kosygin   I expected this kind of reply from you. We are comrades and are waging a common struggle and that is why we should not stand on ceremony with each other. Everything must be subordinate to this.

■ REFLECTIONS

The Cold War used to be ancient history. It ended at such breathtaking speed and with such pronounced results that few imagined tomorrow would have anything to do with yesterday. The Soviet Union collapsed in 1991, like the Berlin Wall in 1989, into an irretrievable heap of rubble. Commissars became capitalists, the USSR awoke as Russia, Leningrad turned back into St. Petersburg, and the red flag with hammer and sickle was exchanged for a French-like tricouleur of red, white, and blue stripes. Shoppers replaced placeholders as waiting lines disappeared; shelves of pricey foreign delicacies appeared fully stocked.

Whole countries cracked off along the periphery of what had been a great empire. Baltic city-states breathed their own air and minted their own money. Newly independent Central Asian countries built mosques and elected new dictators. These non-Soviet "stans" sent Russians back to Russia, from which they emigrated by the millions to Toledo and Tel Aviv. Some of those who stayed turned nationalized industries into personal possessions. Others lost their jobs, their savings, their homes, and half their life expectancies. New classes emerged—the "Russian mafia" from the KGB, the plutocrats from the bureaucrats—except they were often the same people in better clothes.

So too the view from America. Reagan's "Evil Empire" of 1983 became a partner in peace. In 1990 Michael Gorbachev received the Nobel Prize for ending the Cold War. *Time* magazine—the same magazine that brought America the Cold War—named Gorbachev "Man of the Year." Ex-president Nixon—the same Nixon who had made a career of anticommunism, coming into national prominence in a "kitchen debate" with Khrushchev in 1959—said Gorbachev should have been "Man of the Decade." Times had changed.

But the New World Order of nuclear disarmament, shrunken military budgets, and global cooperation that Gorbachev and Reagan envisioned never quite arrived. A CIA director became president of the United States, shortly followed by his son, and a KGB secret policeman from the old USSR became president of the new Russia. George W. Bush, the son, said he looked into the eyes of Vladimir Putin, the KGB man, and saw his soul. Putin saw a partner. That was in June 2001. In the following years, the United States became more militarized and chose to show it could fight two major wars (in Iraq and Afghanistan) at the same time, while Putin, as president and prime minister, closed down the budding democracy of Russia faster than one could say Ivan the Terrible.

From the vantage point of 2010, the Cold War has certainly not returned. But its history has become more current. Russia and the United States are more often at variance in choosing friends and at odds over global issues than they were in the halcyon 1990s. The United States has lessons to learn from the old Soviet Union's misadventures in Afghanistan. And if Russia is a shadow of its Soviet self, China has become a giant. The give and take of superpowers may not be far ahead. One hopes the lessons will not lag too far behind.

27

Resources and Environment

The Case of Water, 1945 to the Present

■ HISTORICAL CONTEXT

From air pollution to deforestation, from the price of oil to global warming, issues of resource depletion and environmental degradation have grabbed public attention throughout the world in recent decades. Efforts to explain these problems have varied widely. This chapter approaches the problems of resources and environment from a number of different perspectives, offering different explanations. We begin with one of the most venerable explanations of human misery—too many humans. Popularized by Thomas Malthus in the nineteenth century, the view that population growth outpaces food production has enjoyed a revival in the age of the shrinking planet. Does the human reproductive instinct inevitably overpopulate our Garden of Eden? A second reading suggests the answer is maybe not. Is population growth an issue at all? From here we narrow our lens to focus on a particular set of resource problems: fresh water and related issues of sufficient food. The third reading offers a singular case of water depletion in a village in India. Or is it so singular? Next we explore the problem of scarce fresh water more generally and comparatively. What do you think of the argument that water is becoming scarcer than oil? Our final reading explores a new global dynamic caused by the scarcity of water in some places. Is it a new form of imperialism or a sensible sharing of resources?

■ THINKING HISTORICALLY

Evaluating Arguments

Each of the readings in this chapter attempts to explain the causes (and sometimes the consequences) of resource and environmental problems. In doing so, they stress certain causes over others. Population growth is emphasized in the first reading and discounted in the second. The third reading stresses economic factors, and the fourth and fifth different combinations of economic, political, and geographic factors. You will be asked to evaluate these explanations or arguments. You will also be asked to reflect on how you make such evaluations.

1

JUSTIN LAHART, PATRICK BARTA, AND ANDREW BATSON

New Limits to Growth Revive Malthusian Fears

In 1798, in *An Essay on the Principle of Population*, the British economist Thomas Robert Malthus argued that human population growth regularly outpaced the growth of the food supply, leading to periodic famine. In 1972 an influential foundation called the Club of Rome published a report titled *The Limits to Growth,* which updated Malthus for an age of oil dependency and a global population of four billion (compared to one billion in 1798). The report projected that exponential (multiplying) population growth would eventually surpass limited resources like oil and minerals.

In this article from the *Wall Street Journal*, the authors write of new "Malthusian fears." To a great extent these fears are based on rising population, standing at 6.6 billion in 2008 when this article was published and projected to rise to 9.2 billion by 2050. But a rising population is not the only problem. According to the authors, what factors besides population growth make it increasingly likely that we will confront limits to such necessary resources as food and water?

Source: Justin Lahart, Patrick Barta, and Andrew Batson, "New Limits to Growth Revive Malthusian Fears," *Wall Street Journal,* March 24, 2008, http://online.wsj.com/public/article_print/SB120613138379155707.html.

THINKING HISTORICALLY

Over the years, critics have raised various objections to Malthus and the Club of Rome. Some have said that population need not continue to grow by multiples: even though the rate of population increase has been staggering since the time of Malthus, it may slow down. Other critics have argued that, despite population growth, new technologies may increase available resources. Some argue for the effectiveness of market pricing to keep scarce resources available. What evidence would you seek to weigh any of these arguments? What further evidence would you seek to evaluate the view expressed here of contemporary Malthusians?

Now and then across the centuries, powerful voices have warned that human activity would overwhelm the earth's resources. The Cassandras[1] always proved wrong. Each time, there were new resources to discover, new technologies to propel growth.

Today the old fears are back.

Although a Malthusian catastrophe is not at hand, the resource constraints foreseen by the Club of Rome are more evident today than at any time since the 1972 publication of the think tank's famous book, "The Limits of Growth." Steady increases in the prices for oil, wheat, copper and other commodities—some of which have set record highs this month—are signs of a lasting shift in demand as yet unmatched by rising supply.

As the world grows more populous—the United Nations projects eight billion people by 2025, up from 6.6 billion today—it also is growing more prosperous. The average person is consuming more food, water, metal and power. Growing numbers of China's 1.3 billion people and India's 1.1 billion are stepping up to the middle class, adopting the high-protein diets, gasoline-fueled transport and electric gadgets that developed nations enjoy.

The result is that demand for resources has soared. If supplies don't keep pace, prices are likely to climb further, economic growth in rich and poor nations alike could suffer, and some fear violent conflicts could ensue.

Some of the resources now in great demand have no substitutes. In the 18th century, England responded to dwindling timber supplies by shifting to abundant coal. But there can be no such replacement for arable land and fresh water.

---

[1] Pessimists. In Greek mythology Cassandra could see disasters but no one believed her. [Ed.]

The need to curb global warming limits the usefulness of some resources—coal, for one, which emits greenhouse gases that most scientists say contribute to climate change. Soaring food consumption stresses the existing stock of arable land and fresh water.

"We're living in an era where the technologies that have empowered high living standards and 80-year life expectancies in the rich world are now for almost everybody," says economist Jeffrey Sachs, director of Columbia University's Earth Institute, which focuses on sustainable development with an emphasis on the world's poor. "What this means is that not only do we have a very large amount of economic activity right now, but we have pent-up potential for vast increases [in economic activity] as well." The world cannot sustain that level of growth, he contends, without new technologies.

Americans already are grappling with higher energy and food prices. Although crude prices have dropped in recent days, there's a growing consensus among policy makers and industry executives that this isn't just a temporary surge in prices. Some of these experts, but not all of them, foresee a long-term upward shift in prices for oil and other commodities.

Today's dire predictions could prove just as misguided as yesteryear's.

"Clearly we'll have more and more problems, as more and more [people] are going to be richer and richer, using more and more stuff," says Bjorn Lomborg, a Danish statistician who argues that the global-warming problem is overblown. "But smartness will outweigh the extra resource use."

Some constraints might disappear with greater global cooperation. Where some countries face scarcity, others have bountiful supplies of resources. New seed varieties and better irrigation techniques could open up arid regions to cultivation that today are only suitable as hardscrabble pasture; technological breakthroughs, like cheaper desalination or efficient ways to transmit electricity from unpopulated areas rich with sunlight or wind, could brighten the outlook.

In the past, economic forces spurred solutions. Scarcity of resource led to higher prices, and higher prices eventually led to conservation and innovation. Whale oil was a popular source of lighting in the 19th century. Prices soared in the middle of the century, and people sought other ways to fuel lamps. In 1846, Abraham Gesner began developing kerosene, a cleaner-burning alternative. By the end of the century, whale oil cost less than it did in 1831.

A similar pattern could unfold again. But economic forces alone may not be able to fix the problems this time around. Societies as different as the U.S. and China face stiff political resistance to boosting water prices to encourage efficient use, particularly from farmers. When resources such as water are shared across borders, establishing a pricing framework can be thorny. And in many developing nations, food-subsidy programs make it less likely that rising prices will spur change.

This troubles some economists who used to be skeptical of the premise of "The Limits to Growth." As a young economist 30 years ago, Joseph Stiglitz said flatly: "There is not a persuasive case to be made that we face a problem from the exhaustion of our resources in the short or medium run."

Today, the Nobel laureate is concerned that oil is underpriced relative to the cost of carbon emissions, and that key resources such as water are often provided free. "In the absence of market signals, there's no way the market will solve these problems," he says. "How do we make people who have gotten something for free start paying for it? That's really hard. If our patterns of living, our patterns of consumption are imitated, as others are striving to do, the world probably is not viable."

Dennis Meadows, one of the authors of "The Limits to Growth," says the book was too optimistic in one respect. The authors assumed that if humans stopped harming the environment, it would recover slowly. Today, he says, some climate-change models suggest that once tipping points[2] are passed, environmental catastrophe may be inevitable even "if you quit damaging the environment."

One danger is that governments, rather than searching for global solutions to resource constraints, will concentrate on grabbing share.

China has been funding development in Africa, a move some U.S. officials see as a way for it to gain access to timber, oil and other resources. India, once a staunch supporter of the democracy movement in military-run Myanmar, has inked trade agreements with the natural-resource rich country. The U.S., European Union, Russia and China are all vying for the favor of natural-gas-abundant countries in politically unstable Central Asia.

Competition for resources can get ugly. A record drought in the Southeast intensified a dispute between Alabama, Georgia and Florida over water from a federal reservoir outside Atlanta. A long-running fight over rights to the Cauvery River between the Indian states of Karnataka and Tamil Nadu led to 25 deaths in 1991.

Economists Edward Miguel of the University of California at Berkeley and Shanker Satyanath and Ernest Sergenti of New York University have found that declines in rainfall are associated with civil conflict in sub-Saharan Africa. Sierra Leone, for example, which saw a sharp drop in rainfall in 1990, plunged into civil war in 1991.

---

[2] Point at which a process has gone too far to be reversed. [Ed.]

A Car for Every Household

The rise of China and India already has changed the world economy in lasting ways, from the flows of global capital to the location of manufacturing. But they remain poor societies with growing appetites.

Nagpur in central India once was known as one of the greenest metropolises in the country. Over the past decade, Nagpur, now one of at least 40 Indian cities with more than a million people, has grown to roughly 2.5 million from 1.7 million. Local roads have turned into a mess of honking cars, motorbikes and wandering livestock under a thick soup of foul air.

"Sometimes if I see something I like, I just buy it," says Sapan Gajbe, 32 years old, a dentist shopping for an air conditioner at Nagpur's Big Bazaar mall. A month earlier, he bought his first car, a $9,000 Maruti Zen compact.

In 2005, China had 15 passenger cars for every 1,000 people, close to the 13 cars per 1,000 that Japan had in 1963. Today, Japan has 447 passenger cars per 1,000 residents, 57 million in all. If China ever reaches that point, it would have 572 million cars—70 million shy of the number of cars in the entire world today.

China consumes 7.9 million barrels of oil a day. The U.S., with less than one quarter as many people, consumes 20.7 million barrels. "Demand will be going up, but it will be constrained by supply," ConocoPhillips Chief Executive Officer James Mulva has told analysts. "I don't think we are going to see the supply going over 100 million barrels a day, and the reason is: Where is all that going to come from?"

Says Harvard economist Jeffrey Frankel: "The idea that we might have to move on to other sources of energy—you don't have to buy into the Club of Rome agenda for that." The world can adjust to dwindling oil production by becoming more energy efficient and by moving to nuclear, wind and solar power, he says, although such transitions can be slow and costly.

Global Thirst

There are no substitutes for water, no easy alternatives to simple conservation. Despite advances, desalination remains costly and energy intensive. Throughout the world, water is often priced too low. Farmers, the biggest users, pay less than others, if they pay at all.

In California, the subsidized rates for farmers have become a contentious political issue. Chinese farmers receive water at next to no cost, accounting for 65% of all water used in the country.

In Pondhe, an Indian village of about 1,000 on a barren plateau east of Mumbai, water wasn't a problem until the 1970s, when farmers began using diesel-powered pumps to transport water farther and faster. Local wells used to overflow during the monsoon season, recalls Vasantrao Wagle, who has farmed in the area for four decades. Today, they top off about 10 feet below the surface, and drop even lower during the dry season. "Even when it rains a lot, we aren't getting enough water," he says.

Parched northern China has been drawing down groundwater supplies. In Beijing, water tables have dropped hundreds of feet. In nearby Hebei province, once large Baiyangdian Lake has shrunk, and survives mainly because the government has diverted water into it from the Yellow River.

Climate change is likely to intensify water woes. Shifting weather patterns will be felt "most strongly through changes in the distribution of water around the world and its seasonal and annual variability," according to the British government report on global warming led by Nicholas Stern. Water shortages could be severe in parts of Africa, the Middle East, southern Europe and Latin America, the report said.

Feeding the Hungry

China's farmers need water because China needs food. Production of rice, wheat and corn topped out at 441.4 million tons in 1998 and hasn't hit that level since. Sea water has leaked into depleted aquifers in the north, threatening to turn land barren. Illegal seizures of farmland by developers are widespread. The government last year declared that it would not permit arable land to drop below 120 million hectares (296 million acres), and said it would beef up enforcement of land-use rules.

The farmland squeeze is forcing difficult choices. After disastrous floods in 1998, China started paying some farmers to abandon marginal farmland and plant trees. That "grain-to-green" program was intended to reverse the deforestation and erosion that exacerbated the floods. Last August, the government stopped expanding the program, citing the need for farmland and the cost.

A growing taste for meat and other higher-protein food in the developing world is boosting demand and prices for feed grains. "There are literally hundreds of millions of people . . . who are making the shift to protein, and competition for food world-wide is a new reality," says William Doyle, chief executive officer of fertilizer-maker Potash Corp. of Saskatchewan.

It takes nearly 10 pounds of grain to produce one pound of pork—the staple meat in China—and more than double that to produce a pound of beef, according to Vaclav Smil, a University of Manitoba geographer who studies food, energy and environment trends. The number of calories in the Chinese diet from meat and other animal products has more than doubled since 1990, according to the U.N. Food and Agriculture Organization. But China still lags Taiwan when it comes to per-capita pork consumption. Matching Taiwan would increase China's annual pork consumption by 11 billion pounds—as much pork as Americans eat in six or seven months.

Searching for Solutions

The 1972 warnings by the Club of Rome—a nongovernmental think tank now based in Hamburg that brings together academics, business executives, civil servants and politicians to grapple with a wide range of global issues—struck a chord because they came as oil prices were rising sharply. Oil production in the continental U.S. had peaked, sparking fears that energy demand had outstripped supply. Over time, America became more energy efficient, overseas oil production rose and prices fell.

The dynamic today appears different. So far, the oil industry has failed to find major new sources of crude. Absent major finds, prices are likely to keep rising, unless consumers cut back. Taxes are one way to curb their appetites. In Western Europe and Japan, for example, where gas taxes are higher than in the U.S., per capita consumption is much lower.

New technology could help ease the resource crunch. Advances in agriculture, desalination and the clean production of electricity, among other things, would help.

But Mr. Stiglitz, the economist, contends that consumers eventually will have to change their behavior even more than then did after the 1970s oil shock. He says the world's traditional definitions and measures of economic progress—based on producing and consuming ever more—may have to be rethought.

In years past, the U.S., Europe and Japan have proven adept at adjusting to resource constraints. But history is littered with examples of societies believed to have suffered Malthusian crises: the Mayans of Central America, the Anasazi of the U.S. Southwest, and the people of Easter Island.[3]

Those societies, of course, lacked modern science and technology. Still, their inability to overcome resource challenges demonstrates the perils of blithely believing things will work out, says economist James Brander at the University of British Columbia, who has studied Easter Island.

---

[3] Maya centers in northern Mexico declined after 800. Anasazi towns were deserted after 1100. Easter Island went into decline after 1600 (see Chapter 14, selection 7 of this reader). [Ed.]

"We need to look seriously at the numbers and say: Look, given what we're consuming now, given what we know about economic incentives, given what we know about price signals, what is actually plausible?" says Mr. Brander.

Indeed, the true lesson of Thomas Malthus, an English economist who died in 1834, isn't that the world is doomed, but that preservation of human life requires analysis and then tough action. Given the history of England, with its plagues and famines, Malthus had good cause to wonder if society was "condemned to a perpetual oscillation between happiness and misery." That he was able to analyze that "perpetual oscillation" set him and his time apart from England's past. And that capacity to understand and respond meant that the world was less Malthusian thereafter.

2

PHILLIP LONGMAN

Headed toward Extinction?

Phillip Longman is a senior fellow at the New America Foundation, a corporate-funded public policy institute, and the author of *The Empty Cradle: How Falling Birthrates Threaten World Prosperity and What to Do about It*. In this opinion piece, Longman summarizes the argument of the book. How, according to Longman, is global population changing? What are the likely implications of this change?

THINKING HISTORICALLY

How would you evaluate Longman's argument? Does he entirely contradict the argument of the previous reading, or is there some basis for reconciling the two? How might you reconcile the two arguments?

World population will hit 7 billion by 2012, according to a recent United Nations report. Given that we just hit the 6 billion mark in October 1999, it is easy to conclude that there are just too many people in the world. How are we ever going to overcome global warming, feed the masses, get that beachfront property, let alone find parking, if the population keeps jumping by nearly one billion per decade?

Source: Phillip Longman, "Headed toward Extinction?" *USA Today*, op ed page, March 24, 2009.

The good news is that's not going to happen again. If you need another megatrend to worry about, fixate instead on the growing prospects for world depopulation and what it means for you and your children (assuming you have any).

Yes, human population is still growing in some places dramatically so. But at the same time, a strange new phenomenon is spreading around the globe, one whose very existence contradicts the deepest foundations of our modern mind-set.

Darwinism presupposes, and modern biology teaches, that all organisms breed to the limit of their available resources. Yet starting in the world's richest, best-fed nations during the 1970s, and now spreading throughout the developing world, we find birthrates falling below the levels needed to avoid long-term, and in many instances, short-term, population loss. The phenomenon has spread beyond Europe and Asia to Latin America.

Brazil, a land once known for its celebration of dental-floss bikinis and youthful carnival exuberance, is an aging nation that no longer produces enough children to replace its population. The same is true of Chile and Costa Rica. Joining them over the next 10 to 20 years, the U.N. projects, will be many other countries Americans still tend to associate with youth bulges including Mexico, Argentina, Indonesia, India, Vietnam, Algeria, Kuwait, Libya and Morocco. Think we need to build a wall on the southern border? Birthrates have declined so quickly in Mexico that its population of children younger than 15 has been in free-fall since 2000 and is expected to drop by one-third over the next 40 years.

The Spread of Childlessness

Fertility[1] remains high in sub-Saharan Africa, but it is falling there, too, even as infants and children die by the millions. In Sierra Leone, for example, the average woman bears more than five children, but nearly one in six die before reaching age 5 and fewer yet make it to reproductive age. Remaining increases in world population depend critically on reduced mortality in sub-Saharan Africa. But that might well not happen given the high levels of warfare, contagion and economic turmoil throughout the continent.

The U.N. projects that world population could begin declining as early as 2040. Those worried about global warming and other environmental threats might view this prospect as an unmitigated good. But lost in most discussions of the subject is the rapid population aging that accompanies declining birthrates.

Under what the U.N. considers the most likely scenario, more than half of all remaining growth comes from a 1.2 billion increase in the

[1] Fertility rates measure average number of births in a population. [Ed.]

number of old people, while the worldwide supply of children will begin falling within 15 years. With fewer workers to support each elder, the world economy might have to run just that much faster, and consume that much more resources, or else living standards will fall.

In the USA, where nearly one-fifth of Baby Boomers[2] never had children, the hardship of vanishing retirement savings will be compounded by the strains on both formal and informal care-giving networks caused by the spread of childlessness. A pet will keep you company in old age, but it is unlikely to be of use in helping you navigate the health care system or in keeping predatory reverse mortgage brokers at bay.

Even countries in which women have few career choices are not immune from the spreading birth dearth and resulting age wave. Under the grip of militant Islamic clerisy, Iran has seen its population of children implode. Accordingly, Iran's population is now aging at a rate nearly three times that of Western Europe. Maybe the middle aging of the Middle East will bring a mellower tone to the region, but middle age will pass swiftly to old age. China, with its one-family-one-child policy, is on a similar course, becoming a 4-2-1 society in which each child supports two parents and four grandparents.

Where does it end? Demographers once believed that only as countries grew rich would their birthrates decline. And few imagined until recently that birthrates would ever remain below replacement levels indefinitely. To suppose the opposite is to presuppose extinction.

"An Avoidable Liability"

Yet we see sub-replacement fertility remaining entrenched among rich countries for more than two generations and now spreading throughout the developing world as well.

For the majority of the world's inhabitants who no longer live on farms or rely on home production, children are no longer an economic asset but an avoidable liability. At the same time, the spread of global media exposes people in even the remotest corners of the planet to glamorous lifestyles that are inconsistent with the sacrifices necessary to raise large families. In Brazil, birthrates dropped sequentially province by province as broadcast television became available.

As the number of women of reproductive age falls in country after country, world population is acquiring negative momentum and thus could decline even if birthrates eventually turn up. Societies around the globe need to ask why they are engaging in what biologists would surely recognize in any other species as maladaptive behavior leading either to extinction, or dramatic mutation.

[2] People born after World War II, when the return of soldiers and the new culture of child-rearing led to a bulge in population (1945–1960). [Ed.]

3

ALEXANDER COCKBURN

Message in a Bottle

Whether populations rise or fall, many areas of the world are already facing severe shortages in such basic resources as water. This article by a columnist in the liberal weekly *The Nation* explores a water shortage in the Indian state of Kerala. Most of Kerala is a tropical rain forest, receiving especially heavy rains in the summer monsoon season and known, as the author points out, as a breadbasket of India. What, according to the author, occurred to reduce the supply of fresh water available to the people of Plachimada, Kerala? What political and economic forces were responsible?

THINKING HISTORICALLY

As a critic of the excesses of corporate capitalism, Alexander Cockburn might be expected to argue that environmental and resource abuse are caused by corporate exploitation rather than population pressure. But what sort of evidence does he provide in this article? How would you try to determine if this particular case illustrates a common phenomenon or a rare exception?

Plachimada, Kerala

Whizzing along the road in the little Tata Indica, driven prestissimo by the imperturbable Sudhi, we crossed the state line from Tamil Nadu into Kerala, branched off the main road and ended up in the settlement of Plachimada, mostly inhabited by extremely poor people. There on one side of the street was the Coca-Cola plant, among the company's largest in Asia, and on the other a shack filled with locals eager to impart the news that they were now, as of April 2, in Day 1,076 of their struggle against the plant.

Coca-Cola came to India in 1993, looking for water and markets in a country where 170 million people have no access to drinking water, with shortages growing daily. The bloom was on neoliberalism back then, with central and state authorities falling over themselves to lease, sell or simply hand over India's assets to multinationals in the name of economic "reform."

Source: Alexander Cockburn, "Message in a Bottle," *The Nation*, May 2, 2005, p. 9.

Coca-Cola had sound reasons for coming to Plachimada, which has large underground water deposits. The site Coca-Cola picked is between two large reservoirs and ten yards south of an irrigation canal. Coke's plot is surrounded by colonies inhabited by several hundred poor people with an average holding of four-tenths of an acre. Virtually the sole source of employment is wage labor, usually for no more than 100 to 120 days in the year.

Ushered in by Kerala's present "reform"-minded government, the plant duly got a license from the local council, known as the Perumatty Grama Panchayat. Under India's constitution panchayats have total discretion in such matters. Coca-Cola bought a property of some forty acres held by a couple of large landowners, built a plant, sank six bore wells and commenced operations in March 2000.

Within six months the villagers saw the level of their water drop sharply, and the water they did draw was awful. It gave some people diarrhea and bouts of dizziness. To wash in it was to get skin rashes, a burning feel on the skin. It left their hair greasy and sticky. The women found that rice and dal did not get cooked but became hard. A thousand families were directly affected, and well water was tainted a considerable distance from the plant.

The locals, mostly very low in caste status, had never had much beyond good water and a bit of land from the true earth-shaking reforms of Kerala's Communist government, democratically elected in 1957 and evicted two years later with US assistance by a central government terrified by the threat of a good example. On April 22, 2002, the locals commenced peaceful agitation that shut the plant down. Responding to popular pressure, the panchayat rescinded its license to Coca-Cola on August 7, 2003.

All of this was amiably conveyed to us in brisk and vivid detail by the villagers. Then Mylamma, an impressive woman, led us down a path to one of the local wells. It was a soundly built square well, some ten feet from side to side. About five feet from the top we could see the old water line, but no water. Peering twenty feet farther down in the semidarkness, we could see a stagnant glint. Today, in a region known as the rice bowl of Kerala, women have to walk a two-and-a-half-mile round trip to get drinkable water, toting big plastic vessels on their hip or head. Even better-off folk face ruin.

The whole process would play well on *The Simpsons*. It has a ghastly symmetry to it. When the plant was running at full tilt, eighty-five truckloads rolled out of the plant gates, each load consisting of 550 to 600 cases, twenty-four bottles to the case, all containing Plachimada's prime asset, water, now enhanced in cash value by Coca-Cola's infusions of its syrups.

Coca-Cola certainly "gave back" to Plachimada, in the form of profuse daily donations of foul wastewater and stinking toxic sludge from the plant's filtering and bottle-cleaning processes. The company told the locals the sludge was good for them, dumping loads of it in the surrounding fields and on the banks of the irrigation canal and heralding it as free fertilizer. Aside from stinking so badly it made old folk and children sick, people coming into contact with it got rashes and kindred infections, and the crops that it was supposed to nourish died. Several lab analyses done in India and Britain have found the sludge toxic with cadmium and lead and useless as fertilizer, a finding that did not faze Coca-Cola's Indian vice president, Sunil Gupta, who swore the sludge was "absolutely safe" and "good for crops."

Plachimada's member of Parliament in Delhi is Veerendra Kumar, who is also chairman and managing director of *Mathrubhumi*, a newspaper that sells over a million copies a day in Malayalam, Kerala's language. Kumar, a forceful man in his late 60s (and formerly a federal minister), tells me that for the past two years *Mathrubhumi* has refused, with serious loss of revenue, to run ads for Coca-Cola's products. Kumar includes in his ban ads for Pepsi, which he says has a plant six miles from Plachimada that has produced the same problems.

The locals won't let the plant reopen, to the consternation of Kerala's present pro-Coke government, which has tried, unconstitutionally, to overrule the local council and hopes the courts will grease Coca-Cola's wheels. Kerala's High Court did just that in early April, and the panchayat is now taking its case to the Supreme Court of India.

Drive along almost any road here and you'll see coconut palms. What Keralites term tender coconut water really is good for you. Ask any local rat. A trio of biochemists at the University of Kerala recently put rats on it, and their levels of cholesterol and triglycerides sank significantly, with antioxidant enzymes putting up a fine show. For the rats dosed on Coca-Cola the test readings weren't pretty, starting with "short, swollen, ulcerated and broken villi in the intestine [and] severe nuclear damage."

Taking a leaf out of the self-realization catechism, Coca-Cola flaunts its slogan in Hindi, "Jo chahe ho jahe," meaning "Whatever you want, happens," which has been translated by women cursed by another Coca-Cola plant, up in Maharashtra, as "Jo Coke chahe ho jahe," "Whatever Coke wants, happens."

But not in Plachimada.

4

JACQUES LESLIE
Running Dry

This article by a veteran journalist argues that we are facing a deepening global water crisis brought about by population pressures, economic exploitation, and other causes. According to Leslie, what are these other causes? What seem to be the most important causes of water shortage and pollution? What are the effects of the shortage of water? What is the relationship between water and food shortages? What does Leslie believe can be done to address the problem? How does his analysis differ from that of the *Wall Street Journal* article (selection 1)?

THINKING HISTORICALLY

One of the implicit arguments of this article is that the availability of fresh water is as important as that of oil. How would you attempt to evaluate this argument? Another argument is that the shortage of fresh water is a critical issue faced now by the developing world, but one that will also affect the developed world. Where do you see the strengths or limitations of this argument? How well does he support his assertions with evidence? How might you challenge his argument?

We face an unassailable fact: we are running out of freshwater. In the last century we humans have so vastly expanded our use of water to meet the needs of industry, agriculture, and a burgeoning population that now, after thousands of years in which water has been plentiful and virtually free, its scarcity threatens the supply of food, human health, and global ecosystems. With global population hurtling toward roughly 9 billion people by 2050, projections suggest that if we continue consuming water with our habitual disregard all those needs cannot be met at once.

The world's supply of freshwater remains roughly constant, at about 2½ percent of all water, and of that, almost two thirds is stored in ice caps and glaciers, inaccessible to humans; what must change is how we use the available supply. Humans have grown so numerous that the usual response to anticipated water scarcity—to increase supply with dams, aqueducts, canals, and wells—is beginning to push against an absolute limit.

Source: Jacques Leslie, "Running Dry," *Harper's Magazine*, July 2000, pp. 37–40, 43–48, 52.

In the developed world widespread water shortages are projected but not yet broadly experienced. In the developing world the crisis has already arrived. As many as 1.2 billion people—one out of five on the globe—lack access to clean drinking water. Nearly 3 billion live without sanitation: no underground sewage, toilets, or even latrines. More than 5 million people a year die of easily preventable waterborne diseases such as diarrhea, dysentery, and cholera; in fact, most disease in the developing world is water related. . . .

To be sure, the water shortages that give rise to these conditions so far are regional, not global, and often involve inequality of distribution and high pollution levels as much as absolute scarcity. Thus one water basin experiences a shortage while neighboring basins enjoy ample supplies. Water doesn't ship well, except in unusual circumstances, such as the provisioning of some Greek and Caribbean islands by tanker or barge: water is far too cheap and unwieldy to justify long-distance transport. This tends to keep shortages confined to specific areas, but it also means that they can't easily be alleviated with water from another region.

In one way, however, the impact of water shortages has already registered globally, thanks to water's role in agricultural production. Indeed, water experts refer to grain as "virtual water," since many countries facing water shortages respond by importing grain. It takes roughly a thousand tons of water to produce a ton of grain, so importing grain has an obvious shipping advantage. As a result, stockpiling grain is one way to counter water shortages. The billion-dollar question among water and agriculture experts, in fact, is whether, owing in part to water scarcity, the human race in the twenty-first century will lose the capacity to feed itself. For now, the answer is unknowable, since predictions inevitably rest on highly speculative assumptions. One forecaster, Lester Brown of the Washington, D.C.–based Worldwatch Institute, has advanced a dire scenario in which China's water shortage forces it to import so much grain that poorer nations are priced out of the international grain market, inducing widespread starvation. More plausibly, others argue that in many developing countries water scarcity is the most significant component of environmental degradation, which in turn is an underlying cause of mass migration, peasant revolt, and urban insurrection. . . .

Irrigation and Its Discontents

In the Tigris-Euphrates, Indus, and Yellow river basins, ancient civilizations flourished when they devised ways to grow crops with irrigated water and foundered when the systems collapsed, either because sediment clogged their canals or waterborne salt poisoned their soils. We like to think that we've mastered irrigation—indeed, in the last two centuries humans have increased land under irrigation thirtyfold. Yet the daunting obstacles we face in maintaining irrigation systems are not so different from those that brought down the Sumerian and Indus civilizations. "The overriding lesson from history is that most irrigation-based civilizations fail," writes Sandra Postel in her compelling survey of the global water crisis, *Pillar of Sand: Can the Irrigation Miracle Last?* "As we enter the third millennium A.D., the question is: Will ours be any different?"

Now, more than ever, humans depend on irrigation: less than a fifth of the world's cropland is irrigated, but because irrigation typically enables higher yields and two or three crops a year, irrigated land produces two fifths of the world's food. Even so, the planet's reliance on irrigated crops undoubtedly will intensify in the coming decades. The world's food supply comes from three major sources: cropland, rangeland, and fisheries. Livestock have already grown so numerous that 20 percent of the earth's rangeland has lost productivity because of overgrazing, and most of the world's fisheries have been decimated by overfishing. By default, the likely source of food for the roughly 3 billion additional humans expected in the next fifty years will be cropland. Yet the amount of cropland is not likely to grow much: newly cultivated land probably will barely surpass the amount of land lost to agriculture because of erosion, urbanization, and salination. Moreover, the best cropland is already in use; much of the land still awaiting cultivation has the potential to be only marginally productive. The result is that population growth is already outstripping growth of irrigated land. In fact, the area of global per capita irrigated land peaked in 1978 and has dropped 5 percent since then. Projections by international agencies suggest that by 2020, per capita irrigated land will have dropped 17–28 percent from the 1978 peak. Success in feeding all the people who will populate the earth in the mid-twenty-first century therefore depends largely on increasing the productivity of existing cropland. "The difference between the Malthusian pessimists and the cornucopian optimists," says Postel, "comes down to little more than an assumption about grainland productivity over the next several decades—specifically, whether yields will grow at closer to the 1 percent rate of the 1990s or the 2 percent rate of the previous four decades."

There's reason to worry. The 2 percent rate occurred as farmers applied Green Revolution techniques to land irrigated by groundwater or reservoirs, but those techniques have largely fulfilled their promise, and yields in recent years have either stagnated or declined. One reason may be irrigation itself: some scientists believe that soils become depleted when repeatedly subjected to the two or three annual crops that irrigation enables. In addition, Green Revolution agriculture depends on copious applications not just of pesticides and fertilizer but of water:

between 1950 and 1995 grainland productivity increased 240 percent while water use for irrigation increased 220 percent. With global depletion of groundwater and increasing diversions of agricultural water for industrial, urban, and environmental needs, the scarcity of water is likely to become the most important factor in limiting agricultural production. That means that more people may hunger for relatively less food.

Unseen Lakes, Pumped Dry

Compared with the earth's visible freshwater—in lakes, ponds, and rivers—the amount of water stored in underground aquifers is sixty times as large. A stock that immense might seem beyond our capacity to exhaust, yet in many parts of the world groundwater is being depleted at an unsustainable rate. The Ogallala Aquifer, one of the world's largest stores of groundwater, covers 225,000 square miles beneath parts of eight U.S. states, from Texas to South Dakota, and feeds a fifth of the nation's irrigated lands. Although its stock is "fossil water"—water locked underground for thousands of years, with few sources of replenishment—it is being depleted so rapidly that many farmers who once depended on it now must rely on rainwater, significantly lowering yield. The amount of acreage supported by the Ogallala in six states fell from its peak in 1978 by nearly 20 percent in less than a decade; despite efforts to limit use of Ogallala water, substantial withdrawals continue.

Of course, unlike the Ogallala, most aquifers are naturally "recharged"—replenished by rain and runoff—but even these are being depleted dramatically, as the rate of withdrawal easily surpasses the recharged amount. India's volume of annual groundwater overdraft is higher than any other nation's. Almost everywhere in the country, water withdrawals are proceeding at double the rate of recharge, causing a drop in aquifers of three to ten feet per year; in the state of Tamil Nadu, groundwater levels have dropped as much as ninety-nine feet since the 1970s, and some aquifers there have become useless. The cost of land subsidence caused by aquifer depletion in the United States is about $400 million per year, with incidents occurring in Houston, New Orleans, and California's Santa Clara County and San Joaquin valley; Beijing is sinking at an annual rate of about four inches a year; and certain Mexico City barrios sink as much as a foot a year. In both Florida and the Indian state of Gujarat, the water table has dropped so low that seawater has invaded the aquifers, limiting their usefulness for drinking or irrigation. In Palestine's Gaza Strip, which relies almost entirely on groundwater, salt-water intrusion from the Mediterranean has been detected as far as a mile inland, and some experts predict that the aquifer will become totally salinized. . . .

The world's most spectacular saline catastrophe is Central Asia's Aral Sea. Decades ago Soviet planners diverted two major rivers that feed the Aral in order to turn the surrounding desert into a cotton cornucopia. As cotton bloomed, however, the sea wilted: it now contains a third of its former volume and may disappear.

All twenty-four native fish species in the Aral have already vanished, and the fish catch has dropped from 48,000 tons to none. The regional climate has declined, producing less rainfall and greater temperature extremes. Each year windstorms pick up 44 million tons of salt and dust from the dried seabed and scatter them over the river basin. Cotton output is dropping. The drinking water is contaminated with high concentrations of salt and agricultural chemicals. Inhabitants suffer plagues of cancer, respiratory illnesses, and waterborne diseases such as hepatitis and typhoid fever.

All dams cause environmental damage: they fragment the riverine ecosystem, isolating upstream and downstream populations, and, by preventing floods, cut off the river from its floodplain. Within the reservoir lake, water temperature changes dramatically. Deep reservoir water is usually colder in summer and warmer in winter than river water. Thus water leaving Glen Canyon Dam never varies more than a few degrees from its 46 degree average. For 240 miles below the dam the water is too cold for native fish to reproduce.

The reservoir lake traps not just sediment but nutrients. Algae thrive on the nutrients and end up consuming the lake's oxygen, turning the water acidic. It comes out of the dam "hungry," more energetic after shedding its sediment load, ready to capture new sediment from the riverbed and bank. As it scours the downstream river, the bed deepens, losing its gravel habitats for spawning fish and the tiny invertebrates they feed on. Within nine years after Hoover Dam was sealed, hungry water took 89,000 acre-feet of material from the first 87-mile stretch of riverbed beneath. In places the riverbed dropped by more than thirteen feet, and it sometimes took floodplain water tables down with it. In addition, riverbank erosion has undermined some embankments and flood-control levees.

"A dammed river," Wallace Stegner wrote, "is not only stoppered like a bathtub, but it is turned on and off like a tap." Instead of varying with snowmelt and rainfall, its flow is regulated to meet the requirements of power generation and human recreation. Most fluctuations reflect electricity demand: the river level changes hour by hour and is lower on Sundays and holidays. These quick fluctuations intensify erosion, eventually washing away riverbank trees, shrubs, and grasses as well as riverine nesting areas. Riverside creatures lose needed food and shelter.

The changes are registered all the way to the river's mouth and beyond. Because of dams, many major rivers—including the Colorado, the Yellow, and the Nile—flow to the sea only intermittently. Without its customary allotment of sediment, the coastline is subject to erosion. By one estimate, dams have reduced by four fifths the sediment reaching the southern California coast, causing once wide beaches to disappear and cliffs to fall into the ocean. Estuaries, where riverine freshwater mixes with ocean saltwater, are crucial in the development of plankton, which in turn supports a huge abundance of marine life; deprived of large portions of freshwater and nutrients, the estuaries decline, and with them so do fisheries. Migrating fish such as salmon and steelhead trout find their paths obstructed, both as juveniles swimming downstream to mature and as adults going upstream to spawn. For this reason, the Columbia River, where 2 million fish returned annually to spawn just before the dam era began, has hosted half that number in recent years, and most remaining stocks in the upper river are in danger of extinction.

Only by multiplying all these effects by the number of the world's river basins studded with dams — an overwhelming majority — can the full environmental impact of dams be appreciated. The numbers are stunning. The planet accommodates 40,000 large dams — dams more than four stories high — and some 800,000 small ones. They have shifted so much weight that geophysicists believe they have slightly altered the speed of the earth's rotation, the tilt of its axis, and the shape of its gravitational field. Together they blot out a terrain bigger than California.

The most obvious beneficiaries of dams are politicians, bureaucrats, and builders, all of whom profit from the dams' huge price tags. Think of the towering political leaders of the twentieth century — Roosevelt, Stalin, Mao, Nehru. They all loved dams. Dams provide jobs and a generous amount of money to constituents, some of whom don't mind donating a portion back to the politicians. Bureaucrats like dams because that's where the action is: the expense of dams ensures power to its overseers. The constituents include dam builders, road builders, engineers, electricians, carpenters, cooks, plus every sort of professional boomtowns attract, from developers to prostitutes. In fact, dams, which provide nearly a fifth of the world's electricity, are also among the world's costliest public-works projects; by the time China's Three Gorges Dam is completed (in about 2009), it will have become the world's largest and most expensive, with an estimated cost of up to $75 billion.

The attraction of dams to farmers is obvious. Supported by funding from central governments and international agencies, farmers rarely pay more than 20 percent of the real cost of the irrigated water. The subsidies distort the farmers' economic outlook: instead of planting crops that match the hydrology of their fields, farmers take advantage of abundant cheap water to plant crops that guzzle water, even if the crops bring a low return. In the San Joaquin valley of California, the richest irrigated land in the world, some farmers grow water-guzzling cotton, or, worse (because it is fed to cows, the most notorious guzzlers of all), alfalfa. It takes at least 15,000 tons of water to produce a ton of beef and nearly that much to produce a ton of cotton; comparatively, a ton of grain requires 1,000 tons of water. . . .

The biggest losers are people displaced by dams. They're usually minorities, often uneducated and powerless, and therefore hard to count or even notice, particularly by a government's ruling elite. If the government bothers to relocate them, it's usually to inferior land, where settled residents resent them. Rates of illness and death usually increase after relocation. One estimate puts the worldwide total of people displaced by dams at 30 to 60 million. As startling as that sum is, it omits another huge group, the floodplain residents living down-stream from dams whose livelihoods are jeopardized by the sudden loss of regular nutrient-bearing floods or other hydrological changes.

If dams are so destructive in so many ways, why don't we tear them down? The most obvious answer is that we can't afford to; dismantling dams is nearly as expensive as building them. Some dams may be decom-missioned and drained, but in the foreseeable future even those will be few, for the world's reliance on dams for electric power and irrigation has grown too great to do without them: a world abruptly deprived of a fifth of its electricity and a significant portion of its food supply would not remain tranquil for long. Boxed in by the size of our population, we have approached a natural limit, damned if we do dam and damned if we don't dam. . . .

Although most water experts appreciate the destructive impact of dams, few oppose them entirely. IWMI, the World Bank–supported water agency, concluded a gloomy survey of global water needs in 2025 by noting that "medium and small dams will almost certainly . . . be needed." . . .

Rain, Rain, Go Away

Global warming, we know, is here. Some people think the change chiefly involves temperature, but the phrase is misleading—it leaves out water. Nearly every significant indicator of hydrologic activity—rainfall, snowmelt, glacial melt, evaporation, transpiration, soil moisture, sedi-mentation, salinity, and sea level—is changing at an accelerating pace. Alaskan and Siberian permafrost is beginning to thaw; in Antarctica scientists are finding beaches and islands exposed after being covered by ice for thousands of years. The sea level has risen between four and ten inches in the last century. Precipitation is increasing, but so are evapora-tion, floods, and droughts.

Pick any point of the hydrologic cycle and note the disruption. One analysis of 1900–1998 data pegged the increase in precipitation at 2 percent over the century. In water terms this sounds like good news, promising increased supply, but the changing timing and composition of the precipitation more than neutralizes the advantage. For one thing, it is likely that more of the precipitation will fall in intense episodes, with flooding a reasonable prospect. In addition, while rainfall will increase, snowfall will decrease. This means that in watersheds that depend on snowmelt, like the Indus, Ganges, Colorado, and San Joaquin river basins, less water will be stored as snow, and more of it will flow in the winter, when it plays no agricultural role; conversely, less of it will flow in the summer, when it is most needed. Once computer model showed that on the Animas River at Durango, Colorado, an increase in temperature of 3.6 degrees Fahrenheit—the global change predicted from now to 2100—would cause runoff to rise by 85 percent from January to March but drop by 40 percent from July to September. The rise in temperature increases the probability and intensity of spring floods and threatens dam safety, which is predicated on lower runoff projections. Dams in arid areas also may face increased sedimentation, since a 10 percent annual increase in precipitation can double the volume of sediment washed into rivers.

The consequences multiply. Soil moisture will intensify at the highest northern latitudes, where precipitation will grow far more than evaporation and plant transpiration but where agriculture is nonexistent. At the same time, precipitation will drop over northern mid-latitude continents in summer months, when ample soil moisture is an agricultural necessity.

Meanwhile the sea level will continue to rise as temperatures warm, accelerating saline contamination of freshwater aquifers and river deltas. This already has occurred in Florida, Gaza, and the Nile River delta. The temperature rise will cause increased evaporation, which in turn will lead to a greater incidence of drought. In fact, extreme water-related events such as storms, floods, and droughts will become more frequent and intense. . . .

The handy cliché is that sooner or later water will cause war. In a quote that caroms ceaselessly from one water publication to another, World Bank vice president Ismail Serageldin declared in 1995, "The wars of the next century will be over water." . . .

Yet such wars haven't quite happened. Aaron Wolf, an Oregan State University specialist in water conflicts, maintains that the last war over water was fought between the Mesopotamian city states of Lagash and Umma 4,500 years ago. Wolf has found that during the twentieth century only 7 minor skirmishes were fought over water while 145 water-related treaties were signed. He argues that one reason is strategic: in a conflict involving river water, the aggressor would have to be both downstream (since the upstream nation enjoys unhampered access to the river) and militarily superior. As Wolf puts it, "An upstream riparian would have no cause to launch an attack, and a weaker state would be foolhardy to do so." And if a powerful downstream nation retaliates against a water diversion by, say, destroying its weak upstream neighbor's dam, it still risks the consequences, in the form of flood or pollution or poison from upstream.

So, until now, water conflicts have simmered but rarely boiled, perhaps because of the universality of the need for water. Almost two fifths of the world's people live in the 214 river basins shared by two or more countries; the Nile links ten countries, whose leaders are profoundly aware of one another's hydrologic behavior. Countries usually manage to cooperate about water, even in unlikely circumstances. In 1957, Cambodia, Laos, Thailand, and South Vietnam formed the Mekong Committee, which exchanged information throughout the Vietnam War. Through the 1980s and into the 1990s, Israeli and Jordanian officials secretly met once or twice a year at a picnic table on the banks of the Yarmūk River to allocate the river's water supply; these so-called picnic-table summits occurred while the two nations disavowed formal diplomatic contact. . . .

On the other hand, water has often been the goal, tool, or target of conflicts that fall just short of war or that contain non-water-related dimensions. Recent history is full of examples. In 1965, Syria tried to divert the Jordan River from Israel, provoking Israeli airstrikes that forced Syria to abandon the effort. Colin Powell, chairman of the U.S. Joint Chiefs of Staff during the 1991 Gulf War, said in 1996 that the United States considered bombing dams on the Euphrates and Tigris rivers north of Baghdad but desisted, apparently because of the likelihood of high civilian casualties. The allies also discussed asking Turkey to reduce the Euphrates flow at the Atatürk Dam upstream from Iraq. As it was, the allies targeted Baghdad's water-supply system while the Iraqis destroyed Kuwait's desalination plants.

. . . In five of the world's most contentious water basins — the Aral Sea region, the Ganges, the Jordan, the Nile, and the Tigris-Euphrates — rapid projected population growth — up to 75 percent by 2025 — threatens to turn the basins into cauldrons of hostility. For instance, in the Tigris-Euphrates basin, Turkey's position upstream gives it enormous leverage over its downstream neighbors, Syria and Iraq. . . . Turkey is now in the midst of a huge dam-building program that will further diminish the Euphrates's flow into Syria, increasing Syria's grievances.

In the Nile basin the situation is more volatile, because the downstream nation, Egypt, dominates the region. Egypt already diverts so much Nile water that the river barely flows to its mouth in the Mediterranean Sea and the Nile delta is subsiding because sediment no longer reaches it. Nevertheless, Egypt is launching vast new irrigation projects that will divert even more Nile water. . . . At the same time, Ethiopia, the source of 86 percent of the Nile's flow, intends to launch its own irrigation and hydroelectric projects, which could dramatically reduce downstream water. Steve Lonergan, a specialist in water and security issues at the University of Victoria, British Columbia, told me, "I don't doubt that if Ethiopia starts building water projects that restrict the flow of the Nile, Egypt will bomb them."

Even if water wars remain rare, other sorts of water-related violence already occur frequently and are certain to increase. Thomas F. Homer-Dixon, a pioneer in the emerging field of environmental security, cites the Israeli-Palestinian conflict as an example of how environmental scarcity affects politics. . . .

Soon after the occupation of the West Bank in 1967, Israeli authorities instituted a rationing program that by the early 1990s gave four times as much water per capita to Israeli settlers as to Arabs. Israelis also required Arabs to seek permission to drill wells. When Arabs sought approval to drill over the West Bank's "Mountain" aquifer, the biggest aquifer in Israeli-controlled territory, they were invariably turned down; in other areas permission was given to Arabs infrequently. In addition, because Israelis had access to more sophisticated technology, their wells went deeper, often sucking Arab wells dry or exposing them to salt-water intrusion. Partly as a result, irrigated Arab farmland dropped from 27 percent to as low as 3.5 percent of the area of all West Bank cropland. Many Arab farmers abandoned their fields for towns, where they worked as day labours, if at all. When the Palestinians revolted in 1987, the disenfranchised farmers were presumably primed to participate. "It is reasonable to conclude," Homer-Dixon writes, "that water scarcity and its economic effects contributed to the grievances behind the *intifadah*."

In this manner, water scarcity encourages insurgencies. . . . "Water scarcity rarely causes interstate wars," Homer-Dixon writes. "Rather its impacts are more insidious and indirect: it constrains economic development and contributes to a host of corrosive social processes that can, in turn, produce violence within societies."

. . . [S]ooner or later we must acknowledge that our relationship to water is intimate, complex, and primal: if we abuse it, we inevitably suffer the consequences. Remove trees from the watershed, and the river below floods; deplete aquifers, and the land above subsides; pollute or obstruct the river, and the effects flow all the way to the sea. We must accommodate ourselves to water, not the other way around. Neither the pollution of our air and soil nor the destruction of wilderness nor even the probable extinction of a majority of the earth's creatures with the threat of catastrophic climate change has prompted us to change our behavior. Now it is the turn of water, the very foundation of life, to teach us to be good animals.

ANDREW RICE

Is There Such a Thing as Agro-Imperialism?

In the previous selection, the author suggests that food and water are interchangeable and that one of the consequences of food and water shortages has been an increase in global conflicts, especially insurgent movements and civil wars. In this piece from the *New York Times Magazine*, journalist Andrew Rice discovers another consequence of food and water shortages: agro-imperialism. What does he mean by agro-imperialism? Is it something that should be stopped or controlled? If so, how?

THINKING HISTORICALLY

Rice presents people who speak both for and against the practice of outsourcing food production. What are the arguments presented in favor of the practice? What are the arguments presented against it? How do you go about evaluating the practice? What is the difference between investment and imperialism?

Dr. Robert Zeigler, an eminent American botanist, flew to Saudi Arabia in March for a series of high-level discussions about the future of the kingdom's food supply. Saudi leaders were frightened: heavily dependent on imports, they had seen the price of rice and wheat, their dietary staples, fluctuate violently on the world market over the previous three years, at one point doubling in just a few months. The Saudis, rich in oil money but poor in arable land, were groping for a strategy to ensure that they could continue to meet the appetites of a growing population, and they wanted Zeigler's expertise.

There are basically two ways to increase the supply of food: find new fields to plant or invent ways to multiply what existing ones yield. Zeigler runs the International Rice Research Institute, which is devoted to the latter course, employing science to expand the size of harvests. During the so-called Green Revolution of the 1960s, the institute's laboratory developed "miracle rice," a high-yielding strain that has been credited with saving millions of people from famine. Zeigler went to Saudi Arabia hoping that the wealthy kingdom might offer money for the basic research that leads to such technological breakthroughs. Instead, to his

---

Source: Andrew Rice, "Is There Such a Thing as Agro-Imperialism?" *New York Times Magazine*, November 22, 2009. Published November 16, 2009, at http://www.nytimes.com/2009/11/22/magazine/22land-t.html?pagewanted=1&_r=1&hpw.

surprise, he discovered that the Saudis wanted to attack the problem from the opposite direction. They were looking for land.

In a series of meetings, Saudi government officials, bankers and agri-business executives told an institute delegation led by Zeigler that they intended to spend billions of dollars to establish plantations to produce rice and other staple crops in African nations like Mali, Senegal, Sudan and Ethiopia. "They laid out this incredible plan," Zeigler recalled. He was flabbergasted, not only by the scale of the projects but also by the audacity of their setting. Africa, the world's most famished continent, can't currently feed itself, let alone foreign markets.

The American scientist was catching a glimpse of an emerging test of the world's food resources, one that has begun to take shape over the last year, largely outside the bounds of international scrutiny. A variety of factors—some transitory, like the spike in food prices, and others intractable, like global population growth and water scarcity—have created a market for farmland, as rich but resource-deprived nations in the Middle East, Asia and elsewhere seek to outsource their food production to places where fields are cheap and abundant. Because much of the world's arable land is already in use—almost 90 percent, according to one estimate, if you take out forests and fragile ecosystems—the search has led to the countries least touched by development, in Africa. According to a recent study by the World Bank and the United Nations Food and Agriculture Organization, one of the earth's last large reserves of underused land is the billion-acre Guinea Savannah zone, a crescent-shaped swath that runs east across Africa all the way to Ethiopia, and southward to Congo and Angola.

Foreign investors—some of them representing governments, some of them private interests—are promising to construct infrastructure, bring new technologies, create jobs and boost the productivity of under-used land so that it not only feeds overseas markets but also feeds more Africans. (More than a third of the continent's population is malnour-ished.) They've found that impoverished governments are often only too welcoming, offering land at giveaway prices. A few transactions have received significant publicity, like Kenya's deal to lease nearly 100,000 acres to the Qatari government in return for financing a new port, or South Korea's agreement to develop almost 400 square miles in Tanzania. But many other land deals, of near-unprecedented size, have been sealed with little fanfare.

Investors who are taking part in the land rush say they are confront-ing a primal fear, a situation in which food is unavailable at any price. Over the 30 years between the mid-1970s and the middle of this decade, grain supplies soared and prices fell by about half, a steady trend that led many experts to believe that there was no limit to humanity's capacity to feed itself. But in 2006, the situation reversed, in concert with a wider commodities boom. Food prices increased slightly that year, rose by a quarter in 2007 and skyrocketed in 2008. Surplus-producing countries like Argentina and Vietnam, worried about feeding their own populations, placed restrictions on exports. American consumers, if they noticed the food crisis at all, saw it in modestly inflated supermarket bills, especially for meat and dairy products. But to many countries—not just in the Middle East but also import-dependent nations like South Korea and Japan—the specter of hyperinflation and hoarding presented an existential threat.

"When some governments stop exporting rice or wheat, it becomes a real, serious problem for people that don't have full self-sufficiency," said Al Arabi Mohammed Hamdi, an economic adviser to the Arab Authority for Agricultural Investment and Development. Sitting in his office in Dubai, overlooking the cargo-laden wooden boats moored along the city's creek, Hamdi told me his view, that the only way to assure food security is to control the means of production.

Hamdi's agency, which coordinates investments on behalf of 20 member states, has recently announced several projects, including a tentative $250 million joint venture with two private companies, which is slated to receive heavy subsidies from a Saudi program called the King Abdullah Initiative for Saudi Agricultural Investment Abroad. He said the main fields of investment for the project would most likely be Sudan and Ethiopia, countries with favorable climates that are situated just across the Red Sea. Hamdi waved a sheaf of memos that had just arrived on his desk, which he said were from another partner, Sheik Mansour Bin Zayed Al Nahyan, a billionaire member of the royal family of the emirate of Abu Dhabi, who has shown interest in acquiring land in Sudan and Eritrea. "There is no problem about money," Hamdi said. "It's about where and how."

Along the dirt road that runs to Lake Ziway, a teardrop in the furrow of Ethiopia's Great Rift Valley, farmers drove their donkey carts past a little orange-domed Orthodox church, and the tombs of their ancestors, decorated with vivid murals of horses and cattle. Between clusters of huts that looked as if they were constructed of matchsticks, there were wide-open wheat fields, where skinny young men were tilling the soil with wooden plows and teams of oxen. And then, nearing the lake, a fence appeared, closing off the countryside behind taut strings of barbed wire.

All through the Rift Valley region, my travel companion, an Ethiopian economist, had taken to pointing out all the new fence posts, standing naked and knobby like freshly cut saplings—mundane signifiers, he said, of the recent rush for Ethiopian land. In the old days, he told me, farmers rarely bothered with such formal lines of demarcation, but now the country's earth is in demand. This fence, though, was different from the others—it stretched on for a mile or more. Behind it, we could glimpse a vast expanse of dark volcanic soil, recently turned over by tractors. "So," said my guide, "this belongs to the sheik."

He meant Sheik Mohammed Al Amoudi, a Saudi Arabia–based oil-and-construction billionaire who was born in Ethiopia and maintains a close relationship with the Ethiopian Prime Minister Meles Zenawi's autocratic regime. (Fear of both men led my guide to say he didn't want to be identified by name.) Over time, Al Amoudi, one of the world's 50 richest people, according to *Forbes*, has used his fortune and political ties to amass control over large portions of Ethiopia's private sector, including mines, hotels and plantations on which he grows tea, coffee, rubber and japtropha, a plant that has enormous promise as a biofuel. Since the global price spike, he has been getting into the newly lucrative world food trade.

Ethiopia might seem an unlikely hotbed of agricultural investment. To most of the world, the country is defined by images of famine: about a million people died there during the drought of the mid-1980s, and today about four times that many depend on emergency food aid. But according to the World Bank, as much as three-quarters of Ethiopia's arable land is not under cultivation, and agronomists say that with substantial capital expenditure, much of it could become bountiful. Since the world food crisis, Zenawi, a former Marxist rebel who has turned into a champion of private capital, has publicly said he is "very eager" to attract foreign farm investors by offering them what the government describes as "virgin land." An Ethiopian agriculture ministry official recently told Reuters that he has identified more than seven million acres. The government plans to lease half of it before the next harvest, at the dirt-cheap annual rate of around 50 cents per acre. "We are associated with hunger, although we have enormous investment opportunities," explained Abi Woldemeskel, director general of the Ethiopian Investment Agency. "So that negative perception has to be changed through promotion." . . .

Of course, there have been scrambles for African land before. In the view of critics, the colonial legacy is what makes the large land deals so outrageous, and they warn of potentially calamitous consequences. "Wars have been fought over this," says Devlin Kuyek, a researcher with Grain, an advocacy group that opposes large-scale agribusiness and has played a key role in bringing attention to what it calls the "global land grab."

It wasn't until Grain compiled a long list of such deals into a polemical report titled "Seized!" last October that experts really began to talk about a serious trend. Although deals were being brokered in disparate locales like Australia, Kazakhstan, Ukraine and Vietnam, the most controversial field of investment was clearly Africa. "When you started to get some hints about what was happening in these deals," Kuyek says, "it was shocking." Within a month, Grain's warnings seemed to be vindicated when the *Financial Times* broke news that the South Korean conglomerate Daewoo Logistics had signed an agreement to take over about half of Madagascar's arable land, paying nothing, with the intention of growing corn and palm oil for export. Popular protests broke out, helping to mobilize opposition to Madagascar's already unpopular president, who was overthrown in a coup in March.

The episode illustrated the emotional volatility of the land issue and raised questions about the degree to which corrupt leaders might be profiting off the deals. Since then, there has been an international outcry. Legislators from the Philippines have called for an investigation into their government's agreements with various investing nations, while Thailand's leader has vowed to chase off any foreign land buyers.

But there's more than one side to the argument. Development economists and African governments say that if a country like Ethiopia is ever going to feed itself, let alone wean itself from foreign aid, which totaled $2.4 billion in 2007, it will have to find some way of increasing the productivity of its agriculture. "We've been complaining for decades about the lack of investment in African agriculture," says David Hallam, a trade expert at the Food and Agriculture Organization. Last fall, Paul Collier of Oxford University, an influential voice on issues of world poverty, published a provocative article in *Foreign Affairs* in which he argued that a "middle- and upper-class love affair with peasant agriculture" has clouded the African development debate with "romanticism." Approvingly citing the example of Brazil—where masses of indigenous landholders were displaced in favor of large-scale farms—Collier concluded that "to ignore commercial agriculture as a force for rural development and enhanced food supply is surely ideological."

In Ethiopia, Mohammed Al Amoudi and other foreign agricultural investors are putting Collier's theory into practice. Near the southern town of Awassa, in a shadow of a soaring Rift Valley escarpment, sits a field of waving corn and a complex of domed greenhouses, looking pristine and alien against the natural backdrop. On an overcast July morning, dozens of laborers were at work preparing the ground for one of Al Amoudi's latest enterprises: a commercial vegetable farm.

"For a grower, this is heaven on earth," says Jan Prins, managing director of the subsidiary company that is running the venture for Al Amoudi. Originally from the Netherlands, Prins says he assumed that Ethiopia was arid but was surprised to learn when he came to the country that much of it was fertile, with diverse microclimates. The Awassa farm is one of four that Prins is getting up and running. Using computerized irrigation systems, the farms will grow tomatoes, peppers, broccoli, melons and other fresh produce, the vast majority of it to be shipped to Saudi Arabia and Dubai. Over time, he says, he hopes to expand into growing other crops, like wheat and barley, the latter of which can be used to feed camels.

The nations of the Persian Gulf are likely to see their populations increase by half by 2030, and already import 60 percent of their food. Self-sufficiency isn't a viable option, as the Saudis have learned through bitter experience. In the 1970s, worries about the stability of the global food supply inspired the Saudi government to grow wheat through intensive irrigation. Between 1980 and 1999, according to a study by Elie Elhadj, a banker and historian, the Saudis pumped 300 billion cubic meters of water into their desert. By the early 1990s, the kingdom had managed to become the world's sixth-largest wheat exporter. But then its leaders started paying attention to the warnings of environmentalists, who pointed out that irrigation was draining a nonreplenishable supply of underground freshwater. Saudi Arabia now plans to phase out wheat production by 2016, which is one reason it's looking to other countries to fill its food needs.

■ REFLECTIONS

In Europe and the United States, air and water pollution were among the pressing issues of the years immediately following World War II. The Great Smog of London in 1952 led to the British Clean Air Act of 1956. In the United States, the smog of cities like Los Angeles and Pittsburgh, acid rain, river fires, and the loss of oxygen in the Great Lakes led to government regulation and the creation of environmental protection agencies. In Europe, Australia, and New Zealand "Green" political parties were formed, often combining a concern for the environment with peace and social justice issues.

Environmental movements were not limited to the rich countries of the world. In the 1970s, Wangari Maathai of Kenya initiated the Green Belt Movement in which Kenyan women organized in great numbers to plant trees. In 1974 village women in north India acted to preserve their traditional forest rights to gather firewood, fodder, and water against government loggers by hugging trees slated to be cut down—giving the sobriquet "tree-huggers" to the environmental movement. Until he was murdered in 1988, Chico Mendes organized fellow Brazilian rubber tappers in the Amazon against the incursion of cattle ranchers who destroyed forests to supply international hamburger chains.

Neither environmental awareness nor concern for dwindling resources was an entirely new development in the second half of the twentieth century. The Indian tree-huggers of 1974 were inspired by a similar act in 1774. The United States had experienced a popular conservation movement in the beginning of the twentieth century. In 1907 Theodore Roosevelt declared: "The conservation of natural resources is the fundamental problem. Unless we solve that problem, it will avail us little to solve all others."[1] The same spirit led Woodrow Wilson to establish the National Park Service in 1916.

What was new about the environmental movement after 1970 was its global character, a response to a new holistic vision that the environmentalist Buckminster Fuller popularized in the phrase "spaceship earth."[2] The recognition that all humanity shared the same fragile planet was verified by increasing rates of global interaction and such newly recognized threats as the depletion of the ozone protective layer of the atmosphere over Antarctica and global warming. The United Nations and international law were the appropriate new venues for dealing with planetary threats. Efforts to devise a Law of the Sea occupied UN conferences in the 1970s and 1980s, despite the opposition of the United States. Since then, the preeminent issue has become global warming. In 1988 the United Nations called an Intergovernmental Panel on Climate Change to access the state of scientific research on the issue. In 1990 the panel reported the scientific consensus that the Earth was warming because of the accumulation of greenhouse gases caused by human intervention. In 1992 a United Nations "Earth Summit" held in Rio de Janeiro established the United Nations Framework Convention on Climate Change (UNFCCC) in an effort to reduce global warming by limiting the emission of greenhouse gases. A follow-up Kyoto Protocol was set in 1997 to require developed countries to limit emissions to 1990 levels. The only country that expressed no intention of ratifying the treaty was the United States, the source of 36 percent of greenhouse gas emissions in 1990. In 2009 the Obama administration expressed greater interest in the issue of climate change and participated in the UNFCCC meeting in Copenhagen, but the U.S. Congress lagged far behind.

As notable as some of these responses have been, they have lacked a long-term commitment to concerted governmental action, especially in the United States. One of the reasons for this is the failure of public pressure, in part due to a lack of public understanding. Another reason is the tendency of political bodies to address emergencies much better than they grapple with the gradual, long-term problems that threaten future generations. What is needed is an understanding of the history that connects these individual emergencies and underscores long-term change.

[1] Theodore Roosevelt, Address to the Deep Waterway Convention, Memphis, Tennessee, October 4, 1907.

[2] Fuller popularized the term in 1969 with his *Operating Manual for Spaceship Earth*, but the term was the title of an earlier book by the economist Barbara Ward in 1966.

28

Globalization

1960 to the Present

■ HISTORICAL CONTEXT

Globalization is a term used by historians, economists, politicians, religious leaders, social reformers, business people, and average citizens to describe large-scale changes and trends in the world today. It is often defined as a complex phenomenon whereby individuals, nations, and regions of the world become increasingly integrated and interdependent, while national and traditional identities are diminished. Although it is a widely used term, *globalization* is also a controversial and widely debated topic. Is globalization really a new phenomenon, or is it a continuation of earlier trends? Is it driven by technological forces or economic forces, or both? Does it enrich or impoverish? Is it democratizing or antidemocratic? Is it generally a positive or negative thing?

Some limit the definition of globalization to the global integration driven by the development of the international market economy in the last twenty to forty years. Worldwide integration dates back much further, however, and has important technological, cultural, and political causes as well. In fact, all of human history can be understood as the story of increased interaction on a limited planet. Ancient empires brought diverse peoples from vast regions of the world together under single administrations. These empires, connected by land or maritime routes, interacted with each other through trade and exploration, exchanging goods as well as ideas. The unification of the Eastern and Western hemispheres after 1492 was a major step in the globalization of crops, peoples, cultures, and diseases. The industrial revolution joined countries and continents in ever vaster and faster transportation and communication networks. The great colonial empires that developed during the eighteenth and nineteenth centuries integrated the populations of far-flung areas of the world. The commercial aspects of these developments cannot be divorced from religious zeal, technological innovations, and political motives, which were often driving factors.

The current era of economic globalization is largely a product of the industrial capitalist world, roughly dating back to the middle of the nineteenth century. We might call the period between 1850 and 1914 the first great age of globalization in the modern sense. It was the age of ocean liners, mass migrations, undersea telegraph cables, transcontinental railroads, refrigeration, and preserved canned foods, when huge European empires dramatically reduced the number of sovereign states in the world. The period ended with World War I, which not only dug trenches between nations and wiped out a generation of future migrants and visitors, but also planted seeds of animosity that festered for decades, strangling the growth of international trade, interaction, and immigration.

Since the conclusion of World War II in 1945, and increasingly since the end of the Cold War in 1989, political and technological developments have enabled economic globalization on a wider scale and at a faster pace than occurred during the previous age of steamships and telegraphs. The collapse of the Soviet Union and international communism unleashed the forces of market capitalism as never before. Jet travel, satellite technology, mobile phones, and the World Wide Web have revived global integration and enabled the global marketplace. The United States, the World Bank, and the International Monetary Fund led in the creation of regional and international free-trade agreements, the reduction of tariffs, and the removal of national trade barriers, touting these changes as agents of material progress and democratic transformation. Yet these changes have also elicited wide-ranging resistance in peaceful protests, especially against the West's economic dominance, and violent ones against the West's political and cultural domination, such as the terrorist attacks on September 11, 2001.

Multinational companies are now able to generate great wealth by moving capital, labor, raw materials, and finished products through international markets at increasing speeds and with lasting impact. This economic globalization has profound cultural ramifications; increasingly the peoples of the world are watching the same films and television programs, speaking the same languages, wearing the same clothes, enjoying the same amusements, and listening to the same music. Whether free-market capitalism lifts all boats, or only yachts, is a hotly debated issue today.

■ THINKING HISTORICALLY

Understanding Process

What are the most important ways in which the world is changing? What are the most significant and powerful forces of change? What is the engine that is driving our world? These are the big questions raised at the end of historical investigation. They also arise at the beginning, as the assumptions that shape our specific investigations. *Globalization* is one of the words most frequently used to describe the big changes that are occurring in our world. All of the readings in this chapter assume or describe some kind of global integration as a dominant driver of the world in which we live. This chapter asks you to think about large-scale historical processes. It asks you to examine globalization as one of the most important of these processes. It asks you to reflect on what globalization means, and what causes it. How does each of these authors use the term? Do the authors see this process as primarily commercial and market-driven, or do they view it as a matter of culture or politics? Does globalization come from one place or many, from a center outwards, or from one kind of society to another? Is globalization linear or unidirectional, or does it have differing, even opposite effects? What do these writers, thinkers, and activists believe about the most important changes transforming our world? And what do you think?

1

SHERIF HETATA

Dollarization

Sherif Hetata is an Egyptian intellectual, novelist, and activist who was originally trained as a medical doctor. He and his wife, the prominent feminist writer Nawal El-Saadawi, have worked together to promote reform in Egypt and the larger Arab world. In this presentation given at a conference on globalization, Hetata outlines the global economy's homogenizing effects on culture. Through what historic lens does Hetata view globalization? What links does he make between globalization and imperialism? What do you think of his argument?

Source: Sherif Hetata, "Dollarization, Fragmentation, and God," in *The Cultures of Globalization*, ed. Fredric Jameson and Masao Miyoshi (Durham, NC: Duke University Press, 1998), 273–74, 276–80.

What, according to Hetata, is the main process that is changing the world? Does he think the engine of world change is primarily techno-logical, commercial, or cultural?

As a young medical student, born and brought up in a colony, like many other people in my country, Egypt, I quickly learned to make the link between politics, economics, culture, and religion. Educated in an English school, I discovered that my English teachers looked down on us. We learned Rudyard Kipling by heart, praised the glories of the British Empire, followed the adventures of Kim in India, imbibed the culture of British supremacy, and sang carols on Christmas night.

At the medical school in university, when students demonstrated against occupation by British troops it was the Moslem Brothers who beat them up, using iron chains and long curved knives, and it was the governments supported by the king that shot at them or locked them up.

When I graduated in 1946, the hospital wards taught me how poverty and health are linked. I needed only another step to know that poverty had something to do with colonial rule, with the king who supported it, with class and race, with what was called imperialism at the time, with cotton prices falling on the market, with the seizure of land by foreign banks. These things were common talk in family gatherings, expressed in a simple, colorful language without frills. They were the facts of everyday life. We did not need to read books to make the links: They were there for us to see and grasp. And every time we made a link, someone told us it was time to stop, someone in authority whom we did not like: a ruler or a father, a policeman or a teacher, a landowner, a *maulana* (religious leader or teacher), a Jesuit, or a God.

And if we went on making these links, they locked us up.

For me, therefore, coming from this background, cultural studies and globalization open up a vast horizon, one of global links in a world where things are changing quickly. It is a chance to learn and probe how the economics, the politics, the culture, the philosophical thought of our days connect or disconnect, harmonize or contradict.

Of course, I will not even try to deal with all of that. I just want to raise a few points to discuss under the title of my talk, "Dollariza-tion, Fragmentation, and God." Because I come from Egypt, my vantage point will be that of someone looking at the globe from the part we now call South, rather than "third world" or something else.

A New Economic Order: Gazing North at the Global Few

Never before in the history of the world has there been such a concentration and centralization of capital in so few nations and in the hands of so few people. The countries that form the Group of Seven,[1] with their 800 million inhabitants, control more technological, economic, informatics, and military power than the rest of the approximately 430 billion who live in Asia, Africa, Eastern Europe, and Latin America.

Five hundred multinational corporations account for 80 percent of world trade and 75 percent of investment. Half of all the multinational corporations are based in the United States, Germany, Japan, and Switzerland. The OECD (Organisation for Economic Cooperation and Development) group of countries contributes 80 percent of world production. . . .

A Global Culture for a Global Market

To expand the world market, to globalize it, to maintain the New Economic Order, the multinational corporations use economic power and control politics and the armed forces. But this is not so easy. People will always resist being exploited, resist injustice, struggle for their freedom, their needs, security, a better life, peace.

However, it becomes easier if they can be convinced to do what the masters of the global economy want them to do. This is where the issue of culture comes in. Culture can serve in different ways to help the global economy reach out all over the world and expand its markets to the most distant regions. Culture can also serve to reduce or destroy or prevent or divide or outflank the resistance of people who do not like what is happening to them, or have their doubts about it, or want to think. Culture can be like cocaine, which is going global these days: from Kali in Colombia to Texas, to Madrid, to the Italian mafiosi in southern Italy, to Moscow, Burma, and Thailand, a worldwide network uses the methods and the cover of big business, with a total trade of $5 billion a year, midway between oil and the arms trade.

At the disposal of global culture today are powerful means that function across the whole world: the media, which, like the economy, have made it one world, a bipolar North/South world. If genetic engineering gives scientists the possibility of programming embryos before children are born, children, youth, and adults are now being programmed after

---

[1] Canada, France, Germany, Italy, Japan, the United Kingdom, and the United States meet as the G7. [Ed.]

they are born in the culture they imbibe mainly through the media, but also in the family, in school, at the university, and elsewhere. Is this an exaggeration? an excessively gloomy picture of the world?

To expand the global market, increase the number of consumers, make sure that they buy what is sold, develop needs that conform to what is produced, and develop the fever of consumerism, culture must play a role in developing certain values, patterns of behavior, visions of what is happiness and success in the world, attitudes toward sex and love. Culture must model a global consumer.

In some ways, I was a "conservative radical." I went to jail, but I always dressed in a classical, subdued way. When my son started wearing blue jeans and New Balance shoes, I shivered with horror. He's going to become like some of those crazy kids abroad, the disco generation, I thought! Until the age of twenty-five he adamantly refused to smoke. Now he smokes two packs of Marlboros a day (the ones that the macho cowboy smokes). That does not prevent him from being a talented film director. But in the third-world, films, TV, and other media have increased the percentage of smokers. I saw half-starved kids in a marketplace in Mali buying single imported Benson & Hedges cigarettes and smoking.

But worse was still to come. Something happened that to me seemed impossible at one time, more difficult than adhering to a leftwing movement. At the age of seventy-one, I have taken to wearing blue jeans and Nike shoes. I listen to rock and reggae and sometimes rap. I like to go to discos and I sometimes have other cravings, which so far I have successfully fought! And I know these things have crept into our lives through the media, through TV, films, radio, advertisements, newspapers, and even novels, music, and poetry. It's a culture and it's reaching out, becoming global.

In my village, I have a friend. He is a peasant and we are very close. He lives in a big mud hut, and the animals (buffalo, sheep, cows, and donkeys) live in the house with him. Altogether, in the household, with the wife and children of his brother, his uncle, the mother, and his own family, there are thirty people. He wears a long *galabeya* (robe), works in the fields for long hours, and eats food cooked in the mud oven.

But when he married, he rode around the village in a hired Peugeot car with his bride. She wore a white wedding dress, her face was made up like a film star, her hair curled at the hairdresser's of the provincial town, her finger and toe nails manicured and polished, and her body bathed with special soap and perfumed. At the marriage ceremony, they had a wedding cake, which she cut with her husband's hand over hers. Very different from the customary rural marriage ceremony of his father. And all this change in the notion of beauty, of femininity, of celebration, of happiness, of prestige, of progress happened to my peasant friend and his bride in one generation.

The culprit, or the benevolent agent, depending on how you see it, was television.

In the past years, television has been the subject of numerous studies. In France, such studies have shown that before the age of twelve a child will have been exposed to an average 100,000 TV advertisements. Through these TV advertisements, the young boy or girl will have assimilated a whole set of values and behavioral patterns, of which he or she is not aware, of course. They become a part of his or her psychological (emotional and mental) makeup. Linked to these values are the norms and ways in which we see good and evil, beauty and ugliness, justice and injustice, truth and falseness, and which are being propagated at the same time. In other words, the fundamental values that form our aesthetic and moral vision of things are being inculcated, even hammered home, at this early stage, and they remain almost unchanged throughout life.

The commercial media no longer worry about the truthfulness or falsity of what they portray. Their role is to sell: beauty products, for example, to propagate the "beauty myth" and a "beauty culture" for both females and males alike and ensure that it reaches the farthest corners of the earth, including my village in the Delta of the Nile. Many of these beauty products are harmful to the health, can cause allergic disorders or skin infections or even worse. They cost money, work on the sex drives, and transform women and men, but especially women, into sex objects. They hide the real person, the natural beauty, the process of time, the stages of life, and instill false values about who we are, can be, or should become.

Advertisements do not depend on verifiable information or even rational thinking. They depend for their effect on images, colors, smart technical production, associations, and hidden drives. For them, attracting the opposite sex or social success or professional achievement and promotion or happiness do not depend on truthfulness or hard work or character, but rather on seduction, having a powerful car, buying things or people. . . .

Thus the media produce and reproduce the culture of consumption, of violence and sex to ensure that the global economic powers, the multinational corporations can promote a global market for themselves and protect it. And when everything is being bought or sold everyday and at all times in this vast supermarket, including culture, art, science, and thought, prostitution can become a way of life, for everything is priced. The search for the immediate need, the fleeting pleasure, the quick enjoyment, the commodity to buy, excess, pornography, drugs keeps this global economy rolling, for to stop is suicide.

2

PHILIPPE LEGRAIN

Cultural Globalization Is Not Americanization

Philippe Legrain, an economist, journalist, and former advisor to the
World Trade Organization, takes aim at what he calls the myths of
globalization in the following article. What, according to him, are
these myths? What are the consequences of globalization according
to Legrain? What evidence does he cite to support his argument?
How does his view differ from that of Hetata?

THINKING HISTORICALLY

Does Legrain believe the driving force of globalization is economic
or cultural? How important does he think globalization is? How,
according to the author, is globalization changing the world?

Fears that globalization is imposing a deadening cultural uniformity are
as ubiquitous as Coca-Cola, McDonald's, and Mickey Mouse. Europeans and Latin Americans, left-wingers and right, rich and poor — all of
them dread that local cultures and national identities are dissolving into
a crass All-American consumerism. That cultural imperialism is said to
impose American values as well as products, promote the commercial
at the expense of the authentic, and substitute shallow gratification for
deeper satisfaction.

. . . If critics of globalization were less obsessed with "Cocacoloniza-
tion," they might notice a rich feast of cultural mixing that belies fears
about Americanized uniformity. Algerians in Paris practice Thai box-
ing; Asian rappers in London snack on Turkish pizza; Salman Rushdie
delights readers everywhere with his Anglo-Indian tales. Although — as
with any change — there can be downsides to cultural globalization, this
cross-fertilization is overwhelmingly a force for good.

The beauty of globalization is that it can free people from the tyranny of geography. Just because someone was born in France does not
mean they can only aspire to speak French, eat French food, read French
books, visit museums in France, and so on. A Frenchman — or an American, for that matter — can take holidays in Spain or Florida, eat sushi

Source: Philippe Legrain, "Cultural Globalization Is Not Americanization," *Chronicle of
Higher Education* 49, no. 35 (May 9, 2003): B7.

or spaghetti for dinner, drink Coke or Chilean wine, watch a Hollywood blockbuster or an Almodóvar, listen to bhangra or rap, practice yoga or kickboxing, read *Elle* or *The Economist*, and have friends from around the world. That we are increasingly free to choose our cultural experiences enriches our lives immeasurably. We could not always enjoy the best the world has to offer.

Globalization not only increases individual freedom, but also revitalizes cultures and cultural artifacts through foreign influences, technologies, and markets. Thriving cultures are not set in stone. They are forever changing from within and without. Each generation challenges the previous one; science and technology alter the way we see ourselves and the world; fashions come and go; experience and events influence our beliefs; outsiders affect us for good and ill.

Many of the best things come from cultures mixing: V. S. Naipaul's Anglo-Indo-Caribbean writing, Paul Gauguin painting in Polynesia, or the African rhythms in rock 'n' roll. Behold the great British curry. Admire the many-colored faces of France's World Cup–winning soccer team, the ferment of ideas that came from Eastern Europe's Jewish diaspora, and the cosmopolitan cities of London and New York. Western numbers are actually Arabic; zero comes most recently from India; Icelandic, French, and Sanskrit stem from a common root.

John Stuart Mill was right: "The economical benefits of commerce are surpassed in importance by those of its effects which are intellectual and moral. It is hardly possible to overrate the value, for the improvement of human beings, of things which bring them into contact with persons dissimilar to themselves, and with modes of thought and action unlike those with which they are familiar. . . . It is indispensable to be perpetually comparing [one's] own notions and customs with the experience and example of persons in different circumstances. . . . There is no nation which does not need to borrow from others."

It is a myth that globalization involves the imposition of Americanized uniformity, rather than an explosion of cultural exchange. For a start, many archetypal "American" products are not as all-American as they seem. Levi Strauss, a German immigrant, invented jeans by combining denim cloth (or "serge de Nîmes," because it was traditionally woven in the French town) with Genes, a style of trousers worn by Genoese sailors. So Levi's jeans are in fact an American twist on a European hybrid. Even quintessentially American exports are often tailored to local tastes. MTV in Asia promotes Thai pop stars and plays rock music sung in Mandarin. CNN en Español offers a Latin American take on world news. McDonald's sells beer in France, lamb in India, and chili in Mexico.

In some ways, America is an outlier, not a global leader. Most of the world has adopted the metric system born from the French Revolution; America persists with antiquated measurements inherited from its

British-colonial past. Most developed countries have become intensely secular, but many Americans burn with fundamentalist fervor — like Muslims in the Middle East. Where else in the developed world could there be a serious debate about teaching kids Bible-inspired "creationism" instead of Darwinist evolution?

America's tastes in sports are often idiosyncratic, too. Baseball and American football have not traveled well, although basketball has fared rather better. Many of the world's most popular sports, notably soccer, came by way of Britain. Asian martial arts — judo, karate, kickboxing — and pastimes like yoga have also swept the world.

People are not only guzzling hamburgers and Coke. Despite Coke's ambition of displacing water as the world's drink of choice, it accounts for less than 2 of the 64 fluid ounces that the typical person drinks a day. Britain's favorite takeaway is a curry, not a burger: Indian restaurants there outnumber McDonald's six to one. For all the concerns about American fast food trashing France's culinary traditions, France imported a mere $620 million in food from the United States in 2000, while exporting to America three times that. Nor is plonk[1] from America's Gallo displacing Europe's finest: Italy and France together account for three-fifths of global wine exports, the United States for only a twentieth. Worldwide, pizzas are more popular than burgers, Chinese restaurants seem to sprout up everywhere, and sushi is spreading fast. By far the biggest purveyor of alcoholic drinks is Britain's Diageo, which sells the world's best-selling whiskey (Johnnie Walker), gin (Gordon's), vodka (Smirnoff), and liqueur (Baileys).

In fashion, the ne plus ultra is Italian or French. Trendy Americans wear Gucci, Armani, Versace, Chanel, and Hermès. On the high street and in the mall, Sweden's Hennes & Mauritz (H&M) and Spain's Zara vie with America's Gap to dress the global masses. Nike shoes are given a run for their money by Germany's Adidas, Britain's Reebok, and Italy's Fila.

In pop music, American crooners do not have the stage to themselves. The three artists who were featured most widely in national Top Ten album charts in 2000 were America's Britney Spears, closely followed by Mexico's Carlos Santana and the British Beatles. Even tiny Iceland has produced a global star: Björk. Popular opera's biggest singers are Italy's Luciano Pavarotti, Spain's José Carreras, and the Spanish-Mexican Placido Domingo. Latin American salsa, Brazilian lambada, and African music have all carved out global niches for themselves. In most countries, local artists still top the charts. According to the IFPI, the record-industry bible, local acts accounted for 68 percent of music sales in 2000, up from 58 percent in 1991.

---

[1] British slang for cheap, low-quality alcohol. [Ed.]

One of the most famous living writers is a Colombian, Gabriel García Márquez, author of *One Hundred Years of Solitude*. Paulo Coelho, another writer who has notched up tens of millions of global sales with *The Alchemist* and other books, is Brazilian. More than 200 million Harlequin romance novels, a Canadian export, were sold in 1990; they account for two-fifths of mass-market paperback sales in the United States. The biggest publisher in the English-speaking world is Germany's Bertelsmann, which gobbled up America's largest, Random House, in 1998.

Local fare glues more eyeballs to TV screens than American programs. Although nearly three-quarters of television drama exported worldwide comes from the United States, most countries' favorite shows are homegrown.

Nor are Americans the only players in the global media industry. Of the seven market leaders that have their fingers in nearly every pie, four are American (AOL Time Warner, Disney, Viacom, and News Corporation), one is German (Bertelsmann), one is French (Vivendi), and one Japanese (Sony). What they distribute comes from all quarters: Bertelsmann publishes books by American writers; News Corporation broadcasts Asian news; Sony sells Brazilian music.

The evidence is overwhelming. Fears about an Americanized uniformity are over-blown: American cultural products are not uniquely dominant; local ones are alive and well.

3

MIRIAM CHING YOON LOUIE

Sweatshop Warriors: Immigrant Women Workers Take On the Global Factory

Sherif Hetata and Philippe Legrain highlight the impact of globalization on consumers, but it is also important to examine how it affects workers. Free-trade policies have removed barriers to international trade, with global consequences. An example of such change can be witnessed along the border between Mexico and the United States, especially in the export factories, or *maquiladoras*,* that are run by

* mah kee lah DOH rahs

Source: Miriam Ching Yoon Louie, *Sweatshop Warriors: Immigrant Women Workers Take On the Global Factory* (Cambridge, MA: South End Press, 2001), 65–71, 87–89.

international corporations on both the U.S. and Mexican sides of the border. In the following excerpt, Miriam Ching Yoon Louie, a writer and activist, interviews Mexican women who work in these factories and explores both the challenges they face and the strength they show in overcoming these challenges. What is the impact of liberalized trade laws on women who work in the *maquiladoras*? What is neoliberalism, and how is it tied to globalization? Why are women particularly vulnerable to these policies?

THINKING HISTORICALLY

According to Louie, how far back do neoliberalism and economic globalization date? How does Louie's assessment of economic globalization differ from the views expressed by Legrain? How might they both be right?

Many of today's *nuevas revolucionarias*[1] started working on the global assembly line as young women in northern Mexico for foreign transnational corporations. Some women worked on the U.S. side as "commuters" before they moved across the border with their families. Their stories reveal the length, complexity, and interpenetration of the U.S. and Mexican economies, labor markets, histories, cultures, and race relations. The women talk about the devastating impact of globalization, including massive layoffs and the spread of sweatshops on both sides of the border. *Las mujeres*[2] recount what drove them to join and lead movements for economic, racial, and gender justice, as well as the challenges they faced within their families and communities to assert their basic human rights. . . .

Growing Up Female and Poor

Mexican women and girls were traditionally expected to do all the cooking, cleaning, and serving for their husbands, brothers, and sons. For girls from poor families, shouldering these domestic responsibilities proved doubly difficult because they also performed farm, sweatshop, or domestic service work simultaneously. . . .

Petra Mata, a former seamstress for Levi's whose mother died shortly after childbirth, recalls the heavy housework she did as the only daughter:

> Aiyeee, let me tell you! It was very hard. In those times in Mexico, I was raised with the ideal that you have to learn to do everything — cook, make tortillas, wash your clothes, and clean the house — just

---

[1] New revolutionaries. [Ed.]
[2] moo HAIR ace   The women. [Ed.]

the way they wanted you to. My grandparents were very strict.
I always had to ask their permission and then let them tell me
what to do. I was not a free woman. Life was hard for me. I didn't
have much of a childhood; I started working when I was 12 or
13 years old.

Neoliberalism and Creeping Maquiladorization

These women came of age during a period of major change in the relationship between the Mexican and U.S. economies. Like Puerto Rico,
Hong Kong, South Korea, Taiwan, Malaysia, Singapore, and the Philippines, northern Mexico served as one of the first stations of the global
assembly line tapping young women's labor. In 1965 the Mexican government initiated the Border Industrialization Program (BIP) that set
up export plants, called *maquiladoras* or *maquilas*, which were either
the direct subsidiaries or subcontractors of transnational corporations.
Mexican government incentives to U.S. and other foreign investors
included low wages and high productivity; infrastructure; proximity to
U.S. markets, facilities, and lifestyles; tariff loopholes; and pliant, pro-
government unions. . . .

Describing her quarter-century-long sewing career in Mexico, Celeste
Jiménez ticks off the names of famous U.S. manufacturers who hopped
over the border to take advantage of cheap wages:

> I sewed for twenty-four years when I lived in Chihuahua in big name
> factories like Billy the Kid, Levi Strauss, and Lee *maquiladoras*.
> Everyone was down there. Here a company might sell under the
> brand name of Lee; there in Mexico it would be called Blanca
> García.

Transnational exploitation of women's labor was part of a broader
set of policies that critical opposition movements in the Third World
have dubbed "neoliberalism," i.e., the new version of the British Liberal
Party's program of laissez faire capitalism espoused by the rising European and U.S. colonial powers during the late eighteenth and nineteenth
centuries. The Western powers, Japan, and international financial institutions like the World Bank and International Monetary Fund have
aggressively promoted neoliberal policies since the 1970s. Mexico served
as an early testing ground for such standard neoliberal policies as erec-
tion of free trade zones; commercialization of agriculture; currency de-
valuation; deregulation; privatization; outsourcing; cuts in wages and
social programs; suppression of workers', women's, and indigenous people's rights; free trade; militarization; and promotion of neoconservative
ideology.

Neoliberalism intersects with gender and national oppression. Third World women constitute the majority of migrants seeking jobs as maids, vendors, *maquila* operatives, and service industry workers. Women also pay the highest price for cuts in education, health and housing programs, and food and energy subsidies and increases in their unpaid labor. . . .

The deepening of the economic crisis in Mexico, especially under the International Monetary Fund's pressure to devaluate the peso in 1976, 1982, and 1994, forced many women to work in both the formal and informal economy to survive and meet their childbearing and household responsibilities. María Antonia Flores was forced to work two jobs after her husband abandoned the family, leaving her with three children to support. She had no choice but to leave her children home alone, *solitos*, to look after themselves. Refugio Arrieta straddled the formal and informal economy because her job in an auto parts assembly *maquiladora* failed to bring in sufficient income. To compensate for the shortfall, she worked longer hours at her *maquila* job and "moonlighted" elsewhere:

> We made chassis for cars and for the headlights. I worked lots! I worked 12 hours more or less because they paid us so little that if you worked more, you got more money. I did this because the schools in Mexico don't provide everything. You have to buy the books, notebooks, *todos, todos* [everything]. And I had five kids. It's very expensive. I also worked out of my house and sold ceramics. I did many things to get more money for my kids.

In the three decades following its humble beginnings in the mid-1960s, the *maquila* sector swelled to more than 2,000 plants employing an estimated 776,000 people, over 10 percent of Mexico's labor force. In 1985, *maquiladoras* overtook tourism as the largest source of foreign exchange. In 1996, this sector trailed only petroleum-related industries in economic importance and accounted for over U.S. $29 billion in export earnings annually. The *maquila* system has also penetrated the interior of the country, as in the case of Guadalajara's electronics assembly industry and Tehuacán's jeans production zones. Although the proportion of male *maquila* workers has increased since 1983, especially in auto-transport equipment assembly, almost 70 percent of the workers continue to be women.

As part of a delegation of labor and human rights activists, this author met some of Mexico's newest proletarians[3] — young indigenous women migrant workers from the Sierra Negra to Tehuacán, a town famous for its refreshing mineral water springs in the state of Puebla, just southeast of Mexico City. Standing packed like cattle in the back

[3] Workers, especially exploited ones (a Marxist term derived from Latin for lower classes). [Ed.]

of the trucks each morning the women headed for jobs sewing for name brand manufacturers like Guess?, VF Corporation (producing Lee brand clothing), Gap, Sun Apparel (producing brands such as Polo, Arizona, and Express), Cherokee, Ditto Apparel of California, Levi's, and others. The workers told U.S. delegation members that their wages averaged U.S. $30 to $50 a week for 12-hour work days, six days a week. Some workers reported having to do *veladas* [all-nighters] once or twice a week. Employees often stayed longer without pay if they did not finish high production goals.

Girls as young as 12 and 13 worked in the factories. Workers were searched when they left for lunch and again at the end of the day to check that they weren't stealing materials. Women were routinely given urine tests when hired and those found to be pregnant were promptly fired, in violation of Mexican labor law. Although the workers had organized an independent union several years earlier, Tehuacán's Human Rights Commission members told us that it had collapsed after one of its leaders was assassinated.

Carmen Valadez and Reyna Montero, long-time activists in the women's and social justice movements, helped found Casa de La Mujer Factor X in 1977, a workers' center in Tijuana that organizes around women's workplace, reproductive, and health rights, and against domestic violence. Valadez and Montero say that the low wages and dangerous working conditions characteristic of the *maquiladoras* on the Mexico-U.S. border are being "extended to all areas of the country and to Central America and the Caribbean. NAFTA represents nothing but the '*maquiladorization*' of the region."

Elizabeth "Beti" Robles Ortega, who began working in the *maquilas* at the age of fourteen and was blacklisted after participating in independent union organizing drives on Mexico's northern border, now works as an organizer for the Servicio, Desarrollo y Paz, AC 520 (SEDEPAC) [Service, Development and Peace organization]. Robles described the erosion of workers' rights and women's health under NAFTA:

> NAFTA has led to an increase in the workforce, as foreign industry has grown. They are reforming labor laws and our constitution to favor even more foreign investment, which is unfair against our labor rights. For example, they are now trying to take away from us free organization which was guaranteed by Mexican law. Because foreign capital is investing in Mexico and is dominating, we must have guarantees. The government is just there with its hands held out; it's always had them out but now even more shamelessly. . . . Ecological problems are increasing. A majority of women are coming down with cancer—skin and breast cancer, leukemia, and lung and heart problems. There are daily deaths of worker women. You can see and feel the contamination of the water and the air. As

soon as you arrive and start breathing the air in Acuña and Piedras Negras [border cities between the states of Coahuila and Texas], you sense the heavy air, making you feel like vomiting.

Joining the Movement

Much of the education and leadership training the women received took place "on the job." The women talked about how much their participation in the movement had changed them. They learned how to analyze working conditions and social problems, who was responsible for these conditions, and what workers could do to get justice. They learned to speak truth to power, whether this was to government representatives, corporate management, the media, unions, or co-ethnic gatekeepers. They built relations with different kinds of sectors and groups and organized a wide variety of educational activities and actions. Their activism expanded their world view beyond that of their immediate families to seeing themselves as part of peoples' movements fighting for justice. . . .

Through her participation in the movement, [María del Carmen Domínguez] developed her skills, leadership, and awareness:

> When I stayed at work in the factory, I was only thinking of myself and how am I going to support my family—nothing more, nothing less. And I served my husband and my son, my girl. But when I started working with La Mujer Obrera I thought, "I need more respect for myself. We need more respect for ourselves." (laughs) . . .
> . . . I learned about the law and I learned how to organize classes with people, whether they were men or women like me.

4

BENJAMIN BARBER

Jihad vs. McWorld

Not everyone views the world as coming together, for better or worse, under the umbrella of globalization. Benjamin Barber, a political scientist, uses the terms *Jihad* and *McWorld* to refer to what he sees as the two poles of the modern global system. *McWorld* is the force

Source: Benjamin Barber, *Jihad vs. McWorld: How Globalism and Tribalism Are Reshaping the World* (New York: Ballantine, 1995), 3–9, 17–20.

of Hollywood, fast-food outlets, jeans, and Americanization. *Jihad* (the Arab word for "struggle") is used to symbolize all the nationalist, fundamentalist, ethnocentric, and tribal rejections of McWorld. Barber's argument is that these forces have largely shaped modern culture and that despite their opposition to each other, they both prevent the development of civic society and democracy. According to Barber, in what ways do both Jihad and McWorld stymie this development? What do you think of his argument? Can the world really be divided into these two groups? What sort of future does Barber predict?

THINKING HISTORICALLY

Barber argues that Jihad originated in opposition to McWorld and that the two play off each other in a way that gives them both substance and support. Which is a greater force toward globalization? Does Barber see Jihad and McWorld as primarily cultural or economic forces? How is Barber's idea of the process of global change different from that of the previous authors?

History is not over.[1] Nor are we arrived in the wondrous land of techné[2] promised by the futurologists. The collapse of state communism has not delivered people to a safe democratic haven, and the past, fratricide and civil discord perduring, still clouds the horizon just behind us. Those who look back see all of the horrors of the ancient slaughterbench reenacted in disintegral nations like Bosnia, Sri Lanka, Ossetia, and Rwanda and they declare that nothing has changed. Those who look forward prophesize commercial and technological interdependence—a virtual paradise made possible by spreading markets and global technology—and they proclaim that everything is or soon will be different. The rival observers seem to consult different almanacs drawn from the libraries of contrarian planets.

Yet anyone who reads the daily papers carefully, taking in the front page accounts of civil carnage as well as the business page stories on the mechanics of the information superhighway and the economics of communication mergers, anyone who turns deliberately to take in the whole 360-degree horizon, knows that our world and our lives are caught between what [Irish poet] William Butler Yeats called the two eternities of race and soul: that of race reflecting the tribal past, that

[1] This is a response to the argument of Francis Fukuyama in "The End of History" (1989) that with the downfall of communism, there were no more fundamental conflicts to challenge the universalization of liberal democracy. [Ed.]

[2] Technology. [Ed.]

of soul anticipating the cosmopolitan future. Our secular eternities are corrupted, however, race reduced to an insignia of resentment, and soul sized down to fit the demanding body by which it now measures its needs. Neither race nor soul offers us a future that is other than bleak, neither promises a polity that is remotely democratic.

The first scenario rooted in race holds out the grim prospect of a retribalization of large swaths of humankind by war and bloodshed: a threatened balkanization of nation-states in which culture is pitted against culture, people against people, tribe against tribe, a Jihad in the name of a hundred narrowly conceived faiths against every kind of interdependence, every kind of artificial social cooperation and mutuality: against technology, against pop culture, and against integrated markets; against modernity itself as well as the future in which modernity issues. The second paints that future in shimmering pastels, a busy portrait of onrushing economic, technological, and ecological forces that demand integration and uniformity and that mesmerize peoples everywhere with fast music, fast computers, and fast food—MTV, Macintosh, and McDonald's—pressing nations into one homogenous global theme park, one McWorld tied together by communications, information, entertainment, and commerce. Caught between Babel and Disneyland, the planet is falling precipitously apart and coming reluctantly together at the very same moment.

Some stunned observers notice only Babel, complaining about the thousand newly sundered "peoples" who prefer to address their neighbors with sniper rifles and mortars; others—zealots in Disneyland—seize on futurological platitudes and the promise of virtuality, exclaiming "It's a small world after all!" Both are right, but how can that be?

We are compelled to choose between what passes as "the twilight of sovereignty" and an entropic end of all history, or a return to the past's most fractious and demoralizing discord; to "the menace of global anarchy," to [John] Milton's capital of hell, Pandaemonium; to a world totally "out of control."

The apparent truth, which speaks to the paradox at the core of this book, is that the tendencies of both Jihad *and* McWorld are at work, both visible sometimes in the same country at the very same instant. Iranian zealots keep one ear tuned to the mullahs urging holy war and the other cocked to [Australian media mogul] Rupert Murdoch's Star television beaming in *Dynasty, Donahue,* and *The Simpsons* from hovering satellites. Chinese entrepreneurs vie for the attention of party cadres in Beijing and simultaneously pursue KFC franchises in cities like Nanjing, Hangzhou, and Xian where twenty-eight outlets serve over 100,000 customers a day. The Russian Orthodox church, even as it struggles to renew the ancient faith, has entered a joint venture with California businessmen to bottle and sell natural waters under the rubric Saint Springs Water Company. Serbian assassins wear Adidas sneakers and listen to

Madonna on Walkman headphones as they take aim through their gun-scopes at scurrying Sarajevo civilians looking to fill family watercans. Orthodox Hasids and brooding neo-Nazis have both turned to rock music to get their traditional messages out to the new generation, while fundamentalists plot virtual conspiracies on the Internet.

Now neither Jihad nor McWorld is in itself novel. History ending in the triumph of science and reason or some monstrous perversion thereof (Mary Shelley's Doctor Frankenstein) has been the leitmotiv of every philosopher and poet who has regretted the Age of Reason since the Enlightenment. [W. B.] Yeats lamented "the center will not hold, mere anarchy is loosed upon the world," and observers of Jihad today have little but historical detail to add. The Christian parable of the Fall and of the possibilities of redemption that it makes possible captures the eigh-teenth-century ambivalence—and our own—about past and future. I want, however, to do more than dress up the central paradox of human history in modern clothes. It is not Jihad and McWorld but the relation-ship between them that most interests me. For, squeezed between their opposing forces, the world has been sent spinning out of control. Can it be that what Jihad and McWorld have in common is anarchy: the ab-sence of common will and that conscious and collective human control under the guidance of law we call democracy?

Progress moves in steps that sometimes lurch backwards; in histo-ry's twisting maze, Jihad not only revolts against but abets McWorld, while McWorld not only imperils but re-creates and reinforces Jihad. They produce their contraries and need one another. My object here then is not simply to offer sequential portraits of McWorld and Jihad, but while examining McWorld, to keep Jihad in my field of vision, and while dissecting Jihad, never to forget the context of McWorld. Call it a dialectic[3] of McWorld: a study in the cunning of reason that does honor to the radical differences that distinguish Jihad and McWorld yet that acknowledges their powerful and paradoxical interdependence.

There is a crucial difference, however, between my modest attempt at dialectic and that of the masters of the nineteenth century. Still se-duced by the Enlightenment's faith in progress, both [G. W. F.] Hegel and [Karl] Marx believed reason's cunning was on the side of progress. But it is harder to believe that the clash of Jihad and McWorld will issue in some overriding good. The outcome seems more likely to pervert than to nurture human liberty. The two may, in opposing each other, work to the same ends, work in apparent tension yet in covert harmony, but democracy is not their beneficiary. In East Berlin, tribal communism has yielded to capitalism. In Marx-Engelsplatz, the stolid, overbearing

---

[3] Interaction; *dialectic* is a term borrowed from the German philosopher G. W. F. Hegel and the philosopher and revolutionary Karl Marx that described historical change as the product of competing systems—of ideas for Hegel, and of social-economic systems for Marx. [Ed.]

statues of Marx and [Friedrich] Engels face east, as if seeking distant solace from Moscow: but now, circling them along the streets that surround the park that is their prison are chain eateries like T.G.I. Friday's, international hotels like the Radisson, and a circle of neon billboards mocking them with brand names like Panasonic, Coke, and GoldStar. New gods, yes, but more liberty?

What then does it mean in concrete terms to view Jihad and McWorld dialectically when the tendencies of the two sets of forces initially appear so intractably antithetical? After all, Jihad and McWorld operate with equal strength in opposite directions, the one driven by parochial hatreds, the other by universalizing markets, the one recreating ancient subnational and ethnic borders from within, the other making national borders porous from without. Yet Jihad and McWorld have this in common: They both make war on the sovereign nation-state and thus undermine the nation-state's democratic institutions. Each eschews civil society and belittles democratic citizenship, neither seeks alternative democratic institutions. Their common thread is indifference to civil liberty. Jihad forges communities of blood rooted in exclusion and hatred, communities that slight democracy in favor of tyrannical paternalism or consensual tribalism. McWorld forges global markets rooted in consumption and profit, leaving to an untrustworthy, if not altogether fictitious, invisible hand issues of public interest and common good that once might have been nurtured by democratic citizenries and their watchful governments. Such governments, intimidated by market ideology, are actually pulling back at the very moment they ought to be aggressively intervening. What was once understood as protecting the public interest is now excoriated as heavy-handed regulatory browbeating. Justice yields to markets, even though, as [New York banker] Felix Rohatyn has bluntly confessed, "there is a brutal Darwinian logic to these markets. They are nervous and greedy. They look for stability and transparency, but what they reward is not always our preferred form of democracy." If the traditional conservators of freedom were democratic constitutions and Bills of Rights, "the new temples to liberty," [literary critic and philosopher] George Steiner suggests, "will be McDonald's and Kentucky Fried Chicken."

In being reduced to a choice between the market's universal church and a retribalizing politics of particularist identities, peoples around the globe are threatened with an atavistic return to medieval politics where local tribes and ambitious emperors together ruled the world entire, women and men united by the universal abstraction of Christianity even as they lived out isolated lives in warring fiefdoms defined by involuntary (ascriptive) forms of identity. This was a world in which princes and kings had little real power until they conceived the ideology of nationalism. Nationalism established government on a scale greater than the tribe yet less cosmopolitan than the universal church and in time gave birth to those intermediate, gradually more democratic institutions that would come to constitute the nation-state. Today, at the far end of this history, we seem intent on re-creating a world in which our only choices are the secular universalism of the cosmopolitan market and the everyday particularism of the fractious tribe.

In the tumult of the confrontation between global commerce and parochial ethnicity, the virtues of the democratic nation are lost and the instrumentalities by which it permitted peoples to transform themselves into nations and seize sovereign power in the name of liberty and the commonweal are put at risk. Neither Jihad nor McWorld aspires to resecure the civic virtues undermined by its denationalizing practices; neither global markets nor blood communities service public goods or pursue equality and justice. Impartial judiciaries and deliberate assemblies play no role in the roving killer bands that speak on behalf of newly liberated "peoples," and such democratic institutions have at best only marginal influence on the roving multinational corporations that speak on behalf of newly liberated markets. Jihad pursues a bloody politics of identity, McWorld a bloodless economics of profit. Belonging by default to McWorld, everyone is a consumer; seeking a repository for identity, everyone belongs to some tribe. But no one is a citizen. Without citizens, how can there be democracy? . . .

Jihad is, I recognize, a strong term. In its mildest form, it betokens religious struggle on behalf of faith, a kind of Islamic zeal. In its strongest political manifestation, it means bloody holy war on behalf of partisan identity that is metaphysically defined and fanatically defended. Thus, while for many Muslims it may signify only ardor in the name of a religion that can properly be regarded as universalizing (if not quite ecumenical), I borrow its meaning from those militants who make the slaughter of the "other" a higher duty. I use the term in its militant construction to suggest dogmatic and violent particularism of a kind known to Christians no less than Muslims, to Germans and Hindis as well as to Arabs. The phenomena to which I apply the phrase have innocent enough beginnings: identity politics and multicultural diversity can represent strategies of a free society trying to give expression to its diversity. What ends as Jihad may begin as a simple search for a local identity, some set of common personal attributes to hold out against the numbing and neutering uniformities of industrial modernization and the colonizing culture of McWorld. . . .

McWorld is a product of popular culture driven by expansionist commerce. Its template is American, its form style. Its goods are as much images as matériel, an aesthetic as well as a product line. It is about culture as commodity, apparel as ideology. Its symbols are Harley-Davidson motorcycles and Cadillac motorcars hoisted from the roadways, where they once represented a mode of transportation, to the marquees of global market cafés like Harley-Davidson's and the Hard Rock where they become icons of lifestyle. You don't drive them, you feel their vibes and rock to the images they conjure up from old movies and new celebrities, whose personal appearances are the key to the wildly popular international café chain Planet Hollywood. Music, video, theater, books, and theme parks—the new churches of a commercial civilization in which malls are the public squares and suburbs the neighborless neighborhoods—are all constructed as image exports creating a common world taste around common logos, advertising slogans, stars, songs, brand names, jingles, and trademarks. Hard power yields to soft, while ideology is transmuted into a kind of videology that works through sound bites and film clips. Videology is fuzzier and less dogmatic than traditional political ideology: it may as a consequence be far more successful in instilling the novel values required for global markets to succeed.

McWorld's videology remains Jihad's most formidable rival, and in the long run it may attenuate the force of Jihad's recidivist tribalisms. Yet the information revolution's instrumentalities are also Jihad's favored weapons. Hutu or Bosnian Serb identity[4] was less a matter of real historical memory than of media propaganda by a leadership set on liquidating rival clans. In both Rwanda and Bosnia, radio broadcasts whipped listeners into a killing frenzy. As *New York Times* rock critic Jon Pareles has noticed, "regionalism in pop music has become as trendy as microbrewery beer and narrowcasting cable channels, and for the same reasons."[5] The global culture is what gives the local culture its medium, its audience, and its aspirations. Fascist pop and Hasid rock are not oxymorons; rather they manifest the dialectics of McWorld in particularly dramatic ways. Belgrade's radio includes stations that broadcast Western pop music as a rebuke to hard-liner Milosevic's supernationalist government and stations that broadcast native folk tunes laced with antiforeign and anti-Semitic sentiments. Even the Internet has its neo-Nazi bulletin boards and Turk-trashing Armenian "flamers" (who assail every use of the word *turkey*, fair and fowl alike, so to speak), so that the abstractions of cyberspace too are infected with a peculiar and rabid cultural territoriality all their own.

The dynamics of the Jihad-McWorld linkage are deeply dialectical. Japan has, for example, become more culturally insistent on its own traditions in recent years even as its people seek an ever greater purchase on McWorld. In 1992, the number-one restaurant in Japan measured by volume of customers was McDonald's, followed in the number-two

---

[4] This is a reference to the attempted genocide of Tutsis by Hutus in Rwanda (1994) and of Muslim Bosnians by Serbian Bosnians in what was Yugoslavia (1992–1995). In both cases the "other" was so indistinguishable that the perpetrators demanded identity cards. [Ed.]

[5] Jon Pareles, "Striving to Become Rock's Next Seattle," *The New York Times,* July 17, 1994, Section 2, p. 1.

spot by the Colonel's Kentucky Fried Chicken. In France, where cultural purists complain bitterly of a looming Sixième République ("la République Américaine"),[6] the government attacks "franglais" even as it funds EuroDisney park just outside of Paris. In the same spirit, the cinema industry makes war on American film imports while it bestows upon Sylvester Stallone one of France's highest honors, the Chevalier des arts et lettres. Ambivalence also stalks India. Just outside of Bombay, cheek by jowl with villages still immersed in poverty and notorious for the informal execution of unwanted female babies or, even, wives, can be found a new town known as SCEEPZ—the Santa Cruz Electronic Export Processing Zone—where Hindi-, Tamil-, and Mahratti-speaking computer programmers write software for Swissair, AT&T, and other labor-cost-conscious multinationals. India is thus at once a major exemplar of ancient ethnic and religious tensions and "an emerging power in the international software industry."[7] To go to work at SCEEPZ, says an employee, is "like crossing an international border." Not into another country, but into the virtual nowhere-land of McWorld.

More dramatic even than in India, is the strange interplay of Jihad and McWorld in the remnants of Yugoslavia. In an affecting *New Republic* report, Slavenka Drakulic recently told the brief tragic love story of Admira and Bosko, two young star-crossed lovers from Sarajevo: "They were born in the late 1960's," she writes. "They watched Spielberg movies; they listened to Iggy Pop; they read John le Carré; they went to a disco every Saturday night and fantasized about traveling to Paris or London."[8] Longing for safety, it seems they finally negotiated with all sides for safe passage, and readied their departure from Sarajevo. Before they could cross the magical border that separates their impoverished land from the seeming sanctuary of McWorld, Jihad caught up to them. Their bodies lay along the riverbank, riddled with bullets from anonymous snipers for whom safe passage signaled an invitation to target practice. The murdered young lovers, as befits émigrés to McWorld, were clothed in jeans and sneakers. So too, one imagines, were their murderers.

Further east, tourists seeking a piece of old Russia that does not take them too far from MTV can find traditional Matryoshka nesting dolls (that fit one inside the other) featuring the nontraditional visages of (from largest to smallest) Bruce Springsteen, Madonna, Boy George, Dave Stewart, and Annie Lennox.

In Russia, in India, in Bosnia, in Japan, and in France too, modern history then leans both ways: toward the meretricious inevitability of

---

[6] "Sixth Republic"; the present French government is the Fifth Republic. [Ed.]

[7] National Public Radio, *All Things Considered,* December 2, 1993, from the broadcast transcription.

[8] Slavenka Drakulic, "Love Story: A True Tale from Sarajevo," *The New Republic,* October 26, 1993, pp. 14–16.

McWorld, but also into Jihad's stiff winds, heaving to and fro and giving heart both to the Panglossians and the Pandoras,[9] sometimes for the very same reasons. The Panglossians bank on EuroDisney and Microsoft, while the Pandoras await nihilism and a world in Pandaemonium. Yet McWorld and Jihad do not really force a choice between such polarized scenarios. Together, they are likely to produce some stifling amalgam of the two suspended in chaos. Antithetical in every detail, Jihad and McWorld nonetheless conspire to undermine our hard-won (if only half-won) civil liberties and the possibility of a global democratic future. In the short run the forces of Jihad, noisier and more obviously nihilistic than those of McWorld, are likely to dominate the near future, etching small stories of local tragedy and regional genocide on the face of our times and creating a climate of instability marked by multimicrowars inimical to global integration. But in the long run, the forces of McWorld are the forces underlying the slow certain thrust of Western civilization and as such may be unstoppable. Jihad's microwars will hold the headlines well into the next century, making predictions of the end of history look terminally dumb. But McWorld's homogenization is likely to establish a macropeace that favors the triumph of commerce and its markets and to give to those who control information, communication, and entertainment ultimate (if inadvertent) control over human destiny. Unless we can offer an alternative to the struggle between Jihad and McWorld; the epoch on whose threshold we stand—postcommunist, postindustrial, postnational, yet sectarian, fearful, and bigoted—is likely also to be terminally postdemocratic.

[9] Extreme optimists and pessimists, respectively. [Ed.]

5

KWAME ANTHONY APPIAH

The Case for Contamination

The author, born in Ghana of English and Asante families, is a philosopher at Princeton University. This essay and his recent book *Cosmopolitanism* (2007) address ethical issues associated with globalization. What does he mean by caring for people rather than cultures, and for individuals rather than "peoples"? What does Appiah mean by *cosmopolitanism*?

Source: Kwame Anthony Appiah, "The Case for Contamination," *New York Times Magazine*, January 1, 2006, http://www.nytimes.com/2006/01/01/magazine/01cosmopolitan.html.

THINKING HISTORICALLY

How does Appiah understand the process of globalization? Compare his view to that of Barber in the previous selection. Does Appiah see economic or cultural forces more instrumental in changing the world? What does he see as the consequences of globalization? How does Appiah's vision of the future differ from that of Barber? Which do you think more likely?

I'm seated, with my mother, on a palace veranda, cooled by a breeze from the royal garden. Before us, on a dais, is an empty throne, its arms and legs embossed with polished brass, the back and seat covered in black-and-gold silk. In front of the steps to the dais, there are two columns of people, mostly men, facing one another, seated on carved wooden stools, the cloths they wear wrapped around their chests, leaving their shoulders bare. There is a quiet buzz of conversation. Outside in the garden, peacocks screech. At last, the blowing of a ram's horn announces the arrival of the king of Asante, its tones sounding his honorific, *kotokohene*, "porcupine chief." (Each quill of the porcupine, according to custom, signifies a warrior ready to kill and to die for the kingdom.) Everyone stands until the king has settled on the throne. Then, when we sit, a chorus sings songs in praise of him, which are interspersed with the playing of a flute. It is a Wednesday festival day in Kumasi, the town in Ghana where I grew up.

Unless you're one of a few million Ghanaians, this will probably seem a relatively unfamiliar world, perhaps even an exotic one. You might suppose that this Wednesday festival belongs quaintly to an African past. But before the king arrived, people were taking calls on cellphones, and among those passing the time in quiet conversation were a dozen men in suits, representatives of an insurance company. And the meetings in the office next to the veranda are about contemporary issues: H.I.V./AIDS, the educational needs of 21st-century children, the teaching of science and technology at the local university. When my turn comes to be formally presented, the king asks me about Princeton, where I teach. I ask him when he'll next be in the States. In a few weeks, he says cheerfully. He's got a meeting with the head of the World Bank.

Anywhere you travel in the world—today as always—you can find ceremonies like these, many of them rooted in centuries-old traditions. But you will also find everywhere—and this is something new—many intimate connections with places far away: Washington, Moscow, Mexico City, Beijing. Across the street from us, when we were growing up, there was a large house occupied by a number of families, among them a vast family of boys; one, about my age, was a good friend. He lives in London. His brother lives in Japan, where his wife is from. They have another brother who has been in Spain for a while and a couple more brothers who, last I heard, were in the United States. Some of them still live in Kumasi, one or two in Accra, Ghana's capital. Eddie, who lives in Japan, speaks his wife's language now. He has to. But he was never very comfortable in English, the language of our government and our schools. When he phones me from time to time, he prefers to speak Asante-Twi.

Over the years, the royal palace buildings in Kumasi have expanded. When I was a child, we used to visit the previous king, my great-uncle by marriage, in a small building that the British had allowed his predecessor to build when he returned from exile in the Seychelles to a restored but diminished Asante kingship. That building is now a museum, dwarfed by the enormous house next door—built by his successor, my uncle by marriage—where the current king lives. Next to it is the suite of offices abutting the veranda where we were sitting, recently finished by the present king, my uncle's successor. The British, my mother's people, conquered Asante at the turn of the 20th century; now, at the turn of the 21st, the palace feels as it must have felt in the 19th century: a center of power. The president of Ghana comes from this world, too. He was born across the street from the palace to a member of the royal Oyoko clan. But he belongs to other worlds as well: he went to Oxford University; he's a member of one of the Inns of Court[1] in London; he's a Catholic, with a picture of himself greeting the pope in his sitting room.

What are we to make of this? On Kumasi's Wednesday festival day, I've seen visitors from England and the United States wince at what they regard as the intrusion of modernity on timeless, traditional rituals—more evidence, they think, of a pressure in the modern world toward uniformity. They react like the assistant on the film set who's supposed to check that the extras in a sword-and-sandals movie aren't wearing wristwatches. And such purists are not alone. In the past couple of years, Unesco's[2] members have spent a great deal of time trying to hammer out a convention on the "protection and promotion" of cultural diversity. (It was finally approved at the Unesco General Conference in October 2005.) The drafters worried that "the processes of globalization . . . represent a challenge for cultural diversity, namely in view of risks of imbalances between rich and poor countries." The fear is that the values and images of Western mass culture, like some invasive weed, are threatening to choke out the world's native flora.

The contradictions in this argument aren't hard to find. This same Unesco document is careful to affirm the importance of the free flow of ideas, the freedom of thought and expression and human rights—values

---

[1] British legal societies that have sole right to confer certain law degrees. [Ed.]
[2] United Nations Educational, Scientific, and Cultural Organization. [Ed.]

that, we know, will become universal only if we make them so. What's really important, then, cultures or people? In a world where Kumasi and New York—and Cairo and Leeds and Istanbul—are being drawn ever closer together, an ethics of globalization has proved elusive.

The right approach, I think, starts by taking individuals—not nations, tribes or "peoples"—as the proper object of moral concern. It doesn't much matter what we call such a creed, but in homage to Diogenes, the fourth-century Greek Cynic and the first philosopher to call himself a "citizen of the world," we could call it cosmopolitan. Cosmopolitans take cultural difference seriously, because they take the choices individual people make seriously. But because cultural difference is not the only thing that concerns them, they suspect that many of globalization's cultural critics are aiming at the wrong targets.

Yes, globalization can produce homogeneity. But globalization is also a threat to homogeneity. You can see this as clearly in Kumasi as anywhere. One thing Kumasi isn't—simply because it's a city—is homogeneous. English, German, Chinese, Syrian, Lebanese, Burkinabe, Ivorian, Nigerian, Indian: I can find you families of each description. I can find you Asante people, whose ancestors have lived in this town for centuries, but also Hausa[3] households that have been around for centuries, too. There are people there from every region of the country as well, speaking scores of languages. But if you travel just a little way outside Kumasi—20 miles, say, in the right direction—and if you drive off the main road down one of the many potholed side roads of red laterite, you won't have difficulty finding villages that are fairly monocultural. The people have mostly been to Kumasi and seen the big, polyglot, diverse world of the city. Where they live, though, there is one everyday language (aside from the English in the government schools) and an agrarian way of life based on some old crops, like yams, and some newer ones, like cocoa, which arrived in the late 19th century as a product for export. They may or may not have electricity. (This close to Kumasi, they probably do.) When people talk of the homogeneity produced by globalization, what they are talking about is this: Even here, the villagers will have radios (though the language will be local); you will be able to get a discussion going about Ronaldo, or Tupac; and you will probably be able to find a bottle of Guinness or Coca-Cola (as well as of Star or Club, Ghana's own fine lagers). But has access to these things made the place more homogeneous or less? And what can you tell about people's souls from the fact that they drink Coca-Cola?

It's true that the enclaves of homogeneity you find these days—in Asante as in Pennsylvania—are less distinctive than they were a century ago, but mostly in good ways. More of them have access to effective medicines. More of them have access to clean drinking water, and more

---

[3] An African ethnic group, mainly in northern Nigeria and southern Niger. [Ed.]

of them have schools. Where, as is still too common, they don't have these things, it's something not to celebrate but to deplore. And whatever loss of difference there has been, they are constantly inventing new forms of difference: new hairstyles, new slang, even, from time to time, new religions. No one could say that the world's villages are becoming anything like the same.

So why do people in these places sometimes feel that their identities are threatened? Because the world, their world, is changing, and some of them don't like it. The pull of the global economy—witness those cocoa trees, whose chocolate is eaten all around the world—created some of the life they now live. If chocolate prices were to collapse again, as they did in the early 1990s, Asante farmers might have to find new crops or new forms of livelihood. That prospect is unsettling for some people (just as it is exciting for others). Missionaries came a while ago, so many of these villagers will be Christian, even if they have also kept some of the rites from earlier days. But new Pentecostal messengers are challenging the churches they know and condemning the old rites as idolatrous. Again, some like it; some don't.

Above all, relationships are changing. When my father was young, a man in a village would farm some land that a chief had granted him, and his maternal clan (including his younger brothers) would work it with him. When a new house needed building, he would organize it. He would also make sure his dependents were fed and clothed, the children educated, marriages and funerals arranged and paid for. He could expect to pass the farm and the responsibilities along to the next generation.

Nowadays, everything is different. Cocoa prices have not kept pace with the cost of living. Gas prices have made the transportation of the crop more expensive. And there are new possibilities for the young in the towns, in other parts of the country and in other parts of the world. Once, perhaps, you could have commanded the young ones to stay. Now they have the right to leave—perhaps to seek work at one of the new data-processing centers down south in the nation's capital—and, anyway, you may not make enough to feed and clothe and educate them all. So the time of the successful farming family is passing, and those who were settled in that way of life are as sad to see it go as American family farmers are whose lands are accumulated by giant agribusinesses. We can sympathize with them. But we cannot force their children to stay in the name of protecting their authentic culture, and we cannot afford to subsidize indefinitely thousands of distinct islands of homogeneity that no longer make economic sense.

Nor should we want to. Human variety matters, cosmopolitans think, because people are entitled to options. What [the philosopher] John Stuart Mill said more than a century ago in "On Liberty" about diversity within a society serves just as well as an argument for variety across the globe: "If it were only that people have diversities of taste, that is reason enough for not attempting to shape them all after one model. But different persons also require different conditions for their spiritual development; and can no more exist healthily in the same moral, than all the variety of plants can exist in the same physical atmosphere and climate. The same things which are helps to one person towards the cultivation of his higher nature, are hindrances to another. . . . Unless there is a corresponding diversity in their modes of life, they neither obtain their fair share of happiness, nor grow up to the mental, moral, and aesthetic stature of which their nature is capable." If we want to preserve a wide range of human conditions because it allows free people the best chance to make their own lives, we can't enforce diversity by trapping people within differences they long to escape.

Even if you grant that people shouldn't be compelled to sustain the older cultural practices, you might suppose that cosmopolitans should side with those who are busy around the world "preserving culture" and resisting "cultural imperialism." Yet behind these slogans you often find some curious assumptions. Take "preserving culture." It's one thing to help people sustain arts they want to sustain. I am all for festivals of Welsh bards in Llandudno financed by the Welsh arts council. Long live the Ghana National Cultural Center in Kumasi, where you can go and learn traditional Akan dancing and drumming, especially since its classes are spirited and overflowing. Restore the deteriorating film stock of early Hollywood movies; continue the preservation of Old Norse and early Chinese and Ethiopian manuscripts; record, transcribe and analyze the oral narratives of Malay and Masai and Maori. All these are undeniably valuable.

But preserving culture—in the sense of such cultural artifacts—is different from preserving cultures. And the cultural preservationists often pursue the latter, trying to ensure that the Huli of Papua New Guinea (or even Sikhs in Toronto) maintain their "authentic" ways. What makes a cultural expression authentic, though? Are we to stop the importation of baseball caps into Vietnam so that the Zao will continue to wear their colorful red headdresses? Why not ask the Zao? Shouldn't the choice be theirs?

"They have no real choice," the cultural preservationists say. "We've dumped cheap Western clothes into their markets, and they can no longer afford the silk they used to wear. If they had what they really wanted, they'd still be dressed traditionally." But this is no longer an argument about authenticity. The claim is that they can't afford to do something that they'd really like to do, something that is expressive of an identity they care about and want to sustain. This is a genuine problem, one that afflicts people in many communities: they're too poor to live the life they want to lead. But if they do get richer, and they still run around in T-shirts, that's their choice. Talk of authenticity now just amounts to telling other people what they ought to value in their own traditions.

Not that this is likely to be a problem in the real world. People who can afford it mostly like to put on traditional garb—at least from time to time. I was best man once at a Scottish wedding at which the bridegroom wore a kilt and I wore kente cloth. Andrew Oransay, the islander who piped us up the aisle, whispered in my ear at one point, "Here we all are then, in our tribal gear." In Kumasi, people who can afford them love to put on their kente cloths, especially the most "traditional" ones, woven in colorful silk strips in the town of Bonwire, as they have been for a couple of centuries. (The prices are high in part because demand outside Asante has risen. A fine kente for a man now costs more than the average Ghanaian earns in a year. Is that bad? Not for the people of Bonwire.)

Besides, trying to find some primordially authentic culture can be like peeling an onion. The textiles most people think of as traditional West African cloths are known as Java prints; they arrived in the 19th century with the Javanese batiks sold, and often milled, by the Dutch. The traditional garb of Herero women in Namibia derives from the attire of 19th-century German missionaries, though it is still unmistakably Herero, not least because the fabrics used have a distinctly un-Lutheran range of colors. And so with our kente cloth: the silk was always imported, traded by Europeans, produced in Asia. This tradition was once an innovation. Should we reject it for that reason as untraditional? How far back must one go? Should we condemn the young men and women of the University of Science and Technology, a few miles outside Kumasi, who wear European-style gowns for graduation, lined with kente strips (as they do now at Howard and Morehouse, too)? Cultures are made of continuities and changes, and the identity of a society can survive through these changes. Societies without change aren't authentic; they're just dead.

6

Cartoons on Globalization

The following are editorial cartoons. Each addresses economic components of globalization, and each in some way addresses the relationship between those in the most developed part of the world and those in the developing world.

Figure 28.1, "As an Illegal Immigrant," raises questions about increased labor and capital mobility, allowing the import of migrant workers and the export of capital for foreign factories. What is the point of the cartoon? How would you describe its attitude toward globalization?

Figure 28.2, "Help Is on the Way, Dude," focuses on an irony of some well-intentioned efforts to protect the environment and exploited foreign laborers. What is the irony? How might you solve the problem posed by the cartoon?

Figure 28.1 "As an Illegal Immigrant."
Source: Gary Markstein.

Figure 28.2 "Help Is on the Way, Dude."
Source: By permission of Chip Bok and Creators Syndicate, Inc.

Figure 28.3 "Cheap Chinese Textiles."
Source: Patrick Chappatte/Globe Cartoon.

Figure 28.4 "Keep the Europeans Out."
Source: Bruce MacKinnon/artizans.com.

Figure 28.5 "I Don't Mean to Hurry You."
Source: J. McGillen/Cartoonstock.com.

Figure 28.3, "Cheap Chinese Textiles," explores the problem of low-cost manufacturing countries flooding global markets with cheap products. What is the meaning of the comment by the representative of the European Union (EU)? What is the meaning of the cartoon?

Figure 28.4, "Keep the Europeans Out," examines a concern of North American farmers, here expressed on a placard of a Canadian farmer. What is that concern, and what is the farmer's solution? What is the point of the cartoon? What does this cartoon say about the use of tariffs, quotas, or other protectionist barriers to limit global competition? Compare this cartoon to the previous one on this issue.

Figure 28.5, "I Don't Mean to Hurry You," asks about the wishes of people in the developing world. What is the point of the cartoon? Compare the cartoon with the analysis of Barber or Appiah.

THINKING HISTORICALLY

All of these cartoonists explore a process of economic globalization. What are the economic forces that bring about the globalization depicted in these cartoons? To what extent does the humor in these cartoons depend on a realization that globalization is inevitable? To what extent is that attitude shared by the authors of the other selections in this chapter?

■ REFLECTIONS

Globalization is not one process, but many. It is as technological as the Internet, smart phones, and the latest flu vaccine. It is as cultural as international film festivals, sushi, and disappearing languages. It is as political as the United Nations, time zones, and occupying armies. Perhaps most important, it is economic. People migrate for jobs, factories move for cheaper labor, and neither consumers nor corporations care about country of origin. Since the end of communism, the entire world has become a single market.

Is this a good thing? It depends on whom you ask. Sherif Hetata sees overcommercialization undermining national traditions. Philippe Legrain applauds the new menu of possibilities. Life is clearly hard for the women working in the sweatshops of international corporations, as Miriam Ching Yoon Louie points out; but is economic globalization responsible for their suffering, or does it provide women like them with new opportunities? Benjamin Barber explains why some choose jihad in response to the effects of world trade. More than any of the other authors, he is skeptical of the inevitability of globalization, but his prognosis is not pretty. Kwame Anthony Appiah offers a far more hopeful view from the palace veranda.

It is the duty of citizens, not historians, to decide what outcomes are good or bad, better or worse. But historians can help us decide by showing us where we are—by deepening the temporal dimension of our awareness.

Understanding the process of change is the most useful "habit of mind" we gain from studying the past. Although the facts are many and the details overwhelming, the historical process appears to us only through the study of the specifics. And we must continually check and revise our interpretations to conform to new information. But like a storyteller without a plot, we are lost without some overall understanding of how our world is changing.

More important, understanding change does not mean that we have to submit to it. Of the processes of globalization discussed in this chapter—trade and technological transfers, cultural homogenization and competition, commercialization and market expansion—some may seem inevitable, some strong, some even reversible. Intelligent action requires an appreciation of the possible as well as the identification of the improbable.

History is not an exact science. Fortunately, human beings are creators, as well as subjects, of change. Even winds that cannot be silenced can be deflected, harnessed, or made to chime. Which way is the world moving? What are we becoming? What can we do? What kind of world can we create? These are questions that can only be answered by studying the past, both distant and recent, and trying to understand the overarching changes that are shaping our lives. Worlds of history converge upon us, but only one world will emerge from our wishes, our wisdom, and our will.

Acknowledgments

Chapter 15

1   Nicholas D. Kristof. "1492: The Prequel" from *The New York Times Magazine* (June 6, 1999). Copyright © 1999 by The New York Times Company. Reprinted by permission. All rights reserved.

2   Ma Huan. Excerpt from *The Overall Survey of the Ocean's Shores*, edited and translated by Feng Ch'eng Chun (London: The Hakluyt Society, 1970). Reprinted with the permission of David Higham Associates, Limited.

5   Kirkpatrick Sale. Excerpt from *The Conquest of Paradise*. Copyright © 1990 by Kirkpatrick Sale. Used by permission of The Joy Harris Literary Agency.

Chapter 16

1   Bernal Díaz. Excerpt from *The Conquest of New Spain*, translated by J. M. Cohen. Copyright © 1963 by J. M. Cohen. Reprinted with the permission of Penguin Books Ltd.

2   Miguel Leon-Portilla (ed.). Excerpt from *The Broken Spears: The Aztec Account of the Conquest of Mexico*, translated by Lysander Kemp. Copyright © 1962 by Beacon Press. Reprinted with the permission of Beacon Press, Boston.

3   Bartolomé de Las Casas. Excerpt from *The Devastation of the Indies: A Brief Account*, translated by Herma Briffault. Reprinted with the permission of The Continuum International Publishing Group.

5   Nzinga Mbemba. "Appeal to the King of Portugal" from *The African Past*, edited by Basil Davidson. Copyright © 1964 by Basil Davidson. Reprinted with the permission of Curtis Brown Ltd.

Chapter 17

1   Jonathan D. Spence. "Emperor K'ang-Hsi on Religion" from *Emperor of China: Self-Portrait of K'ang-Hsi*. Copyright © 1974 by Jonathan D. Spence. Used by permission of Alfred A. Knopf, a division of Random House, Inc.

2   David J. Lu. "Japanese Edicts Regulating Religion" from *Japan: A Documentary History,* edited and translated by David J. Lu. Translation copyright © 1997 by David J. Lu. Reprinted with permission from M. E. Sharpe, Inc.

3   Abdul Qadir Bada'uni. "Akbar and Religion" from *Muntakhab ut-Tawarikh*, Volume 2, translated by G. S. A. Ranking and W. H. Lowe. Edited and reprinted in *Sources of Indian Tradition*, edited by Ainslie T. Embree. Copyright © 1988 by Columbia University Press. Reprinted with permission of the publisher.

4   Ira M. Lepidus. "Ottoman State and Religion" from *A History of Islamic Societies*. Copyright © 2002 by Ira M. Lepidus. Reprinted with the permission of Cambridge University Press.

5   Benjamin J. Kaplan. "European Faiths and States" from *Divided by Faith: Religious Conflict and the Practice of Toleration in Early Modern Europe*. Copyright © 2007 by Benjamin J. Kaplan. Reprinted by permission of Harvard University Press.

Chapter 18

1   Patricia Buckley Ebrey. "Family Instructions for the Miu Lineage" from *Chinese Civilization: A Sourcebook*, Second Edition, by Patricia Buckley Ebrey. Copyright © 1993 by Patricia Buckley Ebrey. Reprinted with the permission of The Free Press, a Division of Simon & Schuster, Inc. All rights reserved.

2   Patricia Buckley Ebrey. "How Dong Xiaowan Became My Concubine" from *Chinese Civilization: A Sourcebook*, Second Edition, by Patricia Buckley Ebrey. Copyright © 1993 by Patricia Buckley Ebrey. Reprinted with the permission of The Free Press, a Division of Simon & Schuster, Inc. All rights reserved.

3   Anthony Reid. Excerpt from "Female Roles in Pre-Colonial Southeast Asia" from *Modern Asian Studies* 22:3 (1988): 629–645. Copyright © 1988. Reprinted with the permission of Cambridge University Press.

4   John E. Wills Jr. Excerpt from "Sor Juana Inés de la Cruz" from "The Empire of Silver" in *1688: A Global History*. Copyright © 2001 by John E. Wills Jr. Used by permission of W. W. Norton & Company, Inc.

5   Anna Bijns. "Unyoked Is Best! Happy the Woman without a Man" from *Women and Writers of the Renaissance and Reformation*, edited by Katharina M. Wilson. Copyright © 1987 by The University of Georgia Press. Reprinted by permission of The University of Georgia Press.

6   Mary Jo Maynes and Ann Waltner. "Childhood, Youth, and the Female Life Cycle: Women's Life-Cycle Transitions in a World-Historical Perspective: Comparing Marriage in China and Europe" from *Journal of Women's History* 12, no. 4 (Winter 2001). Copyright © 2001 by Indiana University Press. Reprinted with the permission of The Johns Hopkins University Press.

Chapter 19

1   Jack Goldstone. Excerpt from *Why Europe? The Rise of the West in World History 1500–1850*. Copyright © 2009 by Jack Goldstone. Reprinted with the permission of The McGraw-Hill Companies, Inc.

3   Sir Isaac Newton. Excerpt from *The Mathematical Principles of Natural Philosophy*, translated by Andrew Motte, revised and supplemented by Florian Cajori. Copyright © 1934, © 1962 by the Regents of the University of California. Published by the University of California Press.

4   Bonnie S. Anderson and Judith P. Zinsser. *A History of Their Own: Women in Europe from Prehistory to the Present*, Volume II. Copyright © 1988 by Bonnie S. Anderson and Judith P. Zinsser. Reprinted by permission of HarperCollins Publishers.

6   Lynda Norene Shaffer. "China, Technology, and Change" from *World History Bulletin* 4, no. 1 (Fall/Winter 1986–1987): 1–6. Reprinted with the permission of the author.

7   Sugita Gempaku. "A Dutch Anatomy Lesson in Japan" from *Japan: A Documentary History,* Volume I, edited by David Lu. Translation copyright © 1997 by David J. Lu. Reprinted with permission from M. E. Sharpe, Inc.

Chapter 20

7   Simón Bolívar. "A Constitution for Venezuela" from *Selected Writings of Bolivar,* edited by Harold A. Bierck Jr. (New York: Colonial Press, 1951), pp. 175–191, translated by Lewis Bertrand. Copyright © Banco de Venezuela. Reprinted with permission.

8   Dipesh Chakrabarty. "Compassion and Enlightenment" from *Provincializing Europe: Postcolonial Thought and Historical Difference.* Copyright © 2000 by Princeton University Press. Reprinted by permission of Princeton University Press.

Chapter 21

1   Arnold Pacey. "Asia and the Industrial Revolution" from *Technology in World Civilization.* Copyright © 1990 by Arnold Pacey. Reprinted with the permission of The MIT Press.

4   Karl Marx and Friedrich Engels. Excerpt from *Manifesto of the Communist Party.* Copyright © 1955. Reprinted with the permission of Harlan Davidson, Inc.

5   Peter N. Stearns. Excerpt from *The Industrial Revolution in World History.* Copyright © 1993 by Peter N. Stearns. Reprinted with the permission of Perseus Books Group.

6   Oreste Sola. Excerpts from Letters 1–4 from *One Family, Two Worlds: An Italian Family's Correspondence across the Atlantic,* edited by Samuel L. Bailey and Franco Ramella, translated by John Lenaghan. Copyright © 1988 by Rutgers, the State University. Reprinted by permission of Rutgers University Press.

Chapter 22

1   George Orwell. Excerpt from *Burmese Days.* Copyright © 1934 by George Orwell. Reprinted by permission of Houghton Mifflin Harcourt Publishing Company.

3   Chinua Achebe. From "An Image of Africa: Racism in Conrad's *Heart of Darkness*" from *The Massachusetts Review* 18 (1977). Reprinted with the permission of *The Massachusetts Review.*

4   Joyce Cary. From *Mister Johnson.* Copyright © 1939 by Joyce Cary. Reprinted with the permission of the Andrew Lownie Literary Agency, Ltd.

5   Francis Bebey. From *King Albert,* translated by Joyce A. Hutchinson (Westport, Conn.: Lawrence Hill, 1981). Reprinted with the permission of Kidi Bebey.

Chapter 23

1   Fukuzawa Yukichi. "Datsu-a Ron (On Saying Goodbye to Asia)" (1885) in *Japan: A Documentary History,* Volume II, edited by David J. Lu. Translation copyright © 1997 by David J. Lu. Reprinted with permission from M. E. Sharpe, Inc.

3   Jun'ichirō Tanizaki. Excerpt from *In Praise of Shadows*, translated by Thomas J. Harper and Edward G. Seidensticker. Copyright © 1977. Reprinted with the permission of Leete's Island Books.
4   Mohandas K. Gandhi. From *Hind Swaraj*. Copyright © 1938 by The Navajivan Trust. Reprinted with the permission of The Navajivan Trust.
5   Jawaharlal Nehru. "Gandhi" from *Toward Freedom: The Autobiography of Jawaharlal Nehru* (New York: John Day Co., 1942). Reprinted by permission.
7   Hassan al-Banna. "The Tyranny of Materialism over the Lands of Islam" from "Six Tracts of Hasan Al-Bana" from *Majmu'at Rasa'il al-Iman al-Shahid Hasan al-Banna*. Copyright © 2006. Reprinted with the permission of the International Islamic Federation of Student Organizations.

Chapter 24

1   Stephen O'Shea. Excerpt from *Back to the Front: An Accidental Historian Walks the Trenches of World War I*. Copyright © 1997 by Stephen O'Shea. Reprinted with the permission of Walker and Company.
2   Erich Maria Remarque. Excerpt from *All Quiet on the Western Front*, translated by A. W. Wheen. Copyright © 1928 by Ullstein A.G., renewed © 1956 by Erich Maria Remarque. Copyright © 1929, 1930 by Little, Brown and Company, renewed © 1957, 1958 by Erich Maria Remarque. Reprinted with the permission of the Estate of Paulette Goddard Remarque, c/o Pryor, Cashman, Sherman & Flynn, New York, NY. All rights reserved.
5   Joe Lunn. From *Memoirs of the Maelstrom: A Senegalese Oral History of the First World War*. Copyright © 1999 by Joe Lunn. Reprinted with the permission of Heinemann, Portsmouth, NH. All rights reserved.

Chapter 25

1   Joachim C. Fest. Excerpts from "The Great Dread" from *Hitler*, translated by Clara and Richard Winston. Copyright © 1973 by Verlag Ullstein. English translation copyright © 1974 by Harcourt, Inc. Reprinted with the permission of Houghton Mifflin Harcourt Publishing Company.
2   Heinrich Himmler. "Speech to the SS" from Lucy Dawidowicz (ed.), *A Holocaust Reader*. Copyright © 1976 by Lucy Dawidowicz. Reprinted with the permission of Behrman House, 235 Watchung Avenue, West Orange, NJ.
3   Jean-François Steiner. From *Treblinka*. English translation copyright © 1967 by Simon & Schuster. Reprinted with the permission of Simon & Schuster, Inc.
4   Timothy Snyder. "Holocaust: The Ignored Reality" from *The New York Review of Books* 56, no. 12 (July 16, 2009). Copyright © 2009. Reprinted with the permission of *The New York Review of Books*.
5   Iris Chang. From *The Rape of Nanking*. Copyright © 1997 by Iris Chang. Reprinted with the permission of Basic Books, a member of Perseus Books, LLC.
7   Akihiro Takahashi. "The Voice of Hibakusha" from Testimony of Akihiro Takahashi in the video *Hiroshima Witness*, produced by Hiroshima Peace Cultural Center and NHK. Reprinted with the permission of Hiroshima Peace Culture Foundation and Akihiro Takahashi.

Chapter 26

1   Odd Arne Westad. Excerpt from *The Global Cold War: Third World Interventions and the Making of Our Times*. Copyright © 2007. Reprinted with the permission of Cambridge University Press.

2   X (George F. Kennan). "The Sources of Soviet Conduct" from *Foreign Affairs* (July 1947). Copyright © 1947 by the Council on Foreign Relations, Inc., www.ForeignRelations.com. Reprinted by permission.

3   Ho Chi Minh. "The Vietnamese Declaration of Independence" from *Ho Chi Minh, Selected Works*. Reprinted with the permission of Foreign Languages Publishing House, Hanoi.

4   Edward Lansdale. Excerpts from "Report on CIA Operations, 1954–1955" in *The Pentagon Papers, Abridged Edition*, edited by George C. Herring. Reprinted by permission of The McGraw-Hill Companies, Inc.

5   *Time Magazine*. "Nikita Khrushchev: We Will Bury You" from *Time Magazine* (November 26, 1956). Copyright © 1956. Reprinted with the permission of Time, Inc.

7   Mao Zedong. Excerpts from *Quotations from Chairman Mao Tsetung*. Copyright © 1972. Reprinted with the permission of Foreign Languages Press, Beijing.

Chapter 27

1   Justin Lahart, Patrick Barta, and Andrew Batson. "New Limits to Growth Revive Malthusian Fears" from *The Wall Street Journal* (March 24, 2008): 1. Copyright © 2008. Reprinted with the permission of Copyright Clearance Center for The Wall Street Journal.

2   Phillip Longman. "Heading Toward Extinction?" from *USA Today* (March 24, 2009), Op-Ed. Copyright © 2009. Reprinted with the permission of the author.

3   Alexander Cockburn. "Message in a Bottle" from *The Nation* (May 2, 2005). Copyright © 2005. Reprinted with the permission of the author.

4   Jacques Leslie. Excerpt from "Running Dry: What Happens When the World No Longer Has Enough Freshwater?" from *Harper's* (July 2000). Copyright © 2000 by Harper's Magazine. All rights reserved. Reproduced by special permission.

5   Andrew Rice. Excerpt from "Is There Such a Thing as Agro-Imperialism?" from *The New York Times Magazine* (November 22, 2009). Copyright © 2009 by The New York Times Company. Reprinted with permission.

Chapter 28

1   Sherif Hetata. Excerpt from "Dollarization, Fragmentation, and God" in *The Cultures of Globalization*, edited by Fredric Jameson and Masao Miyoshi. Copyright © 1998 by Duke University Press. Used by permission of the publisher.

2   Philippe Legrain. "Cultural Globalization Is Not Americanization" from *The Chronicle of Higher Education* (May 9, 2003). Reprinted with the permission of the author.